THE HAND-BOOK OF GAMES.

THE

HAND-BOOK OF GAMES:

COMPRISING

NEW OR CAREFULLY REVISED TREATISES ON

WHIST, PIQUET, ECARTÉ, LANSQUENET, BOSTON, QUADRILLE, CRIBBAGE, AND OTHER CARD GAMES;

FARO, ROUGE ET NOIR, HAZARD, ROULETTE;

Backgammon, Draughts;

BILLIARDS, BAGATELLE, AMERICAN BOWLS;

ETC., ETC.

WRITTEN OR COMPILED BY PROFESSORS AND AMATEURS.

EDITED BY HENRY G. BOHN.

LONDON:

HENRY G. BOHN, YORK STREET, COVENT GARDEN

M.DCCC.L.

Detroit: Reissued by Singing Tree Press, Book Tower, 1969

795.4
B 63 h
70865
July 1970

ADVERTISEMENT.

THE present Handbook comprises, it is believed, the most complete directions for playing games of skill and science, yet presented to the English public. Its great predecessor, Hoyle, for more than half a century the only authority, has now become obsolete or imperfect in respect to several of the principal games, and more likely to mislead than instruct.

The want of a comprehensive and practical Manual of this description, having frequently been pressed on the attention of the Publisher, he determined to undertake it, and confided the task to Mr. J. W. Carleton. That gentleman is responsible for the elaborate treatise on WHIST, and its arrangement in four parts. Three of the four parts, as will be seen, are revised editions of previous treatises; the fourth is partly original and partly compiled, and, as a whole, is new. The Publisher, in his anxiety to render this important portion of the work as perfect as possible, submitted it, while at press, to several distinguished Whist-players, and by their kind co-operation, has been enabled to settle several rules, which seemed either to conflict with themselves, or were at variance with those currently received. Many of the notes have arisen out of this mode of proceeding. To these four parts of Whist are prefixed (by another hand) Bob Short's rules, and something of an index, by way of guiding the student through the mazes of so elaborate a treatise.

Mr. Carleton is likewise responsible for the articles on Ecarté, Hazard, Backgammon, and most of the games adopted from Hoyle or other printed authorities.

PIQUET is by a gentleman, who has long ranked as one of our best players, and has won many considerable matches.

CRIBBAGE is condensed from Mr. Walker's very comprehensive treatise, which is by far the best extant.

The treatise on DRAUGHTS comprises the entire work of Sturges, as revised and edited by Walker; together with some additional games and problems, contributed by Mr. Martin, a professional player of considerable skill. The article on Polish

Draughts is by the Publisher, written from memory, for want of materials at hand.   He is likewise responsible for the BILLIARDS, which, though compiled from Mr. White's celebrated work, has been so extensively altered and corrected, as to become almost a new treatise.   In Mr. White's time the simple white ball games were almost the only ones played in this country, which circumstance will account for the necessity of the numerous alterations.   The elementary part is entirely re-written, and the instructions are, it is hoped, conveyed so explicitly, that a person who never before played a game, may acquire sufficient knowledge of it from the present pages to teach himself, without falling into erroneous modes or habits.   In conducting this rather arduous part of the volume through the press, the Publisher has been favoured with the assistance of several distinguished players, amateur and professional, both in London and Brighton. Mr. Thurston also, eminent for his billiard and bagatelle tables, has rendered every assistance, as well by his own valuable advice as by granting the use of his splendid edition of Kentfield's work.

The GERMAN POOL GAMES (*Wurst-Parthie, &c.*) are contributed by an accomplished amateur, who has frequently played them on the Continent.

VINGT-UN, and two other of the minor games, are by another friend; and AMERICAN BOWLS has been drawn up by the Editor, assisted by the proprietor of the Strand Rooms, Mr. Thomas Robson.

No means have been spared, either by taxing friendships or the liberal application of funds, to render this volume perfect, and now that after nearly two years' lingering at press, it is finally launched, the Publisher entertains a hope that it will be found deserving of sufficient patronage to reimburse a disproportionately large outlay.

It is in contemplation to publish a companion volume of Athletic and Defensive Exercises, extensively decorated with wood-cuts; in which considerable progress has already been made.

York Street, Jan. 1854   H. G. B.

CONTENTS.

a 3

CONTENTS TO WHIST.

INDEX TO WHIST.

BOB SHORT'S RULES,

By way of finger-post to the elaborate Treatise which follows : with occasional references to the same rules, as given by Mathews, Hoyle, Deschapelles, and the Editor.)

---

1. Lead from your strong suit, and be cautious how you change suits, and keep a commanding card to bring it in again.

M. p. 29; H. p. 39; Ed. p. 167, et seq.

2. Lead through the strong suit and up to the weak, but not in trumps, unless very strong in them.

M. p. 29; H. p. 29; Ed. p. 167, et seq.

3. Lead the highest of a sequence, but if you have a quart or cinque to a king, lead the lowest.

M. p. 29; H. p. 29; Ed. p. 167, et seq.

4. Lead through an honour, particularly if the game is much against you.

M. p. 29; H. p. 40, 52; Ed. p. 170, 171, 190,

5. Lead your best trump, if the adversaries are eight, and you have no honour; but not if you have four trumps, unless you have a sequence.

M. p. 29; H. p. 41, 44, 57; Ed. p. 168.

6. Lead a trump, if you have four or five, or a strong hand; but not if weak.

M. p. 29; H. p. 41; Ed. p. 169.

7. Having ace, king, and two or three small cards, lead ace and king, if weak in trumps; but a small one if strong in them.

M. p. 29; H. p. 40, 41; Ed. p. 168.

8. If you have the last trump, with some winning cards, and one losing card only, lead the losing card.

M. p. 26, 29, H. p. 41; Ed. p. 159.

9. Return your partner's lead, not the adversary's; and if you had only three originally, play the best; but you need not return it immediately when you win with the king, queen, or knave, and have only small ones; or when you hold a good sequence, have a strong suit, or have five trumps.

M. p. 27; H. p. 39; Ed. p. 74.

10. Do not lead from ace queen or ace knave.

M. p. 14; H. p. 41; Ed. p. 172.

11. Do not lead an ace unless you have a king.

M. p. 15; H. p. 41; Ed. p. 168, 199.

12. Do not lead a thirteenth card unless trumps are out.

M. p. 15; Ed. p. 171.

13. Do not trump a thirteenth card, unless you are a last player, or want the lead.

M. p. 10, 15; H. p. 61; Ed. p. 172.

14. Keep a small card to return your partner's lead.

M. p. 16.

15. Be cautious in trumping a card when strong in trumps, particularly if you have a strong suit.

M. p. 11, 17; H. p. 40.

16. Having only a few small trumps, make them when you can.

M. p. 14; H. p. 39.

17. If your partner refuses to trump a suit of which he knows you have not the best, lead your best trump

M. p. 13; Ed. p. 170.

18. When you hold all the remaining trumps, play one, and then try to put the lead in your partner's hand.

M. p. 17; H. p. 41; Ed. p. 176.

19. Remember how many of each suit are out, and what is the best card left in each hand.

H. p. 72.

20. Never force your partner if you are weak in trumps, unless you have a renounce, or can ensure the odd trick.

M. p. 10; H. p. 49.

21. When playing for the odd trick, be cautious of trumping out, especially if your partner is likely to trump a suit; and make all the tricks you can early, and avoid finessing.

M. p. 15; H. p. 39.

22. If you take a trick and have a sequence, win it with the lowest.

M. p. 20.

SECOND HAND.

23. Having ace, king, and small ones, play a small one, if strong in trumps, but the king if weak; and having ace, king, queen, or knave only, with a small one, play the small one.

H. 44, 51; Ed. p. 171.

THIRD HAND.

24. Having ace and queen, play the queen, and if it wins, return the ace, and in all other cases play the best, if your partner leads a small one.

Ed. p. 174.

25. Neglect not to make the odd trick, when in your power.

H. 40, 66, 67.

26. Attend to the score, and play the game accordingly.

D. p. 112, 113; Ed. p. 157.

27. Retain the card turned up as long as possible.

D. p. 100.

28. When in doubt, win the trick.

H. p. 40.

WHIST,

IN FOUR PARTS:

I. BY MATHEWS.

II. BY HOYLE.

III. BY DESCHAPELLES.

IV. BY J. W. CARLETON.

WHIST.

PREFATORY CHAPTER.

Age cannot wither it, nor custom stale
Its infinite variety.

WE do not purpose in treating of this noble game to offer any new theories, or promote any novel systems. That such will arise in process of time, there can be little doubt; for Whist admits of endless variety. According to an article on "Probability" in the Library of Useful Knowledge, it appears that if the entire population of the world were to deal packs of cards, whist-fashion, never quitting their employment, and thus continue for a hundred millions of years, accomplishing sixty deals every hour, they would not have exhausted one hundred thousandth part of the essentially different ways in which fifty-two cards can be distributed in equal numbers in four divisions. The possible combinations are almost beyond arithmetic, and absolutely out of the reach of words: the figures are thus given: 16,250, 563, 659, 176, 029, 962, 568, 164, 794, 000, 749, 006, 367, 006, 400: a pretty little array of numbers, the sum whereof is left to the reader's readiness in logarithms. These pages will treat of the game as it now exists; borrowing from the best authorities of the past, and from the *chef d'œuvres* of modern science, as communicated by the most distinguished players of the present day. A few preliminary words may not be deemed irrelevant.

Little is at present known of the origin of Whist. It is however in evidence that it was in vogue nearly two centuries ago in this country; the land most probably of its birth. "Ruff and Honours (*alias* Slam) and Whist," says Cotton, (printed 1680) "are games so commonly known in England, in all parts thereof, that every child of eight years old hath a competent knowledge of that recreation—these games differ very little from one another." In 1715, Pope thus addressed Martha Blount in one of his epistles:—

> Some squire, perhaps, you take delight to rack
> Whose game is *Whist:* whose drink, a toast in sack:
> Whose laughs are hearty, though his jests are coarse:
> Who loves you best of all things—but his horse.

An early mention of the game occurs in the " Beaux Stratagem" (published in 1707), when Mrs. Sullen thus apostrophizes the delights of a rural life : "Country pleasures! racks and torments! Dost think, child, that my limbs were made for leaping of ditches and clambring over styles? or that my parents, wisely foreseeing my future happiness in country pleasures, had early instructed me in the rural accomplishment of drinking fat ale, *playing at Whist*, and smoking tobacco with my husband?"

Thomson, in his Seasons, introduces it as the Squire's autumnal resource against *ennui*.

> To cheat the thirsty moments, *Whist* awhile
> Walk'd his dull round, amid a cloud of smoke,
> Wreathed, fragrant, from the pipe.

Sir Roger de Coverley was in the habit every Christmas of sending a string of hog's puddings, and a pack of cards to every poor family in his parish.*

A modern French writer on this game has the following conjecture as to its origin " It is well known," he says, " that the Peers of the Three Kingdoms after having spoken all day and a portion of the night in parliament on state affairs, found a *mute game* necessary to rest their wearied tongues, and that hence sprung *Whist!* "

The first edition of Hoyle was published in 1743. At that period he gave instructions in Whist for a guinea a lesson, and most probably it then began to be a scientific game, and has gone on advancing to its present perfection. There are many authorities existing for the opinion, that it was not till the latter part of the eighteenth century, that Whist, as it is now played, was known among us. According to Daines Barrington, who had his information from a player much advanced in years, it was not played upon recognized

---

* Swift alludes to it as a favourite pastime for clergymen. He says " the clergymen used to play at whist and swabbers."

principles till about 1730, "when it was much studied by a party that frequented the Crown Coffee-House in Bedford Row," of whom the first Lord Folkstone was one. Even then, it should seem that merely the skeleton of the game was in existence; there were but few rules, and its theory was undefined.

Since then, many treatises and commentators on the great original's volume, have seen the light, but not one that took up the subject *de novo* till Mr. Mathews published his "Advice to the young Whist Players" at Bath, early in the present century. This soon run through a number of editions and in a great measure displaced Hoyle. The fifth is dated 1811, but it has frequently been reprinted since then, though without improvement. Miscellaneous volumes, treating of Whist and other games, appeared, indeed, from time to time, during the latter portion of the last century and the beginning of this, some with dates and some without, as "Maxims for Playing the Game of Whist, London, 1778," "The New Pocket Hoyle, 1800," "Pigott's Hoyle," no date, and others; but their lore is as out of fashion as the taste for pastorals; and as little suited to Brooks's or the Travellers' as Alexis, or Corydon to Regent Street, or the Ring in Hyde Park.

The reader must bear in mind that Whist is not like Chess, essentially a game of science; nor like Billiards an essay of manual skill. It is a game in which chance and skill unite: chance distributes the cards, and skill controls their destiny. Lord William Manners, who seems to have been the best player of his time, insisted that there was no more than five per cent. odds between two of the best and two of the worst players. The degree in which Whist is arbitrarily affected by the cards, may be gathered from the following fact. After a mis-deal, on dealing again with the same pack, one of the players will, nine times out of ten, hold at most but one card of one of the four suits. How this comes to pass, is a problem that remains to be solved; whether the fact be so or not, is of very simple proof.

It has been well said that no fixed rules can make a first-rate Whist player, the game being so "infinite" in its "variety." He is a good player who, upon a sound theory, analyses and proves the best written systems, making them the machinery of his schemes; but he is the superior player, who, equally practical, and as well informed of existing rules, sees when they ought to be violated, and has no hesitation in departing from them. Still that it is a game of system and method is beyond all question; certainly more so than any game that is played with cards.

In the acquirement of any art or science, the learner seeks to become master of its first principles at the outset. Thus the young whist-player having read that with two or more of a sequence (as king and queen) of his partner's lead, he should put on the lowest—he does so. Thereupon, his queen having passed, it becomes evident to his partner that the king is not amongst his right hand adversary's cards, nor the knave in *his*, and this gives him great consequent advantages in the disposition of his suit. The golden rule for the young player is to begin with the beginning. In the whole economy of life there is no truth more worthy of observance than that it is easier to acquire good habits, than to get rid of bad ones. For this reason let the pupil ever remember the prudence, nay the absolute necessity, of proceeding gradually. Before he ventures to take his place at the Whist-table, he should become familiar with the various modes of leading, playing the sequences, and all the fundamental principles. When he feels that he has in some degree mastered the theory, then let him begin to practice it with the best players he can meet with. Let him by degrees cultivate a knowledge of the more intricate combinations, carefully noting when or wherefore the general rules are to be observed or departed from, otherwise they will as frequently puzzle, as help him. It was by this means, by advancing gradually, and always cautiously, that Whist became what it is; a wonderful development of human patience and ingenuity. We will follow in the same course, (as the surest path to conduct us to our end,) the practical working of this fine game up to the constitution of the present system, the most finished specimen of high art in the science of card-playing.

Long Whist, both on the grounds of earlier origin and intrinsic excellence, is entitled to the precedence we shall accord to it. That it was the first of its class needs no proof: that it is the most scientific has been shewn by an erudite and elaborate investigator of the game, *M. Deschapelles*; who thus treats the inquiry :—

Is Short Whist as difficult as Long Whist?

In playing the long game, when both sides mark five, they are precisely in the same position with those parties who are beginning the short game*.

The latter, therefore, is but a portion of the former.

Now the part is less than the whole.

Therefore the question is solved—consequently we begin with the recognised authorities on Long Whist, and will with the reader's leave, first lay before him Mr. Mathews' system, as not only being the most elementary, but replete with excellent matter. Mathews is to the new school what Hoyle was to the old. He is a master of the theory and management of the fifty-two cards, and is eminently free from all unnecessary technicalities. Hoyle, of course, is the key-stone of the arch. Mr. Mathews's game is, in spirit, the same as that of his great predecessor, while its letter omits what could no longer be useful, substituting much that both embellishes the system and assists the practice of the fundamental principles of Whist. It is, in every respect, the book for the beginner, inculcating nothing that he will have occasion to wish he had not learnt, and furnishing a store of that sterling *matériel* which constitutes the stuff whereof the finished player is made. When we come to *M. Deschapelles* we shall find our master of the ceremonies by whom the whole phalanx will be marshalled, and all the preliminary arrangements appropriately set forth. In the meanwhile we cannot place before the young Whist-player any system more admirable and well-considered than that of Mathews, which will direct and amply repay the aspirant who may study its theory, and essay its practice—Pope supplying the introductory motto.

> Behold four kings, in majesty revered,
> With hoary whiskers and a forky beard :
> And four fair queens, whose hands sustain a flower—
> The expressive emblem of their softer power :
> Four knaves in garbs succinct, a trusty band,
> Caps on their heads, and halberts in the hand :
> And party-coloured troops, a shining train,
> Draw forth to combat on the velvet plain.

---

* Excepting that honors cannot be *called* at any period of shorts.

PART THE FIRST.

INTRODUCTION.

Whist is a game of Calculation, Observation, and Position or Tenace.

Calculation teaches you to plan your game, and lead originally to advantage; before a card is played, you suppose the dealer to have an honour and three other trumps; the others each an honour and two others. The least reflection will show, that as it is two to one, that your partner has not a named card, to lead on the supposition he has it, is to play against calculation. Whereas, the odds being in favour of his having one of two named cards, you are justified in playing accordingly. Calculation is also of use on other occasions, which the maxims will elucidate; but after a few leads have taken place, it is nearly superseded by observation. Where the sets are really good players, before half the cards are played out, they are as well acquainted with the material ones remaining in each other's hands as if they had seen them. Where two regular players are matched against two irregular ones, it is nearly the same advantage as if they were permitted to see each other's cards, while the latter were denied the same privilege.

It is an axiom, that the nearer your play approaches to what is called the dumb man the better.

These may be called the foundation of the game, and are so merely mechanical, that any one possessed of a tolerable memory may attain them.

After which comes the more difficult science of position, or the art of using the two former to advantage; without which, it is self-evident, they are of no use. Attentive study and practice will, in some degree, ensure success; but genius must be added before the whole finesse of the game can be acquired—however,

Est quiddam prodire tenus, si non datur ultra.

DIRECTIONS AND MAXIMS FOR BEGINNERS.

STUDY all written maxims with the cards placed before you, in the situations mentioned. Abstract directions puzzle much oftener than they assist the beginner.

Keep in your mind that general maxims pre-suppose the game and hand, at their commencement; and that material changes in them frequently require that a different mode of play should be adopted.

Do not attempt to practice till you have acquired a competent knowledge of the theory; and avoid as much as possible, at first, sitting down with bad players. It is more difficult to eradicate erroneous, than to acquire just ideas.

Never lead a card without a reason, though a wrong one; it is better than accustoming yourself to play at random.

Do not at first puzzle yourself with many calculations. Those you will find hereafter mentioned are sufficient even for a proficient.

Do not accustom yourself to judge by consequences. Bad play sometimes succeeds when good would not. When you see an acknowledged judge of the game play in a manner you do not comprehend, get him to explain his reasons, and while fresh on your memory, place the same cards before you; when once you can comprehend the case, you will be able to adapt it to similar situations.

Before you play a card, sort your hand carefully, look at the trump card, and consider the score of the game, the strength of your own hand, and form your plan on the probable situation of the cards; subject, however, to be changed should any thing fall to indicate a different one; after which, never look at your hand, till you are to play; without attending to the board, no maxims or practice can even make a tolerable Whist player.

Observe silently and attentively, the different systems of those with whom you commonly play; few but have their favourite one, the knowledge of which will give you a constant advantage; one leads by preference from an ace, another never but through necessity. [This will often direct you in putting on the king second.] The players of the old school

never lead from a single card without six trumps; many do so
from weakness; some have a trick of throwing down high
cards to the adversary's lead, and then, by way of deception,
affect to consider, although they have no alternative.   Observation will enable you to counteract this, and turn it to your
own profit.

The best leads are from sequences of three cards or more.
If you have none, lead from your most numerous suit; if
strong in trumps, lead rather from one headed by a king
than a queen; but with three or four small trumps, I should
prefer leading from a single card to a long weak suit.

☞ This is contrary to the usual practice, especially of the players of
the OLD SCHOOL.

The more plainly you demonstrate your hand to your
partner the better.   Be particularly cautious not to deceive
him in his or your own leads, or when he is likely to have
the lead—a concealed game may now and then succeed in
the suits of your adversaries; but this should not be attempted
before you have made a considerable proficiency; and then
but seldom, as its frequency would destroy the effect.

At the commencement of a game, if you have a good hand
or if your adversaries are considerably advanced in the score,
play a bold game; if otherwise, a more cautious one.

Be as careful of what you throw away as what you lead;
it is often of bad consequence to put down a tray with a
deuce in your hand.—Suppose your partner leads the four,
your right-hand adversary the five, and you put down the
tray, it ought to be to a certainty, that you ruff it next time;
but if he find the deuce in your hand, and you frequently
deceive him by throwing down superior cards, it will destroy
his confidence, and prevent his playing his game on similar
occasions.   I would wish to inculcate these minor qualifica-
tions of whist playing to the beginners, because they are
attainable by every body; and when once the great advantage
of this kind of correctness is seen, the worst player would
practice it as constantly as the best—attention being all that
is necessary.

Do not lead trumps merely because an honour is turned
up on your left, or be deterred from it, if on your right-hand.
Either is proper, if the circumstances of your hand require
trumps to be led; but neither, otherwise.

Finesses are generally right in trumps, or (if strong in them) in other suits; otherwise they are not to be risked but with caution.

Never ruff an uncertain card, if strong, or omit doing so if weak in trumps; this is one of the few universal maxims, and cannot be too closely adhered to, even did you know the best of the suit was in your partner's hand: it has the double advantage of making a useless trump and letting your partner into the state of your hand, who will play accordingly.

Keep the command of your adversary's suit as long as you can with safety; but never that of your partner.

Do not ruff a thirteenth card second lead, if strong; but always if weak in trumps.

Always force the strong, seldom the weak, never the two; otherwise you play your adversaries' game, and give the one an opportunity to make his small trumps, while the other throws away his losing cards. It is a very general as well as fatal error; but the extent of it is seldom comprehended by unskilful players, who, seeing the good effect of judicious forces, practice them injudiciously, to their almost constant disadvantage. The following effect of a force is too obvious not to be instantly comprehended. I have only to tell the student, that the same principle operates through the fifty-two cards, however various their combinations; and that a steady consideration of it is one of the first necessary steps towards an insight into the game.

A has a seizieme major in trumps, a quart major in the second, and a tierce major in a third suit.—B his adversary, has six small trumps, and the entire command of the fourth suit; in this case it is obvious that one force on A, gains the odd trick for B, who without it loses a slam. Though so great an effect may seldom be produced, still there is scarcely a rubber where the truth of the maxim is not experimentally proved.

When, with a very strong suit, you lead trumps in hope your partner may command them, shew your suit first. If you have a strength in trumps in your hand, play them originally.

With the ace and three other trumps, it is seldom right to win the first and second lead in that suit, if made by your adversaries, unless your partner ruffs some other.

With a strong hand in trumps, particularly if you have a long suit, avoid ruffing your right hand adversary, as much as possible. As this is a maxim less understood, less practised, and more indispensably necessary, than almost any other, I will endeavour to explain it to beginners, as clearly as I am capable of doing:—Cards being nearly equal, the point to which all the manœuvres of good Whist players tend, is to establish a long suit, and to preserve the last trump, to bring it into play, and to frustrate the same play of their adversaries. With an honour (or even a ten) with three other trumps, by well managing them, you have a right to expect success. In this case do not over-trump your right-hand adversary early in the hand; but throw away a losing card, by which, there remaining but twelve trumps, your own hand is strengthened, and your partner has the tenace, in whatever suit is led; whereas, had you over-ruffed you would have given up the whole game, to secure one trick. But there are reasons for breaking this rule:—1st, if your left-hand adversary has shown a decided great hand in trumps, (in which case make your tricks while you can;) or 2nd, if your partner decidedly means to force you;—to understand if this be the case, you are to observe if your partner plays the winning or losing card of the suit you have refused. If the former, it is by no means clear he means to force you, and you play your own game. If the latter, you are to suppose him strong in trumps, and depend on this, to protect your long suit; a due reflection on this will convince you of the value of that maxim, which enjoins you never to play a strong game with a weak hand, or vice versâ. A few deviations from this effectually destroy that confidence necessary between partners, and introduces a confusion and consequences, that cannot be too carefully avoided or too strenuously deprecated.

If the circumstances of your hand require two certain leads in trumps, play off your ace, let your other trumps be what they may.

It is a general maxim not to force your partner, unless strong in trumps yourself. There are however, many exceptions to this rule: as

1st. If your partner has led from a single card.
2nd. If it saves or wins a particular point.
3rd. If great strength in trumps is declared against you.

4th.   If you have a probability of a saw.
5th.   If your partner has been forced and did not trump out.
6th.   It is often right in playing for an odd trick.

It is difficult to judge when to lead trumps. The following situations will assist the beginner to reason, and in general direct him properly;

1st.   With six trumps, on supposition your partner has a strong suit.
2nd.   If strong in other suits, though weak in trumps yourself.
3rd.   If your adversaries are playing from weak suits.
4th.   If your adversaries are at the point of eight, and you have no honour, or probability of making a trump by a ruff.

It is easy soon to discover the different strengths of good players, but more difficult with bad ones. When your adversary refuses to trump, and throws away a small card, you conclude his hand consists of a strong suit in trumps, with one strong and another weaker suit. If he throws an honour, you know he has two suits only, one of which is trumps. In the latter case win tricks when you can. Avoid leading trumps, or to his suit; force him, and give your partner an opportunity to trump if possible. This maxim cannot be too maturely considered, as this is a fault which is constantly committed by bad players, and is amongst those most fatal in their consequences. The moment an adversary refuses to ruff, though a winning card, they, in violation of common sense, trump out, and not unfrequently give away five or six tricks, which a judicious force would have prevented.

If you are strong in trumps, and have the ace, king, and two more of your right-hand adversary's lead, there are two ways to play; either to pass it the first time, or else to put on the ace, and play the suit on to force your partner. If weak in trumps, put on the ace, but do not continue the suit.

If you win your partner's lead with the queen, unless in trumps, do not return it; it is evident the ace or king lies behind him, and you give the tenace to the adversary.

To lead from only three cards, unless in sequence, is bad play, and only proper when you have reason to think it is your partner's suit; in which case play off the highest, though the king or queen.

N. B.   This is contrary to the general practice, but undoubtedly right.

The first object should be to save the game, if it appears in probable danger; the next to win it, if you have a reasonable hope of success, by any mode of play, though hazardous. If neither of these is the question, you should play to the points or score of the game. In other words, you should not give up the certainty of the odd trick, or scoring five or eight, for the equal chance of two, six, or nine; whereas you should risk an equal finesse that will prevent your adversaries from these scores by its success.

It is generally right to return your partner's lead in trumps unless he leads an equivocal card, such as a nine or ten. These are called equivocal, because they are led with propriety, both from strong and weak suits. With a quart or a king—or nine, ten, knave, and king of a suit, you lead nine, as you do when it is the best of two or three of a suit.

With only four trumps, do not lead one, unless your strong suit is established, except that with a tierce-major and another trump, and a sequence to the king of three more, it is good play to lead trumps twice, and then the knave of your suit, and continue till the ace is out.

If you remain with the best trump, and one of your adversaries has three or more, do not play out, as it may stop the suit of your other adversary. If they both have trumps and your partner none, it is right to take out two for one.

If strong in trumps, with the commanding card of the adversaries' suit, and small ones, force your partner, if he has none of that suit, with the small ones, and keep the commanding card till the last.

If your partner leads the ace and queen of a suit, of which you have the king and two others, win his queen that you may not stop his suit.

If your right-hand adversary wins, and returns his partner's lead, should you have the best and a small one, play the latter. If your partner has the third best he will probably make it. If your adversary is a bad player, I would not advise this, as they never finesse when they ought to do it.

☞ If weak in trumps, you should not venture this in other suits.

If your right-hand adversary calls, and, your partner, leads through him, with ace or king, the nine and a small one, you should finesse the nine.

If your partner calls before his turn, he means you should

play a trump. Take every opportunity to show your partner that you can command the trumps. In this case he will keep his own strong suit entire: whereas, if the strength of trumps is with the adversaries, his play would be to keep guard on their suits, and throw away from his own.

With ace, knave, and another trump, it is right to finesse the knave to your partner's lead; and if strong in them you should do the same in any suit. If he leads the ten of any suit, you pass it invariably with the ace and knave; unless one trick saves or wins any particular point.

It is better to lead from ace nine, than ace ten, as you are more likely to have a tenace in the latter suit, if led by your adversary.

If your partner, to your winning card, throws away the best card of any suit, it shows he wishes you to know he commands it; if the second best, it is to tell you he has no more of that suit.

If very strong in trumps, it is always right to inform your partner of it as soon as possible. If fourth player you are to win a small trump, and if you have a sequence of three or more, win it with the highest, and play the lowest afterwards.

If strong in trumps, do not ruff the second best of any suit your partner leads, but throw away a losing card, unless you have an established saw.

If ten cards are played out, and there remains one entire suit, and your partner lead, if you have a king, ten, and another, and six tricks, you have a certainty to make the odd one, if you play right, let the cards lie how they will; should your right-hand adversary put on an honour, you must win it, if not, put on the ten; with five tricks, put on the king.

Many good players, in playing tierce majors, begin with the king and queen. This is often productive of mischief; as when played at other times from king and queen only, the ace is kept up, and while each thinks his partner has it and has played accordingly, it unexpectedly appears from the adversary, and disappoints their whole plan.

If the fourth player wins his adversary's lead, it is better to return it than open a new suit unless strong enough in it to support his partner.

With ace, knave, and another, do not win the king led by

your left-hand adversary. You either force him to exchange his lead, or give you tenace in his own suit.

With ace, queen, &c., of a suit, of which your right-hand adversary leads the knave, put on the ace invariably. No good player with king, knave, and ten, will begin with the knave; of course it is finessing against yourself, to put on the queen, and as the king is certainly behind you, you give away at least the lead, without any possible advantage.

With only three of a suit, put an honour on an honour; with four or more you should not do it—except the ace should not be put on the knave.

With king and one more, good players sometimes put it on a second, sometimes not; if turned up it should invariably be put on, and generally in trumps. But queen or knave should never be played, unless a superior honour is turned up on the right.

In playing for an odd trick, you play a closer game than at other scores. You lead from single cards and force your partner, when at another time you would not be justified. It is seldom in this case proper to lead trumps; and few finesses are justifiable. It is a nice part of the game, and experience, with attention, will alone teach it with effect.

If the trumps remain divided between you and your partner, and you have no winning card yourself, it is good play to lead a small trump, to put in his hand to play off any that he may have, to give you an opportunity to throw away your losing cards.

A remains with two or more trumps, and two losing cards; his partner with a better trump, and two winning cards. It is evident, if he plays off a losing card, he will take merely his own trumps, but if he plays an inferior trump, and puts it into his partner's lead, he will play off his winning cards, and give A an opportunity to throw away his losing ones.

N.B. This continually occurs, and it is necessary to be comprehended.

When your partner leads, win with the lowest of a sequence, to demonstrate your strength in his suit; but it is often right to win your adversary's lead with the highest, to keep him in ignorance.

When your partner plays a thirteenth card, and most of the trumps are unplayed, he generally means you should put a high trump to strengthen his own hand.

When you have a moderate hand yourself, sacrifice it to your partner; he, if he be a good player, will act in the same manner.

With three, return the highest; with four, the lowest of your partner's lead. This answers two purposes, by giving your partner an opportunity to finesse, and showing him you have but three at most in his suit.

With the ace, queen, and others of your right-hand adversary's lead, put on a small one, except he leads a knave, in which case put on the ace.

When at eight, with two honours, look at your adversary's score, and consider if there is a probability they should save their lurch, or win the game, notwithstanding your partner holds a third honour; if not you should not call, as it gives a decided advantage against you in playing for tricks.

Finessing in general is only meant against one card. There are, however, situations when much deeper are required: but theory alone, can never enable the beginner to discover these.—Supposing it necessary you should make two out out of the last three cards in a suit not yet played, your partner leads the nine, you have ace, ten, and a small one—Query, what are you to do?—Answer, pass it, though the finesse is against three; for if your partner has an honour in the suit, you make two tricks.   If not, it is impossible by any mode of play whatever.

With king, queen, &c., of your right-hand adversary's lead, put on one of them; with queen, knave, and another, the knave; with two or more small ones, the lowest.

The more critically you recollect the cards the better; at least you should remember the trumps and the commanding card of each suit.   It is possible to assist the memory by the mode of placing the cards remaining in your hands—viz., place the trumps in the back part of your hand, your partner's lead the next, your adversary's next, and your own on the outside.   It is also right to put thirteenth cards in some known situation.

It is highly necessary to be correct in leads.—When a good player plays an eight and then a seven, I know he leads from a weak suit; the contrary, when he plays the seven first; the same even with a tray or a deuce.   This is what bad players always err in, as they never can see the difference.

If left with the last trumps, and some winning cards, with one losing one, play this first, as your adversary on the left may finesse, and the second best in your partner's hand make the trick which could not be kept till the last.

Should your partner refuse to trump a certain winning card, try to get the lead as soon as you can, and play out trumps immediately.

Good players never lead a nine or ten, but for one of these reasons:

1st. From a sequence up to the king.
2d. From nine, ten, knave, and king.
3d. When the best of a weak suit not exceeding three in number.

If you have either knave or king in your own hand, you are certain it is for the latter reason, and that the whole strength of the suit is with your adversary, and play your game accordingly.

If your partner leads the nine or ten, and you have an honour, with only one more, put it on; if with two or more, do not; with the ace and small ones, win it invariably; for it is better that he should finesse in his own suit, than you.

Unless you have a strong suit yourself, or reason to suppose your partner has one, do not trump out unless you have six trumps.

There are situations where even good players differ; if a queen is laid on your right hand, and you have ace or king and two small ones, you should certainly win it; but having king or ace, ten, and a small one, I invariably pass it, and for the following reasons—by passing it, if your partner has the ace or king, you clearly lie tenace, and the leader cannot possibly make a trick in the suit, which he must have done, had you even the first trick, as he would lay tenace over your partner; if your partner has the knave you lose a trick; but the odds are greatly against this.

It is seldom right to lead from a suit in which you have a tenace. With ace, queen, &c., of one suit—king, knave, &c., of a second—and the third a weak one—the best play is to lead from the latter.

When it is evident the winning cards are betwixt you and your adversaries, play an obscure game; but as clear a one as possible, if your partner has a good hand.

It is equally advantageous to lead up to as through an ace;

C

not so much so to a king; and disadvantageous to the queen turned up.

Avoid at first playing with those who instruct, or rather find fault, while the hand is playing. They are generally un- qualified by ignorance, and judge from consequences; but if not, advice while playing does more harm than good, by con- fusing a beginner.

It is seldom right to refuse to ruff when your partner, if a good player, visibly intends you should do it. If a bad one, your own hand should direct you.

If you have ace, king, and two more trumps, and your partner leads them originally, insure three rounds in trumps; but if he leads (in consequence of your showing your strength) a nine, or any equivocal card, in that case, pass it the first time; by which you have the lead after three rounds of trumps, a most material advantage.

There is often judgment required in taking the penalties of a revoke. Before the score is advanced, if the party revoking has won nine tricks, the least consideration will show, that the adversaries should take three of them, for if they add three to their own score, they still leave the odd trick to the former; but if the revoking party be at eight, it is better for the adversary to score three points, as the odd trick leaves the former at nine, which is in every respect a worse point than eight. On other occasions, it is only to calculate how the different scores will remain after each mode of taking the penalty; and it will be obvious which will be the most advan- tageous—never losing sight of the points of the game, *i.e.*, scoring eight or five yourself, or prevent your adversary from doing so.

With ace, queen, and ten, of your right-hand adversary's lead, put out the ten.

When your left-hand adversary refuses to trump a winning card, for fear of being over-trumped by your partner, and throws away a losing card, if you have the commanding card of the suits he discards, play it before you continue the former.

When all the trumps are out, if you have the commanding card of your adversary's suit, you may play your own as if you had the thirteenth trump in your own hand.

If A, your right-hand adversary, leads a card, and his part- ner B, putting on the knave or queen, yours wins with the king—should A lead a small card of that suit again, if you have the ten put it on. It is probable, by doing this, you keep the commanding card in your partner's hand, and prevent the second best from making.

If weak in trumps, keep guard on your adversary's suits. If strong, throw away from them, and discard as much as possible from your partner's strong suits, in either case.

Should your left-hand adversary lead the king, to have the finesse of the knave, and it comes to your lead, if you have queen and one more, it is evident the finesse will succeed. In this case, play the small one through him, which frequently will prevent him from making the finesse, though he has originally played for it.

If your partner shows a weak game, force him, whether or not you are otherwise entitled to do it.

When you are at the score of four or nine, and your adversaries, though eight, do not call, if you have no honour, it is evident your partner has two at least. It is equally so if you have one, that he has at least another. If both parties are at eight, and neither calls, each must have one.

A little reflection will enable the beginner to make a proper advantage of these data.

When your partner leads a card, of which you have the best and third, and your right-hand adversary puts on the fourth, the second only remaining—it is a commonly-received, but erroneous opinion, that the chance of succeeding in the finesse is equal; but here calculation will show, that as the last player has one card more than his partner, it is that proportion in favour of his having it. With three cards, it will be three to two against making the finesse.

Moderate players have generally a decided aversion to part with the best trump, though single; thinking that as they cannot lose it, and it can make but one trick, it is immaterial when it does so—this is a dangerous fault.—When your adversary plays out his strong suit, ruff it immediately, before you give his partner an opportunity to throw off his losing cards. Do not, however, go into the contrary extreme, or trump with the best trump, with small ones in your hand, for fear of being over-trumped.—This is a nice part of the game, and can only be understood by practice and attentive reasoning.

It frequently happens that your partner has an opportunity to shew his strong suit, by renouncing to a lead. If you have a single card in this, play it before you force him, let your strength in trumps be what it may; as it is the way to establish the saw, which is almost always advantageous, should the second player put on the ace to prevent it; still it is of great utility by establishing your partner's suit.

A has ace, knave, ten, and a small card of the suit led by his right-hand adversary.—*Query*—Which is he to play? *Answer*—In trumps the ten; in other suits, the small ones, For this reason—In trumps, a good player, with king, queen. &c. leads the lowest; in other suits the king: and in the latter case, of course an honour must be behind you; and be it in either hand you can do no good by putting on the ten; by keeping the three together you render it impossible for your adversary to make one trick in the suit.

It often happens that with only three cards remaining in his hand, the leader has the worst trump, and ace, queen, or some tenace of another suit. In this case he should lead the trump, to put it into his adversary's hand to play. By these means, he preserves the tenace. This, though self-evident on proper consideration, is what none but good players ever think of.

Though it is certainly more regular to win your adversary's as well as partner's lead with the lowest of a sequence, still I recommend occasional deviations from that maxim; as it is of the greatest advantage to give your partner every information in his, or your own, so it is often to deceive your adversaries in their suits. It will now and then deceive your partner also; but if done with judgment, it is, I think, oftener attended with good than bad effect.

There are also other situations, where it is highly necessary to deceive the adversary. A, last player, has a tierce-major and a small trump; a tierce-major with two others of a second suit; king, and a small one of a third; with queen or knave, and a small one of the fourth; of which his adversary leads the ace. It is so very material for A to get the lead, before he is forced, that he should without hesitation throw down the queen, as the most likely method to induce his adversary to change his lead. But this mode of play should be reserved for material occasions, and not by its frequency give cause for its being suspected.

Beginners find it difficult to distinguish between original and forced leads. When a player changes his original suit, he commonly leads his strongest card of another, to give his partner the advantage of a finesse. In this case you are to play this, as if it was your own or adversary's lead—keep the commanding card, tenace, &c., and do not return it, as if it was an original lead.

There is nothing more necessary to be explained to the beginner, than what is usually denominated under-play, as it is a constant engine in the hands of the experienced, to use successfully against the inexperienced player. In other words, it is to return the lowest of your left-hand adversary's lead, though you have the highest in your hand, with a view of your partner's making the third best, if he has it, and still retaining the commanding card in your hand.

To explain this farther, suppose A, fourth player, has ace and king of his left-hand adversary's lead; to under-play, he wins the trick with the ace, and returns the small one, which will generally succeed, if the leader has not the second and third in his own hand. You will see bv this, if you lead from a king, &c. and your right-hand adversary, after winning with a ten or knave, return it, you have no chance to make your king, but by putting it on.

The following is another situation to under-play; A remains with the first, third, and fourth cards of a suit, of which he has reason to suppose his left-hand adversary has the second guarded; by playing the fourth, it is often passed, and A makes every trick in the suit.

N.B. This sort of play is always right in trumps; but if weak in them, it is generally the best play to make your certain tricks as fast as you can; for if you have not your share of them, somebody must have more than their own, and of consequence be weak in some other suit, which probably is your strong one.

Keep the trump card as long as you can, if your partner leads trumps; the contrary, if your adversary leads them. In the former instance, supposing the eight turned up, and you have the nine, throw away the latter; in the last (though you have the seven or six) play the card you turned up.

When your partner is to lead, and you call before he plays, it is to direct him, if he has no honour, to play off the best trump he has.

Though according to the strict laws of Whist, all words and gestures are prohibited; yet, like all other laws not enforced by penalties, they are continually violated. There are, indeed, few players who do not discover, in some degree, the strength of their game, or their approbation or disapprobation of their partner's play, &c. As this is on one side often a material advantage to the party transgressing, so it is quite allowable for the adversaries to make use of it. Attentive and silent observation will frequently give an early insight into the game, and enable you to play your hand to more advantage than by adhering to more regular maxims.

Though tenace, or the advantage of position, cannot be reduced to a certainty, as at piquet; and that it is often necessary to relinquish it for more certain advantages; still no man can be a whist player who does not fully understand it. The principle is simple, but the combinations are various. It is easily conceived, that if A has ace, queen, and a small card of a suit, of which B has king, knave, and another; if A leads the small card, he remains tenace, and wins two tricks; whereas, if he plays the ace, he gives it up and makes but one. But if B is to lead, he has no tenace, and lead which card he will, he must make one trick, and can make no more. This easy instance, well considered, will enable the player, with some practice, to adapt it to more apparently intricate situations.

The following cases, which happen frequently, will further explain this: A is left with four cards and the lead, viz. the second and fourth trump, and the ace and a small card of a suit not played. Nine trumps being out, B, his left-hand adversary, has the first and third trump, king and a small one of the suit of which A leads the ace. *Query*, what card should B play? *Answer*, the king; by which he brings it to an equal chance whether he wins three tricks or two, but if he keeps the king he cannot possibly win three.

By placing the cards you will perceive, that if B's partner has a better card than A's, it prevents A from making either of his trumps, which, had B retained the king, he must have done.

A has three cards of a suit not played, (the last remaining) viz. king, queen, and ten; B, ace, knave, and another; A leads the king; if B wins it he gives up the tenace, and gets but one trick; whereas if he does not, he makes his ace and knave by preserving it.

A has ace, knave, and ten, of a suit which his partner leads. *Query*, which should he put on? *Answer*, the ten, particularly if it is a forced lead; by this he probably wins two tricks. If he puts on the ace, and his partner has no honour in the suit, he gives up the tenace, and can only win one.

Tenace is easily kept against your right-hand, but impossible, without great superiority of skill, against your left-hand adversary.

To explain what is meant by playing to points, place the following hand before you: A has the two lowest trumps, and two forcing cards, with the lead. The two best demonstrably in the adversary's hands; though uncertain if in the same or divided. Nine cards being played, and no trump remaining —*Query*, what is A to play? *Answer*,—this can only be decided by the situation of the score, and whether or no it justifies the hazarding two tricks for one. The least consideration will convince the player, that before the score is much advanced, it would be highly improper for A to play a trump, because he manifestly ventured two tricks for one; of course he should secure two tricks by playing a forcing card. But suppose A to be at the score of seven, and that he has won six tricks, he should then as clearly venture to play the trump, because if the trumps are divided, he wins the game, or otherwise remains at seven, which is preferable to the certainty of scoring nine. But if the adversary is at nine, this should not be done, as by hazarding the odd trick, you hazard the game.

N.B. This mode of reasoning will in general direct you where and when finesses are proper or improper. For there is scarcely one, though ever so right in general, but what the different situations of the score and hand may render dangerous and indefensible.

The following critical stroke decided one of the most material rubbers that ever was played, and is recommended to the attentive perusal even of proficients.

The parties were each at nine. A had won six tricks, and remained with knave, and a small trump, and two diamonds with the lead. B, his left-hand adversary, with the queen and ten of trumps, and two clubs. C, his partner, with two small trumps, and two diamonds. D, last player, with ace and a small trump, a club, and a heart. A led a diamond, which being passed by B, was to be won by D. *Query*— How is he to play, to make it possible to win the odd trick? *Answer*—D saw it was not possible, unless his partner had either the two best trumps, or the first and third, with a successful finesse. He therefore trumped with the ace, led the small one, and won the game.

N.B. In another score of the game, this would not be justifiable, as the chance of losing a trick is greater than that of gaining one by it.

The attentive perusal (in the mode prescribed) of these maxims, will, I think, with a little practice, enable a beginner to play with very good cards to advantage. The difficulty of the game does not consist in this; for aces and kings will make tricks, and no skill can make a ten win a knave. But there are hands which frequently occur when skilful players win, where bunglers lose points; and (unless when the cards run very high) it is on the playing of such, success depends, viz. ace or king, and three other trumps, a tierce-major, with others of a second suit with a probable trick in a third—the player's plan should be to remain either with the last trump, or with the last but one, with the lead: and to accomplish this last, he must not win the second lead with the commanding trump, but reserve it for the third. Nothing then but five trumps in one hand can probably prevent his establishing his long suit, for he forces out the best trump, and the thirteenth brings in his suit again, which (without the lead after the third round of trumps) would be impossible.

As this maxim is of the utmost consequence, the following cases, which happen frequently, are added, to make it more clearly understood:—

A has ace and three trumps, a strong suit, headed by a tierce-major, and a probable trick in a third, and lead. *Query*—How should this hand be played? *Answer*—A should lead a trump; but if his partner wins and returns it, A should not put on his ace, but suffer it to be won by his adversary. When either A or his partner gets the lead, he of course plays a trump, which being won by A, he remains with the lead, and one, but not the best trump, though they should not be equally divided. This (his strong suit having forced out the best) establishes it again, notwithstanding the adversary may command the other suits, which are by these means prevented from making.

N.B. Had the ace been put on the second lead, the force would have been on A, and his strong suit entirely useless.

A, with a similar hand, has ace, king, and two small trumps. If the adversaries lead trumps, he should not win the first trick, even if last player. By this, after the second lead, he still retains the best for the third, according to the maxim, and establishes his suit (though the best trump keeps up against him) unless there are five in one hand originally.

With ace, queen, and two small trumps, do not win the knave led on your left-hand, but let it be played again, according to the same maxim.

As the following, or nearly similar situations frequently occur, I recommend them to the attentive perusal of those students who, feeling within themselves that they comprehend what I have called the alphabet, wish to procure a gradual insight into the game, the whole combinations of which, I cannot too often repeat, proceed from very plain and simple principles; but it requires much reflection to comprehend the same maxim, when applied to inferior cards, that appears self-evident in the superiors. There is scarcely a player, who if he has the ace, king, and knave of the suit of which his right-hand adversary turns up the queen, but will lead the king, and wait for the return to the finesse his knave. But with ace, queen, and ten, (the knave being turned up on his right-hand) the same player will not see that his lead, if he plays a trump, is the queen, and that one and the same principle actuates the players on both occasions, and so through the suit.

It constantly happens that the adversary on the right-hand having won his partner's lead with the ace or king, returns the knave. In this case do not put on the queen, as the probability is against its being finessed. But on all these occasions, play without hesitation, which constantly directs a skilful adversary where to finesse to advantage.

It frequently happens when you have led from six trumps, that after your second lead you remain with three or four trumps, the best in your adversary's hand, in these situations play a small trump, which has these two advantages.—1st. To prevent the stopping of your partner's suit—and 2d, to give you the tenace, in whatever suit is led by the adversary. This, *mutatis mutandis*, will shew that it is bad play to put out the best trump, leaving others in the hand of one of your adversaries. It may do good to keep it up, by stopping a suit, and can answer no good purpose whatever to play it out.

A remains with the best trump (say the ten) and a small one, with some losing cards, B, his partner, having clearly the second best, (say the nine) with some winning cards; the adversaries having one small trump and winning cards of the other two suits. A is forced. *Query*—How is he to play? *Answer*—A is to ruff with his best, and lead out his small trump, by which he puts it into his partner's hand to make his winning cards, and renders those of his adversaries of no use whatever. This mode of play would sometimes be right, even when it was not certain whether the second best trump were in his partner's or his adversary's hand; but the fine player alone can be expected to distinguish on so nice an occasion.

There are points where good players disagree. Some play what is called a forward—others a more timid game. Some commonly put on a king, second; others but rarely. In these cases a man may play either way, without committing error; but where all good players are of the same opinion, it should be received as an axiom—no good player puts on a queen, knave, or ten, second; of course, it should on all occasions be carefully avoided.

The possession of the last trump is of most material advantage in the hands of a good player. A has the thirteenth trump, with the ace and four small ones of a suit not played, of which the adversary leads the king and queen; by passing them both, A probably makes three tricks in the suit; but had he won the king, he could not possibly make more than one.

When it is at your option to be eight or nine, it is material always to choose the former score.

Observe carefully what is originally discarded by each player, and whether at the time, the lead is with the partner or adversary. If with the former, it is invariably meant to direct the partner—if with the latter, it is frequently intended to deceive the adversary, and induce him to lead to his strong suit.

You are not only to take every method to preserve the

tenace or advantage of the position to yourself, when it is evident that the winning cards lie between you and your adversary, but also to give it as much as possible to your partner, when you perceive the strength in any suit is in the hands of him and your left-hand adversary; always keeping in your mind, that when the latter or you lead, the tenace is against, if your partner lead, it is for the adversary. It frequently happens, that by winning your partner's trick, when last player, you accomplish this. A has king, knave (or any other second and fourth card), with a small one of a suit, that B, his left-hand adversary, has the first and third, and another with the lead. If A leads his card, and B, your partner, wins it; you, last player, should, if possible, win the trick, though it is your partner's. By which means you prevent A from making a trick, which he must have done, had the lead remained with B.

As I have ventured to recommend occasional deviations from what is considered as one of the most classic maxims; *i. e.* leading from single cards, without that strength in trumps, hitherto judged indispensably necessary to justify it; I give the reasons that influence my opinion, in favour of this practice, with those generally alleged against it, leaving the reader to determine between them. Two objections are made, which, it cannot be denied, may and do happen. The first, that if your partner has the king of the suit guarded, and the ace behind it, he loses it; which would not be the case, if the lead came from the adversary. The second, and most material, is, that your partner, if he wins the trick, may lead out trumps, on the supposition it is your strong suit, or the adversaries from suspecting your intention. On the contrary, the constant and certain advantages are the preservation of the tenace in the other two suits, which I suppose you to have, and the probable one of making your small trumps, which you could not otherwise do. A has four small trumps, ace, queen, &c. of the second suit; king, knave, &c. of a third: and a single card of the fourth. In these sort of hands, I am opinion, that the chance of winning, by leading the single card, is much greater than of losing tricks; and I appeal to those who are in the habit of attending whist tables, whether they do not frequently see the players who proceed more exactly according to the maxims of Hoyle, &c. after

losing the game, trying to demonstrate that this ought not to
have happened, and that they have been vanquished, by the
bad, not good play of their adversaries.   I do not recommend
in general leading from single cards, unless very strong in
trumps; but with such hands as I have mentioned, I am
convinced it may be occasionally done with very great,
though not certain advantage.   It may not be unnecessary
to inform the reader, that most of Hoyle's maxims were
collected during what may be called the infancy of Whist;
and that he himself, so far from being able to teach the game,
was not fit to sit down even with the third-rate players of the
present day.

I shall conclude these maxims by a short recapitulation of
the most material ones, by way of fixing them in the minds of
the readers.

Let them be assured that without comprehending the leads,
modes of playing sequences, and an attentive observation of
the board, it is as impossible to make any progress in the
science of Whist, as to learn to spell before they know their
alphabet.

That accustoming themselves to reason by analogy, will
alone teach them to vary their play according to circumstances; and shew them, that the best play in some, is the
worst in different situations of the game.   It is common to
see even good players hazard the game, merely to gain the
applause of ignorant by-standers, by making as much of their
cards as they are capable of; but this pitiful ambition cannot
be too much guarded against.   Avoid also the contrary
extreme, the faults of the old, and many of the imitators, of
the new school.   These never part with a tenace, or certain
trick, though for the probability of making several; and are
like fences who parry well the attack.   No player of this kind
can ever excel, though he may reach mediocrity.

I must also repeat my advice to proficients, to vary their
play according to the set they are engaged with; and recollect that it would be of no advantage to speak French like
Voltaire, if you lived with people who are ignorant of the
language.

On Leads.

The safest leads are, from sequences of three or more cards

lead the highest, and put on the lowest to your partner's lead; but the highest on your adversary's. With a tierce to the king and several others, begin with the knave.

With ace, king, knave, and three small trumps, play out the ace and king—with only two the king, and wait for the finesse of the knave. In other suits, without great strength in trumps, or with the hopes of a particular point, do not wait for the finesse.

Ace, king, and five others, lead the ace in all suits. With four or less, the lowest, if trumps. In other suits, always the ace, unless all the trumps remaining are with you and your partner; in this case a small one.

Ace, queen, knave, &c., in all suits the ace. Ace, queen, ten, with others, in trumps, a small one; but if with three, unless very strong in trumps, lead the ace in other suits.

Ace, knave, with small ones, lead the lowest in trumps; in other suits, if with more than two, lead the ace, unless very strong in trumps.

Ace, with four small ones, in trumps, lead the lowest. If with four or more in other suits, and not very strong in trumps, the ace.

N.B. It is the general custom with ace and one other, to lead the ace —this is right if you have reason to think it your partner's suit, otherwise lead the small one.

King, queen, ten, &c., in all suits, lead the king; but if it passes, do not pursue the lead, as certain the ace is in your partner's hand as it is often kept up, but change your lead, and wait for the return from your partner when you have the finesse of the ten, if necessary.

King, queen, and five others, in all suits, the king. With four or less in trumps, lead the lowest. In other suits, always the king, unless you have the two only remaining trumps; if so, you may play a small one.

King, knave, ten, &c., in all suits, lead the ten. King, knave, and two or more small ones, the lowest.

NB. You should not lead from king, knave, and a small one, unless it is clearly your partner's suit, in which case, play off your king and knave.

Queen, knave, nine, and others, lead the queen. Queen, knave, with one other, the queen. Queen, knave, with two more, the lowest.—Queen, ten, and two others, the lowest.

Queen, and three small ones, the lowest.   Queen, or knave, with only two, the queen, or knave.

N.B. The trump card sometimes occasions a deviation from these rules. A has the ace or king, with a sequence from the ten downwards, of the suit of which his left-hand adversary turns up knave or queen. A should lead the ten. If the knave or queen be put on, you have a finesse with the nine; if not, your partner, with an honor, will pass it, and is either way advantageous.

The following calculations are sufficient for a beginner; deeper ones frequently puzzle even the proficient:—

That either player has not one named card, not in your hand, is .... 2 to 1

   5 to 4 in favour of his having............................. 1 of 2

   5 to 2 .... 1 in 3

   4 to 1 .... 1 in 4

N.B. The odds are so considerable, that no player has two or more named cards, that scarce any situation justifies playing on this supposition, except the impossibility of saving or winning the game otherwise; of course further calculations are more for curiosity than utility.

The odds of the game are calculated according to the points, and with the deal:

   1 love .... 10 to 9

   2 love .... 10 to 8

and so on, except that 2 is considered as something worse than 8. It is 3 to 1 in favour of the first game.

N.B. Notwithstanding that calculations are in general accurate, it is difficult to conceive that 10 in 20 is 3 to 1, while 5 in 10 is but 2 to 1, and even 6 in 10 is but 5 to 2. I am convinced whoever bets the 3 to 1, will lose on the long run; and on the contrary, he who bets the 2 to 1, and 5 to 2, will gain in the same proportion.

The odd trick has always been supposed in favour of the leader; but this is an error, as the dealer has the advantage in this, as in every other score.

———

** It will be perceived that the *Laws* of the game are not given in the preceding pages; they will be found in Part II, according to Hoyle; in Part III, according to Deshapelles; and in Part IV, according to the Editor.

PART THE SECOND.

THOUGH not the first writer on the game of Whist, Hoyle was undoubtedly the first of any authority. Long before he wrote, there existed certain rules for ordering its economy, as well as for playing it upon system. Like most other samples of " the good old times," Whist, as practised in the days of our forefathers, was no such shining light of the *prisca fides*. We take it up at an epoch in which the game must have attained a certain amount of respectability, namely, in the year 1734, when Richard Seymour, Esquire, published the fifth edition of his " Compleat Gamester, for the use of the Young Princesses." If his record be true, which there is good reason to believe was the case, society in the reign of George the Second was by no means in a state of chivalry as to morals. He shall tell his own tale, and in his own fashion.

Whist, vulgarly called "Whisk."

" This is a very ancient game among us ; and is said to be the foundation of all the English games upon the cards.

" Very few persons play correctly at it ; though there are many pretenders, who are the easiest to be made, and generally are made, the greatest bubbles.

" Considerable sums of money are played away at this game ; which has put sharpers upon inventions to deceive and cheat unwary players, as will be shewed in the sequel.

" Formerly it was usual to deal four cards together ; but it is demonstrable there is no safety in that method ; but now the cards are dealt round one and one at a time, as the securest and best way.

" In playing your cards, you must have recourse altogether to your own judgment ; and though you have but mean cards

in your hand, yet you may (by observing the course of the
cards) play them so suitable to those in your partner's hand,
that he may either trump them or play the best of that suit on
the board.

"You ought to have a strict eye on what cards are played
out, that you may know by that means either what to play, if
you lead, or how to trump securely and advantageously.
Renouncing, or not following suit when you have it in your
hand, is very foul play; and he that doth it ought to forfeit
one, or the game upon a game, and he that loseth dealing
loseth one, or a trick, as you make it.

"At ruff and honours, by some called slam, you have in the
pack all the deuces, and the reason is, because four persons
playing having dealt twelve a-piece, there are four left for the
stock, the uppermost whereof is turned up, and that is trumps,
He who hath ace of trumps ruffs, that is, he takes in those
four cards, and lays out four; the four honours are the ace,
king, queen, and knave; he who hath three honours in his
hand, his partner not having the fourth, sets up eight by
cards, that is, two tricks; if he hath all four, then sixteen,
that is, four tricks.   It is all one if the two partners make
them three or four between them, as if one had them.   If the
honours are equally divided among the gamesters of each side,
then they say honours are split.   If either side are at eight
groats, he hath the benefit of calling, Can ye?   If he hath
two honours in his hand, and if the other answers one, the
game is up, which is ten in all; but if he hath more than two
he shows them, which is the same thing; but if he forgets to
call, after playing a trick, he loseth the advantage of calling
for that deal.

"All cards are of value as they are superior one to another,
as a ten wins a nine, if not trumps; so a queen a knave in
like manner; but the least trump will win the highest card of
any other card: where note, the ace is the highest.

"Some play at two-handed, or three-handed Whist.   If
three-handed, always two strive to suppress and keep down
the rising man.   They deal to each twelve a-piece, and the
trump is the bottom card.   The manner of crafty playing, the
number of the game ten, honours and dignity of other cards
are all alike; and he that wins most tricks is most forward to
win the set.

"He that can by craft overlook his adversary's game, hath a great advantage; for by that means he may partly know what to play securely; or if he can have some petty glimpse of his partner's hand. There is a way by making some sign by the fingers, to discover to their partners what honours they have, or by the wink of one eye, it signifies one honour, shutting both eyes two; placing three fingers or four on the table, three or four honours. For which reasons all nice gamesters play behind curtains.

" Dealing the cards out by one and one round to each person, is the best method of putting it out of the dealer's power to impose on you. But we shall demonstrate that, deal the cards which way you will, a confederacy of two sharpers will beat any two persons in the world, though ever so good players, that are not of the gang, or in the secret; and three poll one is as safe and secure as if the money was in their pockets, All which will appear presently. The first necessary instructions to be observed at Whisk, as principals of the secret, which may be likewise transferred to most other games at cards, are

> Breef Cards.
> Corner-bend.
> Middle-bend (or Kingston-bridge).

" Of breef cards there are two sorts: one is a card longer than the rest; the other is a card broader than the rest.

"The long sort are such as three, four, five, six, seven, eight, and nine; the broad sort are such as aces, kings, queens, and knaves. The use and advantage of each are as follows.

Example.

"When you cut the cards to your adversary, cut them long or end-ways, and he will have a three, four, five, six, seven, eight, or nine at bottom. When your adversary cuts the cards to you, put them broadside to him, and he will naturally cut (without ever suspecting what you do) ace, king, queen, or knave, &c., which is sufficient advantage to secure any game. It is a fine manner, especially in the old bet that the dealer does not score two that deal, since shuffling is of no signification here. And in case you cannot get cards of the proper sizes ready made to mix with others, you may shave them with a razor or penknife from the threes to the nines each

D

side, and from the aces to the knave each end; then put them up in the same case or cover, and if they are done as they ought to be, they will pass upon anybody. As Whisk is a tavern game, the sharpers generally take care to put about the bottle before the game begins, so quick that a bubble cannot be said to see clearly even when he first begins to play.

"The next is the corner-bend, which is four cards turned down finely at one corner, a signal to cut by.

"The other is vulgarly called Kingston-bridge, or the middle-bend : it is done by bending your own or adversary's tricks two different ways, which will cause an opening or arch in the middle, which is of the same use and service as the other two ways, and only practised in its turn to amuse you.

"After a deal or two is formally played, A and B will begin to operate in the following manner :

"When A or B are to deal, they observe (the preceding deal) to take up the tricks thus :

  1. A bad card.   2. A good card.
  3. A bad card.   4. A good card.

[Meaning the best and worst that fall in that lift.]

"When C or D deals, they must be taken up thus:

  1. A good card. 2. A bad card.
  3. A good card. 4. A bad card.

" By this rule it is very plain that the best cards fall to A and B every deal. How is it possible, therefore, that C and D should ever win a game without permission? But it would be deemed ill policy, and contrary to the true interest of A and B, to act thus every deal : I will therefore suppose it is practised just when they please, according as bets happen in company ; though the rule with gamesters, in low life, is at the first setting out to stupify you with wine and the loss of your money, that you may never come to a perfect understanding of what you are doing. It may be truly said, that many an honest gentleman has been kept a month in such a condition by the management and contrivance of a set of sharpers.

" Now you may imagine it not in the power of A and B to cause the tricks to be taken up after the manner aforesaid; but there is nothing so easy or so frequently practised, especially at three poll one; for in playing the cards, the confederates will not only take care of their own tricks, but also of yours ; for the cards may be so played and shoved together in such a manner, as will even cause you to take them right yourself; and if a trick should lie untowardly upon the table, A or B will pay you the compliment of taking it up for you, and say, Sir, that's yours.

" This operation will the more readily be apprehended by seeing it practised half a score times ; when once you are aware of it, it will otherwise (I may safely say) pass upon any person that has not been let into the secret. This being allowed, the next point and difficulty is to shuffle and cut.

" I say, that either A or B are such curious workmen, and can make a sham shuffle with a pack of cards so artfully, that you would believe they were splitting them, when at the same time they will not displace a single card from its order.

" Now to cut the cards, a bend is prepared for you to cut to; the middle is best, and it is odds but you unwarily cut to it ; if not, Slip is the word ; but if you have no opportunity to do that neither, then deal away at all hazards, it is but an equal bet that they come in your favour; if right, proceed ; if otherwise, miss a card in its course, and it brings the cards according to your first design; it is but giving two at last where you missed ; and if that cannot be conveniently done, you only lose the deal, and there is an end of it.

" But when A or B are to cut, they make it all safe ; for then they make the corner-bend, which any one that knows may cut to, a hundred times together.

Piping at Whisk.

"By piping I mean, when one of the company that does not play (which frequently happens) sits down in a convenient place to smoke a pipe, and so look on, pretending to amuse himself that way. Now the disposing of his fingers on the pipe, whilst smoking, discovers the principal cards that are in the person's hand he overlooks; which was always esteemed a sufficient advantage to win a game by another way, viz., Indeed, signifies diamonds ; Truly, hearts ; Upon my word, clubs ; I assure you, spades : but as soon as these methods become known new ones are invented ; and it is most certain that two persons may discover to each other what sort of cards they have in hand, and which ought to be first played, many different ways, without speaking a word. Talking is not allowed at Whist ; the very word implies, Hold your tongue."

Mr. Seymour's whole book indeed indicates a very truculent social condition at the date of its indicting. "The games," he says, " are always precarious, and betting money that way was thought to be like licking honey off thorns . . . I have been told of one of these sharpers who caused a box to be made, not as they are usually, screwed within, but smooth, and procured it to be so well painted and shadowed within, that it looked like a screwed box; now this box was but half board, wide at the top and narrow at the bottom, that the dice might stick, and the box being smooth, would come out without tumbling. With this box he went and played at Inn and Inn*, by virtue whereof, and his art of taking up and throwing his dice into the box, he got the first night £1000, and the next night £200 a year, with a coach and six horses, and enjoys the estate to this day with great improvements, and never would handle a dice since, well knowing how many worthy families it hath ruined." Moreover we read, as no doubt "the young princesses" read also, how that at the " Game of Nazarene," the knave of clubs is called Knave-Knocker, and he that hath it challengeth two a piece. If women play among men, it is customary for Knave-Knocker to kiss Queen Nazarene, a practice that would extend of course to a royal lady of any kith or country.

In 1743, was published, as we have already said, the treatise ascribed to Hoyle, the great father of the game. It saw the light when obviously it was much needed. Public taste seems just then to have taken up Whist as a necessary accomplishment, for persons of condition. There is the following passage in " A Lady's Letter," in the " Rambler," of May 8, 1750. " Papa made me drudge at whist till I was tired of it; and Mr. Hoyle, when he had not given me above forty lessons, said I was one of his best scholars." The anonymous " Treatise" may however be spared quotation beyond the advertisement, a curious document, helping us to a view of the period, in relation to such matters as came within compass of its observation.

" As some people in particular may be anxious to know,

---

* This was one of those gambling contrivances, known in those days as " Games without the Tables." Hazard belonged to this class.

and the public in general may be glad to be informed, by what means the following Treatise came to be ushered into the world in this manner, we think they cannot be better satisfied on this head, than by making public the following letter from a gentleman at Bath to a friend of his, and hope they will not take it amiss if the gentleman's name is concealed, since we are not at liberty to publish it.

" ' Dear Sir,

" ' In an age where the ignorant and the unwary, as well as the plain downright honest man of sense, are so exposed to the tricks of sharpers of all denominations, from the counter up to the most sacred and respectable offices and institutions, I thought it would be doing no inconsiderable service to many of my countrymen, if I contributed a little to put them upon their guard and preserve their purses, while they are indulging themselves in what is elegantly called killing time. It were indeed to be wished that less time was killed in the manner which has put me upon this undertaking, but as the itch of gaming is likely to prevail as long as we preserve anything of what is now-a-days called polite taste; and as it seems to be an almost necessary evil, which keeps people of a certain disposition from employing their time worse, so I hope I shall deserve the thanks of a great many, for having been instrumental in rescuing them from the snares which they are but too frequently caught in, by being over-matched in these sorts of amusements.

" ' I myself, as you very well know, am one of those unfortunate beings, that being possessed of a pretty handsome fortune, and having a great deal of idle time upon their hands, constantly spend a little portion of it in gaming. The game of Whist is that which I take most delight in, and till of late, fancied myself all along a pretty good master of it. But to my vexation, it is not long since I lost a considerable sum of money one night at it, and yet I could not perceive that the cards run extraordinary cross against me; so that I could not but conclude I was beat by superior skill. This put me upon inquiring into the cause, for I was very far from imputing my misfortune to unfair play; and at last I found that there was a treatise on the game of Whist lately dispersed among a few hands at a guinea price. How to come at one of these books I knew not; but at length I wrote to an acquaintance of mine in London to purchase it for me by all means, which he accordingly did, with no small difficulty. As soon as I had perused it, I found I had heretofore been but a bungler at this game, and being thoroughly sensible of the advantage which those that are possessed of this book have over the innocent player, I thought I could not oblige my friends better than by printing a few of them to make presents of. Accordingly I applied to a stationer, who offered to make me a present of half a hundred of them, provided I would allow him to print a few more for his own use. This I readily complied with, especially in consideration of the imposition and hardship the public lay under; first, by not being able to get the said book under a guinea, and then by its being reserved only in a few hands, that might make a bad use of it: for though a man of superior skill in these amusements, that takes an advantage of an ignorant player, cannot, according to the common acceptation of the word, be deemed a sharper, yet, when he pursues that advantage, after he has found out the weakness of his antagonist, it must be confessed that if he is not a sharper, he is at least very near akin to one.

" ' Thus much I have thought fit to acquaint you with, in regard to my conduct in this affair, which I hope will receive the commendations of every honest well-meaning man and fair gamester, and your's in particular, which is the greatest ambition of your sincere friend, and humble servant.' "

We now come to deal with Hoyle in *propriâ personâ*, the professor who took up an art which society had adopted, with all the enthusiasm that fancies it has discovered a specific against *ennui*. He arose a benefactor of his race. Poetry never sung of patience so tried as it has been, and ever will be, at the Whist table.

> " Sir, I protest, were Job himself at play,
> He'd rave to see you throw your cards away :
> Not that I care a button, not a pin,
> For what I lose—but we have cards to win.
> A saint in heaven would grieve to see such hand,
> Cut up by one who will not understand."

We start with Hoyle at the commencement of the present

century, when the game had assumed most of its principles.
A century before, it differed essentially in several respects
from the fundamental rules now established, and fifty years
ago, recognized.   For instance in Swift's time, it went
generally by the double title of "Whist" and "Swabbers."
These "swabbers" were certain cards, the possession of which
entitled the holders to a part of the stakes; in the same way
that now a claim is made for the aces at quadrille.   In like
manner, there was no bar to counting honours, they reckoned
at nine, as well as at any other score.   It is not clear when
the existing custom of their not counting after eight first
obtained.   M. Deschapelles calls it "a fashionable embellishment."   His observatons, always most pertinent, will be read
with much interest, on this and many other modern innovations   Our text of Hoyle has been carefully collated with
the different editions, some of which are faulty.   We omit
for the present the *mise en scene*, which will be minutely
detailed in Part the Third.

HOYLE'S GENERAL RULES FOR BEGINNERS.

WHEN you lead, begin with the best suit in your hand; if
you have a sequence of king, queen, and knave, or queen,
knave, and ten, they are sure leads, and gain the tenace
to yourself and your partner in other suits.   Begin with the
highest of a sequence, unless you have five in number; in
that case play the lowest (except in trumps, when you must
always play the highest) in order to get the ace or king out of
your partner's or adversary's hand, to make room for your
strong suit.

If you have five of the smallest trumps, and not one good
card in the other suits, trump out, which will make your
partner the last player, and by that means give him the
tenace.

If two small trumps only, with ace and king of two other
suits, and a deficiency of the fourth suit, make as many tricks
as you can immediately; and if your partner refuses either of
your suits, do not force him, because that may weaken his
game too much.

You need seldom return your partner's lead immediately,
if you have good suits of your own to play, unless it be to

endeavour to save or win a game; what is meant by good suits is, sequences of king, queen, and knave, or queen, knave, and ten.

If you have each five tricks, and you are assured of getting two tricks in your own hand, win them, in expectation of scoring two that deal; because if you lose the odd trick, it makes two difference, and you play two to one against yourself.

An exception to the foregoing rule is, when you see a probability either of saving your lurch or winning the game; in either of which cases risk the odd trick.

When you have a probability of winning the game, always risk a trick or two, because the share of the stake, which your adversary has by a new deal, will amount to more than the point or two which you risk.

If your adversary is six or seven love, and you are to lead, in that case risk a trick or two, in hopes of putting the game upon an equality; therefore, admitting you have the queen or knave, and one other trump, and no good cards in other suits, play out your queen or knave of trumps; by which means you will strengthen your partner's game, if he is strong in trumps; if weak, you do him no injury.

If you are four of the game, play for an odd trick, because it saves one-half of the stake; and, in order to win the odd trick, though you are pretty strong in trumps, be cautious how you trump out. What is meant by strength in trumps, is, 1 honour and 3 trumps.

If you are nine of the game, and though very strong in trumps, yet if you observe your partner to have a chance of trumping any of your adversary's suits; then do not trump out, but give him an opportunity of trumping those suits. If your game is scored one, two, or three, you must play the reverse; and also five, six, or seven; because in these two last recited cases, you play for more than one point.

If you are last player, and find that the third hand cannot put on a good card to his partner's lead, admitting you have no good game of your own to play, return the lead upon the adversary; which gives your partner the tenace in that suit, and often obliges the adversary to change suits, and consequently gives the tenace in that new suit also.

If you have ace, king, and four small trumps, begin with a

small one; because it is an equal wager that your partner has a better trump than the last player; if so, you have three rounds of trumps; if not, you cannot fetch out all the trumps.

If ace, king, knave, and three small trumps, begin with the king, and then play the ace, (except one of the adversaries refuses trumps,) because the odds are in your favour that the queen falls.

If king, queen, and four small trumps, begin with a small one, because the odds are on your side that your partner has an honour.

If king, queen, ten, and three small trumps, begin with the king, because you have a fair chance that the knave falls in the second round, or you may finesse your ten upon the return of trumps from your partner.

If queen, knave, and four small trumps, begin with a small one, because the odds are in your favour that your partner has an honour.

If queen, knave, nine, and three small trumps, begin with the queen, because you have a fair chance that the ten falls in the second round; or you may wait to finesse the nine.

If knave, ten, and four small trumps, begin with a small one.

If knave, ten, eight, and three small trumps, begin with the knave, in order to prevent the nine from making a trick; and the odds are in your favour that the other three honours fall in two rounds.

If six trumps of a lower denomination, begin with the lowest, unless you should have ten, nine, and eight, and an honour turns up against you; in that case, if you are to play through the honour, begin with the ten, which obliges the adversary to play his honour to his disadvantage, or leave it in your partner's option, whether he will pass it or not.

If ace, king, and three small trumps, begin with a small one.

If ace, king, and knave, and two small trumps, begin with the king, which, next to a moral certainty, informs your partner that you have ace and knave remaining; and by putting the lead into your partner's hand, he plays you a trump; upon which you are to finesse the knave, and no ill consequence can attend such play, except the queen lies behind you single.

If king, queen, and three small trumps, begin with a small one.

If the queen, knave, and three small trumps, begin with a small one.

If queen, knave, nine, and two small trumps, begin with the queen.

If knave, ten, and three small trumps, begin with a small one.

If knave, ten, eight, and two small trumps, begin with the knave, because in two rounds of trumps it is odds but that the nine falls; or upon the return of trumps from your partner, you may finesse the eight.

If five trumps of a lower denomination, it is the best play to begin with the lowest, unless you have a sequence of ten, nine, and eight; in that case begin with the highest of the sequence.

If ace, king, and two small trumps, begin with a small one.

If ace, king, knave, and one small trump, begin with the king.

If king, queen, and two small trumps, begin with a small one.

If king, queen, ten, and one small trump, begin with the king, and wait for the return of trumps from your partner, when finesse your ten, in order to win the knave.

If queen, knave, nine, and one small trump, begin with the queen, in order to prevent the ten from making a trick.

If knave, ten, and two small trumps, begin with a small one. one.

If knave, ten, eight, and one small trump, begin with the knave, in order to prevent the nine from making a trick.

If ten, nine, eight, and one small trump, begin with the ten, which leaves it in your partner's discretion whether he will pass it or not.

If ten, and three small trumps, begin with a small one.

SOME PARTICULAR RULES.

If you have ace, king, and four small trumps, with good suit, play three rounds of trumps, otherwise you may have your strong suit trumped.

If king, queen, and four small trumps, with a good suit, trump out with the king, because when you have the lead again, you will have three rounds of trumps.

If king, queen, ten, and two small trumps, begin with the king.

If king, queen, ten, and three small trumps, with a good suit, trump out with the king, in expectation of the knave's falling at the second round; and do not wait to finesse the ten, for fear your strong suit should be trumped.

If queen, knave, and three small trumps, with a good suit, trump out with a small one.

If queen, knave, nine, and two small trumps, with a good suit, trump out with the queen, in expectation of the ten falling at the second round; and do not wait to finesse the nine, but trump out a second time, for the reason assigned above.

If knave, ten, and three small trumps, with a good suit, trump out with a small one.

If knave, ten, eight, and two small trumps, with a good suit, trump out with the knave, in expectation of the nine falling at the second round.

If ten, nine, eight, and one small trump, with a good suit, trump out with the ten.

PARTICULAR GAMES.

Suppose you are elder hand, and that your game consist of king, queen, and knave of one suit; ace, king, queen, and two small cards of another suit; king and queen of the third suit, and three small trumps. You are to begin with the ace of your best suit (or a trump) which informs your partner that you have the command of that suit; but you are not to proceed with the king of the same suit, but play a trump next; and if you find your partner has no strength to support you in trumps, and that your adversary plays to your weak suit, *viz.* the king and queen only, in that case, play the king of the best suit: and if you observe a probability of either your adversaries being likely to trump that suit, proceed then and play the king of the suit of which you have king, queen, and knave. If it should so happen that your adversaries do not play to your weakest suit, in that case, though apparently your partner can give you no assistance in trumps, pursue your scheme of trumping out as often as the lead comes into your hand; by which means, supposing your partner to have but two trumps, and that your adversaries have four each, by three rounds of trumps, there remain only two trumps against you.

ELDER HAND.

Suppose you have ace, king, queen, and one small trump, with a sequence from the king of five in another suit, with four other cards of no value. Begin with the queen of trumps, and pursue the lead with the ace, which demonstrates to your partner that you have the king : and as it would be bad play to pursue trumps the third round, till you have first gained the command of your great suit, by stopping thus, it likewise informs your partner that you have the king, and one trump only remaining; because if you had ace, king, queen, and two trumps more, and trumps went round twice, you could receive no damage by playing the king the third round. When you lead sequence, begin with the lowest, because if your partner has the ace he plays it, which makes room for your suit. And since you have let your partner into the state of your game, as soon as he has the lead, if he has a trump or two remaining, he will play trumps to you, with a moral certainty that your king clears your adversaries' hands of all then trumps.

SECOND PLAYER.

Suppose you have ace, king, and two small trumps, with a quint-major of another suit; in the third suit you have three small cards and in the fourth suit one. Your adversary on your right hand begins with playing the ace of your weak suit, and then proceeds to play the king : in that case do not trump it, but throw away a losing card ; and if he proceeds to play the queen, throw away another losing card ; and do the like the fourth time, in hopes your partner may trump it, who will in that case play a trump, or will play to your strong suit. If trumps are played, go on with them two rounds, and then proceed to play your strong suit; by which means, if there happens to be four trumps in one of your adversaries' hands, and two in the other, which is nearly the case, your partner being intitled to have three trumps out of the nine ; your strong suit forces their best trumps, and you have a probability of making the odd trick in your own hand only; whereas if you had trumped one of your adversaries' best cards, you had so weakened your hand as probably not to make more than five tricks, without your partner's help.

Suppose you have ace, queen, and three small trumps; ace, queen, ten, and nine of another suit; with two small cards of each of the other suits: your partner leads to your ace, queen, ten, and nine; and as this game requires rather to deceive your adversaries, than to inform your partner, put up the nine, which naturally leads the adversary to play trumps if he wins that card. As soon as trumps are played to you, return them to your adversary, keeping the command in your own hand. If your adversary, who led trumps to you, puts up a trump which your partner cannot win, if he has no good suit of his own to play, he will return your partner's lead imagining that suit lies between his partner and your's: if this finesse of yours should succeed, you will be a great gainer by it, but scarcely possible to be a loser.

Suppose you have ace, king, and three small trumps, with a quart from a king, and two small cards of another suit, and one small card to each of the other suits; your adversary leads a suit of which your partner has a quart-major; your partner puts up the knave, and then proceeds to play the ace; you refuse to that suit by playing your loose card; when your partner plays the king, your right hand adversary trumps it. Suppose with the knave or ten, do not overtrump him, which may probably lose you two or three tricks by weakening your hand: but if he leads to the suit of which you have none, trump it, and then play the lowest of your sequence, in order to get the ace either out of your partner's or adversary's hand; which accomplished, as soon as you get the lead, play two rounds of trumps, and then proceed to play your strong suit. Instead of your adversary playing to your weak suit, if he should play trumps, do you go on with the two rounds, and then proceed to get the command of your strong suit.

GAMES TO BE PLAYED, WITH CERTAIN OBSERVATIONS, WHEREBY YOU ARE ASSURED THAT YOUR PARTNER HAS NO MORE OF THE SUIT PLAYED EITHER BY YOURSELF OR HIM.

Suppose you lead from queen, ten, nine, and two small cards of any suit, the second hand puts on the knave, your partner plays the eight: in this case, you having queen, ten, and nine, it is a demonstration, that he can have no more of that suit. Therefore you may then play your game accordingly, either by forcing him to trump that suit, if you are strong in trumps, or by playing some other suit.

Suppose you have king, queen, and ten of a suit, and you lead your king, your partner plays the knave, this demonstrates he has no more of that suit.

Suppose you have king, queen, and many more of a suit, and you begin with the king, in some cases it is good play in a partner, when he has the ace, and one small card in that suit only, to win his partner's king with his ace; for suppose he is very strong in trumps, by taking his partner's king with the ace, he trumps out, and after he has cleared the board of trumps returns his partner's lead; and having parted with the ace of that suit, has made room for his partner to make that whole suit, which possibly could not have been done if he had kept the command in his hand.

And supposing his partner has no other good card besides that suit, he loses nothing by the ace taking of his king; but if it should so happen that he has a good card to bring in that suit, he gains all the tricks which he makes in that suit, by this method of play. And as your partner has taken your king with the ace, and trumps out upon it, you have reason to judge he has one of that suit, to return you; therefore do not throw away any of that suit, even to keep a king or queen guarded.

PARTICULAR GAMES, BOTH TO ENDEAVOUR TO DECEIVE AND DISTRESS YOUR ADVERSARIES, AND TO DEMONSTRATE YOUR GAME TO YOUR PARTNER.

Suppose I play the ace of a suit of which I have king, and three small ones; the last player does not choose to trump it, having none of the suit; if I am not strong enough in trumps, I must not play out the king, but keep the command of that suit in my hand by playing a small one, in order to weaken his game.

If a suit is led, of which I have none, and a moral certainty that my partner has not the best of that suit, in order to deceive the adversary, I throw away my strong suit; but to clear up doubts to my partner when he has the lead, I throw away my weak suit. This method of play will generally succeed, unless against very good players; and even with them, you will oftener gain than lose by this method.

PARTICULAR GAMES TO BE PLAYED, BY WHICH YOU RUN
THE RISK OF LOSING ONE TRICK ONLY TO GAIN THREE.

Suppose clubs to be trumps, a heart is played by your
adversary; your partner having none of that suit, throws
away a spade; you are then to judge his hand is composed of
trumps and diamonds; and suppose you win that trick, and
being too weak in trumps, you dare not force him; and
suppose you shall have king, knave and one small diamond;
and further, suppose your partner to have queen, and five
diamonds; in that case, by throwing out your king in your
first lead, and your knave in your second, your partner and
you may win five tricks in that suit; whereas if you had led
a small diamond, and your partner's queen having been won
with the ace, the king and knave remaining in your hand
obstructs the suit: and though he may have the long trump,
yet by playing a small diamond, and his long trump having
been forced out of his hand, you lose by this method of play
three tricks in that deal.

Suppose, in the like case of the former, you should have
queen, ten, and one small card in your partner's strong suit;
which is to be discovered by the former example; and
suppose your partner to have knave and five small cards in
his strong suit; you having the lead are to play your queen,
and when you play again, you are to play your ten; and
suppose him to have the long trump, by this method he
makes four tricks in that suit; but should you play a small
one in that suit, his knave being gone, and the queen
remaining in your hand in the second round of playing that
suit, and the long trump being forced out of his hand, the
queen remaining in your hand obstructs the suit, by which
method of play you lose three tricks in that deal.

In the former examples you have been supposed to have
had the lead, and by that means have had an opportunity of
throwing out the best cards in your hand of your partner's
strong suit, in order to make room for the whole suit: we
will now suppose your partner is to lead, and in the course of
play, it appears to you that your partner has one great suit;
suppose ace, king, and four small ones, and that you have
queen, ten, nine, and a very small one of that suit; when
your partner plays the ace, you are to play the nine; when

he plays the king, you are to play the ten; by which means you see, in the third round, you make your queen, and having a small one remaining, you do not obstruct your partner's great suit; whereas if you had kept your queen and ten, and the knave had fallen from the adversaries, you had lost two tricks in that deal.

Suppose in the course of play, as in the former case, you find your partner to have one great suit, and that you have king, ten, and a small one of the same; your partner leads the ace; in that case play your ten, and in the second your king: this method is to prevent a possibility of obstructing your partner's great suit.

Suppose your partner has ace, king, and four small cards in his great suit, and that you have queen, ten, and a small card, in that suit; when he plays his ace, do you play your ten, and when he plays his king, you play your queen; by which method of play you only risk one trick to get four.

Now suppose you have five cards of your partner's strong suit; viz. queen, ten, nine, eight, and a small one; and that your partner has ace, king, and four small ones; when your partner plays the ace, do you play your eight; when he plays the king, do you play your nine; and in the third round, nobody having any of that suit, except your partner and you, proceed then to play the queen, and then the ten; and having a small one remaining, and your partner two, you thereby gain a trick.*

PARTICULAR GAMES TO BE PLAYED WHEN EITHER OF YOUR ADVERSARIES TURNS UP AN HONOUR.

Suppose the knave is turned up on your right-hand, and that you have king, queen, and ten; in order to win the knave, begin to play with your king; by which method of play, your partner may suppose you to have a queen and ten remaining, especially if you have a second lead, and that you do not proceed to your queen.

The knave being turned up as before, and that you have ace, queen, and ten, by playing your queen, it answers the like purpose of the former rule.

If the queen is turned up on your right-hand, and that you have ace, king, and knave, by playing your king it answers the like purpose of the former rule.

* These directions imply that the trumps are out.

Suppose an honour is turned up on your left-hand, and you hold no honour, in that case you are to play trumps through that honour; but in case you should hold an honour, (except the ace) you must be cautious how you play trumps, because in case your partner holds no honour, your adversary will play your own game upon you.

A CASE TO DEMONSTRATE THE DANGER OF FORCING YOUR PARTNER.

Suppose A and B partners, and that A has a quint-major in trumps, with a quint-major, and three small cards of another suit, and that A has the lead; and let us suppose the adversaries C and D to have only five trumps in either hand; in this case, A having the lead, wins every trick.

Suppose, on the contrary, C has five small trumps with a quint-major and three small cards of another suit, and that C has the lead, who forces A to trump first, by which means A wins only five tricks.

A CASE TO DEMONSTRATE THE ADVANTAGE BY A SAW.

Suppose A and B partners, and that A has a quart-major in clubs, they being trumps, another quart-major in hearts, another quart-major in diamonds, and the ace of spades. And let us suppose the adversaries C and D to have the following cards; viz. C has four trumps, eight hearts, and one spade; D has five trumps and eight diamonds; C being to lead, plays an heart, D trumps it; D plays a diamond, C trumps it, and thus pursuing the saw, each partner trumps a quart-major of A's, and C being to play at the ninth trick, plays a spade, which D trumps; thus C and D have won the nine first tricks, and leave A with his quart-major in trumps only.

Whenever you can establish a saw, it is your interest to embrace it.

VARIETY OF CASES, INTERMIXED WITH CALCULATIONS, DEMONSTRATING WHEN IT IS PROPER, AT SECOND HAND, TO PUT UP THE KING, QUEEN, KNAVE, OR TEN, WITH ONE SMALL CARD OF ANY SUIT, &c.

Suppose you have four small trumps, in the three other suits you have one trick secure in each of them: and suppose your partner has no trump, in that case the remaining nine trumps must be divided between your adversaries; suppose five in one hand, and four in the other; as often as you have the lead, play trumps: and suppose you should have four leads, in that case, your adversaries make only five tricks out of nine trumps; whereas if you had suffered them to make their trumps single, they might possibly have made nine.

This example shews the necessity of taking out two trumps for one upon most occasions.

There is an exception to the foregoing rule; if you find in the course of play, that your adversaries are very strong in any particular suit, and that your partner can give you no assistance in that suit, in such a case you are to examine your own, and also your adversaries' scores; because by keeping one trump in your hand to trump such suit, it may be either a means to save or win a game.

Suppose you have ace, queen, and two small cards of any suit, your right-hand adversary leads that suit; in that case, do not put on your queen, because it is an equal wager that your partner has a better card in that suit than the third hand; if so, you have the command of that suit.

An exception to the foregoing rule is, in case you want the lead, then you are to play your queen.

Never choose to lead from king, knave, and one small card in any suit, because it is two to one that your partner has not the ace, and also thirty-two to twenty-five, or about five to four, that he has ace or queen; and therefore, as you have only about five to four in your favour, and as you must have four cards in some other suit, suppose the ten to be the highest, lead that suit, because it is an equal wager that your partner has a better card in that suit than the last player; and if the ace of the first mentioned suit lies behind you, which is an equal wager it should so happen, in case your partner has it not; in this case, on your adversaries leading this suit, you probably make two tricks in it by this method of play.

Suppose in the course of play it appears to you that your partner and you have four or five trumps remaining, when your adversaries have none, and that you have no winning card in your hand, but that you have reason to judge that your partner has a thirteenth card or some other winning card in his hand; in that case play a small trump, to give him the lead, in order to throw away any losing card in your hand, upon such thirteenth or other good card.

SOME DIRECTIONS FOR PUTTING UP AT SECOND HAND, KING, QUEEN, KNAVE, OR TEN OF ANY SUIT, &c.

Suppose you have the king, and one small card of any suit, and that your right-hand adversary plays that suit; if he is a good player, do not put up the king, unless you want the lead, because a good player seldom leads from a suit of which he has the ace, but keeps it in his hand to bring in his strong suit after the trumps are played out.

Suppose you have a queen, and one small card, of any suit, and that your right hand adversary leads that suit; do not put on your queen, because, suppose the adversary has led from the ace and knave, in that case, upon the return of that suit, your adversary finesses the knave, which is generally good play, especially if his partner has played the king, you thereby make your queen; but by putting on the queen, it shews your adversary that you have no strength in that suit, and consequently puts him upon finessing upon your partner throughout that whole suit.

In the former examples you have been informed when it is thought proper to put up the king or queen at second hand; likewise observe, in case you should have the knave or ten of any suit, with a small card of the same, it is generally bad play to put up either of them at second hand, because it is five to two that the third hand has either ace, king, or queen, of the suit led; it therefore follows, that as the odds against you are five to two, and though you should succeed sometimes by this method of play, yet in the main you must be a loser; because it demonstrates to your adversaries, that you are weak in that suit, and consequently they finesse upon your partner throughout that whole suit.

Suppose you have ace, king, and three small cards of any suit that your right hand adversary leads; upon which you play your ace, and your partner the knave. In case you are strong in trumps, return a small one in that suit, in order to let your partner trump: and this consequence attends such play, viz. you keep the command of that suit in your own

E 2

hand, and at the same time it gives your partner an intimation that you are strong in trumps; and, therefore, he may
play his game accordingly, either in attempting to establish a
saw, or by trumping out to you, if he has either strength in
trumps, or the command of the other suits.

Suppose A and B's game is scored six, the adversaries C
and D is scored 7, and that nine rounds are played out, of
which A and B have won seven tricks, and suppose no
honours are reckoned in that deal; in this case A and B have
won the odd trick, which puts their game upon an equality;
and suppose A to have the lead, and that A has two of the
smallest trumps remaining with two winning cards of other
suits: and suppose C and D have the two best trumps between
them, with two other winning cards in their hands.   It is
eleven to three that C has not the two trumps; and likewise
eleven to three that D has them not; the odds being so much
in A's favour to win the whole stake, it is his interest to
play a trump; for suppose the stake to be £70 depending,
A and B win the whole, if he succeeds by this method; but,
on the contrary, should he play the close game, by forcing C
or D to trump first, he having won the odd trick already, and
being sure of winning two more in his own hand.   By this
method his game will be scored nine to seven, which is about
three to two, and, therefore, A's share of the £70 will amount
only to £42, and A only secures £7 profit; but in the other
case, upon supposition that A and B have eleven to three of
the stake depending, as aforesaid, A, by playing his trump,
is entitled to £35 out of the £70 depending.

The foregoing case being duly attended to, may be applied
to the like purpose in other parts of the game.

DIRECTIONS HOW TO PLAY WHEN AN ACE, KING, OR QUEEN, ARE TURNED UP ON YOUR RIGHT-HAND.

Suppose the ace is turned up on your right-hand, and that
you have the ten and nine of trumps only, with ace, king, and
queen, of another suit, and eight cards of no value.   *Query*,
How must this game be played?   Begin with the ace of the
suit of which you have the ace, king, and queen, which is an
information to your partner that you have the command of
that suit; then play your ten of trumps, because it is five to
two that your partner has king, queen, or knave of trumps;

and though it is about seven to two that your partner has not two honours, yet, should he chance to have them, and they prove to be the king and knave, in that case, as your partner will pass your ten of trumps, and as it is thirteen to twelve against the last player for holding the queen of trumps, upon supposition your partner has it not, in that case, when your partner has the lead, he plays to your strong suit, and upon your having the lead, play the nine of trumps, which puts it in your partner's power to be almost certain of winning the queen if he lies behind it.

The foregoing case shews, that turning up of an ace against you may be made less beneficial to your adversaries.

If the king or queen are turned up on your right-hand, the like method of play may be made use of; but you are always to distinguish the difference of your partner's skill, because a good player will make a proper use of such play, but a bad one seldom.

Suppose the adversary on your right-hand leads the king of trumps, and that you should have the ace and four small trumps, with a good suit; in this case it is your interest to pass the king; and though he should have king, queen, and knave of trumps, with one more if he is a moderate player, he will play the small one, imagining that his partner has the ace: when he plays the small one, you are to pass it, because it is an equal wager that your partner has a better trump than the last player. If so, and that he happens to be a tolerable player, he wil judge you have a good reason for this method, and consequently, if he has a third trump remaining, he will play it; if not, he will play his best suit.

A Critical Case to win an Odd Trick.—Suppose A and B partners against C and D, and the game to be nine all, and suppose all the trumps are played out, A being the last player, has the ace and four other small cards of a suit in his hand, and one thirteenth card remaining; B has only two small cards of A's suit; C has queen and two other small cards of that suit; D has king, knave, and one small card of the same suit. A and B have won three tricks, C and D have won four tricks; it therefore follows, that A is to win four tricks out of the six cards in his hand, in order to win the game. C leads this suit, and D puts up the king: A gives him that trick, D returns that suit; A passes it, and C puts

up his queen: thus C and D have won six tricks, and C
imagining the ace of that suit to be in his partner's hand,
returns it; by which means A wins the four last tricks, and
consequently the game.

Suppose you should have the king and five small trumps,
and that your right-hand adversary plays the queen; in that
case do not put on the king, because it is an equal wager that
your partner has the ace; and suppose your adversary should
have queen, knave, ten, and one small trump, it is also an
equal wager that the ace lies single, either in your adversary's
hand or partner's; in either of which cases it is bad play to
put on your king; but if the queen of trumps is led, and that
you should happen to have the king, with only two or three
trumps, it is the best play to put on the king, because it is
good play to lead from the queen and one small trump only:
and in that case should your partner have the knave of trumps,
and your left-hand adversary hold the ace, you neglecting to
put on the king lose a trick.

THE TEN OR NINE BEING TURNED UP ON YOUR RIGHT-HAND.

Suppose the ten is turned up on your right-hand, and that
you should have king, knave, nine, and two small trumps,
with eight other cards of no value, and that it is proper for
you to lead trumps; in that case, begin with the knave, in
order to prevent the ten from making a trick; and though it
is but about five to four that your partner holds an honour,
yet if that should fail, by finessing the nine on the return of
trumps from your partner, you have the ten in your power.

The nine being turned up on your right-hand, and that you
should have ten, eight, and two small trumps, by leading the
knave it answers the like purpose of the former case.

You are to make a wide difference between a lead of choice,
and a forced lead of your partner's; because, in the first case,
he is supposed to lead from his best suit, and finding you
deficient in that, and not being strong enough in trumps, and
not daring to force you, he then plays his next best suit; by
which alteration, it is next to a demonstration that he is
weak in trumps; but should he persevere, by playing off his
first lead, if he is a good player, you are to judge him strong
in trumps, and play your game accordingly.

There is nothing more pernicious than to change suits often, because in every new suit you run the risk of giving your adversary the tenace; and, therefore, though you lead from a suit of which you have the queen, ten, and three small ones, and your partner puts on the nine only, in that case, if you should happen to be weak in trumps, and that you have no tolerable suit to lead from, it is your best play to pursue the lead of that suit by playing your queen, which leaves it in your partner's option whether he will trump it or not, in case he has no more of that suit; but in your second lead, in case you should happen to have the queen or knave of any other suit, with one card only of the same suit, it would be better play to lead from your queen or knave of either of these suits, it being five to two that your partner has one honour at least in either of those suits.

When you have ace, king, and one small card of any suit, with four trumps; if your right-hand adversary leads that suit, pass it, because it is an equal wager that your partner has a better card in that suit than the third hand; if so, you gain a trick by it; if otherwise, as you have four trumps, you may not lose, because when trumps are played, you probably will have the long trump.

CAUTIONS NOT TO PART WITH THE COMMAND OF YOUR ADVERSARY'S GREAT SUIT, &c.

In case you are weak in trumps, and it does not appear your partner is very strong in them, be very cautious how you part with the command of your adversary's great suit; for suppose your adversary plays a suit of which you have the king, queen, and one small card only, the adversary leads the ace, and upon playing the same suit again you put on your queen, which makes it almost certain to your partner that you have the king; and suppose your partner refuses to that suit, do not play the king, because if the leader of that suit, or his partner, have the long trump, you risk the losing of three tricks to get one.

Suppose your partner has ten cards remaining, and it appears to you that they consist of trumps and one suit only; and suppose you should have king, ten, and one small card of his strong suit, with queen and two small trumps; in this case, you are to judge he has five cards of each suit, and therefore you ought to play out the king of his strong suit; and if you win that trick, your next play is to throw out the queen of trumps; if that likewise comes home, proceed to play trumps: this method of play may be made use of at any score of the game, except at four and nine.

The Trump turned up to be remembered.—It is so necessary that the trump turned up should be remembered, both by the dealer and his partner, that the dealer should always so place that card, as to be certain of having recourse to it; for suppose it to be only a five, and that the dealer has two more, viz. the six and nine, if his partner trumps out with ace and king, he ought to play his six and nine; because suppose your partner to have ace, king, and four small trumps; in this case, by your partner knowing you have the five remaining, you may win many tricks.

Your right-hand adversary leads a suit of which you have the ten and two small ones; the third hand puts up the knave, your partner wins it with the king; when your adversary leads that suit again, and plays a small one, do you put on your ten, because it may save your partner's ace, upon supposition that your right-hand adversary led from the queen.

Suppose you have the best trump, and that the adversary A has one trump only remaining, and that it appears to you that your adversary B has a great suit; in this case, though you permit A to make his trump, yet by keeping the trump in your hand, you prevent the adversary B from making his great suit; whereas, if you had taken out A's trump, it had made only one trick difference; but by this method you probably save three or four tricks.

The following Case happens frequently:—That you have two trumps remaining when your adversaries have only one, and it appears to you that your partner has one great suit; in this case always play a trump, though you have the worst, because by removing the trump out of your adversary's hand, there can be no obstruction to your partner's suit.

Suppose you should have three trumps when no one else has any, and that you should only have four cards of any certain suit remaining; in this case play a trump, which shows your partner that you have all the trumps, and also gives you a fair chance for one of your adversaries to throw away one card of the aforesaid suit; by which means, supposing that suit to have been once led, and one thrown away, makes five, and four remaining in your hand makes nine, there being only four remaining between three hands, and your partner having an equal chance to hold a better card in that suit than the last player it therefore follows that you have an equal chance to make three tricks in that suit, which probably could not otherwise have been done.

Suppose you have five trumps, and six small cards of any suit, and are to lead; then lead from the suit of which you have six, because, as you are deficient in two suits, your adversary will probably trump out, which is playing your own game; whereas, had you begun with playing trumps, they would force you, and consequently destroy your game.

THE MANNER OF PLAYING SEQUENCES FURTHER EXPLAINED.

In trumps play the highest of your sequences, unless you should have ace, king, and queen; in that case play the lowest, in order to let your partner into the state of your game.

In suits which are not trumps, if you have sequence of king, queen, and knave, and two small ones; whether you are strong in trumps or not, it is the best play to begin with the knave, because by getting the ace out of any hand, you make room for the whole suit.

And in case you are strong in trumps, supposing you should have sequence of queen, knave, ten, and two small cards of any suit; play the highest of the sequence, because, if either of the adversaries should trump that suit in the second round, you, by being strong in trumps, fetch out their trumps, and consequently make the remainder of that suit.

The like method may be taken in a sequence by knave, ten, nine, and two small cards of any suit.

If you have a sequence of a king, queen, knave, and one small card of any suit, whether you are strong in trumps or otherwise, play your king, and do the like by any inferior sequences, if you have only four in number.

But if you are weak in trumps, always begin with the lowest of the sequence in case you have five in number; for suppose your partner to have the ace of that suit, he then

makes it; and if you have the ace and four small cards of any
suit, and are weak in trumps, and led from that suit, play the
ace; and if you are very strong in trumps, you may play your
game as backward as you please; but if you are weak in
trumps, you must play the reverse.

Let us explain what is meant by being strong or weak in
trumps.

If you have ace, king, and three small trumps.

King, queen, and three small trumps.

Queen, knave, and three small trumps.

Queen, ten, and three small trumps.

Knave, ten, and three small trumps.

Queen, and four small trumps.

Knave, and four small trumps.

In any of the aforesaid cases, you may be understood to be
very strong in trumps, and therefore play by the foregoing
rules, being morally assured of having the command.

If you have two or three small trumps only, you are weak
in them.

What strength in trumps entitles you to force your partner
at any point of the game?

Ace, and three small trumps.

King, and three small trumps.

Queen, and three small trumps.

Knave, and three small trumps.

If, by accident, either you or the adversaries have forced
your partner (though you are weak in trumps) if he has had
the lead, and does not choose to trump out, force him as often
as the lead comes into your hand, unless you have good suits
of your own to play.

If you should happen to have only two or three small
trumps, and that your right-hand adversary leads a suit of
which you have none, trump it, which is an information to
your partner that you are weak in trumps.

Suppose you have ace, knave, and one small trump, and
that your partner trumps to you, suppose from the king and
three small trumps, and suppose your right-hand adversary
has three trumps, and that your left-hand adversary has the
like number; in this case, by finessing your knave, and playing your ace, if the queen is on your right-hand, you win a
trick; but if queen is on your left-hand, and you should play

the ace, and then return the knave, admitting your left-hand
adversary put on the queen, which he ought to do, it is above
two to one that one of the adversaries has the ten, and consequently you gain no tricks.

If your partner has led from the ace of trumps, and you
have king, knave, and one small trump, by putting on your
knave, and returning the king, it answers exactly the like
purpose of the former rule.

In other suits practise the like method.

If you are strong in trumps, and have king, queen, and two
or three small cards in any other suit, lead a small one, it
being five to four that your partner has an honour in that
suit, but if you are weak in trumps, you ought to begin with
the king.

If your right-hand adversary leads a suit of which you have
king, queen, and two or three small cards of the same suit,
you being strong in trumps, may pass it, because it is an
equal wager that your partner has a better card in that suit
than the third hand; if not, by your strength in trumps, you
need not fear making that suit.

If your right-hand adversary leads a suit of which you have
king, queen, and one small card, whether in trumps or not,
put on the queen: also, if you have queen, knave, and one
small card, put on the knave: and if you have knave, ten, and
one small card, put on the ten: by putting up the second
best, as aforesaid, your partner has an expectation of your
having a better card or cards in the same suit: and by the
calculations annexed to this treatise, he may judge what are
the odds for or against him.

When you have ace, king, and two small cards in any suit,
being strong in trumps; if your right-hand adversary leads
that suit, you may pass it, because it is an equal wager that
your partner has a better card in that suit than the third
hand; if so you gain a trick by it, if otherwise you need not
fear to make your ace and king by your strength in trumps.

If you have the ace, nine, eight, and one small trump, and
your partner leads the ten; in that case pass it, because,
unless the three honours lie behind you, you are sure of
making two tricks; do the like, if you should have the king,
nine, eight, and one small trump; or the queen, nine, eight,
and one small trump.

In order to deceive your adversaries, if your right-hand adversary leads from a suit of which you have ace, king, and queen, or ace, king, and knave, put on the ace; because that encourages the adversaries to play that suit again: and though you deceive your partner by this method of play, you also deceive your adversaries, which is of greater consequence in this case; because if you had put on the lowest of the tierce-major, or the knave, your right-hand adversary had made a discovery that the strength of that suit was against him, and consequently would have changed suits.

Suppose you have ace, ten, and one small card, in any suit; also the ace, nine, and one small card of another suit to lead; from the suit of which you have the ace, nine, and one small card; it being an equal wager that your partner has a better card in that suit than the last player; if not, let us then suppose that your right-hand adversary leads from the king or queen of the suit of which you have the ace, ten, and one small card; in that case it is an equal wager that your partner has a better card in that suit than the third hand; if that happens to be the case, upon the return of the suit, you lie tenace, and consequently stand a fair chance for three tricks.

A Case to demonstrate the Tenace.—Let us suppose A and B to play at two-handed whist,* and A to have the ace, queen, ten, eight, six, and four of clubs, which, in case B always leads, are six sure tricks. Let us suppose he has the same hand in spades, which, in case B always leads, are six more sure tricks. We suppose B has the remainder of these two suits.

Suppose B to have the same hand in hearts and diamonds as A has in spades and clubs, and that A has the remainder of the hearts and diamonds, which, in case A always leads, are twelve sure tricks to B.

The foregoing case shows that both hands are exactly equal; and therefore let one of them name his trumps, and lead, he wins thirteen tricks only.

But if one names the trumps, and the other leads, he that names the trumps ought to win fourteen tricks.

He who would play whist to perfection, must not be content only with being a master of the calculations contained in this treatise, and also an exact judge of all the general and particular cases in the same; but be a very punctual observer

* In this example, Hoyle evidently means that the 52 cards should be divided between two players, which would give 26 tricks.

of such cards as are thrown away, both by his partner and adversaries, and at what time.

ADDITIONAL CASES.

When it appears to you that the adversaries have three or four trumps remaining, and that neither you nor your partner have any, never attempt to force one hand to trump, and to let the other throw away a losing card, but rather endeavour to find out a suit in your own partner's hand in case you have no suit in your own; by which means you prevent them from making their trumps separate.

Suppose A and B are partners against C and D, and suppose nine cards are played out; and also that eight trumps are played out; and further suppose A to have one trump only, and his partner B to have the ace and queen of trumps, and the adversaries C and D to have the king and knave of trumps between them. A leads his small trump, C plays the knave of trumps. *Query,* Whether B is to play his ace or queen of trumps upon the knave? because D having four cards in his hand remaining, and C only three, consequently it is four to three in B's favour, that the king is in D's hand : if we reduce the number of four cards in hand to three, the odds then is three to two : and if we reduce the number of three cards in a hand to two, the odds then is two to one in favour of B's winning another trick, by putting on his ace of trumps. By the like rule you may play all the other suits.

Suppose you have the thirteenth trump, and also the thirteenth card of any suit, and one losing card; play the losing card, because if you play the thirteenth card first, the adversaries knowing you to have one trump remaining, will not pass your losing card, and therefore you play two to one against yourself.

Suppose that you have the ace, king, and three small cards, in any suit which has never been played; and that it appears to you that your partner has the last trump remaining, lead a small card in that suit, because, it is an equal wager that your partner has a better card in it than the last player; if so, and that there are only three cards in that suit in any one hand, it follows that you win five tricks; whereas, if you play the ace and king in that suit, it is two to one that your partner does not hold the queen, and consequently you win only two tricks in that suit. This method may be taken in case all the trumps are played out, provided you have good cards in other suits to bring in this, and you may observe that you reduce the odds of two to one against you to an equal chance by this method of play, and probably gain three tricks by it.

If you choose to have trumps played by the adversaries, and that your partner has led a suit to you of which you have the ace, knave, ten, nine, and eight, or the king, knave, ten, nine, and eight, you are to play the eight; which probably leads the adversary, if he wins that card, to play trumps.

Suppose you have a quart-major in any suit, with one or two more of the same, and that it is necessary to let your partner know that you have the command; in that case throw away the ace upon any suit of which you have none in your hand, to clear up his doubts, because the odds are that neither of the adversaries have more than three in that suit: the like method may be taken if you have a quart to a king; the ace being played out, you may throw away the king; also, if you should have a quart to a queen, the ace and king being played out, you may throw away your queen; all which lets your partner into the state of your game; and you may play by the like rule in all inferior sequences, having the best of them in your hand.

There is scarcely anything more common amongst moderate players, in case the king is turned up on the left hand, and they have the queen and one small trump only, to play out their queen, in hopes their partner may win the king if it is put on; not considering that it is about two to one that their partner has not the ace, and admitting he has the ace, they do not consider that they play two honours against one, and consequently weaken their game. The necessity only of playing trumps should oblige them to play thus.

A Case which frequently happens.—A and B are partners against C and D, and all the trumps are played out except one, which C or D has; A has three or four winning cards in his hand of a suit already played, with an ace and one small card of another suit: it is A's best play to throw away one of his winning cards; because, if his right-hand adversary plays to his ace-suit, he has it in his power to pass it, and consequently his partner B has an equal chance to have a better card in that suit than the third hand; if so, and B has **any** forcing card, or one of his partner's suit to play to, in order to force out the last trump, A's ace remaining in his hand, brings in his winning cards; whereas, if A had thrown away the small card to his ace-suit, and that his right-hand adversary had led that suit, he had been obliged to put on his ace, and consequently had lost some tricks by that method of play.

Suppose ten cards have been played out, and it appears very probable that your left-hand adversary has three trumps remaining, viz., the best and two small ones; and you have two trumps only, and your partner no trump; and suppose your right-hand adversary plays a thirteenth or some other winning card, in that case pass it, by which means you gain a trick, because the left-hand adversary must trump.

In order to let your partner into the state of your game, suppose you to have a quart-major in trumps (or any other four best trumps) if you are obliged to trump a card, win it with the ace of trumps, and then play the knave, or win it with the highest of any four best trumps, and then play the lowest, which clears up your game to your partner: and may be the means of winning many tricks: practise the like rule so, in all other suits.

If your partner calls at the point of eight before his time, you are to trump to him, whether you are strong in trumps or suits, or not; because, as he calls before he is obliged to do so, it is a declaration of his being strong in trumps.

Suppose your right-hand adversary turns up the queen of clubs; and, when he has the lead, plays the knave of clubs; and suppose you have the ace, ten, and one club more, or the king, ten, and one small card; when he leads his knave, you are not to win it, because it is an equal wager, you not having the king, that your partner has it: also it is an equal wager, when he leads his knave, you not having the ace, that your partner has it, and consequently you may gain a trick by passing it; which cannot be done, if you either put on your king or ace of clubs.

A Case for a Slam.—Let us suppose A and B partners against C and D; and C to deal; and let us suppose A to have the king, knave, nine, and seven of clubs, they being trumps; a quart-major in diamonds, a tierce-major in hearts, and the ace and king of spades.

B to have nine diamonds, two spades, and two hearts.

Also D to have the ace, queen, ten, and eight of trumps, with nine spades.

And let C have five trumps and eight hearts.

A is to lead a trump, which D is to win, and D is to play a spade, which his partner C is to trump: C is to lead a trump, which his partner D is to win; when D is to lead a spade, which C is to trump; and C is to play a trump which D is to win; and D having the best trump is to play it; which done, D having seven spades in his hand, wins them, and consequently slams A and B.

If your partner leads the king of a suit, and that you have none of that suit, pass it, by throwing away a losing card, (unless your right-hand adversary has put on the ace) because, by so doing, you make room for his suit.

Suppose your partner leads the queen of a suit, and your right-hand adversary wins it with the ace, and returns that suit; in case you have none of it, do not trump, but throw away a losing card, which makes room for your partner's suit. An exception to this is, if you play for an odd trick, and are very weak in trumps.

Suppose you have the ace, king, and one small card of a suit, and that your left-hand adversary leads that suit, and suppose you should have four small trumps, and no suit of consequence to lead from; and your right-hand adversary should put on the nine, or any lower card; in this case win it with the ace, and return the lead upon the adversary by playing the small card of that suit; who will have reason to judge that the king lies behind him, and consequently will not put up his queen if he has it; and therefore you have a fair probability of winning a trick by this method of play, at the same time letting your partner into the state of your game.

If your partner forces you to trump a card early in the deal, you are to suppose him strong in trumps, except at the points of four or nine; and, therefore, if you are strong in trumps, play them.

Suppose you call at the point of eight, and your partner has no honour; and suppose you should have the king, queen, and ten; the king, knave, and ten; or the queen, knave, and ten of trumps: when trumps are played, always put on the

ten, which demonstrates to your partner that you have two
honours remaining, and so he plays his game accordingly.

Suppose your right-hand adversary calls at the point of
eight, and his partner has no honour; and you should have
the king, nine, and one small trump, or the queen, nine, and
two small trumps; when trumps are played by your partner,
put on the nine, because it is about two to one that the ten
is not behind you.

If you lead a suit of which you have the ace, king, and two
or three more, when you play the ace, if your partner plays
the ten or knave, and suppose you should have one single
card in your hand in any other suit, and two or three small
trumps only; in this case lead the single card, in order to
establish a saw; and this consequence attends such play, viz.
upon leading that suit it gives your partner an equal chance
of having a better card in it than the last player; whereas,
had he led that to you, which is probable had been his strong
suit, the adversaries would discover your attempt to establish
a saw, and would trump out.

Suppose you have the ace and deuce of trumps, and strong
in the three other suits; if you are to lead, play the ace, and
next your deuce of trumps, in order to put the lead into your
partner's hand, to take out two trumps for one; and suppose
the last player wins that trick, and that he leads a suit of
which you have the ace, king, and two or three more, pass
it, because it is an equal wager that your partner has a better
card in that suit than the third hand; if so, he will then have
an opportunity of taking out two trumps to one; when the
lead comes into your hand, endeavour to force out one of
the two trumps remaining, upon supposition eleven trumps
are played out, and the odds are in your favour that your
partner has one of the two trumps remaining.

Suppose ten cards are played out, and that you have the
king, ten, and one small card of any suit, which has never
been led; and suppose you have won six tricks, and your
partner leads from that suit, and that there is neither a trump
or thirteenth card in any hand; in this case, unless your
right-hand adversary puts on so high a card as obliges you to
play the king, do not put it on, because upon the return of
that suit you make your king, and consequently the odd
trick, which makes two difference; if there happens to be

F

only nine cards played out, in the like circumstance, play by the like rule. This method is always to be taken, unless gaining two tricks gives you a chance either to save your lurch or to win or save the game.

Suppose A and B partners against C and D, and B has the two last trumps, also the queen, knave, and nine of another suit; and suppose A has neither the ace, king, or ten of that suit, but A is to lead. B should play the nine, because it is only five to four against him that his left-hand adversary holds the ten; and if he plays either the queen or knave, it is about three to one the ace or king is in his left-hand adversary's hands, and consequently he reduces the odds of three to one against him, to five to four only.

Vary the foregoing case, and put the king, knave, and nine of a suit into B's hand, upon supposition that A has neither ace, queen, or ten; when A leads that suit, it is exactly equal whether B plays his king, knave, or nine.

Suppose you have ace, king, and three or four small cards of a suit not played, and that it appears to you that your partner has the last trump; in this case, if you are to lead, play a small card in that suit, it being an equal wager that your partner has a better card in that than the last player; if so, the probability is in your favour that you make five or six tricks in that suit; but if you should play out ace and king of that suit, it is two to one that your partner has not the queen, and consequently it is two to one that you make only two tricks, by which method, you risk the losing of three or four tricks in that deal to gain one only.

If your partner leads a suit of which he has the ace, queen, knave, and many more, and leads his ace, and then plays his queen; in case you have the king and two small cards in that suit, win his queen with the king; and suppose you are strong in trumps, by clearing the board of trumps, and having a small card of your partner's great suit, you do not obstruct his suit, and consequently win many tricks.

HOW TO PLAY FOR AN ODD TRICK.

Suppose you are elder hand, and that you have the ace, king, and three small trumps, with four small cards of another suit, three small cards of the third suit, and one small card of the fourth suit; lead the single card, which, if it is won by the last player, puts him upon playing trumps, or to play to your weak suit; in which case your partner and you gain the tenace.

THE LIKE CASE FOR AN ODD TRICK, AND THAT YOUR PARTNER IS TO LEAD.

Suppose he plays the ace of the suit, of which you have only one, and proceeds to play the king of the same suit, and that your right-hand adversary trumps it with the queen, knave, or ten; do not overtrump him, but throw away a small card of your weakest suit; because it makes your partner the last player, and gives him the tenace in your weak suits.

THE LIKE CASE, UPON SUPPOSITION YOU WANT FOUR OR FIVE POINTS, AND THAT YOU ARE ELDER HAND.

Play a small trump, and if your partner has a better trump than the last player, and returns the lead, put on the king of trumps, and then proceed to play the suit of which you have four in number.

These examples being duly attended to, on all parts of the game, must be of great consequence to the player; because when he has no good suit to play, his partner being the last player gains the tenace in his weak suits.

A and B are partners against C and D, twelve trumps are played out, and seven cards only remain in each hand, of which A has the last trump, and also the ace, king, and four small cards of a suit.

A ought to play a small card of that suit, because it is an equal wager that his partner has a better card in it than the last player; and in this case, if four cards of that suit should happen to be in either of his adversaries' hands, he will be able to make five tricks in that suit: when if he played off his ace and king, he had made only two tricks. If neither of the adversaries have more than three cards in that suit, A has an equal chance to win six tricks in it.

Suppose A and B are partners against C and D, and that eight trumps are played out, and that A has four of those trumps remaining, C having the best trump, and to lead. C onght not to play his trump to take out one of A's trumps, because he would leave three trumps in A's hand; but in case A's partner has any great suit to make, C, keeping the trump in his own hand, can prevent him from making that suit by trumping it.

A Case of Curiosity.—Suppose three hands of cards, containing three cards in each hand: let A name the trumps, and let B choose which hand he pleases, A having his choice of either of the other two hands, wins two tricks.

Clubs are to be trumps.

First hand, ace, king, and six of hearts.

Second hand, queen, and of ten hearts, and ten of trumps.

Third hand, nine of hearts, and two and three of trumps.

The first hand wins of the second.

The second wins of the third.

And the third wins of the first.

THE LAWS OF WHIST.

OF DEALING.

If a card is turned up in dealing, it is in the option of the adverse party to call a new deal; but if either of them have been the cause of turning up such card, in that case the dealer has his option.

If a card is faced in the deal, there must be a new deal, unless it is the last card.

Every person ought to see that he has thirteen cards dealt therefore, if any one should happen to have only twelve, and does not find it out till several tricks are played, and that the rest of the players have their right number. the deal stands good; and also the person who plays with 12 cards is to be punished for each revoke, in case he has made any; but if any of the rest of the players should happen to have fourteen cards, in that case the deal is lost.

The dealer ought to leave in view upon the table his trump card, till it is his turn to play; and after he has mixed it with his cards, nobody is entitled to demand what card is turned up, but may ask what is trumps. This consequence attends such a law that the dealer cannot name a wrong card, which otherwise he might have done.

None of the players ought to take up or look at their cards, while any person is dealing; and if the dealer should happen to miss deal, in that case he shall deal again, unless it arises from his partner's fault; and if a card is turned up in dealing, no new deal shall be called, unless the partner has been the cause of it.

If the dealer, instead of turning up the trump, puts the trump card upon the rest of his cards, with the face downwards, he is to lose his deal.

OF PLAYING OUT OF TURN.

If any person plays out of his turn, the card so played may be called at any time in that deal, provided it does not cause a revoke; or either of the adversaries may require of the person who ought to have led, to play the suit the said adversary may choose.

A and B are partners against C and D; A plays the ten of a suit, the adversary C plays the knave of the same suit, B plays a small card of the same suit, but before D plays, his partner C leads another card, the penalty shall be in the option of A or B to oblige D to win the trick if he can.

A and B are partners against C and D; A leads a club, his partner B plays before the adversary C; in this case D has a right to play before his partner C, because B played out of his turn.

If the ace, or any other card of a suit is led, and it should so happen that the last player plays out of his turn, whether his partner has any of the suit led or not, provided you do not make him revoke, he is neither entitled to trump it, nor to win the trick.

OF REVOKING.

If a revoke happens to be made, the adversaries may add three to their scores, or take three tricks from the revoking party, or to take down three from their score; and the revoking party, provided they are up, notwithstanding the· penalty, must remain at nine: the revoke takes place of any other score of the game.

If any person revokes, and before the cards are turned discovers it, the adverse party may call the highest or lowest card of the suit led, or have their option to call the card then played, at any time when it does not cause a revoke.

No revoke to be claimed till the trick is turned **and**

quitted, or the party who revoked, or his partner have played again.

If any person claims a revoke, the adverse party are not to mix their cards, upon forfeiture of the revoke.

No revoke can be claimed after the cards are cut for a new deal.

OF CALLING HONOURS.

If any person calls at any point of the game, except eight, either of the adverse parties may call a new deal; and they are at liberty to consult each other whether they will have a new deal.

After the trump card is turned up, no person must remind his partner to call, on penalty of losing a point.

If the trump card is turned up, no honours in the preceding deal can be set up, unless they were before claimed.

If any person calls at the point of eight, and his partner answers, and both the opposite parties have thrown down their cards, and it appears that the other side had not two by honours; in this case they may consult with one another about it, and are at liberty to stand the deal or not.

And if any person answers when he has not an honour, the adverse party may consult one another about it, and are at liberty to stand the deal or not.

If any person calls at eight, after he has played, it shall be in the option of the adversaries to call a new deal.

OF SEPARATING AND SHEWING THE CARDS.

If any person separates a card from the rest, the adverse party may call it, provided he names it, and proves the separation; but in case he calls a wrong card, he or his partner are liable for once to have the highest or lowest card called in any suit led during the deal.

If any person throws his cards upon the table with their faces upwards, upon supposition that he has lost the game, the adversaries have it in their power to call any of the cards when they think proper, provided they do not make the party revoke, and he is not to take up his cards again.

If any person is sure of winning every trick, he may show his cards upon the table; but he is then liable to have all his cards called.

OF OMITTING TO PLAY TO A TRICK.

A and B are partners against C and D; A leads a club, C plays the ace of clubs, B plays a club, and D, partner to C, takes up the trick without playing any card; A, and the rest of the players, play on, till it appears D has one card more than the rest: penalty to be in the option of the adversaries to call a new deal.

RESPECTING WHO PLAYED ANY PARTICULAR CARD.

Each person in playing ought to lay his card before him; after he has done so, if either of the adverse parties mix their cards with his, his partner is entitled to demand each person to lay his card before him; but not to enquire who played any particular card.

AN EXPLANATION OF THE TERMS, OR TECHNICAL WORDS, IN THIS TREATISE.

Finessing, means endeavouring to gain an advantage thus: When a card is led, and you have the best and third best of that suit, you put your third best card upon that lead, and run the risk of your adversary having the second best; if he has it not, which is 2 to 1 against him, you are then sure of gaining a trick.

Forcing, means obliging your partner or adversary to trump a suit, of which he has none. The cases mentioned in this Treatise will shew when it is proper to force either of them.

Long Trump, means having one or more trumps in your hand, when all the rest are out.

Loose Card, is a card of no value, and, consequently, the properest to throw away.

Points, ten of them make a game; as many as are gained by tricks or honours, so many points are set up to the score.

Quart is a sequence of any four cards immediately following one another in the same suit.—Quart-major is a sequence of ace, king, queen, and knave.

Quint is a sequence of any five cards immediately following one another in the same suit.—Quint-major is a sequence of ace, king, queen, knave, and ten.

Reverse, means only playing the hand in a different manner; that is, if you are strong in trumps, you play one way; if weak in trumps, you play the Reverse, viz. another.

See-saw, is when each partner trumps a suit, and plays those suits to one another to trump.

Score, is the number of points set up, ten of which make a game.

Slam, is when either party win every trick.

Tenace, is having the first and third best cards, and being last player, and, consequently, catching the adversary when that suit is played: as, for instance, in case you have ace and queen of any suit, your adversary leads, you must win those two tricks; and so of any other tenace in inferior cards.

Terce or Tierce, is a sequence of any three cards immediately following one another in the same suit. Terce-major is a sequence of ace, king, and queen.

AN ARTIFICIAL MEMORY, FOR THOSE WHO PLAY AT THE GAME OF WHIST.

Place, of every suit in your hand, the worst to the left hand, and the best (in order) to the right; and the trumps, in the like order, always to the left of all the other suits.

If in the course of play you have the best card remaining in any suit, put the same to the left of your trumps.*

And if you find you are possessed of the second best card of any suit, place it on the right of your trumps.

And if you have the third best card of any suit, place a small card of that suit between the trumps and that third best, to the right of the trumps.

To remember your partner's first lead, place a small card of that suit in the midst of your trumps, and if you have but one trump, on the left of it.

When you deal, put the trump turned up to the right of all your trumps, and keep it as long as you can, that your partner may, knowing you have that trump left, play accordingly.

TO FIND WHERE OR IN WHAT SUIT YOUR ADVERSARIES REVOKE.

Suppose two suits on the right-hand to represent your

* This conspicuous mode of arrangement is hardly suitable to the present day; players have become too sharpsighted.

adversaries in the order they sit, as to your right and left hand.

When you suspect either of them to have made a revoke, clap a small card of that suit amongst the cards representing that adversary, by which you record not only that there may have been a revoke, but also who made it, and in what suit.

If the suit representing the adversary that made the revoke, happens to be the same he revoked in, change that suit for another, and put a small card of the suit revoked in the middle of that exchanged suit, and if you have not a card remaining of that suit reverse a card of any other you have, (except diamonds) and place it there.

As you have a way to remember your partner's first lead, you may also record in what suit either of your adversaries made their first lead, by putting the suit so led in the place which in your hand represents that adversary; and if other suits were already placed to represent them, then exchange those for the suits in which each of them makes his first lead.

The foregoing method is to be taken when more necessary to record your adversary's first lead, than to endeavour to find out a revoke.

CALCULATIONS WHICH DIRECT WITH MORAL CERTAINTY HOW TO PLAY WELL ANY HAND, BY SHEWING THE CHANCES OF YOUR PARTNER HAVING 1, 2, OR 3, CERTAIN CARDS.

☞ Read with attention those marked N. B.

FOR EXAMPLE.

What is the chance of your friend having one certain card?

Answer.	against him	for him
That he has it not, is, N. B.	2 to	1

What is the chance of having two certain cards?

Answer.

That he has one of them only, is	31 to	26
That he has not both of them	17 to	2

<table>
<tr><td></td><td>against
him</td><td>for
him</td></tr>
</table>

But that he has one or both, is about 5 to 4, or
N. B. .... 25 to 32

What are the chances of having 3 certain cards?

Answer.

That he holds one of them only is 325 for him to
378 against him, or about .... 6 to 7

That he has not 2 of them only, is 156 for him to
547 against him, or about .... 2 to 7

That he has not all 3 of them, is 22 for him to 681
against him, or about.. 1 to 31

But that he has 1 or 2 of them, is 481 for him to
222 against him, or about .... 13 to 6

And that he has 1, 2, or all 3 of them, is about
N. B. .... 5 to 2

AN EXPLANATION AND APPLICATION OF THE CALCULATIONS
NECESSARY TO BE UNDERSTOOD BY THOSE WHO READ
THIS TREATISE.

First Calculation.

It is 2 to 1 that my partner has not one certain card.

To apply this calculation, suppose the right-hand adversary
leads a suit, of which you have the king and one small card
only; observe that it is 2 to 1, by putting on your king, that
the left-hand adversary cannot win it.

Again, suppose that you have the king and three small
cards of any suit, likewise the queen and three small cards of
any other suit, lead from the king, because it is 2 to 1 that
the ace does not lie behind you; but it is 5 to 4 that the ace
or king of any suit lies behind you, and consequently, by
leading from your queen suit, you play to a disadvantage.

2nd Calculation. It is 5 to 4, at least, that your partner
has one out of any 2 certain cards; the like odds are in
favour of your adversaries; therefore, suppose you have two
honours of any suit, and knowing it is 5 to 4 that your
partner holds one of the other two honours, you do by this
play your game to a greater degree of certainty.

Again, suppose that you have the queen and one small
card in any suit only, aud that your right-hand adversary
leads that suit, if you put on your queen, it is 5 to 4 tha

your left-hand adversary can win it, and therefore you play 5 to 4 to disadvantage.

3rd Calculation. It is 5 to 2 that your partner has one out of any three certain cards.

Therefore, suppose you have the knave and one small card dealt, and that you right-hand adversary leads from that suit, if you put on the knave, it is 5 to 2 that your left-hand adversary has either ace, king, or queen of the suit lead, and therefore you play 5 to 2 against yourself; besides, by making a discovery to your right-hand adversary, he finesses upon your partner throughout the whole suit.

And, in order to explain the necessity there is of putting on the lowest of sequences in all the suits led, suppose that your adversary led a suit of which you have the king, queen, and knave, or queen, knave, and ten; by putting on your knave of the suit of which you have the king, queen, and knave, it gives your partner an opportunity of calculating the odds for and against him in that suit, and also in all inferior suits of which you have sequences.

A farther use to be made of the foregoing calculation: suppose that you have the ace, king, and two small trumps, with a quint-major or five other winning cards in any other suit, and that you have played trumps two rounds, and each person followed trumps; in this case there are eight trumps out, and two trumps remaining in your hand, which make ten, and three trumps divided between the remaining three players, of which three, the odds are 5 to 2 that your partner has one; and, therefore, out of seven cards in your hand, you are entitled to win five tricks.

SOME COMPUTATIONS FOR LAYING WAGERS.

All with the Deal.

The deal	is 21 to 20	6			5	to	2
1 love	11 — 10	7			7	—	2
2	5 — 4	8			5	—	1
3	3 — 2	9 is about			9	—	2
4	7 — 4						
5 is 2 to 1 of the			2 to 1	is	9	to	8
game, and 1 of			3 — 1		9	—	7
the lurch	2 — 1		4 — 1		9	—	6

5 to 1......................	9	to	5	5 to 4.....................is 6	to	5
6 — 1...................	9	—	4	6 — 4................... 6	—	4
7 — 1...................	3	—	1	7 — 4................... 2	—	1
8 — 1...................	9	—	2	8 — 4................... 3	—	1
9 — 1 is about	4	—	1	9 — 4 is about 5	—	2

3 to 2.....................is 8	to	7	6 to 5.....................is 5	to	4
4 — 2..................	4	—	3	7 — 5................... 5	—	3
5 — 2..................	8	—	5	8 — 5................... 5	—	6
6 — 2..................	2	—	1	9 — 5 is about 2	—	1
7 — 2..................	8	—	3			
8 — 2..................	4	—	1	7 to 6.....................is 4	to	3
9 — 2..................	7	—	2	8 — 6................ 2	—	1
			9 — 6 is about 7	—	4

4 to 3.....................is 7	to	6			
5 — 3...................	7	—	5	8 to 7 is above 3	to	2
6 — 3...................	7	—	4	9 — 7 is about 12	—	8
7 — 3...................	7	—	3			
8 — 3...................	7	—	2			
9 — 3 is about	3	—	1			

8 to 9 is about 3 and a half in the hundred, in favour of 8 with the deal; against the deal, the odds are still, though small, in favour of 8.

CALCULATIONS FOR THE WHOLE RUBBER.

Suppose A and B are at play, and that A is 1 game, and 8 love of the second game, with the deal.

Query. What are the odds throughout the whole rubber?

1 Game love and 9 love of the second game (upon supposition of 9 love with the deal) being nearly 6 to 1.

First game and 9 love of the second game is nearly 13 to 1

First game and 8 love of the second game is a little more than the former.. 13 — 1 &c.

First game and 7 love of the second is nearly .... 10 — 1

Ditto and 6 love of the second is nearly .... 8 — 1

Ditto and 5 love of the second is nearly .... 6 — 1

Ditto and 4 love of the second is nearly .... 5 — 1

Ditto and 3 love of the second is nearly .... $4\frac{1}{2}$— 1

Ditto and 2 love of the second is nearly .... 4 — 1

Ditto and 1 love of the second is nearly .... 7 — 2

The above calculations are made with the deal.

AGAINST THE DEAL.

Suppose A and B are at play, and that A is one game, and any number of points in the second deal.

First game and 9 love of the second is nearly	11 to 1
Ditto and 8 love of the second game, is a little more	11 — 1
Ditto and 7 love of the second game is...............	9 — 1
Ditto and 6 love of the second game is...............	7 — 1
Ditto and 5 love of the second game is...............	5 — 1
Ditto and 4 love of the second game is...............	4½— 1
Ditto and 3 love of the second game is...............	4 — 1
Ditto and 2 love of the second game is...............	7 — 2
First game and 1 love of the second is nearly	6½— 2

The use which is to be made of the foregoing calculations, may be made by dividing the stake, according to the tables herewith set down.

PART THE THIRD.

WHIST : FROM THE TEXT OF DESCHAPELLES.*

THE most elaborate and philosophical treatise in existence on the game of Whist, is that written by the distinguished Frenchman, to whom we are indebted for this portion of our *matériel*. He tells us that one Chapter is the result of twenty years' experience—which may serve to illustrate the amount of practical detail contained in the complete work. As it would be impossible in this place to attempt more than a slight epitome of the whole, we have culled such portions as seemed most suited to our purpose. The infinite variety of this noble game, renders it impossible to apply any system to it, which would be available on every occasion of doubt and difficulty. It abounds with instances wherein the patient must minister to himself. For this reason we the less regret that we cannot follow *Mr. Deschapelles* through the rich wilderness of hypotheses which fill and fructify his pages. The suggestions that are strewn through this selection from them, however, will supply general instructions by which a competent understanding of the fundamental elements of whist, may be acquired—fine play of any kind is alone the result of personal application and peculiar fitness. As most available, then, I take up his analysis of its Rules. He proves to us that they not only form the basis of its principle, but that they are a code of maxims for the player. He insists that their honourable observance is the best policy, and that when departed from, whatever may be the temporary advantage, ultimate evil is sure to come of it. Here, whatever may be the nature of the theory, is at least a moral of account: and if it be gracious to find sermons in stones, surely none will quarrel with the philosophy which extracts a precious jewel from " a game at whist!"

* The student must bear in mind that Deschapelles' " Laws and Regulations" are not established as authority in England. They are principally applicable to French Whist, and are given here in extenso only on account of their interest and merit.

DESCHAPELLES' LAWS AND REGULATIONS.

SECTION I.—PRELIMINARY ARRANGEMENTS.

Article 1.—A complete whist table is composed of six persons.

The first four are chosen by lot, (see Article 6,) for the first rubber, and the two others take their turn for the succeeding ones.

Art. 2.—If the table be not complete, new players take their turn in the order of their arrival; and afterwards fill up, in their turn, whatever vacancies may occur.—(See Article 13.)

Art. 3.—If more than six persons present themselves to form a table, the four first players are chosen by lot.—(See Article 7.)

Art. 4.—Every one is entitled to play two rubbers, after which he must quit the table, to make room for those whose turn it is to replace him; the two players who are to leave at the expiration of the first, or opening rubber, are fixed on by lot.

Art. 5.—When the rubber is finished, if there are parties waiting to play, a table is compelled to admit two of them, but never three.

Art. 6.—The lot is decided by a single pack of cards, each party drawing one.

Art. 7.—It may be necessary to draw lots twice, before a table is completely made up.

Firstly, to decide on the six persons of whom it is to be composed, and on the four who are to commence.

And, secondly, to determine the choice of partners.

Art. 8.—The person who draws the lowest card chooses his place, and the pack to deal with.

Art. 9.—When once seated at the table, there can be no changing seats, nor can there be any change of cards when once cut.

Art. 10—The dealer's partner takes his seat opposite him, the adversaries may take their places as they please, without reference to the cards which they may have respectively drawn.

Art. 11.—At the beginning of a rubber, the parties who are to complete it being absent, may take their seats if they arrive before the trump card of the first deal has been turned up.

Art. 12.—If they do not arrive in time, (see Article 11,) they must take their turn at the bottom of the list.

Art. 13.—Persons who are in the habit of playing, are to be considered as inscribed for their turn at the table from the time they approach it.

Art. 14.—The four persons composing the first rubber determine the amount of the points, and other necessary conventions (according to the practices of the game).

Art. 15.—After drawing for partners, or in the course of the rubber, a party may withdraw, on paying for himself and his partner all that may have been lost.

Art. 16.—A player compelled to leave the room for a short time, may, with the consent of the other three players, give his hand to another to play for him.

If he be not returned at the expiration of the rubber, his place is to be taken by the next in order of succession, without favour.—(See Article 12.)

Art. 17.—A person playing at one table, loses his turn at all the others for which he may be inscribed

Art. 18.—In case a party be inscribed for several tables, he may make his choice in the event of another party desiring admission.

Art. 19.—When the time arrives for a table to change, the parties composing it cannot continue unless there are no applicants to replace them.

Its condition changes immediately, at the will of any member of the society who may put his name down to take his turn.—(See Articles 2 and 13.)

SECTION II.—THE DEAL.

ART. 20.—The dealer may shuffle the cards or not, at his option.

He must hand them to his right-hand adversary to cut.

Art. 21.—In case of an irregular cut, or the dealer omitting to have the cards cut, the adversaries, on proving the fact, may demand a new deal. This right is however lost, if not demanded before the first card has been played.

Art. 22.—If the cards are not cleanly cut, the dealer may instantly demand another cut, or a new deal.

Art. 23.—He has the same right (Article 22,) if the cut contain less than four cards.

Art. 24.—Each player is entitled to shuffle the cards once before they are cut.

Art. 25.—If the turn-up or trump card is shown, either,

1. in cutting, or,
2. in taking up the cards,

the opposite party has a right to demand a new deal.

Art. 26.—If the dealer look at the turn-up card before it is turned, or show it before the cards are all dealt, it is a lost deal, and the cards pass to the next hand.

Art. 27.—If the dealer disarrange the cards, or drop one, the deal is lost.

Art. 28.—The cards are to be dealt,

1. From left to right;
2. Deliberately;
3. Detached by the centre, and distributed one at a time.

Art. 29.—Each player has the right, before he has shown a card, (see Article 34,) to make observations on the deal. (See Article 133.)

Art. 30.—If (see Article 29,) the bystanders decide that the dealing ought to be more regular, the deal is lost.

Art. 31.—If the dealer, in distributing the cards,

1. Show more than one card, either through his own fault, or that of his partner;
2. Give more than two cards wrong;
3. Touch the hand of one of the players to count the cards;
4. Or place the trump-card on the other cards without having turned it up;

the deal is lost.

Art. 32. During a deal, when a card is seen, owing to the the fault of one of the players, (see Article 31,) the opposite party may have the card retained, or demand a new deal.

In case of a new deal, the deal is not lost.

Art. 33. The partner of the dealer is to collect the cards for the following deal, and place them on his right.

If he neglect this duty before the turn-up card be seen, the deal is lost.

Art. 34.—The dealer's adversary, who, during the time of his dealing, shall touch the cards dealt him, or the pack intended for the following deal, loses for himself, and causes his partner to lose the rights conferred by Articles 29 and 32.

Art. 35.—Before the hand is commenced playing, (see Article 129,) should there occur any mixing of the cards; if any mistake, or irregularity in the number of cards, arise from the fault of the dealer; the deal is lost.

If these mistakes be occasioned by the adverse party, or by any other cause, there must be a new deal.

Art. 36.—The fifty-two cards having been regularly dealt out; the last, which is the trump card, must remain turned up before the dealer. (See Articles 80 and 115.)

Art. 37.—If a card is faced in the pack, even if it be the last, there must be a new deal.

Art. 38.—Should a player deal out of his turn, if it pass unnoticed until he has turned the trump card, the deal holds good.

Art. 39.—No one has a right to change the cards, (except as provided in Article 38,) but each player may, at his own expense, take a fresh pack.

SECTION III.—OF IRREGULARITIES IN THE HANDS AND THE PACKS.

Art. 40.—After the trump card has been turned, and before the lead, (see Article 35,) any irregularity in the hands will be rectified according to the provisions of Article 133.— (See Articles 43, 44, and 48.)

Art. 41.—If, after the lead, a player find that he has one 'ess than his proper number of cards, and the missing card be found in his adversary's hand, the deal is lost.

Art. 42.—If the missing card be found in his partner's hand, the adverse party has a right to claim the provisions of Article 127.

N.B.—This error is corrected by drawing indiscriminately from the upper part of the hand, one card to complete the hand which has one deficient.

Art. 43.—If a hand be found short of its complement, and the missing cards be discovered on the ground or elsewhere, (except as specified in the Articles 41, 42, and 45) the missing cards shall be placed on the table with the faces upwards. (See Articles 127 and 131.)

Art. 44.—If the missing cards cannot be found, they shall be searched for by some one not engaged in the game; and, when found, laid on the table, except as provided in Article 45.   (See Article 131.)

Art. 45.—If the missing cards be found in the tricks with have been played,

It causes a revoke.   (See Article 47.)

Art. 46.—A hand having too many cards, except in cases specified in Articles 41 and 42, constitutes a revoke.   (See Article 47.)

Art. 47.—The revoke (Articles 45 and 46,) is marked at the moment when claimed; the other circumstances of the deal are annulled.   (See Articles 107, 127, 131.)

Art. 48.—If the pack of cards be faulty, the deal in which it is discovered, is null, though the previous ones hold good. (See Articles 49.)

Art. 49.—A pack of cards is faulty, when it contains more or less than fifty-two cards; or when there is a duplicate card in the pack.

This is a circumstance which should not be passed over by those interested in the game, without strict inquiry.

SECTION IV.—OF THE STAKES, AND OF THE SCORE.

Art. 50.—The rubber, which is two out of three games, is reckoned at four points; the party who first win two games, gain the rubber.

Art. 51,—The game consists of ten points; when no points are marked by the losing partners, it is treble, and reckons three points*; double, if one, two, or three points be marked; and single, when more than four.

Art. 52.—When six tricks have been made, (*le devoir,*) each trick afterwards made, counts for one point.

Art. 53.—If the whole thirteen tricks are won by one side, it is called a slam, and is equal to a full rubber (ten points.)

There is nothing marked for the game.

* This is called a lurch.

Art. 54.—Four honours count four points; three honours count two points only.

Art. 55.—Tricks count before honours, except as specified in Article 68, and in cases where one party is entitled to the call.

Art. 56.—The points gained by one side can only be marked by one of the players.

Art. 57.—In the event of two partners marking the game, and their score not agreeing; when the second trick has been turned, their adversaries, on noticing the error, may insist on which score they choose being retained.

Art. 58.—Points neglected to be marked before the second trick has been turned, are lost.

Art. 59.—If a player, by mistake, mark more points than he is entitled to, he has the right of correcting the error at any time before the termination of the game. (See Article 135.)

SECTION V.—THE HONOURS.

Art. 60.—Honours are to be announced audibly; those marking them, without signifying that they have them, and who do not rectify their error before the second trick is turned, must take them off their score. (See Article 133.)

Art. 61.—If a player hold four honours, it must be announced, or rectified within the delay specified in Article 60, on pain of losing two points out of four which should have been marked. (See Article 133.)

Art. 62.—Honours cannot count, unless they have been announced or marked before the trump card of the following deal has been turned up.

Art. 63.—They cease to count when a party is in the well, that is to say, when at nine, and have only one point to win the game. (Except as provided in Article 68.)

Art. 64.—At the point of eight, the party who hold more than two honours in their hands, win the game on showing them. (See Article 66.)

Art. 65.—At the point of eight, he who has two honours in his hand, has the privilege of calling; if his partner reply by showing one honour, the game is won. (See Article 66.)

Art. 66.—If the honours are shown, or called.

1. At any other point of the game than at eight.

2. Or after a card has been played; they are not counted, and must be turned up on the table, and considered in the light of exposed cards.

Art. 67.—If a player call without having two honours in his hand, or reply without holding one, the adversaries will have the rights conferred by Article 127.

In case of correction, if cards are shown, they must be turned up on the table as exposed cards.

Art. 68.—If a player call without having two honours, and if it so happen that three or four honours are in the hands of his adversaries, the latter will become possessed of the rights conferred by Article 127.

And in case they avail themselves of them, all the honours will count before the tricks.

Art. 69.—The call must be made so as to be audible to all at the table; a player endeavouring to call so as to be heard only by his partner, will be liable to the penalties laid down in Article 127.

Art. 70.—At the point of eight, when the trump card has been once turned up, if a player tell his partner not to forget to call he is subject to the regulations of Article 127.

Art. 71.—When a player calls, and his partner refuses to answer, although he has the power, they cannot gain a slam. Honours take their usual place. (See Article 55.)

Art. 72.—If, when the round has commenced, (see Article 129,) a player discover who holds the honours, and make known his observation, he will be liable to the provisions of Article 127.

SECTION VI.—EXPOSED CARDS.

Art. 73.—Cards seen by your partner, and not played immediately, shall be turned up, and laid on the table.

Art. 74.—A card intentionally drawn out from the hand to more than half its extent, (see Article 133,) will come within the meaning of Article 73.

Art. 75.—When a card is exposed, the adverse party have the right—

1. Of either demanding or refusing its being played;
2. Or of demanding that the highest or lowest card in the suit shall be played. (See Article 76.)

Art. 76.—An exposed card may be called for several

times, and does not become free until it shall have satisfied either one or the other of the provisions of Article 75. (See Article 85.)

Art. 77.—A player having a card exposed, if it be his turn to play, or to lead off the trick, (see Article 85,) may demand the card to be called for, but should wait until the trick which precedes it be put in its place, and the hand removed from it.

Art. 78.—A player having a card exposed, if his right-hand adversary play without calling for the card, is at liberty to play what card he chooses. (See Article 85.)

Art. 79.—If a person play more than one card to a trick, his adversaries may choose which of them shall remain on the table, (see Article 123,) and can cause the others to be placed as exposed cards.

Art. 80.—The turned-up, or trump card, should be left in view on the table until the first card of the second trick has been played, But if it be not taken up before that trick is finished, it must be considered as an exposed card. (See Article 115.)

SECTION VII.—CARDS PLAYED OUT OF TURN, AND OF THE CALL FOR THEM.

Art. 81.—A lead made out of turn holds good, when the party, whose proper turn it was to play, has led, or played to, the following trick. (See Articles 119 and 120.)

Art. 82.—If the player, whose turn it was to play, (Article 81,) claim his right in time, he will have the choice:

1. Of approving of the card played;
2. Of considering it as an exposed card;
3. Or of calling for a particular suit, either for that or the following trick. (See Article 119.)

Art. 83.—A person playing his card out of turn, his partner having already played; the adverse party may consult upon taking or leaving it.

Art. 84.—If a person play his card out of his turn, and before his partner has played, the adverse party may demand of the latter his highest or lowest card in the suit played; and, in default, trump or not trump. (See Articles 85 and 88.

Art. 85.—If a card be played too precipitately before the

call; (see Articles 77, 78, and 84,) the card thus played shall be also considered as an exposed card, and subject to the call. (See Article 119.)

Art. 86.—In case of two parties leading simultaneously, Article 82 is applicable to the player who is in fault; (see Article 119;) if both be wrong, the one fault cancels the other.

Art. 87.—A party having a suit called for, which he does not hold in his hand, may play as he chooses; the fault in this case is atoned for. (See Article 88.)

Art. 88.—A player called upon,

1. For his best or worst card, and consequently trump or not trump;
2. Or to play a particular suit; must obey, and in default, will be considered to have made a revoke. (See Articles 107 and 109.)

SECTION VIII.—THE REVOKE.

Art. 89.—A revoke is made, when a player having in his hand a card of the suit led, does not play it. (See Article 107.)

Art. 90.—The revoke is complete:

1. When the trick in which it has occurred has been put in its place, and the hand removed from it;
2. Or when the party who has revoked, having the lead, has played a card for the next trick. (See Article 118.)

Art 91.—The demand of the partner, made in time, if replied to, annuls the revoke; only as far as the fact is unperceived by the adverse party.

Art. 92.—A player perceiving in time that he has made a revoke, may take up his card, and must play his best or worst card, at the option of the adverse party; besides which, the card taken up is to be considered as an exposed card. (See Articles 75 and 119.)

Art. 93.—The side which has made a revoke, loses three points for each revoke.

Art. 94.—The adverse party profit by the revoke, in one of the three following ways:

1. By adding three points to a score; or

2. By deducting three points from their adversaries' score, (or all their points, if they have less than three;)
3. Or in taking from them three of their tricks. (See Article 104.)

N.B.—They cannot, however, divide their advantages by, for instance, adding one and a half points to their own score, and deducting one and a half from that of their adversaries.

Art. 95.—Those who claim a revoke, are bound to prove that it has occurred. (See Article 117.)

Art. 96.—The revoke is proved, by pointing out the trick in which it has occurred. (See Article 117.)

Art. 97.—The revoke may be claimed the moment it is perceived to have been made, but cannot be established and marked for, until the expiration of the deal, except as provided in Article 107.

Art. 98—Those who have made a revoke, on playing to the end of the deal, may gain enough points to save themselves a double or a treble.

Art. 99.—Those who might gain by their own score, may take advantage of the revokes of their adversaries, to put back their score, and gain double or treble.

Art. 100.—Those who can claim several revokes, may make use of some to add to their own score; and of others to diminish the score of their adversaries, but without dividing them. (See Note on Article 94.)

Art. 101.—Should a revoke not have been claimed, (Article 97,) and the four hands are played out, the tricks may be thrown together, and the revoke is cancelled.

Art. 102.—Before a player loses his right, (Article 101,) by playing his last card, if he suspect a revoke has been made, he may put down his card, and require that the other players should do the same.

Art. 103.—If any one (Article 102,) cause a confusion in the lost trick, and afterwards be not able to draw his own card, he shall be considered to have revoked.

Art. 104.—The penalty for one or more revokes, cannot be inflicted until the deal is quite finished, or at least within one trick of it. (See Article 94.)

Art. 105.—The side making a revoke, can neither count a slam, nor win the game in the deal in which the revoke is made; they must remain at nine, " in the well," if they have made points enough to reach it or pass it.

Art. 106.—Should revokes be made by both parties, even though the numbers of them be not equal on both sides, there must be a new deal.

Art. 107.—In the event of revokes by assimilation, (see Articles 45, 46, 88, and similar,) the provisions of this Section 8, are in all respects applicable, as far as they may concern them, unless otherwise specially provided for.

Art. 108.—At the end of the deal, a revoke cannot be claimed. (See Articles 127 and 131.)

SECTION IX.—INTIMATIONS BETWEEN PARTNERS, AND OF THEIR LIMITS.

Art. 109.—The right of asking questions rests entirely with your partner, and may be used for avoiding or alleviating error.

Art. 110.—" What are trumps?"   " Draw your card."
" Can you not follow suit?"   " I think there is a revoke."

The above remarks, or those analogous, are the only ones allowed to be used, and they only by the person whose turn it is to play.

Art. 111.—During the continuance of the deal, nothing beyond what is allowed by the rules of the game should be said or done, which may be detrimental to the interests of the adverse party. (See Article 116.)

Art. 112.—A winning card can only be played as any other card. (See Article 116.)

Art. 113.—No player may draw his card for his partner, unless he require it.   (See Articles 110 and 116.)

Art. 114.—No player is allowed to look at the tricks taken up, except the last.   (See Article 116.)

Art. 115.—After the second trick is turned, and the trump, or turn-up card has been taken up, it cannot be named or shown.   (See Articles 80 and 116.)

Art. 116.—In case of any violation of the Articles 111, 112, 113, 114, and 115, the adverse party has the right of demanding a new deal.

SECTION X.—GENERAL RULES.

Art. 117.—In taking up the tricks, it is essentially necessary that they should be placed in distinct order, under pain of being condemned in case of dispute.

Art. 118.—A player wholly detaching a card from his hand in order to play it, or intentionally throwing down his hand, is considered to have played. (See Articles 74, 90, and 124.)

Art. 119.—In case of cards being played precipitately or unintentionally;—

From the party in fault, those which shall not be played for the trick shall be considered as exposed cards, (see Article 82); if otherwise, they shall remain at the disposition of the party to whom they belong.

Art. 120.—If one side take up a trick belonging to the adverse party, the right of recovery holds good until the end of the deal. (See Articles 81, 130, and 135.)

Art. 121.—A player who is able from the cards in his hand to make the rest of the tricks, may throw down his hand. (See Article 124.)

Art. 122.—Should a player say, " I can win the rest;" " I have won the game;" or make signs to that effect, his hand shall be thrown down. (See Article 124.)

Art. 123.—Should a player, from any cause whatever, show more than half the cards he holds in his hand, his hand shall be thrown down. (See Article 124.)

Art. 124.—A player having thrown down his hand, his partner must do the same; then one of the two hands at the option of those who shall have made the error, shall be played at command; the exposed cards shall still remain so.

Art. 125.—If a player throw down and give up his cards, and his adversary throw his cards on them, the round is at an end.

Art. 126.—If a deal become very much disordered, through the fault of either side, or from any other cause (see Article 133,) there must be a new deal.

Art. 127.—If the confusion alluded to in Article 126, proceed from one side only, the adverse party will have the choice:

    1. Of retaining the same hands, and rectifying the error:

    2. Or of having a new deal.

Art. 128.—In case of a new, or a lost deal; the deal cancelled is considered as not having taken place, with regard to circumstances not specified.

Art. 129.—A lead is begun when one party has played to it. (See Article 130.)

Art. 130.—The game is finished, when one side having gained it without dispute, the cards are reunited in one mass.

Art. 131.—With regard to a fault of any kind, the opposite party have the following rights:—

1. To look for revokes if there have been any;
2. Or, waving the infliction of any penalty, to demand that the deal be rectified, and played according to the rules of the game. (See Article 127.)

SECTION XI.—BYSTANDERS.

Art. 132.—In all cases of dispute, the bystanders shall act as umpires.

Art. 133.—In case of complaint of those interested, a majority of the bystanders will decide upon the fact, that the law, if necessary, may be applied to the case.

Art. 134.—If any difficulty arise, which cannot be settled by the rules, the case shall be stated, (see Articles 132 and 133,) and the parties concerned shall be free to choose their own arbitrators.

Art. 135.—If any points be marked, which have not been gained, it is the duty of the bystanders to mention the circumstance, and to have the error rectified.

Art. 136.—During the continuance of a deal, the bystanders are forbidden, either to warn a player of a fault, to refresh his memory, or, in fact, to say or do anything which may favour the players. (See Article 139.)

Art. 137.—Questions relative to the game, (Articles 110 and similar,) are not allowed to be asked by the bystanders. (See Article 139.)

Art. 138.—No bystander has a right, either,

1. To walk round the table at which the game is playing;
2. Or even to place himself so as to be able to look over two hands. (See Article 139.)

Art. 139.—In case of any violation of these preceding articles, the players who feel themselves aggrieved, have the right, (see Articles 132 and 133,) of rendering the person in fault responsible, and placing whatever loss may have arisen to his charge.

THE PRINCIPLE OF THE LAWS OF WHIST.

SECTION I.—PRELIMINARY OBSERVATIONS.

Rules are to games what laws are to society; they are those enactments, the infringement of which entails penal infliction.

Rules, however, from a variety of causes, either from a desire of perspicuity, or from a weak or erroneous conception in principles, have, in all sciences, become so multiplied, and so mixed up with precepts which should be wholly separated from them, that they have served only to fatigue attention by their bulk, and to distort all natural principles of logic and equity.

Without attempting to evade the difficulties of our position, we shall venture to lay down the following maxim:— Law will never be perfect until it shall contain nothing but what is sanctioned by authority.

There are two great obstacles to the enforcement of a law of this kind; one proceeding from the party required to submit to it, and the other from the legislator himself.

But where shall we find one who seriously applies himself to the rules of a game; and who, engages, of his own accord, in a pursuit, the more difficult on account of its apparent futility?

Where shall be found a majority of individuals, who are willing to submit their learned acuteness to the tediousness of repetitions; who will patiently endure a concise brevity, and employ their intellectual powers in unravelling difficulties; and who will condescend to relax from their logical gravity, and admit reforms and innovations, in order to arrive by degrees, at the solution of perplexities?

We will venture to affirm that the second of the two parties above alluded to, does not exist. If it did, of what use would be the former? He would in vain labour to produce a work of no utility, and which rejected by the world, might moulder for years in his desk without any chance of ever being brought to light.

Having offered these excuses to succeeding generations, and made this appeal to corrections whenever their want shall be felt and acknowledged, we profess to work for those who will avail themselves of our labour; to save the indolent the necessity and tediousness of research; in fine, to exert ourselves to form a compendium, which shall be independent of other works, and deemed a sufficient authority on the subject. Here, as in other cases, we shall conform to relative circumstances, following, at the same time, the direction of that absolute power which we assume to ourselves in matters in which our skill is acknowledged.

The nineteen Articles of which this first section is composed are only directions; but their importance, the necessity of rendering them authentic, and the tendency to confusion which it is their office to repress, have induced us to bring them forward, and invest them with all the powers of law.

When once out of this Section, it will be seen how religiously we shall adhere to principles, and should the reader again meet with any directions, he must excuse them, in consideration of their fewness, and the light they throw upon the articles of law which follow them, and with which they are connected.

DIRECTIONS.

Articles 1, 2, and 3.—Four persons are seated at the table, and the game is arranged; nevertheless, the table is not complete and perfect; there is an integral portion of it waiting for their turn; there are two prepared to take their seats, with the same rights and privileges as those already seated; and behind these there is a number of candidates anxiously waiting to take their part in the contest. This ensures it a long continuance, and prevents the least abatement of the excitement arising from the game. Neither fatigue, nor absence, nor even discouragement, throws a damp on the scene, or allows the slightest traces of languor to appear. The ranks are constantly filled up without allowing a moment's interval of rest, and fresh combatants, animated with a noble ardour, successively present themselves to seize the weapons and continue the contest.

Such are the resources of the game of Whist as it has been established. Such is its life, its movement, and its pleasures. If to these be added the social interests alluded to in Chapter I., that ardour for the game which renders us indifferent to the person of the party filling the first vacancy at the table, provided he plays; and who, in the midst of hopes and dangers incident to all, makes us forget all misplaced prejudice, we shall be compelled to admit that this game has been invented for the delight of man, since it affords him a no less useful than agreeable pastime.

Articles 4 and 5.—Thus, after the termination of the first rubber, chance decides the right which every person has to play two successive rubbers. This is only necessary at the beginning; it is the fertilizing principle, it is like the power of water, or the force of steam, which gives life and energy to the machine, and sets it in motion.

We have admitted, as a general principle, the rights of a party to play two consecutive rubbers, although in some societies it is otherwise arranged. The winners remain, and the two losers resign their seats. This is a means of checking extensive losses; convenient enough when a desire of gain is the ruling passion in the game, but very misplaced when the game is considered in a proper light, merely as a pastime.

Art. 6.—The drawing is of importance, whether it be the means of procuring the partner wished for, or of conferring the advantage of the deal.

In order to avoid confusion, one pack of cards only is to be made use of; therefore, a card drawn from another pack is useless, and recourse must be had only to the pack chosen.

The pack should be laid on the table untouched, several cards cut successively, and the bottom one shown. By cutting neatly from an entire pack, the least suspicion of having selected a card is avoided, and by immediately showing the card cut, a lesson is given to those who are less inclined to be polite.

Art. 7.—In the drawing among six persons, the holders of the four lowest cards commence the first rubber, and the other two cut in for the one following. If a greater number of persons be concerned in the drawing, as the complement for the table is only six, the others take their turn in the succession and order determined by the cards they have drawn.

At the second drawing, the holders of the two lowest cards become partners. Here a difficulty may sometimes occur, but one which ought not to produce any serious discussion.

Suppose three persons draw each an ace, and the fourth a deuce. A fresh drawing takes place between the holders of the three aces, the deuce loses the deal and becomes the partner of the highest of the next drawing. This is the just and reasonable decision of this and all similar cases.

Art. 8—The rule is, that the person who draws the lowest card becomes the dealer. The ace, although highest in playing, is conventionally considered the lowest in cutting.

We disapprove extremely of all ceremonious etiquette in the player who has the privilege of choosing his seat. Let him take his seat promptly, for the politeness he wishes to show to one individual, operates to the annoyance of the other party in the game, who are waiting for his being seated to take their places.

A certain prince is said to have made the following sensible remark, " Promptitude is the politeness of kings." The drawer, therefore, of the lowest card, possessing for the time being the rights of royalty, his prompt decision dispels all anxiety, and removes every idea of subjection to his will. It is the custom without its abuse.

Art. 9.—The right of choosing a seat can be acquired, and should be enforced only in the sense of the game : the moment this right shall have been made use of by the dealer taking his place, the said right becomes extinct. The rules will not allow of the revival of this privilege from any change of mind or caprice in an individual; they will not permit three persons to be disturbed or removed.

Art. 10.—It frequently happens that drawing by lot occupies a considerable time, in consequence of cards of equal value being cut, either for choosing the players to commence, or for determining the partners, or for choosing places. This causes a momentary delay to which every player should submit with a good grace, because it tends to decide a question of equal importance to all parties, and because it is unavoidable. But for a player purposely or uselessly to prolong that delay, or wilfully to offer unnecessary obstacles to the progress of the game, is not to be endured.

Articles 11 and 12.—A game should not suffer interruption from the absence or wilful negligence of parties cutting in, neither should the exclusion of the latter appear to have been effected precipitately.

As soon as the rubber is over, the parties next in order of succession should be called; if they do not immediately answer the summons, the parties present may immediately proceed to form another rubber; the time which elapses between the rubbers in changing places or partners, with the addition of a few minutes' grace, which continues to the moment of turning the trump card, is surely amply sufficient to allow of parties cutting in, who may then be at the farthest extremity of the room, to reach the table and prevent the forfeiture of their turn.

Art. 13.—Whist tables may be said to be regulated in degree by the amount of stakes; every player approaches that table at which his circumstances may allow, or his taste may incline him to play; therefore, whoever has been in the habit of joining a certain whist party, soon becomes acquainted with its company, and consequently soon knows the amount of stakes that the company play for; in the same way, his habits of play are soon known to the other frequenters of the table; his presence is, therefore, equivalent to an inscription on the list of players. This is so much an established custom, that when one person enters the room after another, he hardly ever thinks of applying to cut in until the latter has declined. That which has been acknowledged as an established rule of etiquette, we have laid down as a fixed law.

Art. 14.—It has often occurred at the close of a rubber, that a player has found himself the winner of a much larger sum than he had expected; or, which happens still more frequently, he has discovered that he has been playing higher points than would have suited him had he been aware of their price, and has consequently complained of his losses.

The rules declare, that the party cutting in shall, on taking his seat at the table, inquire the price of the points; and that the said party has no right to find fault in that particular, provided the stakes be no higher than is customary.

Art. 15.—It may occur, from motives more or less justifiable, that one of the players refuse to sit out the rubber.

The rules have provided for this case, by preserving for such a player the full enjoyment of his rights, till he be again able to join the table.

Art. 16.—This Article comes within the limits of Article 15, except with regard to extreme cases; every player should be lenient, and willingly make allowances for an unforeseen incident which may cause a momentary interruption, and which may happen that very evening to himself; he should be indulgent to others, since he may, at some future period, stand in need of indulgence for himself.

We shall here explain a case, the minor importance of which has not allowed of its being stated sooner.

Before the partners are drawn for, can a person give up his turn to another, and still retain the privilege to take his turn afterwards?

We answer, he certainly can, provided the person who takes his place be one of the six required to compose the table.

Art. 17 & 18.—To justify the admission of Article 17, it is necessary to have witnessed how far every other feeling is sometimes sacrificed to an insignificant point of personal interest.

Article 18 is a corollary which fully fixes and determines its signification, and definitively silences all argument.

Art. 19.—A turning table, or one in which the partners are changed at stated intervals may be considered as a close game, to which no one can be admitted.

It is formed under certain peculiar circumstances; these are, when only four players are present, and there is no hope of a fifth to relieve them; in which case, in order to avoid that the same partners should play opposite each other throughout the evening, certain regulations for changing partners should be determined upon instanter. This, in case of need, will be a very convenient expedient and will provide the table with a resource within itself, which can be no longer expected from without. But if a fifth player arrive, the case alters, and the game should be as soon as possible made subject to the standing rules.

SECTION II.—THE DEAL.

The deal is the distribution of the cards; a mere mechanical operation, but sometimes one of great fatigue, and attended with much annoyance.

It is often accompanied with mistakes; one party from innate awkwardness is liable to continued errors; another, perhaps, from some natural infirmity or stupidity, for we must not expect to find the intellect and talents of the Lycæum at a Whist table.

The deal gives two advantages to the dealer, the trump-card, and the last play. The first is calculated mathematically, the second depends upon circumstances. The former possesses a positive value, whilst the latter is enhanced or diminished by various causes, and particularly by the cards held by the leader.

Before proceeding to the consideration of the Articles, we would again repeat our earnest advice that all discussion be discontinued from the moment the deal commences, that the former deal be reconsidered, that the points marked on both sides be examined, and that the dealing of the cards be watched, in order to avoid, as well as profit by, the faults made by the adverse party. At a later period of the game there will not be so much time to repair the effects of negligence, and attention will be drawn into another channel.

Art. 20.—Cards are shuffled because they are new, to remove any symmetrical arrangement of them; or because each trick taken up being of the same suit, the cards should be mixed; we shuffle the cards by way of distraction, and from pure habit.

The pack is presented to be cut, because it is the usual practice.

Abstractedly, these two operations of shuffling and cutting may be considered as reciprocal guarantees; although but little attention is paid to this fact by players who only practise them mechanically.

The necessity of the cut is not entirely arbitary, it is evidently reasonable; we cannot suppress it as a guarantee, nor leave it optional without rendering it in some measure injurious, by being at one time used, and at another rejected.

It is not the same with regard to the shuffle; that is a power which every one has a right to partake of, and the cut is used as a last resource. The adversary, who has collected the cards, has also shuffled them before putting them in their place; if the dealer be therefore satisfied, and present them in that state to be cut, what can there be said on the subject? To require a person, against his inclination, to perform an action which is perfectly useless, is an act of tyranny; the game already recognises a sufficient number of commands, without introducing those which are superfluous; we disapprove of any tendency of this kind, and, if that demand were replied to, we think it would imply great rudeness in the person demanding.

We have seen a person who, after availing himself of his

right of shuffling the cards, required the dealer to re-shuffle them, and for that purpose presented him with the pack reversed. The latter asked for fresh cards, and the hint was taken, for the other never repeated the act.

We should be continually on our guard against any feeling of ill-temper which may lead us to transgress the rules of good breeding. If we are the first to act wrong, we shall bear all the blame.

Art. 21.—A cut is called irregular when it is not made by the dealer's right-hand adversary.

The cut is enforced by rule; it is the business of the law to regulate its mode, and to punish its omission.

The acknowledgment of this power of the law which concerns the cut, is a matter of some consequence, for frequently its irregularity does not strike us until we see the turn-up card or our own hand.

In case of complaints (which do not so often occur), it will be necessary, even in so insignificant an affair to quote some precedent to obtain a judgment. (See Article 133.)

Art. 22.—The cut is not clean if there be any hesitation or awkwardness in performing it. It is not clean if one card be dragged after the rest; the cut should be made neatly, and the cards fairly lifted up.

Art. 23.—A cut must be at least to the depth of four cards, the number composing a trick. This is the custom at all games. Some limit must be fixed, and this is as easily adopted as any other: besides, it could not well be fixed lower; if only one card were cut, it might be suspected that it had been seen.

In this, as in the preceding article, the dealer should declare his right before he avails himself of it; that is, if he would not run the risk of losing his deal, which must necessarily ensue, if any dispute should arise, and the matter be referred to the decision of the bystanders.

Art. 24.—The right of shuffling the cards is a guarantee which belongs equally to each player.

The proper way to do this is, to shuffle them over the table, and not to allow the whole of the pack to be, at one time, in the hand.

Art. 25.—If we were to show the turn-up or trump card, at the moment of cutting, it might operate to the disadvantage of those who have made bets during the deal. Some even go so far as to request a delay in the turning of the card, which is granted them by placing the card aside, and not allowing it to be seen by any one.

If the turn-up card be accidentally seen, the deal holds good, and must continue; this may be scarcely worth mentioning, for we can hardly conceive how such a thing can happen.

By the old regulations, when it was permitted to show the turn-up card in cutting, we have seen players endeavour to discover it, and even stoop during the deal, to catch sight of it. This practice was then attended with no inconvenience, but is no longer allowed by the rules of the game.

Art. 26.—As the dealer has no right to show the turn-up card before it is turned, he has still less right to look at it himself. He is then more guilty than another in yielding to a spirit of cavilling; he deserves a more severe punishment, and we have inflicted it on him by making him lose his deal.

Art. 27.—By accepting the cut, you have abdicated your claim, and have no longer any rights to exercise; fulfil then the task which falls to your lot as mechanical distributor, with all its risks and perils; if you are inattentive and careless in the fulfilment of your duty, you will pay the penalty for it.

If the cards be shuffled when the right of doing so is passed by, and if they be dealt in that state, the dealer is answerable if I hold bad cards; for I am not satisfied that I have received the cards which properly belong to me; if a new deal ensue, the same blame will be attached to the dealer, added to the delay caused by his want of dexterity. Was the card which you have turned up the one really cut? There is too much interest attached to this question, to allow a doubt to exist of the identity of the trump card.

Arts. 28, 29, and 30.—These three articles we shall condense into one.

Article 28; it is merely a precept, and affects the progress of the game; Article 29, appears here to establish the rights, and Article 30, as the deciding judge. The matter of these articles is interesting, and should be regulated with exactness.

In whatever manner the deal be made, it is necessary to pay attention in dealing, that each player may feel convinced he has taken up the card which properly belongs to him. From the moment the slightest doubt exists, the law comes into operation. The question which is addressed to the by-standers (Article 133), is as explicit as its answer; it affects the three divisions laid down in the article, and any other cases which may arise from peculiar circumstances. It is essentially necessary to lay every possible obstacle in the way of innovations which bad taste may introduce. We are even justified in rendering assistance to the delinquent, if it will prevent a repetition of the fault.

Art. 31.—If a card be seen, owing to the fault of the party dealing, application must be made to the provisions of Article 32; if a second card be seen from the same cause, the deal is lost. If it were otherwise, it might happen that the dealer, taking advantage of Article 34, would withdraw as many cards as he thought proper, without making himself liable to be called upon for a new deal.

One card dealt irregularly, may be either right or wrong. As long as the irregularity is confined to two cards, the error is easily rectified; but when it extends to three, the possibility of correctness becomes doubtful, and the established rule is, that the deal is lost.

It frequently happens, that, in consequence of some interruption, the dealer loses the thread of his deal. The rules of the game will not allow him to touch the different hands in order to correct his mistake, and the only resource he has is to judge by his eye, or to continue the deal with the chance of finding himself right.

Sometimes the turn-up, or trump card, is thrown down without being turned up or shown; this card is of such importance, that the punishment of making the deal lost cannot be dispensed with in this case.

Art. 32.—As long as the deal is in hand, the option of continuing it, or re-shuffling the cards, remains with the dealer, in case of any irregularity arising on the part of the adverse party. In fact, the latter have nothing to attend to on the table, and it is, on the contrary, to their interest that mistakes should occur, which must be to their advantage.

Art. 33.—Deals out of turn frequently arise from the pack for the following deal being improperly placed. Habit, which becomes with us second nature, ends by being the ruler of all our minor actions; we find a pack of cards on our left hand, and we naturally make use of them; however, there is an injury done; where then is the delinquent? He is easily pointed out; it is he whose duty it was to collect the cards and place them in their proper position, and as a just punishment for his unpardonable negligence, he loses his deal.

This penalty makes players careful, and becomes a reward for attention to the game; for those who fail in this respect incur a loss of their right, conformably to the provisions of Article 38.

The point in question is properly discussed at the end of the rubber, when the bets are being settled, and before the players have begun to move from the table.

During the round, the question "who dealt?" is not permitted, although parties may be much interested in knowing it, in order to direct them, either with regard to their lead or their play. If the cards be misplaced, you are thereby led into error. Sometimes necessity refreshes the memory, and the thing is rectified. Our rules have an equal tendency to punish negligence, and to favour the exercise of the memory.

Art. 34.—He who is compelled to deal, and who is punished for the slightest irregularity by the loss of an advantage should be subjected to no annoyance, and guaranteed from all interference.

It is the duty of the dealer's partner to collect and shuffle the cards for the following deal; with this the law has no concern; but if he proceed further, and take upon himself to correct the deal, it is to his own disadvantage, and that of the party with whom he is jointly responsible.

Art. 35.—In principle, it is admitted that the dealer may cancel the deal, but that this right is not enjoyed by his adversaries.

The deal lost by one party is to the advantage of the other; whatever may be the cause of it, the forfeit must be paid; it is the general custom, and established practice.

Art. 36.—It is singular enough that the plan of dealing out an entire pack of cards one by one, should have been ever adopted. It is sometimes a great fatigue, and one which has been imposed on a class of persons who would willingly dispense with it, as we show by our observations on the deal. This plan, to say the truth, possesses no advantage, it even exposes the card to be seen, on account of their being singly separated.

The rule of leaving the turned-up card before you, is determined by the application of the law in Articles 80 and 115.

Art. 37.—" Cards seen, cards thrown down. This is a proverb, it is a general practice, and, in order to deprive it of its efficacy, or to admit of one single exception to it, there must be adduced at least twenty reasons to one.

According to the old rule, should there be in the pack a faced card, which from the cutting has become the trump card, the cut held good. This rule was made to save time, and also for this reason, that as the trump card was intended to be seen, its original position was immaterial. Experience has taught us that when a card has been found turned in the pack, it is possible so to manage the deal as to make that the trump card. It was then in the dealer's power to give one card more chance than another, this was unjust. Let us, therefore, abolish this irregularity, and return to the principle, which we believe we shall have the credit of reinstating, since custom has already repealed this Article among players who pride themselves on understanding the logical principles of the game.

Art. 38.—A player has a right, if he choose, to allow his deal to be taken from him; but never, designedly, to take that of others.

Art. 39.—As a whist-table is furnished with two packs of cards, it was necessary to decide whether their use should be regulated by caprice or by some established rule. If, for instance, it should happen that, from caprice, each party make use of the same pack, one will be used, whilst the other will remain untouched. It was more natural that the packs should be used alternately; the rule intervened, and the change was prohibited.

When in playing with the same cards, we have lost several games in succession, we at length conceive a sort of antipathy to them, and if we were not allowed to change them, we should probably quit the table. We are then allowed to take new cards. It is useless to endeavour to restrict this privilege, as it may be rendered necessary by the destruction of a single card.

Perhaps it would be convenient to change the cards even oftener than is usually done. At short whist, cards which have been played during six rubbers are thrown aside; this is an article or regulation which I recommend.

The phase, or change, is severely prohibited by the English; I know not what reason they have to complain of it, nor what harm it has done them. Before 1814, the French phased; at present it is not done; and it is well that the custom is discontinued.

SECTION III.—IRREGULARITIES IN THE HANDS AND THE PACKS.

As soon as the cards are all dealt out, each player takes up the hand which belongs to him. In this, as in all other acquisitions, it seems proper that our first care should be to acquaint ourselves with what we have obtained possession of; we arrange them according to their suits, or, at least, sort them in the manner we are accustomed to; the essential point being to impress them well on the memory. We have seen players who hold their cards in their hands just as they have taken them up from the table, and, if this mode lead them not into error, we consider it the best. We have seen others who sort their suits so carelessly as to be heedless of the notice of others, or whether their adversaries may be thus made acquainted with a part of that of which they ought to be ignorant. Another goes still farther; with the greatest candour and *sang froid*, he places each colour by itself, either invariably in the same position, or in accordance with a system, the key to which is very easily discovered. Thus he classes the cards according to their sizes or value, he then carefully turns the court cards, so that the figures may appear to stand on their legs, as if he feared that by keeping them with their heads downwards, they might be attacked with a fit of apoplexy; he next proceeds to turn all the spades, the hearts, and clubs, as if afraid that the points might be broken by being improperly placed; not suspecting that, during all these preparations, his actions are noticed by others; that every other player at table has, for some time, finished arranging his hand, and that the round has commenced. At length, the visionary begins by saying, with the most unaccountable indifference, "Gentlemen, draw your cards." Thus, from being absorbed in a childish operation, in a sort of monomania, he enters on the business of the game, not only without the preliminary knowledge so necessary for success, but with the great disadvantage of having, in a manner, exposed his own game to his adversaries.

When it is an adversary who acts in this manner, it is needless to avoid looking at him; it is useless, from an affectation of modesty, to endeavour to keep the eyes averted from his hand; in spite of ourselves we become initiated into the knowledge of facts. But when it is our partner who acts in the way above mentioned, and who thus acts in spite of the looks of those who are well disposed to profit by his imprudence, we have more cause for despair.

After the final arrangement of the cards, comes the plan of the campaign. Every one should have a plan of some sort, good or bad. No one should ever play a card without some motive for it. This motive must proceed from a principle common to all players; the knowledge of the strength or weakness of our own hand, and of suits of which it is composed.

After these two important and general operations are finished *i. e.* the arrangement of the cards, and the plan of playing them, we can scarcely imagine that a player, so far and so well instructed in the game, should not perceive whether he have in his hand more or less than his proper complement of thirteen cards; and that he could enter into action without having reviewed his forces, and acquainted himself with whom he is to contend; this, however, has happened, and not unfrequently. We mention the fact, in order that parties may guard against so serious a fault.

Art. 40.—This article treats of irregularities which may be noticed during the short inferval between the turning of the trump card and the lead; it is necessary to offer to the attentive player a possibility of escaping the serious consequences of a fault to which it is probable he has not been, in the least degree, accessary. This interval begins for him when he takes up his hand, and this he may be compelled to do precipitately, by the hurry with which his partner plays his card.

Art. 41.—When once entered into the spirit of the contest, a sort of passion takes possession of the combatants. The vicissitudes of fortune and the agitation of the struggle make them forget all the minor details of the game; but which, however, should never be lost sight of by the player, since a neglect of them would end in the destruction of all his labour and all his projects.   Of these details a register should be kept in his memory; from the moment he sits down to play, he should bestow a part of his attention upon the peculiar circumstances arising out of the game he is playing, and which should be considered apart from the action and progress of the game itself.

Art. 42.—There is here a double fault, and on the same side; the punishment should therefore be exemplary. The law, which is suspicious and severe, will regard only the intention and connivance; nothing can destroy that spirit which appears to form part of its essence; it does not take into consideration the cards of the guilty party who would have won the game, if one of their hands had not been found to contain a card which was missing in those of their adversaries.

The application of Article 127, excludes the right of looking for revokes which may have been previously made.

Arts. 43 and 44.—The moment a player perceives that he has not his proper complement of cards, he should quietly look around him, and search wherever there is a probability of their being found. If we succeed, we are aware that he will still be liable to the danger of having made a revoke, in consequence of the absence from his hand of the cards which he has recovered, but revokes themselves often escape observation, particularly if nothing is said or done to direct attention to the subject.

But if the player do not succeed in finding the missing cards, if there be no means of avoiding the difficulty which arises on calling for the assistance of the bystanders, still it would be far more desirable to decide the point at once, than to suffer the mischief to be increased by delay, and to incur a severe punishment, in that penalty which is the inevitable effect of several revokes.

In the case of Article 44, any one not engaged in the game, may take upon himself to examine the other pack, which stands close to the tricks, and, in case of need, to procure the missing card from any pack whatsoever.

Art. 45.   It may be easily ascertained whether the missing cards are in the tricks which have been turned, by counting the tricks without turning the cards, and if five cards instead of four be found in one of the tricks, there arises a strong presumption that the party who finds his hand short of one card, has played two cards to a trick. To rectify this fault in the spirit of Article 127, is rather difficult; it would be necessary to turn all the tricks, which is expressly forbidden by the rules; it would involve an endless discussion on which card should be played, and which should be taken back; it would be even necessary to recommence the deal; by which proceedings, the memory, as well as the tricks, would be disturbed. And after all this labour, we might not escape one or perhaps several revokes, as authorised by Article 131. On the other hand, if we do not explicitly provide for the case, it would then be possible for a bad hand to make that deal good, which would be otherwise lost.

Art. 46 —What penalty should be inflicted on him who has his hands full of cards, when the hand of the three other players are exhausted? Can he have forgotten to play to some of the tricks? or has he taken up the tricks or the neighbouring pack to mix them with his own hand? If he has not played to the trick, it is a *bonâ fide* revoke; if he has mixed the cards, he loses his turn to deal. When any one has involved himself in such a dilemma, he may congratulate himself at escaping from it at the price of a revoke.

In a case of importance, the adversaries may have recourse to Articles 127 and 131; the rights acquired by the first of these Articles are often of greater value than the acquisition of three points; when, for instance, a strong hand would have put you three to nine by the application of a revoke, whilst it leaves you nothing to nothing, by causing a new deal, without taking into consideration the possible acquisition of the deal. Article 131 interposes its assistance, and ratifies Article 127 in a case of great importance, or of a slam, which a revoke would have prevented.

Among practised players, the faults alluded to in Articles 45 and 46 should but very rarely occur. No rule has hitherto been laid down to meet these exigencies. The loss of the game ought to be a sufficient punishment for them. To remedy this want, we have neglected no means in our power to supply the deficiency.

A case of a very singular nature, relating to Article 46, was once referred to our arbitration. One party held the ace of trumps; and the others, notwithstanding, wished to make a slam.

It must be understood that, in a trick containing five cards, in which the ace had become accidentally mixed, those who demanded the rectification of the error, thought they had a right to choose which of the five cards should be returned to the hand, in order to make up the complement.

Art. 47.—These revokes are privileged, and are marked immediately. As to the time when they are made, their value, and the manner of benefiting by them, we refer our readers to the provisions of Section VIII. Whatever may be the number of cards which has occasioned the confusion, the penalty is not increased or doubled in proportion, but remains the same.

Arts. 48 and 49.—If a pack of cards be faulty, from containing more or less than 52 cards (which is of rare occurrense), he who deals first will scarcely fail to detect it, unless fearing that he has committed a mistake and will lose his deal, he distributes the last cards at hazard. In all cases, as there will be too many or too few cards, it is probable that the correction will immediately take place.

The pack may also be faulty, when it contains a duplicate card. This error is not so easily detected as the other, and may long remain undiscovered. In fact, if the duplicates are of trifling importance, they will, on the one hand, escape those who count the cards of a suit, and on the other, those who will not see them together. Suppose a pack contains two fours of spades, instead of a four and a five; this is unimportant, and might remain long undetected. At length they are played together, and immediately perceived; yes, and ten to one that it has not been the best player who has first made the discovery. This affair has been often made a subject for a joke, and perhaps a bystander would be wrong to interfere in such a case. We have seen it carried to great lengths; the players certainly were very unskilful, but it was strange that out of four players, not one should have discovered the defect. It lasted a long time, and would have continued much longer, but for the shouts of laughter from the lookers-on. For two hours the party had been playing with two packs, one of which had no aces, and the other no kings. It was amusing to hear the discussions at every round on the odd trick and the honours; at every moment they appeared on the point of discovering the deficiency, and then again their attention was diverted into another channel.

These precedents hold good; the rule is ancient, and universally applied. If we refuse to acknowledge it, we must go back to the flood. The game is finished. (See Article 130.) It is the same for every round, except when specially provided for otherwise.

SECTION IV.—THE STAKES AND THE SCORE.

Before mentioning the faults committed under this head, or entering on the penalties which they involve, it will be proper here to detail the general system of the game, and to determine what are the means we employ, and the object we wish to attain. It is necessary to explain the technical terms; a Rubber, a Game, a Trick, a Slam, and the Honours; also, how these are acquired; and when acquired, how they are to be made use of. All this will be treated of in Sections 4 and 5.

With regard to all these objects, a system and an authority which shall be universally acknowledged is requisite for the general interest, so that no change of place or country may involve the necessity of a fresh apprenticeship to acquire a knowledge of the game. These points will be therefore found laid down in a law, and by a system which should become universal and obligatory.

There are some places where the rubber pays only two points; others where the game counts only two points; others where the slam is reckoned as the half of a full rubber, and counts for the game; others again, where the penalties are not fixed, and where the customs of the game appear to be regulated only by that spirit of contradiction and caprice which is so common, and so much to be regretted.

At length, sound principles, receiving the sanction of good society, gradually prevail, and obtain ascendancy as soon as they become thoroughly explained and understood.

This, therefore, seems to be the point at which we have now arrived; general opinion is directed towards a system to which it unanimously appeals, and which, when found, it proclaims aloud, and acknowledges as genuine and undoubted authority.

Art. 50.—An English dictionary has defined a Rubber to be " a game, revenge, and the whole." To say the least of it, this is a truly singular definition; it is incomprehensible

to us, and we should even say that it is the definition of a
person who has never made one at a whist table. This,
however, does not astonish us; it is of a piece with what
we witness every day, and in every species of business. It is
a great chance that a work is confided to one specially devoted
to it. This reminds us that in the edition of 1788, of the
dictionary of the French Academy, the definition of the word
" beefsteak," is laid down as " a mutton chop broiled on a
gridiron."

The rubber is the winning of two games out of three; every
nation in which the game is played understands the term in
this sense. When one game has been won on each side, a
third is required to decide the rubber: if, on the contrary,
the two games have been won by the same side, the rubber
is finished, and a fresh one is commenced.

This then is what is expressed by the word Rubber. Nevertheless, it would seem to imply something more, otherwise we should not have introduced the word into our
language, which is repugnant to the admission of synonymous
terms, and which requires a rigorous reform in many of those
words which it has admitted. A rubber means two out of
three consecutive games.

Art. 51.—Strictly speaking, a fish might have been fixed
as the value of each point; games might then have been
gained against the point of nine, which would have counted
only one point, and others (lurches) which would have been
worth ten points. It would be necessary to raise considerably
the value of the rubber, to prevent the winning party finding
themselves, notwithstanding, losers; the result of this would
be, a great difference in the gain or loss of different rubbers;
it would be necessary to win twelve or fifteen rubbers to com-
pensate for one which had been lost; we should no longer
know for what we were playing, nor to what loss we were
exposed; and when any one was heard to say, " I have lost
or won four rubbers," it would not be known whether he had
lost or won 8 points, or 120.

The present arrangement was admirably conceived; it
creates no alarm in the minds of amateurs by the prospect of
aggravated extravagance, at the same time that it leaves them
room to hope for alternatives of sufficient variety to prevent
monotony; it appears that it has been admitted, with a de-

sign of preventing heavy losses. One fault which has been found with it, is in our opinion a positive recommendation; this is, that in certain cases, the winning of one game may increase the loss of points. We see nothing to object to in the fact, that while the interest is kept up, and the rubber is not finished, the chances should multiply and increase in favour of a sudden change of fortune.

The word lurch is a term used in backgammon; in passing into other games, its signification is a little changed; it is used when the losing partners have not made one point, *i. e.* when they have lost everything that can be lost.

Art. 52.—A trick at whist consists of four cards played consecutively.

We count as tricks, those *levées* which are won after six have already been made. Each trick then counts one point; thus he who has taken up nine *levées*, counts three tricks, or three points. The word *levée* in this case used is only as a periphrasis, and we may say: we are three by tricks, as we say two by honours, which in fact signifies, that we have gained that number of points by tricks, or by honours.

The word "duty" (devoir), applied to the complement of tricks necessary to be made before we can gain the odd trick, is a happy expression; the application carries with it the precept it implies, that we have something to reproach ourselves with when we have not attained that point, and that our efforts must be redoubled to prevent our being deprived of it.

Art. 53.—The Slam is considered of the same value as a full rubber, on condition that it shall not count in the game. This custom we have adopted, at the same that we are perfectly aware of the varieties introduced at different places.

As long as Whist had no written laws, every one regulated the game according to the dictates of his own caprice. In some places they count five honours, others, twelve tricks are reckoned a slam; in a third, in *L'Ambogue* for instance, no traces of the original game can be recognized; and it would be a thankless and dangerous task to attempt to enumerate and follow the various deviations to which it has been subjected. It is high time that this sublime game should have a fixed and invariable form, and we repeat our exhortations to its numerous and intelligent amateurs, to rally round our laws, and not to suffer the slightest deviation from them to be attempted.

Art. 54.—Every honour counts one point; this is a generally admitted practice. If we hold four honours, by a simple inference, we consequently mark four points. When we hold three honours, two points only are marked; here instead of one deduction, two are necessary; we may be supposed to calculate thus: "from three honours which I hold, I must subtract one which is held by my adversaries, and I mark only two."

Art. 55 —The discord of principles between chance and skill is not at an end; law, occupied by other subjects, returns at intervals to lend assistance to one and the other alternately. Article 55 pronounces the opinion openly in favour of skill—it declares that the properties of the latter give it a decided superiority over its enemy. This is the least that can be expected when there is a question of making the trick, which is the result of reflection, and which, though it may sometimes yield to the breath of fortune, is always prepared to take every advantage, and will not fail to recover its superiority if the struggle be continued.

Moreover, the same Article 55, probably with a view to favour the contest, and that an adversary may not be immediately driven to despair, admits two restrictions; by the call it abridges the privilege of the trick, and by Article 68 it limits to finessing.

Art. 56.—This is the established rule of the game; it prevents remark, and silences bad temper.

Art. 57.—The inconvenience attending any difference between two scores of partners, is a strong argument against the practice, and in favour of one score only. We are, however, by no means inclined to lay this down as an arbitrary law.

With respect to the disarrangement of the scores, a question arises which it is necessary to solve.

" If during a round, the two scores should become confused, are the points lost?"

If one score alone has been strictly marked, and a second be afterwards set up and not regularly kept, any concession of the former to the latter, must be a matter of voluntary compliance; but when two scores made according to rule, and progressing together, are found to disagree, justice must be done. Should one player wish to establish that three points have been gained, although his partner has marked only two, the rule is positive on the subject, two points alone can be marked, and those must be scored immediately, or otherwise the penalty may be doubled, if it be put off until the termination of the game; as the point becomes the odds, if the game should stand at eight to nine.

Art. 58.—Points, from whatever source they may arise, should strictly be considered as lost, unless marked at the moment they are made. There is the following weighty reason in support of this rule; that the players combine their efforts, and regulate their play according to the points which they see marked. In fact, different combinations are favourable to different modes of play, which may very materially prejudice a person unacquainted with his adversary's play. The fault will then operate in favour of the party forgetting to mark his game, and to the disadvantage of his adversary, which is just the reverse of the principle we wish to establish. However, by delaying until the turning of the second trick, that fatal moment when points neglected to be marked, are lost; and by allowing forgetfulness or distraction, a respite which reason does not strictly command, we have thought proper to conform to the old law, and the customs to which it has given birth. This law has determined that honours are lost, unless declared before the next lead; but in the event of their being declared, it specifies no period at which it shall no longer be allowed to mark them. That period cannot precede the lead, for that is close on the turning of the trump card. By extending the marking of every sort of point to the end of the second trick, we have chosen that which we consider the fairest course, and which seems to meet every exigency of the case.

Art. 59.—Here the case is quite different; there is no longer a question of harmless omission, this is an encroachment which must be vigorously repressed. We call it an encroachment, for truly it does not deserve a more severe appellation, to judge by the thousand times that we have witnessed its occurrence. Nevertheless, however innocent it may really be, we must not allow the forgetful or ignorant to retain possession of what they have improperly acquired.

SECTION V.—THE HONOURS.

In its original state, Whist was a four-handed game, in which, in admitting only the hierarchy of the cards in their order and class, two players were matched against two others to decide which party should gain the greater number of tricks.

In this simple state the game existed for a long period, the favourite pastime of the cooling portico and the magnificent saloon; there appeared no intention or opportunity of adding to it any embellishment worthy of its fame. It was not till it had passed its infancy, and had attained the mature age of manhood, that it was invested with the additional charm of the trump, and received successively those other attractive accessories, the honours, the call, &c. &c.

The trump is an ancient invention; and is found in most games played with cards. Sometimes a whole suit is invested with its power, sometimes its authority is restricted to one single card, which then appears as a type of civil power, and like a magistrate entrusted with the preservation of public order. The term "honour" is applied to the game of Whist only, and although of such ancient date, it would appear as belonging to a more advanced stage of improvement. It is so well chosen, and so happy an expression, that it has been admitted or adopted in all countries. The terms, "the call" and "the well" (point of nine) are simple, but full of meaning. If the latter in some languages is considered a homely expression, we must at any rate allow it the merit of being most expressive of a place from which there is but one outlet.

Art. 60 and 61.—It may appear a hard case, that a player who holds the honours and marks them, should still be liable to be deprived of this advantage, because he has not announced them. He might object, that his marking them is a stronger proof that he holds them in his hand, than if he had merely announced them—No, the law is explicit, and the rule has been infringed. "Your law," rejoins he, "is not common sense; it is full of contradiction and absurdity: the rules impose silence on the players, and yet require them to announce facts." To this we reply, that our law is perfectly equitable. If honours be marked which are not held, the custom of the game does not allow the adversaries, even if they perceive it, any opportunity of retaliating; they can only oblige the party in fault to take them off their score; thus no equilibrium is established with the case in which they are not seen. The law, thus forced to yield to custom, has employed every means in its power to prevent the commission of injustice; it has declared that honours shall be audibly announced, and publicly marked; it has prevented all clandestine and underhand dealing; and, to obviate the possibility of unjust possession, it has subjected the privilege to the prescribed formalities of the game.

Art. 62.—This is a general practice; and however unreasonable it may appear, the law must be obeyed. It would have been desirable to have but one period fixed for deciding the points; for instance, "when the trump-card is once seen, whatever points have not been marked, are forfeited;" or, when the second trick is taken up, &c.

This latter rule is an introduction of our own, and we shall have occasion to speak of it hereafter; though of so short a duration, its functions are of considerable importance. When no received custom, or habitual practice, is formally acknowledged, the authority of the law is paramount: but when an unjust decision results from universally-received opinions, it then becomes our duty to labour hard to correct them, and thus promote the advancement of the game. For want of courage to declare, that parties marking honours improperly shall be liable to the penalty of retaliation, we have been drawn into several articles, which must be well studied in order to avoid confusion.

Art. 63.—"The well" (the point of nine) is a fashionable embellishment, which belongs to the decorations of which we spoke at the beginning of this section. An intellectual embellishment, when considered in connexion with the assistance which it renders to good players; since it offers them a port of refuge against all the storms of fortune, with a means of self-defence proportioned to the strength of some players, or of the weakness of others. A rational embellishment, in regard to the distinction between even and odd, this being the only point at which the honours are compelled to stop short in their career. An original embellishment, in which point of view it has become inherent to the game of

Whist, which it accompanies through all its deviations. At Short Whist its power has not been curtailed; it has there even increased; it there comes into action ten times in an hour instead of once, and there acquires a different degree of importance; for by a skilful defence of the single point, it gives the possibility of winning the game with a moderate hand in the following round.

Art. 64.—The rule of the game says, that honours are counted only at the end of a round or deal; but in this case the party at the point of eight, holding three honours, mark them, and win the game without playing. This is an exception, and is another embellishment. It would appear strange that the game of Whist does not so strongly insist upon the application of this rule, as it does upon that of the former. This is to be accounted for only by that extraordinary perversion of the mind which attaches itself more closely to its own caprices, than to its rational desires.

The call is not known at Short Whist. Some pretend that the scope of the game is so confined, that there is no room for its introduction; others see in this arrangement an effort of reason and sagacity; of reason, as far as it is a proof of virtue to relinquish our inventions when no longer necessary; of sagacity, inasmuch as the call, which holds the balance between the odds and "the well," become superfluous and useless at the moment when the latter is as it were filled up by the making of five points, which deprives it of all its resources of power and extent.

Art. 65.—By an extension of the advantage granted by Article 64, the holder of two honours is authorised to call; if his partner answer to the call, the object is obtained, and the game won. But if his partner cannot answer, a great disadvantage has arisen to the party calling, because it has discovered to his adversaries the state of his hand. This circumstance, and that of the slam, are the only reasons which would prevent a player from calling; he fears that his hand, which is already weak, may be still further weakened by a disclosure of two cards. Without rejecting this view of the case, we think this occasion very rarely occurs; and we add that it should not be attempted but by a first rate player. We have witnessed a game lost by three or four tricks which might have been gained by the call, and even if the game be not lost by this means, it involves a loss of points, because it favours the adversaries winning a double or a treble.

The term "call," (perhaps the day is not far distant when it will disappear in Long Whist) is used to signify the announcement in an audible voice that we hold two honours. It is the only positive indication permitted, for all other demands or intimations are expressly forbidden, since they are liable to different interpretations, and may materially affect the interests of the adverse party.

Art. 66.—The rule of the call, which at a specified time grants an enjoyment by anticipation, evinces at the same time great jealousy of all encroachments; it seems to fear that its invention would not be sufficiently appreciated, it permitted to be attached to any thing else which might be confounded with it.

The fixing a time after which the call is not allowed, was a matter of necessity; it might indeed be deferred, but that would increase the advantages of the party who ought to call, and the law has not permitted it; delay would also have caused confusion by raising an uncertainty. In fact, if too great a latitude were permitted, if the call were allowed after playing, it would follow that each party being at the point of eight, he who held two honours would defer calling as long as possible, with the view of allowing his adversary to call, should he by chance also hold two honours. Procrastinating and temporising modes of attack are the very antipodes of Whist, and would produce frequent dilemmas similar to the one above mentioned.

Calling at any other point of the game except at eight is so flagrant a breach of all rule, that necessity becomes the common law of the case.

The two cases pointed out in the Article, have not appeared to us of extreme importance, and we have refrained from the application of Article 127.

If a player announce two cards in his hand, it amounts to an exposition of them, and they must therefore be turned up on the table; the loss of their value is to be added to the account of their importance, and to the intention which has caused the fault.

To call after having played, is a fault of slighter importance and ought not to be often punished. Nevertheless, the laws are here transgressed, though the punishment should not be too severe. The rule would have no limits, if separate articles were required for every case.

Art. 67.—A player holding only one honour might call, and his partner might answer with one or two; 2nd. he might call through mistaking the colour of the trump card; and his partner, from the same error, might answer the call. We do not enter into all the varieties of this fault; the errors are similar to the one just mentioned, and the results the same. Article 127 provides for all cases, the more particularly as it must have been remarked, that we are not scrupulous in the application of penalties incurred by all faults of whatsoever nature.

The right of demanding a new deal, conferred by Article 127, is only optional; if a party will not avail themselves of the privilege, the deal must be taken up and played. It is difficult to apply to the rule for the mode of rectification. There are a thousand different ones if we could detail them. In these cases, we must refer to Article 133, and the equitable application of its principle.

Art. 68.—We have frequently been an eye-witness to this fault, and it has always appeared to us to proceed from mistaking the suit of the trump-card. Independently of the case before quoted, where the game was lost through negligence, it would cause a serious prejudice during the playing of the round, if it were not severely punished. At the point of eight, the adversaries would not call; and at every other point, they would play badly, from mistaking the situation of the strong cards.

The error would not be discovered till the middle or the end of the deal; then, with every motive for applying it, the powers of Article 127 for a new deal, would be rarely found satisfactory. Nevertheless, those persons who would wilfully lead others into error, though their intentions be not always crowned with success, and their intended victims escape the snares laid for them, should indemnify those whom they would have led astray, and should suffer a punishment in proportion to their fault. Now, it is not easy to determine upon a penalty proportioned to this exigency. This is the excuse we offer those who would find fault with the innovation introduced by our article; we beg then to remark,—

First, that the law is paramount in cases which are not entirely ruled by custom.

Secondly, that we are not opposed to natural tendencies, since, in playing whist in which ten points made the game, those who marked six and held two or three honours, were entitled to the call; and,

Lastly, that we favour the spirit of the game which is prodigal of chances in the colour of the trump, and which seems inexhaustible in combination.

Having made this defence of our principles, we have no fear of explaining our intended innovation to its fullest extent. We are of opinion that honours should count at all points of the game, even when the party holding them mark nine; that to win the game they should take precedence of tricks made by the adverse party; and that in all other cases, they should be admitted as mitigating the loss of the vanquished.

On the other hand, as we think our conduct perfectly justified, we shall not make a bad use of our triumph, and by way of consolation to the loser, we may hint that the first of the above-mentioned cases is of very rare occurrence; that the circumstances which make it appear so alarming, are still less frequent; and there is no great reason to fear for that which can happen but by mere chance, and which may be considered as an almost impossible coincidence.

Art. 69.—The understanding between partners forms the very spirit of the game, and the basis of all improvement; the law protects and encourages them, provided their conduct be legal and impartial. The telegraph is at their disposal— let them work it, and draw from it every possible advantage; but let the signals be open and apparent, and the key to it always on the table, within reach of those who wish to make use of it in all its bearings. This same law abhors everything approaching to clandestine dealing, and provides against forgetfulness; for, on the slightest apparent symptoms of distraction, it fails not to awaken our attention and strengthen the memory; and it reminds us that, at no great distance, there is an abyss into which our negligence may plunge us headlong.

Art. 70.—The appearance of the turn-up card is the signal for action, and puts an end to all conversation. The game is again put in motion; all distraction disappears, and the attention of the players is redoubled.

The rules applied to the deal before the trump-card is turned, differ from those which affect the round when once begun. Cards turned during the deal authorise a new deal, whilst those shown afterwards are exposed on the table; the same occurs where the packs are incomplete, or faulty. When the trump-card is turned, honours which have not been announced, are lost. The turning of the trump, therefore, is a critical moment, which gives birth to a new era in the game.

In the old law, we find no prescription with regard to points forgotten to be marked. If the honours have been declared in time, but neglected to be scored, or if tricks have not been marked, till what time does the law extend the power of marking them? In discussions which have arisen on this subject, for want of being able to quote one article of law on the case, the delinquents have always ended by assuming the points in dispute; and we have seen, even in the middle of a round, a neglected score recover three or four points, by tricks or honours, in this manner. The prejudice in this case to the adverse party is evident, for they, seeing nothing marked, have regulated their play accordingly; and the moment the new score makes its appearance, they find their whole system of play disturbed. This result, which creates an advantage from a fault, and consequently is directly opposed to the spirit of the game, has obliged us to establish a limit beyond which no points forgotten to be marked can be recovered.

Art. 71.—There can be but one motive in not replying to the call; that of gaining a slam: the law will not allow this to exist. This act, thus deprived of its effect, comes under the denomination of caprice; the adversaries have so much the less reason to complain of it, as by waiving this privilege, they are in a position to make profitable tricks.

Art. 72.—To intimate to our partner during the deal that " we have the honours," is the same as if we said: " in order to win the game, we must gain so many tricks; therefore manage your game, and do not seek to gain more than sufficient to attain that point." To say to him: " we have not the honours," " our adversaries have or have not the honours," is the same as making any other remarks; it is exposing our hand to him, and amounts to a consultation, which the rule of the game strictly prohibits.

At whist, no remarks are permitted but those which are necessary and indispensable to the progress of the game. Thus, when there is an obstruction in the play, it is natural for a player to exclaim: "Whose play is it?" &c., but we earnestly advise all players to refrain from many other remarks frequently made during the play: the following for instance: "I play a heart," "It is my play," "I will not take it," "I take it," and all such expressions, which, though they appear inoffensive, we highly disapprove of; we even think that they are susceptible of being denounced and punished, as tending to convey hints between partners.

SECTION VI.—EXPOSED CARDS.

The law of the game is very strict with regard to shown cards; and nevertheless, cases occur every day which do not appear to us to be punished with sufficient severity. A card is shown either intentionally or through awkwardness; it may either serve to discover the weakness of a hand, or it may not be of any material consequence. It appears unjust to apply undue correction to this fault, but on the other hand, too great lenity will encourage speculation, which it is of the greatest importance to repress by every possible means. It would be inconvenient to make it an affair of conscience, because it would be so often excused on the score of error: besides, those cases which occur in what is called playing a fine game, invariably affect the interest of those who possess the greatest modesty and delicacy; and it is therefore a tax from which the law cannot deliver them but by severity, and a rigorous and constant application.

Art. 73.—In two-handed games, that is, where parties are single, if cards be shown through awkwardness or finesse, an adversary has no right to call for them. On what grounds could he acquire that right? No one is prejudiced except him who exposes the card, and it is the adversary who derives advantage from the fault.

But in playing at games with partners, circumstances are materially altered. If you have shown your cards from speculation, it is very evident that you will expose those only, the discovery of which would produce no advantage to your adversaries, but would convey important information to your partner. We do not pretend that what we here state is exactly true as regards the fact, but we maintain that the principle is incontestible.

It has been established—That an exposed card may be called for; but that if there be a mistake made in the card, 1st. That card shall be considered free; and, 2nd. The error shall give the right of a new deal, or the loss of one point.

Thus, on a four being shown, but quickly recovered, if the party seeing it, and unfortunately mistaking it for a five, under that impression call for it as such, not only do they lose their rights, but they become involved in a multitude of dangers and penalties, that are equivalent to a loss of the game.

This is really absurd. We have had no difficulty in expunging such a law from all the societies that we have frequented, and we hope that these remarks will everywhere expose its inconsistency.

To return to the rule; we approve of indulgence in all doubtful cases; we will even make every conscientious allowance for awkwardness; but if the error be intentional (see Article 74,) or if a player should have evidently availed himself of his partner's fault, no favour should be shown.

Art. 74.—Whenever a card is drawn out, a partner may see it, either from its transparency, or from his own peculiar keenness of sight. The law declares, that to constitute the fault, the card must have been drawn out to more than half its extent, because some line must be drawn, and a discussion upon whether two-thirds or three-fourths of it were exposed, would be puerile. The word intentionally must also be justly appreciated, to provide for cases of accident or awkwardness. The rule is more particularly directed against undecided players, who mix up all their cards together; detach, sometimes, three or four at a time, and are long in determining on what card they will play.

Art. 75.—There is no universally established rule with regard to cards which have been shown; every society introduces its own customs, and scarcely a day passes but we are consulted on difficulties or disputes arising from this question. We believe that our article will fix the law on this point;

in the first place, because it is lenient, and secondly, because it is a reasonable adjustment of the matter, and prevents it, as much as possible, from becoming a source of profit.

The option which we give to adversaries, of demanding or refusing the card, and of calling for the highest or lowest card in the suit, appears to provide completely against all danger of a card negligently shown; if the danger be increased (as is seen by Section VII.), by cards played out of turn and intentionally, we shall there find a more powerful system of repression, and the employment of more rigorous means.

Art. 76.—A little explanation on the mode of proceeding does not appear to us entirely superfluous in this place; for instance, suppose one of your cards, the queen of hearts, has been seen, and has therefore fallen under the denomination of an exposed card; a spade is played; your right-hand adversary, before playing his card, says to you: "If you have no spade, I refuse;" or, "I demand the queen of hearts;" if you hold no spade, you must obey, and the card will be played or liberated; but if you hold a spade, and therefore follow suit according to the rules, your queen of hearts must remain an exposed card until there is a possibility of the call being obeyed.

But, again, we will suppose hearts to be played; independently of the right of demanding or refusing your queen, your adversary also possesses that of demanding your highest or lowest heart; whatever call may be made, your queen is thrown down or liberated. There is a case in which your queen may remain as an exposed card, from not having been demanded, but that would be your own fault, for you ought to have played it yourself, to avoid a consequence against which you could not provide.

Articles 77 and 78.—These two cases are similar as regards the fault committed. The first limits the time till the trick has been laid in its place, and the second, till the right-hand adversary has played. It was desirable to restrain this right within a fixed period,—first, to avoid the necessity of a discussion; and, secondly, to prevent its neglect. A discussion is quite superfluous, particularly in a game where silence is so strictly enjoined; to submit to it is attended with sufficient inconvenience, but to exact it would be too great a tax on our patience. It would be strange indeed to be called upon to suffer for the negligence of others; for it is altogether repugnant to the spirit of the law itself. It amounts to this: " I have an exposed card, do not forget to avail yourself of the advantage you may derive from it, and of the mischief that you may do me in consequence."

A card is often shown through inattention. If the adversary neglect to apply the law for its punishment, the one fault cancels the other, and the account is balanced.

It is well understood, by the trick being put in its place (Article 77), or by the right-hand player throwing down his card (Article 78), that there is no longer any demand against the exposed card, and that he to whom it belongs may dispose of it as he pleases.

Art. 79.—It frequently occurs that several cards are played together on a trick, either through haste or awkwardness; as it is impossible to decide on the one that has fallen or been seen first, the application of this article prevents all discussion.

Art. 80.—The principle of this rule has been universally adopted, although no law has hitherto sanctioned it, since it has never been specifically declared. This will no longer be the case, and every turn-up, or trump-card, that shall not have been taken up before the completion of the second trick, will most certainly be considered as an exposed card, and treated as such.

We should here observe that a partner has a right to watch the turn-up card, and that he may warn the dealer to take it up in time.

SECTION VII.—CARDS PLAYED OUT OF TURN, AND OF THE
RIGHT OF CALLING FOR THEM.

The fault of playing out of turn has appeared to us of sufficient weight, and of such frequent occurrence, as to demand particular notice, and require a special treatment; and we have considered it our duty to make it the subject of a separate section, and to combine it with the case of calling for cards so played, which has not necessarily been noticed elsewhere, and on which the former case exercises a considerable influence.

Art. 81.—When the four players have each played their cards, the said cards form a complete trick; this is the law.

In the case of a revoke, we have granted to the party in fault
the means of retrieving their error, by extending the time
for so doing until the trick has been put in its place, and one
card has been played to the following trick. We have acted
in the same spirit of extension towards a lead made out of
turn. We have been anxious to allow the right of recovery
to exist as long as possible; because independently of a breach
of the rules, a false lead frequently involves pecuniary interests. An irregular lead generally proceeds from a false
notion entertained by one of the players, that he has won the
previous trick; which he consequently takes up, though it
properly belongs to his adversaries. In this case there is an
illegal act, un usurpation of the right of another, an injury
which must be repaired by a fine imposed on the offender.

Art. 82.—If it were lawful to play out of turn wilfully,
(which it is not, being merely a case to which the law submits
from want of power to reach it), and if an account were taken
of the results of such play, it is probable, that out of six
times, four would be successful; and that, in these four times,
there would be two in which a trick would be unjustly taken
from the adverse party. Besides the advantage of the lead,
and the chance of winning a trick, there still remains, in all
cases, even when detected in the act, the hint given to your
partner, of the suit which your play requires him to lead.

The right of demanding any suit, is the penalty of retaliation; you have exposed your game, I will expose mine. We
have doubled this privilege by extending it to the following
trick, optionally; for otherwise this right would be reduced
to a mere trifle, and even with this extension, it is not always
attended with advantage. When there is no profit found in
the immediate application of this right, it may be convenient
to wait for the change of suit, in order to accommodate the
partner's hand. In fine, if, even after this delay, the adversaries find no profit accruing to them, they may still have
recourse to the exposed cards. To prevent mistakes, we
should here mention, that only one of the three penalties can
be applied, and that when the choice has been once made, it
must be maintained.

Art. 83.—To play out of turn when a partner has already
played, is but a trifling fault; it is a manner of intimating to
your partner the state of your hand, which the law has not

actually prohibited, and for which it has provided but a slight punishment. A player's hand is shown in many ways; suppose, for instance, that your partner has played a queen, you play before your turn because you have the king, or the ace and king, or perhaps none of the suit; your partner learns by the fate of the trick, how you are situated. This species of intimation is against the spirit of the game; and does come within reach of the arm of the law; but as there is nothing in it repugnant to honour, and as every one indulges in it without scruple, it has become a common practice.

The penalty laid down by our article is not very severe: "Small crimes deserve but a small punishment." The consultation, on whether the card shall be taken or left, is almost always insignificant; nevertheless, as the fault in question has in general, not been calculated on, and as it is a matter of inattention, there are cases in which it acquires some degree of importance. Suppose, for instance, that the partner of the leader has played directly after the latter, the second player and his partner wait until the hand passes from one side or the other, which may become very advantageous. We remark, *en passant*, that in all cases where called for, the call should never be pressed, and above all things should be left to the most skilful player, for we have observed that a call, badly made, has frequently increased an advantage instead of punishing a fault.

Art. 84.—A player invariably and without exception has a right to play when his right-hand adversary has played; if, therefore, it be the latter who has committed the fault the provisions of Article 83 must be applied to the case.

But, in this instance, there is a double fault; a player has played before the two others who should have preceded him.

For this reason, and on account of the advantage which it almost invariably confers on the partner, the law is very severe on the case.

Art. 85.—There has been here a fault committed, and a penalty must follow. The law will apply it deliberately; and if the adversary would interrupt it by precipitation, the only effect of such interruption will be, to double its power.

Art. 86.—When the right is on one side, the article operates naturally. But as it will sometimes happen that the lead is out of order on both sides, we think that the faults should then cancel each other. The principle of reciprocity is defined in Article 106, where it carries with it the necessity of the new deal, which we do not consider it necessary to introduce here, as the fault is not sufficiently weighty.

Art. 87.—If a suit be called for, to which we cannot reply, the weakness of our hand is thus made known, and the fault is thereby punished. In point of fact, it becomes evident that we are short of a particular suit, or even of trumps, which, in almost every case, must be very prejudicial. If, after this punishment, the party were not liberated, if they remained still under the ban of the law, would it not amount to injustice?

Art. 88.—In this fault we find obstinacy or infatuation carried to the very highest degree. You are required to play your highest or lowest card in a suit, and you refuse to obey: you are called upon for one suit, and you play another; this is a real revoke, and no one can complain of the injustice of its punishment. How shall we judge of it otherwise, and by what other penalty can the fault be resisted?

The forfeiture of three tricks is by no means too heavy a penalty to atone for this fault, and to avoid confusion; whatever may have been its origin, the injury it causes increases its bad effects, changes its appearance, and makes it assume the character of absolute rebellion.

SECTION VIII.—THE REVOKE.

In this game, the exertion required of the mind is divided under numberless heads, each simple and intelligible in itself, but which, when combined, present difficulties too great for any single individual to surmount. If it were impossible to consider these obstacles separately, no efforts of the mind would be able to overcome them, and every amateur, after vainly endeavouring to comprehend them, would retire dispirited from the contest, or would at least confine himself to playing with those of his own strength; but the facility with which he masters them in detail, prevents him from perceiving his own want of capacity. He may argue with himself thus: "In this particular, I have been mistaken, perhaps through want of attention; I perceive my error, and will guard against it for the future." Thus he proceeds, and, by degrees, conquers all the difficulties of the game. To return to the subject of the revoke; it may be perceived at once, that it is an exception to the regular course of play, and not an inherent quality, and that the vigilance required to discover it is totally different from that attention so necessary to bestow on the game itself; this is so true, that we frequently find it escape the observation of practised players, whilst others, far less advanced in the game, never let it pass unnoticed.

We have no hesitation in declaring, that there is no circumstance which tends more to confusion in whist, than a revoke. It is altogether repugnant to the principles of the game. This fault requires a severe chastisement, on account of the disorders which it occasions, and also because of the facility with which it may escape notice.

Art. 89.—This article cannot claim the honour of being a precept; it is merely a definition, but nevertheless, indispensable, and for this reason, that a question should be plainly laid down before the consequences dependent on such question be admitted.

Art. 90.—The great difficulty to be here provided against, is when a player who has revoked, objects to the penalty; a dispute ensues on the facts of the case, or on the meaning of the rules; the offending party of course opposes the infliction of the penalty, and refuses to own himself in the wrong, or to yield to the decision of his adversaries; and if he be subsequently obliged to succumb to a majority of voices against him, he endeavours to come to some arrangement, or to refer the matter to arbitration.

The frequent recurrence of such cases has induced us to draw up regulations, based on the evidence of the parties present, the unanimous adoption of which method probably takes its date from the very origin of the game of Whist.

We are decidedly of opinion, that the trick in which a revoke has been made, should not only be replaced, that is to say, returned to the pack, but be turned up and thrown aside. A revoke cannot be considered as made, unless it be accompanied by all the circumstances mentioned in the first paragraph of the article; but if these circumstances have existed but for one second, they are sufficient to convict the offender; nor could any doubt be thrown on the case, by attempting to replace the hand when once removed from the trick.

A person revokes, and is discovered at the moment when the trick is put in its place; but this trick which belonged to the person revoking, is taken up by the adverse party, and the error immediately rectified. It may be asked, is the question of the revoke set at rest, or can it be returned to? The revoke is not destroyed, because the trick taken up by another hand, is not really replaced in its proper position until it be claimed.

He who plays to the card led, is not in the same position; he revokes, and renders himself liable to the penalties contained in Articles 83 and 84, for this reason, that his right-hand adversary can thereby regulate the leading card as he pleases.

The second remark regards the case in which a person is considered to have played; such cases come under Article 118.

Art. 91.—Partners being mutually responsible for each other's faults, a penalty is frequently incurred by an innocent party, even when the latter has employed all his rights, and used his utmost endeavours to avoid it.

Article 91 may be enforced either as a standing rule, or as a mutual agreement. We may make use of our right, by putting our partner on his guard, or by compelling him to count his cards. During these investigations, the adversaries take up the trick, put it in its place, and even lead off the next trick; the case then becomes clear, as one revoke cannot be made by two persons. But if the offence be completed by the party in fault, it will be irremediable, in spite of all discussion on the subject. With regard to the inquiry, we must further remark that, if delayed, it becomes null and void.

Art. 92.—If your partner be warned in time, he may withdraw the card which is wrongly played; but then he is not permitted to play as he chooses; he must take up his card, and wait till he is called upon for his best or worst card of the suit led; if he play without waiting for the call, this second card, improperly played, will be con-

K

sidered as an exposed card. The following reason strongly exemplifies this view of the case.—A player holding the knave and nine of spades is much interested in passing the ten which remains in hand. His right-hand adversary plays a small spade; he plays a diamond—having discovered by the play of his left-hand adversary where the ten of spades lay, he plays a sure game; his diamond taken up in time, will be, in truth, an exposed card, but of what consequence is that to him? he will be sure to win the round, if they have not the right of forcing him to play his best or worst. We have seen this happen precisely as it is here quoted, though the same thing may occur under many different forms and with other cards.

When our right-hand adversary has played, we have the right of doing the same; that is the rule. But, in the above case, will it be an infringement of the rule to prevent our playing? We believe not. This right has been cancelled by playing the diamond.

One more observation—you inflict a double penalty on the same deal. Must I submit to have one card turned up, and another called for? That is true, but a double fault deserves a double punishment, and this is the only means of restraining it.

Art. 93.—In this article, the expression "loses" is not quite precise, but it is true, and cannot be misunderstood by reason of the articles which precede and follow it, and which explain its various meanings. Strictly speaking the score must be considered in the light of an equation; whatever is added on one side is a loss to the other.

Art. 94.—If the revoke gave three points to the adverse party only in one manner, it would not confer any certain advantage upon those who are entitled to profit by it; and, consequently, would not operate to the disadvantage of those who have been guilty of the error.

The right of adding to their own score is of no service to those who have gained sufficient by their own game.

The right of causing their adversaries' score to be put down is of no detriment to those adversaries who have gained nothing;

And the taking of three tricks is inapplicable to those games in which three tricks beyond the gaining point have been already made.

The option granted by the law, was then an indispensable provision; but even this would have been insufficient, but for the addition of Article 105.

But, notwithstanding all these efforts to frame a law, so complete and so perfect as to provide against every contingency, and we could quote instances without number where the revoke is attempted with impunity. Let us suppose a case in which one party has scored nothing, and let us suppose that the said party has discovered that their adversaries hold in their hands a means of winning, to which, in the regular course of the game, no legal opposition can be made with any probability of success: it is evident, in that case, that they run no risk in thwarting their adversaries' game by revokes. The law, foreseeing the probable occurrence of this case, has departed from its usual tenor of mildness, and, employing its last resource, has launched forth its anathema by which it strictly prohibits the revoke, and calls upon all players conscientiously to abstain from it.

Arts. 95 and 96.—This is a general practice. Before entering on the possession of an estate, a good title to it should be proved, and it is also necessary that the title deeds be carefully preserved, since they are the documents by which the right of possession is supported.

Art. 97.—A legal revoke (*esquiche*) is an essential right in Whist, and is caused by inability to follow suit. This, however, may sometimes occur by mistake, as in the case of cutting the cards. An attentive player never fails to detect this error; during the rest of the round he carefully notices the playing of the thirteen cards in each suit, and, on the least apparent irregularity, he exclaims instinctively, "There has been a revoke." He is allowed to make this remark on mere suspicion; it injures no one, because the result must be known to all, and it serves to prevent forgetfulness at the end of the deal. On instituting an investigation for the purpose of proving a revoke, it is required to show the trick in which it was made; and as it probably may be necessary to turn up several of the recently made tricks, it cannot take place in the middle of the round; firstly, because it is forbidden by the law; secondly, because the tricks might become mixed with the hands of the players, which would render the provisions of Section III. unjust; and lastly, because it would give the crafty player an undue advantage over his adversaries; since, in order to ascertain if a certain card had been played, he would only have to declare a revoke to gain a sight of the tricks already made.

Arts. 98 and 99.—We have already remarked that those who profit by a revoke are in justice bound to prove the fact, which can be done only by pointing out the trick in which it has occurred; and we have also shown in the preceding remarks, that the tricks must not be inspected before the end of the round; now, these two regulations comprehend some weighty consequences and deductions.

In the middle of a round a revoke is proved; sometimes this decides the game, in which case it would appear fastidious to continue to play out a quantity of cards, when there is no interest for so doing. But a powerful motive for continuing the play does exist, for a pecuniary loss may be much diminished by winning an additional number of points. We may remark, *en passant*, that here the adept shows his great skill; he struggles hard, and strains every nerve to dispute the ground inch by inch, whilst on the other side, the careless player, intoxicated with his success, voluntarily concedes his advantage, without even troubling himself to contest the point. If he has marked three and holds the honours, or if he has made two points and has proved a revoke, of what importance is it to him to win a double or a treble!

Another interested motive for continuing the round may be discovered, in the hope that a revoke on the other side may cancel the first; or in the fear that a fresh act of inattention may make the losing party amenable to the provisions of Article 99.

Art. 100.—The law provides for the possibility of several revokes: This was a necessary measure, for otherwise, a party having once offended, and paid the forfeit, might consider themselves privileged to revoke during the remainder of the game. It has, therefore, been found necessary to provide a remedy for any repetition of the fault.

Art. 101.—A moment arrives in the course of the game when the claim of a revoke is no longer admitted; this may be easily guessed—it is when the cards are all thrown together, or when the proof (see Article 96) is destroyed. Our article admits this axiom; the more cards the stronger the

right.   It is undeniable if no claim has been made before the
last card is played.

Articles 102 and 103.—It frequently occurs that a revoke
is detected by the last card in the round; the axiom laid down
in the preceding remarks, gave rise to Article 102; and
again, this latter Article required to be sanctioned and supported by Article 103.

Art. 104.—We once witnessed a circumstance which led to
a discussion on a point extremely difficult to decide, and in
which, for want of reasonable principles to guide us, and
from the silence of the ancient law of the game on the subject, we were reduced to the expedient adopted by the judges
of Pantagruel, and drew lots for it.

The following is the case alluded to:—One party had made
a revoke, and either from bad play or from holding bad cards,
had taken up only three tricks; their adversaries, on discovering a revoke, insisted on claiming the penalty, as declared
in the third paragraph of Article 94, *i. e.* by taking their
three tricks and adding them to their own score.   By enforcing this penalty, they made the whole of the thirteen tricks,
and therefore, by the provisions of Article 53, they claimed
a slam, and its value.

Art. 105.—It is a general practice, that the party which
makes a revoke, cannot win the game in the same round in
which it has been made.   We have therein united a prohibition against counting the slam, which, although hitherto
tacitly understood, appeared an indispensable addition to the
rule.

To deprive a party of the power of winning the game, when
they have the means of doing so, appears a punishment of
extreme severity.   This is no longer one single forfeiture, but
becomes a most formidable accumulation of penalties.   If
the said party be in the "well," they must remain there,
even though they hold strong cards, the four honours, and
most of the trumps; nor is this all; their adversaries mark
their three points in spite of the mortification it causes to the
other party.   It is hoped that these considerations will operate with sufficient weight to ensure the caution of all players
against so grave a fault as a revoke.

Art. 106.—When revokes are made on both sides, it is not
an easy matter to detect them.   How many times has such a

side revoked? And what influence has one revoke had upon others? Besides, of what use is it to continue a game, which cannot be finished, unless the text of Article 105 be changed, and a new law introduced? This, however, cannot be done, particularly when we take into calculation the skill of the players to whom such a case may happen. On reflection, we shall see that we have but one course to pursue, that the discussion must be put an end to, and the proceeding terminated. The fault of both parties is proved, and the guilt cancelled. We shall not inquire which side has been the more culpable, nor shall we seek even to ascertain whether the revokes are direct or by assimilation; in the eye of the law they are the same, it is on the fact only that we decide. There must be a new deal, and therefore no points can be marked, and the party who had the deal must take it again.

Art. 107.—The revoke by assimilation has never yet been specified in the laws of the game, though it appears to have always been contemplated, otherwise what decision could have been arrived at, in the case of Articles 47, 88, and others similar? When we reflect that every time a card is called and consequently that every card liable to be so called, may become the cause of a revoke, we cannot see how it is possible to elude an enactment so consonant to justice.

With the exception of Article 47, where revokes are immediately marked, and terminate the round, it appears that all revokes by assimilation are in every respect applicable to Section VIII., and subject to the same rules with revokes properly so called.

Art. 108.—Notwithstanding all the precautions which the law has taken, and in spite of the numerous and heavy denunciations uttered against any transgressions of its rules, cases are constantly occurring in which the revoke eludes its grasp, and is placed altogether beyond its power.

A wilful and well-calculated revoke may sometimes advance a party without any danger, especially where a game is considered as lost, or where a revoke alone may change its doom. These cases are of common occurrence, and are closely allied to others, not perhaps so flagrant, though, in these latter, the profit always equals, if it does not exceed the loss, since there is always a chance that the revoke will not be discovered;

and this very chance, which is greater or less, according to the skill of the players, possesses a certain value.

It is possible that a revoke may operate greatly to the advantage of the party revoking; let us suppose the following example:—

You hold in your hand four honours, and nine best spades; with these you might make a slam, because no hand could hold five trumps.*

Your adversary holds four trumps, and nine best clubs; at the fourth round of trumps, he revokes, and afterwards trumps your suit, and wins nine tricks.

In this case, how could Article 108 be dispensed with? The example above quoted, is perhaps an extreme case, but there are others analogous to it, of frequent occurrence.

SECTION IX.—INTIMATIONS BETWEEN PARTNERS AND OF THEIR LIMITS.

Art. 109.—Since all right of communication between partners is founded on their mutual and individual responsibility, it is, consequently, necessary to adopt some means of obviating that punishment in which a player may be involved by the ignorance or inattention of his partner. We may consider these rights as existing, in a different degree, during three different periods of time. The first period is that which precedes the turning of the trump-card, during which time, intimations are limited in no other way than by the rules of common politeness.

During the second period, which commences from the time that the trump-card is seen, and extends to the termination of the round, communication is much more restricted. This is the period which the law affects; it admits of parties acting on the defensive, but prohibits all acts of aggression. It authorises us to check an excess of vivacity; allows us to caution our partner to hold his cards in a better position, and to abstain from asking questions which are contrary to the rules of the game; to request him to make the necessary claim in case of a revoke, and to examine his hand for our more complete satisfaction. It also allows us, either by voice or gesture, to prevent our partner from throwing down his cards; but, at the same time, it expressly forbids any

* This position is exactly as M. Deschapelles has stated it.—ED.

observation which may be detrimental to the interests of the adverse party. The rights of the third period come into operation during the interval between one round and another. These consist of a review of what has taken place, and what might have been done. An increased degree of amenity is here required, in order that no harsh expression be made use of; each player is supposed to have done his best, and the want of success should be considered a sufficient punishment for any error that may have been committed.

Art. 110.—An old rule of the game requires that each player should keep before him the card which he has played, and enjoins the strict observance of this practice. This custom, however, is neither reasonable nor necessary. A card, when once played, ceases to belong to any particular hand; it forms a component part of a trick, and the player from whose hand it has proceeded, has no more right to keep it in any particular position, than he has to take it up again. This remark, of course, does not apply to a card which may have slid away, and is removed from its proper place. In this case, any one has a right to replace it. The privilege of touching this latter card, when once played, might be a means of collusion between partners, which is contrary to the spirit of the law, as giving a preponderating advantage to one side. With respect to the necessity of the case, it can affect him only whose turn it is to play; it is his business to put the question, and to act accordingly. The other players must look upon it as an exception to the general course of the play, and it can serve them only as a hint; if, however, they have not seen it in time, it is their own fault; why have they averted their eyes from the table? of what use is attention if its reward must be divided with the careless and negligent?

We are acquainted with persons who, when it is their turn to play, make a point of asking every question which the law does not positively forbid; not that they require information, but they act in this manner merely to show their authority, and stretch their prerogative to the utmost.

Questions at whist are allowed to be addressed only to our partner; if they prove injurious to him, or cause mistakes, he has no remedy. It is only when a doubt or discussion arises, that the question is laid for decision before the bystanders.

Art. 111.—Every one knows how much the significancy of

an expression depends on circumstances which precede or accompany it. There are a thousand phrases which take their sense and bearing only from the incidents which have preceded them, or with which they are connected.

At whist, words derive their significancy from numerous accidental circumstances, which are intelligible only to the experienced. Words are frequently accompanied by gestures which have a powerful influence on nervous temperaments; a player becomes agitated and exasperated because his partner does not return his lead, or does not follow his suit. " What, Sir, you have played me a diamond! for the last quarter of an hour I have been giving you every possible hint to play spades!" He then raises himself on his chair, and holds up his hand, to intimate that he would take the trick over which his partner is hesitating.

No excuse can be admitted for any word or gesture intelligible to the partner, which may exercise the slightest influence, either on the round in hand, or on those consequent to it.

Articles 112, 113, 114, and 115.—These prohibitory articles define the limits allowed to intimations; they are tacitly understood in Article 111, but we have judged it necessary to lay them down as separate Articles, in order to serve as a reference, and to explain the exact spirit and signification of the law.

We should look with an unfavourable eye on him who plays a winning card in such a manner as to signify to his partner not to trump it; but from the moment that this act is repressed, he who has committed it feels no annoyance from it, because, as the profit bears no proportion to the detriment, the act can be attributed only to negligence or thoughtlessness.

It is not now allowed to draw your card for your partner unless he request it. The cause of this prohibition is evident; here is the boundary within which intimations are confined; the abuse of the custom was feared; the legislator was afraid lest this abuse would tend to make one player too attentive, and render the partner careless.

As long as the trick has not been turned, the preceding one may be looked at, unless the first card of the next round has been played; conformably to the maxim that nine cards must not be seen at once. When any one wishes to see the trick which has been taken up, it is usual to make the request to the player before whom it is placed. In the event of seeing another, (not the last) trick, it is customary to refrain from all further examination, on the principle that the right of inspection no longer exists.

In order to apply the provisions of Article 115, we must suppose the trump-card taken up; for if it be allowed to lie on the table after the second trick, as very frequently happens, it will then fall under the denomination of an exposed card, by the provisions of Article 80.

This is a judgment will be followed by immediate application in case of Articles 112, 113, 114, and 115, since they bear upon positive facts affected by a special law.

There appears here some defect; the privilege of a new deal will be of no use to those who hold good cards, from which it might be inferred that of two faults, only one will be punished. This is true. But it is a great point gained to restrain the abuse of advantages. Another circumstance increases our confidence that this law will prove beneficial; every appeal will cause an interruption of the game, which will increase the difficulty of recollecting the previous play; this will make players on both sides cautious of giving occasion for those delays, and thus the general interests of the game will be promoted.

SECTION X.—GENERAL RULES.

We have devoted each Section to the special consideration of certain laws.

Art. 117.—It is the duty of one player on each side to take up the tricks which are won, and place them near him, in such a manner that each of them may cover the half of the one preceding; the last being placed at the top, and seen wholly.

This arrangement, firstly, will facilitate the inspection for faults; secondly, it will considerably shorten the calculation of those whose play is directed by the tricks already made; and, thirdly, when the last trick is required to be shown, it will prevent the possibility of the wrong trick being turned.

Order is a duty which we should exercise, were it only because it tends to fix our attention. The slightest confusion becomes an excuse for error. Thus, if your tricks appear to consist of four instead of five, it may prove a fertile source of mistakes to your adversary. He has a right to accuse you of infringing Article 111, and to call for the application of Article 116. In Section II., under Article 33, a penalty is inflicted for a similar fault.

If your tricks are crowded together in a heap, if they are divided with your partner, or are in any way disordered, you act contrary to the prescribed rules of the game, and you give rise to errors which an intelligent adversary will not fail to turn to your disadvantage. In the event of a discussion, your interests must suffer, as you are subjected to all the disagreeable effects of a quarrel; and if your property be contested, how will you be able to prove your title?

Art. 118.—This case is included in Article 74, as regards a card detached from the hand, and in Article 124 with respect to the hand thrown down. Circumstances, however, frequently prevent the application of both these Articles.

A player shows his card, or throws down his hand when he thinks that, by so doing, the round will be finished. This is only another way of expressing that he can make the rest of the tricks, or win the game, which, in most cases, proves true. If, however, a revoke has preceded the act, it may be contended that the revoke is not complete; for this error is punished with sufficient severity by adhering to the letter of the law, without aggravating the penalty by forcing its interpretations.

In this Article, the completion of the revoke, or of other faults, is the same in principle as that laid down in Article 90. When any one has wholly detached a card from his hand for the purpose of playing it, or when he has voluntarily exposed his hand to view, we consider, in both cases, that he has played.

This fault often occurs: frequently, though he holds cards of the same suit in his hand, a player will trump the suit, and throw down his hand. In this case, there is an evident revoke.

This mistake is frequently made in another manner, which must be here explained, in order that a just decision be applied to it.

Suppose that spades are trumps; a player holds the ace

and the two of hearts, and the two of spades; the suit played is
hearts, and it is his turn to play; instead of playing, he throws
down his hand, and exclaims, " I trump, and play the ace of
hearts." Under these circumstances has he revoked?—
Decidedly not.

Art. 119.—When a card is played in consequence of
another player's mistake (and this be rectified), it is said to
be played precipitately.—(See Articles 82, 86, 92, and
others.)

Suppose a player has played a club, and the three others
have also played to the trick; it is discovered in time (see
Article 82) that he has played out of turn. In this case the
lead must return to the proper player, and the fault be dealt
with according to the rules.

But there are here three cards which have been improperly
seen. We have before declared, and our reasons for it are
evident, that the card belonging to the party in fault, must
remain exposed, unless, by chance, the suit be led in the
following trick, in which case the card can be played.

The two other cards must remain at the disposal of those
who have, in reality, committed no fault, but who have been
unwittingly led into error.

Art. 120.—If a player take up, or allow his partner to take
up, a trick which he erroneously thinks to belong to himself,
he is thereby led into a second error; he plays to the next
trick, and consequently is liable to the application of Articles
81 or 82.

Have players a right, knowingly, to appropriate to their
own use a purloined trick?

No, they should return it to the rightful owners, when the
fault has been atoned for.

Are the bystanders authorised to interfere?

Certainly, it is their duty to do so, when the fault has been
expiated.

Art. 121 and 122.—Hitherto, no law has existed which prohibited cards or hands from being voluntarily thrown down.

It was only necessary, however, to object to this right, to
procure its condemnation; since, as no written law could be
produced in its favour, the assailants had recourse to those
articles of law by which shown cards are placed at the disposal of the adversaries.

In accordance with our regulations for throwing down the hand, whoever (see Article 121) shall have done so correctly will thereby incur no risk; but on the contrary, will exert his own privilege, and economise the time of the players.

Art. 123.—If when you hold thirteen cards in your hand, you allow six of them to be seen, those six become exposed cards; if seven be seen, your hand must be thrown down. Whether this be done through awkwardness, or purposely, the law must take its course. In case of the fault occurring from some external or reciprocal cause, Article 126 may be referred to; if it be the fault of the adverse party, a remedy will be found in Article 127.

When very bad cards are held, it may be advantageous that the partner should see them, in order to demonstrate the impossibility of co-operating with his friend's plans, and to caution him against speculation. Thus, thrown back upon his own resources, he will foresee the necessity of employing them so as to soften the severity of his disaster.

We must here observe, that if the hand not subject to the call, should contain any cards previously exposed, such cards are disposed of by the usual regulations. (Article 73.)

Art. 124.—We have already shown, that a hand thrown down involves a necessity of the same act on the side of the partner, and that were it otherwise, the fault might be productive of advantage to its authors.

In order to obviate the slightest mistake in the application of the law, we repeat; Firstly, that in all cases where the hand is thrown down, the partner must do the same; Secondly, that one of the two hands, at the option of the delinquent, is played at command; and Thirdly, that the other hand cannot be called for, with the exception of whatever cards may have been previously exposed.

Art. 125.—If a player throw up his hand, and an adversary do the same, the cards become so mixed that it is impossible to continue the game, and there must be a new deal; but if his partner should prevent it in time, by removing the hand thrown up before the cards become mixed, the fault must then be compensated by applying to Article 124.

Art. 126.—Our rules contain many Articles which are vaguely and indefinitely expressed. Article 126 is liable to

this exception. What is to be understood by the expression
" very much?" How are we to provide for the case when
the fault is on both sides? And in what acceptation are we
to take " from any other cause?"

The strongest and most serious objections are as nothing
when weighed in the scale against necessity. The removal of
the Article will create a deficiency in the rules; if the expression be struck out, it will be the cause of endless discussions;
if we were to specify every sort of mutual fault, we should fill
volumes.

Art. 127.—This is merely a corollary to the preceding
Article. In the last, we pronounced a penalty upon extra-
neous or reciprocal faults, by declaring the necessity of a new
deal; here we apply the same penalty to special faults, and
fix the punishment upon the guilty party.

Art. 128.—If a player should have forgotten to declare
honours till after the trump-card is turned, the honours
cannot be marked. Suppose, however, that, in consequence
of some fault, the deal be lost, or a fresh deal be necessary:—

In this case he might assume that, as the round was annulled, he had a right to resume all his privileges of the
preceding round.

In the case of a new deal, no objection could be raised to his
pretensions, for a round which is annulled, can be productive
of no effects.

But, in the case of a lost deal, it might be maintained that
the round was not altogether without effect, since it produced
a gain to one party, and a loss to the other.

Under these circumstances, the legislator considered himself
authorised to decide the two cases differently, though, at the
same time, he found it convenient to combine them in one article, and under the same law. The only effect produced by this
arrangement, is a slight increase in the value of the honours.

This rule, which regards honours, may be applied by analogy to other cases.

Art. 129.—On the principle of mutual responsibility, when
a player has played or put down his card, the round is, to all
intents, led off, as far as it may affect his own or his partner's
rights.

A round is finished in the same way as the game (see Article 130).

To play to a trick, is to put down your card on those which have been played before your turn.

Art. 130.—If one party assert that they have won the game, and if their adversaries, without any dispute, assent to the assertion, the game is finished. The circumstance of the cards being again put together is no additional proof of the fact.

Art. 131—It is contrary to the rules, not to follow suit when you are able to do so. Thus, to put a heart upon a spade, when you have a spade in your hand, is an infringement of the law.

To deal, or to play out of turn, are also illegal acts; but they are not such serious offences against the law, because they produce no evil consequences, and do not act to the prejudice of either party. Indeed, though they interrupt, they do not perplex the game. If they escape the notice of the players, or if they be remarked, and suffer the consequent penalty, it is too late to rectify them, and the game must proceed.

SECTION XI.—THE BYSTANDERS*.

Art. 132.—If a dispute arise between two players, one positively affirming that an error has been committed, and the other as positively denying the fact; it is evident, that, in such a case, all continued discussion would be useless.

Under these circumstances, the dispute must be settled by arbitration or by lot. The umpires are the bystanders, or witnesses. They are the best judges of the fact, as they have seen it, and, consequently, there is no appeal from their decision. Every man of sense will think himself too fortunate to have such a tribunal to refer to; even if unjustly condemned, he will submit without murmuring; for where shall we look for him who has never discovered, after an argument, that he has been all the while in error, though he was positive, at the time, of being in the right?

The drawing by lot is a concession on both sides. Each party gives up the half of his rights; a proceeding which it is necessary to adopt in the absence of witnesses. By this concession, the interests of neither side are injured, consequently there can be no oppression exercised.

* This section has been greatly reduced; the author has indulged in details far too diffuse for a work of general reference.—ED.

Art. 133.—Whenever a player thinks that he perceives, in the course of the game, an act unauthorised by the law, he has a right to remark upon it, and consequently to refer to the bystanders for their opinion.

The bystanders are not allowed to express their opinion, except at the express request of the players. The only exception to this remark is the case of Article 135.

Art. 134.—We have already declared that, with regard to the fact, the decision of the bystanders is paramount. They have the power of maintaining, specifying, and determining the fact; but players are privileged to refuse to submit to their opinion, though this is an extreme case, which we would advise all persons to avoid, because the power vested in the bystanders is of great advantage to players, even though they be not always very competent, or very impartial judges.

The following rules will serve as a supplement to, or correction of, the law as it now stands.

Firstly,—If an unforeseen case should occur in any whist club, it shall be submitted to the decision of players of acknowledged skill, and be made the subject of deliberate consideration.

Secondly,—It shall be reduced to writing, and posted for public inspection.

Thirdly,—It shall be communicated to all neighbouring clubs.

Fourthly,—It shall be submitted to foreign clubs in those countries where the game of Whist is well played.

Fifthly, and Lastly.—The decision shall be delivered to the club where the dispute originated, and be held binding.

Art. 135.—Customs which are purely the result of habit, should not be allowed to offer any obstacle to discussion: their foundations have been long since sapped by the gradual improvement of the game, and the day is at length arrived when they must give way to rational institutions. Article 135 creates a revolution in the former usages of the game, and restores to the bystanders the rights of which a long and inveterate habit had deprived them; it re-establishes equity in decisions, it animates the progress of the game, and raises those, who were before considered a hindrance, into powerful protectors of the player's interests.

Art. 139.—No engagement can be more binding than a

mutual contract: when a benefit is conferred, every one should acknowledge the obligation, and take the first opportunity of making a return. Thus the privileges with which we have invested the bystanders authorise us to impose upon them certain restrictions. These are laid down in Article 139.

Here we breathe from our labours. We have, at length, arrived at a point we have long wished to reach. We confess that this accumulation of articles has been very trying to our patience; indeed, we scarcely think we should have undertaken the work, had we been aware of the necessity of so many explanations. To show, however, how far we are influenced by a conscientious feeling, we shall not shrink from the task, but shall conclude with some general remarks, which are necessary to the completion of the work, and which our readers have a natural right to expect.

The study of games resembles that of languages; they both employ the more prominent faculties of the mind, memory, reflection, &c. In infancy, this occupation tends to the development of the mental powers, and the progress of reason; but in after-life, it interrupts the growth of ideas; thus it becomes a pleasing and useful study for young people, but disagreeable and unintellectual for those of a more advanced age.

The saying of a celebrated diplomatist is well known: " *Vous ne savez pas le whiste, jeune homme? quelle triste vieillesse vous vous préparez!* "

PART THE FOURTH.

WHIST BY THE EDITOR.

ACCORDING TO THE BEST MODERN AUTHORITIES.

It has been said by one of our most popular poets that

"Troy owes to Homer what Whist owes to Hoyle."

The magician of the Iliad, whose individual existence and identity are questions upon which the learned are at issue, from vague and vagrant traditions moulded the most entire and perfect epic that poetry has produced. So did Hoyle, from elements as indefinite and dispersed, model the most complete and peerless game that is played with cards: the most elaborate and finished of all the essays of science, skill, and memory, whereof they are the instruments. This talent for distinguishing and turning to account the beautiful and rare stands in the same relation to the embellishments of life as knowledge and energy to its more important offices. The sage discover and the diligent apply the mines of wisdom and wealth, which are the moral and material inheritance of civilization; the imaginative and the speculative weave their fancies and their schemes from the rich legacies of the ideal and the subtle contrivances of art.

The origin of playing cards is as unsettled, as it is obscure. There are several volumes on the subject extant, but they leave this vexed question where they found it. One antiquarian ascribes it to Arabia, another to Persia, a third to China. Were I writing a history, I should make bold to borrow from them, but I am not. The purpose of this treatise is to trace the game of whist from its seedtime to the ripe harvest of its present maturity. Any attempt to find out by whom the germ was first planted or whence it was derived, would be as difficult, if not as impossible, as to search out the source of its machinery. Whether descended from "Ruff and Honours," from "Slam," or from "Whist and Swabbers," is an inquiry that may conveniently be bequeathed to posterity. We made

our acquaintance with the game when, after an ordeal of
several seasons at Bath, it had obtained *entrée* to the clubs and
salons of London.   Here we have watched its progress and
recorded its changes and improvements.   We have in the previous pages exhibited the results of its introduction among the
élite of the French capital.   It now remains to specify its
changes at home during the last half century, and more especially to record the revolution which overthrew the ancient
" Long" dynasty, under the title of " Short Whist." *

A popular writer upon this game, in alluding to the
necessity for a generally understood and acknowledged code
applicable to it, observed, some ten or a dozen years ago,
"The whist of Brookes's, White's, and Graham's Clubs, is no
more like country play, than Phillidor's game of chess is like
that of Mrs. Grundy."   Such a remark, indeed, could not have
referred to players of any pretension, who would necessarily
be on terms with the changes that time, even an hour, brought
about.   Nevertheless a record or register of the rules and
regulations adopted in the circles distinguishad for whist
playing, more especially the leading card clubs and societies,
would at all times and under all circumstances have been a
manual of great convenience in disputed cases, as well as
furnishing the best means of preventing much misunderstand-
ing.   But while the system was yet crude in theory, and
scantily developed by practice, a work of the kind was not to
be expected.

Whist was in general favour as a game of skill and
great interest a century ago, but it seems very doubtful
whether the game spoken of by Farquhar, Pope, Thomson,
and others of their contemporaries, is the same as that
at present known.   " We may, on many accounts, regret,"
says an amateur, who published, a few years since, a
pretty little illustrated *brochure* on the subject, " that Whist
was not generally known nor played throughout England
at an earlier period, in the days of Elizabeth, or rather
in those of Shakspeare, for it is fair to compute epochs

---

* The game was cut in half one night to give a chance to Lord Peter-
borough of recovering a heavy loss.   Hoare, the great Picquet player,
lately deceased at Bath, at a very advanced age, was one of the party.
This must have been nearly sixty years ago.

from the highest in intellect as well as the highest in rank. Had it been so ordained, and our immortal bard had loved his innocent rubber, what inimitable allusions to it might have been scattered through his works. Conceive his criticisms on the Prince's lead or Poins's finesse, delivered the more earnestly that he might cheat unobserved. How figurative had ancient Pistol been on kings, queens, knaves, and deuces! How accomplished a trickster, in another sense, had Autolycus shown himself! How Sir Toby Belch would have expressed his detestation of a mean and meagre hand, next in his sober abhorrence to 'an unfilled can,' or to a sot in his drunken reprehension!"

Hoyle, then, furnished the text of the game now known as Whist, an embodiment derived, and to a certain extent completed, during the latter part of the seventeenth century, from certain games previously distinct and specific. In 1680 Cotton thus spoke of the rules observed in playing Ruff and Honours, by some called Slam or Whist. "If either side are at eight groats, he hath the benefit of calling Can ye? If he hath two honours in his hand, and the other answers 'One,' the game is up, which is nine all; but if he hath more than two, he shows them, and then it is one and the same thing; but if he forgets to call, after playing a trick, he loseth the advantage of Can ye for that deal." In another place he says, "He that hath three honours in his own hand, his partner not having the fourth, sets up eight by cards, that is two tricks; if he hath all four, then sixteen, that is four by tricks: it is all one if the two partners make their three or four between them, as if one had them." To Hoyle we are indebted for the existing single abstract game, formed out of the above-named compound; to the various editions of that great master we owe our knowledge of its elemental progress and amended systems. "Honour to Edmund Hoyle," exclaims one of his least aspiring, though not one of his least discerning followers, "honour to Edmund Hoyle! If he was not exactly the first who reduced this sport into a science, he was the first who rescued its rules from the vagueness of oral tradition, and gave them a systematic arrangement, a printed existence." The pith of their lore and philosophy was given in the Second Part of this Treatise, and that transcript may be regarded as the text book of whist down to the introduction of the Short Game.

It is true he had many disciples, but these are rather commentators than historians of any new facts or principles. We reckon among his successors Mathews, Admiral Burney, Arnaud the *savant* of modern Athens, and a host of small deer, *servum pecus.* We find in them the most meagre and unsatisfactory allusion to that re-organization of the game which was indeed slowly, but still surely going on, and which, about five-and-twenty years ago, resulted in the introduction of that new system which is destined at no very distant day to supersede altogether the custom, if not the memory, of its predecessor.

"It is a great desideratum," observes Deschapelles, "that the game should be curtailed in a definite, constant, and uniform manner; but at the same time that its principles should remain unchanged, and that, in this state, it should appear invested with the same charm, and offering the same attraction as before. After various attempts that plan was adopted, which, from its simplicity, should have first offered itself. The game *was cut in two*, and thus became short whist. The increased importance of the honours, which had at first given cause for alarm (since, from being four-tenths they became four-fifths), was not in reality so meant to be feared, as they held the same relation to the tricks, which rose in an equal proportion; and the penalty inflicted on the revoke, which was doubled, and thus better adapted to the short game, did not appear exorbitant in practice. The punishment of the revoke, in fact, should be always proportioned to the mischief it might cause should it pass unperceived; and if the legislator had inflicted the loss of the game as a penalty for the fault, no one could have murmured at his decision.

"These two circumstances, respecting the honours and the revoke, the only obstacles to the adoption of short whist, had already been sanctioned by experience. In the game of *Favourite*, four honours had marked eight points, and the revoke six points, without exciting any opposition. The path being thus cleared, short whist had but to present itself to be received with universal acclamation.

"By the assistance of a simple regulation, the essential

clause, regarding double and treble games, is maintained; and by abolishing the 'call,' a means has been found of compensating the skilful player for the advantages of which he was deprived. With these few exceptions, short whist was found to possess all the essential qualities of its parent, and to resemble it in every respect; and indeed it is an excellent substitute for long whist, whenever excitement and vivacity are required, or when business may make it necessary to economise time.

"Except these illustrations, and some shades of difference in the manner of playing, long and short whist are identically the same, and all the remarks made in this treatise are equally applicable to both games. In order to explain the spirit which distinguishes them, we shall adopt Plutarch's system, and draw a parallel between them. An opportunity for adopting this plan is offered in the solution of two very interesting questions, which are subjects of continual discussion. This solution is of some importance: it is a conscientious discussion, and the result of long reflection; and to insure its general adoption, we shall here present it to our readers.

"Is short whist as difficult as long whist?*

"In playing the long game, when both sides mark five, they are precisely in the same position with those parties who are beginning the short game.

"The latter, therefore, is but a fraction of the former.

"Now the part is less than the whole.

"Therefore the question is solved.

"At short whist the points are marked from one to five.

"At long whist they are extended as far as ten.

"The calculation, confined to the number of points to be won in a single round,† increases in a geometrical progression. In this respect long whist is exactly similar to the new game, as it is possible in the same round [hand] to make eleven points, by seven tricks and four honours. Hence it follows that, in this point of view, and with this progression in the

* This is a repetition, the question having being already put and answered; but it is necessary to the context.

† The translator continually applies the word "round" to playing out four cards or the whole fifty-two indifferently.

calculation, the difference and increased difficulty of the latter game must be immense.

"We engage our readers not to draw a rash conclusion from these two corollaries, but first to listen to the modifications on the other side, which will set the question in a new light, and correct their first impressions.

"The state of the game from five to five cannot be identified with short whist, because the latter still has the chances of winning a double or a treble.

"Whence it follows that all the combinations of the game which concern the number of five, are not affected by its extension, and remain unchanged in both games. The intrinsic merit of the game is equally unaltered. The merit, combined with skill, becomes irresistible in the hands of the proficient.

"The calculation itself, which is generally considered to increase in proportion with the number of points marked by the game, only does so by exception: it will be frequently disturbed by peculiar combinations of the cards, and even sometimes completely confused for want of co-operation on the side of the timid and unenterprising partner.

"Having thus neutralized the chief objections, we shall return to the question, and here we shall find that the reduction of the game from ten to five points is one great cause of its excellence, since the very fact of its being circumscribed gives occasion for a greater exertion of intellect: this is more especially true with regard to those things of which we cannot be certain, but in which probability of possession is increased in proportion to the intelligence employed in acquiring them. We find that the distribution of the cards easily admits the possibility of making five points in one round [hand], a possibility which is increased, both by the eargerness of those who, having scored nothing, desperately run all hazards, and by the backwardness of others who, having made three or four points, are afraid of venturing too far, and act on the defensive.

"These two-fold principles of action open a field for energy, decision, and ardour, in which the excited feelings of the player are, as it were, counterbalanced by his caution and skill, by which means talents are developed which are wholly unknown in long whist. . . . ." "Long whist is more difficult than short whist in the ratio of twenty to nineteen."

This latter axiom justifies our placing the long game, with such modern changes and improvements as have grown up since Hoyle's time, in the reader's possession before he is introduced to the practice and polity of its successor. No startling variations, indeed, are to be looked for: no deviations from the principles as already detailed: no departure from the fundamental rules, but such a treatment of them as best tends to get rid of intricacy and perplexity. Where the law was found defective of course such provision has been made for the imperfection as experience and practical skill suggested. But while the principles of the game remain almost precisely as detailed by Hoyle, it has become more scientific and more elaborate than it was. Refinements, it is true, are not to be acquired by studying maxims or systems, but an improved method is capable of being imparted, and "tact" may be taught by example as instruction is conveyed by precept.

LONG WHIST.—LAWS.

ACCORDING TO THE BEST MODERN AUTHORITIES.

"It is true that what is settled by custom, though it be not good, yet at least it is fit."—BACON.

CUTTING IN.

This of course only applies to cutting; where the cards are drawn, one need only be removed.

A party of four having assembled, two packs of cards are placed upon the table. From one of these each person removes a cut, of not less than four cards:*the two highest and the two lowest become partners; the holder of the lowest is entitled to the deal. If in cutting there be two lowest cards of a like value, the holders cut again for the deal, to which the lowest has the claim.

The ace is the lowest card in cutting.

The dealer and his partner have the choice of seats and cards, which they retain during the rubber. When their opponents have sat down, they cannot alter their position.

* This is a club rule: the usual mode is for the players to draw one card each from the same pack.

Should there be two or more "ties" in the cut, they go for nothing: all three cut again, while the fourth retains its relation, whether of high or low, to the four cards first cut.

The right hand adversary cuts to the dealer.   In doing so he must not cut less than four cards from the top, nor less than three from the bottom.   Should a card be exposed in the operation, there must be a fresh cut, and the dealer has the option to shuffle the pack before it is cut again.

The pack being cut, it cannot be changed for that deal.

At the conclusion of the rubber the players cut again from the same cards, and the two highest retire, should there be two others waiting to come in.   Cutting in or out must be by pairs.   After the round the two that have been in longest must go out.

THE DEAL.

The pack may be shuffled by any of the players; the dealer being entitled to shuffle them last, the cards having been placed during the previous deal on the left hand of the next dealer by his left-hand adversary.   The cards must be shuffled *above* the table.   In shuffling *on* the table there is a chance of the position of the cards being seen: this latter practice is only admissible with a pack that is being opened for the first time.

The deal is performed by the distribution of one card at a time, commencing with the player on the dealer's left hand. Should the bottom card be exposed either in cutting or dealing, the opposite party may claim a new deal.   The trump-card may be retained by the dealer, with the face turned down while bets are being made; but if placed with the face downwards on the table, the deal is lost.

If in the process of dealing the trump-card be in any way exposed, the opponents have the choice of demanding a fresh deal.

Should the dealer look at the bottom card, before it is turned up, it is a lost deal.

The dealer is not at liberty to touch the cards on the table to ascertain how he has disposed of them, but he may count those undealt to see how many remain in his hand.

Should either of the opponents turn up the cards while the

deal is in progress, if a card be accidentally exposed, a misdeal cannot be claimed, nor a fresh deal called.

When the pack is found to be perfect, should any of the players hold more than thirteen cards, the deal is lost.

Should a pack be imperfect, there must be a fresh deal.

If a card be found, though it be the last, still there must be a new deal.

The deal is lost should a card be misdealt.

Should two cards be dealt at one time to one player, and the dealer give a card to the next before correcting himself, he loses his deal; and should he omit a hand and deal to the two following, or should he give the top card where the lower one should have gone, he pays a like penalty.

Should a dealer deal out of turn, so soon as he turns the trump his deal holds good, and the one who was passed loses the deal.

If the dealer does not see that the cards are cut, the adverse party can call a new deal.

It is the duty of the dealer's partner to collect the cards as soon as the score has been arranged, and place them on his own right hand.

If a pack of cards be found faulty, the deal only in which the discovery is made shall be void, but the deal is not lost.

The trump-card should be left on the table till it is the dealer's turn to play, and then be placed in his hand. If it be left till his partner or he himself shall play a second time, it comes within the category of an exposed card, and may be called accordingly.* If taken up before it is his turn to play, he may be required to show it; and should he by accident or otherwise show a wrong card, it can also be called.

THE GAME.

Count your cards as you take them up, for should the first trick be turned, and you then discover that you have not the right number (thirteen), and the other players happen to have their complement, the deal is good; and should you have revoked, you pay the penalty. But if the pack be found imperfect, and without the missing card, no revoke can be claimed, neither is the deal a lost one. But if the missing card be in the hand of one of the players, the deal is lost.

---

* This penalty is seldom enforced.

If a card be led out of turn, it can be called during any portion of the game, provided it does not cause a revoke; or any other suit may be required from the same player, or his partner, should it be his turn to play. But should the player not have a card of the suit named, he cannot be called upon to play a card of another. Should your adversaries call different suits, you may play which you please.

A lead made out of turn cannot be objected to after the person whose turn it was to play has led or played to the next trick.

Should you play out of your turn, your partner having also played, the adversaries have the option of consulting whether the cards shall remain or not.

Should you play out of turn, before your partner has played, the opposite party may call on him to play his highest or lowest card of the suit played; and should he have none of that suit, then a trump or any other suit.

A player having won a trick, should he lead again before his partner has played, the card so shown becomes an exposed one, and his partner may be compelled, if he can, to win the trick over again.

If two cards have been played together, or if the player shall have played twice to the same trick, the opposite party can select which of the two shall remain, and the other may at any time be called, provided it does not cause a revoke; if the trick is turned with the two cards in it, that gives a right to the adversary to call a fresh deal, or most likely leads to a revoke.

When your partner does not play to the suit you have led, you are entitled to inquire whether he holds any of that suit or not.

Should two players answer the lead simultaneously, the player whose turn it was may either allow his adversary's card to remain, or he may treat it as an exposed card, or call for a particular suit either for the next trick or the following one.

" Who dealt ?" is a question that is not permitted; but you may inquire whether the cards are placed right for the next deal.

All cards played out of turn, whether one, two, or more, become " exposed," and must be left on the table at **the** demand of the adverse party, who may "call" them all in turns.

Before playing, the request "Draw your card" may be put to your partner; but you cannot inquire who it was that played any particular card.

You are not entitled to see a trick after it has been turned.

Should the third player play before the second, the fourth is entitled to play before the second; should the fourth play before the second and third, the second may be compelled to win the trick, if he can, or not, at the option of the leader or his partner.

Should a card be trumped in error, and thereby you have been induced to play as you would not otherwise have done, the mistake being corrected, you have a right to take up your card, without the penalty of being called, and may claim from the person so playing erroneously the highest or lowest of the suit previously led; or at any future period of the game you may call for the exposed card.

Being called on to play your best or your worst card, consequently a trump or not a trump, or to play any suit you may hold, should you fail to do so, you have made a revoke, and become liable to the penalty.

You cannot transfer your cards to another to play for you under any circumstances, save with the consent of the other three players.

You may call for new cards during any portion of the rubber, before dealing, upon paying for them: this latter condition, of course, is only applicable to play at a public establishment.

THE REVOKE.

If a suit is led and any one of the players having a card of the same suit shall play one of another suit to it, and the trick has been turned and quitted, that constitutes a revoke; but the error being discovered before the trick is quitted, or before the party having so played a wrong suit, or his partner, shall play again, the penalty only amounts to the card being treated as "exposed," and being liable to be called.

Having discovered before the trick is turned that you have revoked, you may take up your card, and you must then play your best or your worst card of the suit, at the demand of your adversaries, and the card you have exposed may be called.

Should a revoke be claimed, in searching the tricks turned for it, the opposite party pay the penalty as for a revoke, if they mix their tricks before you have examined them.

The revoke being complete, the parties by whom it has been committed forfeit three points for each revoke, should there be more than one; the adversaries having the option of deducting them from their antagonists' score, or adding three to their own score, or taking three of their adversaries' tricks and adding them to their own.

The party that claims a revoke must prove that it has been made before the cards are cut for the next deal.

The party against whom a revoke has been proved cannot under any circumstances win the game in that hand.

It is the custom at many whist clubs, that when a rubber has been lost by a revoke, the party making it pays his partner's points.*

The party revoking, should their score exceed the points which constitute the game, remain at nine.

When there are revokes on both sides, there must be a new deal.†

THE SCORE.

The game of Long Whist consists of ten points.

For each trick after six one point is scored.

The honours are ace, king, queen, and knave of trumps.

In reckoning, tricks have precedence of honours.

If the four honours are in one hand, or held by partners, they count four; should there be three honours in one hand or between partners, they reckon two points; the one held by their adversaries being deducted from their three. If partners hold two between them, either in one hand or one each, honours are said to be divided.

Honours do not reckon when the score is nine.

Honours do not count unless they have been claimed and scored before the trump-card of the succeeding game has been turned.

When the score is eight on your side, should you hold more than two honours, you win the game by showing them.

At the point of eight, having two honours in your own

---

* At the Blenheim Club, this law has been established for many years.
† See Deschapelles, Rule 106, at page 134.

hand, you have the privilege of calling on your partner to produce another. Should he do so, you win the game.

If through error you call without holding two honours, and your adversaries hold two or more, they may either demand a new deal, or play out that in which the error has been made, with the privilege of counting honours before tricks.

Should a player at the point of eight remind his partner of his right to call, after the trump-card is turned, the opposite side may, at their option, demand a new deal.

When a player calls, and his partner neglects to answer, though he has the power, they cannot make a " slam;" the honours in that case take their usual place.

Should both partners score, and their scores differ, their adversaries can compel them to abide by that which they may choose.

Should honours be marked without the right of being so, the other side may deduct them from the adversaries' score, and add them to their own at any period of the game.*

Honours shown after the lead has taken place, or at any point except eight, do not count, and may be dealt with as exposed cards.

The rubber consists of two games out of three. They who first win two games, gain the rubber, which may be from one to five points at long, and from one to eight points at short whist.

The term " point" relates to the numbers scored for tricks and honours, as well as for the games of a rubber: five points of the game reckon as one point in the rubber.

A game consists of ten points. Should you score these before your adversaries have marked five, you win a double : if they have scored more than four points, then it is a single.

When the other side have not scored at all, and you have won the game, it is a " lurch," for which you count three. (But only if this is agreed on before the game begins.)

Should you win the whole thirteen tricks in one hand, it is called a " Slam." The effect of the slam is dependent upon custom or arrangement; there is no fixed rule, or generally adopted practice, that the game which it decides shall or shall

---

* Adding the score to your own in this manner is by no means universal, but is properly recommended by Deschapelles. It is in keeping with the law in cribbage.

not be an integral part of the rubber, or be treated as a perfect rubber in itself. According to Deschapelles, "it is considered of the same value as a full rubber." That clever writer has some admirable observations on this anomaly which we have given in the extracts from his "Principles of the Rules of Whist."

No points can be marked after the second trick of the following deal has been turned.

If you have scored more than you are entitled to, you have the right to correct the error at any time before the termination of the game.

If, after winning a game you neglect to score the points of which it consisted, and another game has been played, you cannot score at all, as already observed, unless your adversaries admit that you have won, and in that case you can only score one point. At the closing point of the game also, as before stated, the court cards in trumps go for nothing. A smart commentary was once made upon this loss of privilege. It was observed to Talleyrand, during a rubber at whist, that a certain elderly lady of quality had married her footman. "Ah," said the courtier, "*at nine we don't count honours.*"

The score with coins or counters is thus made on the principle that the unit placed above counts for three and below for five.

1	2	3	4	5	6
0	00	000	0000	0	0
				00	000

7	8	9	or	9
00	000	0		0
0	0	0		0 0
		0		0

INTIMATIONS BETWEEN PARTNERS.

You are entitled to question your partner upon the points: "What are trumps?" "Draw your card." "Can you not follow suit?" "Is there not a revoke?" But these can only be put when it is your turn to play.

You are not entitled to draw your own card, unless required by your partner.

MISCELLANEOUS RULES.

You have no right to look at the trick that has been taken up, unless you are the last player.*

When the first trick of the deal is turned, and the trump turned up has been taken into the dealer's hand, it cannot be shown or named.

The tricks should be placed in an orderly manner as they are taken up, otherwise in cases of dispute the arrangement is liable to challenge.

A card drawn distinctly out of the hand may be dealt with as a card actually placed upon the table.

No penalty attaches to taking up a trick which belongs to the adverse party, but they can claim it at any part of the deal.

If the player intimate that he can win all the remaining tricks, he may be required to throw up his cards; his partner must then do the same, and one of the two hands shall be "called," that is, treated as exposed cards, and called seriatim.

If a player throw up his cards, and the next player follow his example, the hand is at an end. Such is the law, as it at present exists; but there is a laxity in the practice, a breach of system that should not be permitted in a game whose principle is order. All the written authorities that I have consulted are silent upon the point except Deschapelles, who leaves it, after his comment, worse than he found it. " Our expressions," he says, " are sometimes designedly indefinite, because, upon reflection, having found it necessary to be vague, we make a duty of necessity." Most assuredly his paragraph is a perfect example of his philosophy.

The lead is complete as soon as it has been played to.

The game is terminated when no dispute has been raised as to its progress and result, and the cards are again mingled together.

LOOKERS ON.

The office, if any, of bystanders at a whist table, is according to the adopted practice, altogether dependent on the reference made to them. Upon this head, however, the authorities are point blank opposed to each other. Mr. Watson, in his " Short Whist," distinctly states that the rules

---

* This is a French rule, based on a correct principle of play, but not generally enforced in this country.

regarding bystanders relate " to all whist." His dictum, on this point is, " Should a trick be scored wrongly, or parties during play take up a trick they are not entitled to, or honours omitted to be scored, or scored when they had them not, or a revoke made and not noticed, &c., the bystander must remain silent, whatever may be his interest therein." On the other side, Deschapelles declares, " If any points be marked which have not been gained, it is the duty of the bystanders to mention the circumstance, and to have the error rectified." Mr. Watson represents the English school; Deschapelles the French. We incline to the former, as silence is essentially the attribute of Whist.

TERMS USED IN THE GAME OF WHIST.

Bumper—Winning two games in succession before your adversaries have scored.

Cutting In—Selecting partners and deciding who shall deal, at the commencement of a rubber.

Cutting Out—Deciding by the lowest cards cut which of two persons shall remain in, when one or two are required to go out.

Call, the—When at eight and having two honours in his hand, one partner inquires of the other, " Can you one?" " Have you an honour?"

Deal, the—The distribution of the cards from left to right, one by one.

Deal, fresh—When, in consequence of an accident, you are entitled to deal again.

Deal, lost—*Deal, miss*—The forfeiture of the deal is the result of an error coming under the title of mis-deal, as specified in the laws.

Double—Having scored ten before your adversary scores five, in the long game; or five before he scores three, in the short game.

Eldest Hand—The player on the dealer's left hand.

Finesse—Literally passing by your best card, and playing one of less value.

Forcing—Playing a card that compels your adversary or your partner to part with a trump.

Hand—The thirteen cards dealt to each player.

Honours—Ace, king, queen, and knave of trumps.

King Card—The highest card unplayed of a suit.

M

Lead, the—The commencement of the play by the person on the dealer's left, or the card played by the winner of a trick immediately after having won it.

Long Trumps—The last of the suit of trumps.

Longs—The game of long whist.

Love—When you have scored and your adversaries have not.

Love Game—A game won in which one side does not score at all.

Loose Cards—Those of any suit, except trumps, which from the strength of the other hands are useless.

Points—The score made by tricks or honours.

Quart—Sequence of any four cards.

Quart Major—Sequence of ace, king, queen, and knave.

Quint—Sequence of five, the quint major being the sequence of the five highest cards of a suit.

Renounce—Not holding a card of the suit led.

Revoke—Playing a different card from the suit led, though it is in the player's power to follow suit.

Rubber—Two games won consecutively, or two out of three games, constitute winning the rubber.

Ruffing—Playing a trump to any other suit.

Sequences—Cards that follow in regular order of value.

See-Saw—Partners trumping each a suit and playing to each other for that purpose

Score—The points marked by coins or counters, as described under the head of the score.

Shorts—Short whist.

Slam, a—One side winning all the tricks.

Single—(at long whist)—Scoring the game after your adversary has scored five or more; at short whist, after he has scored four.

Tenace—When the last to play holds the best and third best of a suit.

Treble—(at short whist)—is scoring five before your adversary scores one.

Tricks—Four cards, that is, the three played to a card led, constitute a trick.

Trump, the—The card turned up by the dealer.

Trumps—Cards of the same suit as that turned up by the dealer.

Under-play—The leader playing a small card, though he holds the best of the suit.

> "If Hercules and Lychas play at dice,
> Which is the better man? The greater throw
> May turn by fortune from the weaker hand:
> So is Alcides beaten by his page."—SHAKSPEARE.

Though not altogether exempt from the operations of fortune or chance, this "sublime game" is more an essay of skill and science than any played with cards. For this reason, if the utilitarian will insist upon classing it among the frivolous pursuits of life, he cannot deny that it has many properties which, in a degree, make amends for its want of high end and purpose. The lists then being arranged, and entered according to the preliminaries already set forth, let us imagine the first blow about to be struck: *Le premier pas qui coûte*. This is the lead. "The first card that is played in a deal is generally a mistake." So, according to our French professor of whist, said a player of the game, so famous for his skill, that before the last trick was played, he could name every card of which it would consist. Whatever force attaches to this opinion, I cannot do better than follow M. Deschapelles in his analysis of this important step.

Deschapelles loquitur:—" The difference which exists between the beginning and the end of a deal at whist is incalculable. It sets out in ignorance and obscurity, guided by instinct and chance, supported by invention and talent. It finishes in experience, guided by positive evidence, and supported by the light of mathematical deduction. A deal at whist may, therefore, be considered as a graduated scale or intelligence, beginning with the inventive faculty, and ending with mathematical demonstration; and we may easily imagine that the intellectual powers are not unemployed during its continuation. Every single faculty of the mind, one by one, is successively engaged in the operation; every class of mental agency, and every shade of intelligence is in some degree called into action; and the continual change in the faculty employed prevents too laborious an exertion of intellect, keeps up excitement to the end, and produces the highest degree of pleasure.

" To explain this more clearly, and following the degree of division adopted by geographers and natural philosophers, we shall divide a deal of whist into two parts. Let us suppose a

* Many English players not only do this, but can also tell from what hands the cards will come.

M 2

parabola described by the fall of a cannon-ball, whose culmi-
nating point shall be the seventh or odd trick. On this side
of the above point invention is the ruling agent of the game;
beyond it calculation. Attention and memory are seated at
its base, and sagacity, placed at its summit, portions out the
task, invokes, by turns, all the instruments which contribute
to its completion, urges on or circumscribes their endeavours,
and prescribes to them, at the appointed time, the repose
necessary to maintain their vigour.

   " The beginner at whist is not entirely destitute of some
notion of the game. Firstly, he has before his eyes his thirteen cards, the trump card, and the position of the game;
and again, he is acquainted with the strength of the players,
and has some idea of a system of play. But these advantages
are trifling, when compared with what remains to be learnt;
and with those probabilities which arise from the fall of every
card as the round advances. To the indolent these advantages will ever remain a hidden talent; nor is it likely that
chance will improve them; to the hesitating and doubtful, as
they do not appear in a sufficiently tangible form, they will
be lost in imagination and caprice; but when placed in the
hands of the investigating and sagacious, they will increase
with study and practice; they will grow with the growth of
genius, and at length invest it with a regular and palpable
system, which, gradually disengaging itself from the obscure
and probable, will at length be enabled to draw inferences
amounting to almost a positive certainty.

   " The leading of the round should be preceded by reflection.
Some time may be found for the latter, an excuse for which
may be made in arranging the cards, and reviewing the
strength of our hand. This, of course, will not confuse the
memory, that great organ by which our game is regulated,
because it is not yet called into action. This interval will be
well employed, as it will give an opportunity of laying down
the frame-work of that web whence all the threads of action
proceed, and from which an effect is to be produced. The
time thus spent in reflection will be well repaid, and the
sequel will yield most beneficial results; for every second
thus employed, will afterwards produce a ten-fold interest.
The cards will flow in such rapid succession from your hand,
that your adversaries will be wholly unable to draw any in-

ductions from them injurious to your game; and your partner, excited by your calm and collected manner, and attentively seconding your efforts, will feel sometimes inspired by
a spark of that feeling of concord which destroys all separate
existence, and makes us consider ourselves as parts of a
whole; that feeling which is so instantaneous in its action,
and so surprising in its effects; so subtile in its essence, and
yet productive of such miracles!

"A round at whist sometimes appears like a shapeless mass,
in which common right seems to possess little or no influence.
Under these circumstances, we must view it in a summary
manner, and consider its general tendencies, by which means
we shall acquire a guide to enlighten us in that obscurity in
which nothing can be distinctly perceived.

" If you play the king when you hold the ace, or lead with
a tierce to the king, by king and queen, or even by the true
invite, you thus make a parade of your means without rendering them available; you give information to the enemy,
who by this means can proceed to action with a greater degree of certainty; and who thus boldly plays out his suits
according to his knowledge of your strength; besides this,
your position renders it impossible for you to gain the same
information of the weakness or strength of your adversaries;
for, when you have the lead, you will often be puzzled to
decide upon what card to play, and thus you will commence
the contest, deprived of all your resources, and hampered in
your expedients. Then perhaps you will regret that you did
not entice your antagonists into some act by which the state
of their hands would have been exposed, or their weakness
revealed to your knowledge.

" Suppose you lead with a queen, knave, or ten with a
sequence; then the trick will be taken by the ace on your
left, although the same hand should hold the king, or the
tierce major; or else the lead will fall to your right-hand
adversary, without your acquiring, in either case, the slightest
idea of where the cards lie. In the case above stated, your
partner, at any rate, is informed, but here it will be frequently
the enemy; and when the lead returns to your hand, at the
risk of being entrapped by your antagonists and incurring a
double loss of time, you will be perplexed about changing
the suit.

" If you lead by a false invite, or by a queen or knave; in the former case, you may deprive your partner of his best means of defence, and in the latter, you may fall into the adversaries' strongest suit, and involve yourself in utter ruin.

" Suppose you lead by a true invite; here again, your chance of success may be weak, especially if it be true, that, in order to discover the state of your partner's hand, you must play from a weak suit; besides, such a mode of play, even when successful, is not accompanied with important results, and if you are not supported, your means are crippled for the remainder of the round.

" Suppose you lead a trump; if you are strong in trumps, they are weakened by the lead, and thus, giving your antagonists timely notice of your strength, they will unite their efforts, and strain every nerve to save the game; if, on the other hand, you are weak in trumps, you have thus initiated your adversaries, and taught them their own power; you have been the first to provoke the contest, and draw upon yourself the inevitable and disastrous consequences of your indiscretion, and every succeeding moment of the round, by contributing to expose your weakness, will confirm your impending fate, and at length complete your destruction.

" The lead of a deal at whist is directed by invention in a descending scale of progression, from the first trick down to the seventh.

" The second part of the deal begins between the sixth and the eighth trick. All plans of finessing and stratagems disappear now that the action of the game itself comes into play. The scheming of the players is now revealed, the position of the cards more palpable, and the fate of the game, to a certain degree, evident. This moment comes sooner or later to different players, in proportion to the attention they bestow on the game; it depends, in a great measure, on the will of the player, on the interest which he takes in playing, and, consequently, on his desire or indifference for gain."

Before he shows his card, the dealer will bear in mind that the object he has in view is two-fold—to win the game, and to prevent his adversary from doing so. Let him give no clue to the adverse party by the fashion in which he sorts his suits. Eschew a uniform mode of arrangement, at all events.

Do not always place your trumps to the right or left, and your strongest suit next to them. Establish a habit of playing your cards as you take them up; it will not cost you much effort, and you will find it, like virtue, its own reward. With bad cards lead them so as least to damage your partner's hand. Opinions differ as to the policy of leading from a single card, when there is a weakness in trumps. Still, when you are weak, there is the more probability that your partner may be strong. The following table of the odds as to the probable arrangement of the pack, after it is dealt, will serve to demonstrate the balance of chances.

It is just 2 to 1 against your partner holding any one card.

It is rather more than even that he holds one card out of any two.

It is nearly 3 to 1 that he does not hold two of any three.

It is 5 to 2 in favour of his having one out of three.

It is 6 to 4 against his having two cards out of four.

It is 4 to 1 in favour of his holding one card of any four.

It is nearly 8 to 1 against his holding any two cards.

These odds refer to the occasion in which you are the dealer. If your partner deal, it is 26 to 12 against his holding any particular card, and a fraction of odds less against either of your adversaries. Many other points in the odds will suggest themselves, such as that it is 13 to 1 against the dealer having four by honours in his own hand, and so forth. Still there are refinements of calculation that cannot be brought to bear upon a general system of whist practice. Returning to suggestions for the leader, if he hold good cards, let him begin with his best suit; best as regards the value of the cards and their number. But if you have a sequence, begin with that. "From sequences are safe leads, and generally good," says Admiral Burney. "The safest leads are from sequences," reiterates Major A. Failing these, but being strong in trumps, as well as cards of other suits, out with the trumps, that your strong suits may be secured from all possible peril.

THE LEAD.

Should you have the ace and four small cards, not in trumps, lead your ace, and then play a small one. If your lead be from a sequence, play the highest, unless the sequence be to a king. In that case begin with a small one, which will compel your partner to part with his ace; or the left-hand adversary may pass it, should he hold it, and then you have the lead again. It is impossible, however, to give precise rules for playing sequences of every kind.

With ace, king, and three others in trumps, and you have another five suit, or strong suit, play the king of trumps, and then show your partner your long suit, which if he wins, he will immediately return a trump, thereby enabling you to finesse or not, as you may deem advisable by the fall of the cards.

If you are compelled to lead either from a queen or a knave, lead the strongest card; it will serve to throw more strength into your partner's hand.

With only ace, king, queen, lead the king; then play the queen, and you tell your partner where the ace is.

With king and queen unguarded, should you make your king, play the queen forthwith, lest it fall to your partner's ace.

With king, queen, and three others of a suit not trumps, lead the king.

With ace, king, and some small ones of a suit not trumps, when your partner drops the knave to either of your high cards, lead him a small card of the same suit. By this means he makes his queen, should he hold it, or a small trump.

But if you are weak in trumps yourself, it is best to go on with your winning card; but with strong suits not in trumps, show your partner your game, and then play trumps whatever your number. By this means you have a better chance of making tricks.

If with only one trump and a good hand, play one of your winning cards, and then the trump. When it is discovered you have no more, your partner should get them out as fast as he is able, and give you the chance of your long suit.

If compelled to lead from weak cards, such as queen, knave, or a ten, play the highest, as the only means you have of strengthening your partner's hand.

Avoid, when in your power, leading from ace, queen, or any tenace. It is, however, better to lead from ace, queen, or ace, knave, and others of a suit, than to open a weak suit.

Do not keep back the highest card of your partner's best suit, lest he imagine that it is in an adversary's hand, and it should hinder him from carrying out his prospect for playing his hand.

It is by no means essential that a lead should be immediately returned. Let the player work out his own plans, always bearing in mind his partner's lead, and returning it when the best opportunity presents itself.

Mark your adversaries' strength, and, if possible, retain a card that shall command it. But do not keep a card that you have any reason to suppose might fall to your partner's trump.

If your left-hand adversary pass a winning card, without trumping it, note the suit he throws away, and on the first opportunity play a winning card of the same suit, should you hold one.

When you have reason to think your right-hand adversary weak in any suit, but holding small cards of it, lead it the moment you can.

Should you win a trick as last player, you may more safely play the same suit than lead one in which you know both yourself and your partner to be weak; as it is bad policy to open a new suit, when the hand is advanced, unless you have good cards in that suit.

Do not lead from ace, queen, or from ace, knave, unless the suit be a long one, as the probable consequence will be that you do not score more than one point; whereas by waiting till led up to, you have a fair prospect of making a couple of tricks.

It is, however, better to lead from ace, queen, or ace, knave, than to open a weak suit.

With ace and four small trumps, lead the lowest; in all other suits, lead the ace, unless when you have a command in trumps.

Never lead a king when it is the only card of a suit you hold. Even should the ace be against you, there is still a chance of its passing, should it be led to you, when last player.

Some risk the last card of a suit when the trumps are nearly exhausted.

It is a miserable experiment to lead out a small card, being the only one of the suit, with a view to making your small trumps. When you hold but one of a suit, some one else must have several. Should this be an adversary, he will at once detect your object, and set to work to draw out the trumps. Moreover, it may ruin your partner's hand, for as soon as the trumps are all exhausted, he will probably return your lead. But though to be condemned as a habit, it may sometimes be judicious in a player who adopts it rarely, and is therefore not suspected.

Nevertheless, with five or six small trumps, you make certain to lead from a single card.

Should you hold five trumps, get out two rounds of them: this will leave you three; and should your partner hold two, your adversaries at the most will have but two left between them. This ensures the command to your hand, with the means of carrying out your partner's game.

But should you possess a strong hand in trumps, and a long suit of other small cards also, lead from the latter, and thus endeavour to make something of what remains to you of it. Being short in two suits, you must presently be forced, which will materially affect the chance of your bringing in your long suit. Being forced, then pursue your suit, and this may cause the opposite side, should they get the lead, to lead trumps. This still favours your chance of making your suit much more than if you had begun with trumps.

Unless some positive mischief or risk attach to it, return your partner's lead in trumps.

Should a king or queen be turned up on your left hand, lead through it: if your partner desire to get the trumps out, he must, under the circumstances, attempt it at a disadvantage.

Having a long suit, which you wish to bring in, lead from that first, and then lead a trump; your partner will comprehend your purpose.

With the four suits equally distributed, do not hesitate to begin with the trumps.

With ace, king, queen of trumps, and a small one, having another strong suit, though the cards be inferior, do not force more than one round of trumps before you commence with your long suit.

Should your partner not trump a winning card, played by an adversary, and he have none of the suit, then play a trump the moment the lead falls to you.

If left with but one trump, and that the ace, and your adversaries are strong in the suit, play your ace.

Seeing your partner is best in trumps, do not force him, without some important point be at issue. But if he has been forced, without returning trumps, then do not spare him.

With four trumps, lead one : should your partner lead up to a suit in which you are out, with a view to establish a ruff, give him credit for a good hand of trumps also.

If an adversary leads trumps, and from your own hand you know that he must be weak in them, do not return his lead, his object being to get out the trumps, to get in a suit in which he is strong.

If three trumps only remain out, and of these you hold two, play one of them, so that, should the lead fall to you or your partner, his suit shall run no risk of being stopped.

Having the "long trumps," play one, to ascertain what suit your partner throws away to it.

Suppose yourself and partner without a trump between you, and each of the opposite party furnished with them, do not play a thirteenth card, or any that may enable them to make their trumps separately.

Having ace, king, knave, of trumps, only, play the king, and then stop. This will tell your partner how the honours lie, and you may finesse your knave, as the queen may be on your right hand.

At the point of eight, should you hold two honours, unless from the advanced state of your adversaries' score, or weakness of your other suits, you have fears for the game, it is the better policy not to call.

With but a single trump in your hand, unless it be king, or there be other urgent reasons to the contrary, lead it: when your partner returns it, he takes two for his one.

Never lose sight of the fact, that the lead is the great move in the game of whist: have ever in mind the saying, not more trite than true, " the first blow is half the battle."

SECOND HAND.

When your suits are strong, play small cards as a principle. If you hold ace, king, and some small ones, make the first and second trick, as the odds are in favour of the third round being trumped.

Should you, as second player, have ace, king, and knave, of a suit only, win with the ace, and wait. If your right-hand adversary repeat the same lead with a higher card than his first, then finesse with your knave, as he led, you may be sure, from his queen. And even if he did not, you remain with the command of his suit.

If you hold a sequence in a suit led, play the lowest card in it.

Having ace, king, and queen, win with the ace; this will induce your left-hand adversary to return his partner's lead.

If you hold the ace, ten, and a lower card, should the queen be led, play the lowest, as should your partner win it, it may enable you to make up the other tricks of that suit. But should the card led win, do not, on the next round, finesse with your ten, as most probably the king is with your right-hand adversary.

Having ace, knave, and another, when the king is led, it is sometimes as well to pass it, as the adversary supposing the ace to be in his partner's hand, may repeat the lead, and thereby enable you to make both. But this mode of play is dangerous out of trumps, and like many other niceties, requires caution and experience.

With king and queen, play the queen: with queen and knave, play the smaller; and so with the other cards.

Holding the ace and another, in most cases play the lowest.

If you have ace, queen and ten, and the lead, put on the queen; by playing the ten, it is five to four that you lose it; but if in trumps, put on the ten, which if the third player wins, may induce him to return the suit to your tenace.

If a knave is led, and you hold the queen, put it on; if lost, you draw two honours to your one.

Should you trump a thirteenth card, it must be with your highest trump.

With the ten and two smaller cards, put on a small one, if it be the first round. But if it be the second, and your right-hand adversary leads a low card, play your ten; it may save or strengthen your partner's hand.

If strong in trumps, avoid trumping uncertain cards; but

if your hand be weak in trumps, trump the adverse lead whenever you can do so, unless you know that your partner has the best of the suit. Never throw away the chance of a trick; for your trumps would, as a matter of course, be sacrificed, when trumps were led; and even should your partner hold winning cards of the suit you ruff, they will most probably come into play before the hand is finished.

It is generally good to trump the second round of a suit led by your adversary, especially if you are weak in trumps.

If your hand be strong in trumps, and you can win the right-hand lead of trumps once only, it is good to pass it, as you give your partner the chance of gaining that trick, and in any case you will hold the command of the adversaries' lead.

With king and one other, or " king singly guarded," as it is called, it is usual to play the king, the chances being that your adversary leads from the ace.

With only queen and one other, not trumps, play the lesser card, because the chances are that your right-hand adversary did not lead from two honours in the suit; and then if your left-hand adversary has the king, and your partner the ace of the suit, the latter wins the trick, and you make your queen; therefore winning two tricks in your adversary's suit. The old jingle of " King ever, Queen never," is a sound maxim, although many of the old players (Aubrey, Tippoo, Smith, Lind, Franco, Pacey, and others) disapprove of all play by the second hand beyond covering the card led.

Should the highest remaining card of a suit be led to you, and you cannot follow suit, trump it, notwithstanding you know your left-hand adversary will over-trump you. But in case you fear the same lead may again occur, should your right-hand adversary again have the power of leading, win it if possible, and go on with trumps.

If you cannot win, play your worst card: if you cannot follow suit, or trump, throw away the least likely card to be made available by any circumstances of the game.

THE THIRD HAND.

With ace, queen, finesse with the queen, and if it wins, play the ace. In all other cases, when your partner leads a small card, put on your best, and having won, return the suit, unless you are strong in it.

Should the second best card of a suit be led by your partner (we are now speaking of the opening rounds of a deal), if it be the first or second round, and you cannot follow suit, do not ruff it, but play a card of your weakest suit, unless your hand be very strong, and you have no cards to throw away. In the event of your trumping, the best would be reserved, and your partner would be prevented getting a command in the suit through the deal.

The third hand has the best and most frequent opportunities for finessing. As that, the most scientific principle of the game, is elsewhere fully treated, it is only alluded to in these maxims when absolutely necessary for the matter at issue. Thus with ace queen, and others, the third player usually finesses with his queen, and returns the ace.

Should your partner lead an ace, and then play a queen, the probabilities are the knave and some others are in his hand. If you have the king put it on his queen, and this will leave his suit open, then if you have a good command in trumps play them.

Should your partner play a thirteenth card to you, if the left-hand adversary has shown a weakness in trumps, put on a good one and win the trick. If this be not so, reserve your trump, should the suit be at all exhausted, and let the fourth hand be forced. Occasionally, a thirteenth card is led, to enable a partner to make his strong trumps separately: occasionally you should sacrifice your own trump to his lead, that his best remaining trump may be good.

When a right-hand adversary calls, should your partner lead through him, and you have ace, king, nine, and others, finesse the latter: if a left-hand adversary neglect to call when at eight, or does not answer the call of his partner, then finesse the ten, if you have it.

THE FOURTH HAND.

Should the trick be against you, win it, if you can.

In the event of the third player having answered his partner's lead with a good card unsuccessfully, should the winner of the trick have no good suit of his own to lead from, let him return the lead of his adversary. His own partner may be strong in it, and he knows his adversary's partner has parted with the best he had.

It is a most important policy to lead through a hand strong in a suit, in which the last player is known to be weak. Such an opportunity is well worth purchasing at the cost of winning your partner's trick, more especially towards the latter part of the deal.

Having but two cards of a suit, win your partner's trick with one, and return the other.

Should you hold a sequence, win with the lowest, and return the highest.

Do not be forced to play trumps unless it suits your hand; it is better to throw away a loose card.

SEQUENCES.

Whether you lead, or play second, or third hand, should you hold the two highest cards of the suit, sequences, play one of them, if a higher card has not been played already.

With king and queen of a suit in your hand, it would be poor policy to let the knave win; in like manner all sequences may be beneficially dealt with.

With king, queen, and three small trumps, lead the king. Should it win, and your object be to force trumps, go on with a small one, taking the chance of your opponents having reserved the ace.

In all cases where you lead from a sequence, commence with the best, save only with a long sequence to the king, when, by beginning with a low card, you give your partner the opportunity of making his ace, or rather of getting it out of your way. If you wish your partner not to finesse, you should lead the lowest of a sequence.

With tierce to the queen, you lead the queen; the second player puts on his king; your partner, having the ace, plays it, of course, which he would not have done, had the king not have been played. Thus you place the king in jeopardy, from which he cannot escape. Had you led the ten, the second player would have reserved his king, and your partner, all the same, have put his ace on.

When your sequence is led up to through, play the lowest of it, that your partner may be taught your strength in the suit.

INDICATIONS AND INFERENCES.

Should the ace fall from the second hand in the first round of a suit, it is fair to conclude that he is either very strong in it, or has only the one card.

Should there be a renounce in which a court card is thrown away, it indicates that the holder of it has a high sequence in the suit, or perhaps no other, or wishes a trump played.

When you have cleared away all your trumps, avoid playing a suit from which your partner threw away, when he could no longer follow your trump lead. He is weak in that suit. If he has thrown away more than one suit, play that which he threw away last.

When a suit is ruffed, and he who wins plays the ace of trumps and then stops, be sure that is the last of his trumps.

Should you hold the next best of a sequence that has been led, you may suspect the lead was from a single card, and with a view to a ruff.

When there is no call at the point of eight, and you do not hold an honour yourself, the odds are your partner has two. You may model your game by that presumption.

With ace, king, win with the king; if leader, begin with the king; and if it be trumped, or you think right to change the suit, your partner may shrewdly guess where the ace is.

The call at eight is a hint to your partner to play trumps, whatever else come of it.

When the last player wins with a high card, and then leads a lower one with the same suit, with which he might equally have taken the trick, it is assumed that he has all the intermediate cards.

A SYNOPSIS OF THE ODDS.

These calculations, of course, are based upon the supposition that the players are of equal skill. They are, by no means, put forth as absolutely accurate in their estimate; but merely as offering a fair average of the chances which may serve to guide those who speculate on a rubber at whist, and rather to add to its interest, than with a view to gain or gambling.

ODDS IN THE POINTS SCORED.

With the Deal.

1 point to "love" ..11 to 10	9 — 2	7 —	2
2 .. .. 5 — 4	4 — 3	7 —	6
3 .. .. 3 — 2	5 — 3	7 —	5
4 .. .. 7 — 4	6 — 3	7 —	4
5 .. .. 7 — 3	7 — 3	7 —	3
6 .. .. 5 — 2	8 — 3	7 —	2
7 .. .. 7 — 2	9 — 3	3 —	1
8 .. .. 5 — 1	5 — 4	6 —	5
9 .. .. 9 — 2	6 — 4	6 —	4
2 to 1 .. .. .. 9 — 8	7 — 4	2 —	1
3 — 1 .. .. .. 9 — 7	6 — 4	3 —	1
4 — 1 .. .. .. 9 — 6	9 — 4	5 —	2
5 — 1 .. .. .. 9 — 5	6 — 5	5 —	4
6 — 1 .. .. .. 9 — 4	7 — 5	5 —	3
7 — 1 .. .. .. 9 — 3	8 — 5	5 —	2
8 — 1 .. .. .. 9 — 2	9 — 5	2 —	1
9 — 1 .. .. .. 4 — 1	7 — 6	4 —	3
3 — 2 .. .. .. 8 — 7	8 — 6	2 —	1
4 — 2 .. .. .. 4 — 3	9 — 6	7 —	4
5 — 2 .. .. .. 8 — 5	8 — 7	3 —	2
6 — 2 .. .. .. 2 — 1	9 — 7	12 —	8
7 — 2 .. .. .. 8 — 3	9 — 8	100 —	103¼
8 — 2 .. .. .. 4 — 1			

Having the deal is one point in twenty in your favour at long whist, and 6 to 5 in the short game. Having won the first game at long or short is 3 to 1 in your favour. At long whist whatever points you are over your adversaries, if the eighth, make the calculation as from ten downwards. Thus, when you are at seven, and they have scored two, the odds are 8 to 3 on your side: if you are five to their three, they are 7 to 5 on you. At nine love, however, the odds are only 9 to 2, for then you are "in the well," as the phrase goes, you

N

have forfeited the right to score honours. At short whist, with the first game one, and four points before your adversaries have scored, it is 5 to 1 you win the rubber.

DUMBY, OR THREE-HANDED WHIST.

This game is played exactly in the same manner as four-handed Whist, with the exception that one of the hands, that called Dumby, lies exposed and spread on the table throughout the game, and is played by the partner to whom it is allotted, in conjunction with his own.

Three persons draw from the pack in the usual manner, and he who draws the lowest card takes Dumby as his partner, and the deal, with the choice of cards and seat.

When the rubber is over, it becomes the turn of the party who had cut the next lowest card to take Dumby, with all its privileges, choosing another seat or keeping his own.

When the second rubber is finished, the third player takes the Dumby, and this is called having a round at Dumby.

In distributing the cards, the hand of Dumby is dealt as usual, and then the partner arranges them as he pleases, with the faces upwards. Dumby has his deal in turn.

The advantage which the partner of Dumby is supposed to derive from playing a hand which he can see, and therefore adapt to his own, is generally supposed to be about one point in ten in the long game, and five to four in the short, in the rubber; and sometimes a point is given by Dumby's partner on each rubber.

Deschapelles says, "Among players of moderate pretensions, the defender has a trifle the best of it; among good players, it is equal; and among first-rate players, the assailants have the best by a trifle."

The same authority says, that "In playing this game, decisive strokes are in favour of the defence (*i. e.* Dumby) in the first rounds, after which the advantage gradually leans to the assailants." He therefore recommends that the defender should act with energy in the commencement, having little or nothing to hope when the play assumes its regular course. On the other side, it behoves the assailants to watch with patience till they see clearly the best course open for their adoption.

It will be self-evident to a whist player, that the adversary who sits on the left of Dumby should always lead or play up to what he sees to be the weak suits, and that he who sits on the right should lead or play through the strong ones.

The laws and regulations are, with two or three exceptions, and these not quite agreed, the same as those of the parent game. The principle of three-handed whist, as regards the acts and liabilities of Dumby, is a spirit of mutual responsibility, and this should influence the game in all its bearings. Dumby may fairly be exempted from fines which arise from errors committed in sight of, and therefore it may be said with the acquiescence of, both parties. A new deal, in most cases, is as much as the adversaries should have a right to claim against Dumby.

If Dumby's partner lead out of turn, the adversaries may either insist upon the card led, or call a suit from either hand. By special exception, Dumby cannot make a revoke; the oversight may be remedied by a new deal.

As regards the other players, more particularly as respects acts not dependant on Dumby, there seems no reason why they should be allowed any exemptions.

DOUBLE DUMBY,

Is when two persons only play, each having his partner's cards laid faced upon the table.

Each player and the two Dumbies take the deal in turn, and are liable to all the laws previously stated.

Although cards will " beat their makers," the game of Double Dumby is more in favour of the best player than any other at whist. It undoubtedly is very instructive to the novice, and has been recommended by high authorities as the best mode of studying the game.

Dumby is rarely played, excepting in default of a fourth to make up the battle, and then the dead hand is usually taken by the three players turn about. The French name for this game is La Mort.

SHORT WHIST: ITS SYSTEM AND SCIENCE.

About thirty years or more ago*, this refinement upon the popular game of whist became current, and among the more exclusive circles soon took the lead of its predecessor. " We anticipate the time," observes Deschapelles, " in which this modification will get so much the upper hand of the original game as entirely to supersede it, and cause its articles of law to be referred to only as ancient and forgotten archives. To this usurpation we have no objections to offer, both games possess powerful attractions; and the pleasure of re-adopting the slam and honours would be much diminished by the loss of that excitement which short whist promotes. . . . When we consider the sociable feeling it engenders, the pleasure and vivacity it promotes, and the advantages it offers to the less skilful player, we cannot help acknowledging that short whist is a decided improvement, because, however it may lose in theory, it is infinitely superior to the other game in practice. Some persons, perhaps, imagine that there is a vast difference between the rules of the two games. This is not true; they are positively the same. To divide the game into two parts does not divest it of any of its essential qualities; it is still treble, double, or single, and is quite as amusing as before. The ' call' is not admitted, but what does that signify? It was at best but a trifling gratification, and its absence will soon be forgotten. The call was, indeed, a matter of insignificance, and certainly did not deserve the consideration bestowed upon it in the articles. And, besides, it was a privilege of such small importance that we cannot, in any point of view, regret its abrogation. . . . But what shall we say of the slam? This is, indeed, a real loss. The slam is wanting to the completion of the game, without it whist is imperfect, and in this particular is inferior to many other games, even *écarté* has its *vôle*. . . . But as the mischief is done, all we have to do is to console ourselves for our loss, and bear it with equanimity. The slam did not count

* See anecdote of its introduction, page 147.

for the game : players have been known to avoid winning the game, and thus betray their partners, because their bets made it more advantageous. Rubbers have been sometimes prolonged to a tedious length by means of repeated 'slams,' thus fatiguing both the betters and players. Players have been known to diminish their stakes by three-fourths, from the remembrance that the slam involved them in a greater loss than they were inclined to incur ; or, fearing their own want of skill, have declined playing, from an opinion that the slam gave an unfair advantage to the experienced player."

" One thing is beyond a doubt, that the delay caused by the slam is a constant disadvantage to the game. Without it the superior force of the enemy is frequently discovered after two or three cards are out, and the game, consequently, thrown up. Sometimes eight or ten hands are thrown up, by which proceeding much time is gained. This frequently occurs, especially at short whist, when the game is so soon decided that it may be given up at any point. The admission of the slam was directly opposed to these advantages, and the delays and tediousness which it caused, are, by no means compensated by any equivalent. Short whist, however, though somewhat shorn of its proportions, is still a very interesting game. But we must refrain from further comment. . . . If we were to enter into the intricacies and minor points, there would be no end of the subject. We might write whole chapters on the ' little slam,' or the ' five honours,' of those tricks and honours which may be paid for, and on that load of silly inventions which have obtained a reputation merely because they are foreign importations, but which, in reality, are as devoid of merit as they are innumerable."*

The laws of this game are, as already said, in principle identical with those of long whist. It differs from it in the score, inasmuch as the game is five up in lieu of ten, one point saves a triple game; three points a double. The rubber reckons two points, making eight points altogether. Honours do not count at four, neither can they be " called " at any period of the game. Its rules of practice, according to the most generally adopted system among modern players of authority, vary, in some respects, from the laws of Hoyle and his followers. These differences I proceed to specify, with

* The great French authority seems here at issue with himself as regards the value of the slam : we give it as he writes.—ED.

this suggestion, afforded in all earnestness, that their recognition as a standard of reference is almost the only desideratum now wanted to make entire and perfect that noble national game of whist.

Cards that have been but just opened and are quite new may be shuffled upon the table; new cards are found to run so much in suits, that the necessity for this plan of separating them is generally admitted.

When a card becomes exposed, or is seen in cutting, the pack is re-shuffled and cut again.

Should one player have but twelve cards, and the others their right number, the deal is good, and the holder of the twelve, in the event of the pack being perfect, is subject to the penalty of a revoke, if he have made one. If either of the three others holds fourteen cards, the deal is lost.

If the dealer should drop the trump card with the face downwards, before it has been seen, he loses deal.

Before a trick is taken up, or put together for that purpose, every player may demand to know who played each card of which it is composed, but not after they are turned.

The adversaries may call a new deal at their pleasure, when one of their opponents has not played to the trick, and retains one card more than the rest in his hand.

After the four cards have been played no error of playing out of turn can be rectified.

A card may be called should the holder name or hint that it is in his hand.

If a player assert that he can win the game, or win so many tricks, or give his partner to understand that he holds either good or bad cards, he may be compelled to lay his hand upon the table to be " called."

In the event of a revoke the opposite party has the option of taking three tricks from their adversaries, adding three points to their own score, or deducting three points from that of their opponents. And in whatever way the penalty be enforced, the side making the revoke must remain at four, though, in spite of the forfeit, they had points enough left to make the game. The revoke may thus be turned to the best account. Suppose that you have not scored, and that the revoking parties are at four, add three to your own score, and you are three to their four, (the point at which honours do not count,) while you save two points certainly.

A player making any intimation of approval or disapproval to his partner during the progress of the game, or who shall put a question not authorised by the recognised laws of whist, shall forfeit a point, to be deducted from his own score, or added to that of his adversaries, at the option of the latter.*

At several of the metropolitan clubs, when honours are scored by those who do not hold them, they are mulcted for doing so of as many points as they marked in error.*

You cannot insist upon seeing the last trick, upon the principle recognised at long whist.*

I pass by the vexed question as to the influence of skill upon the two games. The principle upon which it should be worked, I take it, is that which is known upon the turf as " strong running." Five tricks and an honour save the game; there are but five points to be got, instead of ten, *carpe diem.*

" If it were done, when 'tis done, then 'twere well
It were done quickly.———

With a bad hand never risk losing a fifth trick, but play a winning card, if you hold one.

You have four tricks, your adversaries five, the lead is yours; you hold king, three of a suit, and a small card of a suit in which you know the other side is strong. Lead the latter, your best chance to make your king is that your adversaries lead to it.

Rather than lead from a bad suit play a card that is worthless, the other side may then lead from the weak suit, and your partner, being last to play, may make a trick in some way or other.

Bear in mind the proverb of *le premier pas qui coûte.* If your own hand is so bad that you cannot count on making a trick, you must calculate the probabilities that may affect that of your partner. Do not exhaust his resources by leading from a suit of low cards. If you have a king, with one or two others, play the highest. Should you have a high card, and a few poor trumps, do not play it out for the sake of a ruff. It will, most probably, lead a good card of your partner's into trouble. Moreover he will probably attribute your game to strength in the suit you lead, and return it, in lieu of leading trumps.

Still the likelihood is, no doubt, that your partner may be

* These three are French rules, and though very good, are not recognized in this country, excepting by a few disciples of Deschapelles.

strong in the suit in which you are weak, and he may have a good finesse; also bear in mind the scale of odds, given in the observations on the long game, as to the probabilities of his holding any particular card.

And, above all, never lose sight of the fact that you are not engaged in a game of mere chance.   Remember that there is a power of intrinsic command, equivalent, if not superior to, mere strength.   I mean *the tenace*, that arrangement which places the first and third best cards of any suit in the hand of the player, whose turn to play follows that of his adversary, who holds the intermediate one, *and that the finesse is the art of attaining that position.*   I cannot do better than quote Mr. Deschapelles' treatise on this the most important of all the scientific agents at whist.

PASSING THE TRICK, OR FINESSING.

" If, when a suit is played, each party were to hasten to force it with their best card, the most skilful player would be he who is best furnished with that suit; the strongest card would, in all cases, determine the fortune of the players; all science and skill would entirely disappear from the game, and the empire of brute force, operating in all cases with the same power, would be firmly established.   Ennui would soon give rise to new reforms, the useless trouble of dealing the cards would be discontinued, and thus, that beautiful problem, whist, would be degraded into the common and ignoble game of *Rouge ou Noir.*

" All this is, however, prevented by the finesse.

" The principle of this practice, which forms an essential part in all the various combinations we are here investigating, and which is based upon acute discernment and a well-calculated doctrine of chance, is diametrically opposed to *mere* chance.   It deprives the latter, one by one, of all those solid, and apparently, enormous advantages it possesses, and eventually completes the triumph of mind over matter.

" It appears here indispensably necessary to define the various and different acceptations in which the word finesse may be taken; qualifying each of them by an epithet which will facilitate our progress, and render our meaning more intelligible to the reader.

" We shall commence by designating the principal circumstances of the finesse, annexing definitions and examples illustrative of their nature, and characteristic of their peculiarities.

1. The finesse proper.
2. The returned finesse.
3. The finesse by trial,
4. The forced finesse.
5. The finesse by speculation.
7. The finesse on the partner.

" *The Finesse Proper.*—When, upon the invite of your partner, you refuse to force with your strongest card, or one of equal strength, you are in the case of the finesse proper.

"Holding the ace, queen, and ten, and taking with the queen, is a simple finesse; that is, a finesse to the king.

" If your left-hand adversary hold the king, the finesse will have been unsuccessful, but you cannot be called to account for bad playing, for the chances were three to one in your favour; that is, that the king was held by your right-hand adversary, or, more probably, by your partner. Even in this latter case, the finesse is not without some consequence, because it affords you the opportunity, after you have made your ace, of returning your partner's lead, by a low card of that suit in which, by his invite, he may be presumed to hold strong cards.

" If, instead of taking the trick with the queen, you only forced with the ten, or even let pass a nine or eight played by the partner, the finesse would be double, treble, or quadruple, without losing its denomination.

" When your partner leads in a certain suit, it may be presumed that he does so with some intention; he is desirous of assisting you to make as many tricks as possible in that suit. However vague it may be, it is your business to interpret his meaning. Has he played in this manner to rid himself of the suit, or to favour another suit and get the last play? Or is his motive to favour your play, as he has no opportunity of making tricks himself? If his intention be to get rid of the suit, return his lead, and do not forget to play out your highest cards; if he wish to get the last play, return the suit, and preserve your low cards to continue the play; if he wish to favour your play, the suit is then confided to your care, make the best use of it and exert all your skill to make it last as long as possible. The difference between these answers, and the evil resulting from mistaking either of his motives, are evident. Nothing therefore should be neglected which may give you a chance of discovering his intention. To attain this end requires, however, considerable reflection, without which no one can expect to succeed.

" Firstly, We must consider the skill and mode of playing of our partner, together with the interest and attention he bestows on the game; we must next endeavour to remember the cards already played, and the particular circumstances o the round. We must always be prepared to take advantage of every information we may acquire; and, in all instances, to make allowances for those circumstances which may modify or change our position.

" The motives for a peculiar system of play rest entirely with the player; it is here that proficients display their great skill. Much might be said on this question, so much indeed, that we think it more advisable to refrain from entering on the subject, as we have already demonstrated the danger of over-charging the memory with the peculiarities of each case, and as the position of the player is continually changing in form and circumstances.

" It will be observed, once for all, that the cases which we quote as examples are purely hypothetical; and that our precepts are equally applicable to every stage of the game.

" When strong cards are played, the finesse is a general practice, which no one omits to employ. There are, however, many cases in which it should not be used. We should keep our attention continually on the stretch to guide us, after well weighing its advantages, in the pursuit of that plan which others practise as a matter of course. One moment of inattention or distraction is sufficient to draw us into some absurd fault, which will sacrifice our reputation for ever. We have seen very skilful players pass a trick which would have won them the game; and we have known others commit the same error upon the last trick but one, although they still held a trump.

" The finesse is also a dangerous experiment with a bad hand, because as only weak cards are then held, every new lead must become a fresh source of injury to your game; it is also very unsafe to try it upon a trick which may save the game.

" *The returned Finesse.*—This finesse takes place on the lead of the left-hand adversary; but it is not definitive, since your partner has not yet played, and he may be in a condition to take the trick. With a good hand, this finesse may continue some time; and we may thus procure an opportunity for making an advantageous counter-invite; the same occurs when it is to our interest to give our partner the lead, but we should assist him when he holds weak cards, and support him in a suit of which he may probably hold none; holding ace and queen, put down the queen; the danger is then in the false invite.

" A false invite is easily discovered, by comparing the card played with those already out; it is also known by an acquaintance with the player's game, by his necessity of inviting with a low card for want of a stronger, or by that description of play which is interested in deceiving all parties. The point of time in which this occurs, and its coincident circumstances, are our chief assistance in the solution of the problem. For this, we refer our readers to our remarks on the subject of the true invite. Whether it be that the elements of analysis are not sufficiently numerous, or that they are improperly applied, or whether our attention is distracted by some new stratagem of the enemy, it must be confessed that the meaning intended to be conveyed by invites is frequently mistaken. To this we can only remark with the physician in Molière, ' Sometimes, however, all this will not prevent the patient's dying; but, at any rate, you will be consoled by reflecting that you have done something for him.'

" Frequently, when your partner is short of a suit, your right-hand adversary, presuming upon the weakness of his hand, will not fail to play a low card, and his partner, understanding his intention, will take it with his strongest, contrary to the usual practice; this manœuvre will be repeated a second time, and if you allow the trick to be taken, in hopes of preserving your resources, you will lose a point; sometimes, also, it may be to your interest to take the lead, in order to play some strong card, or to get the lead again into your partner's hand. In all these cases, it is advisable not to finesse, since, in general, all the strongest cards should be played out, by which there may be any hope of making a trick.

" The same may be remarked of every description of finesse, when there is question of a trick of importance, which may cause the winning, or prevent the losing of the game.

" *Of the Finesse by Trial.*—If, holding king, knave, and ten, you put down the latter, on the invite either of your right-hand adversary or partner, and if it be taken by the ace on your left, you are justified in concluding that the queen is not there; whence it follows, that on the return of the suit, you may securely put down your knave, as the finesse has been fairly tried.

" This deduction may be considered certain upon the invite of the partner, for the last player would never have taken with the ace, and made the king the best card, if he could have taken the trick with the queen, unless by a mistake, which you cannot, of course, be expected to take into account. If the invite had originated from your right-hand antagonist, your security would not be so good, because it might happen that your left-hand player would not choose to risk a trick in a very long suit, or because it might be to his interest to take the trick at all events; from which it follows, that this finesse can never be tried beyond a certain point, and we should place no dependance upon it, except when admitted by the game, or when the trick is of minor importance.

" With regard to the important trick above mentioned, we must here remark, that when it may win the game, it should never be allowed to pass.

" We have seen some persons play with this trick, as a cat plays with a mouse; even letting it escape them, blindly confident that another opportunity would present itself, and that they could take the trick whenever they pleased. Their folly, however, frequently suffered a just punishment; for the opportunity never occurred again, and they lost not only the game, but, perhaps, the rubber, and did not dare to reply to the irritated looks of a partner, who was prevented only by politeness, from bestowing a severe rebuke. Besides so disagreeable a dilemma, there is another circumstance of some weight, which is, that when the game is on the point of being lost, the moment of suspense should not be prolonged.

" With respect to the trick which prevents the loss of the game, we are not of opinion that it should always be taken on the first opportunity.

" But let us be understood : this trick is not of such import-ance, either when you hold in your own hand, or when you know that your partner possesses the means of winning it, nor when, instead of a certainty, you have three or four probable chances of saving the game ; these latter chances are more especially to be weighed in the scale against the hopes you may entertain of making the trick by playing with less timidity. In this case we should be well acquainted with the number of trumps not yet played, the thirteenth card of each of the four suits, the best cards remaining in the four hands, and where they lie, &c., &c. It is the knowledge of these facts which makes this trick of comparative insignificance to the proficient.

" We have already given it as our opinion, that the only case in which this trick should not be exposed to risk, is between the points of three and four.

" It is not necessary to lay down any further directions on the use of the finesse by trial. We have here mentioned it merely in order to explain its meaning, and place it under its proper class."*

I now return to the practical details of a game supposed to be in progress, and that you are leader, with a sequence of four from the knave downwards, and the two in clubs, five small trumps, one small diamond, and two small spades. I borrow the proposition from Major A———. According to the scale of odds already referred to, it is 5 to 2 that your partner has an honour. Play your nine of clubs, and you have the best chance of clearing your suit. Should your partner hold no honour (that is, no court card, according to the absolute phraseology), your nine will draw one, and there will then be the ace and king against you. This will make your partner last in play in your two next suits, and should he ruff the clubs, and you get rid of your small diamonds, there is a " saw" established between you. Should your adversaries return a club, from any indisposition to touch a new suit, your command of trumps will enable you to bring in your suit. The same result would come of your leading the lowest from king, knave, ten.

Holding a sequence, you lead off the highest, should your partner hold a higher card of the suit he finesses it. Should

* Deschapelles.

the lead come from your partner, you put on the lowest of
your sequence, and return him the highest.   If you lead from
king, queen, knave, play the lowest, and your partner will
take it with the ace, if he has it.

Lead the best, having king, queen, ten, and if it succeed
change your suit.   Your ten may then serve you, when the
deal comes to wind up.

Should you hold four trumps, not honours, lead the lowest
of them; with king, queen, and three other trumps, lead the
highest; with king and three others, lead the small one,
unless you have all the trumps that are left; in that case, lead
the lowest.

Should you be compelled to lead from king, knave, and a
small card, begin with the lowest.

Should you hold queen, or queen and knave and three
small cards, lead the worst.

Still these rules must give place to circumstances; to the
trump turned, for instance.   Should you have ace, or king,
ten, nine, or some others of a suit, lead your ten through an
honour; if your partner holds the queen or knave, he may
finesse : should it answer his game, for instance.   In the
event of his playing either of those cards, when the suit
comes to you again, you have your nine to do the same with.

With ace, king, knave, and two small trumps, play the
king, and wait for the finesse; with these honours and three
small ones, begin with the two highest cards.   Do not wait
for the finesse in any other suit, without the command in
trumps.

If you hold ace, king, and three others, lead the highest;
if the suit be trumps and you hold four, lead the worst.   Do
the same under the same circumstances with every suit, when
you have the trumps that are left in.

With ace, queen, knave, and one or two more, always lead
the best; with ace, queen, ten, and two small ones, lead the
lowest, in trumps; but the best in every other suit.   It is not
a rule without an exception that you should wait till your
tenace is played to.   Rather than begin a weak suit, lead
from ace, queen, and another or two others of the suit.

Lead the lowest from ace, knave, and three small trumps;
in other suits, begin with the best, unless the probability is
that you can bring in the suit by your strength in trumps.

With ace and four small ones, lead the ace; the reverse with trumps.

With ace and but one other, lead the small one, if you doubt your partner being strong in the suit.

With a weak hand in trumps, get as many tricks as you can early in the game.

These sketches of leads are not given so much as guides for playing the game, as to induce the reader to study and apply the system in which they originate. The leader has certain advantages; but in most cases the command is with his right-hand adversary—the dealer. The leader will, however, remember that he has no need of all the cards he holds to obtain the purpose he has in view. He has but five points to get, and there are eleven points out of which they may be made. This furnishes him with a freedom of action that greatly enhances the interest of the game. Let him always bear in mind what he has to do—first to save, and then to win the game; and let him set about it in such wise as shall soonest and surest bring that result to pass.

With a good suit, and a strong hand of trumps, let him not ruff upon compulsion. His trumps will presently enable him to establish his suit.

Having won a trick, with the game open, lead a small card, and this gives your partner a chance of making his next best, should he hold it, for you may calculate on your best making it in the third round: the ace of trumps should be thus dealt with in almost every instance.

"Strength in trumps," says Major A———, "can alone justify deep finessing in other suits*. But, as at short whist, scarcely a hand is played in which the game may not be either saved or won, there is, contrary to the received opinion, more scope for finessing judiciously than with the old game." Nothing can be more true, than that it is not a game for faint hearts; the motto of short whist should be *Audaces Fortuna juvat.*

RULES FOR LEARNERS.

Rules are mere axioms, not laws. Those who adopt the study of whist, should set out with the understanding that

* Another, and even greater authority than Major A———, seems to be at issue with him on this point, and says:—"If weak in trumps finesse deep in your partner's weak suit, and protect his hand."

they may read to become good but not fine players. They
may be taught to play correctly; but not with the genius
that exults in the possession of a bad hand. Still it is essential that they should learn the rudiments, whatever brilliancy
of talent they may bring to the service of their game. People
don't dance the polka without being instructed in the first
steps, and does not the head stand in need of a tutor as well
as the heels?

I suppose you with the thirteen cards already in your
grasp. It is your lead; do not send out a single card
on an errand, without an object. It is better to des-
patch it on mischief than for no purpose at all. Mark well
the cards you hold, the progress of the game, the probabilities
on your own part and on that of your partner, and observe
cautiously the direction the deal assumes. Play with reference
inclining more to your partner than yourself: he cannot see
the premises of your policy; let him have every indication you
can give, by your playing as open a game as may be consistent with safety. Should the score be critical, and against
you, go point blank for every trick that offers by possibility
to be within your reach; desperate cases require desperate
remedies. In ordinary cases adopt a more cautious course.
To show you the necessity for having a reason for every move
at whist, I quote the following proposition from the work of
Major A———, already referred to. "Your partner leads a
four; your right-hand adversary plays a five; if you put
down a tray, it ought to be *certain* that you have no more of
the suit; but if the deuce make its appearance afterwards, it
will destroy all confidence in your play, and you will be justly
set down for a spoon." A stronger case than this is the following. The most important working machinery in whist is
the tenace. You know full well its importance when you see
the ace and queen in your hand, but does it strike you that at
certain portions of a game, the four and two may do you as
much good service? Five and seven are as effective against
four and six as ace, queen, against king, knave. During the
time cards are being played the utmost application of thought
and the keenest address of judgment will find more to do
than they are in general prepared for.

I do not think it necessary to recapitulate here the **maxims
of practical** detail already given in the general **system and**

science of whist. The peculiarities of the short game, however, call for special appliances, and these are offered, not
indeed in the character of specifics, but rather as cordials to
give the patient nerve and vigour; as stimulants to exite his
emulation, and rouse his energy. Let circumstances guide
you more absolutely than the recognised order of routine,
applicable to the cards you hold. Thus should an honour
turn up on your left, or lie on your right, do not permit those
accidents to operate for or against a lead of trumps, if there
be a good suit to be brought in by the latter course. Trumps
should be your rifle company; use them literally in your
manœuvres; have copious reference to them in finessing, to
enable you to maintain a long suit. Should you be weak in
trumps, ruff a doubtful card at all times; with a command in
them be very chary of that policy. Let your great principle
always be to keep the control of your adversaries' suit, and
leave that of your partner free. If you see the probable good
effect of forcing, decide which of your adversaries you will
assail, but do not attempt them both at once. Let it be the
stronger if possible; when you force both hands opposed to
you, one throws away his useless cards; while the chance is,
the other makes trumps that, under other circumstances,
would have been sacrificed. Major A——— puts the policy
of forcing very *forcibly*. " A has six minor trumps and a
septième major in another suit, with the lead. B, his adversary, has a *sixième* major in trumps, a *quart* major, and a
tierce major, of the other suits. If A, relying upon his six
trumps, lead a trump (as many say, with six trumps, always
lead one), he loses *every trick;* if, on the contrary, he forces
B once, he inevitably gains the odd trick. The same principle operates throughout every combination of the fifty-two
cards; a conviction of it is one of the first necessary steps
towards an insight into the game, and although so great an
effect may be seldom produced, and our example may be
regarded as a very extreme case, there is scarcely a rubber
wherein the soundness of the principle of forcing is not
experimentally proved." . . . .
With the command of trumps, and a long suit to bring in,
begin with trumps; if weak in them, show your suit, that
your partner may do it for you, if he can. With four trumps,
headed by the ace, should your adversaries lead them, do not

o

win the first or second trick, unless you have seen reason to
suspect the adversary's weakness in the suit. Never ruff your
right-hand adversary's leads, should you be strong in trumps,
and have a suit you desire to maintain.   I take my example
for this axiom from Major A———.   "The cards being
nearly equal, the object of the good whist player is to establish a long suit; to keep the long trump to bring it in, and to
frustrate the same plan of his adversaries.   With an honour,
or even the ten, and three other trumps, you may by good
management succeed.   Do not over-trump your right-hand
adversary early, but throw away a losing card; one trump thus
gone strengthens your hand, and your partner, as last player,
has that advantage in whatever suit is led.   For instance, had
you over-trumped, you would have given up the whole chance
of the game to secure one trick.   But this, like all rules, is
not without exception; namely, if your left-hand adversary
has shown a great superiority in trumps, then make whatever
tricks you can.   If your partner, a good player, means obviously to force you, of which you may judge by his playing
a winning or losing card of the suit to be trumped; if the
former, he may not intend to force you; if the latter, you
may give him credit for strength in trumps to protect your
long suit.   In short, it is bad to play for a great game with
a weak hand, or a weak game with a strong hand, when
the state of the scores requires the reverse."   According to
the old rule, you should never force your partner without
having a command in trumps yourself; this maxim may,
however, be occasionally departed from with advantage; as,
for example, should your partner indicate by his lead that he
wishes to be forced, as from a single card, when an over-
whelming strength of trumps is on the opposite side, when a
" saw" threatens to be established, when your partner refuses
to lead trumps after being forced, or when you are playing
only for the trick.

   With respect to the policy of leading trumps, a few general
hints may be given.   By all means lead them when you have
four or five, with a long suit besides, and the impression that
your partner may have another.   If the adversaries evince
weakness in their general cards, but with good trumps; if
they have scored three, and you hold no honour, and suits
that make the establishment of a ruff in your behalf impro-

bable, judge your adversaries' cards by the policy you would adopt yourself, if holding such cards as you may presume constitute their hands. Thus they decline a ruff, or throw away a good card; they hold long suits in trumps, as they have but two suits, trumps being one of them. In the former case, force them if you can, but do not lead them a trump. If the adversary on your right lead the suit of which you hold ace, king, and four cards, win with your king, and do not return the suit, should you have commanding trumps. In leading from a sequence of three trumps, when you cannot help yourself, play the best; but avoid such a lead when you can. When your partner leads off trumps so as to assure you his suit in them is strong, fail not to return the lead, as soon as the opportunity offers. But should you have any doubt as to his motive, consult your own hand for an aid in solving it. Let the possession of the long, or odd trump, have much weight with the method of your lead in that suit. With a strong suit to establish, and a tierce major in trumps, lead them twice before you begin your long suit. If you hold only four small ones, keep them back till your suit is established. Should your partner's trumps be exhausted, and your adversary's the reverse, play a trump if you have it, as you will be repaid *cent. per cent.* If possible, reserve the last trump for a great *coup;* it may stop your opponent's long suit, and give you the lead, which he may not again recover. Thus, with a command in trumps and the best card of your adversary's suit, lead small trumps to force him, keeping your best of his suit *in petto.* Your right-hand adversary having returned his partner's lead of trumps, if you have the best and a small one remaining, play the latter, looking to the probability of a finesse on your left, and your partner's position as last player. Should your partner lead from a tenace of ace and queen of trumps, and you hold king and some small cards, win his queen and keep up his lead by returning it. Let your partner understand that you are strong in trumps, when such is the case; this will make him preserve his best suit in all its force, instead of watching for his adversaries' long suit. If your partner lead the ten of trumps, and you hold ace, knave, and another, pass it, unless the state of the score should make the finesse

dangerous. However, if you have a direct object in getting
out two leads of trumps, play your ace. Ace, nine is a
safer lead than ace, ten. When a best card of a suit is
thrown away to a partner's winning card, it is clear the
command is in your hand; the second best so disposed of
shows that it is the only one you have got. When your
partner leads the second best of a suit, if you have a command in trumps pass it, unless you can, by winning, make a
saw.

When you and your partner have all the trumps between
you, play a small one, if you wish to throw the lead into his
hand. When you turn up the king, the sooner you make him
the better. It is sometimes politic to win your adversaries'
leads whenever you can with the highest of a sequence, if
you can do so without deceiving your partner; they wonder
what has become of the lower honours. Holding ace, ten,
and a small one, your partner leading the nine of the suit,
pass it; for if he holds an honour, you make two tricks,
counting your ace for a certain trick. With king, queen, or
queen and knave, and another, play one of the high cards in
all cases when you are second hand. With an average remainder of trumps and good cards, having one certain loser,
throw it away at your first opportunity, it may enable your
partner to make his second best of the suit. It is peremptory
notice to you to play trumps, whatever may be the state of
your hand in reference to that suit, when your partner does
not trump a winning card. Should the queen come from
your right, in a lead, with ace or king, ten or another, pass it,
this gives you a tenace, as if your partner have either ace or
king, you make three tricks in the suit. Players, however,
f the old school think it best to cover the queen. It is bad
licy to lead up to queen or knave; the contrary with respect
the ace or king; the same holds with reference to leading
through those several cards. If your partner leads trumps
and you have four high trumps, endeavour to make sure of
three rounds in that suit; should his lead, however, be a nine,
pass it, you will then have the lead after the third round.
When the lead comes from your right-hand adversary, put on
your queen, should you hold ace, queen, and ten. Should
your left-hand adversary pass a winning card, throwing away a

losing one, lead him the suit he has discarded, should you have the opportunity. The commanding card will serve you as well as trumps when they are exhausted. When you have strength in trumps, throw away from your adversaries long suits; if weak, preserve such cards as will check them. Upon all occasions when you discover your partner's hand to be weak, force it. So, when a strong suit has been established by the opposite side and you have the opportunity to stop it, do so with the best trump, should you hold it, and it happens to be the only one you have. It is better to play to your partner's strong suit, if he has one, than immediately to lead a suit you know he will ruff. It is better also, when you have a small trump, with ace, queen, or any other tenace, to play the losing one, in order that your tenace may be led up to. Mark well whether your partner's lead be of his free will or on compulsion. If the latter, treat it as though it were an adversary's or your own: avoid returning it.

It is a point of high science to keep back a high card, and play a low one in return to a left-hand adversary's lead. "Suppose," says Major A———, "the fourth player to have ace, king, and a small one of his left-hand adversary's lead. If he wins with the ace and returns a small one, his partner will make the third best, unless the second and third are both against him. It is indeed from this, if you lead from the king and your right-hand adversary, after winning with the ten or knave, return your lead, that the best chance to make your king, is to put it on." With king, knave, and others against ace, queen, and one other, the only remaining card of the suit, lead the king; for if the queen is unguarded, you bring out the ace, and every other trick is your own. In like manner, your left-hand adversary having the second best of a suit guarded, if you remain with ace, queen, and four others, by playing the lowest, it is most probably passed, and you win all the rest.

I have already shown the effect of the tenace and the importance of keeping up its combinations in cards of every value. I take the liberty of appropriating a sample or two of its operation from the authority that I have made frequent reference to. "A, the leader, has four cards left, viz., the second and fourth trump, and the ace and five of clubs. B, the left-hand adversary, has the first and third trump, and the king and six of clubs. The ace of clubs, being led by A, the king should be put down to it by B. A will then probably lead trumps; if so B inevitably makes three tricks: by keeping the king of clubs he cannot possibly make more than two. A has king, queen, ten of a suit, B ace, knave, and another. A, leading the king, B wins it with the ace, he makes but one trick; by passing the king and thus preserving the tenace, he makes two. Tenace is more easily kept against the right-hand than against the left-hand adversary: the latter, in fact, requires good skill." It is unnecessary to multiply these instances, or nothing would be more easy. The principle pervades the cards, and memory and observation will furnish the material to any amount. The influence that experience and art exercise upon this game may be calculated by such *data*.

One more case of system and science, and I leave this cause in the reader's hands, with little doubt as to the result. The score is four. A, with six tricks turned, remains with ten and seven of trumps, and two hearts, he leads one of the latter. B, the left-hand adversary, has knave and eight of trumps, and two clubs. C, A's partner, has two small trumps, and two hearts. D, the last player, has the king, and a small trump, a club, and a diamond. D, seeing it is necessary to win every trick, and that there is no hope of doing so unless his partner has either the two best trumps, or a successful finesse in them, trumps A's lead of hearts with his king, returns the small one, and thus wins a most critical game (presuming that B finesses the eight of trumps).

And thus we have arrived at the refinements of the game, attainments to be taught neither by example nor precept, and but by practical experience alone. Upon some of its leading points even the best players are still divided in opinion; they disagree as to the principle of leading single cards, for instance. These and many such moot points and mysteries are *per force* left to the student's research and the practical player's solution. Our pages are but pioneers for the beginner, with here and there a hint from which the proficient may peradventure reap instruction and guidance. But Whist has higher properties than may be learnt by rote. It has subtle contrivances and cunning secrets that whoso would unfold and appropriate must " minister to himself." It is well worth the essay—*Le jeu vaut les chandelles.*

FLOREAT SCIENTI

PIQUET.

HOYLE, in his account of this game, as well as of several others in his very popular treatise, begins as if he were addressing those who had already made considerable progress in the matters under discussion. As we have no right to assume any such anterior knowledge, but rather the contrary, seeing that our purpose is equally to teach the unpractised as to minister to more mature study, we shall commence with the first elements of the game.

The game of Piquet, then, is played by two persons, with thirty-two cards, namely ace, king, queen, knave, ten, nine, eight, and seven of each suit, and these cards rank according to the succession in which they are here placed, the ace being higher than the king, the king than the queen, the queen than the knave, and so on. In reckoning what is called the point, the ace counts eleven, the king, queen, knave, ten each, and the other cards according to the number of their respective pips, ten, nine, eight, or seven. Having agreed on the amount of the stakes, the next step is to cut for the deal. He that cuts the lowest piquet card deals; having first shuffled the pack he presents it to his adversary, who if he pleases may shuffle also. Should he do so, the dealer may shuffle them again; and having done so, he places them before the other who cuts them. If in this operation a card shall drop, the dealer has the right to shuffle over again. It is always advisable for the elder hand to shuffle, especially when the dealer's pack is running in his (the dealer's) favour, for though there must of course be a great deal of luck in a run of good cards, yet this luck is frequently owing to the neglect of effectual shuffling, because in the course of play the cards naturally drop into such a position as to cause this run. For the same reason, if the run continues against him, he should change his method of shuffling, alternating them by one at a time, or three. It is an established rule that, the cards in being shuffled, may not be laid on the table.

It is a rule with all good players to have two packs, each deals with his own pack throughout the game or partie, unless either of them chooses to call for new cards at his own expense; at the end of the partie the choice of cards is usually cut for, the highest being entitled to the choice.

The number of points in each game is now one hundred, it used to be one hundred and one: fifty saves the lurch.

The cards are to be dealt two by two, and in no other numbers. In this manner each player is to have twelve cards dealt him and there will then remain eight cards, which are called "the stock," and are to be placed on the board, directly between the two players.

The penalties for misdealing will be found in the rules appended to this treatise.

When the cards are dealt, each player should sort his own hand, placing together those of each suit. The first thing to be observed by each, is, whether he has a carte-blanche, that is, whether he has no picture cards in his hand; these are, the king, queen, and knave. Should the eldest hand have a carte-blanche, he is to tell the dealer to discard for a carte-blanche, and when that is done he shows it by counting his cards one by one on the table, with the faces uppermost. If the younger hand has a carte-blanche, he is to wait till the elder has made his discard, and then, before he takes in, shew his cards as above. The great advantage of a carte-blanche is, that the player who has it counts ten, which takes precedence of every other score, and not only counts towards the pique or repique but prevents the adversary from having either one or the other; and if the player who holds it is at the point of ninety or upwards, he wins the game.

When the players have sorted their cards, the elder hand makes his discard, that is to say, he throws out not more than five of such cards as he considers of least value, and exchanges them for a corresponding number of cards taken from the stock in their natural order. The general rules as to discarding by the elder hand are two: first, he must exchange one card at least, and secondly he must leave three cards in the stock for dealer. If he takes in a smaller number than five, he has a right to look at such of the five as he leaves.

The dealer is not bound to discard at all, but if he does he must take in first, those that are left by the elder hand, and then his own three which are at the bottom of the stock; and though these be his rightful number, he is at liberty to take in not only those three, but also all that his adversary has left. Should he leave any cards, he has a right to look at them, but if he does so, the elder hand, after he has led a card, or declared the suit that he intends to lead, may look at them also, but if the dealer does not look at them neither may the elder hand do so. Here it may be observed, that it is often for the advantage of the dealer not to look at the cards he leaves; as, for instance, if he has in his hand a king unguarded, if the adversary has all the rest of the suit, there is no help for it; but it may happen that there are one or two cards of that very suit left in the stock, if so, it is better they should be unseen, as the elder hand will be thereby led to conclude that the king is guarded. Should the dealer leave any cards and mix them up with his own discard, the elder hand has a right to see the whole, after having first named the suit he intends to lead.

In either of the above cases, should the elder hand lead a different suit from that which he named, the dealer may require him to lead any suit he pleases.

A novice at the game will naturally think that he ought to throw out those cards which are of least numerical value; but the case is constantly otherwise. He must, therefore, well consider the object he has in view and how to attain it. Now, for this purpose, he must be well acquainted with the value of the various combinations of cards, and of their relative importance in counting the score.

The various denominations of the score (so to speak) are as follows; and they are reckoned in the following order. After the carte-blanche already spoken of, there is 1, the Point; 2, the Sequence; 3, the Quatorze; 4, the Cards; 5, the Capot.

1. *The Point.*—This counts first. Whoever has the greatest number of cards in a suit has the point; but if both players have an equal number of cards in the same or different suits, then whichever has the greatest number of pips, reckoning the ace as eleven, and the court cards as ten each, wins the point. It will be readily seen that, in this view of the matter, the five lowest cards must be superior to the four highest, the former amounting to forty-four, the latter to forty-one. Whoever has the point counts one for each card, unless the number ends in four, in which case the party holding it counts one less than the number of cards.

2. *The Sequence.*—A sequence is the having several cards in the same suit following consecutively, as ace, king, queen, or knave, ten, nine, eight; of these, there are six different kinds; 1, a Tierce, three in sequence; 2, a Quart, four in sequence; 3, a Quint, (commonly called "a Kent,") five in sequence; 4, a Seizième, six in sequence; 5, a Septième, seven in sequence; 6, a Huitième, eight in sequence, that is, a whole suit. Of these, the most numerous is the most valuable, and where the numbers of cards are equal, that which is the highest is most valuable; for instance, a tierce to an ace, which is called a "tierce major," is more valuable than any other tierce, though it is inferior to a quart to a ten, because the latter contains four cards. A sequence counts next to the point; the tierce being worth three, a quart four, a quint fifteen, a seizième sixteen, and so on. Now, supposing the elder hand to have five cards (which are good) for his point, he counts five, and if these five form a sequence, he counts twenty, that is, five for the point and fifteen for the quint; but if he have a quart major (that is, a quart to an ace,) and a nine, and the dealer has a quint to a knave, the former counts five and the latter fifteen; and note that the player, who holds the highest sequence, is entitled to count all lower sequences that he may happen to hold in the same or other suits.

3. *The Quatorze.*—A player holds a quatorze when he has four cards of equal value in the four different suits; that is to say, four aces, kings, queens, knaves, or tens, no lower cards count. Whichever player holds the highest quatorze counts fourteen, those which are highest taking precedence, and preventing any inferior quatorze from being of value. In like manner, if neither party holds a quatorze, then three of equal value, as three aces, &c., count three, and next in order to the sequence. But the lowest quatorze, that of tens, is superior to the highest three, that of aces. And it is to be observed, that whoever has the highest quatorze is entitled to count any other inferior ones, even though his adversary should have an intermediate one. Thus, the quatorze of aces annuls all the others; and the player who has them counts a quatorze of tens, though his adversary should have quatorze of kings, queens, or knaves. If there is no quatorze, he may count three aces, kings, queens, knaves, or tens; and it is to be observed,

that three aces are superior to three kings, and so of the rest; and that by virtue of a good quatorze, you not only count inferior ones, but also three tens, or any other threes except those of nine, eight, or seven; although your adversary should have three of a superior value. The least practice will make all this, which may seem a little difficult at first, quite familiar.

Before proceeding to describe the two remaining modes of scoring, namely, the cards and the capot, it will be as well, as we are at present considering the method or object of discarding, to point out to the beginner what he has to aim at, and what to avoid. He is to know, then, that if the elder hand counts in his hand and play thirty, before the dealer counts one, he at once leaps from thirty to sixty, which is called a pique; and if, without playing a card, he counts thirty in his hand, he jumps from thirty to ninety, which is called a repique. This will be best explained by example: and, first, for the pique. Supposing the elder hand to have a quint to an ace, in other words a quint-major, which is good as a point, it is consequently good, also, as a sequence, and counts twenty; suppose him, also, to have three aces, which must be good, because he has a quint-major, that is, one of each of the cards that can constitute a quatorze, that makes him twenty-three; well then, in playing the cards his quint-major and the two additional aces must also count one each, as will presently be seen, making up a total of thirty, upon which the player, instead of saying in his play twenty-nine, thirty, says twenty-nine sixty. This is a pique. Again, as to a repique. Supposing the elder hand to have the same point, good, as above, and four aces besides instead of three, he counts in his hand, without playing a card, first, five for his point, fifteen for his quint-major, and fourteen for his four aces, that is to say, thirty-four in hand, which is ninety-four, in fact, the game in one hand. Again, supposing the dealer to have the same hand in the two several cases above mentioned: in the former case he counts only twenty-three, that is, his point, quint and three aces, and then the elder hand plays a card and counts one, which prevents the dealer gaining a repique; whence it will be observed that the dealer cannot win a pique, but may win a repique, because a pique is won by playing up to the number thirty before the adver-

sary has counted one, but the eldest hand when he plays his
first card must count one: and in the latter case the dealer
would win a repique, because by means of his point, quint
and four aces, he counts thirty before the elder hand counts
one; for all scores made in the hand without playing out
count before cards played on the table. For instance, if the
elder hand is ninety-nine towards the game, and the younger
hand ninety-four, still though the elder hand must play one
to begin with, yet the younger hand, if he has a good point of
six cards, wins the game.

4. *The Cards.*—We now recur to the fourth of our five
methods of scoring, called "The cards." Two cards, one from
each player, make a trick; if each player has six tricks the
cards are divided, but if either wins seven or more tricks he
has "the cards," that is, he counts ten beyond the number he
has already scored. It is scarcely necessary to observe that,
as in other games, the higher card wins a lower, and makes
a trick.

5. *The Capot.*—Whichever player wins all the tricks wins
what is called a capot, and, instead of ten, adds forty to his
score.

With reference to the playing of the cards, it must be
noticed that the first player counts one for each card he plays,
provided it be of the value of a ten at least, and that the
second player, if he wins a trick also counts one, subject to
the same limitation. Whoever wins the last trick of the
twelve counts one extra, or, as it is called, " one for the last
card;" a game very often depends on the winning of this
trick, whence the young player will soon discover how important it is to win this last trick.

It is impossible to give any general rules for discarding,
which shall be applicable in all cases, inasmuch as the number of points which you are to aim at securing is continually
varying according to the varying position of the game. The
ordinary and correct calculation is that the elder hand will
make twenty-seven points and the younger thirteen. Keeping this in view, we will suppose that the game is at its commencement; then each player should endeavour to procure
his proper number. To begin with the elder hand; if his
cards do not show a very strong probability of his gaining a
pique or repique, he should discard so as, in the first place,

to gain the point, and, secondly, the cards. He has seventeen cards against fifteen, and may reasonably calculate on attaining both these ends; but of the two the latter is the most important. To gain the point, the most obvious plan is to keep the suit of which he has the most, but in doing so he will often lose the cards; he must, therefore, very frequently discard from his most numerous suit, in order to retain that which is strongest for play. And, in doing so, he should never forget that he has more chance of taking in to his weaker suit than to his stronger one. To give an instance, supposing him to have a tierce-major in one suit, and a quint to a knave in another. If he is to discard five cards he must clearly break up one suit or the other; if he keeps the quint to the knave he will probably lose the cards, for he cannot reasonably calculate on taking in the ace and another honour in that suit, and unless he has two other aces he will almost to a certainty lose the cards. With still more force does this reasoning apply if he has a small quint in one suit and forty-one in another, because another tenth card in the latter suit will give him a quint-major. To multiply instances would be useless. We therefore pass on to the general method of playing the younger hand.

We have already said that the dealer ought to make thirteen points. But inasmuch as the elder hand has a great advantage over him, because, in addition to having more cards, he has also the chance of a pique, as well as a repique; he therefore ought first of all and especially to consider what his opponent can possibly make, and to defend himself accordingly. Supposing him then to have, as above stated, a tierce-major in one suit and a quint to a knave in another, in any case, except that of having three aces, he should keep his small quint; for, if it is good at starting, it prevents the pique, and, if not good, the only chances he has of preventing the pique are, that he shall take in the queen of that suit, which will give him a seizième, or take in so as to break both his adversary's strong suits, which is a piece of luck he can scarcely calculate upon. These are strong, but by no means uncommon, cases, given by way of illustration. If any general rule can be given at the commencement of a game, it is this, that the elder hand (being safe) should play an offensive game, the younger hand a defensive game.

But when the game is further advanced, the principles on which the discard is to be made vary exceedingly, and are frequently quite the reverse of those above given. In the former case, as we have seen, the player commonly gives up the chance of a great game in order to make good his average score, unless, indeed, he can play for a great game without much risk; but in the latter case, he abandons the certain winning of his average score with the very slender hope of making a pique or repique. For instance, supposing the dealer to be within ten of game, and the elder hand to have scored only twenty, it is clear that the latter must play for a repique. Let him have, then, a tierce-major in clubs, a quint to a knave in diamonds, king, knave of spades, and knave, nine of clubs, he should discard his tierce-major, his king of spades, and the nine of clubs, because, if he takes in the fourth knave and any card to his quint suit, he will probably win the repique. Whereas, with the same cards at the beginning of the game, he should discard his four lowest diamonds and the nine of clubs, which would give him a safe game. But it is unnecessary to multiply instances in this place. The General and Particular Rules that follow, accompanied with constant play and careful observation, will best teach the learner the most advantageous method of discarding.

When both parties have discarded and taken in, the elder hand declares his point, and asks if it is good; if his adversary has not so many, he answers, "It is good;" and if the same number, he says "Equal;" in which case neither counts anything for the point; but if the younger hand has more, he answers "Not good." Whichever gains the point is bound to show it on the table, and if he fails to do so he cannot count it; in like manner, if the points are equal both must show them, and if either fails to do so, before he has played a card on the table, his adversary may count the point which he has shown.

The point being decided, the elder hand next declares his best sequence, and if that is admitted to be good, he then reckons all minor sequences, showing them or declaring what suit they are in; failing to do this, he is not entitled to count them.

In like manner, the elder hand proceeds to call his quatorze, or three aces, &c.; these he is not bound to show, though his adversary may require him to do so, as it sometimes happens

that the player has discarded one of a quatorze, and if he calls
it improperly he reckons nothing that hand, or if he only calls
three, his adversary is entitled to know which of the four has
been discarded.

When the elder hand has thus counted his game, he plays a
card on the table, and thereupon, the dealer, before he plays in
answer to that card, is bound to count his own game, that is
to say, point, sequence, and quatorze, or whichever of them he
may happen to have got. If the younger hand takes the
trick he leads in his turn, and so the game proceeds till all
the cards are played out.

Having thus introduced the beginner to the general method
of playing this game, we now direct his attention to Edmund
Hoyle's

GENERAL RULES FOR PLAYING PIQUET.

I. You should play by the stages of your game; that is
when you are backward in the game, or behind your adversary, play a pushing game, otherwise you ought to make
twenty-seven points elder-hand, and thirteen points younger-
hand; and you should in every hand compare your game with
your adversary's, and discard accordingly.

II. Discard in expectation of winning the cards, which is so
essential a part of the game, that it generally makes twenty-
two or twenty-three points difference; therefore do not discard for a low quatorze, such as four queens, four knaves, or
four tens, because in any of these cases, the odds are three
to one, elder-hand, and seventeen to three younger-hand, that
you do not succeed; for let us suppose you should go for a
quatorze of queens, knaves, or tens, and throw out an ace or a
king; by so doing you run the risk of losing above twenty
points, in expectation of winning fourteen.

III. At the beginning of a party, play to make your game,
which is twenty-seven points elder-hand, and thirteen points
younger-hand; therefore, suppose you are elder-hand, and
that you have a tierce-major, and the seven of any suit: it is
five to two but that you take in one card out of any four certain
cards; therefore, suppose you should have three queens, three
knaves, or three tens, in this case discard one of them preferably to the seven of your long suit, because it is three to one

that you do not take in any one certain card, elder-hand, to make you a quatorze, and consequently you would discard the seven of such a suit to a great disadvantage.

IV. If your adversary is considerably before you in the game, the consideration of winning the cards must be put quite out of the question; therefore suppose you should have a quart to a queen, or a quart to a knave; in either of these cases it is only about five to four, being elder-hand, but that you take in a card to make you a quint, and about three to one but that you take in a queen, a knave, or a ten; and should you have three of either dealt you, make a push for the game, particularly if it is so far advanced as to give you but little chance for it in another deal; and in this, and other cases, you may have recourse to the calculations ascertaining the odds.

V. Gaining the point, generally, makes ten points difference; therefore, when you discard, endeavour to gain it but do not risk losing the cards by so doing.

VI. Saving your lurch, or lurching your adversary, is so material, that you ought always to risk some points to accomplish either of them.

VII. If you have six tricks, with any winning card in your hand, never fail playing that card; because, at least, you play eleven points to one against yourself by not playing it, unless in the course of the play you discover what cards your adversary has laid out, or unless by gaining the additional point you save the lurch or win the game.

VIII. If you are greatly advanced in the game, as suppose you are eighty to fifty, in that case it is your interest to let your adversary gain two points for your one as often as you can, especially if in the next deal you are to be elder-hand; but if, on the contrary you are to be younger-hand, and are eighty-six to fifty or sixty, never regard the losing two or three points for the gaining of one, because that point brings you within your show.

IX. The younger-hand is to play upon the defensive; therefore, in order to make his thirteen points, he is to carry tierces, quarts, and especially strive for the point: but suppose him to have two tierces to a king, queen, or knave, as it is twenty-nine to twenty-eight that he succeeds, he having in that case four certain cards to take in to make him a quart to either of them, and perhaps, thereby save a pique, &c., he ought preferably to go for that which he has the most chance to succeed in : but if he has three queens, knaves, or tens, and should attempt to carry any of them preferably to the others, the odds that he does not succeed being seventeen to three against him, he consequently discards to a great disadvantage.

X. The elder or younger-hand, should sometimes sink one of his points, a tierce, or three kings, queens, knaves, or tens, in hopes of winning the cards; but that is to be done with judgment, and without hesitating.

XI. It is often good play for a younger-hand not to call three queens, knaves, &c., and to sink one card of his point, which his adversary may suppose to be a guard to a king or queen.

XII. The younger-hand having the cards equally dealt him, is not to take in any cards, if thereby he runs the risk of losing them, unless he is very backward in the game, and has then a scheme for a great game.

XIII. If the younger-hand has a probability of saving or winning the cards by a deep discard. As for example : suppose he should have the king, queen, and nine of a suit; or the king, knave, and nine of a suit ; in this case he may discard either of those suits, with a moral certainty of not being attacked in them ; and the odds that he does not take in the ace of either of those suits being against him, it is not worth his while to discard otherwise in expectation of succeeding.

XIV. The younger-hand having three aces dealt him, it is generally his best play to throw out the fourth suit.

XV. The younger-hand is generally to carry guards to his queen-suits, in order to make points, and to save the cards.

XVI. When the younger-hand observes that the elder-hand, by calling his point, has five cards which will make five trick in play, and may have the ace and queen of another suit, he should throw away the guard to the king of the latter suit, especially if he has put out one from it, which will give him an even chance of saving the cards.

XVII. If the elder-hand has a quart to a king dealt him, with three kings and three queens (including the king to his quart) and is obliged to discard, either one of his quart to the king, or to discard a king or queen.

Q. Which is best for him to discard?

A. The chance of taking in the ace or nine to his quart to

P

a king, being one out of two certain cards, is exactly equal to the taking either a king or a queen, having three of each dealt him; therefore he is to discard in such a manner as will give him the fairest probability of winning the cards.

The foregoing case may be a general direction to discard in all cases of the like nature, either for the elder or younger-hand.

XVIII. Suppose the elder-hand has taken in his five cards, and that he has the ace, king, and knave of a suit, having discarded two of that suit: and has also the ace, king, knave, and two small cards of another suit, but no winning cards in the other suits,

Q. Which of these suits is he to play from, in order to have the fairest chance of winning, or saving the cards?

A. He is always to play from the suit of which he has the fewest in number; because, if he finds his adversary guarded there, the probability is in his favor that he is unguarded in the other suit; and should he play from the suit of which he has the most in number, and find his adversary's queen guarded, in that case he has no chance to save or win the cards.

XIX. If the elder-hand is sure to make the cards equal, by playing them in any particular manner, and is advanced before his adversary in the game, he should not risk losing them; but if his adversary is greatly before him, in that case it is his interest to risk losing the cards, in expectation of winning them.

Particular Rules and Cases.

I. Suppose you are elder-hand, and that you have dealt you a quart-major, with the seven and eight of clubs, the king and ten of diamonds, the king and nine of hearts, with the ten and nine of spades,

Q. Whether are you to leave a card, by carrying the quart-major and two more of the same suit for the point, with two other kings; or to throw out one card from your point?

A. If you throw out one card from your point, there is a possibility that you reckon only five points, and that your adversary may win the cards, by which event he gets eleven points, besides his three aces, &c., which gives you a bad chance for the game: but by leaving a card, and admitting that one card of consequence lies in the five cards which you are entitled to take in, it follows, that you have four chances to one against leaving that card, and, consequently it is your interest to leave a card; the odds are also greatly in your favor, that you take in some one of the following cards in your four cards, viz., there are two to your point, three aces, and one king.

II. If you should happen to have the ace, king, and four small cards of any suit, with two other kings, and no great suits against you, the like method may be practised.

III. Suppose you should have the king, queen, and four of the smallest clubs, the king and queen of diamonds, the ace and knave of hearts, and the king and nine of spades,

Q. How are you to discard, with a probability of making the most points?

A. You are to throw out the queen and four small clubs, and to carry three entire suits, with the king of clubs; for this reason, because the chance of your taking in the fourth king, is exactly the same as the chance of taking in the ace of clubs; in either of which cases it is three to one against you: but if you fail of taking in the fourth king, by discarding thus, you have a fair chance to win the cards, which will probably make twenty-two points difference. But should you discard with an expectation of taking in the ace of clubs, and should happen to fail, being obliged to throw out some of your great cards, you would have a very distant chance of either saving or winning the cards.

IV. Suppose you should have the king and queen of clubs, a tierce-major in diamonds, queen and knave of hearts, and a quint to the knave in spades,

Q. How are you to discard with a probability of making the most points?

A. You are to throw out the quint to a knave in spades, in order to make the most points; because, let us admit that your quint is good for every thing, after you have taken in, you in that case only score nineteen points, if you carry it, and you probably give up the cards, and also the chance of a quatorze of queens, beside a great number of points in play; and consequently, by carrying the quint, you would discard to a great disadvantage.

V. Suppose you have the king, queen, seven, eight, and nine

of clubs; the queen and knave of diamonds; the queen, ten, and nine of hearts, with the ace and nine of spades,

Q. How are you to discard?

A. You are to discard the king, seven, eight, and nine of clubs, and the nine of spades; by which means you do not only go for three suits, but you have the same chance for taking in the fourth queen, as you have to take in the ace of clubs: besides, the probability of winning the cards is greatly in your favor, by this method of discarding.

VI. Suppose you have the queen, ten, nine, eight, and seven of clubs; the knave and ten of diamonds; the king, queen, and knave of hearts, with the ace and nine of spades,

Q. How are you to discard?

A. You are to discard the five clubs; because it is three to one that you do not take in the knave of clubs, and the carrying three entire suits gives you a fairer chance to score more points.

VII. Suppose you have the ace, queen, and knave of clubs; the king, queen, and knave of diamonds; the queen and knave of hearts, with the ten, nine, eight, and seven of spades,

Q. How are you to discard?

A. You are to discard the ace of clubs and the four spades, because it is only five to four but that you take in a queen or a knave; it is also about three to two that you take in an ace: you have also three cards to your tierce to a king to take in, viz. the ace and ten, or the ten and nine, to make you a quint; all which circumstances considered, you have a fair probability of making a great game; whereas, if you should leave a card, by throwing out the four spades only, you run the risk of leaving one of the following cards, viz. the king of clubs, the ace of diamonds, the ace, queen, or knave of spades; in any of which cases you would probably lose more points than by throwing out the ace of clubs; and if you should carry two suits, viz. three clubs, three diamonds, and the queen of hearts, you run the risk of putting out fourteen points; and it is only five to four against your taking in a queen or a knave, and therefore you would discard to a great disadvantage.

VIII. Suppose you have the king, queen, and ten of a suit, and that your adversary has the ace, knave, and one small card of that suit; and that you have only those three cards left, and you are to make three points of them,

Q. What card are you to play?

A. You are to play the ten.

IX. Suppose you have the ace, queen, ten, and nine of clubs; also the king, queen, ten, and nine of diamonds,

Q. Which of these suits are you to carry, in order to have the fairest probability of scoring the greatest number of points?

A. You are to carry the king, queen, ten, and nine of diamonds, because the chance of taking in the ace of diamonds is exactly equal to that of taking in the king of clubs; and also the chance of taking in the knave of diamonds is equal to that of taking the knave of clubs; by which manner of discarding, you have a probability of scoring fifteen points, for your quint in diamonds, instead of four points for the quart in clubs, and the chance of winning the cards is better, because by taking in the ace of diamonds you have seven tricks certain, which cannot happen by taking in the king of clubs.

X. Suppose you have four aces and two kings dealt you, younger-hand, in order to capot the elder-hand, you are to make a deep discard, such as the queen, ten, and eight of a suit; by which means, if you happen not to take in any card to such suit, you may probably capot the adversary.

XI. Suppose, being elder-hand, that you have the ace, queen, seven, eight, and nine of clubs; also the ace, knave, seven, eight, and nine of diamonds,

Q. Which suit are you to carry, in order to make the most points?

A. You are to carry the ace, knave, seven, eight, and nine of diamonds, because the taking in the king of diamonds is equal to the taking in of the king of clubs, and consequently as good for winning the cards; but you have the chance of taking in the ten of diamonds to make you fifteen points, which event cannot happen by taking in any one certain card in clubs.

XII. Suppose, elder-hand, that you have the ace, queen, seven, eight, and ten of clubs; also the ace, knave, seven, eight, and ten of diamonds.

Q. Which suit is best to carry?

A. You are to carry the ace, knave, seven, eight, and ten of diamonds, because the chance of taking in the king of diamonds is equal to the chance of taking in the king of clubs, and consequently as good for winning the cards; but you have an additional chance of taking in the nine of diamonds to make your fifteen points, which event cannot happen by taking in one certain card in clubs.

XIII. Suppose you have the ace, queen, ten, and two more of a suit; also the ace, queen, and ten of another suit only. And let us suppose, that your adversary has shewn six cards for his point; suppose the ace, queen, and four small ones, and suppose you are guarded in that suit; as soon as you have the lead, you are to play from the suit of which you have the fewest in number, because if he is guarded in that suit, he is probably ungarded in the other suit; but should you begin with the suit of which you have the most in number, if he happens to be guarded there, you have then no chance to win the cards; which may prove otherwise, if you begin with the suit of which you have the fewest in number. If he is guarded in both suits, you have no chance to win the cards.

SOME COMPUTATIONS, DIRECTING, WITH MORAL CERTAINTY HOW TO DISCARD ANY HAND WELL.

I. The chance of an elder-hand's taking in one certain card is three to one against him.

II. That of his taking two certain cards is 18 to 1 against him.

III. I would know what are the odds that an elder-hand takes in four aces?

			Against him.		For him.
A. That he takes in 4 aces is	-	-	968	to	1
At least 3 of them is about	-	-	33	to	1
2 of them	-	-	3	to	1
1 of them	-	-	5	to	2

IV. If an elder-hand has one ace dealt him, what are the odds that he takes in the other three?

			Against him.		For him.
A. That he takes in the 3 aces	-	-	113	to	1
At least 2 of them about	-	-	6	to	1
1 of them	-	-	2	to	3

V. If an elder-hand has two aces dealt him, what are the odds that he takes in the other two?

		Against him.		For him.
A. That he takes in the other 2 aces is		18	to	1
At least 1 of them is near 5 to 4				
against him, or	- - -	21	to	17

VI. In case the elder-hand has two aces and two kings dealt him, what are the odds that he takes in either the two aces or two kings remaining?

	Against him.	For him.
A. It is about - - - - -	17	to	2

VII. Elder-hand having neither ace nor king dealt him, what is his chance to take in both an ace and a king in 2, 3, 4, or 5, cards?

	Against him.	For him.
A. In 2 cards is about - - -	11	to	1
In 3 cards - - -	4	to	1
In 4 cards - - -	9	to	5
In 5 cards - - -	33	to	31

VIII. What are the odds that a younger-hand takes in two certain cards?

	Against him.	For him.
A. - - - - - - -	62	to	1

What are the odds that a younger-hand takes in three certain cards?

	Against him.	For him.
A. - - - - - -	1139	to	1

IX. The younger-hand having no ace dealt him, what chance has he for his taking one?

	Against him.	For him.
A. It is - - - - - -	28	to	29

X. If the younger-hand has one ace dealt him what are the odds of his taking in one or two of the three remaining aces?

	Against him.	For him.
A. That he takes in two of them is about	21	to	1
At least one of them - - -	3	to	2

XI. What are the odds that the younger-hand takes in one certain card?

	Against him.	For him.
A. That he does not take it in is -	17	to	3

What are the odds of a carte-blanche?

	Against him.	For him.
A. - - - - - - -	1791	to	1

AN EXPLANATION AND APPLICATION OF THE FOREGOING CALCULATIONS.

I. As by the first calculation it is three to one, that, being elder hand, you do not take in one certain card? you have, therefore, a better chance of advancing your game, by carrying two suits for points and the cards, than by aiming at quatorze of queens, knaves, or tens.

II. Second calculation; to take in two certain cards, elderhand, is eighteen to one against you.

Therefore suppose you have a quart-major, and two other aces dealt you, the odds that you do not take in the ten to your quart-major, and the other ace, is eighteen to one against you; but that you take in one of them, is only twenty-one to seventeen against you. And suppose you have three aces and three kings dealt you, the odds are eighteen to one against your taking in the other ace and the other king; yet it is not much above five to four, but that you take in one of them. This example shews, how you are to discard in cases of the like nature.

III. The odds in taking in four certain cards, as four aces, &c. being nine hundred and sixty-eight to one by the third calculation, is so great a chance of not succeeding, that it is scarce worth further notice.

But that you take in three out of four certain cards, elderhand, is only thirty-three to one against you.

Example.—Suppose you have two aces and two kings dealt you, the odds of taking in three of them out of four certain cards, such as two kings and one ace, or two aces and a king, are only thirty-three to one against you.

But suppose you should want to take in any two out of four certain cards, such as the queen of clubs, the ten of diamonds, the ace of spades, and knave of hearts, being elder-hand, it appears by the calculation to be three to one against you; and the odds are the same as to any two out of four certain cards.

But if, being elder-hand, you only want one card out of four, the odds are five to two in your favor that you take it in. Therefore, if you have four tens, or any inferior quatorze dealt you, and no ace, it is great odds in your favor, that, being elder-hand, you take in one ace, and ought to play your game accordingly. But you must always consider the disadvantage either of losing the cards, or running the risk of a capot, which you do by keeping four tens when they are not good.

IV. By the fourth calculation; if you have one ace dealt you, it is one hundred and thirteen to one, that you do not take in the three others; forty-nine to eight, or about six to one, that you do not take in two out of the three; but that you take in one out of the three, is about three to two in your favor, or one hundred and thirty-seven to ninety-one.

As for Example.—If you have a quart to a king, and two other kings dealt you; as it is three to two that you take in either ace or nine to your quart to the king, or the fourth king, and you have the chance of reckoning fourteen or fifteen points by this method of discarding, you ought to play accordingly. And this method shews you how to play any hand of the like sort.

But if you should discard, with an expectation of taking in two out of three certain cards, the odds against such an event being above six to one, your game must indeed be very desperate, if you attempt to discard with that view. The chance of taking in three certain cards, being one hundred and thirteen to one, is a very distant chance; yet even such does happen sometimes, but ought never to be ventured upon, but when a man has no other resource in the game.

V. The fifth calculation is, that if you have two aces dealt you, it is eighteen to one that you do not take in the two other aces, but only seventeen to twenty-one that you take in one of them. Let us illustrate the use of this by an example; suppose you have a quart-major dealt you, and a quart to a king, and that you are greatly behind your adversary in the game: to take in the ten to your quart-major is three to one against you; but to take in the ace or nine to your quart to the king, is only about five to four against you.

Also, by the same rule, suppose you have three kings and three queens dealt you, the odds of your taking in both a king and a queen, are eighteen to one against you; but that of your taking one of them, is only five to four against you.

All other cases of the like nature may be discarded by this method of calculation

VI. As by the sixth calculation, it is seventeen to two that you do not take in two certain cards out of four, such as two kings, two queens, &c., you must not, therefore, confound this with the third calculation, where the odds are not above three to one that you take in two cards out of the four.

VII. Having neither an ace nor a king dealt you, what are the odds of your taking in both an ace and a king in two, in three, in four, or in five cards?

A. To take in an ace and a king.

	Against you.		For you.
In 2 cards is about - - -	11	to	1
In 3 cards - - - -	4	to	1
In 4 cards - - - -	9	to	5
In 5 cards - - - -	33	to	31

You may observe, by the foregoing calculation, what are the odds of taking in two, three, four, or five cards, out of any eight certain cards, and consequently discard to the greatest advantage.

The foregoing calculation is either for the elder or younger-hand.

Example. Let us suppose the younger-hand to have two quatorze against him, he may observe, that it is not above four to one but that he takes in one of each of them. The like rule may serve for any other eight certain cards.

VIII. As by the eighth calculation it is sixty-two to one, that the younger-hand does not take in two certain cards, he ought not therefore to run so great a hazard except when his game is desperate, and does not promise him another deal.

IX. By the ninth calculation, as it is twenty-nine to twenty-eight that the younger-hand takes in one ace, having none dealt him: the calculation is the same for any card out of four certain cards.

As for Example. Suppose you have two quarts dealt you from the king or queen of any suit, there are the same odds of twenty-nine to twenty-eight, but that you take in a card to make one of them a quint, and therefore you are to discard accordingly.

As also, that you take in either ace, king, queen, knave of any one suit, when a pique or a repique is against you.

X. The tenth calculation is, that if the younger hand has one ace dealt him it is twenty-one to one that he does not take in two aces, and about three to two that he does not take in one of them; which calculation holds good in the taking in any three other certain cards. Therefore, for example, let us suppose, that as it is but three to two against the younger-hand's taking one card out of three to save a pique, or a repique, it would generally be reckoned good play, either to throw one from his point, or discard a king, &c., for the event of such a chance.

XI. By the eleventh calculation it is seventeen to three, younger-hand, against your taking in any one certain card; therefore, the odds of not succeeding in this case are so greatly against you, that it ought not to be attempted, especially if the winning or saving the cards is risked by so doing, except in desperate cases.

CASES OF CURIOSITY AND INSTRUCTION.

I. Suppose you are younger-hand, and that you have the queen, knave, seven, eight, and nine of clubs; also the seven, eight of diamonds, the seven of hearts, and the ten, nine, eight, and seven of spades; and that the elder-hand has left a card,

Q. How are you to discard, to put it in the power of the cards to repique the elder-hand.

A. You are to carry the five clubs and the four spades, and to leave a card; and by taking in the ace, king, and ten of clubs, you repique your adversary.

II. Suppose you have eight clubs, the ace and king of diamonds, the ace of hearts, and the ace of spades,

Q. Whether do you repique the younger-hand, or not?

A. The younger-hand may have a carte-blanche, by having three quarts to a ten, which reckons first; and therefore he is not repiqued.

III. What is the highest number to be made of a pique?

A. Eighty-two points.

What are the cards which compose that number?

A. A quart-major in two suits, ace, king, and ten of the third, with the ace of the fourth.

This is only upon the supposition that the quart-major is good for every thing.

IV. What is the highest number to be made of a repique and capot?

A. A hundred and seventy points.

What are the cards which compose that number?

A. The four tierce-majors, which are supposed to be good for every thing.

V. Suppose you are elder-hand, and that you want eight points of the game, and that the younger-hand wants twenty-three points? and suppose you have dealt you the ace, king, and queen of clubs, the ace, king, and ten of diamonds; the ace, knave, and nine of hearts; the knave, nine, and seven, of spades,

Q. How are you to discard, to prevent any possibility of the younger-hand's making twenty-three points, without his reckoning a carte-blanche?

A. You are to discard the king and queen of clubs, and the knave, nine, and seven of spades ; by which method of discarding you are certain to make eight points, before the younger-hand can make twenty-three points.

VI. Suppose you have the ace, queen, and knave of clubs with the king and ten of diamonds ; and suppose your adversary has the ace, queen, and knave of diamonds, and the king and ten of clubs, your adversary being to lead, is to make five points, or to lose the game.

Q. How shall you play to prevent him from making five points?

A. When he plays his ace of clubs, you are to play your king of clubs ; by which means he can make only four points.

VII. A and B play a partie at Piquet.

They are one game each of the partie.

A has it in his power to win the second game ; but then he is younger-hand at the beginning of the next game.

A has it also in his power to reckon only ninety-nine points of the second game, and B is to be seventy :

Q. Whether it is A's interest to win the second game, or not?

A. It is A's interest to win the second game, in the proportion of fourteen to thirteen in his favor.

SOME COMPUTATIONS FOR LAYING MONEY AT THE GAME OF PIQUET.

I. It is five to four that the eldest-hand wins the game.

II. It is about two to one that the eldest-hand does not lurch the younger-hand.

III. It is near four to one that the younger-hand does not lurch the elder-hand.

SUPPOSE A AND B MAKE A PARTIE AT PIQUET.

I. A has the hand; what are the odds that A wins the partie ?

A. It is about twenty-three to twenty.

II. If A has one game, and B one game, he who is eldest-hand has above five to four to win the partie.

III. If A has two games love, and A has the hand, the odds are about five to one that he wins the partie.

IV. If B has the hand when A has two games love, the odds in favor of A are about three and a half to one.

V. If A has the hand, and two games to one, the odds are about eleven to four.

VI. If B has the hand, when A is two games to one, the odds in favour of A are about nine to five.

VII. If A is one game love, and elder-hand, the odds in favor of A is about seventeen to seven.

VIII. If A is one game love, and younger-hand, the odds in favor of A is about two to one.

LAWS OF THE GAME AT PIQUET.

I. THE elder-hand is obliged to lay out at least one card.

II. If the elder-hand takes in one of the three cards which belong to the younger-hand, he loses the game.

III. If the elder-hand, in taking his five cards, should happen to turn up a card belonging to the younger-hand, he is to reckon nothing that deal.

IV. If the elder or younger-hand play with thirteen cards, he counts nothing.

V. Should either of the players have thirteen cards dealt, it is at the option of the elder-hand to stand the deal, or not; and if he chooses to stand, then the person having thirteen is to discard one more than he takes in; but should either party have above thirteen cards, then a new deal must take place.

VI. If the elder or younger-hand reckons what he has not, he counts nothing.

VII. If the elder-hand touches the stock after he has discarded, he cannot alter his discard.

VIII. If a card is faced, and it happens to be discovered either in the dealing, or in the stock, there must be a new deal, unless it be the bottom card.

IX. If the dealer turns up a card in dealing, belonging to the elder-hand, it is in the option of the elder-hand to have a new deal.

X. If the younger-hand, takes in five cards, he loses the game, unless the elder-hand has left two cards.

XI. If the elder-hand calls forty-one for his point, which happens to be a quart-major, and it is allowed to be good, and only reckons four for it, and plays away, in this case he is not entitled to count more.

XII. If the elder-hand shews a point, or quart, or tierce, and asks if they are good, and afterwards forgets to reckon any of them, it bars the younger-hand from reckoning any of equal value.

XIII. Carte-blanche counts first, and consequently saves piques and repiques: It also piques and repiques the adversary in the same manner, as if those points were reckoned in any other way.

XIV. Carte-blanche need not be shewn till the adversary has first discarded; only if you are eldest-hand, you must bid the younger-hand discard for carte-blanche; which, after he has done, you shew your blanche by counting your cards down one after another.

XV. You are to cut two cards at the least.

XVI. If the elder-hand calls a point, and does not shew it, it is not to be reckoned; and the younger-hand may shew, and reckon his point.

XVII. If you play with eleven cards, or fewer, no penalty attends it.

XVIII. If the elder-hand leaves a card, and after he has taken in, happens to put to his discard the four cards taken in, they must remain with his discard, and he only plays with eight cards, viz., those added to his discard.

XIX. If the younger-hand leaves a card or cards and mixes it with his discard before he has shewn it to the elder-hand, who is first to tell him what he will play, the elder-hand is entitled to see his whole discard.

XX. If the younger-hand leaves a card or cards, and does not see them, nor mixes them to his discard, the eldest-hand has no right to see them; but then they must remain separate whilst the cards are playing, and the younger-hand cannot look at them at all.

XXI. If the younger-hand leaves a card or cards, and looks at them, the elder-hand is entitled to see them, first declaring what suit he will lead.

XXII. If the dealer deals a card too many, or too few, it is in the option of the elder-hand to have a new deal; but if he stands the deal, he must leave three cards for the younger-hand.

XXIII. You are, in the first place, to call your point; and if you have two points, and design to reckon the highest, you are to call that first, and are to abide by your first call.

XXIV. You are to call your tierces, quarts, quints, &c., next; and to call the highest of them, in case you design to reckon them.

XXV. You are to call a quatorze, preferable to three aces, &c., if you design to reckon them.

XXVI. If you call a tierce, having a quart in your hand, you must abide by your first call.

XXVII. Whoever deals twice together and discovers it previous to seeing his cards, may insist upon his adversary dealing, although the latter may have looked at his cards.

XXVIII. Should the pack be found erroneous in any deal, that deal is void; but the preceding deals are valid.

XXIX. The player who at the commencement does not reckon or shew carte-blanche, his point, or any sequence, &c., is not to count them afterwards.

XXX. No player can discard twice, and after he has touched the stock, he is not allowed to take any of his discard back again.

XXXI. When the elder hand does not take all his cards, he must specify what number he takes or leaves.

XXXII. Whosoever calls his game wrong and does not correct himself before he plays, is not to reckon anything that game; but the adversary is to reckon all he has good in his own game.

XXXIII. Any card that has touched the board is deemed to be played unless in case of a revoke.

XXXIV. If any player names a suit, and then plays a different one, the antagonist may call a suit.

XXXV. The player who looks at any card belonging to the stock, is liable to have a suit called.

TERMS USED AT PIQUET.

CAPOT is when either of the players makes every trick, for which he scores forty.

Cards signify the majority of tricks, which reckon for ten points.

Carte Blanche means a hand without a court card in the twelve dealt, which counts for ten, and takes place of everything else.

Huitième, eight successive cards of the same suit, counts eighteen points.

Pique, is when the elder hand has reckoned thirty in hand and play before the adversary has gained one; in which case, instead of thirty it is called sixty, adding thereto as many points as are obtained above thirty.

Point, the greatest number on the cards of the same suit in hand after having taken in, reckoned by their pips, scores for as many points as cards.

Quart, four cards in sequence of the same suit counts four points: there are five kinds of quarts, the first, called quart-major, consists of ace, king, queen, and knave; the second quart from a king, of king, queen, knave, and ten; the third, quart from a queen, of queen, knave, ten, nine; the fourth, quart from a knave, of knave, ten, nine, eight; the fifth, a basse-quart of quart-minor, of ten, nine, eight, and seven.

Quatorze, the four aces, kings, queens, knaves, or tens, scores fourteen points.

Quint means five cards of the same suit in sequence, and reckons fifteen points: there are four sorts of quints; a quint-major of ace, king, queen, knave, and ten, down to knave, ten, nine, eight, and seven, styled a quint-minor.

Repique signifies when one of the players counts thirty or more in hand, before the adversary obtains one, then it is called ninety, reckoning as many points above ninety as were gained above thirty.

Sixième, or six cards of the same suit in sequence, reckons for sixteen points: there are three sorts of sixièmes, viz., sixième-major from the ace, sixième from the king, and sixième-minor from the queen.

Septième, or seven of the same suit in sequence, counts for seventeen points, there are two septièmes; one from the ace, the other from the king.

Threes of aces, &c., down to tens, reckon three points.

Talon, or *Stock*, means the eight remaining cards after welve are dealt to each player.

Tierce, or sequence of three, reckons for three: there are ix kinds of tierces, tierce-major, of ace, king, queen; down o nine, eight, seven, styled tierce-minor.

QUADRILLE.

The game of Quadrille is played by four persons. The number of cards required are forty; the four tens, nines, and eights, being discarded from the pack. The deal is made by distributing the cards to each player, three at a time, for two rounds, and four at a time, for one round; commencing with the right hand player, who is the elder hand.

The trump is made by the player, with or without calling, by naming spades, clubs, diamonds, or hearts, and the suit so named becomes trumps.

The two following tables will show the rank and order of the cards, when trumps, or when not so.

The Rank or Order of the Cards when not Trumps.

Clubs and Spades.	Hearts and Diamonds.
King,	King,
Queen,	Queen,
Knave,	Knave,
Seven,	Ace,
Six,	Deuce,
Five,	Three,
Four,	Four,
Three,	Five,
Deuce,	Six,
——In all 9.	Seven,——In all 10.

The Rank and Order of the Cards when Trumps.

Clubs and Spades.	Hearts and Diamonds.
Spadille, the ace of spades.	Spadille, the ace of spades,
Manille, the duce of spades or of clubs,	Manille, the seven of hearts, or of diamonds,
Basto, the ace of clubs,	Basto, the ace of clubs,
	Punto (or Ponto), the ace of hearts or of diamonds,
King,	King,
Queen,	Queen,
Knave,	Knave,
Seven,	Duce,
Six,	Three,
Five,	Four,
Four.	Five,
Three, ——In all 11	Six,——In all 12.

From these tables it will be observed that spadille and basto are always trumps, and that the red suits have one trump more than the black; the former twelve, the latter only eleven.

There is a trump between spadille and basto, which is called manille, and is in black the deuce, and in red the seven: they are the second cards when trumps, and the last in their respective suits when not trumps. Example: the deuce of spades being second trump, when they are trumps, and the lowest card when clubs, hearts, or diamonds are trumps; and so of the rest.

Ponto, is the ace of hearts or diamonds, which are above the king, and the fourth trump, when either of those suits are trumps; but are below the knave, and called ace of diamonds or hearts, when they are not trumps. The two of hearts or diamonds is always superior to the three; the three to the four; the four to the five; and the five to the six: the six is only superior to the seven when it is not trumps, for when the seven is manille, it is the second trump.

There are three matadores, viz., spadille, manille, and basto; whose privilege is, that when the player has no other trumps but them, and trumps are led, he is not obliged to play them, but may play what card he thinks proper, provided, however, that the trump led is of an inferior value; but if spadille should be led, he that has manille or basto only, is compelled to play it, which is the case with basto in respect to manille, the superior matadore always forcing the inferior.

Although, properly speaking, there are but three matadores, yet all those trumps which succeed the three first without interruption, are also called matadores; but the three first only enjoy the privilege above stated.

TERMS USED IN THE GAME OF QUADRILLE.

To ASK LEAVE, is to ask leave to play with a partner, by calling a king.

BASTO, is the ace of clubs, and always the third best trump.

BAST, is a penalty incurred by not winning when you stand your game, or by renouncing: in which cases you pay as many counters as are down.

CHEVILLE, is being between the eldest hand and the dealer.

CODILLE, is when those who defend the pool make more

tricks than those who defend the game, which is called winning the codille.

CONSOLATION, is a claim in the game, always played by those who lose, whether by codille or remise.

DEVOLE, is when he who stands the game makes no trick.

DOUBLE, is to play for double stakes, with regard to the game, the consolation, the sans prendre, the matadores, and the devole.

FORCE; the ombre is said to be forced, when a strong trump is played for the adversary to over-trump. He is likewise said to be forced, when he asks leave, and one of the other players obliges him to play sans prendre, or pass, by offering to play sans prendre.

FORCED SPADILLE, is when all have passed, he who has spadille is obliged to play it.

FORCED SANS PRENDRE, is, when having asked leave, one of the players offers to play alone, in which case you are obliged to play alone, or pass.

FRIEND, is the player who has the king called.

IMPASSE. To make the impasse, is when, being in cheville, the knave of a suit is played, of which the player has the king.

MANILLE, is, in black, the deuce of spades or clubs; in red, the seven of hearts or diamonds; and is always the second best trump.

MARK, means the fish put down by the dealer.

MILLE, is a mark of ivory, which is sometimes used, and stands for ten fish.

MATADORES, or matts, are spadille, manille, and basto, which are always the three best trumps. False matadores, are any sequence of trumps, following the matadores regularly.

OMBRE, is the name given to him who stands the game, by calling or playing sans appeller, or sans prendre.

PARTY, is the duration of the game, according to the number of tours agreed to be played.

PASS, is the term used when you have not a hand either to play alone, or with calling a king.

PONTO or PUNTO, is the ace of diamonds, when diamonds are trumps; or hearts, when they are trumps; and is then the fourth trump.

POOL. The pool consists of the fishes, which are staked for the deals, or the counters put down by the players, or the basts which go to the game. To defend the pool is to be against him who stands the game.

PRISE, is the number of fish or counters given to each player at the commencement of the game.

REGLE, is the order to be observed at the game.

REMISE, is when those who stand the game do not make more tricks than they who defend the pool, and then they lose by remise.

RENOUNCE, is not to play in the suit led when you have it : likewise when not having any of the suit led, you win with a card that is the only one you have of that suit in which you play.

REPRISE and REPORT, are synonymous with Party.

ROI RENDU, is the king surrendered when called, and given to the ombre, for which he pays a fish. In which case the person to whom the king is given up, must win the game alone.

SPADILLE, is the ace of spades ; which is always the best trump.

SANS APPELLER, is playing without calling a king.

SANS PRENDRE, is erroneously used for sans appeller, meaning the same.

TENACE, is to wait with two trumps that must make, when he who has two others is obliged to lead ; such as the two black aces against manille or punto.

TOURS, are the counters, which they who win put down, to mark the number of coups played.

VOLE, is to get all the tricks, either with a friend or alone, sans prendre, or declared at the first of the deal.

MANNER OF PLAYING THE GAME AND DEALING THE CARDS, OF THE STAKES, OF SPEAKING, OF THE BAST, &c., &c.

1. Every person is to play as he thinks proper, and most advantageously to his own game.

2. No one is to encourage his friend to play; but each person should know what to do when he is to play.

3. The stakes consist of seven equal billets or contracts, as they are sometimes called, comprising the ten counters and

fishes, which are distributed to each player. A mille is equal to ten fish, and every fish to ten counters: the value of the fish is according to the players' agreement, as also the number of tours; which are usually fixed at ten, and marked by turning the corners of a card.

4. After each player has received his ten cards, he that is on the left hand of the dealer, upon examining his hand, must declare whether he plays; and if he has not a good hand, he passes, and so the second, the third, and fourth. All four may pass: but he who has spadille, after having shewn or named it, is compelled to play by calling a king.

5. If the deal is played in this manner, or one of the players has asked leave, and no one choosing to play without calling, the eldest hand must begin; previously naming his suit, and the king he calls; he who wins the trick must play another card, and the rest of course, till the game is finished. The tricks are then reckoned, and if the ombre, meaning him who stands the game, has, together with him who has king called, six tricks, they have won, and are accordingly paid the game, the consolation, and the matadores, if they have them, and divide what is upon the game, and the basts, if there be any.

6. Should they make only six tricks, it is a remise, and they are basted, what goes upon the game; paying to the other players the consolation and the matadores. When the tricks are equally divided between them, they are also basted; and if they make only four tricks between them, it is a remise. Should they make less, they lose codille, and in that case pay their adversaries what they should have received if they had won; namely, the game, consolation, and matadores, if they have them, and are basted what is upon the game; and if they win codille, divide the stakes. The bast, and everything that is paid, arise equally from the two losers; one-half by him who calls, and the other by him who is called; equally the same in case of codille as a remise, unless the ombre does not make three tricks, in which case, he who is called is not only exempt from paying half the bast, but also the game, consolation, and matadores, if there are any, which, in that case, the ombre pays alone, and likewise in case of a codille as a remise. This rule is enforced to prevent unreasonable games being played.

7. A single case may occur, in which if the ombre makes only one trick, he is not basted alone; which is, when not having a good hand, he passes, and all the other players have passed likewise, and he having spadille is compelled to play. In this case, it would be unjust to oblige him to make three or four tricks; wherefore he who is called pays a moiety of the losing; and, for the same reason, he who has spadille, with a bad hand, should pass, in order that if he is afterwards obliged to play by calling a king (which is called forced spadille), he may not be basted singly.

8. The player who has once passed, cannot be allowed to play: and he who has asked leave cannot refuse to play; unless another should propose playing without calling.

9. When a person has four kings, he may call a queen to one of his kings, but not that which is trumps. He who has one or more kings may call himself, that is one of those kings; but in this case he must make six tricks alone, and therefore wins or loses singly. The king of the suit in which he plays cannot be called.

10. When he who is not eldest of hand has the king called, and plays spadille, manille, or basto, or even the king called, in order to show that he is the friend, having other kings that he is apprehensive the ombre may trump, he is not to be allowed to go for the vole; and he is basted, if it should appear it is done with that design.

11. No hand is allowed to be shown, though codille may already be won, in order that it may be seen whether the ombre is basted singly. Should the ombre or his friend show his cards, before he has made six tricks, judging that he might have made them, and there should appear a possibility of preventing his making them, the other players may compel him to play his cards in what order they choose.

12. Whoever plays without calling must himself make six tricks to win; all the other players being united against him, and therefore exert their combined efforts to distress him. Whoever plays without calling, is permitted to play in preference to any other, who would play with calling: nevertheless, if he who has asked leave will play without calling, he has the preference of him who would force him. These are the two methods of play without calling, which are called *forced*.

13. He who plays without calling, not dividing the winnings with any other player, consequently when he loses pays all himself. Should he lose by remise, he is basted, and pays each other player the consolation, the sans appeller (commonly, though erroneously, called the sans prendre), and the matadores. should there be any. Should he lose codille, he is also basted, and pays each player what he would have received from them if he had been the winner. Those who win codille divide the gains; and if there be any remaining counters, they belong to the player of the three who may have the spadille, or the highest trump in the succeeding deal. The same rule operates with respect to him who calls one of his own kings; he wins or loses alone, as in the other case, except the sans appeller, which he pays if a loser, or receives as a winner, although he plays singly.

14. Should he play sans appeller, though he may have a sure game, he is compelled to name his suit; which neglecting, showing his cards, and saying, " I play sans appeller," in this case, either of the rest of the players can oblige him to play in which suit he chooses, though he should not have a trump in that suit.

15. No player is compelled to trump, when he is not possessed of any of the suit led, nor obliged to pay a higher card in that suit if he has it; it being optional to him, although he is the last player, and the trick belongs to the ombre; but he is compelled to play in the suit led if he can, otherwise he renounces. Should he separate a card from his game and show it, he is compelled to play it; if, by not doing it, the game should be prejudiced, or give any intelligence to his friend, but particularly if it should be a matadore. He who plays sans appeller, or by calling himself, is not subject to this rule.

16. One player may turn the tricks made by the others, and reckon what has been played; but only when it is his turn to play. Should he, instead of turning a player's tricks, turn and see his game, or show it to the other players, he is basted, together with him whose cards he turned; each paying a moiety of the loss.

17. He who renounces is basted as often as detected; but no renounce takes place till the trick is turned. Should the renounce be discovered before the deal is finished, and has

proved detrimental to the game, the cards must be taken up again, and the game replayed from that trick where the renounce began. But should all the cards be played, the bast is still made, and the cards must not be replayed, unless there should be several renounces in the same deal. In this case they are to be played again, unless the cards should have been previously mixed together. When several basts appear in the same deal, they all go together, unless a different agreement is made; and in cases of bast, the greatest is first reckoned.

SHORT RULES FOR LEARNERS.

1. When you are the ombre, and your friend leads from a mat, play your best trump, and then lead the next best the first opportunity.

2. If you possess all the trumps, continue leading them, except you hold certain other winning cards.

3. If all the mats are not revealed, by the time you have six tricks, do not run a risk in playing for the vole.

4. When you are the friend called, and hold only a mat, lead it; but if it is guarded by a small trump, lead that. But when the ombre is last player, lead the best trump you possess.

5. Punto in red, or king of trumps in black, are good cards to lead when you are best, and should either of them succeed, then play a small trump.

6. If the ombre leads to discover his friend, and you have king, queen, and knave, put on the knave.

7. Preserve the suit called, whether friend or foe.

8. When playing against a lone hand, never lead a king, unless you have the queen; nor change the suit; and prevent, if possible, the ombre from being last player.

9. You are to call to your strongest suits, except you have a queen guarded: and if elder hand, you have a better chance than when middle hand.

10. A good player may succeed better with a weaker hand, when either elder or younger, than if middle hand.

PARTICULAR GAMES.

Having made the learner acquainted with the rules necessary to a knowledge of the game of quadrille, we shall now present him with a copious collection of such cases as give a fair chance of winning the game by calling a king; with directions at the end of each case, what trump it is necessary to lead.

Games in Red, which may be played, calling a King.

I. Spadille, manille, two small hearts or diamonds, the queen of clubs and one small one, and four small cards of the other suits. Lead a small trump.

II. Spadille, manille, two small hearts or diamonds, with the knave and two small clubs, and three small cards of the other suits. Lead a small trump.

III. Spadille, manille, two small hearts or diamonds, three small clubs, and three small cards of the other suits. Lead a small trump.

IV. Spadille, punto, king, queen, and one small heart or diamond, three small clubs, the queen, and one spade. Lead punto.

V. Spadille, punto, king, knave, and one small heart or diamond, the knave and two small clubs, and two small spades. Lead punto.

VI. Spadille, king, queen, knave, and one small heart or diamond, with the queen, knave, and one small club, and two small spades. Lead the king of trumps.

VII. Spadille, three, four, five, and six of hearts or diamonds, king of clubs and one more, queen and two small spades; whether elder or any other hand, when you have the lead play a small trump, in the second lead play spadille.

VIII. Manille, basto, punto, and two small hearts or diamonds, three small clubs, and the knave and one spade. Lead manille.

IX. N.B. Manille, basto, king, and two small hearts or diamonds, queen, and one small club, and three small spades. Lead manille.

X. N.B. Manille, basto, queen, and two small hearts or diamonds, queen, and two small clubs, knave, and one spade. Lead manille.

XI. Manille, basto, with the three smallest hearts or diamonds, queen, and one small club, knave, and two small spades. Play a small trump.

XII. N.B. Manille, Punto, king, and two small hearts or

diamonds, queen, knave, and one small club, king and one small spade. Lead manille.

XIII. Manille, punto, queen, and two small hearts or diamonds, queen and one small club, king and two small spades. Play a small trump.

XIV. Manille, punto, and three small hearts or diamonds, knave and one small club, king, queen, and one small spade. Play a small trump.

XV. Manille, and the four smallest hearts or diamonds, queen, and one small club, king, queen, and one small spade. Play a small trump.

XVI. N.B. Basto, punto, king, and two small hearts or diamonds, king and queen of clubs, queen, and two small spades. Lead basto.

XVII. N.B. Basto, punto, queen, and two small hearts or diamonds, queen, knave, and one small club, king and queen of spades. Lead basto.

XVIII. N.B. Basto, punto, and three of the smallest hearts or diamonds, king and queen of clubs, queen, knave, and one small spade. Play a small trump.

XIX. Basto, and the four smallest hearts or diamonds, king and queen of clubs, queen, knave, and one small spade. Play a small trump.

XX. N.B. Punto, king, queen, and two small hearts or diamonds, king and queen, of clubs, queen, knave, and one small spade. Lead punto.

XXI. Punto, king, and three small hearts or diamonds, king and queen of clubs, queen, knave, and one small spade. Play a small trump.

You are to observe that those cases which are marked thus, (N.B.) are very good games to play, and that you have the odds of your side, to win those which are not marked.

Games in Black, which may be played, calling a King.

I. Spadille, manille, and two small clubs or spades, the knave, and two small hearts, and three small diamonds. Lead a small trump.

II. N.B. Spadille, manille, and two small clubs or spades, queen, and two small hearts, and three small diamonds. Lead a small trump.

III. Spadille, manille, and two small clubs or spades, three small hearts, three small diamonds. Lead a small trump.

IV. N.B. Spadille, king, queen, and two small clubs or spades, with the queen and one small heart, three small diamonds. Lead the king of trumps.

V. Spadille, king, knave, and two small clubs, queen, and two diamonds, two small hearts. Play a small trump.

VI. Spadille, queen, and three small clubs or spades, queen, and two small hearts, two small diamonds. Play a small trump.

VII. Spadille, and the four smallest clubs or spades, king, and one small heart, queen and two small diamonds. Play a small trump.

VIII. Manille, basto, king, and two small clubs or spades, three small hearts, and two small diamonds. Lead manille.

IX. Manille, basto, queen, and two small clubs or spades, three small hearts, queen, and one small diamond. Lead manille.

X. Manille, basto, knave, and two small clubs or spades, knave and one heart, three small diamonds. Lead manille.

XI. Manille, basto, and three small clubs or spades, queen and two small hearts, knave and one small diamond. Lead manille.

XII. N.B. Manille, king, queen, and two small clubs or spades, king, and one small heart, queen, knave, and one small diamond. Lead manille.

XIII. N.B. Manille, king, knave, and two small clubs or spades, king and one small heart, queen and two small diamonds. Lead manille.

XIV. Manille, king, and three small clubs or spades, queen, and two small hearts, king and one small diamond. Play a small trump.

XV. Manille, and the four smallest clubs or spades, king, queen, and one small heart, two small diamonds. Play a small trump.

XVI. N.B. Basto, king, queen, and two small clubs or spades, queen and two small hearts, king and one small diamond. Lead basto.

XVII. N.B. Basto, king, knave, and two small clubs or spades, knave and one heart, king and two small diamonds. Lead basto.

XVIII. N.B. Basto, king, and three small clubs or spades,

king and queen of hearts, queen and two small diamonds. Play a small trump.

XIX. Basto, and four of the smallest clubs or spades, king and queen of hearts, queen, knave, and one small diamond. Play a small trump.

XX. N.B. King, queen, knave, and two small clubs or spades, king and queen of hearts, knave and two small diamonds. Lead the king of trumps.

XXI. King, queen, seven, six, and five of clubs or spades, king and queen of hearts, queen, knave, and one small diamond. Lead the king of trumps.

You are to observe, that those cases which are marked thus, (N.B.) are very good games to play, and you have the odds of your side to win those which are not marked.

N.B. You are to call to your strongest suits, except you have a queen guarded. And if you are elder hand, you have a fairer chance to win the game than if middle hand, because you have an opportunity of leading a trump, which frequently makes your Adversaries play against each other.

CASES CALCULATED, SHOWING THE PLAYERS THE ODDS OF WINNING THE FOLLOWING GAMES AT QUADRILLE, SANS PRENDRE; AND ALSO SUCH GAMES AS OUGHT NOT TO BE PLAYED SANS PRENDRE.

Games in Black, Elder Hand.

I. Three matadores in clubs, king and six of diamonds, king and six of hearts, king, five and six of spades. Play trumps to all the elder-hand games. The above game wins 27 to 4.

II. Three matadores and the three of clubs, king and six of diamonds, king and six of hearts, and two small spades. The above game wins 215 to 162, or about 4 to 3.

III. Three matadores, three and four of clubs, king and six of diamonds, three small hearts. Wins 291 to 86, or above 10 to 3.

IV. Three matadores, with the three, four, and five of clubs, two small diamonds, and two small hearts. Wins near 10 to 1.

V. Spadille, manille, king, knave, three and four of clubs, two small diamonds, two small hearts. Wins 4895 to 3022 or about 8 to 5.

VI. Spadille, manille, king, three, four and five of clubs, two small diamonds, two small hearts.   Wins about 8 to 5.

VII. Spadille, manille, king, three and four of clubs, king and six of diamonds, and three small hearts.   Loses 1514 to 1125, or about 4 to 3.

VIII. Spadille, manille, three, four, five, and six of clubs, two small diamonds, and two small hearts.   Loses 1514 to 1125, or about 4 to 3.

IX. Spadille, manille, three, four, and five of clubs, king, and one small diamond, and three small hearts.   Loses 2234 to 405, or about 11 to 2.

X. Three false matadores and three of clubs, king and six of diamonds, king and six of hearts, king and six of spades. Wins 215 to 162, or about 4 to 3.

XI. Three false matadores, three and four of clubs, king and six of diamonds, king, six and five of hearts.   Wins 291 to 86, or above 10 to 3.

XII. Three false matadores, three, four and five of clubs, king, and six of diamonds, two small hearts.   Wins 1025 to 106, or near 10 to 1.

XIII. Manille, basto, queen, three, four and five of clubs, king and one small diamond, two small hearts.   Wins 4895 to 3022, or above 8 to 5.

XIV. Manille, basto, knave, three, four and five of clubs, king and one small diamond, two small hearts.   Loses 4162 to 3755, or almost 10 to 9.

XV. Spadille, three, four, five, and six of clubs, king and one small diamond, king of spades, king and one small heart. Lead a small trump, and the chance for winning is 1749 to 890; or near 2 to 1.

XVI. Spadille, three, four, five, six and seven of clubs, king, and one diamond, king of spades and king of hearts. Wins about 275 to 2.

XVII. Manille, king, queen, two small spades or clubs, king, and a small heart, queen, knave, and one small diamond.

XVIII. Manille, king, knave, two small spades, or clubs, king and a small heart, queen and two small diamonds.

XIX. Basto, king, queen, two small spades or clubs, queen and two small hearts, king and a small diamond.

XX. Basto, king, knave, two small clubs or spades, king and queen of diamonds, queen and two small hearts.

Games in red, Elder Hand.

I. Three matadores in hearts, king and one diamond, king and one spade, king and two clubs. Wins 24 to 11, or about 2 to 1.

II. Three matadores and three of hearts, king and one small diamond, king and queen of clubs, and two small spades. Wins 7010 to 1661, above 4 to 1; besides the chance that his kings and queen pass, though he should not fetch out all the trumps.

III. Three matadores and three and four of hearts, king and one small club, three diamonds. Wins almost 4 to 3.

IV. Three matadores, three, four and five of hearts, two small diamonds, two small clubs. Wins 291 to 86, or above 10 to 3.

V. Spadille, manille, punto, queen, three and four of hearts, two small diamonds, and two small clubs. Loses 1706 to 1339, or above 5 to 4.

VI. Spadille, manille, punto, three, four and five of hearts, two small diamonds, two small clubs. Loses 1514 to 1125, or above 4 to 3.

VII. Spadille, manille, king, three, four and five of hearts, two small diamonds, two small clubs. Loses 278 to 99, or about 14 to 5.

VIII. Spadille, manille, three, four, five and six of hearts, two small diamonds, two small clubs. Loses above 3 to 1.

IX. Spadille, manille, three, four, five and six of hearts, king and one club, two small diamonds. Wins 1845 to 794, or above 9 to 4.

X. Spadille, manille, two, three, four, five, six of hearts, two small diamonds, one small club. Wins above 9 to 1, nearer 10 to 1.

XI. Four matadores in hearts, king and two small clubs, king and two small spades. Wins about 16 to 1. That he fetches out the trump is 7206 to 1465, near 5 to 1; besides the chance for his king's passing, though the trump should not fall.

XII. Three false matadores and three of hearts, king and one small club, king and one diamond, king and one small spade. Loses 5791 to 2880, or above 2 to 1.

XIII. Three false matadores, three and four of hearts, king

and one club, king and two spades. Wins 215 to 162, or about 4 to 3.

XIV. Three false matadores, three, four and five of hearts, king and one small club, two small spades. Wins 291 to 86, or above 10 to 3.

XV. Three false matadores, with the knave, the three, four and five of hearts, one small diamond, two small spades. Wins 1025 to 106, near 10 to 1; provided the lead comes into your hand a second time, without trumping with a matadore.

XVI. Three false matadores, with the queen, the three, four and five of hearts, one small diamond, two small clubs. (As the former) wins near 10 to 1.

XVII. Manille, basto, king, three, four and five of hearts, king and one diamond, two small clubs. Loses 1514 to 1125, or about 4 to 3.

XVIII. Manille, basto, queen, three, four and five of hearts, king and one club, two small spades. Loses 278 to 99, or near 3 to 1.

XIX. Manille, basto, three, four, five and six of hearts, king and one diamond, two small clubs. Loses 2639 to 405, or about 6 to 1.

XX. Spadille, two, three, four, five and six of hearts, king and one diamond, king of spades, and the king of clubs. That spadille fetches out three trumps, is above 4 to 1, and consequently above 4 to 1 for winning.

XXI. Spadille, three, four, five and six of hearts, king and one diamond, king and one spade, and the king of clubs. That three sure tricks in trumps lie against the player is 1384 to 1255, and consequently the odds is against his winning the game.

If he plays the game, he must begin with leading a small trump; for if he plays spadille, he has no chance at all.

At his second lead he ought to play spadille, having the fairest probability of winning the game by that method of play.

In all the games of false matadores, we have supposed the player is not over-ruffed or trumped before the lead comes again into his hand.

N.B If you should have a sans prendre game, and it should be 5 to 4 for winning it, you are to consider that the calling a king makes it a sure game won, besides the chance of winning a vole; and therefore, upon a strict calculation, it is found to be more advisable to call a king in such a case.

N.B. A good player may play a weaker game, either elder or younger hand, than middle hand.

LAWS AT QUADRILLE.

I. Whoever names any suit for trumps, he must abide by it, though it should happen to be his worst suit.

II. If a card happens to be faced in dealing, you must deal again, except it is the last card.

III. If you play with eleven cards you are basted.

IV. If you play sans prendre, or have matadores, you are to demand them before the next dealer has finished his deal, otherwise you lose the benefit of them.

V. If any body names his trump without asking leave, he is obliged to play sans prendre, unles he is the younger hand, and all the rest have passed.

VI. If any body plays out of his turn, that card played may be called at any time in that deal, provided he does not revoke; or the adversaries may demand the partner of him, who played out of his turn, or his own partner, to play any suit he thinks fit.

VII. After the game is won, if the person who won the sixth trick plays the seventh card, he is obliged to play for the vole.

VIII. If you have four kings dealt you, you are at liberty either to call a queen to one of your kings, or to call one of your kings; but you are not to call the queen of trumps.

IX. If anybody separates a card from the rest, he ought to play it, if the adverse party has seen it, unless he plays sans prendre.

X. If the king called, or his partner plays out of his turn, no vole is to be played for.

XI. No person is to be basted for a renounce, unless the trick is turned and quitted; and if any person renounces, and it is discovered, if the player should happen to be basted by such renounce, all the parties are to take up their cards, and play them over again.

XII. Forced spadille is not obliged to make three tricks, nor is allowed to play for the vole.

XIII. Whoever undertakes playing the vole, has the prefer-ence of playing before him who offers to play sans prendre.

XIV. If all parties agree to it, before you begin to play, let the person have the preference of playing who plays for the most tricks; which will prevent small games from being played.

XV. The ombre is entitled to know his king called, before he declares for the vole.

XVI. When six tricks are won, he who won the sixth trick ought to say, I play the vole; or I do not play the vole; or, I ask—and nothing else.

XVII. He who wins the vole is to take double the stake played for out of the pool.

XVIII. He who asks leave (if elder hand) may play sans prendre, in preference to any of the other players.

XIX. If you have one king only, you may call yourself, but must win six tricks.

XX. If you play the king surrendered, he must win six tricks who demands the king of any person.

XXI. He who has passed once, (unless he has spadille) has no right to call afterwards; also, he who has asked is obliged to play, unless some body else plays sans prendre.

XXII. If the ombre, or his friend, shew their cards before they have won six tricks, the adversaries may call their cards as they please, specifying each card.

XXIII. Whoever has only asked leave, cannot play sans prendre, unless he is forced.

XXIV. You are at liberty to look at all the tricks turned, when you are to lead, but not otherwise.

XXV. Whoever undertakes playing for the vole, and does not succeed, has a right to the stakes sans prendre, and mata-dores if he has them, having won his game.

XXVI. If any person discovers his game, he is not entitled to play for the vole.

XXVII. If there happen to be two cards of the same sort, and found out before the deal is ended, the deal is void, but not otherwise.

XXVIII. No body is to declare how many trumps are played out.

XXIX. He who calls, and does not make three tricks, is to be basted alone, unless he plays forced spadille,

R

ADDITIONS TO THE GAME AT QUADRILLE.

In order to vary this game, some introduce the Mediateur, either with or without the Favourite suit; the first term signifies a king, which any person may demand, in order to play *sans prendre*, giving in return some other card and a fish; but if the king is of the favourite suit, then two fish are to be paid. The favourite suit is determined either by drawing a card, or otherwise fixing upon a suit at the commencement of the party; and during the whole game, each player, asking leave in that, has a preference before others who have a good hand in a different suit, unless a mediateur is demanded, then it takes the lead; and if in the favourite suit, first; those who play alone, without the mediateur, precede even that, and, when in the favourite, take place of all.

Solitaire quadrille is where it is agreed not to call, but always play *sans prendre*, with or without the mediateur; and if in any deal no one can play alone, then the cards are to be dealt again, and such additions made to the stake as may have been settled.

Solitaire quadrille by three, or tredille, is excepting the king, throwing out all of one red suit, and the six of the other; each person playing on their own account, as at three-handed whist.

In Lancashire, where this game is very much in vogue, it is customary to play with a purchased king, and preferable suit (always hearts) in a manner similar to what is styled the Mediateur and Favourite suit, as may be fully perceived by the following table of

REWARDS AT PREFERENCE.

1. An Ask-leave in a common suit: the same as at plain quadrille; viz. one a piece.

2. An Ask-leave in hearts: double from the pool, that is two a piece besides the aces; if matadores two a piece from the adversaries; double mats four a piece.

3 A purchased king in a common suit: one from each antagonist; mats two; double mats three.

4. A Purchase in hearts: two from each; mats four; double mats six.

N B. Pay two for the purchased-king, when the suit is in hearts.

5 A Solo, common suit: two from each; mats three; double mats four.

6. A Solo in hearts: four from each; mats six; double mats eight.

7. A Vole, common suit, with a friend: the game and five a piece out of the pool; and from the adversaries two a piece; if mats three; double mats four.

8. A Vole in hearts: the game and ten each out of the pool; four a piece from the adversaries: with mats six; double mats eight.

9 A Purchase-vole, common suit: the game and ten out of the pool; three from each adversary; mats four; double mats five.

10. A Purchase-vole in hearts: the game and twenty out of the pool: six a piece from the opponents; mats eight; double mats ten.

11. A Solo-vole, common suit: the game and twenty out of the pool, six from each antagonist: mats seven; double mats eight.

12. A Solo-vole in hearts: the game and forty out of the pool; twelve from each adversary; mats fourteen; double mats sixteen.

13. A Baste in hearts: pay two a piece to the board, and put four more out of the pool; if the next game be in hearts, take double out of the pool, but if in common suit, only what lies upon the table, excepting the aces; always pay double to a baste if it happens to be an eight board, and when basted with a friend-called, pay eight a piece, making the next a sixteen board; should another baste succeed, pay thirty-two, and the next sixty-four.

N.B. In common suits never take any more than what lies on the table, excepting the aces, nor pay more for a baste, unless in hearts, and then in that suit always pay and receive double.

A Baste off the board is always paid out of the pool; if in playing alone you are basted off upon an eight or sixteen board, the adversaries are to receive four or eight a piece, and so on in proportion to the baste upon the table, but if in hearts double.

A Lost-vole in hearts: pay four to each adversary.

A Lost-vole with mats: four, that is, two to the two the adversaries should otherwise pay you.

A Lost-vole with double mats : the four to be returned you were to have received.

Quadrille is in fact ombre, played by four persons. The latter being now obsolete, it is not our design to speak of it practically, but as there is reference to it in our article on Whist and elsewhere, we take leave to touch on the subject once more through the medium of Mr. Pope's very elegant paraphrase.

> Belinda now, whom thirst of fame invites,
> Burns to encounter two advent'rous knights
> At Ombre, singly to decide their doom,
> And swells her breast with conquests yet to come.
> Straight the three bands prepare in arms to join ;
> Each band the number of the sacred Nine.
> Soon as she spread her hand, th' aërial guard
> Descend, and sit on each important card :
> First Ariel perch'd upon a matadore,
> Then each, according to the rank they bore ;
> For sylphs, yet mindful of their ancient race,
> Are, as when women, wond'rous fond of place.
>
> Behold, four kings in majesty rever'd,
> With hoary whiskers, and a forky beard :
> And four fair queens, whose hands sustain a flower,
> Th' expressive emblem of their softer pow'r ;
> Four knaves in garb succinct, a trusty band,
> Caps on their heads, and halberds in their hand ;
> And party-colour'd troops, a shining train,
> Draw forth to combat on the velvet plain.
> The skilful nymph reviews her force with care ;
> "Let spades be trumps" she said ; and trumps they were.
>
> Now move to war her sable matadores,
> In show like leaders of the swarthy Moors.
> Spadilla first, unconquerable lord !
> Led off two captive trumps, and swept the board.
> As many more Manillia forced to yield,
> And march'd a victor from the verdant field.
> Him Basto follow'd, but his fate more hard,
> Gain'd but one trump, and one plebeian card,
> With his broad sabre next, a chief in years,
> The hoary majesty of Spades appears ;

Puts forth one manly leg, to sight reveal'd;
The rest, in many colour'd robe conceal'd.
The rebel-knave, who dares his prince engage,
Proves the just victim of his royal rage.
Ev'n mighty Pam, that kings and queens o'erthrew,
And mow'd down armies in the fights of Loo,
Sad chance of war! now, destitute of aid,
Falls undistinguish'd by the victor spade.

Thus far both armies to Belinda yield;
Now to the baron, fate inclines the field.
His warlike Amazon her host invades,
Th' imperial consort of the crown of spades.
The club's black tyrant first her victim dy'd.
Spite of his haughty mein, and barb'rous pride!
What boots the regal circle on his head,
His giant limbs, in state unwieldly spread;
That long behind he trails his pompous robe,
And, of all monarchs, only grasps the globe.

The baron now his diamonds pours apace;
Th' embroider'd king who shows but half his face,
And his refulgent queen, with powers combin'd,
Of broken troops an easy conquest find.
Clubs, diamonds, hearts, in wild disorder seen,
With throngs promiscuous strew the level green.
The knave of diamonds tries his wily arts,
And wins (O shameful chance!) the queen of hearts.
At this, the blood the virgin's cheeks forsook,
A livid paleness spread o'er all her look;
She sees and trembles at th' approaching ill,
Just in the jaws of ruin, and Codille.

And now, (as oft in some distemper'd state)
On one nice trick depends the gen'ral fate;
An ace of hearts steps forth: the king unseen
Lurk'd in her hand, and mourn'd his captive queen;
He springs to vengeance with an eager pace,
And falls like thunder on the prostrate ace.
The nymph exulting, fills with shouts the sky.
The walls, the woods, and long canals* reply.

* Scene, Hampton Court.

ECARTE.

THE following treatise, for which we are indebted to the kindness of the Author, was written ten years ago; in the first instance merely for the use of a circle of friends among whom he was at the time residing, and by whom the game was frequently played. A long residence on the Continent, where it was in very general esteem, and a personal aptitude for games of calculation, peculiarly fitted him for the self-imposed task. The spirit and style of his essay are evidences that it is the production of one on the best of terms with his subject, and by no means without confidence in himself. " For convenience of reference," as he tells us, "it is divided into parts. The first Part lays down clear and concise Rules for the Game, as played and acknowledged by the 'Académie de Paris.'

"The Second Part relates to the probabilities of chances, with tables for calculating the relative value of any card. The reader by studying these tables, which are extremely simple, may acquire, in a short period, a scientific method of play.

"The Third Part gives some examples of difficult games, and the method of playing them: by an attention to which the reader may get an insight into the niceties of Ecarté. There are a few passages marked, which refer to rules necessary to be observed when playing with Foreigners; but which scarcely apply to the game as played in our clubs and drawing-rooms. Further notice will be taken of this peculiarity.

" The Author confidently offers this little treatise to the public as a *safe guide*—long experience of the game having made him acquainted with all its mysteries. Said a worldly Parisian to his son, whom he discovered lamenting over an empty purse, ' My son, until you have four eyes in your head, risk not your gold at Ecarté.'—The Author has but one better counsel to offer—

' PLAY NOT AT ALL!'"

PART I.—ON THE RULES.

OF all Games of Commerce, the most fashionable at this moment is Ecarté; yet, strange to say, we have never yet been furnished with a complete Treatise on its Rules—still less has any writer indicated the method of playing, or explained its niceties and different combinations. * Hence was the author determined to compile a Treatise, in which should be layed down, not only the rules recognized and adopted by the clubs, but also be pointed out, how to detect and punish the different errors which might be committed in the course of the rubber.

It became necessary to give an example of the ordinary games, and the manner of playing them; hence he has added to this Treatise directions how the cards ought to be played in different games, whether with a view to win points, or to avoid losing them,—taking for his basis, every probable combination which the doctrine of chances presents in a game composed of thirty-two cards.

ON THE GAME OF ECARTE.

1. Ecarté is played by two persons, with a pack or game of thirty-two cards,—the deuce, three, four, five, and six of each suit being discarded.

2. Five points scored are game,—unless there be any mutual agreement to the contrary.

3. The score is always marked on the side of the stakes.

4. The money, whether stakes or bets is always put on the table.

5. Whoever wins three tricks, scores *one* point: whoever wins *all* the tricks, scores *two*. This is called in French, making the "*vole.*"

6. Only two points can be scored in a single deal, unless one of the parties hold or turn up the king.

7. It may be either played in games or rubbers. A rubber consists in winning two games out of three.

* No person really understanding cards will aver that there is "no play in Ecarté." This is a silly sophistry, arising from the false data that it is easier to manage five cards than thirteen; and a person acting on this principle will soon find his mistake to his cost.

8. The winner cannot refuse giving "a revenge;" the loser is not obliged to accept it.

9. It is usual to have two packs of cards, used alternatively: to prevent mixing them, the backs of one are generally dotted or coloured: the latter method is preferable.

10. The king is the highest card; the ace ranks next after the knave.

ON CUTTING, AND CUTTING FOR DEAL.

1. First see who is eldest hand: at this game the eldest hand deals: there is a slight advantage in dealing, because the king turned up, scores a point, as we shall see presently.

2. Many players imagine it is as advantageous to be younger, as elder hand; in other words, as advantageous to play first, as to be played up to; * they are in error,—for it is only 7 to 1 against the king being turned up and it is more than 7 to 1 against the first player making the point, from the sole reason that he is first player, *i.e.*, with cards which win because he is first, and which would lose were he last.

3. Another advantage in dealing is, that if the first to play (younger hand)proposes, the dealer presumes that his adversary has a weak hand, and can profit by this knowledge by refusing to give cards, whilst the younger hand, playing without throwing out, (écarté, signifies "thrown out,") can have no clue to the strength of the dealer's cards.

4. The eldest hand has choice of cards: this choice once made must last throughout the game, unless fresh cards be called for, which is allowable.

5. The deal is decided by cutting into the pack and showing the last card of the cut; highest deals.

6. If in cutting for deal, several cards are shown, the lowest of those turned up is accounted the cut.

7. Whoever neglects to show his cut, is supposed to have cut lowest of all.

8. The cut holds good, even if the pack be incomplete.

* As in Ecarté the eldest deals, and consequently plays last, (contrary to the usual mode,) to avoid the confusion which the terms "elder hand" and "younger hand" would make, the two players are throughout this work called the one "dealer," the other "player,"—the latter designating him who leads the first card.

9. When a pack of cards is discovered to be incorrect, all preceding deals—even that in which the discovery is made, provided the deal be already played out—hold good.

10. A cut must consist of more than one card.

ON DEALING.

1. The cards are dealt by two and three, or by three and two. Five are given to each player, and the eleventh is turned up.

2. The turned up card indicates the suit of the trumps.

3. A trump is superior to every other card of a different suit.

4. When once the cards are dealt by two and three, or by three and two, this order cannot be changed during the game, unless by giving notice to the adversary previously to his cutting.

5 If this order of dealing should be changed, the adversary has a right to call a fresh deal, provided he has not seen his hand. Once, however, the hand seen, the deal holds good.

6. The residue of the pack (Fr. *talon*) is placed on the right of the dealer, and the écart (or cards rejected) on the left, both to avoid confusion, and to show, if forgotten, which party was dealer.

7. The dealer ought always to shuffle the cards, and the adversary always cut; but the latter is entitled to shuffle also before cutting, and the dealer to re-shuffle afresh, or to present the pack for the cut without re-shuffle, or to call for fresh cards.

8. It is allowable to shuffle the cards each time they are presented for cutting, but not to do so twice following in the same deal.

9. The party receiving cards plays first.

10. The king counts as one point in favor of the person either turning it up or holding it.

[Note. The following rule is important, and ought to be read with attention, as an ignorance of it gives rise to frequent discussions.]

11. It is not sufficient that the holder of the king mark it; he ought to distinctly announce "that he has the king." If the holder is also "the player," he ought to make this announcement before he leads his first card, except when he plays king first, and in that case it is allowable to announce it *after* it is on the table, but *before* it is covered by the adversary's

card. This rule is only applicable to the younger hand (or first to play;) the second to play (or eldest hand) should invariably announce the king just before covering his adversary's first card, otherwise he cannot score it; for his own interest he ought not to announce it until just after the opponent's first card is played.

12. When a player deals out of his turn, and the error is perceived before the trump is turned up, there is a fresh deal by the proper dealer; if the trump is turned up, the deal is put aside, and is a good deal for the next time; if the error is only perceived after the hand is played, the deal holds good, since the fault lies between the two players, the one in having dealt, the other in having allowed the deal.

13. A player who plays before his turn is only obliged to take back his card; if however it is covered, the *coup* (or trick) is good, this fault also being commited through the negligence of both players.

14. When the player is not satisfied with his hand, he proposes to take other cards, saying "I throw out" or "I propose" (usually however the French terms are adopted in this game, "*J'écarte*" or "*Je propose*;") the dealer accepts or refuses, according to whether satisfied or not with what he holds; if he accept, he gives as many cards as his adversary requires, and then serves himself with as many as he may want.

15. Whoever plays without changing cards, or whoever refuses to change cards, loses two points if he make not three tricks; and making them, scores but one.

16. When a proposition is once made or refused, there can be no retracting; also, when once a certain number of cards are asked for, that number can neither be diminished nor increased.

17. If after the second time of giving cards, the player still wishes to propose, he has the power of so doing; likewise after the third, and so on until the pack is exhausted; but the dealer in refusing, no longer loses two points if he does not make three tricks.

18. When after having changed (or écarté'd) several times, the player proposes again, without paying attention as to whether sufficient cards remain or not, and that the dealer inconsiderately accepts, the former takes as many cards as he needs; so much the worse for the latter if there remain not

sufficient for him, or even none at all—as he dealt, it was his duty to pay proper attention; in this case he keeps his own hand and if he has already écarté'd, takes at hazard, from the cards thrown out, the necessary number to complete his hand.

OF FAULTS IN GENERAL.

1. Each player previously to receiving fresh cards, puts his écart (or those he rejects) on one side, and once this écart made can no longer touch it. Should either happen to look at the rejected cards, even his own, not only is it forbidden to retake them, were they even trumps, but he is obliged to play with his cards on the table, being supposed to have cognizance of his adversary's écart.

[Note. The following rules (2 and 3) apply to Foreigners, who are often vociferous in their play, calling out the suit of the card before they throw it on the table. To our quiet and gentlemanly English habits, this rule can never be but a dead letter. But as many who read this little treatise may perhaps either play with Foreigners abroad or at home, I insert the rule, in order that they may not fall into the very commonly laid trap of a false card being called.]

2. It is obligatory to play the colour announced: thus any one calling "club," and playing spade or any other suit, is obliged, if the adversary desire, to retake his card and to play the suit announced; if he has none the adversary can call a suit.

3. If, however, the adversary deem the card played more favorable to him than the suit announced, he has the right to hinder its being taken back.

4. Whichever from mistake, or otherwise, announces "the king," and has it not, loses one point independently of the result of that *coup* or deal: that is to say, instead of marking the king thus falsely announced, the adversary marks it unless the mistake is declared previously to a card being played. It is easy to see the necessitiy of this forfeit, since a *ruse* of this nature might cause the other party to lose the point or miss the *vole*, from not daring to lead trump, thinking the king to be in his adversary's hand.

[Note. Although the following is the rule, it is seldom attended to, as players generally omit to take up their tricks.]

5. It is not allowable to look at the adversary's tricks under pain of playing with cards on table.

6. Whichever through error, or purposely, throws his cards on the table, loses one point, if he have already made a trick, and two points if he has not.

7. The cards are considered as thrown on the table, if being embarassed to keep a suit, a player lowers them so as to shew them to his adversary; since it is possible by this movement, to make him believe that the *coup* is abandoned, and induce him to shew *his* cards also.

8. A player who quits the game, loses it.

9. If a faced card is found in the pack, and it is perceived in dealing, the deal is null, except when the faced card happens to be the eleventh, because in that case there is no interference with its destiny, which was "to have been turned up."

10. If it be only detected after the écart, and the faced card falls to the party receiving cards, he may either keep it, or begin the deal afresh, *and take the deal*, the fault lying with the dealer, it being possible to have been committed purposely, with a fraudulent intention, by an unscrupulous player.

11. If the faced card fall (after the écart) to the dealer, the deal holds good; equally good is it should the faced card remain unperceived till both players have finished taking in cards.

ON REVOKING OR UNDER-FORCING.

1. It is forbidden to either revoke or under-force (*sous-forcer.*) This term means the answering a card with one of the same suit, but inferior value to those remaining in hand; for instance—putting the nine of clubs on the ten, having the ace in hand.

2. When a player revokes or underforces, he is obliged to retake his card, and the hand is played over again; but a player commiting this fault does not score if he make the point, and only scores one if he make the *vole*.

[*Note.* Some persons imagine that there is nothing gained by sub-forcing, and that they are only obliged to withdraw their card, and take with a stronger, without punishment; they are wrong,—for there are games which are lost because of this necessity of taking, and games which might be won if this practice were allowed.]

ON BETS.

1. It is allowed to bet on either player, and the betters have the right of advising; but their advice, and what they say, is counted for nothing by the adversary, so long as the player has not spoken:—thus, if a better calls "the king," and the player has not announced it before playing his card, he no longer has the right to score it, save in the case already cited in the chapter on "Dealing."

2. The players have the privilege of taking all bets on the opposite side, in preference to the *gallery*, which can only take the amount of what the player has declined to cover.

[*Note.* The gallery is a technical term, used for all except the two players.]

3. It is forbidden to look over the hand of the party betted against.

4. The betters have no right to speak about the hand of their "partners" (or player whom they back), and when they advise, they ought to *point* at the card to be played or kept, but they ought neither to *name* the card nor its suit.

5. Bets can be made on the rubber, the game, and the point; also when either or both players are at the two, three, or four first points; on the king and the queen of trumps; or on the suit of the trump.

6. The gallery has a right to give notice of all errors which would be frauds, could it be supposed they were done intentionally:—for example, if a player scored a point too many, or took tricks not belonging to him.

7. We have said further back, that a player who quits the game loses it; but in this case, one of the betters is obliged by his own interest, and that of the others, to take the vacant seat and finish the game.

8. At the end of each game the winning player first takes whatever is due to him, and then divides the remainder amongst the betters, giving to each his due, without however being responsible for errors which may result from the inexactitude of the accounts; the deficit (if any) must be borne by the betters amongst them.

ON MIS-DEALING.

1. When the dealer turns up two or more cards instead of one, the player has the right to pick out that which ought to be the trump; or to put aside the cards thus exposed and take the next remaining on the pack for trump; or to recommence the hand, taking the deal; but he has only this last choice provided he has not seen his hand.

2. When the dealer shows or turns up one or more cards of his adversary's hand, he must finish dealing, and the adversary has then the choice of recommencing the hand, taking the deal, or counting the deal good.

3. If the cards exposed belong to the dealer, neither party has the choice of recommencing the deal, the fault being prejudicial to the dealer who has chosen his cards, and advantageous to the player who has seen them.

4. If, however, this happen after the écart, (or change,) the party who has exposed the cards can only require another or others, but cannot recommence the deal.

5. If the dealer after changing, turn up a card as if he were turning up the trump at the beginning of the hand, he can neither refuse a fresh change to his adversary, nor to give him the card thus turned up.

ON MIS-DEALING THE ENTIRE HAND.

[*Note.* The entire hand (called in French *D'Emblée*), is the *first hand* dealt by each dealer; when five cards are given to each party and one turned up, making the full number of eleven.]

1. If the dealer gives one or more cards too many, the player has the right either to look at his hand and throw out the supernumerary cards, first showing them to the dealer, or to recommence the hand, taking to himself the deal.

2. If he has given too few, the player has the right to take the number wanting from the *talon* or residue of the pack, without however changing the trump; or to recommence, taking the deal.

3. If, on the contrary, the dealer has dealt himself too many cards, the adversary has a right either to pick out at hazard the supernumerary cards; or to recommence the hand, taking the deal.

4. If the dealer deals himself too few cards, the adversary has a right either to make him take the number wanting from the *talon*; or recommence the hand, taking the deal.

5. If one of the two players, having too many, or too few, cards, should écart without giving notice to his adversary, and if the latter should perceive it, either from counting the cards thrown out, or in any other way, the player who thus makes a false écart, loses two points, *and the right of marking the king, even if he had turned it up.*

ON MIS-DEALING AFTER CHANGING CARDS.

1. If the dealer gives more or less cards than asked for, he loses the point and the right of marking the king if he has it in his hand, but not if he has turned it up, the turn up being anterior to the mis-deal.

2. If the dealer deals himself more cards than he has thrown out, he loses the point and the right of marking the king if he has it in his hand.

3. If he deals himself fewer, he completes his hand from the first cards of the *talon*, since they are his by right.

4. If he only perceives it when he has played, the player counts as tricks those cards which cannot be covered.

5. If, however, the fault is not the dealer's, as in the case where the player has asked for more or less cards than he has thrown out, then the player loses one point and the right of marking the king. But if he has too few cards he may mark it, for the simple reason, that holding the king with too few cards, he would of course have equally held it, if he had asked for his proper number.

6. Whichever (after having changed cards) holds more than five, loses a point, and the right to score the king.

7. Any case not mentioned in this treatise, ought always to be decided against the player who commits the fault.

There only now remains to treat of the principles of the game, the manner of playing it, its niceties or *finesses*, its combinations, and the advantages to be derived from a knowledge of these points.

PART II.—ON THE PRINCIPLES.

All Games of Hazard are subject to an analysis founded on mathematical principles.

Many calculators have exercised their talents in analysing different games, but not one has entered into any details on the game of Ecarté, either because it is but lately in fashion, or because it has not attracted their attention.

The following are the fundamental principles of this game :—

1. As five cards are dealt to each, and one turned up, it is evident that a player after having looked at his hand, has a knowledge of six cards, and that there remain twenty-six unknown to him, viz.,—twenty-one in the *talon*, and five in his adversary's hand, making altogether thirty-two, of which number the pack is composed.

2. It is then on the six known, and the twenty-six unknown cards, that he must reason, and base his calculations.

For example :—if in the six known cards there are two of the same colour turned up, (or trumps,)there remain six trumps in the twenty-six unknown.

Hence—if in the twenty-six unknown, there are six trumps, or rather less than a quarter, it is probable that in the adversary's five cards there is, at most, but one trump, since one is also a trifle less than the quarter of five.

This principle is the basis of all; from it arise all others; and in order to place it in a more obvious light, and more copious in consequences, we have given in the following table, the number of the principal combinations of twenty-six cards, calculated mathematically.

Twenty-six cards can form 65,780 combinations of five cards,—or in other words, 65,780 different hands of five cards each.

	IF IN THE SIX KNOWN CARDS						
	there is not one club.	there is one club.	there are two clubs.	there are three clubs.	there are four clubs.	there are five clubs.	there are six clubs.
The science of combinations teaches that the number of hands of five cards, which will be with-out a club, in the twenty-six unknown cards, is	8568	11628	15504	20349	26334	33649	42504
With one club..	24480	27132	29070	29925	29260	26565	21252
With two clubs	22848	20349	17100	13300	9240	5313	2024
With three clubs	8568	5985	3800	2100	924	253	..
With four clubs	1260	665	300	105	22	..	..
With five clubs	56	21	6	1	..	..	..
Total	65780	65780	65780	65780	65780	65780	65780

To point out the method of using this table.—suppose the player has but one club in the hand first dealt him, and that the trump card is also a club, making *two known* clubs, and that it is desired to ascertain what are the chances of probability which can also give two or more to the adversary.

It will be seen in the third column, that of the 65,780 hands which the twenty-six unknown cards can form, there are—

Without one club 15.504
With one club 29,070

Total of hands which have not two clubs   44,574
Hands with two clubs................... 17,100
  ,,   three clubs 3,800
  ,,   four clubs............................ 300
  ,,   five clubs 6

Total of hands which have two or more clubs   21,206

Total of hands which twenty-six cards can form   65,780

s

From these combinations we may draw the conclusion that a player can risk, with probability of success, a first hand, (called in French *"un jeu d'emblée,"*—being the first five cards dealt previously to changing, and which, for brevity's sake, we shall denominate a first hand,) which ought to win the point if it does not encounter two trumps in that of his adversary, (such as will be seen in the paragraph which treats of the *"Jeux de Regles,"* see p. 247) since the odds are 44,574 against 21,206, or reduced to simple terms, a little more than 2 to 1 that two clubs will not be found in the adversary's first hand.

The kings being superior cards, and that turned up of double importance, (as the king gives one point, moreover as a trump taking all other trumps,) it is an interesting enquiry, how many, according to the doctrine of chances, there are likely to be in the adversary's hand after the cards have been distributed to each of the players, and the trump ascertained.

To resolve this question we have compiled the following table.

	IF IN THE SIX KNOWN CARDS				
	there is not one king.	there is one king.	there are two kings.	there are three kings.	there are four kings.
The number of hands without a king in the 26 unknown cards is ..	26334	33649	42504	53130	65780
With one king	29260	26565	21252	12650	..
With two kings.. ..	9240	5313	2024	..	..
With three kings ..	924	253	..	..	..
With four kings ...	22	..	..	..	..
Total	65780	65780	65780	65780	65780

Hence—if there were one king in the six known cards, it would be seen in the second column that in 65,780 different hands which the adversary can have, there will be 33,649, that is to say, more than half, which are without kings. and consequently it is probably that he has no king in his hand.

This rule about kings, applies also to queens, knaves, &c.

This same table serves to ascertain the probability of finding the king of trumps in the adversary's hand; it is sufficient to glance down the fourth column where it is seen that when one king only fixes the attention, there are 12,650 games that contain it, and that there are 53,130 which do not.

Consequently the odds are 53.130 against 12,650, or in simple terms, 21 against 5, that the adversary has not the king of trumps, first hand.

It will perhaps be noticed that the three first columns of the last table, are the same as the three last of the preceding table; this arises from the circumstance that when there are four, five, or six clubs known, and that there consequently remain four, three, or two, in the twenty-six unknown cards, the case as to the probability of finding four clubs is exactly similar to that of finding four kings.

We will not swell this little work with more tables. Volumes might be written, and it would be easy to lose oneself in endless calculations; we must leave to players the task of appreciating these principles *by practice*, without a further demand on their memory and attention.

PART III.—ON THE METHOD OF PLAYING.

GENERAL RULES.

When a player holds (comprising the king of trumps) three cards which ensure the point, *he ought always to propose*, if the two remaining cards are not sufficiently strong to give reasonable expectation of the *vole*. It is even good play to propose, were it only for *one card*, in order to hazard receiving a refusal, or to make the *vole* if the proposal is accepted, and there should be five cards in the *rentrée* (or take in).

When a player has hopes of making the *vole*, and the adversary cannot answer a lead of trumps, it is better to play a king if single, than to continue trump; because the system of the game being to play double cards (*i. e.* two or more of a suit), if the adversary is dubious which to retain, he will by preference keep the suit in which he was attacked. If the player is engaged with an adversary who is acquainted with this *ruse*, it may be still advantageous to act in a similar manner, but in an inverse sense; that is to say, equally play the king, although guarded, before continuing trump, because imagining that it is done to induce him to keep the suit of the king already played, he will part with it more readily than any other suit.

When a player expects to make the *vole*, and has not trumps sufficiently strong to begin by playing them, he must be careful to keep changing his suit, in order not to be roughed, and to be able to make a trump, whatever it may be, at the fourth card after having secured the point.

When a player has made two tricks, and remains with the queen of trumps and two small ones, knowing the king to be in the adversary's hand, he ought to lead with one of the small trumps, and wait with the queen guarded. Nothing could prevent his making the odd trick even against king third.

When there is a fear lest the adversary should make the *vole*, and the player has but one trump and four weak cards, without any hope of making the point, he must play his strongest single card, in order to get a chance of employing his trump in case the suit of his single card should be lead up to him.

When the game is three against four, and the player who is at four makes his adversary play, or plays himself without changing, the one who is at three, if he have the king, would do well *not to announce it*, in order to draw his antagonist into the error of leading trump to *pass* his good cards, and be taken by the king which he did not expect, thus losing the point which he would perhaps have won, had he known that the king was in the adversary's hand: in this case it is the less consequence for the player who is at three to announce his king and mark it, inasmuch as he gains two points, that is,—the game, if he make three tricks; his adversary having played, or forced him to play, without changing.

[*Note.* To *pass* a card, means to lead it and make a trick with it, without its being taken by a higher of the same suit or roughed. By some writers this latter word is spelt "ruffed,"—but we think erroneously.]

HANDS TO BE PLAYED WITHOUT CHANGING; AND METHOD OF PLAYING THEM.

These are termrd "*Jeux de Regles.*" No hand ought to be played without changing, excepting when the odds are 2 to 1 that the player make three tricks, for the risk is 2 to 1 against him if he do not make them, excepting the cases where the adversary is at four, because as he then wants but one point to win, the risk is no longer 2 to 1, and by playing without a change the chance of giving him the king is avoided.

On this principle all "*Jeux de Regles*" are played without changing (although there be a few which can scarcely reckon in their favor 2 to 1).

The following are "*Jeux de Regles:*"—all those hands which cannot fail making three tricks, except from finding two trumps (first hand) in the adversary's hand.

Example 1st.—A has one trump, no matter how small; a tierce major, and a small card of either remaining suit; the odds are more than 2 to 1 that he wins the point;—the probability is demonstrated in the first table.

Method of playing.—Begin with the king of the tierce, and continue the suit, if not roughed, until you are roughed; if it happens at the second card, your trump will bring you back to your suit, and enable you to make the third trick

Example 2nd.—Two trumps,— a queen second, and a small card. This hand ought always to be risked by the player, although the odds are scarcely 2 to 1.

Method of playing.—If the trumps are small, begin by playing the single card, being certain if it is taken, the adversary will not return the suit, and that he will prefer playing a king if he has one; should it be of that suit of which you hold queen second, you make her, later, with the two trumps, supposing he has not superior ones.

But if one of the two trumps is strong, for instance, the queen or the knave, you must then begin with the queen guarded; because you hope if she is roughed, to regain the lead with one of your trumps, and then make a trick with your knave or queen of trumps, in order to pass the second card of the queen which has been roughed.

Example 3rd.—Two trumps; a knave and ace of another suit; and another knave.

Method of playing,—Begin with the knave guarded; if it passes, and the trumps are sequences, and pretty high, risk one; if that makes, play the other, and then your ace, &c.

ᶠ*Note.* Generally speaking, a player ought to commence with a card which is guarded, except when he fears the *vole*, or when he can only hope for the point *by being played up to*.]

Example 4th.—Two kings, and queen second.

Method of playing.—As necessarily one king is guarded,

begin with this; if it makes a trick, continue the suit; should it be roughed, the chance remains of regaining the lead through the other king, or through the queen, and returning afterwards to the suit of the king first played.

Example 5th.—One trump; a king single; and a queen third.

[*Note.* This is a weak hand if the player has not the lead.]

Method of playing.—If you have the lead, commence with the queen; if she passes, continue the colour; if she is roughed, immediately you regain the lead, again play the suit of the queen that has been roughed.

Example 6th.—One trump, and king fourth.

Method of playing.—If your trump happen to be the queen, play her; for the odds are 21 to 5, that is, rather more than 4 to 1, that the king is not in the adversary's hand; more than 2 to 1, that he has not two trumps; and 55,594 to 10,186, or more than 5 to 1, that he has not two cards of the suit of which you hold king fourth; but it is especially necessary when you are at three, and your adversary four, that you should not hesitate playing the hand in this manner. For be it observed, that in every other position, probabilities which would appear only to offer favorable chances isolatedly, present also the contrary when united: for, firstly, you may encounter the king of trumps; and then probably lose two points: you would likewise lose if you encountered two cards of the suit of which you hold the king; and if the adversary is enabled to take, you might equally lose against an adversary who has no trump; whilst by beginning with the king fourth, you can win against an adversary who has two trumps, if after having roughed, he should lead trump in order to pass a king.

Example 7th.—Two trumps, and three cards of a suit.

[*Note.* This is a very strong hand, and ought *always* to be risked by the player.]

Method of playing.—Having the lead, you commence with the highest card of your suit; if it is roughed, your adversary must have three trumps in order to get the point.

Example 8th.—Four court cards; provided they be not the four knaves, nor the card second, the knave of trumps.

Method of playing.—Very often the way to play this is, to begin with trump, even if it is single; the order in which hands like this ought to be played, can scarcely be pointed out; it depends on the nature of the court cards, more particularly of that which is guarded.

Example 9th.—All hands which require only two cards to be thrown out.

In this class are found those " *Jeux de Regles*" of which we have spoken, where the odds are not 2 to 1 that they will win the point; and yet they are played, because in two cards a player has much less chance of taking in advantageously, than has his adversary in the five which he perhaps requires, and amongst which he may find the king; hence there are very few hands and very few cases wherein a player ought to change for two cards only.

If you play with two trumps and a king unguarded, begin with a low card and *never with the king*, in order to avoid getting it roughed; but on the contrary to be enabled to regain the lead with one trump, play the other to protect the king, and then pass it.

Holding three trumps, especially when sequences, it is almost always the game to lead trump, no matter how inferior they may be.

There are so very few hands which can be reckoned more advantageous to be led up to, than to lead, that we will not mention them; with such sort of hands, never refuse to change *once* and never accede to it a *second time*.

ON HANDS WHICH WIN OR LOSE THE POINT, ACCORDING TO THE MANNER IN WHICH PLAYED.

Example.—Suppose a club the trump. The dealer has ace of trumps, king and nine of diamonds ; knave and nine of spades.

The player has queen of trumps, queen of spades, ace of hearts, eight and seven of diamonds.

The right game of the player is, to lead his eight of diamonds, as it is guarded by the seven; if the dealer take with the nine, he ought to lose the point. and if he take with the king. he ought to win it; because taking with the king. he intimates that he has no other diamond, and as he is certain that the adversary led the strongest of his suit he runs no risk in employing this *ruse ;* then he plays his knave of spades which is also his guarded card; the player takes with the queen, and then leads queen of trumps, in order to pass his seven of diamonds, which he imagines to be a sure card, the eight having brought out the king, and he loses the point; whereas if the dealer, who took with the king, had taken with the nine, the player, after having played the queen of trumps, would have preferred endeavouring to pass his ace of hearts, which had but three cards superior to it, rather than his seven of diamonds, which had five, and he would thus have gained the point.

As it is necessary to make three tricks in order to win the point, it often happens that after having trumped once, it is advisable to *lead trumps*, in order to pass a king, or some high card;—again, there are cases where this would be bad play, as is demonstrated by the following example:—

Suppose a spade the trump card:—the player has the knave and ten of trumps; the king of clubs; and the king and ten of diamonds. The dealer has queen and nine of trumps; knave and ten of hearts; and seven of diamonds.

Should the player not find the king of trumps in his adversary's hand, he has a game which warrants his hoping to make the *vole:* he ought then to commence by playing his king single, in preference to his king second; having more chance of escaping the rough with it, than with that which is guarded; and of being able afterwards to win a trick with a lead from the knave of trumps, having only to fear the queen, (if the dealer has not announced the king,) and endeavour to get the *vole;* the right play therefore is, to commence with the king of clubs; if the dealer trump it, adieu to all hopes of the *vole:*—there only remains to secure the point; the adversary then leads the knave of hearts, which the player takes with his ten of trumps: and *now* comes the nicety; he loses the point if he lead knave of trumps in order to pass his king of diamonds,—whereas he gains it, if he plays his king first. For if he lead his knave of trumps, the dealer takes it with the queen, and makes his second heart; whereas had he played his king of diamonds, it would have been answered with the seven:—he plays diamonds again—the ten,—the adversary is obliged to trump with queen, and then play his ten of hearts, which the player takes by roughing it with his knave of trumps, thus making the third trick.

We have given one reason why it was preferable to play the king of clubs, rather than that which was guarded; we may add another which confirms the rule, that king single ought to be played first; which is, that if the adversary with two diamonds to the queen, and two clubs to the queen in hand, has any hesitation which suit to keep, he will prefer keeping the queen of clubs, which is his suit first attacked, to keeping the queen of diamonds second.

Final Example.—Be particular in holding your cards well up, so that none can see them but yourself, for fear of any indiscreet exclamations on the part of the betters,—as the following *coup* is not so easy that it can be learnt by every player.

The object is to win the point with a hand which would infallibly lose if it were played naturally, that is to say, without *finesse.*

Suppose a heart the trump. The player has the king, ace, and ten of trumps; the king of diamonds; and the king of spades. The dealer has the queen, knave, and seven of trumps; the eight and seven of clubs.

The player would feel almost sure of making the *vole,* if to his king of trumps, with which he ought to open the game, he sees fall the queen; and yet this would cause him to lose the point, if the dealer is sufficiently adroit to throw her away, instead of the seven, on the king; because the player would then continue leading trumps, by playing his ace, and the dealer take it with his knave, and then play his eight of clubs, which the player would rough with his ten of trumps, and play one of his kings,—the dealer would rough this with his seven of trumps, and then pass his second club; the player having no more trumps to rough with, loses the point; whereas had the dealer thrown the seven, instead of the queen of trumps on the king, the player, fearful of meeting the queen and knave of trumps accompanied by clubs, would not have continued leading trumps, but played one of his kings, and would necessarily have won the point.

CONCLUSION.

It would exceed the limits of this little work to give more examples of hands which are susceptible of *finesse;* it being essential only to cite a few of the most remarkable, in order to lay down the principles; to establish fixed and complete rules; to indicate the method of playing the cards to advantage; and to give the power, by means of a recognized code, of avoiding, smoothing down, or settling all the discussions which continually arise in society, where this game is undoubtedly very fashionable; disputes having hitherto been generally decided according to the usages of localities; which a traveller would find to vary very much.

This is the object we have aimed at; whether successfully, the Reader must decide.

RULES FOR CALCULATING BETS ON ANY EVENT.

Add together the odds for and against; divide the given sum : or, (as a general example,) say—£1 into as many parts as there are odds, and give to each party as many shares as he has chances.

Example.—Odds 5 to 1 against A.—7 to 3 against B.—11 to 4 against C.

What are the odds between the field and the favorites?— $5 + 1 = 6$. Divide £1 by 6; then A.'s value will be one-sixth, or 3s. 4d.—B.'s value three-tenths, or 6s.—and C.'s value four-fifteenths, or 5s. 4d.,—being altogether, 14s. 8d. for the favourites, leaving 5s. 4d. for the field; or, reduced to fractions, 11 to 4 against the field.

The odds, A. against B., will be 3s. 4d. to 6s. = 18 to 10, or 9 to 3 against A. The same rule can be applied in comparing the value of any of the other odds. The odds may be readily computed by the following rule:—reduce the odds, in each case, to a vulgar fraction; then multiply all the denominators for a common denominator, and each numerator by all the denominators, except its own, for a new numerator.

In the last case, A.'s value = one-sixth, B.'s = three-tenths, and C.'s = four-fifteenths.—giving a new denominator of 900 : and A.'s numerator = 150, B.'s = 270, and C.'s = 240 ; leaving the remainder, or 240, for the field; or, reduced to 30ths, A. = 5, B. = 9, C. = 8, and field = 8.—Total 30.

The value which ought to be paid to cancel a bet, where either party has betted too high, is found as follows:—deduct the value which ought to be staked, from the amount actually staked ; then divide the surplus stakes by the total odds between the parties, and the party in whose favor the bet stands, will be entitled to receive such a proportion of the surplus as is equal to his odds on the event.

Example.—I bet 9 to 6 against C., the odds being as above.

In this case my opponent ought to stake four-fifteenths, or 5*s.* 4*d.*, instead of six-fifteenths, or 8*s.*, and, consequently, he stakes 2*s.* 8*d.* beyond the correct amount; and the odds in my favor being eleven-fifteenths, I am entitled to that proportion of the 2*s.* 8*d.*, or surplus amount staked, to cancel the bet.

VOCABULARY OF THE PRINCIPAL TERMS USED IN PLAYING .ECARTE.

[*Note.* Those marked with an * are words which are commonly used even amongst English at this game; the rest are useful to be acquainted with when playing with foreigners.]

Abattre—To lower the cards and show them.
* *Atout*—Trump.
Avoir la main—The action of dealing.
Battre—To shuffle the cards before dealing.
Carte doublée }
Carte Gardée } Two cards of the same suit.
* *Couper*—To cut.
Défausser—To refuse a suit.
* *Donner*—To deal.
* *Ecart*—The cards which are thrown aside.
Etre à la devine—To be embarrassed which suit to keep.
Faire—The same as "*donner*" to deal.
Faire un main—To make a trick.
* *Forcer*—To play a superior card on an inferior.
La Belle—The highest card of any suit.
* *La Vole*—To make all the tricks.
* *Le Point*—One score of the five which compose the game.
Levée—One trick made whilst playing.
* *Proposer*—The asking fresh hands, or part of fresh hands.
Refaire—To recommence distributing the cards.
* *Renoncer*—Not to answer the suit led.
* *Retourner*—When the cards are dealt to turn up the first of the *Talon.*
Sous-forcer—To play a card inferior to what remains of some suit in hand.
Talon—What remains of the pack after there has been distributed to each player what he requires.

CRIBBAGE.

CRIBBAGE is a game played by two persons, with a complete pack of 52 cards. We shall commence by treating of the five-card game, which, besides being the parent stem, affords the greatest scope for the exercise of skill, and is the most generally played. Sixty-one points constitute the game. These points are scored on a Cribbage Board, of which the following is a representation. It has, as will be seen, sixty-one holes, and in these. the points aforesaid, are marked; the whole table being subdivided into compartments of five holes each.

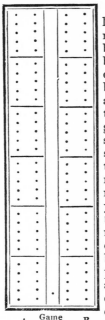

A   Game hole.   B

The board is placed either across or lengthways, between the players. It is a matter of indifference how the end of the board from which you commence is placed; but you must count from that end which contains the sixty-first, or game hole; beginning at the outside edge, (A or B) and passing along it to the top, then down the inside row to game. To mark the game, each player has two pegs; if the first score be two, stick a peg and leave it in the second hole, and when next it becomes your turn to mark, place the other peg in the number that gives the points you have to mark, counting from your first peg. When you have to mark a third score, take out the back peg, and reckon from the foremost, which must never be disturbed during the progress of the game, the scores being invariably marked by the hindmost peg of the two. Thus, the foremost peg always keeping its hole, the players can detect the amount that is marked, and check each other's score. To avoid confusion it is usual for the pegs of each party to be of different colours; although the one player never in any way, touches his adversary's half of the board. Before stating out of what results the points so scored arise, it is fit to give the relative value of the cards.

All the Kings, Queens, Knaves, and Tens, count as ten each; the rest of the cards according to their ordinary value, as sixes for six, eights for eight, and so forth; Aces reckon one only. This means merely their value as cards. The points which count for the game are made by Fifteens, Sequences, Flushes, Pairs, &c. The board being duly prepared, the players cut for the deal, the lowest cribbage card winning the cut. If you play games, you must cut at the termination of each; not so when playing rubbers. The winner of the crib then shuffles the pack, the dealer being entitled to do so the last. How this shall be done, together with all the minutes of proceeding, will be given in the Laws.

The first move of account, is the marking of three holes, by the player who loses the deal, as a make-weight for the adversary's advantage. He is entitled, indeed, to mark them at any part of the game. Five cards, in alternate succession, are then dealt with the faces downwards, one at a time; the rest of the pack being then placed faces downwards also on the table. The players then gather up their cards, and each having taken out two, they are placed by themselves on the table, with the faces down. These four cards are what is called the " Crib," which becomes the property of the dealer, under certain conditions. Each player having put out his two crib cards, which of course have not been seen by his adversary, the non-dealer cuts the remainder of the pack, and the dealer turns up the top card of it.

These preliminaries thus settled, the game commences by the non-dealer leading, and his adversary playing to him, and announcing the nature of his card. Suppose it a king, he calls "ten," and the dealer replying with an "eight," he, the latter, cries " eighteen," as the amount of the ten and eight. The dealer having thus made eighteen, his opponent plays again, and announces the increased aggregate, and thus the play proceeds till the whole amount reaches exactly thirty-one, or as near it, without exceeding, as can possibly be accomplished by the cards in either hand. He who makes up thirty-one, or, as before said, who comes the nearest to it that the cards permit, scores two, the remaining cards in hand, if any, are thrown up.

The better to convey a view of a hand in process of being played, let us suppose the leader plays a three, and calls " three;" the dealer then puts on it a tenth card, and cries " thirteen," upon this the first leader plays another tenth card, and exclaims " twenty-three," his antagonist rejoins with a five, and proclaims the total " twenty-eight." The first player finding his third or last card will not come within the prescribed limits of thirty-one, declares his inability to play, by the word "go," and exposes his card by throwing it upon the table. Should the opposite player hold a three, and thus be enabled to make out thirty-one, he plays this card and scores two points; but failing, he throws up his card, but scores one for the " go," because it was he who made twenty-eight, the nearest number to thirty-one. If, however, his last card should be an ace or deuce, he must play it, as it does not exceed the thirty-one; still, however, scoring one for the "go." It is to be understood that at Cribbage, there is no restraint upon the player, as to what card he shall play.

The points which each party has made, during the playing out the hand, having been all taken at the time they were gained ; and, the deal being finished, each party now completes his score, and marks that number of points towards game, to which he is entitled. The non-dealer reckons first ; and, having marked his gains, if any, on the board, the dealer in his turn counts—first, his hand, and then his crib, for the crib belongs to the dealer.

Another deal then takes place, and is conducted in a similar manner ; and so on, until either one of the parties has completed the required number of sixty-one, when he is proclaimed the victor, and the game is finished.

FOR WHAT YOU MARK AT CRIBBAGE.

Points in *play* can only be made by one of the seven following ways :—

Firstly, by Fifteens—Secondly, by Sequences—Thirdly—by Pairs—Fourthly, by Pairs-royal—Fifthly, by Double-pairs-royal—Sixthly, by the Knave being turned up—and Seventhly, by making thirty-one, or the nearest number thereunto.

Points on *reckoning* the hand and crib, after the hand is played out, can only be made by one of the seven following ways :—

Firstly, by Fifteens—Secondly, by Sequences—Thirdly, by *Flushes* — Fourthly, by Pairs — Fifthly, by Pair-royal — Sixthly, by Double-pairs-royal—and Seventhly, by the Knave being of the same suit as the card turned up. The various points you are entitled to, under either of these several denominations, being added together, form the whole number contained in your hand or crib; and you score accordingly.

And first of the Fifteens; as often as you make the number fifteen in playing, you score two. The leader, for instance, plays an eight, you put a seven on it, cry "fifteen," and straightway you score two points. The result is the same whenever you make fifteen, whether in one or more leads or rounds. As already observed, all tenth cards count for ten. The hand being played, you now set about summing it up, taking two points for every fifteen you can make by means of reckoning the cards together of which it consisted. The turn-up, or "start" card, is common property, and available to both players in computing their hands, and to crib also. All this is wholly without reference to any thing that occurred while the hands were being played; and by whatever combination fifteen can be made out of the cards as above enumerated, two points are added to the score. Should you hold king, knave, and a five, you count for two fifteens; should a tenth card turn up, in this case you score three "twos," that is to say, a third for the combination of your five with such tenth card; and if, instead of being a tenth card, the turn up should be a five, then you count eight, having four fifteens on the cards. The dealer calculates the crib for fifteens, in the same manner that he does his hand, and uses the turn-up with both, that is separately, he cannot combine his hand with his crib.

Thirty-one.—Every time you make this amount in the course of the game, you score two. But this only applies to the game when in progress of being played, it has nothing to do with the subsequent summing up.

End-hole.—If neither party make up thirty-one, then he who plays the card that makes up the nearest number to it, without exceeding it, as already stated, scores one; this is "one for the go."

Pair or Pairs.—Every pair made in the play or the hand, reckons for two points. To pair is to play a card of the same description, not of the same suit only. If a tenth card be played, and you can answer it with a similar tenth card during any part of the same hand, without exceeding thirty-one, it is a pair, and counts two. But in these pairs, all tenth cards do not count alike. It must be king for king, queen for queen, and so forth. At the end of the deal, you take the turn-up card to assist you in pairing, and count two for all pairs made by its assistance.

Pair Royal, or Prial.—This consists of three cards of a similar sort, held either in the hand or crib, or occurring in the course of the game, as three Kings, three Aces, three nines, &c. It scores six. Thus:—if the leader play a six, you put another six on it, and score two for the pair; he then returns a six, makes a pair-royal, and counts six points. If you have a pair-royal in your hand or your crib, you also score six for it; and should you only hold a pair, and turn up the third, it reckons also for six. It is needless to say these combinations do not count for points, when other cards have been played between them.

Double Pair Royal.—Four cards of a sort make this combination, for which the score is twelve; alike, whether made in play, or in the hand, or in the crib. The turn-up card reckons with hand and crib, in this, as in every other case. Moreover, should your opponent have made a pair-royal, by playing a third of a sort, you are entitled to the double-pair-royal, if you answer him with a fourth.

In taking six for a pair-royal, or twelve for a double-pair-royal, you are not to suppose that the six and the twelve are merely increased numbers, bestowed as premiums for such combinations of the cards, and settled by arbitrary arrangement, independent of the rule that two points are allowed for every pair. A pair reckons for two, and the same principle, applied to a pair-royal, produces six; because, as a pair-royal contains three distinct pairs, you score two for each pair. Place, for instance, three sixes in a row on the table, and mark them 1, 2, and 3, thus:—

1	2	3
Six	Six	Six

Here Nos. 1 and 2 form the first pair, Nos. 1 and 3 the second pair, and Nos. 2 and 3 the third pair; without the same two cards having ever been reckoned more than once together.

Having analyzed this example, there will be little difficulty in ascertaining the number of pairs to be found by *taking in pieces* a double pair-royal. The readiest way to attain demonstration is to place the four sixes in a row on the table, as you did the three sixes, and number them 1, 2, 3, and 4, thus:—

1	2	3	4
Six	Six	Six	Six

Nos. 1 and 2 combined together, form a pair, and
    yield two points, for which carry out -   -   2
— 1 and 3 form the second pair, and give two
    more -   -   -   -   -   -   2
— 1 and 4 form the third pair -   -   -   2
— 2 and 3 form the fourth pair -   -   -   2
— 2 and 4 form the fifth pair -   -   -   2
— 3 and 4 form the sixth pair -   -   -   2

Total -   - 12

Thus we have six distinct pairs in a double pair-royal, which, of course, are thereby entitled to twelve points. Observe, that in making these points, although we reckon the cards over and over again, they always unite in different associations, and the same two cards are never reckoned twice together.

Sequences—Consist of three or more cards following in successive numbers, whether of the same suit or otherwise. He who holds them scores one point for every card in the combination, whether it take place in playing or in counting the hand or crib. But there cannot be a sequence under three cards. As in certain other cases, the court cards, king, queen, and knave, rank in sequences, after their usual classification as to rank, and not all alike as tenth cards. To form a sequence in play, it matters not which of the cards is played first, or last, provided the sequence can be produced by a transposition of the order in which they fell. Thus, you lead the five of hearts, your adversary returns the three of diamonds, you then play the four of any suit, and score three

T

for the sequence; he then plays six, and makes four, and so
on, as long as the continuous sequence can be made. The
spirit of this rule may be applied to all combinations occurring in regular successions.

You here observe that it does not matter of what suit are
the cards forming the sequence, nor does the order signify in
which they are played. You must not pass thirty-one in
making a sequence. If a sequence in play is once broken, it
must be formed afresh, or cannot be acted on.

In reckoning your sequences at the close of the deal, you
use the card turned-up along with your hand and crib; and
reckon them every way they will. A single example of this
will here suffice :—

Suppose the crib to consist of two Kings, (Clubs and
Diamonds,) and two Queens, (Hearts and Spades,) the Knave
of Spades being the card turned-up;—how many can you take
for sequences ?

Twelve, being four sequences of three each; to be computed
by reckoning the Knave with the Kings and Queens; ringing
the changes on the latter, somewhat in a similar manner to
the mode in which you have been taught to form a double
pair-royal. To simplify this, take the Knave, the two Queens,
and the two Kings, and spread them before you; when they
will count thus :—

Knave, with Queen of Hearts and King of Clubs   3
Knave, with Queen of Spades and King of Clubs   3
Knave, with Queen of Hearts and King of Dia-
monds   -   -   -   -   -   -   - 3
Knave, with Queen of Spades and King of Dia-
monds   -   -   -   -   -   -   - 3
                                               ——
Points for the four sequences   -   -   - 12
                                               ——

THE KNAVE.—If you hold a Knave of the same suit as the
card turned-up, you are entitled to one point, which you take
on reckoning your hand   Should there be, in the crib, the
Knave of the suit turned-up, the dealer, to whom the crib belongs, takes one point on reckoning his crib. In the eupho-
nious phraseology of some cribbage-players, this is termed
" one for his nob."

Should the turn-up card itself be a Knave, the dealer immediately scores two points ; which, by way of antithesis with " his nob," are called " two for his heels." Similar phrases are, after all, rather to be considered as quaint, than vulgar. They recall to our minds the recollection of the once popular game of QUADRILLE, played by the Lady Teazles of the past century, in which the verb " TO BEAST" is so indefatigably conjugated.

A FLUSH.—A Flush cannot happen in play, but occurs only in computing the hand or crib. A Flush signifies that all the cards in hand, or crib are of the same suit, in which case you are allowed to mark one point for every card of which the Flush is composed. Thus, if your hand comprise three hearts, you will take, on scoring for your hand, three for the flush in hearts ; and should the turn-up card chance to be also a heart, you will add another point for that, making four altogether. You are not permitted, however, to reckon a flush in the crib, unless the cards, of which the crib is composed, are of the same suit as the card turned up. It is essential to recollect the difference between a flush in the hand, and a flush in the crib.

In reckoning the hand and crib after the deal, you have been already informed that the non-dealer counts first. It will facilitate your reckoning, if you sum up the amount of points to which you are entitled, in the following order: Firstly, Fifteens—Secondly, Sequences—Thirdly, Flushes— Fourthly, Pairs; Pairs - Royal, or Double Pairs-Royal— Fifthly, the point for the Knave. Reckoning up the hand, or crib, is technically termed " showing." Thus the non-dealer is said to have " the first show," a point of immense importance at the final stage of the game; since he may thus be enabled just to " show out," and consequently win the game; while the dealer may hold in his hand, and crib, points enough to make him out three times over, but altogether useless, since he has not the first show.

The non-dealer having summed up his score, under the observation of his opponent, the latter then performs the same operation, as relates to his own hand. He then turns up crib, which has up to this time lain *perdue,* and scores all to which it may entitle him.

T 2

THE LAWS.

I.—In single games there must be a fresh cut for each game; but not so when rubbers are played. The lowest cribbage card wins the cut: when both players cut alike, it is a tye, and there must be another cut.

II.—In cutting for the deal, not less than four cards should be removed, and not more than half the pack, that a fair and proper cut may remain for him who cuts last.

III.—The cards are to be dealt out one by one, and they must not be touched till the deal has been completed.

IV.—The dealer may expose his own cards in dealing if he please, but if he shows one of his adversary's, the latter scores two points, and may demand a new deal, provided he does so before turning his cards. When a faced card occurs in dealing, there must be a fresh deal, including all the formalities of cutting, shuffling, &c.

V.—If the dealer mis-deal without being aware of it till one of the hands has been taken up, the opposite party may score two, and the cards must be dealt over again. Should his adversary expose a card during the progress of the deal, the dealer may deal over again if he pleases, provided he has not seen his hand.

VI.—Though both players have the privilege of shuffling the pack previous to the cards being dealt, the dealer has the right to do so last.

VII.—Should the dealer give his adversary more than five cards, the non-dealer may mark two points, and there must be a fresh deal; but, in such case, the non-dealer must discover the error, before he takes up his cards, or he cannot claim the two, though there must still be a new deal. Should the dealer, in dealing, give himself more than five cards, his adversary may mark two points, and either call a fresh deal, or draw the extra card, or cards, from the hand of his opponent. Should the dealer give to either party less than five cards, there must be a fresh deal; and should the dealer deal two cards at once to either party, there must be a new deal, unless his adversary consent to his withdrawing the surplus card; in which case it must be placed on the top of the pack.

VIII.—Should either player find that his adversary has more

than five cards in his hand, he can claim two points and a new deal.

IX.—Should the pack, being dealt from, be touched previous to being cut for the "start," the party so offending forfeits two points.

X.—In cutting for the start, the non-dealer must remove at least three cards, and leave not less than four behind.

XI.—Should the dealer turn up a Knave, and neglect scoring the two points for such Knave, until he has played his first card, he cannot take the two points.

(He is, however, in time to take the two points, after his adversary has played his first card; a distinction of some consequence, since we are all at times liable to forgetfulness.)

XII.—The non-dealer must turn out for the crib first. A card once so laid out, cannot be taken up again. Either player confusing his cards with the crib, forfeits two points, and his opponent may claim a fresh deal. The dealer alone is entitled to touch the crib, but he may not do so until he takes it up to count it.

XIII.—He who takes more points than he is entitled to, when reckoning his hand or crib, or scoring for a penalty, may be put back as many points as he has over-scored, and then his adversary may add the same amount to his own account.

XIV.—No penalty attaches to a neglect of making points, to which the player is entitled.

XV.—One player cannot demand of another his aid to make out a score.

EXAMPLE.—Suppose K to say to L, " am I not twelve?"— L replies, properly enough, "I shall neither tell you, nor shall I pass any opinion on the subject. If you take more than you ought, I shall take you down;" *et voilà tout!*

XVI.—If one player touch the pegs of his adversary, save to correct an error of the score, he shall forfeit two points. If a player touch his own pegs, save when he has a right to score, he forfeits two points. When both pegs have been displaced by accident, the opposite player must be allowed to restore them to their places; or in the event of being refused, he can claim the game. When the foremost peg has been displaced by any chance, it must be put into the hole behind the back peg, of the player to whom it belongs.

XVII.—He who scores a game as won, that he has not won, forfeits it.

XVIII.—A player who detects his adversary with more or fewer cards in his hand than he has a right to, can score two points and call a new game.

XIX.—A lurch cannot be claimed, unless it be specified in the first instance. When the "lurch" has been agreed to between the players at the commencement of a game, it reckons as a double game; it consists in one player having marked sixty-one before the other has scored thirty-one

XX.—When scoring points, if the pegs be quitted, that score cannot be altered. If two cards be played, and any points remain unreckoned, they become forfeited. Should a player put his cards away without taking for them, he forfeits any points he might have claimed for hand or crib.

XXI.—When a card that may legally be played has been shown, it cannot be recalled. If it cannot be played according to the laws of the game, no penalty attaches to the exposure.

XXII.—If a player neglects to play, when he can come in under thirty-one, his opponent may score two.

XXIII.—In reckoning a hand or crib, it must be plainly set out, and remain till the other side fully understands the nature of the claims made on account of it.

XXIV.—There is no penalty for a number called in mistake in the progress of the game.

XXV.—As already said, the three points appropriated by the non-dealer may be claimed by him during any part of the game; but if his adversary be permitted to score his sixty-one points, it is then too late, for the game is at an end.

XXVI.—If either player refuse to pay a penalty that he has incurred, by infringing the rules of play, his adversary may claim the game.

XXVII.—Bystanders shall not in any way interfere with the progress of the game.

XXVIII.—In cases of disputes that do not come within the provisions of these rules, a third party may be appointed as umpire, by consent of the players, and his decision must be adopted as final.

ON LAYING OUT FOR THE CRIB.

How to discard in the best manner for the Crib is one or

the most scientific parts of the game; and consequently one of the most important.

Firstly, When it is NOT your own crib, you will lay out such cards as are likely to be, in an average number of cases, of the least possible advantage to your opponent, in the production of pairs, fifteens, sequences, &c.

Secondly, When it is your own crib, you will lay out favorable cards for the crib.

Thirdly, It being your own crib to which you are about to discard, you will prefer consulting the interests of the crib, in preference, even to those of your hand.

The most advantageous cribbage-cards are fives, sevens, eights, &c., when so assorted as to form fifteens, sequences, pairs, or flushes. The five is, of all others, the most useful card, since it makes fifteen equally with either one of the tenth cards; of which there are no fewer than sixteen in the pack. Fives must therefore be in general the most eligible cards to lay out to your own crib, and the least eligible (for you) to lay out to your adversary; since, in so doing, you are almost certain to give him points. To discard a pair of any cards, again, is mostly bad play, unless it is for your own crib; and cards which follow each other in order, as a three and four, or nine and ten, being likely to be brought in for sequences, are generally bad cards to lay out in the case of its being your adversary's crib. The same calculation should, in its principle, be carried out as far as possible. Suppose you discard, to your opponent's crib, two hearts, when you might with equal propriety have laid out a heart and a club instead,—you here give him the chance, however remote you may fancy it, of making a flush in his crib; which could not be effected by him, had you laid out the heart and club.

To lay out cards, purposely, which are disadvantageous for the crib, is called in the "cribbage dialect" of our ancestors "baulking" or "bilking" the crib.

The least likely cards to reckon for points in the crib, and therefore generally the best to discard for our adversary, are kings; since a sequence can only be made up to, or as it may be termed, on one side of them; and cannot be carried beyond them. A king is therefore a greater baulk in the crib than the queen. So, again, of an ace,—a sequence can only be made from it, and not up to it; and an ace is, therefore, frequently a great baulk to a crib; though in discarding an ace some judgment is required to be exercised, being often a good card to hold for play; and forming a component part of fifteen, particularly when combined with sixes, sevens, and eights, or with fours and tenth cards.

The cards, then, best adapted to baulk our antagonist's crib, are, a king with a ten, nine, eight, seven, six, or one; a queen, with a nine, eight, seven, six, or ace, or cards equally distinct, or far off, and therefore certain not to be united in sequence by meeting with any other cards whatever. Of course, particular hands require particular play, and general principles must give way before their exceptions. "Circumstances alter cases;" throughout this work, as in all similar works, the author writes for what may be called "average hands of cards;" and recommends that play which would be most conducive to success in the largest proportion of events.

Never lay out a knave for your adversary's crib, if you can, with propriety, avoid it; as the probability of the turn-up card being of the same suit as the knave, is 3 to 1 against it. Consequently, it is only 3 to 1 but the retaining such knave in your hand gains you a point; whereas, should you discard it to your opponent's crib, it is only 3 to 1 against the chance of its making him a point; hence the probable difference of losing a point by throwing out your knave, is only 3 to $2\frac{1}{3}$; or 9 to 7,—that is to say, in laying out a knave for your antagonist's crib, when you could equally keep the same in your hand,—sixteen times—you give away just seven points; it being only 9 to 7, but you give away a point every time you play in this manner; and every single point is of consequence, if contending against a good player. As I just now remarked, there may, of course, occur exceptions to this and every other rule.

The cards which are usually the best to lay out for your own crib, are, two fives, five and six, five and tenth card, three and two, seven and eight, four and one, nine and six, and similar couples. If you have no similar cards to lay out, put down as close cards as you can; because, by this means, you have the greater chance of either being assisted by the cards laid out by your adversary, or by the turn-up; and further, you should uniformly lay out two cards of the same suit for your own crib, in preference, *cæteris paribus*, to two other cards of the same kind, that are of different suits, as this gives you the probable chance of flushing your crib; whereas, should you lay out two cards of different suits, all gain under the head of a flush is at once destroyed. It is mostly good play, to retain a sequence in hand, in preference to cards less closely connected; more especially should such sequence be a flush; and once more remember that the probable chance of points from the crib is something nearly approaching to twenty per cent. over the hand. It is therefore indispensably your duty, if you wish to win, to give the lead to your crib at the expense of your hand.

In general, whenever you are able to hold a Pair-royal in hand, you should lay out the other two cards, both for your own, and your adversary's crib; some few cases, however, excepted. For example, should you hold a Pair-royal of any description, along with two fives,—it would be highly dangerous to give your antagonist the brace of fives, unless in such a situation of the game that your Pair-royal would make you certainly out, having the first show;—or else that your adversary is so nearly home, himself, that the contents of the crib are wholly unimportant. Many other cards are very hazardous to lay out to your adversary's crib, even though you can hold a Pair-royal; such as two and three, five and six, seven and eight, and five and tenth card; therefore, should you have such cards combined together, you must pay particular regard to the stage of the game. This caution equally applies to many other cards, and particularly when, the game being nearly over, it happens to be your own deal, and that your opponent is nearly home, or within a moderate show-out. Here then should be especial care taken to retain in hand cards which may enable you to play "off," or wide of your adversary; and thus prevent his forming any sequence or Pair-royal. In similar positions you should endeavour, also, to keep cards that will enable you to have a good chance of winning the end-hole; which frequently saves a game.

GENERAL DIRECTIONS FOR PLAYING THE GAME SCIENTIFICALLY.

Never, at any period of the game, make a pair, fifteen, sequence, &c., without glancing your eye first at the relative places of the cribbage-pegs, to know whether you are justified in playing a forward or backward game. I repeat, that on this the whole art may be said to turn, of playing Cribbage scientifically.

To gain the end-hole, or point nearest to thirty-one is, among professed players, justly esteemed a considerable advantage, and should be proportionately kept in view. By attaining the end-hole yourself, you not only score a point, but save a difference of two points by snatching it from your opponent. In playing for this, there is much scope for judgment.

Should you hold a three and a two, it is frequently the best play to lead off the three, on the chance of your adversary's playing a tenth card (*of which never forget that there are sixteen*), making thirteen; when your two " drops in," and produces two points for the fifteen. The same principle applies to the leading from a four and an ace, and has this additional advantage, that should you thus succeed in forming fifteen, your opponent can form no sequence from your cards.

Remember, that when your adversary leads a seven or eight, should you make fifteen, you give him the chance of coming in with a six or a nine, and thus gaining three holes against you. Sometimes this would even tend to your advantage, by allowing of your rejoinder with a fourth card in sequence. For instance, your opponent leads an eight, and you make fifteen by answering with a seven; he plays a six, making twenty-one, and scores three for the sequence; but having a nine, or ten, you play it, and score after him. In all such cases, play to the state of your game; for what would be at one time correct, would be, at another, the worst possible play.

To lead from a pair is mostly good; because, should your opponent pair you, you form a Pair-royal, making six holes; while the chance of his rejoining with a fourth is too small to be taken into consideration. It would rarely, though, be correct, to lead from a pair of fives.

When your adversary leads a card which you can pair, it is mostly better to make fifteen, in preference, should you be able so to do; as you will naturally suspect he wishes you to pair him, in order to make a Pair-royal himself. But here, as elsewhere, your chief guide is the relative state of the scores.

When you can possibly help it, consistently with your cards, do not, in play, make the number twenty-one; for your antagonist is then likely to come in with a tenth card.

Should you hold a nine and three, it is good play to lead the three; because, should it be paired, you form fifteen by playing the nine. The same applies to the holding of a four and a seven, in which case, should your four be paired, you make fifteen with the seven.

The following style of play facilitates your obtaining frequently the end-hole. Should you hold two low cards, and one high card, lead from the former; but should you hold one low card, and two high cards, lead from the latter; like other general directions, all this being subject to contingencies.

Holding a ten and five, and two holes being at the moment an object of great importance, lead the tenth card, in hopes of your adversary's making fifteen, when you can pair his five.

Holding a seven and four, it is good play to lead the four; because, if paired, your seven comes in for fifteen: the same direction applies to your holding a six and three, and three and nine, or other cards similarly related.

When compelled to lead from a sequence of three cards, play off the lowest, or highest, in preference to the middle card.

In laying out for your own crib, suppose you hold a pair of fives, and no tenth card, discard them both. Bear in mind that of all the tenth cards, the knave is of the most importance; and that those cards which tell best in counting the hand, are not always the best for playing.

If in play, you throw down a four, making the number twenty-seven, your adversary has the chance of pairing your four, and of making at the same time, thirty-one. If you make twenty-eight with a three, you incur the same risk. These apparent trifles must be studied, and similar points, if possible, avoided on your part; while you should be constantly on the watch to grasp them for yourself, should your antagonist leave an opening.

As the dealer plays last, his chances are greater than those of the leader, for making the end-hole, or other desirable points in play. The dealer has also in his favor the chance of gaining the two points by lifting a knave. (The knave is called by many Cribbage-players "the Jack.")

The phrase "playing off," is used to denote playing cards which are wide apart, in contradistinction to its reverse, termed "playing on." Thus, should your opponent lead a four, and you answer with a two, three, five, or six, you "play on;" because you give him the option of making a sequence, should he hold the fitting card. But if, in answer to his four, you play a high card, you "play off," since he can have no card capable of forming a sequence. Whether to play "off," or "on," is half the battle, and depends entirely, should you hold the option, on the relative state of the scores.

It is frequently your game, to allow of your adversary's forming a sequence, in order to come in yourself for a longer one. To tempt him to this, play a card close to his, instead of playing off. Suppose you hold a three, four, and five, and your opponent leads a seven:—in this case, should it be to your interest to bestow a certain number of points, in order to realize the same amount for yourself, you play the five; for if he answers with a six, marking three, you play your four, and score for the sequence and fifteen accordingly.

ODDS OF THE GAME.

The chances of points in a hand are calculated at more than 4, and under 5; and those to be gained in play are reckoned 2 to the dealer, and 1 to the adversary, making in all about 6 on the average, throughout the game; and the probability of those in the crib are estimated at 5; so that each player ought to make 16 in two deals, and onward in the same proportion to the end of the game; by which it appears that the first dealer has rather the advantage, supposing the cards to run equal, and the players likewise equally matched in skill. By attending to the above calculation any player may judge whether he is at home or not, and thereby play his game accordingly, either by making a push when he is behind and holds good cards, or by endeavouring to baulk the opponent when his hand proves indifferent.

IN FAVOR OF THE DEALER.

Each party being even 5 holes going up, is 6 to 4
at 10 holes each . . . 12 11
15 each 7 4
20 each 6 4

Each party being at	25 each . . . . . is 11 to 10
	30 each 9 5
	35 each 7 6
	40 each 10 9
	45 each 12 8
	50 each 5 2
	55 each 21 20
	60 each 2 1

When the dealer wants 3 and his opponent 4 . 5 4
In all situations of the game, till within 15 of
the end, when the dealer is 5 points a-head . 3 1
But when within 15 of the end 8 1
And if the dealer wants 6, and the adversary 11 . 10 1
Should the dealer be 10 a head, it is . . 4 or 5 1
And near the end of the game . . . 10 or 12 1
When the dealer wants 16 and the antago-
nist 11 . . . . 21 20

Both players being even at 56 holes each, is . 7 to 5
 57 . . . . . . 7 4
 58 . . . . . . 3 2
If the dealer wants 20, and his opponent 17 . 5 4
When the dealer is 5 points behind, previous
to turning the top of the board 6 5
When he is 31, and the antagonist 36 . . . 6 4
When 36, and the adversary 41 . . . . . 7 4

When at 59 holes each player.
In all points of the game, till within 20 of the end, if the
non-dealer is three a-head.
The dealer wanting 14, and his antagonist 9.
Ditto . . . . . 11, Ditto . . . . 7.

SIX CARD CRIBBAGE.

This game is also played with the whole pack, but both in
skill and scientific arrangement, it is vastly inferior to that
played with five cards. Still it is a pleasant resource in a
dull hour, and abounds with amusing points and combinations.
without taxing the mind much. It is played on the same

board, and according to the principal portion of the rules of the preceding game: its leading peculiarities may be thus summed up.

The dealer gives six cards to himself and his adversary. Each player lays out two of these for crib, retaining four in his hand. The deal and the "start" card is the same as at the five card game, in like manner the pairs, sequences, fifteens, &c., operate, and the game point is sixty-one. The non-dealer, however, is not allowed any points at the beginning. The main difference between the games, is, that in the game already described, the object is to get thirty-one, and then abandon the remaining cards; at the six card game, the whole are played out. There are more points made in the play, while at five cards, the game is often decided by the loss or gain of one point. At six card Cribbage, the last card played scores a point. This done the hands and crib are scored as at the five card game; then another deal is played, and the victory is gained by the party who first gets sixty-one.

As all the cards must be played out, should one party have exhausted his hand, and his adversary have yet two cards, the latter are to be played, and should they yield any advantage, it must be taken. For instance, C has played out his four cards, and D having two left (an eight and seven), calls fifteen as he throws them down, and marks three points: two for the fifteen, and one for the last card. Again, should D's two cards have been a pair (threes, for instance), he marks two for the pair, and a third point for the last card. Speculating on this, and other probabilities, you will always endeavour when you are last player, to retain as close cards as possible, for this will frequently enable you to make three or four points, by playing your last two cards, when you would otherwise make but a single point. But this demands further illustration, as it is of paramount importance. For example:—

Suppose you to hold for the last two cards a seven and eight, and that your adversary has only one card remaining in his hand, the probable chance of its being either a six or a nine (in either of which cases you come in for four points), is eleven to two; therefore it is only eleven to two, but you gain three points by this play, exclusive of the end-hole;—whereas, were you to retain as your last two cards, a seven, with a ten, or any two cards similarly wide apart, you have no chance to score more for them than the end-hole, as there is no probability of their coming in for any sequence; or if you can retain a pair of any kind for the last two cards (your adversary having only one card, and he being the first player), you by this means make a certainty of two points, exclusive of the end-hole. By the same rule you ought always to retain such cards, as will (supposing your adversary to have none left) make a pair, fifteen, &c., for by this means you gain many points which you otherwise could not possibly get.

The calculations for throwing out at the five card game, are, for the most part, applicable to this. Still there is not quite so much temptation to sacrifice the hand for the sake of the crib, as they do not both contain a similar number of cards. At this game the hand scores more than the crib, as there is one player always on the look out to baulk crib, while so many points being open to the play, offers a greater inducement to keep together a good hand. As soon as thirty-one, or the number nearest to it, be made in playing the hand, the cards should be turned down, that no confusion may come of their being mixed with the succeeding cards.

As before explained, in speaking of Five-Card Cribbage, your mode of conduct must be governed uniformly by the state of your game. Play to your score, and put the final result partially out of view. Whether it is your policy to play "on" or "off," must be ever the question in making up your judgment.

On an average, a hand, the moderns say, ought to yield about seven, and a crib five points. It is useful to remember this in laying out, and to note the difference between the odds of seven to five in favor of the hand here, and the superiority of the crib to the hand at Five-Card Cribbage.

The average number of points to be made each time by play, is from four to five. The dealer has the advantage here, because he plays last. Pasquin considered that you were only entitled to twenty-five points for three shows and play, and that the dealer is at home if when he make his second deal, he is twenty-five points up the board, and when he deals for the third time, within eleven holes of game. The present system of calculation is to allow twenty-nine instead of twenty-five holes for the three shows, and to consider that at the end of the second round each player is at home at twenty-nine holes.

As you are on a parity at starting, being both at home, you will play with moderate caution your first hand; making fair risks, but not running into too wide speculations. On taking up your second hand, you will adapt your play to the relative scores on the board, as you have been told in relation to the other variety of the game, and will play "on" or "off," according to the dictates of policy. The same rule will govern your conduct during the remainder of the game; and should your adversary have gained the preference, or should you be more than home, both cases must be taken into consideration in playing your hand. If your cards present a flattering prospect, and you are by no means home, it is your duty to make a push, in order to regain the lead by running; whereas, should your adversary be better planted than you, and should you take up bad cards, it will be the best play to keep off, and only endeavour to stop your antagonist as much as possible, and thereby have a probable chance of winning the game, through his not being able to make good his points.

As so many points are to be gained in play, by the formation of long sequences, you will frequently find it advantageous, having eligible cards for the purpose in view, to lead, or play, so as to tempt your adversary to form a short sequence, in order that you may come in for a longer. And this opportunity is particularly to be sought for, when a few holes are essential to your game, though gained at any risk. If you hold, as leader, a one, two, three, and four, the best card to lead is the four, since if paired, you answer with the ace, and your adversary's second card may not form a fifteen.

ON THREE-HANDED CRIBBAGE.

The game of Three-handed Cribbage is not often practised. It is played, as its name imports, by three persons; the board being of a triangular shape, to contain three sets of holes of sixty each, with the sixty-first or game hole. Each of the three players is furnished separately with pegs, and scores his game in the usual manner.

Three-handed Cribbage is subject to the same laws as the other species of the game. The calculations as to discarding and playing are very similar, but it must be remembered that as all three are independent. and fight for themselves alone, you have two antagonists instead of one.

Five cards compose the deal. They are delivered separately, and after dealing the fifteenth, another, or sixteen.th card is dealt from the pack to constitute the foundation of the Crib. To this, each of the three players adds one card, and the Crib therefore consists of four cards, while each individual remains with four cards in hand. The deal and crib are originally cut for, and afterwards pass alternately.

It is obvious, that you will be still even, if you gain only one game out of three, since the winner receives a double stake; which is furnished by the two losers to him who first attains the sixty-first hole. It has been computed that he who has the second deal has rather the best chance of victory, but there seems very little difference.

Occasionally, at this game, some amusement arises from the complicated sequences formed in play, but ordinarily it is a poor-enough affair. It will frequently happen that one of the three players runs a-head of the two others so fast, that it becomes their interest to form a temporary league of union against him. In this case they will strive all they can to favor each other, and regain the lost ground; and in general, players will do well not to lose sight of this principle, but to prefer favoring the more backward of the adversaries, to giving the chance of a single point to the other. Such leagues, however, are a good deal resembling those between higher authorities; in the making of which, each enters a mental caveat to break it the first moment it suits his convenience.

ON FOUR-HANDED CRIBBAGE.

The game of Four-handed Cribbage is played by four persons, in partnerships of two and two, as at Whist; each sitting opposite to his partner. Rubbers or single games are played indifferently. Sixty-one generally constitute the game, but it is not unusual to agree, in preference, to go twice round the board, making the number of game one hundred and twenty-one.

At the commencement of the sitting, it is decided which two of the four players shall have the management of the score, and the board is placed between them. The other two are not allowed to touch the board or pegs, though each may prompt his partner, and point out any omissions or irregularities he may discover in the computation. The laws which

U

govern Five-Card Cribbage are equally applicable here, as to the mode of marking holes, deficiencies in the counting, the taking too many points, &c. He who marks has a troublesome task, arising from the constant vigilance requisite to be exercised, in order not to omit scoring points made by his partner; his own gains he seldom forgets to take. He who does not mark should acquire the habit of seeing that his partner marks the full number he requires. Partners may assist each other in counting their hands or cribs; their interests being so completely identified.

It is most usual to play rubbers, and to cut for partners every rubber. The two highest and two lowest play together. The ace is always lowest. In some circles they consider all tenth cards equal in cutting for partners: in others they allow of preference, according to rank, as at Whist. This would, however, be only applicable to cutting for partners. Also, in some cases, it is the practice for the deal to go to the two who cut the lowest cards for partnership; but in general, the deal is decided by a subsequent cut between the two parties who are to score ; the ace being the lowest card, and all tenth cards being equal. If it is decided not to change partners after a game or rubber, there must be a fresh cut still for the deal. Each may shuffle the cards in turn, according to the laws which regulate this operation at Whist.

The deal and crib pass alternately round the table as at Whist, from right to left. The usual laws of Cribbage regulate the act of dealing, as to exposing cards and so forth; and no one is suffered to touch their hands until the deal is complete. Before dealing, the cards must be cut in the ordinary way by your right hand antagonist.

The dealer delivers five cards to each, in the usual mode, from right to left, one card at a time. The remainder of the pack he places on his left hand, Each person then lays out one card for the crib, which is of course the property of the dealer. The left-hand adversary must discard first, and so round the table; the dealer laying out last. There is no advantage in this. but such is the custom. It is hardly necessary to say that the crib always belongs to the dealer.

As there is but one card to be laid out from the five received by each player, there is seldom much difficulty in making up your choice. Fives are the best cards to give your own cribs, and you will never, therefore give them to your antagonists. Low cards are generally best for the crib, and Kings or Aces the worst. Aces sometimes tell to great advantage in the play at this game. When your partner has to deal, the crib being equally your own, as if you had it in your proper possession, must be favored in the same way. Before discarding, always consider with whom the deal stands.

When all have laid up for the Crib, the pack is cut for the start-card. This cut is made by your left-hand adversary's lifting the pack, when you, as dealer, take off the top-card, as at Five-Card Cribbage. Observe that it is the left-hand adversary who cuts this time, whereas, in cutting the cards to you at the commencement of the deal, it is your right-hand adversary who performs the operation.

Having thus cut the turn-up card, the player on the left-hand of the dealer leads off first, the player to his left following, and so on round the table, till the whole of the sixteen cards are played out according to the laws. Fifteens, sequences, pairs, &c., reckon in the usual way for those who obtain them. Should either player be unable to come in under thirty-one, he declares it to be " a go," and the right of play devolves on his left-hand neighbour. No small cards must be kept up, which would come in, under a penalty. Thus should A play an ace, making the number twenty-eight, and should each of the other three pass it without playing, not having cards low enough to come in,—on its coming round to A, he must play if he can under thirty-one, whether he gain any additional points by so doing, or not. Example:—

B plays an ace and makes thirty. Neither of the other three can come in, and on the turn to play coming round again to B, he plays another ace, and marks four points ; two for the pair of aces, and two for the thirty-one.

Many similar examples might be adduced, and there frequently arise difficult and complicated cases of sequences made this way out of low cards. Indeed, the playing out of the hand requires constant watchfulness on all sides; much more so than in Six-Card Cribbage. So many points are made by play in Four-handed Cribbage, that it is essential to play as much as possible to the points, or stages, of the game; sufficient data respecting which will be presently given.

In leading off, great care is necessary; not only at first starting, but after every "rest," or thirty-one. A five is a bad lead, because the chances of a ten succeeding it, are so numerous; and an ace is seldom a good lead, since should the second player pitch what is highly probable, a tenth card, your partner cannot pair him without making the ominous number of twenty-one; a number equally bad at every description of Cribbage, since the next player has thus so good a chance of converting it, by another tenth card, into thirty-one. A nine, again is a bad lead, for should your left-hand adversary make fifteen with a six, he cannot be paired by your partner, without making twenty-one. Bear this constantly in mind, and when possible to avoid it by equally good play, never either make the number twenty-one yourself, nor lead so as to compel your partner to do so. Threes, or fours form safe leads.

The second player will observe caution in pairing a card, so as not to give away the chance of six for a paltry couple, unless particularly wanting; or, from some collateral reasons, he may consider it a safe pair; as in the case of the turn-up's being a similar card,—his holding a third of the same in his hand—the having seen one of the same already dropped, and so on. The same care must be shown in not playing closely on, unless compelled by the cards. Suppose your right-hand adversary leads a three, it is obvious, that if you reply with a two or four, you give your left-hand antagonist a good cnance of forming a sequence, which he could not do, had you played off. On the other hand, there frequently arise cases in which you feel justified in playing "on," purposely to tempt your adversary to form the sequence; in order to give your partner the chance of coming in for a still longer sequence. In many situations, a few holes may be of paramount value, gained at any risk. If the second player can make fifteen, it is generally better play than pairing the card led. Towards the end of the game it is sometimes important to retain cards all wide apart, when the object is merely to prevent your antagonist from making points in play; but as you only lay out one card, you have little chance of assorting your hand as you could wish.

The third player should aim at making the number below

twenty-one, in order to give his partner a good chance of gaining the end-hole for the "go," or the two for thirty-one.

The dealer knowing he will have to play last the first round, will sometimes find it advantageous to hold aces, or low cards, for the purpose; particularly when it is essential to score a few holes in play, or when the only chance of game arises from the possibility of playing out. Holding aces, it is frequently better play, when you have the option, to make twenty-seven or twenty-eight, than thirty, in order to have a chance of bringing in your aces, which sometimes yield a heavy amount of points at that stage of the computation. When it is certain that the game will be decided in the course of the playing out of the hand, without coming to your show, you will keep good cards for playing at all hazards.

When the hand is played out, the different amounts are pegged, the crib being taken last. He who led off must score first, and so on round to the dealer. Each calls the number, to which he considers himself entitled, and watches to see that they are scored properly; while at the same time he does not fail to scan his adversaries' cards with an observant eye, to see that, *through mistake*, they do not take more than their due.

The amount of points to be expected, on an average, from each hand, is seven, and from the crib about four to five. From the play, it is computed that each of the four players should make five points every time. Reasoning on these data, the non-dealers are at home, at the close of the first round, should they have obtained nineteen or twenty points, and the dealers are at home at the end of the first round, should they have acquired twenty-three or twenty-four. At the finish of the second round, with their average number, each set of players would be forty-two to forty-three. At the close of the third round, the non-dealers should be just out, or else the dealers will win. You must not, however, suppose there is any advantage to be gained from not having originally the deal; the chances are so various that the parties start fully equal; no matter whether with, or without the deal. From the above calculation, the game, going only once round the board, should be over in three rounds, both parties having a crib inclusive. Those who have not the first deal, have the original chance of winning, *if they can keep it*, by holding

average cards throughout the game. Should they fail in
making this good, the dealers (those who dealt originally are
here signified), will generally sweep all, having their second
crib, and first show afterwards. As I have before intimated,
it is quite as likely that the non-dealers will fail in holding
"their own," as not. The non-dealers should observe moderate caution in the first hand, but under this head it is needless to say more to either party, than to impress it upon them
again and again, to become thoroughly acquainted with the
number of points which form medium hands; as well as the
different stages of the game, and play accordingly. Moderate
attention is all that is required to play Four-handed Cribbage
well. It is a pleasant lively game and when well conducted
yields considerable amusement. Good Cribbage is universally
preferable to bad Whist.

[Those who wish to study the game more fully, will do well
to read MR. WALKER's *Cribbage Player's Handbook.*]

BOSTON.

This game very much resembles Whist, and is somewhat like Quadrille. The players put 8 fish each into a pool, and the dealer 4 more. The cards are distributed as at Whist, except that the last is not to be turned up. During every deal, the player opposite the dealer, should shuffle a pack to be cut by his right hand neighbour, and turn up a card, for the *first Preference;* the suit of the same colour, whether red or black, is styled the *second Preference*, and the other two are common suits. The player who misses deal does not lose his turn; but as a punishment is to put 4 more fish into the pool.

When the eldest hand thinks he can get 5 or more tricks, he is to say '*Boston;*' if otherwise, he says '*Pass*,' unless he plays *Misère*, that is, so as to lose every trick. *Petite Misère* is to put out a card, and lose every remaining trick; *Grande Misère* is to lose them without putting one out; *Petite Misère Ouverte* is to put out a card, and lay the others down, and then lose all; *Grande Misère Ouverte* is the same without laying one out. When the eldest hand has '*Passed*' the second may proceed as the eldest; or if the eldest has said '*Boston,*' the second, or after him the third, and the dealer, may also say '*Boston*,' if he will engage to win 5 tricks with either Preference for the trump; or the second and other hands may say '*Petite*' or '*Grande Misère*,' or undertake to get 6 or more tricks, the trump being any suit, for these declarations will supersede that of Boston simply, as appears by the table at page 299; where all are arranged according to the order in which they take place of each other; the highest, called *Grand Slam*, is, undertaking to get 13 tricks. By engaging to *do more*, the elder hand may, as at Quadrille, supersede the younger. If all pass, the cards must be thrown up, and dealt by the person to the left of the former dealer, the new dealer putting 4 fish into the pool; and the new eldest hand, unless he has previously passed, may also supersede the declaration of any other, or say '*Pass*;' and so on, till at length every person, except one, has '*Passed*,' and that person (if he has declared '*Boston*') is to name the trump, always in the choice of the player; and also (unless he has undertaken more than 7 tricks) whether he chooses a partner. In the last case, any person who engages to get the required number of tricks may answer ' *Whist*:' the right of answering begins with the next eldest hand to him who has declared. The partner must undertake to get 5 tricks if the player undertakes 7; 4, if the player undertakes 6; and 3 if he undertakes 5, as is in the table. When this is settled the playing begins, as at Whist, except that the partners may be differently placed, and each is to take up his own tricks.

If the player obtains, or the player and partner jointly get the proposed number of tricks, or more, he or they are entitled to the fish in the pool, called the *Bets*, and besides, the number of tricks which they have won together, added to the number of honours they both held, is to be multiplied by the number in the table at page 299, over against the tricks they undertook, and under the name of the suit the trump was in; whether in the Preference or common suits; the product must then be divided by 10, and the quotient shows the number of fish to be paid to each of the successful players, by the other two; or in the event of a *Solo* to be paid him by each of the three others: should the product happen to be less than 10, one fish is to be paid nevertheless; if 15 or upwards, and under 20, it is to be considered as 20, and two fish to be paid; if 25 or upwards, and less than 30, as 30, and so on, viz:

Suppose the player and partner have undertaken 5 and 3 tricks, the trump in a common suit; they get 8, their proposed number, this, if they have no honours, is to be multiplied by one, (because in a common suit) the product is only 8, which cannot be divided by 10, but one fish is, however, paid to both player and partner by the other two. If they undertake 5 and 3 tricks, and get 9, the trump in Second Preference, no honours, then 9 multiplied by 2 producing 18, is considered as 20, and divided by 10, making two fish to be paid to each of them. Should they undertake and win 6 and 4 tricks, the trump in a common suit, having two by honours; 2 and 10 are 12, which multiplied by 2, as stated in the table, make 24, that is, two fish to be paid; the remainder not being taken notice of.

But if the player, or player and partner do not get their tricks, then the number they are deficient, added both to what they undertook, and the honours they held, is to be multiplied

by the number found in the table, and divided by 10, to show
the fish to be paid by them to their antagonists; for instance,
when they undertake 5 and 3 tricks, having 2 by honours, the
trump in a common suit, suppose they get only 6 tricks, then
6 subtracted from 8 leave 2, which, added to 8, the number
they undertook, and 2, the honours they held, make 12; this
multiplied by one, and divided by 10, gives one fish.   If they
undertake 5 and 3 tricks, having 2 by honours, the trump in
Second Preference, should they get but 7, then 1 they are
deficient, added to 8 they undertook, and 2 honours, make 11;
this multiplied by 2, the number in the table, makes 22, which
divided by 10, leaves 2, the fish to be paid.   Should they
undertake 6 and 4 tricks, having 4 honours, the trump in the
First Preference; suppose they get but 8 tricks, 8 from 10,
leave 2, which, added to the 10 they undertook, and 4
honours, form 16, that multiplied by 8, as in the table, make
128, then 130 divided by 10, gives 13 fish to be paid by
them.

When the player and partner each fail to get their proposed
number of tricks, then the fish to be paid by them is to be
defrayed in equal proportions between them; exactly the
reverse of what would have been done, had they been successful.   But if one gets his number of tricks, and the other fails,
then the unsuccessful person bears the whole of the loss, and
when the player is alone, he pays the allotted number of fish
to each of his three opponents.

In all failures, whether the player has a partner or not, he
or they pay a *Bast* to the pool, equal to the number of fish
they would have taken from it, had they proved successful;
this is the invariable rule for assessing the *Basts*, which are
not to be directly put into the pool, but laid aside, to be
brought into the same at a future period, when some successful person has emptied it of the *Bets*, and all succeeding
Basts are to be kept separately, to supply the pool at the
end of different deals, and till all are exhausted the game
cannot end, unless after any round is completed, the parties
agree to share the *Basts*.

In respect to playing *Misère*, when a person has any kind
of hand that he thinks will enable him to lose all the tricks,
the method is as follows: if he thinks it requisite to get rid
of any particular card, then the declaration must be only

'*Petite Misère;*' if this is not superseded by the other players,
he puts out a card without showing it, and the game commences, as at Whist, by the eldest hand, but in playing
Misère of any kind there are no trumps.   The parties (still
endeavouring to lose their tricks) proceed as at Whist, except
that the general rules with regard to playing are reversed at
Misère.

Whenever the *Misère* player is obliged to win a trick, the
deal is at an end, and he is Basted, exactly as in playing
Boston; and moreover, is to pay to each of the other persons
4 fish, as appears in the table: on the contrary, if the 12
tricks are played without winning one of them, he is entitled
to the contents of the pool, and also to 4 fish from each of his
antagonists. After a similar manner, *Grande Misère* is played,
with the difference of not putting out a card, and having, of
course, to lose 13 tricks; which, if effected, entitles him to
the pool, and 8 fish from each of his adversaries; if otherwise, he must pay 8 fish to each of them, and a bast to the
pool, equal to what he would have taken out, had he gained
his point.   *Petite Misère Ouverte*, and *Grande Misère Ouverte*
differ from the foregoing, merely by laying down the cards
to be played on the table, so as to be seen by all parties (except the card put out, in the case of *Petite Misère Ouverte*),
and the playing is nearly the same; the only variation in the
reckoning consists in paying or receiving 16 or 32 fish, explained in the Boston table, at the end.

When the deal is concluded and settled according to the
afore-given directions, one or two persons will have won and
taken the contents of the pool, or some, on the contrary, have
been basted.   In the former case, all the parties must furnish
the pool afresh, as at the beginning: but when either of the
players is basted, the new dealer has only to add 4 fish to the
old pool, and so on till some one wins, who is entitled to the
bets, and then the bast of greatest value (if there are more
than one) is brought into the pool.   The basts may be of
different value, because they are to be equal to the contents
of the pool at the time of paying each of them, as already
mentioned.

If there are several basts, and the players wish to finish
the game, it will be necessary to put two or more basts into
the pool at once, or else the parties must share the fish on
the table.

THE BOSTON TABLE.	Tricks to be won by the		Reckoning for the Game.			
	Player.	Partner	First Prefer-ence.	Second Prefer-ence.	Com-mon Suits.	Misère.
Boston	5	3	4	2	1	....
Petite Misère	....	....	....	....	....	4
	6	4	8	4	2	....
	7	5	12	6	3	....
Grande Misère....	....	....	....	....	....	8
	8	....	16	8	4	....
	9	....	20	10	5	....
Petite Misère Ouverte	....	....	....	....	....	16
	10	....	24	12	6	....
	11	....	28	14	7	....
Grande Misère Ouverte	....	....	....	....	....	32
	12	....	32	16	8	....
Grand Slam	13	....	36	18	9	....

REVERSIS.

AS PLAYED WITH TWO QUINOLAS.

REVERSIS is played by four persons, with a box, contain-ing* thirty-six fish, twenty-four counters, and six contracts; likewise with two pools, viz., the great and the little Quinola pools, (the great one to be under the little) they are always to be placed on the dealer's right hand.

For reversis the tens must be taken out from a pack of cards; the deal is to the right, giving three cards to each player the first round, and four to the dealer, afterwards always four, so that each of the three players will have eleven cards, and the dealer twelve, with three cards remaining

* Six fish make one counter, and eight counters one contract, or square.

36 fish		36
24 counters, each 6 fish .	.	144
6 contracts, each 48 fish	.	288

which are to be placed singly in the middle of the table opposite to each player, who will put out a card from his hand, under the pools, and will replace it with the card that is on the table, opposite to him; the dealer likewise puts out a card, but having none to take in, he will find himself with eleven cards, like the rest of the players : these four cards form the party : should, however, there be three remises or stakes in the pools, (as it is convenient to prevent mistakes to have some distinguishing mark for each pool, when there are three remises or stakes in them; *it is not unusual* to have flags for that purpose, a red one to distinguish the great quinola, and a blue one the little quinola ;) then it is in the player's option to take a card or not, if he does not, he has on declaring his intention, permission to see the card, and to place it to the discard under the pools.

Before a card is played, the opposite parties exchange a card with each other.

The ace takes the king, the king the queen, and so on.

The points in the tricks are forty, each ace reckoning four, king three, queen two, and knave one.

The most interesting parts in this game, are the quinolas, the party, the reversis, and the espagnolette.

THE QUINOLAS.

The great quinola pool, is to consist of twenty-six fish, which number is to be renewed every time the pool is cleared, or has fewer in it than the twenty-six fish; this stake is attached to the knave of hearts or great quinola, and is one of the most important cards in the game ; the great quinola cannot be put to the discard, unless there are three stakes or a hundred fish in the pool.

The little quinola pool consisting of thirteen fish, is attached to the queen of hearts, as little quinola, which is to be renewed in the same manner, in proportion to the stake as the great quinola, and the little quinola cannot be put to the discard, unless there are three stakes, or fifty fish in the pool.

Each time the quinolas are placed, or played on a renounce, they are entitled to the stakes attached to them, except when there are three stakes in the pool, in which case the great quinola is entitled to receive only a hundred fish, and the little quinola fifty ; and on the contrary, each time the quinolas are forced, led out, or gorgé, the stakes are paid in the same proportion as they would have been received, except in the single instance of the person who played the quinolas making the reversis; and then in order to derive any benefit from the stakes, the quinola which is to be entitled to such benefit, must be played before the two last tricks.

THE PARTY.

The points in the discard, (to which add four for the party,) reckon as in the tricks, with the exception of the ace of diamonds, and the knave of hearts as great quinola; the former reckoning five, and the latter four.

He who has the fewest points wins the party. It will frequently happen, that two players will have the same number of points; then he who has the fewest tricks, has the preference; if points and tricks are equal, then he who is best placed wins; the best placed is he who dealt last; but he who has no trick, has the preference of him who has no trick without points; in general in cases of equality the best placed has the preference.

When the espagnolette is played, and won, he wins the party in preference to the best placed.

When every trick is made by one person, there is no party; and this is called (by way of excellence) making the reversis.

THE REVERSIS.

Every trick without exception must be made by one person to make the reversis.

The reversis is undertaken when the first nine tricks are made by the same person; there is then an end of the party and of the quinolas; the great quinola being only as the knave of hearts, and the little quinola as the queen of hearts, except the person who wins the reversis, plays his quinolas at any time before the two last tricks, he is then entitled to the stakes; but on the contrary, should the reversis be broken by one of the players winning either of the two last tricks, he then not only pays the reversis broken, but the stakes to the pools, for the quinolas he may have played before the reversis was undertaken.

All consolations paid for aces or quinolas, by the person undertaking the reversis, is to be returned on his winning it.

THE ESPAGNOLETTE, OR THE FOUR ACES.

The espagnolette is either simply four aces, three aces, and one quinola, or two aces and two quinolas.

The player having the espagnolette, has a right to renounce in every suit, during the whole game, and if he can avoid winning any trick, and there is no reversis, he of course wins the party in preference to him who is better placed; but if he is obliged to win a trick, he then pays the party to him who would otherwise have received it, and returns the consolations he may have received for aces or quinolas; and if he has a quinola, he will pay the stake to the pool, instead of receiving it, unless a reversis is made upon him.

The player having the espagnolette, is at liberty to waive his privilege, and to play his game as a common one, but loses that privilege the moment he has renounced playing in suit.

The espagnolette receives consolation in any part of the game, if he forces the quinola, and this can only happen in three instances :—

I.—By playing a heart eldest hand, and the quinola being single in some other hand.

II.—If having through inattention, made a trick during the course of the game, he returns a heart, and forces.

III.—If by being obliged to enter at the tenth trick, or choosing to enter sooner, he should have a heart to play, and by that means forces it.

If any person wins the reversis, the espagnolette pays singly for all the company.

If any person undertakes a reversis, and another breaks it, the espagnolette pays the whole to the person who broke it.

The person holding the four aces or espagnolette, can likewise break the reversis, and is payed as before mentioned, by the person whose reversis he broke ; he can likewise undertake the reversis, but then his hand must be played as a common game, for he cannot renounce.

If the espagnolette has placed his quinola, and there is a reversis either made or broken, he is not to receive the stake : according to the general rule, viz., when the reversis takes place, the pools are neither received or paid, except by him who undertakes the reversis.

If another player having the ace or king of hearts, the espagnolette has in any part of the game, either of his quinolas forced, he pays the stake, and his consolation the same as the two other players, which is due to him that forces, except there is a reversis.

PAYMENTS.

The dealer always puts two fish into the great quinola pool, and one into the little, over and above his common stake of six and three, besides which every one puts into the former, for the first stake six fish, and into the latter three; so that the great quinola pool, will consist of twenty-six fish, and the little quinola pool of thirteen fish; each time the stakes are drawn, or when there are fewer fish in the pool than the first original stake, the pool must be replenished as at first.

The person who gives an ace upon a renounce, receives a fish from the person who wins the trick; if the ace of diamonds, he will receive two.

The person who forces an ace, receives the same payments from each of the players, as well as from the person forced.

The great quinola placed upon a renounce, receives six fish; the little quinola placed upon a renounce, receives three fish; and if either of them is forced, the person who forces, receives the same payment from each player.

These payments should be made immediately, without being asked for.

One or more aces, or either of the quinolas played or gorgé, that is, led out, pay the same as if they had been forced, and are paid to the person who wins the party, but it is for him to recollect and demand them.

When either ace or quinola are placed, played, or gorgé the last card, it is called à la bonne, and payed double, and all payments whatever, are double to the person who sits opposite.

The payment for the reversis made or broke, is eighty fish; each player paying twenty, and the opposite party forty, when the reversis is made; but when it is broken, the whole is paid to the person who breaks it, by the person whose reversis is broken; that is, he pays the persons breaking it, exactly the same number of fish he would have received from the whole table, had he won it.

LAWS OF THE GAME OF REVERSIS.

I.—The eldest hand ought to take care that all the players have put their stakes into the pools; if not, he will pay for those whom he has not called upon to pay their stake.

II.—The person who misdeals. loses his deal.

III.—If the player takes his card without having put out to the discard, the deal goes for nothing.

IV.—The discard is not to be changed after it is once put out.

V.—The eldest hand should be attentive not to play a card till the discard is complete ; should he have played one, he is permitted, if nobody has played to it, to take it up and play another.

VI.—No person must play before his turn.

VII.—He who flings down his game, thinking he has the rest of the tricks, is to pay for any ace or quinola that has or can be placed or given ; but, in case of a reversis, the person who might break it, can oblige him to take up his cards, and play them one after another, as the person who can break it shall direct.

VIII.—When a player thinking he has won the party, or willing to favor the person who has won it, asks for the aces or quinolas led out, before the person who has won the party has demanded them, he is to pay for him who might have been called upon to pay them.

IX.—If at the end of the game, it is perceived there is an error in the discard, either by putting out too many cards or too few, the deal goes for nothing and must be made again ; and if it is discovered that a quinola has been put to the discard, without there being three remises in the pool of the quinola so put out ; the person from whose hand such quinola was put out to the discard, pays the party, and the stake to the pool. the same as if his quinola had been forced or gorgé.

X.—When the cards are cut, it is too late to ask for the payment of any ace or quinola, which may have been played or gorgé ; as likewise for the party or the stake in the pools.

XI.—Before you play your cards, it is always permitted to ask how the cards have been played, but it is not permitted to observe it to others who may not make the inquiry.

XII.—If any player, not having the espagnolette, revokes,

he shall pay a counter to each of the pools; and can neither receive the party or any payment.

XIII.—The player is permitted to examine all his own tricks at any time, but not to look at the tricks of any other person, the last trick excepted.

A FEW HINTS TOWARDS PLAYING THE GAME OF REVERSIS.

There seem to be four great objects in this game; the first, winning the party; the second, placing the quinolas; the third, making the espagnolette; and the fourth, making the reversis : there is likewise a lesser object, viz., that of placing the different aces on a renounce.

In playing your cards you should endeavour to give your quinolas, your aces, and great cards on a renounce, when the person who sits opposite to you is likely to make the trick, as all the payments are double from him; if you win the party, he may by that means lose it; and if you lose the party, most probably you will not have it to pay to him.

In order to gain the party, you must avoid, if possible, winning a trick, for which purpose keep all the lowest cards in your hand, such as two's and three's.

AN ELDER HAND LIKELY TO WIN THE PARTY.

Suppose the elder hand to be dealt the ace, seven, four, and two of spades; the king, four, and three of clubs; four and two of hearts; and six and five of diamonds.

The ace of spades should be put to the discard, because you hope from your hand to win the party; and by discarding a high card, you increase its value; suppose the card you take up from the table to be the seven of diamonds, you should then give the seven of diamonds to the person who sits opposite to you, in preference to the king of clubs, with which you would have much less chance of winning a trick than with the seven of diamonds, because your lowest card in this suit is only a five, while that in clubs is a three; suppose you receive in exchange for the seven of diamonds, the queen of spades, with this hand you will play your four of hearts to force the quinolas : the person who wins the trick will most probably do the same, to which you must play your two of hearts; if another heart should be played, then part with your six of diamonds, which is a worse card to keep than the king of clubs or the queen of spades; because having the latter with three small spades, and the former with two small clubs, you have very little chance of winning a trick in those suits, and with a five or six of any suit, when hearts have been played three or four times, you have a very good chance to win a trick with one of them, as every player will of course, fling away their highest cards, unless they suspect a reversis is attempted to be played.

AN ELDER HAND LIKELY TO LOSE THE PARTY.

An elder hand composed of the king, nine, and eight of hearts; queen, seven, and five of diamonds; knave, eight, and seven of spades; ace and nine of clubs; with this hand it is most probable you will lose the party; therefore you should put to the discard a card of no value; for which reason the seven of diamonds would be the best card; suppose in the place of which you take up the seven of clubs, having three high hearts, it would be highly dangerous to part with one of them, as you might receive a quinola from the person who sits opposite to you, as well as take one in from the table. The queen of diamonds should be given to the person who sits opposite to you, which will leave you with only the five of diamonds, and give you the best chance should the person who is opposite to you give you a quinola to get the lead out of your hand. Suppose the person who is opposite to you gives you the nine of spades, with this hand you have nothing to do, but lead out your king of hearts, and to follow with the nine and eight, if not taken, in hopes of forcing the quinolas. If they are not forced by your three hearts, and you have still the lead, you should play the spades, till all those spades lower than your own are out; then you will play your nine of clubs, and then your five of diamonds, which if taken and played again, you should immediately place your ace of clubs upon the renounce. If the diamond was not taken, then play your seven of clubs, and with winning that trick in all probability you will make the reversis, as you will have the ace of clubs, and most probably the best spade remaining.

AN ELDER HAND WITH THE QUINOLAS.

An elder hand composed of the knave, seven, six, five, four, and two of hearts; four and five of diamonds; four, three, and two of spades : with this hand the five of diamonds should be put to the discard; suppose in return you take up the two of clubs, you will then give the four of diamonds to the person who is opposite to you, who in return gives you the queen of hearts; which with your hand, becomes a valuable present, as most probably you will not get a trick, and are sure of placing both your quinolas upon a renounce, and cannot possibly have them forced; with this hand you should lead the seven of hearts, which most probably will be taken; you are then sure of winning no trick, and of placing your quinolas, and which you will take care to do with the great quinola the very last card, which is called *à la bonne*, and for which you are payed double what you would receive if played at any other part of the game.

A quinola should never be kept in your hand, unless accompanied with three other hearts; therefore if you have two quinolas, and only one heart, you must give that quinola which has the greatest remise to the person who is opposite to you. If you have both quinolas, and one or two hearts, and there are three remises in one pool, or in both, the quinola, whose three remises are in the pool, should be put to the discard, and the other to the person who is opposite to you; if both quinolas have three remises, the great quinola should be put to the discard.

AN ELDER HAND WITH THE ESPAGNOLETTE.

An elder hand composed of the ace, king, queen, knave, four, and two of hearts; the ace of diamonds; the queen and knave of spades; the four and three of clubs: this hand having the espagnolette, or four aces, you should put the king of hearts to the discard, to make the party as great as you can ; because if you win the espagnolette, you are sure of gaining the party, in preference to the person who is better placed ; suppose you take up in return the five of spades, you will then give the five of spades to the person who sits opposite, (as giving him too high a card, might assist him in making a reversis against your espagnolette) and in return receive the seven of clubs; with this hand you should play the four of clubs to get the lead out of your hand : and when hearts are played, you must, if possible, not discover too soon, by renouncing your espagnolette; but play a heart in suit once, preserving, however, the two, which may be a card of much more consequence to you; and if more hearts should be played, get rid of your spades, and if a second player wins a trick, (by which means the reversis cannot be made against your espagnolette) give your aces, and if all the hearts have been played, give your great quinola *à la bonne;* but if there are yet hearts remaining, you must give it away, and keep your lowest cards for the two last tricks.

AN ELDER HAND PLAYING FOR THE REVERSIS.

An elder hand composed of the ace, king, queen, knave, nine, seven, and four of hearts ; king and two of diamonds; queen and knave of clubs; with this hand in expectation of winning the reversis, you should discard the two of diamonds: suppose in return you take up the eight of spades; you will then give up the eight of spades to the person who sits opposite to you, who in return gives you the king of clubs. You will then begin playing your ace and king of hearts, and then your nine, which will most probably take out all the hearts ; but you should still play one more, in hopes the ace of clubs will be thrown away upon a renounce, (if not already discarded,) you will then play your king, queen and knave of clubs ; then your queen of hearts, taking care to play the knave of hearts before the two last tricks ; because when the reversis is made, that quinola which is played in either of the two last tricks, does not receive the stakes out of the pool, but becomes simply the knave or queen of hearts.

THE YOUNGEST HAND WINNING THE PARTY, AND PLACING THE QUINOLAS.

Suppose the youngest hand or dealer to have the king, knave, eight, six, four, three, and two of hearts; knave, seven, five, three, and two of spades. The dealer having twelve cards has the advantage of putting to the discard, without taking up a card in return ; having seven hearts the quinola cannot be forced; therefore put out the king of hearts to the discard, as from your hand and situation in being best placed, you are almost sure of winning the party; except the espagnolette should be played and won. You will then give the knave of spades to the person who sits opposite to you, who in return

gives you the little quinola : with this hand you are sure of
placing both your quinolas, and of not taking a trick; the
only thing therefore (on account of your quinolas) you have to
fear, is one of the players making the reversis ; which would
then prevent your having the remises out of the pool.

MINOR CARD GAMES.

THE catalogue of the Minor Card Games has been far more
reduced by those which have become obsolete within these last
hundred years than the list of those played and introduced
during the ninteenth century will seem to balance. "The
Compleat Gamester," published in 1734, contains treatises upon
Ombre, Quintille, Basset, Gleck, French Ruff, Five Cards*,
Costly Colours, Bone-Ace, Wit and Reason, Art of Memory,
Plain Dealing, Queen Nazarene, Peneech, Post and Pair,
Bankafalet, Beeste, the famous game of Verquere, the noble
and courtly game called Grand Trick Track, Tick Tack,
Doublets, Sice Ace, Catch Dolt, Inn and Inn, and Passage;
games scarcely known by name in the present day, and
never played. Many of the lesser games popular now, are,
no doubt, indebted for their existence to the notices of them
written by Hoyle, and left by him as a revertive legacy to
those who seek relief from *ennui*, and the still graver visita-
tions of life. These "small deer" of the card-player enjoy
a roving commission. At a loo table you will find as many
versions of the matter for discussion as men to propose
and propound them. Commerce is variously conducted
in various places,—and Matrimony is constantly a source
of difference of opinion......................As the best course in
this dilemma, we have chosen that which seems the most
apt. A more convenient principle than that which Hoyle
has adopted in founding his systems has not been suggested by any who have followed him. For this reason we
give most of them from his text, departing from him only in
a few instances, where we have been able to improve.

* Five Cards is still played in Ireland under the name of **Five Fingers,**
or Spoilt Five.—ED.

CASSINO.

CASSINO is generally played by four people, but occasionally by three or two; the points consist of eleven, and the lurch is six.

The points are thus calculated:

That party which obtains the great cassino (or ten of diamonds) reckons	2	points.
Ditto, little cassino (the deuce of spades)........	1	,,
The four aces one point each............................	4	,,
The majority in spades	1	,,
The majority of cards......................................	3	,,
Besides a sweep before the end of the game, when any player can match all on the board, reckons	1	,,

In some deals at this game it may so happen, that neither party wins any thing, as the points are not set up according to the tricks, &c. obtained, but the smaller number is constantly subtracted from the larger both in cards and points, and if they both prove equal, the game commences again, and the deal goes on in rotation: when three persons play at this game, the two lowest add their points together, and subtract from the highest; but when their two numbers together either amount to or exceed the highest, then neither party scores.

LAWS.

The deal and partners are determined by cutting, as at whist, and the dealer gives four cards by one at a time to every player, and either regularly as he deals, or by 1, 2, 3, or 4, at a time, lays four more face upwards on the board, and after the first cards are played, four others are to be dealt to each person till the pack is concluded; but it is only in the first deal that any cards are to be turned up.

The deal is not lost when a card is faced by the dealer, unless in the first round before any of the four cards are turned up, on the table; but if a card happens to be faced in the pack before any of the said four are turned up, then the deal must be begun again.

Any person playing with less than four cards must abide by the loss, and should a card be found under the table, the player whose number is deficient is to take the same.

Each person plays one card at a time, with which he may not only take at once every card of the same denomination on the table, but likewise all that will combine therewith; as for instance, a ten takes not only every ten, but also nine and ace, eight and deuce, seven and three, six and four, or two fives; and if he clears the board before the conclusion of the game he scores a point, and whenever any player cannot pair or combine, then he is to put down a card.

The number of tricks are not to be examined or counted before all the cards are played, nor may any trick but that last won be looked at, as every mistake must be challenged immediately.

After all the pack is dealt out, the player who obtains the last trick sweeps all the cards then remaining unmatched on the table.

RULES.

The principal objects are to remember what has been played; and when no pairs or combinations can be made, to clear the hand of court cards, which cannot be combined, and are only of service in pairing or in gaining the final sweep: but if no court cards are left, it is best to play any small ones, except aces, as thereby combinations are often prevented.

In making pairs and combinations a preference should generally be given to spades, for obtaining a majority of them may save the game.

When three aces are out, take the first opportunity to play the fourth, as it then cannot pair; but when there is another ace remaining, it is better even to play the little cassino, that can only make one point, than to risk the ace, which may be paired by the opponent, and make a difference of two points; and if great cassino and an ace be on the board prefer the ace, as it may be paired or combined, but great cassino can only be paired.

Do not neglect sweeping the board when opportunity offers; always prefer taking up the card laid down by the opponent, also as many as possible with one, endeavouring likewise to win the last cards or final sweep.

While great or little cassino is in, avoid playing either a ten or a deuce.

When you hold a pair, lay down one of them, unless when there is a similar card on the table, and the fourth not yet out.

Attend to the adversaries' score, and, if possible, prevent them from saving their lurch, even though you otherwise seemingly get less yourself, particularly if you can hinder them from clearing the board.

At the commencement of a game, combine all the cards possible, for that is more difficult than pairing; but when combinations cannot be made, do not omit to pair, and also care-fully avoid losing opportunities of making tricks.

QUINZE.

THIS is a French game. It is usually played by only two persons, and is much admired for its simplicity and fairness; as it depends entirely upon chance, is soon decided, and does not require that attention which most other games on the cards do: it is, therefore, particularly calculated for those who love to sport upon an equal chance.

It is called Quinze from fifteen being the game; which must be made as follows:

1. The cards must be shuffled by the two players, and when they have cut for deal, which falls to the lot of him who cuts the lowest, the dealer has the liberty at this, as well as at all other games, to shuffle them again.

2. When this is done, the adversary cuts them; after which the dealer gives one card to his opponent, and one to himself.

3. Should the dealer's adversary not approve of his cards, he is entitled to have as many cards given to him; one after the other, as will make fifteen, or come nearest to that num-ber; which are usually given from the top of the pack: for example, If he should have a deuce, and draws a five, which amount to seven, he must continue going on, in expectation of coming nearer to fifteen. If he draws an eight, which will

make just fifteen, he, as being eldest hand, is sure of winning the game. But if he overdraw himself, and make more than fifteen, he loses, unless the dealer should happen to do the same; which circumstance constitutes a drawn game, and the stakes are consequently doubled. In this manner they persevere, until one of them has won the game, by standing, and being nearest to fifteen.

4. At the end of each game, the cards are packed and shuffled, and the players again cut for deal.

5. The advantage is invariably on the side of the elder hand.

CONNEXIONS.

THIS game may be played by either three or four people; if the former number, ten cards each are to be given; but if the latter, then only eight a-piece, which are dealt and bear the same import as at whist, except that diamonds are always trumps here.

The connexions are formed as follows,—

1. By the two black aces.
2. The ace of spades and king of hearts.
3. The ace of clubs and king of hearts.

For the first connexion 2s. are drawn from the pool; for the second 1s.; and for the third, and by the winner of the majority in tricks, 6d. each is taken. These sums are supposing guineas staked, but when only silver is pooled, then pence are drawn.

A trump played in any round where there is a connexion wins the trick, otherwise it is gained by the player of the first card of connexion, and after a connexion any following player may trump without incurring a revoke, and also whatsoever suit may be led, the person holding a card of connexion is at liberty to play the same, but the others must, if possible, follow suit, unless one of them can answer the connexion, which should be done in preference.

No money can be drawn till the hands are finished, then the possessors of the connexions are to take first, according to precedence, and those having the majority of tricks take last.

LOTO.

For this game, which may be played by an unlimited number of persons, boxes containing 100 counters; 14 fishes, every one reckoned as ten counters; 12 contracts, valued at ten fish a-piece; a pack of 24 very large cards, with fifteen different numbers marked on each, and in a bag 90 knobs or balls, numbered from 1 to 90; besides a board with ten cavities cut therein, for the purpose of placing the knobs as drawn; are sold at the Tunbridge ware or turners' shops. Fresh covers for the cards may be purchased, ready printed, and any bookbinder can easily make a new or repair the old pack.

RULES.

1. Every player should draw two cards, and deposit a stake previously agreed upon; and if the party is not too numerous, then any may take four or six cards, laying down a double or treble stake accordingly; and when the players are more than twelve, then some are only to have one card, paying half a stake, and likewise should the players not take all the cards among them, the remainder of the pack is to be laid aside until some other persons join the set From the cards not taken, players may exchange one or more of those drawn, or they may change with one another; similar exchanges, if the company consent, may also be made previous to each drawing, and likewise prior to replenishing the pool. Cards may be thrown up, or additional ones drawn from those put by; stakes being paid proportionably.

2. The stakes are to be put together in a pool, placed on the middle of the table, and also on the table a quantity of counters sufficient for the number of cards taken; upon the counters a value is to be fixed adequate to the stakes first deposited, from the whole of which a sum must be reserved, enough to pay, at the conclusion of the game, all the counters laid upon the table.

3. Then after counting the 90 knobs so as to be certain they are right, the eldest hand shall first shake them well together in the bag, and afterwards draw out ten successively,

not only declaring the number of each as drawn, but also placing the same conspicuously on the board.

4. As soon as the number is declared, each player having the same on one or more cards, is to take up counters sufficient to lay one upon that number every time it occurs, and so on until the ten knobs are drawn.

5. When only part of the pack is taken, and a number drawn happens not to be upon any player's card, then the players may put away that knob till some person takes the card on which it is printed.

6. When ten knobs are drawn out, every player examining the cards separately, and having only one counter upon any horizontal line, wins for that no more than the said counter, which is styled gaining by *abstract;* where two counters are on the same horizontal line of a separate card, the player gains an *ambo*, and becomes entitled to five counters, besides the two; when three are upon the same line, the player obtains a *terne*, and is to receive 25 additional counters; if four are on the same line, that is called a *quaterne*, winning 100 counters additional; when five occur on the same line, that makes a *quinterne*, gaining 250 additional counters, and the player is entitled to payment out of the pool for all the above-mentioned acquisitions previous to another drawing. Instead of giving counters, payment for the same may at once be made from the stock in the pool.

7. The knobs are then to be returned, and the bag given to the next player in rotation, who is to shake the same, and draw, &c. as before stated.

8. Whenever the pool is exhausted, the players must contribute again, according to the number of cards taken; and when it is resolved to finish the game, they agree among themselves to have only a fixed number of drawings more.

9. At the last drawing each player proceeds as heretofore directed, but the drawing concludes when no more counters are left on the table. The players then beginning with the eldest-hand, are to be paid out of the pool, as far as the money will go; and when that is expended, the others remain unpaid, which is styled a Bankruptcy; next the players are to re-unite the counters with those that were on their cards, and receive payment for them out of the fund reserved at the commencement of the game.

10. There are also cards of a new combination, which may be played by 6=12=18=or 24, observing that when six cards only are taken, but one counter is given; if 12, two; if 18, three; and when 24, four counters; and also when but six cards are taken, they must be either from 1 to 6—7 to 12—13 to 18—or 19 to 24; if 12 cards, from 1 to 12—or 13 to 24—for 18 cards, from 1 to 18; and when 24, the whole number.

11. The counters may refer for the payment to the amount of the stakes deposited in the stock.

For 24 cards	.	. . . .	.	144	times	10
„ 18 „	.	. . . .	.	108	„	10
„ 12 „	.	. . . .	.	72	„	10
„ 6 „	.	. . . .	.	36	„	10

There are other methods of playing at Loto, but the before-mentioned is the most approved.

POPE, or POPE JOAN.

POPE, a game somewhat similar to that of Matrimony, is played by a number of people, who generally use a board painted for this purpose, which may be purchased at most turners' or toy shops.

The eight of diamonds must first be taken from the pack, and after settling the deal, shuffling, &c. the dealer dresses the board by putting fish, counters, or other stakes, one each to ace, king, queen, knave, and game; two to matrimony, two to intrigue, and six to the nine of diamonds, styled Pope. This dressing is in some companies at the individual expense of the dealer, though in others the players contribute two stakes apiece towards the same.

The cards are next to be dealt round equally to every player, one turned up for trump, and about six or eight left in the stock to form stops; as for example, if the ten of spades is turned up, the nine consequently becomes a stop; the four kings and the seven of diamonds are always fixed stops, and the dealer is the only person permitted in the course of the game to refer occasionally to the stock for information what other cards are stops in that respective deal.

If either ace, king, queen, or knave, happens to be the turned-up trump, the dealer takes whatever is deposited on that head; but when Pope is turned up, the dealer is entitled both to that and the game, besides a stake for every card dealt to each player. Unless the game is determined by Pope being turned up, the eldest hand begins by playing out as many cards as possible; first the stops, then Pope if he has it, and afterwards the lowest card of his longest suit, particularly an ace, for that never can be led through; the other players are to follow when they can, in sequence of the same suit, till a stop occurs, and the party having the said stop, thereby becomes eldest-hand, and is to lead accordingly, and so on, until some person parts with all his cards, by which he wins the pool (game), and becomes entitled besides to a stake for every card not played by the others, except from any one holding Pope, which excuses him from paying; but if Pope has been played, then the party having held it is not excused, having already received the stakes for that card.

King and queen form what is denominated matrimony, queen and knave make intrigue, when in the same hand; but neither they, nor ace, king, queen, knave, or pope, entitle the holder to the stakes deposited thereon, unless played out, and no claim can be allowed after the board is dressed for the succeeding deal; but in all such cases the stakes are to remain for future determination.

This game only requires a little attention to recollect what stops have been made in the course of the same; as for instance, if a player begins by laying down the eight of clubs, then the seven in another hand forms a stop, whenever that suit is led from any lower card, or the holder when eldest may safely lay it down in order to clear his hand.

VINGT-UN.

Vingt-un, or twenty-one, is very similar to Quinze, and may be played by two or more people. It is essentially a family game, and when played as such, the stakes are usually represented by counters, which may be of any value; say, sixpence the dozen, or more. It is common to limit the

stakes to be laid to a dozen of counters, or the amount in
money which they represent. As the deal is advantageous,
and often continues long with the same person, it is usual to
determine it at the commencement by the first ace turned
up, or any other mode that may be agreed upon.

The deal is retained by the person who commences, until
a natural vingt-un occurs, when it passes to the next in rotation*. (The old mode of play, however, is, that in the case of
a natural vingt-un the deal passes to the holder, and many
still adhere to this custom. This item of the game must,
therefore, be regulated by the custom of the table, or be previously agreed.) The poney or youngest hand should collect
the cards that have been played, and shuffle them together
ready for the dealer against the period when he shall have
distributed the whole pack.

The dealer begins by giving two cards, one at a time, face
downwards, to each player, including himself. After the
first card has been dealt round, each places his stake upon it
(which may, if he chooses, be as low as a single counter), and
then receives the second card; but the dealer, upon the stakes
being all laid, and before proceeding with the deal, looks at
his own card, and if he thinks proper (having perhaps an ace,
ten, or court card), he may double the stakes, which he
announces by crying 'double.' He then distributes a second
card to each, and lastly to himself. Should he chance to have
a natural vingt-un, he declares it at once, before any more
cards are dealt, and collects the stakes (which, by a vingt-un,
are doubled), but should he have drawn less than 21, the
game proceeds thus:—The dealer enquires of each player
in rotation, beginning with the eldest hand on the left,
whether he stands, or wishes for another card, which, if
required, must be given from off the top (face upwards) of
the pack, and afterwards another, or more, if requested, till
the points of the additional card or cards, added to those
dealt, exceed or make 21 exactly, or such a number less than
21, as the player may choose to stand upon; but when the
points exceed 21, the player is technically said to have over-
drawn, and his cards are to be thrown up forthwith, and the
stake laid on them paid to the dealer. When the dealer has

* Should a natural vingt-un occur in the first round it does not put
out, the dealer being allowed a *misericorde*.

gone the round of the table in this manner, he turns up his own cards to the view of the company, and should he have any number of points, between, say, from 17 to 20, he usually " stands," that is. pits his cards against the other players. Those under his number, as well as ties *, pay, those above it receive. If the dealer should have only 14 or 15 points in his first hand, the chances would be against him, were he to stand on so small a number. He would therefore draw another card, and should this be a very low one (an ace or a deuce), and he have reason to suppose, by the extra cards dealt round, that he had to contest high numbers, he would draw again, and if he obtained 19 or 20 points would then probably win on more than he loses; the average of chances being in his favor; if by drawing he should happen to make up 21, he would receive double from all, excepting from the ties and those who had already thrown up; if more than 21, he would have to pay all who stand, paying the vingt-uns double.

Should either the dealer or a player happen to turn up two cards of the same denomination, for instance, two aces, deuces, or any other number, or two kings, two queens, &c., he would have the choice of going on both, and should the next card he draws be a triplicate, he may go on all three. If the cards happen to be aces, which count either as 1 or 11, at the option of the player, and if by great luck he should successively draw three tens, or Court cards, thus making three natural vingt-uns, he would obtain double stakes upon each, therefore six times as much as the stakes placed on the various hands, and should he, on laying his first card, have cried " double," the stakes payable, would, in such case, be twice doubled, therefore upon the three cards twelve-fold. This is an extreme case, cited merely to show the nature of the game. It commonly happens, however, that when either dealer or player " goes " on several cards, he loses on one or more, and thus neutralises his gains. Players, as already intimated, have the same right of " going " on several cards, as the dealer.

When any player has a vingt-un, and the dealer not, then the player wins double stakes from him; in other cases, except a natural vingt-un happens, the dealer pays single stakes to

* Ties are the principal advantage of the dealer.

all whose numbers under 21 are higher than his own, and receives from those who have lower numbers; players who have
similar numbers to the dealer pay; and when the dealer draws
more than 21, he overdraws, and has to pay to all who have
not thrown up, as already stated.

Twenty-one, whensoever dealt in the first two cards, is
styled a Natural Vingt-un, and should be declared immediately.   Hoyle says that this entitles the possessor to the deal,
besides double stakes from all the players, unless there shall
be more than one natural vingt-un, in which case the younger
hand or hands so having the same, are exempted from paying
to the eldest.   But this rule, like that mentioned at page 318,
is nearly obsolete.   It is not now customary to allow any
except the dealer to take double stakes from the company, in
respect to his natural vingt-un.

One of the first thoughts of the dealer, after the cards have
been cut, should be to look for BRULET, which is a natural
vingt-un formed by the bottom and top card, when they happen to be an ace and tenth card.   The card or cards looked
at must be thrown out, and mixed with those collected by
the poney.   Brulet either clears the board of the stakes laid,
(usually one or two counters levied on each player, at the
commencement of every game, and collected into a tray),
or takes the amount of the limit (perhaps 6d.) from each, as
may be agreed.

The deal, it should be observed, may be sold to the best
bidder, and, as it is undoubtedly of some advantage, a buyer
will generally be found.   But should a timid player object to
the deal, and no buyer be found, he may decline it, and so let
it pass to the next.

N.B. An ace, as already intimated, may be reckoned either
as 11 or 1: every court-card is counted as 10, and the rest
of the pack according to their points.

The odds of this game merely depend upon the average
quantity of cards likely to come under or exceed 21; for example, if those in hand make 14 exactly, it is 7 to 6 that the
one next drawn does not make the number of points above 21,
but if the points be 15, it is 7 to 6 against that hand; yet it
would not therefore always be prudent to stand at 15, for as
the ace may be calculated both ways, it is rather above an
even bet that the adversary's two first cards amount to more

than 14. A natural vingt-un may be expected once in 7 coups when two, and twice in 7, when four people play, and so on according to the number of players.

LANSQUENET.

THIS game may be played by almost any number of people, although only one pack of cards is used at a time, during each deal*. The dealer, who has rather an advantage, begins by shuffling the cards, and having them cut by any other person of the party; after which he deals out two cards on his left-hand, turning them up; then one for himself, and a fourth, which he places in the middle of the table for the company, called the *rejouissance* card. Upon this card any, or all of the company, except the dealer, may put their money, either a limited or unlimited sum, as may be agreed on, which the dealer is obliged to answer, by staking a sum equal to the whole that is put upon it by different persons. He continues dealing, and turning the cards upwards, one by one, till two of a sort appear: for instance, two aces, two deuces, &c. which in order to separate, and that no person may mistake for single cards, he places on each side of his own card; and as often as two, three, or the fourth card of a sort comes up, he always places them, as before said, on each side of his own. Any single card the company has a right to take and put their money upon, unless the dealer's own card happens to be double, which often occurs by this card being the same as one of the two cards which he first of all dealt out on his left-hand. Thus he continues dealing till he brings either their cards, or his own. As long as his own card remains undrawn he wins; and whichever card comes up first, loses. If he draws or deals out the two cards on his left, which are called the hand-cards, before his own, he is entitled to deal again; the advantage of which is no other, than being exempted from losing when he draws a similar card to his own, immediately after he has turned up one for himself.

* As the game is now played in France, four, and even more, packs of cards are mixed together.

Y

This game is often played more simply without the *rejouis-sance* card, giving every person round the table a card to put their money upon.   Sometimes it is played by dealing only two cards, one for the dealer, and another for the company.

PUT.

WE will borrow the opinions and views of this little con-trivance against time—as broached by Mr. Seymour in his volume written for the especial behoof of the young princesses —and append to them Mr. Hoyle's observations on it.

"Put is the ordinary rooking-game of every place; and seems, by the few cards that are dealt, to have no difficulty in the play; but there is great craft and cunning in it.

" If you play at either Two or Three-handed Put, the best put-card deals. Having shuffled the cards, the adversary cuts them; then the dealer deals one to his antagonist, and another to himself, till they have three a-piece: five up, or a Put is commonly the game. The eldest, if he hath a good game, and thinks it better than his adversary's, puts to him; if the other will not, or dare not see him, he then wins one : but if he will see him, they play it out, and he who wins two tricks, or all three, wins the whole set; but if each wins a trick, and third tied, neither win, because it is trick and tye.

" Sometimes they play without putting; and then the winner is he that wins most tricks.   In playing keep up your cards very close; for the least discovery of any one of them, is a great advantage to him who sees it.

"This game consists very much in daring; for a mettled gamester will put boldly upon very bad cards sometimes, as upon a five, seven, and a nine; the other thinking there are good cards in his adversary's hand, having very indifferent ones in his own, dares not see him; and so by going to stock, loseth one.   He who once hath the confidence to put on bad cards, cannot recal his putting, by which means he frequently pays for his bravado.

" The best Put-cards are, first, the tray, next, the duce, then the ace; the rest follow in pre-eminence, as king, queen, knave, ten, and so onwards, to the four, which is the meanest card at Put.

" Put, played with a complete pack, generally by two people sometimes by three, and often by four, is a game at which the cards rank differently from all others, tray being the best, next the deuce, then ace, king, and so on in the usual order. After cutting for deal, &c. at which the highest Put-card wins, three cards, by one at a time, are given to each player, then the game is played in the following way. If the non-dealer throws up his cards, he loses a point, if he plays, and the dealer does not lay down another to it, he gains a point; but, should the dealer either win the same, pass it, or lay down one of equal value, forming what is styled a tie, the non-dealer is still at liberty to put, that is play, or not, and his opponent then only gains a point; then if both parties agree to go on, whoever gains all the tricks or two out of three, wins five points, which are the game; if each player obtains one trick, and the third is a tie, then neither party scores.

" Four-handed Put differs only in that any two of the players give each their best card to his partner, who then lays out one of his, and the game is afterwards played as in Two-handed Put.

" If the dealer turns up any of his adversary's cards, another deal may be demanded; but, when he shows his own, he is to abide by them: and should a faced card occur, the pack must be shuffled and dealt again: when more cards than necessary are given to the non-dealer, he may either claim a fresh deal, or have the extra cards drawn out; but should the dealer give himself too many, then his opponent is entitled to a point, and may either have another deal, or draw the supernumerary cards. Bye-standers ought never to interfere, under penalty of paying the stakes. Either party saying 'I put,' must abide the event of the game, or pay the stakes."

ALL FOURS.

THIS game, usually played by two people, sometimes by four, with a complete pack, derives its name from the four chances therein, for each of which a point is scored, namely, *high,* the best trump out; *low,* the smallest trump dealt;

jack, the knave of trumps; *game,* the majority of pips reckoned from such of the following cards as the respective players have in their tricks; viz. every ace is counted as 4; king, 3; queen 2; knave 1; and ten for 10. Low is always scored by the person to whom it was dealt; but jack being the property of whoever can win or save it, the possessor is permitted to revoke and trump with that card: and when turned up as trump the dealer scores; it is also allowable for the player who lays down a high or low trump to enquire at the time whether the same be high or low.

After cutting for deal, at which either the highest or lowest card wins, as previously fixed, six cards are to be given to each player, either by three or one at a time, and the 13th turned up for trump; then if the eldest does not like his card, he may, for once in a hand, say, *I beg,* when the dealer must either give a point or three more cards to each, and turn up the 7th for trump; but if that should prove of the same suit as the first turned up, then three cards more are to be given, and so on till a different suit occurs. The cards rank as at whist, and each player should always strive to secure his own tens and court cards, to take those of the adversary, to obtain which, except when commanding cards are held, it is usual to play a low one to throw the lead into the opponent's hand. Ten or eleven points form the game, which may be set up as at Whist, though a very customary method is to draw two cards from the pack, and lay them one on the other, so as to exhibit only the number of pips the player has gained.

When the dealer shews any of his adversary's cards a new deal may be demanded, but in shewing his own he must abide by the same.

If discovered, previous to playing, that too many cards are given to either party, a fresh deal may be claimed, or the extra cards drawn out by the opponent; but should even a single card have been played, then there must be another deal.

With strict players the adversary may score a point whenever his opponent does not trump or follow suit, and each calculates his game without inspecting the tricks, which when erroneously set up must not only be taken down, but also the antagonist either scores four points or one as shall have been agreed on.

SPECULATION.

THIS is a lively round game, that several may play, using a complete pack of cards bearing the same import as at Whist, with fish or counters, on which such a value is fixed as the company agree; the highest trump, in each deal, wins the pool; and whenever it happens that not one is dealt, then the company pool again, and the event is decided by the succeeding coup. After determining the deal, &c. the dealer pools six fish, and every other player four; next three cards are given to each by one at a time, and another turned up for trump; the cards are not to be looked at, except in this manner,—the eldest hand shews the uppermost card, which if a trump, the company may speculate on or bid for; the highest bidder buying and paying for it, provided the price offered is approved of by the seller. After this is settled, or if the first card does not prove trump, then the next eldest shews the uppermost card, and so on, the company speculating as they please, till all are discovered; when the possessor of the highest trump, whether by purchase or otherwise, gains the pool.

The holder of the trump card, whether acquired by purchase or otherwise, has the privilege of keeping his cards concealed till all the rest have been turned up.

To play this game well, little more is requisite than recollecting what superior cards of that particular suit have appeared in the preceding deals, and calculating the probability of the trump offered proving the highest in the deal then undetermined.

LOO.

LOO or Lue, subdivided into limited and unlimited Loo, game, the complete knowledge of which can easily be acquired, is played two ways, both with five and three cards, though most commonly with five cards dealt from a whole pack, either first three and then two, or by one at a time. Several persons may play together, but the greatest number can be admitted when with three cards only.

After five cards have been given to each player another is

turned up for trump; the knave of clubs generally, or some-times the knave of the trump suit, as agreed upon, is the high-est card and styled Pam; the ace of trumps is next in value, and the rest in succession, as at Whist. Each player has the liberty of changing for others from the pack all or any of the five cards dealt, or of throwing up the hand in order to escape being looed. Those who play their cards either with or with-out changing, and do not gain a trick, are looed; as is likewise the case with all who have stood the game, when a flush or flushes occur, and each, except any player holding Pam, or an inferior flush, is required to deposit a stake to be given to the person who sweeps the board, or divided among the winners at the ensuing deal, according to the tricks which may then be made. For instance, if every one at dealing stakes half-a-crown, the tricks are entitled to sixpence apiece, and whoever is looed must put down half-a-crown, exclusive of the deal; sometimes it is settled that each person looed shall pay a sum equal to what happens to be on the table at the time. Five cards of a suit, or four with Pam, compose a flush, which sweeps the board, and yields only to a superior flush, or the elder hand. When the ace of trumps is led, it is usual to say "Pam be civil," the holder of which last-mentioned card is then expected to let the ace pass.

Any player having a flush, or five cards of a suit in his hand, looes all the parties then playing, and sweeps the board.

When Loo is played with three cards, they are dealt by one at a time. Pam is omitted, and the cards are not exchanged nor permitted to be thrown up.

In different companies these games are frequently played with a few trifling variations from the manner as before stated.

One of the most usual variations in three card loo is the laying out of two or three extra hands, which are called Misses. These may be exchanged with their own hands by any of the players, the elder having the first choice, and the others according to their turn, the dealer being last. It commonly happens that the first two or three players avail themselves of their option, so that it rarely comes round to the dealer. The Miss, which is to be taken at a venture, without previous inspection, must be played.

LOTTERY.

Of the minor games of cards, Lottery is without doubt one of the most amusing. A great excellence of this game is, that it is most agreeable when there is a great number of players; for it may be played by ten, twelve, or more; but not well with less than four or five players. Two entire packs of cards are employed, one of which serves for the tricks, and the other for the lots or prizes. Each player should take a certain number of counters, more or less, that and their value depending on the will of the players. These points being settled, every one gives the counters he has, for his stake, and these being collected into a box or purse, on the middle of the table, compose the fund of the Lottery.

The players being all ranged round the table, two of them take the two packs of cards, and as it is of no importance who deals, as there is no advantage in being eldest or youngest, the cards are commonly presented in compliment to some two of the players. The dealers, after well shuffling the cards, have them cut by their left-hand neighbours, and one of them deals a card to each player; all these cards are to remain turned, and are called the *lots;* each player then places on his lot what number of counters he thinks proper; they should observe, however, to make them one higher than the other, that there may be as few as possible of the same value. The lots being thus prized, he who has the other pack deals likewise to each player one card, which are called the *tickets;* each player having received his card, the lots are then turned, and each examines whether his ticket answers to any of the lots; for example, if any of the lots are, the knave of clubs, the queen of hearts, the ace of spades, the eight of clubs, the six of diamonds, the four of hearts, the three of spades, and the two of diamonds; he or they, whose cards correspond to any of those, take up the lot or prize that is marked on that card.

The two dealers then collect those cards that belong to their respective packs, and after having shuffled them, deal again in the same manner as before, the lots being laid down and drawn by the tickets, in the manner we have just mentioned; and such lots as remain undrawn, are to be added to the fund of the lottery. This continues till the fund is all drawn out, after which each player examines what he has won, and the stakes are paid in money by him who drew the lottery; whose business it is to collect and divide it.

If the party should last too long, instead of giving only one card to each, for his ticket, you may give two, three, or even four, one after the other, according as you would have the party continue; the increasing the value of the lots likewise, helps greatly to shorten the party.

Another method is, to take at random three cards out of one of the packs, and place them face downward, on a board or in a bowl on the table for the prizes, then every player purchases from the other pack any number of cards for tickets as may be most agreeable, paying a fixed sum or certain quantity of counters for each, which sums or counters are put in different proportions on the three prizes to be gained by those who happen to have purchased corresponding cards, and such that happen not to be drawn are continued till the next deal.

This game may be played with a single pack, by separating the same into two divisions, each containing a red and black suit.

COMMERCE.

OF this there are two distinct methods of playing, the new and the old mode. The new way is played by any number of persons, from three to twelve, with a complete pack of 52 cards, bearing the same import as at Whist, only the ace is reckoned as eleven. Every player has a certain quantity of counter's on which a fixed value is put, and each, at every fresh deal, lays down one for the stake. Sometimes the game is continued until, or finished when, one of the players has lost all the counters given at the commencement; but in order to prevent it from being spun out to an unpleasant length, or concluded too soon, it is often customary to fix the duration to a determinate number of tours or times, that the whole party shall deal once each completely round.

After determining the deal, the dealer, styled also the banker, shuffles the pack, which is to be cut by the left hand player; then three cards, either altogether or one by one, at the dealer's pleasure, are given to each person, beginning on the right hand, but none are to be turned up. If the pack proves false, or the deal wrong, or should there be a faced card, then there must be a fresh deal.

At this game are three parts: 1st, That which takes place of all others, called the tricon, or three cards of the same denomination, similar to pair-royal at Cribbage: 2dly, the next in rank is the sequence, or three following cards of the same suit, like tierce at Piquet: and lastly, the point, being the greatest number of pips on two or three cards of a suit in any one hand; of all which parts the highest disannuls the lower.

After the cards have been dealt round, the banker enquires, "Who will trade?" which the players beginning with the eldest hand, usually and separately answer by saying, "For ready money," or "I barter." Trading for money is giving a card and a counter to the banker, who places the card under the stock or remainder of the pack styled the bank, and returns in lieu thereof another card from the top. The counter is profit to the banker, who consequently trades with the stock free from expense. Barter is exchanging a card without pay with the next right hand player, which must not be refused, and so on, the players trade alternately, till one of them obtains the object aimed at, and thereby stops the Commerce; then all shew their hands, and the highest tricon, sequence, or point wins the pool. The player who first gains the wished for tricon, &c., should shew the same immediately, without waiting till the others begin a fresh round, and if any one chooses to stand on the hand dealt, and shew it without trading, none of the junior players can trade that deal, and if the eldest hand stands, then of course no person can trade.

The banker always ranks as eldest hand, in case of neither tricon or sequence, when the game is decided by the point. Whenever the banker does not gain the pool, then he is to pay a counter to that player who obtains the same, and if the banker possesses tricon, sequence, or point, and does not win the pool, because another player has a better hand, then he is to give a counter to every player.

Commerce the old way is played by several persons together, every one depositing a certain sum in the pool, and receiving three fish or counters a piece, on which a value is fixed; as suppose sixpences are pooled, the counters then may be rated at 1d. or 1$\frac{1}{2}d$. each, so as to leave a sum for that player who gains the final sweep. After determining the deal, three cards, begining on the left hand, are given to every player, and as many turned up on the board by one at a time.

This game is gained, as at the other, by pairs, sequences, or flushes, and should the three cards turned up be such as the dealer approves of, he may, previous to looking at the hand dealt to himself, take them so turned up in lieu of his own, but then must abide by the same, and cannot afterwards exchange any during that deal. All the players, beginning with the eldest hand, may in rotation change any card or cards in their possession for such as lie turned up on the table, striving thereby to make pairs-royal, sequences, or flushes, and so on round again and again, till all have refused to change, or are satisfied, but every person once standing cannot change again that deal. Finally the hands are all shewn, and the possessor of the highest pair-royal, &c., or the eldest hand if there are more than one of the same value, takes the sum agreed upon out of the pool, and the person having the worst hand, puts one fish or counter therein, called "Going up." The player, whose three are first gone off, has the liberty of purchasing one more, called, "Buying a Horse," for a sum as agread, usually one-third of the original stake, to be put into the pool. After that, every player, whose fish are all gone, sits by till the game is concluded, which finishes by the person who continues the longest on the board, thereby gaining the pool or final sweep.

BRAG.

This is taken from the text of Seymour—whose quaint spirit and phrases are singularly suited to the subject.

At this game, the whole pack is dealt round the table to all who are desirous to share in the gain and diversion. As many play at it as the cards will hold out to supply; he dealing three a-piece to each of the gamesters at one time, turning up the last card all round, belonging to every one present.

Each gamester is to put down three stakes, one for each card, as much, or as little as the humours of the company will consent to; whether three guineas, three crowns, three shillings, three sixpences, or what other stakes, according to their qualities and purposes, is thought convenient: And this being done, the manner of playing the game is as follows:

The best card turned up in the dealing round, in its degree, beginning from ace, king, queen, knave, and so downwards, through all the cards of the players, wins the first stake; and the person who has the luck to have it dealt him, is to demand it from the rest; who pay it accordingly, unless the ace of diamonds be turned up amongst them; which if shewn, by a superior authority in the game, is to be preferred, and wins the stake. And observe, that though the eldest hand, who has an ace, carries it from the rest by a kind of descent, yet the ace of diamonds, by the aforesaid authority, even in the youngest hand which is the last card that is dealt, wins the stake from any other turned up before.

The next principal matter, and the main thing by which the second stake is to be won, is called the Brag, which, by the ingenuity of its management, gives the game its denomination. The nature of it is, that you are to endeavour to impose upon the judgment of the rest who play, and particularly on the person who chiefly offers to oppose you, by boasting of cards in your hand, whether pairs-royal, pairs or others, that are better than his or hers who plays against you. The best cards you can have really to brag of, are a pair-royal of aces, the next of kings, queens, &c. A pair-royal of any sort winning from any pair of the best sort, as a pair of any sort wins of any other cards that are not pairs.

But here you are to observe, that the witty ordering of this brag, is the most pleasant part of the game; for those who by fashioning their looks and gestures, can give a proper air to their actions, as will so deceive an unskilful antagonist, that sometimes a pair of fives, trays, or duces, in such a hand, with the advantage of his composed countenance, and subtle manner of over-awing the other, shall out-brag a much greater pair-royal, and win the stakes with great applause and laughter on his side from the whole company.

The knave of clubs, is here, as principal a favorite as at Loo, and makes a pair with any other card in hand, or with any other two cards a pair-royal, and is often in this game very necessary, to advance the credit of the brag, to him who has the assurance of imposing upon the company; and by such convenient confidence, the advantage of winning the second stake.

The third stake is won by the person who first makes up the
cards in his hand thirty-one, each ace, king, queen, knave,
&c. going for ten, and drawing from the pack, as is usual in
that game: or, instead of the thirty-one, if his fortune will not
oblige him, the nearest to it may win, he having the privilege
to draw, or not to draw, as he pleases, according as he finds it
convenient, by the cards that are in his hand; for if he draws
out, he loses his third stake.

Some very nice players at this game make the nine of diamonds a second favorite card, with the knave of clubs, to
make a pair-royal of aces; so that those two joined with one
natural ace, shall win from any pair-royal of kings, queens,
knaves, or any other cards, but a pair-royal of natural aces.

The person who is so lucky to win all the three stakes, is to
be rewarded by the whole company of gamesters round the
table, with three stakes more, if they play the strictness of the
game; which necessarily makes the winnings and losings
amount to a considerable sum of money. But very often our
modern gamesters waive this particular, and out of a decent regard to their pockets, content themselves with the satisfaction
of the pleasure of the brag, rather than trust to the uncommon
good fortune of winning the three stakes, from the rest of the
disappointed company.

The deal is to go round from person to person; and by the
different management of the brag, you may find very great
diversion, some doing it so awkwardly, with so little cunning,
and so ill an address, that the defects or value of their game
will presently be discovered, whilst others with a more artful
assurance, and by their subtle management, will wittily ban-
ter and impose upon their adversaries, and seldom fail of their
designed profit.

It is not fair for any of the gamesters, that sit near him who
makes the brag, to peep into his hand, or by any mute sign
or token to give the opposer any knowledge of the cards that
he has in his hand; because it may chance that the oppositions,
natural to this game, may draw on a considerable sum of
money, to be staked down, each of the two who are concerned, valuing his own cards, and lessening those of his antagonist, as he thinks he has reason.

A very notable damage, occasioned by one person's peeping
into another's hand, I once chanced to be a spectator of.

Some gentlemen and ladies were playing at this game, when one of the gamesters, who seemed to be very skilful at the game in general, but more particularly so, at the subtle management of the brag, and, by his artful method and cunning manner of behaviour, had induced his competitor to believe that he resolved to out-brag him upon very low and insignificant cards; but it was the gentleman's good luck at that juncture, to have in his hand far otherwise than he imagined, having been dealt two natural aces, and the knave of clubs, which, joined with the other two, made the greatest pair-royal that could then possibly be dealt, and consequently proper to win also the greatest stake that could be laid; he kept his countenance demure, and with a gesture neither overjoyed nor desponding, made a brag of half-a-crown; the other who had in his hand a pair-royal of kings, and, as afterwards was discovered, had, through the imprudence of the dealer, casually seen an ace or two given about to other gamesters, thinking himself also as secure as possible, answers with a crown; his antagonist then sets half-a-guinea, and the opposer, immediately a whole one, and vying with each other, till the same amounted to ten pounds, when as ill fate, for one of them, would have it, a too curious impertinent of the female kind, who sat next him that had the aces, having a furious itch upon her to know whether his repeated brag was upon a sure foundation, or not, could not forbear covertly peeping into his hand, and at the view was so surprized, that on a sudden she, by a violent shriek, gave the gamester, with the pair-royal of kings, warning of his unavoidable loss, giving him reason to cease the brag, and thereby lose the game.

BLIND HOOKEY.

This is purely a game of chance, without any limit as to the number of players, but is best suited to a party of four, six, or ten. Each player cuts for the deal, which is decided in the same manner as at Whist. The pack being then shuffled by the player on the dealer's right hand, may be again shuffled by the dealer himself, and being cut by the right hand player, is placed by the dealer before the player on his left hand. He cuts a parcel for himself, consisting of not less than four cards, nor of more than shall allow an equal

number at least to all the players, and lays them before him
with the faces downwards. All the players having done the
same, and a small parcel being left for the dealer, he also lays
it before him, faced downwards. Each player then places
upon the parcel of cards before him, the stake which he is
inclined to go for, and all the party having followed his
example, the dealer forthwith turns up his parcel, for he is
obliged to set the players in the amount they decide to venture. The dealer having turned up his parcel, the left-hand
player does the same, and whoever turns up the highest card
wins the stake, but should the cards "tie," that is, be of
equal value, the dealer wins. This is a considerable advantage, and consequently the deal is many points in the favor
of the holder. It may be sold, and the buyer being out,
which results from his turn-up card being lower than any that
is turned up by any of the players, it returns to the player on
the left-hand of the dealer who sold it. This is the principle
upon which Blind Hookey is commonly played.

MATRIMONY.

MATRIMONY may be played by any number of persons from
5 to 14. This game is composed of 5 chances, usually marked
on a board or sheet of paper, as follows:

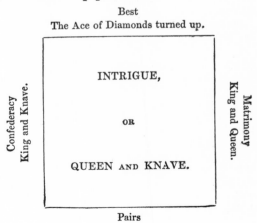

Best

The Ace of Diamonds turned up.

INTRIGUE,

OR

QUEEN AND KNAVE.

Confederacy
King and Knave.

Matrimony
King and Queen.

Pairs

The Highest.

N.B. The ace of diamonds turned up takes the whole pool, but when in hand ranks only as any other ace, and if not turned up, nor any ace in hand, then the king, or next superior card, wins the chance styled best.

The game is generally played with counters, and the dealer stakes what he pleases on each or any chance, the other players depositing each the same quantity, except one; that is, when the dealer stakes twelve, the rest of the company lay down eleven each. After this, two cards are dealt round to every one, beginning on the left, then to each one other card turned up, and he who so happens to get the ace of diamonds sweeps all; if it is not turned up, then each player shews his hand, and any of them having matrimony, intrigue, &c. takes the counters on that point; and when two or more people happen to have a similar combination, the eldest hand has the preference, and should any chance not be gained, it stands over to the next deal.

TABLE GAMES.

FARO.

FARO, Pharo, Pharaoh, or Pharaon, is very similar to Basset, a game formerly much in vogue.

RULES OF THE GAME.

The banker turns up the cards from a complete pack, deliberately, one by one, laying them alternately, first to his right for the bank, and then to his left hand for the punter, till the whole are dealt out.

The punter may, at his option, set any number of stakes, agreeable to the sum limited, upon one or more cards chosen out of his livret, from the ace to the king inclusive, either previous to dealing the cards, or after any quantity of coups are made, or he may masque his bets, or change his cards whenever he pleases, or finally decline punting, except an event is unsettled when not above eight cards are undealt.

The banker wins when the card, equal in points to that on

which the stake is set, turns up on his right hand, but loses when it is dealt to the left.

The punter loses half the stake when his card comes out twice in the same coup.

The last card neither wins nor loses.

The last card but one is called hocly, and forms part of the banker's gain; but now is frequently given up, and generally so in the last deal.

When by accident or design the pack happens to contain more or less than 52 cards, or should the last coup be found deficient, owing to any misdeal, however arising, whether discovered at the end or during the game, the bank must then pay every stake depending at the period when the error is detected, which payment must also be made if the cards are thrown up.

The dealer should hold the cards close in his hand, and always be prepared to inform any punter how many cards remain.

The first card is never valid till the second is dealt.

No person but the dealer or croupier should ever meddle with the cards, unless to cut them.

A paroli, &c., may be purchased by paying a sum equivalent to the stake.

METHOD OF PLAY.

The tailleur and croupier sit opposite each other at a large oval table covered with a green cloth, on which is a line marked by coloured tape, or a wooden rim about an inch high, and eight from the edge of the table, for the purpose of separating those cards punted on from the others. Money is placed either loose in a well, or done up in rouleaus. The tailleur is to deal, while the croupier pays and receives, guards against errors, and shuffles another pack of cards.

The game may be played by any number of persons, each punter being furnished with a livret, from which having chosen a card, or cards, and placed the same upon the table, just within the line, putting the stake either thereon, or upon other cards placed face downwards at the head of those betted on. The stakes are answered by the banker, who usually limits the sums according to his capital; and at public tables has generally two or more croupiers. Then the dealer having

previously counted and shuffled the cards, and had them cut
by a punter, should hold the pack tight in his hand, and
show the bottom card, as a caution to avoid punting on it near
the conclusion of the game, and to prevent mistakes, a similar
card, with the corners cut off, is usually laid in the middle of
the table; next he says play, and proceeds to deal slowly,
first to the right, afterwards to the left, mentioning every one
as he goes on, and stopping between each two cards, while
the croup settles the event.

When a punter gains, he may either take his money or
paroli; if he wins again, he may play sept et le va; should
he then prove successful, he can paroli for quinze et le va;
afterwards for trente et le va; and, finally, for soixante et le
va, which is the highest chance in the game. Should the
punter not like to venture so boldly, he may make a paix, or
pont; afterwards a double or treble paix, &c., or a single,
double, or treble paix-paroli. When doublets are dealt, the
punter may either pay or make a pli.

A reckoning may be kept of the number of times each card
is dealt, by properly placing a livret and bending the corners of
similar cards, one way for the punter, another way for the dealer.

TERMS USED AT FARO.

Banker; the person who keeps the table.

Cocking. See Paroli.

Couche or *Enjeu;* the Stake.

Coup; a Stroke or Pull. Any two cards dealt alternately
to the right and left.

Croupier; Croup. An assistant to the dealer.

Doublet; is when the punter's card is turned up twice in
the same coup, then the bank wins half the stake. A single
paroli must be taken down, but if there are several, only one
retires.

Hocly; a Certainty; signifies the last card but one, the
chance of which the banker claims, and may refuse to let any
punter withdraw a card when eight or less remain to be dealt.

Livret; a small Book. A suit of 13 cards, with 4 others,
called *Figures*, viz. one named the little figure, has a blue
cross on each side, and represents ace, deuce, tray; another
yellow on both sides, styled the yellow figure, signifies, 4, 5,
6; a third with a black lozenge in the centre, named the
black figure, stands for 7, 8, 9, 10; and a red card, called the

great or red figure, for knave, queen, king: these figures are
useful for those who punt on several cards at once.

L'une pour l'autre; One for the other; means a drawn
game, and is said when two of the punter's cards are dealt in
the same coup.

Masque; signifies turning a card, or placing another face
downwards, during any number of coups, on that whereon the
punter has staked, and which he afterwards may play at
pleasure.

Oppose; the Opposite Game; is reversing the game, and
having the cards on the right for the punter; and those on
the left for the dealer.

Paix; Peace.   Equivalent to double or quits; is, when the
punter having won, does not choose to paroli and risk his stake,
but bends or makes a bridge of his card, signifying that he
ventures his gains only.   A double paix is, when the punter
having won twice, bends two cards one over the other.
Treble paix, thrice, &c.   A paix may follow a sept, quinze, or
trente, &c.

Paix-Paroli; is when a punter has gained a paroli, wishes
then to play double or quits, and save his original stake,
which he signifies by doubling a card after making his first
paroli; double-paix-paroli succeeds to winning a paix-paroli;
treble-paix-paroli follows double, &c.

Paroli or *Parolet;* Double.   Sometimes called *Cocking*, is
when a punter, being fortunate, chooses to venture both his
stake and gains, which he intimates by bending a corner of
his card upwards.

Pli; Bending; is used when a punter, having lost half his
stake by a *doublet*, bends a card in the middle, and setting it
up with the points and foot towards the dealer, signifies thereby a desire either of recovering the moiety, or of losing all.

Pont; a Bridge.   The same as Paix.

Ponte or *Punt;* a Point.   The punter or player.

Quinze et le Va; Fifteen and it goes; is when the punter
having won a sept, &c., bends the third corner of the card,
and ventures for 15 times his stake.

Sept et le Va; Seven &c.; succeeds the gaining of a
paroli, by which the punter being entitled to thrice his stake,
risks the whole again, and, bending his card a second time,
tries to win seven-fold,

Soixante et le Va; Sixty-three, &c.; is when the player

having obtained a trente, ventures all once more, which is signified by making a fifth paroli, either on another card, if he has parolied on one only before, or by breaking the side of that one which contains four, to pursue his luck in the next deal.

Tailleur; the Dealer.   Generally the banker.

Trente et le Va; one and thirty; follows a quinze, &c., when the punter again tries his luck, and makes a fourth paroli.

ODDS AT THE GAME OF FARO.

The chances of doublets vary according to the number of similar cards remaining among those undealt.

The odds against the punter increase with every coup that is dealt.

When 20 cards remain in hand, and the punter's card but once in it, the banker's gain is 5 per cent.

When the punter's card is twice in 20, the banker's gain is about the 34th part of the stake.

When the punter's card is thrice in 20, the banker's gain is about 4 per cent.

When the punter's card is 4 times in 20, the banker's gain is nearly the 18th part of the stake.

When only 8 cards remain, it is 5 to 3 in favor of the bank, when but 6 are left, it is 2 to 1; and when no more than 4, it is 3 to 1.

TABLE EXHIBITING THE ODDS AGAINST WINNING ANY NUMBER OF EVENTS SUCCESSIVELY: APPLICABLE TO HAZARD, BILLIARDS, FARO, ROUGE ET NOIR, OR OTHER GAMES OF CHANCE.

That the punter wins or loses the first time is an even bet.

That he does not win twice together, is 3 to 1; three successive times, 7 to 1; four successive times, 15 to 1; five successive times, 31 to 1; six successive times, 63 to 1; seven successive times, 127 to 1; eight successive times, 255 to 1; nine successive times, 511 to 1; ten successive times, 1023 to 1; and so on to any number doubling every time the last odds, and adding one for the stake.

N.B. A punter plays on the square by placing a stake, referring to both at the head of two cards that have been dealt thrice each, and neither of which is the bottom one.

A TABLE FOR FARO, WHEREBY THE SEVERAL ADVANTAGES OF THE BANKER, IN WHATEVER CIRCUMSTANCES HE MAY HAPPEN TO BE, IS SEEN SUFFICIENTLY NEAR AT THE FIRST VIEW.

Number of Cards in the Stock.	The Number of times the Punter's Card is contained in the Stock.			
	1	2	3	4
52	**	**	**	50
50	**	94	65	48
48	48	90	62	46
46	46	86	60	44
44	44	82	57	42
42	42	78	54	40
40	40	74	52	38
38	38	70	49	36
36	36	66	46	34
34	34	62	44	32
32	32	58	41	30
30	30	54	38	28
28	28	50	36	26
26	26	46	33	24
24	24	42	30	22
22	22	38	28	20
20	20	34	25	18
18	18	30	22	16
16	16	26	20	14
14	14	22	17	12
12	12	18	14	10
10	10	14	12	8
8	8	11	9	6

Example I.—To find the gain of the banker when there are 30 cards remaining in the stock, and the punter's card twice in it.

In the first column seek for the number answering to 30, the number of cards remaining in the stock: over against it, and under 2, at the head of the table, you will find 54, which shows that the banker's gain is the fifty–fourth part of the stake.

Example II.—To find the gain of the banker when but 10 cards are remaining in the stock, and the punter's card thrice in it.

Against 10, the number of cards, in the first column, and under number 3, you will find 12, which denotes that the banker's gain is the twelfth part of the stake.

Example III.—To find the banker's profit when the punter's cards remain twice in 22.

In the first column find 22, the number of cards over against it under figure 2, at the head of the table, you will find 38, which shows that the gain is one 38th part of the stake.

Example IV. To find the banker's gain when eight cards remain, and the punter's card thrice among them.

In the first column seek for 8, on a line with which under the 3 stands the figure of 9, denoting the profits to be 1-9th, or 2s. 4d. in the guinea.

Corollary 1,—From the table it appears, that the fewer cards there are in the stock, the greater is the gain of the banker.

Corollary 2.—The least gain of the banker under the same circumstances is, when the punter's card is but twice in hand, the next greater when three times, still greater when once, and the greatest of all when four times.

The profit of the banker is three per cent. upon all the sums adventured, supposing the punters to stop when only six cards remain, but with hocly it is full five per cent.

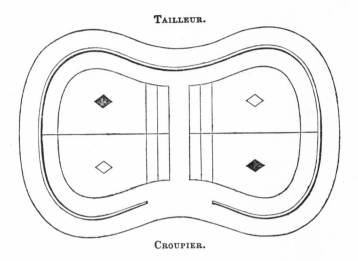

CROUPIER.

ROUGE ET NOIR.

ROUGE ET NOIR, (Red and Black,) or Trente-un, is a modern game, so styled, not from the cards, but from the colours marked on the tapis or green cloth with which the table is covered.

To form the game, it is necessary that there should be a banker, or *tailleur* (DEALER), who represents him, and players, the number of whom are unlimited.

The table usually employed for this game is of an oblong form, thirty feet long, and four feet wide, covered with a green cloth; in the middle of which the bank is placed; in other words, the money that belongs to the banker, and which is destined to pay the fortunate players. The company are at liberty to place their money on the right and left of this table, upon the chances that seems to them most likely to win. Those chances are : —

1st. Le Noir (the black) le Rouge (the red) designated by two large spots on the green cloth, marked red and black, something in the shape of the ace of diamonds, and placed opposite to each other on the cloth; to which is sewn a long strip of yellow border.

2nd. The couleur and the inverse. If the player be desirous to risk his money on the colour, he must put it on a narrow band, which is situated between the two squares of the Rouge and Noir. If he be determined to try his luck on the inverse, he must place his money on a yellow circle, or rather a collection of circles, situated at the extremity of the table.

There are many tailleurs, who are replaced successively; some of whom deal the cards, and others pay the winners, superintend the play, and overlook the players.

The first parcel of cards played, is usually for noir, the second for rouge, though sometimes the cards are cut to determine which shall begin. All the terms of this game are French, and that language is commonly used in playing.

The tailleur and croupier being seated opposite each other, with a basket for receiving the cards of every coup after dealing, placed on the middle of the table, one of the tailleurs commences the game, by unsealing before the company six packs of cards, which are regularly counted in their presence; and, after being shuffled, he passes them to another sitting opposite to him; who also shuffles them in his turn by a handful at a time, and hands them to the punter who happens to be on the right hand, who has the privilege to shuffle them if he pleases: they are ultimately transmitted to the tailleur, whose duty it is to deal, and who again shuffles them by a handful at a time. He then puts the six packs together, shuffles them once more, and gets them cut.

The cut is made by presenting a blank card to one of the players, who places it in any part of the six packs of cards that he thinks proper: he cannot, however, cut less than three cards.

The tailleur completes the cut, by putting those cut under the top cards.

This ceremony being over, the punters place on the Rouge, the Noir, the Couleur, or the Inverse, the sum they wish to risk. No individual can put down less than five francs, nor more than twelve thousand at the same time, except in the two following cases; viz :—

1st. When the banker agrees to an augmentation of the stake, after a proposition made to him by the player.

2nd. When a player is forced to augment his mass, the consequence of a martingale.

During this interval, the tailleur places before him the cards, of which he takes a handful, and cries out, " Le jeu est fait, rien ne va plus:" that is to say,—the deal having commenced, no more money is to be placed on the table than the sum already staked. After those words are pronounced, should any one put money on the table, it will be taken up by one of the tailleurs, and returned to him; for the player putting money down too late can neither win nor lose.

The tailleur now draws a card, which, after showing to the company, he lays on the table : he draws a second; a third, which he places in the same row, right and left, until the number of points on the cards amount to at least thirty-one ; so that if he should happen to count only thirty, he must still draw another.

The cards retain their nominal value. The ace counts as one point; the II, two points; the III, three points; the IV, four points ; the V, five points ; the VI, six points ; the VII, seven points; the VIII, eight points ; the IX, nine points; the X, ten points ; and the court cards ten points each.

The first row of cards, of which the number of points are at least equal to thirty-one, and cannot consequently pass the number of forty, is for the Noir; that is to say, it determines the chance of those who have placed their money upon that part of the cloth where the black mark is ; which we have already described as being in the shape of a diamond.

The tailleur immediately afterwards draws in the same manner another row of cards for the Rouge.

If he has counted thirty-six points in the first row of cards, he calls out, in a loud voice, to the players, six, to avoid the too frequent repetition of the word thirty, which would recur too often, but which is well understood ; and thirty-five points in the second row of cards, which he also announces in like manner by saying five. He adds, " Rouge gagne," red wins ; because it is always the thirty-one points, or those which more closely approach to them, that win. At that moment, the four tailleurs, who are placed opposite each other, gather by the aid of their rakes all the money which is placed on the Noir, and double all that placed on the Rouge, which is immediately withdrawn by the lucky players.

It now only remains to speak of the money placed on the chances, the Couleur and the Inverse. The first card drawn by the banker determines the couleur. If, then, the first card of the preceding cut drawn by the tailleur is Noir, as it is Rouge which gains, the couleur will lose.

The tailleurs have then a right to draw to the bank all the money which was placed upon the chance of the couleur, and double all the money which was placed upon the chance of the inverse.

To make this better understood, a contrary example may be cited ; that is to say, a case in which the Noir and the Couleur win. Let us suppose, that the tailleur turns up for the first row, the king of spades, ten of clubs, seven of diamonds, and four of spades, which count thirty-one, and which he expresses by one, pronounced in a loud voice ; and that he next turns up for the second row, the queen of clubs, nine of hearts, nine of spades, and five of diamonds, which count thirty-three, which he expresses by three. Noir wins ; since the tailleur has turned up in the first row of cards thirty-one ; and, as we have already observed :—

1st. That the first row of cards is for La Noir.

2nd. It is the chance of thirty-one, or the point which approaches the nearest to it, that wins.

The tailleur then cries out, "Rouge perd," red loses, and adds, " et Couleur gagne," and colour wins ; because the first card turned up is a king of spades, consequently black ; and in that case, the colour being black, the colour wins because black wins. If the first card had been the king of diamonds, the colour would have lost because it is the black which has won ; which the dealer would have expressed by saying, "Rouge perd et Couleur," the red and the colour loses.

When the dealer has turned up in the second row of cards, which is for the red, the same number he has turned up in the first row for the black, it is what is called un refait ; that is to say, that the cut is null, and that the dealer must again turn up other cards. The punter can in this case change his game by playing more, less, or not at all ; as he may think proper.

When the points turned up for the black and for the red are thirty-one, half of all the money which may be on the red, or the black, the colour, or the inverse, belongs to the banker, which half, the punters may either pay, or have their stake moved into the middle semicircles of the colour they then choose, called "la première prison," the first prison, to be determined by the next event, whether they lose all or are set at liberty; but if "un refait second trente et un," a second doublet of one-and thirty, should occur in the next succeeding deal, the punters lose only one-half of their remaining moiety, making three-fourths of their original stakes, and are removed into the smallest semicircle, styled "la seconde prison," the second prison, and the next coup determines whether the punter loses all or is to be removed again into "la premiere prison."

Thus if a player had at the first coup one hundred francs, by the first thirty-one turned up he would lose fifty; he has no more then in prison than fifty francs, after the first thirty-one; twenty-five francs, after the second; twelve francs and a half, after the third; and six francs and a quarter, after the fourth.

Happily for the player, it seldom happens, that thirty-one is three or four times successively repeated in favor of the banker.

Punters after winning may paroli, &c. and pursue their luck up to a soixante, as at faro; but as no livrets are used at Rouge et Noir, they cannot make either paix or pont.

At this game a banker cannot refuse any stake not exceeding his fund; which the punter declares, by saying, "Je va la Banque, Va la Banque, or Va Banque," I aim at the Bank.

Bankers generally furnish punters with slips of card paper, ruled in columns, each marked N or R at the top, on which accounts are kept by pricking with a pin, and when "un refait" happens, the same is denoted by running the pin through the middle line.

Some bankers give up the profit of "le refait" during the first deal.

The odds against "le refait" being dealt, are reckoned 63 to 1, but bankers expect it twice in three deals, and there are generally from 29 to 32 coups in each deal.

For the table exhibiting the odds against winning any number of events successively, vide page 340.

EXPLANATION OF THE TERMS USED AT ROUGE ET NOIR.

Banquier, or Tailleur—The dealer.

Fausse Taille—Occurs when the dealer commits a fault, which subjects him to double all the money staked.

To Martingale—Is to play one coup at least more than the stake previously lost. This is the boldest manner of playing at any of the games of chance.

Paroli—Is doubling the stake you have won at the preceding coup. A plan usually adopted by all players.

Paroli et masse en avant—Is double the sum staked the preceding coup, more than the player has risked. If the gamester has played five shillings the first time and has won the second coup, instead of taking up his money, he must add five shillings to his mass, which makes fifteen shillings, and which he risks the second coup: this is called " Faire Paroli et masse en avant." Perhaps this is the safest and best method of playing, especially for a novice. In pursuing this plan it is possible to win; and it is impossible to lose much, provided the first stake does not exceed a crown.

Refait de Trente et un—A coup by which the banquier wins one-half the money staked. It is effected by dealing thirty-one for each colour.

Refait—Occurs when the banquier deals the same sum for both colours, from thirty-two to forty.

Sept et le va—Seven times the amount first staked.

Taille—Is made every time the dealer has turned up all the cards.

Figure—The name given to the kings, queens, and knaves.

Point—The number which results from the sums of the cards dealt by the banquier.

Punter—Those who play against the banquier.

LA ROULETTE.

The table employed for the Roulette is somewhat in the shape of that used for the game of Rouge et Noir; it is of an oblong square form, covered with green cloth. In the centre is a round cavity usually made of mahogany, and resembling in some degree a punch-bowl. The sides are immovable, and around it are placed at equal distances several bands of copper, which commencing at the top descend to the extremity of the machine. In the centre of it, which is movable, a circular bottom is formed, containing thirty-eight holes, to which the copper bands just mentioned are attached, and upon which are painted, alternately, in black and red, thirty-six numbers, from one to thirty-six, a Zero (0), and a double Zero (00).

In the middle is a moulinet (mill) of copper, surmounted by a cross of the same metal, which serves to impress the movable bottom with the rotary motion that any one would wish to give it.

There is a banker, or rather many tailleurs who represent him : the number of players are not limited.

One of the tailleurs puts the machine in motion, by turning with his fore-finger the cross which surmounts it from right to left, thus impressing the bottom that contains the thirty-eight holes, which produces, as before stated, a rotary motion. At this instant, he throws an ivory ball into the concavity of the Roulette, in a direction opposite to the movement which he has given to the movable bottom. This ball moves in the interior with great velocity, making several revolutions; until at length from the feebleness of its motion, and after many irregular bounds, it falls into one of the thirty-eight holes, formed, as already stated, by the copper bands.

It is the hole into which the ball enters that determines the gain or the loss of the numerous chances which this game presents.

To the right and left of this machine are figured on the green cloth, for the accommodation of the players, the thirty-six numbers, and the Zeros, simple and double, in the following manner.

[See Diagram, page 349.]

The other chances are also designated on the green cloth, divergent from its centre, on one side " l'impair, la manque, et le rouge ;" on the other " le pair, le passe, et le noir.

The impair wins, when the ball enters a hole numbered impair. The manque wins, when the ball enters a hole numbered eighteen, and all those under that number. The rouge wins, when the ball enters a hole of which the number is red, and *vice versá*.

This game affords seven chances, comprising that of the

A Roulette Table.

numbers; and this latter chance divides itself into many others, of which we shall presently give a brief detail.

The player puts upon those chances of which he makes choice, any sum he pleases; that is to say, from two francs, the least stake admitted, to 12,000, the highest; unless in the like cases of which we have already spoken respecting the game of Rouge et Noir.

The player who puts his money on one of the numbers, or the Zeros painted on the green cloth (which is called plein), gains thirty-five times the amount of his stake, should the ball fall into the corresponding number, or Zero, marked in the interior of the roulette.

The gamester who plays on the numbers may play the twelve first, the twelve middle, and the last twelve. If the ball enters the hole in the interior, which corresponds with one of those twelve numbers marked on the green cloth, on which the player has put his money, he is paid three times the amount of his stake.

To play the Colonnes, the player places his money in the square, which is at the foot of each column marked on the green cloth. If the ball enters one of the holes corresponding with one of the numbers of the column, the player gains three times the amount of his stake.

He may equally, and at his pleasure, play two, three, four, six numbers, and he wins and loses always in the same proportion; eighteen times the stake for two numbers; twelve times the stake for three numbers; nine times the stake for four numbers; six times the stakes for six numbers; and the rest in the same proportion.

The player who may have put his money on one or the other of the six chances wins double his stake if the chance arrives. If, then, the ball enters a hole of which the number is thirty-six, and rouge, the banker pays double all the money which is placed on the following chances—la passe, le pair, and le rouge, and pays thirty-five times the amount of the sum which was placed on the number thirty-six, and draws to the bank all the money which was placed on the other chances.

If the ball should happen to enter the hole numbered seventeen, noir, the banker pays the player double the amount of the stakes which may have been placed on the following chances, la manque, l'impair, and la noire, and thirty-five times the amount of the stake played on number seventeen, and draws to the bank all the money that may have been placed on the other chances.

When the tailleur perceives that the ball has but a few seconds to roll, he cries out—" Le jeu est fait, rien ne va plus." After this the players cannot put any money on the table: should they do so, their money is taken up by a croupier and returned to them.

E. O.

An E O table is circular in form, but of no exact dimensions, though in general about four feet in diameter. The extreme circumference is a kind of counter, or depôt, for the stakes, marked all round with the letters E and O; on which each adventurer places money according to his inclination. The interior part of the table consists, first, of a kind of gallery, or rolling-place, for the ball, which, with the outward parts above, called depôt, or counter, is stationary or fixed. The most interior part moves upon an axis, or pivot, and is turned about with handles, whilst the ball is set in motion round the gallery. This part is generally divided into forty niches or interstices, twenty of which are marked with the letter E, and the other twenty with the letter O. The lodging of the ball in any of the niches distinguished by those letters, determines the wager. The proprietors of the tables have two bar-holes, and are obliged to take all bets offered, either for E or O; but if the ball falls into either of the bar-holes, they win all the bets upon the opposite letter, and do not pay to that in which it falls; an advantage in the proportion of 2 to 40, or 5 per cent. in their favor.*

* This very gambling game used to be extensively played some fifty or sixty years ago. One of Gillray's early caricatures represents an E O table in the act of being destroyed by the " Westminster Just-asses," as he denominates them.—*See Bohn's Gillray, plate 9.*

HAZARD.

THIS is exclusively a game of calculation and commerce; for it is one that cannot be played at all without considerable knowledge of the disposition and operation of the odds; and which is never played merely with a view to amusement. It is a " keen encounter of wit;" a forlorn hope for those who are rash enough to venture upon it without an ample understanding of its tactics, and a head cool and clear enough to conceive and conduct its combinations. Essentially an essay of demonstrations, calculations, and conclusions, dependant upon a logical adaptation of premises, it has especially been an incitement to the wildest schemes and chimeras, under the name of " systems," that ever laughed mathematics, causes, and consequences to scorn! Hazard is and has been longer, we may say, a standing game at all the houses of play in Great Britain, in the face of a fact,—as capable of proof, as the existence of those who read it here,—that between the amateur and professional player at such a passage of ready reckoning, the odds on a moderate average, are a hundred per cent. In spirit, if not to the letter, it is the arithmetic of dice. He who " throws in" a succession of mains, no doubt wins; but his success is the effect of accident: while he that secures the best of the odds by a mathematical application of the doctrine of chances to the main thrown, and the Caster's probabilities of throwing out or in, wins as a matter of course. It is true, that when seven is the main called, and six is the throw, seeing there are six ways of making seven, and but five of making six, the odds are 6 to 5 in favor of the Caster, and that most players know this, and such as this. But it is the faculty of reducing the effect of the fractions that draws the line,—the mighty demarcation between the professor and the pupil of Hazard.

In George Lowbut's preface to his " Game of Hazard investigated," a work we shall give almost in an entire state; he states that he selects the sum supposed to be staked for the purpose of avoiding the complication of fractions of odds. He says, " The calculations on the different mains, are made on a common stake between Caster and Setter of 36l. or 18l. deposited by each, as that sum from the number of chances on two dice (36) divides *with fewer fractions* than any smaller one. I have let many of the fractions remain unreduced, for the purpose of their showing at first sight, from whence they come: as for instance in the Caster's table of five, the main for the probability of his winning with 7, then put $\frac{6}{36}$ of $\frac{6}{10}$ to shew that the first fraction arises from the number of ways to throw 7 out of the number of all the ways the two dice can come. It is 6 out of 36. Whereas if it had been reduced to its lowest term, which is $\frac{1}{6}$, it might not be quite so clear to many whence it arose. And the same reason applies to the second fraction, which shows that there being ten ways for 7 and 5 to come, and six of those ways are for 7, therefore the probability of 7 coming before the 5 is $\frac{6}{10}$; but which reduced, is $\frac{3}{5}$; and so on with respect to many other fractions, but they are reduced at last into money, or the least odds they admit of. The class of readers whom this subject immediately concerns, the work I hope, will be found valuable, as, by a little reflection, it will remove all doubts concerning the difference between the expectations of Caster and Setter . . . . To those whose object may be mathematical research, it will introduce a branch of the doctrine of chance, and, as far as it goes, show the method of calculating the values of events depending thereon. The arithmetical part of the work, has repeatedly been revised, and the result likewise compared with other authors on the same subject, so as almost to do away with the possibility of an error." Thus having hinted at our own views of the subject, about being presented to the reader, and the fashion in which we propose dealing with it, the reader has but to imagine two boxes and a pair of dice as the properties, and the scene is drawn up for his learning.

It is first necessary, as being the foundation of all calculations on the Game of Hazard, to show the number of ways and different forms in which the chances on two dice can come up. These may clearly be seen in the following table:

2 ▲

Chances.		Number of Ways.		Form.
2	....	1	....	1 and 1
3	....	2	....	1 — 2 2 — 1
4	....	3	....	1 — 3 3 — 1 2 — 2
5	....	4	....	1 — 4 4 — 1 2 — 3 3 — 2
6	....	5	....	1 — 5 5 — 1 2 — 4 4 — 2 3 — 3
7	....	6	....	1 — 6 6 — 1 2 — 5 5 — 2 3 — 4 4 — 3
8	....	5	....	2 — 6 6 — 2 3 — 5 5 — 3 4 — 4
9	...	4	....	3 — 6 6 — 3 4 — 5 5 — 4
10	....	3	....	4 — 6 6 — 4 5 — 5
11	....	2	....	5 — 6 6 — 5
12	....	1	....	6 — 6

Total 36 Ways.

The foregoing table exhibits every form and the number of ways in which every chance on two dice can be produced.

The first column contains the chances or numbers to be thrown, the second the number of ways they may be produced, and the third the forms they may come in.—For example, to produce the chance 7 there are 6 ways, as follow: suppose the dice to be thrown out one at a time, the first die may be an ace and the second a 6—or the first may be a 6 and the second an ace; the first may be a deuce and the second a 5—or the first may be a 5 and the second a deuce.; the first may be a 3 and the second a 4—or the first may be a 4 and the second a 3, making together six different ways as shown in the table; this instance will explain the whole. It may further be seen that any two chances equally distant from the extremes (2 and 12) have an equal number of ways to happen, or any two chances making together the amount of the extremes (14) have an equal number of ways to happen. Thus 5 is the same distance from 2, as 9 from 12, and 5 added to 9, make 14,—also, 6 and 8, 4 and 10, 3 and 11, 2 and 12, are equal chances. This rule holds good let the number of dice be what they may. The odds between these chances connected in any other way, may also be found by referring to the column containing the number of ways for them to come. For example, there are six ways for 7 to come and five ways for 6, it is therefore 6 to 5 in favor of 7, &c. These cases being kept in mind, the calculations in this work will be more readily understood.

I shall now proceed to ascertain separately the Caster's and Setter's expectations on each main, in doing which I shall first estimate the value of every chance singly, and then placing them in one point of view, show their total amount, and the odds between those chances.

THE VALUE OF THE CASTER'S EXPECTATIONS OF WINNING. A STAKE OF 36*l*., WHEN FIVE IS THE MAIN.

First. If the Caster throw 5, he wins the stake, and as there are four ways out of thirty-six for that to happen, the value of his expectation must be four parts out of thirty-six of the stake, or $\frac{4}{36}$ of 36*l*., viz. 4*l*.

Secondly. If he throw 6, for which there are five ways,

2 A 2

his expectation by the same reasoning would be worth five parts out of thirty-six of the stake or 5l. provided he immediately won the stake by it, but he having then to throw the 6 again before the 5 to win it, and there being nine ways to throw the two chances 5 and 6, of which five are for 6, and four for 5, he is entitled to only five parts out of nine, or $\frac{5}{9}$ of 5l. that is $\frac{5}{9}$ of $\frac{5}{36}$ of 36l., or 2l. 15s. 6$\frac{3}{4}d$. as the value of his expectation on 6.

Or, if he throw 6, the value of his expectation on 6 against 5, will be worth five parts out of nine, or $\frac{5}{9}$ of the stake, that is 20l.; but as there are only five ways out of thirty-six, for getting into that situation, the value of his expectation of winning the stake with 6, is only $\frac{5}{36}$ of 20l. or 2l. 15s. 6$\frac{3}{4}d$. as before stated.

Another way of proving the preceding case is by betting. By which method the 2l. 15s. 6$\frac{3}{4}d$. will produce, including itself, 36l. as follows: first, I take the odds to the first sum, at the rate of 31 to 5 that the Caster throws 6 for his chance; this is 17l. 4s. 5$\frac{1}{4}d$. to 2l. 15s. 6$\frac{3}{4}d$. If the Caster throw the 6, I then have the amount of those sums, that is, 20l. I then bet 20l. *at the rate* or in the proportion of 5 to 4, which is 20 to 16 that the Caster throws the 6 before the 5, or that he wins. If he do so, I have then 20l. and 16l., making 36l. If he had failed in either event, I should have lost 2l. 15s. 6$\frac{3}{4}d$. which clearly proves that to be the sum which should be given for the Caster's expectation in this case.

So that it appears the Caster's expectation of winning with 6, here, is compounded of the probabilities of throwing that number for his chance or first after the main five is declared, and again before the 5, that is, $\frac{5}{36}$ of $\frac{5}{9}$ or $\frac{25}{324}$ of the stake to be thrown for. I have enlarged on this case by way of establishing a principle of calculating that applies to all cases where a second throw or chance is concerned. In this manner are the odds of winning two events independent of each other ascertained.

Thirdly. There being the same number of ways for the Caster throwing 8 as 6, the value of his expectation on that must be exactly the same, viz. 2l. 15s. 6$\frac{3}{4}d$.

Fourthly. If the Caster should throw 7, the probability of winning with 7 against 5, is 6 to 4, or $\frac{6}{10}$, there being six ways out of his thirty-six for throwing 7, the probability of that circumstance is $\frac{6}{36}$; consequently the value of his expectation of winning with 7, is $\frac{6}{36}$ of $\frac{6}{10}$ of 36l. or 3l. 12s.

Fifthly. If the Caster throw 9, for which there are four ways, the same as for 5, the probability of his winning will be equal to that of his losing, or $\frac{1}{2}$, the probability of throwing 9 being $\frac{4}{36}$, his expectation is $\frac{4}{36}$ of $\frac{1}{2}$ of 36l. or 2l.

Sixthly. If the Caster should throw 10, for which there are three ways, it will be 4 to 3 against his winning with 10 against 5, his expectation on that is $\frac{3}{7}$ of $\frac{3}{36}$ of 36l. or 1l. 5s. 8$\frac{1}{2}$$d$.

Seventhly. There being the same number of ways for 4 to be thrown, the value of the Caster's expectation on that must be the same, viz. 1l. 5s. 8$\frac{1}{2}$$d$.

Bringing together the preceding values of the Caster's expectations on the different chances by which he can win the stake, we shall find their total amount and comparative values.

Chances.	Probability of winning.		Value of the Caster's Expectation on 36l.		
5	....	$\frac{4}{36}$	£4	0s.	0d.
6	....	$\frac{5}{36}$ of $\frac{5}{9}$ or $\frac{25}{324}$	2	15	6$\frac{3}{4}$
8	....	The same $\frac{25}{324}$	2	15	6$\frac{3}{4}$
7	....	$\frac{6}{36}$ of $\frac{6}{10}$ or $\frac{1}{10}$	3	12	0
9	....	$\frac{4}{36}$ of $\frac{1}{2}$ or $\frac{1}{18}$	2	0	0
10	....	$\frac{3}{36}$ of $\frac{3}{7}$ or $\frac{1}{28}$	1	5	8$\frac{1}{2}$
4	....	The same $\frac{1}{28}$	1	5	8$\frac{1}{2}$
			£17	14	6$\frac{1}{2}$

The sum of the fractions is $\frac{1396}{2835}$ which part of 36l. is equal to 17l. 14s. 6$\frac{1}{2}$$d$. and deducting this from 18l., what the Caster's share would be worth on equal terms, there proves to be a loss to him of 5s. 5$\frac{1}{2}$$d$. which, out of 18$l$., is equivalent to 3$\frac{3}{4}$$d$. and $\frac{1}{3}$ of a farthing out of 1 guinea and to 3$\frac{1}{2}$$d$. and $\frac{1}{2}$ of a farthing out of every 1l., staked by the Caster.

By comparing the values of the different chances, the odds between them, previous to the Caster's chance being thrown, may be readily found; but it must be particularly attended to, that those odds relate only to the expectation that one of the chances in question may happen to be the Caster's chance, that is, being thrown first after the main is declared or determined on.—After the main and chance are fixed or ascertained, the odds between them must be precisely as appear in the table in the second page.—But in this instance, that is, as soon as five is declared to be the main, it is 4*l*. to 2*l*. 15*s*. 6¾*d*. that the Caster nicks or wins by throwing five, against his having 6 for his chance and winning with that.—It is 4*l*. to 2*l*. or 2 to 1 on his nicking against having nine, for his chance and winning.—It is 3*l*. 12*s*. to 1*l*. 5*s*. 8½*d*. that the Caster wins with 7 for his chance against 10, or that he has 7 for his chance and wins against having 10 for his chance and winning with that.—It is 3*l*. 12*s*. to 2*l*. his winning with 7 against his winning with 9,—Also it is 32*l*. to 4*l*. or 8 to 1 the Caster does not nick 5.—32*l*. 8*s*. to 3*l*. 12*s*. or 9 to 1 he has not 7 for his chance and win with it.   It is 34*l*. to 2*l*. or 17 to 1 he has not not 9 and win, and 34*l*. 14*s*. 3½*d*. to 1*l*. 5*s*. 8½*d*. or 27 to 1 he has not 10 for his chance and wins with it.   By adding together the values of the expectations on any two or more chances there may be found, the odds of winning with one of them.—Thus, if five is the main, what are the odds that the Caster has 6 or 7 for his chance and throws in or wins with it. In the last table I find the value of the expectation on 6 to be 2*l*. 15*s*. 6¾*d*. and on 7, 3*l*. 12*s*., these together make 6*l*. 7*s*. 6¾*d*. deducting this sum from 36*l*. (the stake here calculated on) there remains 29*l*. 12*s*. 5¼*d*. which sum it is to the 6*l*. 7*s*. 6¾*d*. or 4*l*. 12*s*. 10½*d*. to 1*l*., that is, rather more than 4 and a ½ to 1 that the Caster has not 6 nor 7 for his chance and throw in, when five is the main.—Adding together the fractions in this table produces one ($\frac{1396}{2835}$) which shews the probability of the Caster winning one main, and multiplying that by itself, we get another which shews the probability of his winning two successively, and by multiplying this last by the first, we find the probability of his winning three successive mains, and so on for any number; thus $\frac{1396}{2835}$ multiplied by $\frac{1396}{2835}$ produces $\frac{1948816}{8037225}$ the Caster's probability of winning twice successively, this reduced to money is 3*l*. 2*s*. 6*d*. to 1 or 25*l*. to 8 the Caster does not throw in twice following when five is the

main. Multiplying this last fraction $\frac{1948816}{8037225}$ by $\frac{1396}{2835}$ produces $\frac{2720547136}{22785532875}$ this is 7*l.* 7*s.* 6*d.* to 1*l.* or 59 to 8 that the Caster does not win three successive mains when five is the main.

THE VALUE OF THE SETTER'S EXPECTATIONS ON A STAKE OF 36*l.*, WHEN FIVE IS THE MAIN.

By way of further proof of the preceding, I shall now estimate the value of the Setter's expectations on the same main and stake; and having already enlarged so far on the method of ascertaining the probabilities and value of the different chances, it will be requisite here only to state them, with very little or no further explanation.

First. If the Caster throw 2, 3, 11 or 12, next after the main is declared, the Setter wins the stake, and as there are six ways for those four chances to come, the Setter's expectations on that must be worth $\frac{6}{36}$ of 36*l.* viz. 6*l.*

Secondly. If the Caster throw 6, as he will then have 6 for his chance against 5 (the main) it will be 5 to 4 in his favor, consequently the Setter's share of the stake will be then only $\frac{4}{9}$ and the value of his expectation on that is $\frac{5}{36}$ of $\frac{4}{9}$ of 36*l.* viz. 2*l.* 4*s.* $5\frac{1}{4}d.$

Thirdly. The value of the Setter's expectation on the Caster having 8 for his chance must be the same as on 6 viz. 2*l.* 4*s.* $5\frac{1}{4}d.$

Fourthly. If the Caster throw 7, the Setter's share of the stake will be $\frac{4}{10}$ the value of his expectation on which is $\frac{6}{36}$ of $\frac{4}{10}$ of 36*l.* viz. 2*l.* 8*s.*

Fifthly. If the Caster throw 9, the Setter's share of the stake will then be $\frac{1}{2}$, or equal to the Caster's, and the value of his expectation on that is $\frac{4}{36}$ of $\frac{1}{2}$ of 36*l.* viz. 2*l.*

Sixthly. If the Caster throw 10, the Setter's share will be $\frac{4}{7}$, the value of his expectation on that is $\frac{3}{36}$ of $\frac{4}{7}$ of 36*l.* viz. 1*l.* 14*s.* $3\frac{1}{2}d.$

Seventhly. The value of the Setter's expectation on 4 must be the same as on 10, viz. 1*l.* 14*s.* $3\frac{1}{2}d.$

Bringing together these probabilities and values, we find the amount of the Setter's expectations and comparative values of the different chances.

Chances.		Probability of winning.		Value of the Setter's Expectation on 36*l.*		
2, 3, 11, 12	....	$\frac{6}{36}$	....	£6	0s.	0d.
6	....	$\frac{5}{36}$ of $\frac{4}{9}$ or $\frac{5}{81}$	....	2	4	$5\frac{1}{4}$
8	....	The same $\frac{5}{81}$	....	2	4	$5\frac{1}{4}$
7	....	$\frac{6}{36}$ of $\frac{4}{10}$ or $\frac{1}{15}$	....	2	8	0
9	....	$\frac{4}{36}$ of $\frac{1}{2}$ or $\frac{1}{18}$	....	2	0	0
10	....	$\frac{3}{36}$ of $\frac{4}{7}$ or $\frac{1}{21}$	....	1	14	$3\frac{1}{2}$
4	....	The same $\frac{1}{21}$	....	1	14	$3\frac{1}{2}$
				£18	5	$5\frac{1}{2}$

The sum of the fractions in the last table is $\frac{1439}{2835}$ which part of 36*l.* is 18*l.* 5*s.* 5½*d.* being a gain to the Setter on 18*l.* of 5*s.* 5½*d.* equal to the loss of the Caster as shewn in his table. By comparing the values of the chances in the two tables, it will be found to be 6 to 4, the Caster crabs by throwing 2, 3, 11 or 12, against his nicking by throwing 5, and adding together the 6 and 4, shows it to be 10 parts out of 36, or 26 to 10, or 13 to 5, that the Caster does neither.

In like manner may all the comparative and joint values of the chances be found.

That the Caster do not throw out or the Setter win twice following is found as before, by multiplying the fraction expressing the amount of the Setter's expectation by itself, that is $\frac{1439}{2835}$ by $\frac{1439}{2835}$, which makes $\frac{2070721}{8037225}$, or 89 to 31, and brought into money, is 2*l.* 17*s.* 5¾*d.* to 1*l.*, or 1*l.* to 6*s.* 11½*d.*

That the Caster do not throw out three times successively is $\frac{2070721}{8037225}$, multiplied by $\frac{1439}{2835}$, that is $\frac{2979767519}{22785532875}$, or 6*l.* 12*s.* 11¼*d.* to 1*l.*, nearly 133 to 20,—a little more than 6⅝ to 1.

By comparing the fractions expressing the probability of the Caster winning the stake $\left(\frac{1396}{2835}\right)$ with that of the Setter's $\left(\frac{1439}{2835}\right)$ it is found to be 1439 to 1396 or 1*l.* to 19*s.* 4¾*d.*, in favor of the Setter. And by comparing the fraction expressing the Caster's probability of throwing in twice successively with that of his throwing out twice, it appears to be 2070721 to 1948816, or 1*l.* 1*s.* 3*d.* to 1*l.* in favor of the latter circumstance. And by the same method we find the odds of throwing in three times successively to those of throwing out the same number of times, is as 2979767519 to 2720547136, or 1*l.* to 1*l.* 1*s.* 10¾*d.* By adding the fraction expressing the probability of the Caster throwing out twice successively to that of his throwing in twice, we get one which shews the probability of his doing either, that is $\frac{4019537}{8037225}$, or 4019537 to 4017688, or 18*l.* 0*s.* 1*d.* to 17*l.* 19*s.* 11*d.* that the Caster does either throw in or out twice successively. By the like method we find the odds that the Caster does not throw in nor out three times successively, to be $\frac{5700314655}{22785532875}$ or 17085218220 to 5700314655, or 26½*l.* 19*s.* 10½*d.* to 9*s.* 0*s* 1½*d.*

The whole of the calculation on Five applies to Nine, when that is the main. I shall therefore proceed to Six.

THE VALUE OF THE CASTER'S EXPECTATIONS OF WINNING A STAKE OF 36*l.*, WHEN SIX IS THE MAIN.

First. If the Caster should throw either 6 or 12, he wins the stake, for which two chances, there being 6 ways out of 36, his expectation must be worth $\frac{6}{36}$ of 36*l.*, viz. 6*l.*

Secondly. Should the Caster throw 5, his share of the stake will be worth $\frac{4}{9}$ of it, and the value of his expectation on that is $\frac{4}{36}$ of $\frac{4}{9}$ of 36*l.*, viz. 1*l.* 15*s.* 6¾*d.*

Thirdly. The value of the Caster's expectation on Nine, is the same as on Five, viz. 1*l.* 15*s.* 6¾*d.*

Fourthly. If the Caster throw 7, his share of the stake will then be worth $\frac{6}{11}$ of it, and the value of his expectation on that is $\frac{6}{36}$ of $\frac{6}{11}$ of 36*l.* viz. 3*l.* 5*s.* 5½*d.*

Fifthly. If the Caster throw 8, his share of the stake will be worth ½, the value of his expectation on that is $\frac{5}{36}$ of ½ of 36*l* viz. 2*l.* 10*s.*

Sixthly. If the Caster throw 10, his share of the stake will be worth $\frac{3}{8}$ of it, the value of his expectation on that is $\frac{3}{36}$ of $\frac{3}{8}$ of 36*l.* viz. 1*l.* 2*s.* 6*d.*

Seventhly. The value of the Caster's expectation on 4 is the same as on 10, viz. 1*l.* 2*s.* 6*d.*

The amount of the preceding probabilities and values of the Caster's expectation when 6 is the main, is, as in the following table.

Chances.		Probability of winning.		Value of the Caster's Expectation on 36l.		
6, 12	....	$\frac{6}{36}$	....	£6	0s.	0d.
5	....	$\frac{4}{36}$ of $\frac{4}{9}$ or $\frac{4}{81}$	....	1	15	6¾
9	....	The same $\frac{4}{81}$	....	1	15	6¾
7	....	$\frac{6}{36}$ of $\frac{6}{11}$ or $\frac{1}{11}$	....	3	5	5½
8	....	$\frac{5}{36}$ of $\frac{1}{2}$ or $\frac{5}{72}$	....	2	10	0
10	....	$\frac{3}{36}$ of $\frac{3}{8}$ or $\frac{1}{32}$	....	1	2	6
4	....	The same $\frac{1}{32}$	....	1	2	6
				£17	11	7

The sum of the fraction in the last table is $\frac{6961}{14256}$ which part of 36l. is equal to 17l. 11s. 7d. (within $\frac{7}{10}$ of a farthing) and deducting this from 18l. proves the loss of the Caster to be 8s. 5d. out of 18l. which is equal to 5½d. and nearly one-half of a farthing out of 1l.—And to 5¾d. and nearly one-fourth of a farthing out of 1 guinea.

By this table is shewn, that previous to the chance being thrown, the probability of the Caster nicking or throwing 6 or 12, is 6 out of 36, that is, 5 to 1 against him.—That it is 6l. to 3l. 11s. 1d. nearly 12 to 7 the Caster nicks against winning with 5 or 9 for his chance.—That it is 6l. to 3l. 5s. 5½d. nearly 24 to 13 the Caster nicks against winning with 7.—That it is 3l. 5s. 5½d. to 1l. 2s. 6d. rather more than 26 to 9, the Caster has 7 for his chance, and wins against his having 10 for his chance and winning with that, &c.

That the Caster does not throw in twice successively when 6 is the main. is $\frac{6961}{14256}$ multiplied by $\frac{6961}{14256}$ that is $\frac{48455521}{203233536}$ or 3l. 3s. 10½d. to 1l.

That the Caster does not throw in three times successively is $\frac{48455521}{203233536}$ multiplied by $\frac{6961}{14256}$ that is $\frac{337298881681}{2897297289216}$ or 7l. 11s. 9½d. to 1l.

THE VALUE OF THE SETTER'S EXPECTATION OF WINNING A STAKE OF £36, WHEN SIX IS THE MAIN.

First. If the Caster should throw 2, 3, or 11, for which there are five ways out of 36, the setter wins the stake, the value of his expectation therefore on that is $\frac{5}{36}$ of 36l. viz. 5l.

Secondly. If the Caster throw 5, the Setter's share of the stake will be $\frac{5}{9}$, and the value of his expectation on that is $\frac{4}{36}$ of $\frac{5}{9}$ of 36l. viz. 2l. 4s. 5$\frac{1}{4}d$.

Thirdly. The value of the Setter's expectation on 9 is the same as on 5, viz. 2l. 4s. 5$\frac{1}{4}d$.

Fourthly. If the Caster throw 8, the Setter's share of the stake will be $\frac{1}{2}$, and the value of his expectation on that is $\frac{5}{36}$ of $\frac{1}{2}$ of 36l. viz. 2l. 10s.

Fifthly. If the Caster throw 7, the Setter's share of the stake will be $\frac{5}{11}$, the value of his expectation on that is $\frac{6}{36}$ of $\frac{5}{11}$ of 36l. viz. 2l. 14s. 6$\frac{1}{2}d$.

Sixthly. If the Caster throw 10, the Setter's share of the stake will be $\frac{5}{8}$, the value of his expectation on that is $\frac{3}{36}$ of $\frac{5}{8}$ of 36l. viz. 1l. 17s. 6d.

Seventhly. The value of the Setter's expectation on 4 is the same as on 10, viz. 1l. 17s.6d.

The amount of the preceding probabilities and values of the setter's expectations on 36l. when 6 is the main.

Chances.		Probability of winning.		Value of the Setter's Expectation on 36l.
2, 3, 11	....	$\frac{5}{36}$	....	£5 0s. 0d.
5	....	$\frac{4}{36}$ of $\frac{5}{9}$ or $\frac{5}{81}$	....	2 4 5$\frac{1}{4}$
9	....	The same $\frac{5}{81}$	....	2 4 5$\frac{1}{4}$
8	....	$\frac{5}{36}$ of $\frac{1}{2}$ or $\frac{5}{72}$	....	2 10 0
7	....	$\frac{6}{36}$ of $\frac{5}{11}$ or $\frac{5}{66}$	....	2 14 6$\frac{1}{2}$
10	....	$\frac{3}{36}$ of $\frac{5}{8}$ or $\frac{5}{96}$	....	1 17 6
4	....	The same $\frac{5}{96}$	....	1 17 6
				£18 8 5

The amount of the fraction in this table is $\frac{7295}{14256}$, which part of 36l. is equal to 18l. 8s. 5d. leaving a surplus or advantage to the Setter of 8s. 5d. on 18l. answering on this and the other sums to what is stated in the Caster's table.

In this table may be seen that it is 31 to 5 the Caster does not throw out by crabbing, that is, by throwing 2, 3, or 11.— And, by comparing it with the Caster's table, will appear that it is 6 to 5 he nicks against crabbing; by adding together these probabilities it is found to be (they making but 11 chances out of 36) 25 to 11 the Caster does neither.

That the Caster does not throw out twice following, is $2l.$ 16$s.$ 4$d.$ to 1$l.$

That the Caster does not throw out three times following is 6$l.$ 9$s.$ 3$d.$ to 1$l.$

That the Caster throws out any one time against throwing in on this main, is 7295 to 6961, or as 1$l.$ to 19$s.$ 1$d.$

That the Caster throws out twice following against throwing in twice following, is 1$l.$ to 18$s.$ $2\frac{1}{2}d.$

That the Caster throws out three times following against throwing in three times following, is 1$l.$ to 17$s.$ $4\frac{1}{6}d.$

That the Caster does throw in or out twice following is 18$l.$ 0$s.$ $2\frac{1}{4}d.$ to 17$l.$ 19$s.$ $9\frac{3}{4}d.$

That the Caster neither throws in or out three times following is 26$l.$ 19$s.$ $8\frac{1}{2}d.$ to 9$l.$ 0$s.$ $3\frac{1}{2}d.$

The same calculations applying to the main of Eight as to Six. I shall proceed to Seven.

THE VALUE OF THE CASTER'S EXPECTATIONS OF WINNING A STAKE OF 36$l.$ WHEN SEVEN IS THE MAIN.

First. If the Caster throw 7 or 11, for which there are 8 ways, he wins the stake, the value of his expectation on that is therefore $\frac{8}{36}$ of 36$l.$, viz 8$l.$

Secondly. If the Caster throw 6, his share of the stake will then be $\frac{5}{11}$ of it, and the value of his expectation on that is $\frac{5}{36}$ of $\frac{5}{11}$ of 36., viz. 2$l.$ 5$s.$ $5\frac{1}{2}d.$

Thirdly. The value of the Caster's expectation on 8, is the same as on 6, viz. 2$l.$ 5$s.$ $5\frac{1}{2}$d.

Fourthly. If the Caster throw 9, his share of the stake will be $\frac{4}{10}$ of it and the value of his expectation on that is $\frac{4}{36}$ of $\frac{4}{10}$ of 36l, viz 1$l.$ 12$s.$

Fifthly. The value of the Caster's expectation on 5 is the same as on 9, viz. 1$l.$ 12$s.$

Sixthly. If the Caster throw 10, his share of the stake will be $\frac{1}{3}$ of it, and the value of his expectation on that is $\frac{3}{36}$ of $\frac{1}{3}$ of 36$l.$, viz. 1$l.$

Seventhly. The value of the Caster's expectation on 4 is the same as on 10, viz. 1$l.$

The amount of the preceding probabilities and values of the Caster's expectations, when 7 is the main.

Chances.		Probability of winning.		Value of the Caster's Expectation on 36l.		
7 or 11	....	$\frac{8}{36}$	....	£8	0s.	0d.
6	....	$\frac{5}{36}$ of $\frac{5}{11}$ or $\frac{25}{396}$	....	2	5	$5\frac{1}{2}$
8	....	The same $\frac{25}{396}$	....	2	5	$5\frac{1}{2}$
9	....	$\frac{4}{36}$ of $\frac{4}{10}$ or $\frac{2}{45}$	....	1	12	0
5	....	The same $\frac{2}{45}$	....	1	12	0
10	....	$\frac{3}{36}$ of $\frac{1}{3}$ or $\frac{1}{36}$	....	1	0	0
4	....	The same $\frac{1}{36}$	....	1	0	0
				£17	14	11

The sum of the fractions in this table is $\frac{244}{495}$, which part of **36**l. is 17l. 14s. 11d. deducting this from 18l., proves the loss of the Caster to be 5s. 1d. out of 18l., which is equal to $3\frac{1}{4}d$. and $\frac{1}{2}$ a farthing out of 1l.—And to $3\frac{1}{2}d$. and $\frac{1}{4}$ of a farthing out of 1 guinea.

By this table is shewn that it is 28 to 8, or 7 to 2 the Caster does not nick 7—That it is 8 to 1 he nicks against winning with 10, and the same against 4, &c. &c.—That the Caster does not throw in twice following, is 3l. 2s. $3\frac{3}{4}d$. to 1l.—That he does not throw in three times following, is 7l. 6s. $11\frac{3}{4}d$. to 1l.

THE VALUE OF THE SETTER'S EXPECTATIONS OF WINNING
A STAKE OF 36l., WHEN SEVEN IS THE MAIN.

First. If the Caster should throw 2, 3, or 12, for which there are 4 ways. the Setter wins the stake; the value of his expectation therefore on that is $\frac{4}{36}$ of 36l., viz. 4l.

Secondly. If the Caster throw 6, the Setter's share of the stake will be $\frac{6}{11}$ of it, and the value of his expectation on that is $\frac{5}{36}$ of $\frac{6}{11}$ of 36l., viz. 2l. 14s. $6\frac{1}{2}d$.

Thirdly. The value of the Setter's expectation on 8 is the same as on 6, viz. 2l. 14s. $6\frac{1}{2}d$.

Fourthly. If the Caster throw 9, the Setter's share of the

stake will be worth $\frac{6}{10}$ of it, and the value of his expectation on that is $\frac{4}{36}$ of $\frac{6}{10}$ of 36l., viz. 2l. 8s.

Fifthly. The value of the Setter's expectation on 5 is the same as on 9, viz. 2l. 8s.

Sixthly. If the Caster thow 10, the Setter's share of the stake will be $\frac{2}{3}$ of it, and the value of his expectation on that is $\frac{3}{36}$ of $\frac{2}{3}$ of 36l., viz. 2l.

Seventhly. The value of the Setter's expectation on 4 is the same as on 10, viz. 2l.

The amount of the preceding probabilities and values of the Setter's expectations.

Chances.		Probability of winning		Value of the Setter's Expectation on 36l.
2, 3, 12	....	$\frac{4}{36}$	....	£4 0s. 0d
6	....	$\frac{5}{36}$ of $\frac{6}{11}$ or $\frac{5}{66}$	....	2 14 6$\frac{1}{4}$
8	....	The same $\frac{5}{66}$	....	2 14 6$\frac{1}{4}$
9	....	$\frac{4}{36}$ of $\frac{6}{10}$ or $\frac{1}{15}$	....	2 8 0
5	....	The same $\frac{1}{15}$	....	2 8 0
10	....	$\frac{3}{36}$ of $\frac{2}{3}$ or $\frac{1}{18}$	....	2 0 0
4	....	The same $\frac{1}{18}$	....	2 0 0
				£18 5 1

The sum of the fractions in this last table is $\frac{251}{495}$, which part of 36l. is 18l. 5s. 1d, being a gain to the Setter of 5s. 1d. on 18l., which is equal to the loss of the Caster, as shewn in his table. It also shews that it is 32 to 4 or 8 to 1 against the Caster's crabbing, and comparing that with the probability of nicking, it is 8 to 4 or 2 to 1 on a nick against a crab, and 24 to 12 or 2 to 1 that the Caster does neither. It is an equal probability that the Setter wins by the Caster's having 10 or 4 for his chance, with that of his winning by the Caster crabbing; the value of the Setter's expectation on 10 and 4 being 4l., and that on 2, 3, and 12, the same.

It is also an equal probability that the Caster loses by crabbing, or by having 10 or 4 for his chance, with that of nicking. And it is 2l. 8s. to 2l., or 6 to 5, the Caster loses by having 5 or 9 for his chance against losing by having 10 or 4.—&c.

The fraction expressing the sum of the Caster's probabilities of winning being $\frac{244}{495}$, and that expressing the Setter's being $\frac{251}{495}$, shews it to be 251 to 244 that the Caster throws out any one time, when 7 is the main.

That the Caster does not throw out twice following, is $2l$. $17s$. $9\frac{1}{4}d$. to $1l$.

That the Caster does not throw out three times following, is $6l$. $13s$. $4\frac{3}{4}d$. to $1l$.

That the Caster throws either in or out twice following, is $18l$. $0s$. $0\frac{3}{4}d$. to $17l$. $19s$. $11\frac{1}{4}d$.

That the Caster throws neither in nor out three times following, is $26l$. $19s$. $10\frac{3}{4}d$. to $9l$. $0s$. $1\frac{1}{4}d$.

That the Setter wins twice following against the Caster's doing so, is $1l$. to $18s$. $10\frac{3}{4}d$.

That the Setter wins three times following against the Caster's doing so, is $1l$. to $18s$. $4\frac{1}{2}d$.

Having gone through the mains of 5, 6, and 7, which calculations include also those of 8 and 9, I shall now proceed to estimate in like manner the values of the Caster's and Setter's expectations on a casual main, or that which may happen to be first thrown. In order to this we must suppose there to be only 5 chances on the two dice and 24 ways for them to come up, which is the number of ways the five different mains 5, 6, 7, 8 and 9 can come, as may be seen in the table, page 2; now out of these 24 ways, there are, first, four ways for 5 to be the main, the probability of that happening is therefore $\frac{4}{24}$, and the value of the Caster's expectations on a stake of $36l.$, when 5 is the main, has been shewn to be $\frac{1396}{2835}$ of $36l.$, or $17l$. $14s$. $6\frac{1}{2}d$. and $\frac{4}{24}$ or $\frac{1}{6}$ of that is $2l$. $19s$. $1d$. which last sum is the value of the Caster's expectation on 5 being the main.

Secondly. The value of his expectations on 9 must be the same as on 5, viz. $2l$. $19s$. $1d$.

Thirdly. There being 5 ways out of the 24 for the main to be 6, the probability of that happening is $\frac{5}{24}$, and the Caster's share, should that happen, being $\frac{6061}{14256}$ of $36l.$, or $17l$. $11s$. $7d$. $\frac{5}{24}$ of that or $3l$. $13s$. $3d$. is the value of the Caster's expectation on 6 being the main.

Fourthly. The value of the Caster's expectation on 8, must be the same as on 6, viz. $3l$. $13s$. $3d$.

Fifthly. There being 6 ways out of 24 for 7 to be the

main, the probability of that happening is $\frac{6}{24}$, and the Caster's share of the stake, should that happen, will be $\frac{244}{495}$ of 36l., or 17l. 14s. 11d., $\frac{6}{24}$ or $\frac{1}{4}$ of that sum, or 4l. 8s. 8$\frac{3}{4}d$. is the value of the Caster's expectation on 7 being the main. Now adding together the preceding values of his chances of winning with every main, we find the exact value of his share of the stake.

Mains.		Probability of winning.		Value of the Caster's Expectation on £36.		
5	....	$\frac{4}{24}$ of $\frac{1396}{2835}$ or $\frac{698}{8505}$	....	£2	19s.	1d.
9	....	The same $\frac{698}{8505}$	....	2	19	1
6	....	$\frac{5}{24}$ of $\frac{6961}{14256}$ or $\frac{34805}{342144}$	....	3	13	3
8	....	The same $\frac{34805}{342144}$	....	3	13	3
7	....	$\frac{6}{24}$ of $\frac{244}{495}$ or $\frac{61}{495}$	....	4	8	8$\frac{3}{4}$

$$£17 \quad 13 \quad 4\tfrac{3}{4}$$

The sum of the fractions is $\frac{1979}{4032}$, which part of 36l., is 17l. 13s. 4$\frac{3}{4}d$. being a loss to the Caster of 6s. 7$\frac{1}{4}d$. out of 18l., which is equal to 4$\frac{1}{4}d$. and $\frac{3}{5}$ of a farthing out of 1l., and to 4$\frac{1}{2}d$. and $\frac{1}{2}$ of a farthing out of 1 guinea, or $\frac{37}{2016}$ of any sum staked by the Caster.

By this table it appears to be before any main is thrown, 33l. 0s. 11d. to 2l. 19s. 1d. or very near 11l. 4s. 0d. to 1l., the Caster has not 5 for a main and wins with it.

That he has not 6 for a main and wins with it, is 32l. 6s. 9d. to 3l. 13s. 3d. or nearly 8l. 16s. 7d. to 1l.

That he has not 7 for a main and win, is 31l. 11s. 3$\frac{1}{4}d$. to 4l. 8s. 8$\frac{3}{4}d$., or nearly 7l. 2s. 3d. to 1l.

That he has 7 and wins against his having 5 and winning, is as 4l. 8s. 8$\frac{3}{4}d$. to 2l. 19s. 3d.

Here it may not be amiss to remark on the difference between the values of the Caster's expectations on an exact calculation and the common supposition of an equality between Caster and Setter; in this latter case the value of the Caster's expectations of winning with 6, would be $\frac{5}{24}$ of $\frac{1}{2}$ of 36l., or 3l. 15s. 0d. making it only 8l. 12s. 0d. to 1l. instead of as above 8l. 16s. 7d. to 1l. And of course in proportion on all the other mains.

That the Caster does not win twice following is 3l. 3s. 0d. to 1l.

That the Caster does not win 3 times following, is 7l. 9s. 1$\frac{3}{4}d$. to 1l.

THE VALUE OF THE SETTER'S EXPECTATIONS OF WINNING A STAKE OF 36l. WHEN THAT IS TO BE THE MAIN WHICH MAY BE FIRST THROWN.

First. Should the Caster throw 5, the Setter's share of the stake will be $\frac{1439}{2835}$, consequently the value of his expectation on that is $\frac{4}{24}$ of $\frac{1439}{2835}$ of 36l., viz. 3l. 0s. 11d.

Secondly. The value of the Setter's expectation on 9, must be the same as on 5, viz. 3l. 0s. 11d.

Thirdly. Should the Caster throw 6, the Setter's share of the stake will be $\frac{7295}{14256}$; the value of his expectation on that is $\frac{5}{24}$ of $\frac{7295}{14256}$ of 36l., viz. 3l. 16s. 9d.

Fourthly. The value of the Setter's expectation on 8, is the same as on 6, viz. 3l. 16s. 9d.

Fifthly, Should the Caster throw 7, the Setter's share of the stake will be $\frac{251}{495}$, and the value of his expectation on that is $\frac{6}{24}$ of $\frac{251}{495}$ of 36l., viz. 4l. 11s. 3$\frac{1}{4}d$.

The amount of the preceding probabilities and values of the Setter's expectation.

Mains.	Probability of Winning.	Value of the Setter's Expectations on £36.		
		£	s.	d.
5	$\frac{4}{24}$ of $\frac{1439}{2835}$ or $\frac{1439}{17010}$	3	0	11
9	The same $\frac{1439}{17010}$	3	0	11
6	$\frac{5}{24}$ of $\frac{7295}{14256}$ or $\frac{36475}{342144}$	3	16	9
8	The same $\frac{36475}{342144}$	3	16	9
7	$\frac{6}{24}$ of $\frac{251}{495}$ or $\frac{251}{1980}$	4	11	3$\frac{1}{4}$
		£18	6	7$\frac{1}{4}$

The amount of the fractions in this last table is $\frac{248413}{487872}$, which part of 36l., is 18l. 6s. 7$\frac{1}{4}d$., making the advantage of the Setter, equal to the disadvantage of the Caster as before

2 B

shewn. Comparing the fractions expressing the amount of the Caster's probabilities with that of the Setter, it will be seen to be 248,413 to 239,459, or 111 to 107 nearly in favor of the Setter before the main is thrown.

That the Caster does not throw out twice following, is $2l.$ $17s.$ $1\frac{3}{4}d.$ to $1l.$

That the Caster does not throw out three times following, is $6l.$ $11s.$ $6d.$ to $1l.$

That the Caster or Setter wins twice following, is $18l.$ $0s.$ $1\frac{1}{4}d.$ to $17l.$ $19s.$ $10\frac{1}{2}d.$

That neither Caster nor Setter wins three times following, is $26l.$ $19s.$ $9\frac{3}{4}d.$ to $9l.$ $0s.$ $2\frac{1}{4}d.$

The Setter's winning twice following against the Caster's doing so, is $1l.$ to $18s.$ $7d.$

The Setter's winning three times following against the Caster's doing so, is $1l.$ to $18s.$ $0\frac{3}{4}d.$

TO PLACE THE CASTER AND SETTER ON AN EQUALITY.

Having shewn the difference between the Caster and Setter's expectations on every main, it will now be proper to ascertain how they may play with little or no disadvantage on either side.

Suppose the Caster takes 7 for a main, the advantage of the Setter on that main is $\frac{7}{495}$, being the difference between $\frac{251}{495}$ the Setter's expectation, and $\frac{244}{495}$ that of the Caster, which is nearly $\frac{1}{70}$ of the money staked by each. Now returning the Caster half of his stake upon the event of a chance or number being thrown, that has but one way out of 36 to come up, will be taking off $\frac{1}{2}$ of $\frac{1}{36}$, that is $\frac{1}{72}$ from the $\frac{7}{495}$, there will then remain $\frac{1}{3960}$ only in favor of the Setter, which is not quite $\frac{1}{4}$ of a farthing in $1l.$ Therefore if it be agreed between the Caster and Setter that should the Caster lose by throwing ames ace, (2 aces) he shall have half of what he staked returned, he would then play at only the above trifling disadvantage. But to find what part of the Caster's stake should be returned to place him exactly on equal terms with the Setter, we must divide $\frac{7}{495}$ by $\frac{1}{36}$, which will give a fraction that being multiplied by $\frac{1}{36}$, will produce $\frac{7}{495}$, the exact difference between the Caster and Setter; and that is $\frac{28}{55}$, for $\frac{28}{55}$ of $\frac{1}{36}$ is equal to $\frac{7}{495}$, therefore if it be agreed that in case the

Caster throws out with ames ace, he is to receive back $\frac{28}{55}$ of his own stake, that is 28l. out of 55l., or 9l. 3s. 3$\frac{1}{4}$$d$. out of 18$l$., or 10$s$. 2$\frac{1}{4}$$d$. out of 1$l$., he will then play on an equality with the Setter. If the main is 6 or 8, the advantage of the Setter will be $\frac{167}{7128}$, and if that is divided by $\frac{1}{36}$, it will give $\frac{167}{198}$, which is equal to 167l. out of 198l. staked by the Caster, or 15l. 3s. 7$\frac{3}{4}$$d$. out of 18$l$., or 16$s$. 10$\frac{1}{4}$$d$. out of 1$l$., to be returned him in case he throws out with ames ace, that he may play on equal terms with the Setter.

If the main should be 5 or 9, the advantage of the Setter will be $\frac{43}{2835}$, and by dividing this by $\frac{1}{36}$ gives $\frac{172}{315}$, which part of the Caster's stake should be returned him in case he throws out with ames ace when 5 and 9 is the main, and is equal to 172l. out of 315l., to 9l. 16s. 6$\frac{3}{4}$$d$. out of 18$l$., and to 10$s$. 11$d$. out of 1$l$., he will then play on an equality with the Setter.

If the Caster is to have the first main that may happen to be thrown, the advantage of the Setter in that instance is $\frac{37}{2016}$, dividing which fraction by $\frac{1}{36}$ gives $\frac{37}{56}$, which part of the Caster's stake should be returned in case he loses by throwing ames ace, and which is equal to 37l. out of his stake of 56l. to 11l. 17s. 10$\frac{1}{4}$$d$. out of 18$l$., and to 13$s$. 2$d\frac{1}{2}$$d$. out of 1$l$.

If two persons, each having 20 guineas, agree that one shall be the Caster and have the first main that may happen to be thrown, and the other be the Setter of a guinea each main till one of them loses his 20 guineas, the odds between them will be the same as those of the Caster's winning 20 times successively against the Setter's doing so. The odds on a casual main having been proved to be 111 to 107 in favor of the Setter; the odds of the above may be found in one way by multiplying each of these last numbers by itself 19 times, and the product will show the proportion of the different expectations of the Caster and Setter to be nearly as 2 to 1 in favor of the latter; his expectations may therefore be stated as $\frac{2}{3}$ of 40 guineas or 28l., from which, deducting his 20 guineas, there remains 7l. advantage or clear gain, and so much does the Caster give away out of his 20 guineas by playing on those terms.

If they have 15 guineas each and play as before mentioned, the odds are to be found by multiplying 111 to 107, each by itself 14 times, and the products are nearly as 1$\frac{3}{4}$ to 1, or the

Setter's exact expectation of the 30 guineas is worth 19*l.* 19*s.* 7*d.*, from which, deducting his 15 guineas, leaves him an advantage of 4*l.* 4*s.* 7*d.*

If they stake 10 guineas each, by the same method the odds are found to be nearly as 36 to 25, and the Setter's exact expectation of the 20 guineas is worth 12*l.* 8*s.* 1*d.*, from which, deducting his 10 guineas, leaves him an advantage of 1*l.*, 18*s.* 1*d.*

If they have 5 guineas each, the Setter's expectation will be worth 5*l.* 14*s.* 7*d.* leaving him a surplus of 9*s.* 7*d.*

De Moivre in his Doctrine of Chances states, that if the chances for A and B winning a stake be as 11 to 10 and they play till one has lost 100 guineas at 1 guinea each stake, the expectations of A will be worth above 99 guineas, 20 shillings, and 1 penny; consequently B's 100 guineas cannot be worth to him when they begin so much as 11*d.*

A very great disparity will be found by 6 multiplications only of 11 and 10 each by itself, which will prove that in staking 7 guineas each, it is nearly 2 to 1 in favor of A winning B's 7 guineas against B winning A's.

ON THE MAIN BEING DECIDED BY DOUBLETS.

For example: when 6 and 4 are concerned, that is when the Caster has 6 to 4, there being 8 ways for throwing 6 and 4 and only 1 way out of those 8 for the two trois to come, the probability of the Caster winning with them is $\frac{1}{8}$, and. which part should be given of any sum to be received on the happening of that event. The probability of the Setter winning by the two deuces is of course the same. On these principles is the following table formed, which shews the sums to be given for the sums therein mentioned to be returned on every main and chance where doublets are concerned.

I have made the calculations on the sums of 7, 8, 9, and 10*l.*, because it is usual to return those sums on the respective mains and chances on receiving 1*l.*, which is more than should be given by from 1*s.* 10*d.* to 2*s.* 10$\frac{1}{4}$*d.*

TABLE.

				£	s.	d.
When 5 and 4 are concerned to receive 6l. on the two deuces, there should be given				0	17	
5 and 6 to receive 8l. on the two Trois				0	17	9_2
5	,, 8	,, 8	,, Fours	0	17	$9\frac{1}{4}$
5	,, 10	,, 6	,, Fives	0	17	$1\frac{1}{2}$
6	,, 4	,, 7	,, Trois	0	17	6
6	,, 4	,, 7	,, Deuces	0	17	6
6	,, 7	,, 10	,, Trois	0	18	$2\frac{1}{4}$
6	,, 8	,, 9	,, Fours	0	18	0
6	,, 8	,, 9	,, Trois	0	18	0
6	,, 9	,, 8	,, Trois	0	17	$9\frac{1}{4}$
6	,, 10	,, 7	,, Fives	0	17	6
6	,, 10	,, 7	,, Trois	0	17	6
7	,, 4	,, 8	,, Deuces	0	17	$9\frac{1}{4}$
7	,, 8	,, 10	,, Fours	0	18	$2\frac{1}{4}$
7	,, 10	,, 8	,, Fives	0	17	$9\frac{1}{4}$
8	,, 4	,, 7	,, Fours	0	17	6
8	,, 4	,, 7	,, Deuces	0	17	6
8	,, 9	,, 8	,, Fours	0	17	$9\frac{1}{4}$
8	,, 10	,, 7	,, Fives	0	17	6
8	,, 10	,, 7	,, Fours	0	17	6
9	,, 4	,, 6	,, Deuces	0	17	$1\frac{1}{2}$
9	,, 10	,, 6	,, Fives	0	17	$1\frac{1}{2}$

ON THE MAIN BEING DECIDED IN TWO THROWS.

When 7 is the main it is 14 to 13 that it is decided or off in two throws, this may be proved by ascertaining the probability of the contrary happening, and by betting.

First, there are 12 ways out of 36 for its coming off the first throw, those are by throwing 7, 11, 12, 2, or 3, consequently there are 24 ways against it, therefore the probability of not coming off the first throw is $\frac{24}{36}$ or $\frac{2}{3}$ or 2 to 1.—Secondly, if it is not off the first throw, the chance to the 7 must be either 4, 5, 6, 8, 9, or 10, for which chances to come there are 24 ways, and dividing 24 by 6, the number of chances, we get an average number of ways which is 4, we may therefore say there are 4 ways for the Caster's chance to come the second throw, and which added to the number of ways for the main, which are six, make 10 ways for the main to be decided the second throw. If then it is not off the first throw, it is 26 to 10 or 13 to 5 that it is not the second throw, which probability is $\frac{26}{36}$ or $\frac{13}{18}$, and multiplying this last fraction by that expressing the probability of not coming off the first throw, gives one which shews the probability of its being decided in two throws, that is $\frac{26}{54}$ or $\frac{13}{27}$, or 13 out of 27 against coming off; consequently 14 out of 27, or 14 to 13 in favor of its coming off in two throws, and which shews that although it is 2 to 1 in favor of one event happening, and 13 to 5 in favor of another, it is 14 to 13 they do not both happen.

This may further be proved by betting. First, I bet 14*l.* to 13 the main is off in two throws; to hedge to which I must bet 13*l.* to 6*l.* 10*s.*, it is not off the first throw, if it is, I lose this last 13*l.* and win the first, which balances.—If it do not come off the first throw, I win 6*l.* 10*s.* which added to my 13*l.* will make 19*l.* 10*s.*, this I bet at the rate of 13 to 5 that it is not off the second throw, now 13 is to 5 as 19*l.* 10*s.* is to 7*l.* 10*s.*, and if it is not off the second throw, I have 19*l.* 10*s.* and 7*l.* 10*s.*, making 27*l.*, but as 13*l.*, out of it was my own, I only win on balance 14*l.*, and which 14*l.* I must pay on account of my original bet of 14 to 13 that the main came off in two throws; now had it come off the second throw, I should have lost 19*l.* 10*s.*, 13*l.* of which was my own, as before observed, but should have won 13*l.* on the original bet, the main being decided in two throws.

When 7 and 8 are concerned together, or main and chance, there being 11 ways out of 36 for them to come, it is $\frac{25}{36}$ or 25 to 11 that the main is not decided the first throw, and the same on the second throw, and $\frac{25}{36}$ multiplied by $\frac{25}{36}$ is $\frac{625}{1296}$ or 671 to 625, or 1*l.* to 18*s.* $7\frac{1}{2}d.$ that it is off in two throws. The same of course when 7 and 6 are concerned.

When 7 and 5 or 7 and 9 are concerned, there being 10 ways for them to come, it is $\frac{26}{36}$ or 13 to 5 the main is not decided the first throw and the same the second, and $\frac{13}{18}$ multiplied $\frac{13}{18}$ in $\frac{168}{324}$ or 169 to 155 or 1*l.* to 18*s.* 4*d.* that the main is not decided in two throws. It is 1*l.* to 11*s.* that it is off in three throws.

When 6 and 8 are concerned the odds are the same as on 7 and 5.

When 5 or 9 is concerned with 4 or 10, it is 841 to 451, or

1*l*. to 10*s*. 8½*d*. that it is not off in two throws, and 109 to 100 nearly, or 1*l*. 1*s*. 10¾*d*. to 1*l*., that it is off in three throws. When 6 or 8 is concerned with either 4 or 10, it is 49 to 32 that it is not off in two throws, and 386 to 343, or 1*l*. to 17*s*. 9*d*.that it is off in three throws.

ON THE GAIN OF THE BOX.

This, if the probability of throwing in and out were equal, would be exactly worth to the box-keeper for every Caster when he first takes the box, ⅛ of what is paid at the end of three mains won successively, as may be proved in the following way : suppose the sum paid on winning three successive mains to be half a guinea, and suppose the Caster when he first takes the box to give the box-keeper ⅛ of half a guinea, that is 1*s*. 3¾*d*. If the box-keeper bet this sum that the Caster throws in and he does so, the box-keeper then has 2*s*. 7½*d*. and one main is thrown in, he then bets 2*s*. 7½*d*. the Caster throws in, which if he do, the box-keeper then has 5*s*. 3*d*., and two mains are thrown in. He then bets 5*s*. 3*d*. the Caster throws in; if that take place, he has 10*s*. 6*d*., and the Caster has thrown in three mains. Had the Caster thrown out any one of those mains the box-keeper would have lost the 1*s*. 3¾*d*., and been in the same situation as had he waited for the half-a-guinea at the end of three successive mains being won. But the probability of winning a main to that of losing it, being as 107 to 111, it reduces the value of the box-keeper's expectations to 1*s*. 2¾*d*. and half a farthing.

THE DIFFERENCE BETWEEN THE ODDS IN CHANCES AND THE ODDS IN MONEY CLEARLY ASCERTAINED AND EXEMPLIFIED IN THE GAME OF HAZARD.

Upon a first thought it may be supposed that there is no difference between odds in stakes and the same odds in the number of ways for winning equal stakes; that is to say, whether a person stakes 6 guineas to another's 5, and plays on equal terms with respect to the number of chances for winning or losing, or whether the chances for winning and losing are as 6 to 5, and they make equal stakes of 5 guineas each; but the difference will plainly be perceived in the following cases : —First, suppose the Caster and Setter to stake each 5 guineas, and the Caster has 7 for the main and 6 for his chance, it is then 6 to 5 against him, and the value of the Setter's expectation on the whole stake of 10l. 10s. is $\frac{6}{11}$ of it, or 5l. 14s. 6½d. nearly, from which deducting his own stake, there remains a clear gain of 9s. 6½d.—But supposing the Setter to propose to the Caster to change the main and chance to such as shall be equal: for instance, to 5 and 9, or 6 to 8, on condition that the Caster shall instead of the origional equal stakes of 5 guineas each, stake 6 guineas to the Setter's 5; this agreed on, the value of the Setter's expectation is now ½ of the whole stake of 11l. 11s. or 5l. 15s. 6d. and from this deducting his stake of 5l. 5s. there remains a clear gain of 10s. 6d. which is 11½ more than before.   Secondly, suppose the Caster has 10 to 7, when playing for the same stake; the value of the Setter's expectation will be then ⅔ of the 10l. 10s. which is 7l., this gives him a gain of 1l. 15s.—But if the Caster agree to stake 10 to 5, and change the main and chance to 6 and 8, or 5 and 9, the expectation of the Setter will be worth ½ of 15l. 15s. or 7l. 10s. leaving him a gain of 2l. 5s., which is 10s. more than before; but supposing the Caster instead of staking 10 guineas to 5, in this last case, says that the whole or common stake between him and the Setter shall be only to the same amount as before, that is 10 guineas, but that he will contribute in the proportion of 2 to 1, he must then stake 7l. and the Setter 3l. 10s; the value of the Setter's expectation will be then 5l. 0s., from which deducting his stake of 3l. 10s. there remains a gain of 1l. 15s. the same sum as in the first instance of the Caster having 10 to 7; but that is only a gain of ⅓ of his stake, which there is 5l. 5s., whereas this is a gain of ½ of what he stakes; the first is a profit of only 33⅓ and the last exactly 50 per cent.

POSTSCRIPT—*From Jones's Edition of Hoyle's Games.*

Any number of persons may play at hazard. The person who takes the box and dice throws a main, that is to say, a chance for the company, which must be above four, and not exceed nine, otherwise it is no main, consequently he must keep throwing till he brings five, six, seven, eight or nine; this done, he must throw his own chance, which may be any above three, and not exceeding ten; if he throws two aces or trois-ace (commonly called crabs) he loses his stake, let the company's chance, called the main, be what it will. If the main should be seven, and seven or eleven is thrown immediately after, it is what is called a nick, and the Caster (the present player) wins out his stake. If eight be the main, and eight or twelve is thrown immediately after, it is also called a nick, and the Caster wins his stakes. The Caster throwing any other number for the main, such as are admitted, and bringing the same number directly afterwards, it is likewise termed a nick, and he then also wins whatever stakes he has made. Every three successive mains the Caster wins, he pays half a guinea to the box or furnisher of the dice.

The meaning of a stake or bet at this game somewhat differs from any other. If a person chooses to lay some money with the Thrower or Caster, he must put his cash upon the table, within a circle which is described for that purpose; when he has done this, if the Caster agrees to it, he knocks the box upon the table at the person's money with whom he intends to bet, or particularly mentions at whose money he throws, which is sufficient, and he is obliged to answer whatever sum is down, unless the staker calls to cover; in that case the Caster is obliged to stake also, otherwise the bets would be void. It is optional in the person who bets with the thrower, to bar any throw which the Caster may be going to cast, provided neither of the dice are seen; if one die should be discovered, the Caster must throw the other to it, unless the throw is barred in proper time.

The common odds, which are absolutely necessary to be understood before any body attempts to play or bet at this game, are as follow: if seven is thrown for a main, and four the chance, it is 2 to 1 against the person who throws: if six to four is thrown, 5 to 3: if five to four is thrown, 4 to 3: seven to nine, 3 to 2: seven to six, 3 to 2, barring the two trois; with the two trois, only 6 to 5: seven to five, 3 to 2; six to five an even bet, barring the doublets or the two trois: with the trois, 5 to 4: eight to five an even bet, barring the two fours; five to four with the two fours: nine to five, even: nine to four, is 4 to 3: the nick of seven is 7 to 2, but often laid but 10 to 3, and 5 to 1 you do not nick six or eight.

To illustrate these calculations still more clearly, the following table will be necessary:

```
7 to 4 is 2 to 1
6 .... 4 .... 5 .... 3
5 .... 4 .... 4 .... 3
7 .... 9 .... 3 .... 2
7 .... 6 { 3 .... 2, barring two trois.
          6 .... 5, with the two trois.
7 .... 5 .... 3 .... 2
6 .... 5 { even, barring two trois.
          5 .... 4 with two trois.
8 .... 5 { even, barring two fours
          5 .... 4 with two fours.
9 .... 5 even
9 .... 4 .... 4 .... 3
```

Against the Caster.

The nick of seven is 7 to 2, often laid 10 to 3.

The nick of six and eight is 5 to 1.

It is necessary to be perfectly master of these odds, in order to play the prudent game, and to make use of them by way of insuring bets in what is called hedging, in case the chance happens to be unlikely; for by taking the odds a ready calculator secures himself, and often stands part of his bet to a certainty. For example, if seven is the main, and four the chance, and he has five pounds depending on the main, by taking six pounds to three, he must either win two pounds or one pound; and on the contrary, if he does not like his chance, by laying the odds against himself he must save in proportion to the bet he has made.

SOME ADDITIONAL CALCULATIONS ON HAZARD.

If 8 and 6 are main and chance, it is very near 11 to 12, that either one or the other is thrown off in two throws.

And if 5 and 7, or 9 and 7 are main and chance, the probability that they will be thrown in two throws is near 11 to 12.

If 5 and 8, or 9 and 8, or 5 and 6, or 9 and 6 are main and chance; the probability of throwing one of them in two throws is as 7 to 9 exactly.

And if 7 and 4, or 7 and 10 are main and chance, the probability that they will be thrown in two throws is also as 7 to 9.

If 7 and 8, or 7 and 6 are main and chance, one may lay 15 to 14 that one of them is thrown in two throws.

But if 5 and 4, or 5 and 10, or 9 and 4, or 9 and 10 are main and chance, he that undertakes to throw either main or chance in three throws has the worst of the lay; for it is as 21 to 23 exceeding near.

If the main be 7, and each person stakes a guinea, the gain of the Setter is about $3\frac{1}{2}d$. per guinea.

If the main be 6 or 8, the gain of the Setter is about sixpence in a guinea.

But if the main be 5 or 9, the gain of the Setter is about $3\frac{3}{4}d$. in a guinea.

However if any person is determined to set up on the first main that is thrown, his chance, supposing each stake to be a guinea, is $4\frac{5}{8}d$. exactly.

Hence the probability of a main, to the probability of no main, is as 27 to 28 very near.

If any one should undertake to throw a six or an ace with two dice in one throw, he ought to lay 5 to 4.

BACKGAMMON.

BLACK.

Black's Home, or Inner Table.   Black's Outer Table.

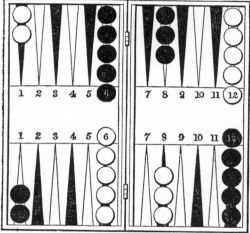

White's Home, or Inner Table.   White's Outer Table.

WHITE.

This is a mixed game, being a combination of chance and calculation. Its derivation is a vexed question, both as to whence it came and how it acquired its present designation. "La Maison des Jeux Académiques" abandons its origin as a desperate problem, and Dr. Henry claims its name as a Welsh compound, from "bach," little, and "cammon," battle. On the other hand, Bp. Kennett and Strutt derive it from the Anglo-Saxon, viz., from "bac," back, and "gamone," a game, that is to say, a game where players are exposed to be sent back. Perhaps this may satisfy the antiquarian and be accepted as a sufficient offering to the etymologist. It would have been a mere recreation in chronology, to have disputed all the probabilities for assigning Backgammon to the antediluvian age. One portion of its machinery consists of dice—now dice defy chronology. Their types are found in Etruscan tombs and in the hieroglyphics of Egypt; and the historian of Chæronea asserts, that Mercury had a throw of the dice once upon a time with the Goddess Luna.

From Chaucer we gather that the early name of Backgammon, or at all events its synonyme was " Tables;" at which period it was played with three dice, and all the " men" commenced their action from the adversary's table. Backgammon has always been a particularly respectable instrument of amusement, like the Organ in " She Stoops to conquer." Even Whist has not escaped defilement, but Backgammon " was never a vulgar game, never beloved of lackeys." Shakspere has used it as a medium for his philosophy, and Bacon has served bail for its good behaviour.

Backgammon is played by two persons, with two boxes and two dice, upon a quadrangular table or board, on which are figured 24 points or *flèches*, of two colours, placed alternately. The board is divided into four compartments, two inner and two outer ones, each containing six of the 24 points (alternate colours). The players are each furnished with fifteen men or counters, black and white (usually draughts). These are arranged upon the board, in the following manner. To play into the left hand table, two of your men are placed upon the ace point of your opponent's inner table, five upon the sixth point in his outer table (numbered 12 in our diagram), three upon the cinque-point in your own outer table numbered 8), and five upon the sixth point, in your own inner table. The adversary's men are to be placed in corresponding order, in a position directly opposite. All this is shown in the diagram annexed, and to facilitate reference the points or flèches are numbered from 1 to 12 of each colour.

The game consists in moving your men from point to point, so as to bring them round into your own inner table (*i. e.*, that on your left hand), and then moving or bearing them off the board. The player who first clears off his men wins.

The moves of the men are determined by the throws of the dice, according to the directions for playing. at page 389. It will there be seen that the most advantageous throw at the outset is that of aces, as it blocks the bar or sixth point in your outer table (numbered 7), and secures the cinque-point in your inner table, so that your adversary's two men **cannot** move if he throw either quatre, cinque, or size. This **throw** is frequently conceded to inferior players, at the commencement of the game, by way of odds.

As the grand object of the game consists in bringing **round** your men into your own inner table, all throws that contribute towards that end, and prevent your adversary from doing **the** same are advantageous, and *vice versâ*. During the progress of the game you should endeavour to block up or detain **a** part of your adversary's men, in your own tables; and **to** obstruct his re-entering such of them as you may happen **to** have taken up, unless all your own men have passed his **main** body, and are so far advanced to your inner table (which **we** will here call home) as to possess the best chance, should **he** seek to win by running away.

At the commencement of the game the players must **agree** towards which end of the board they will play. Each **party** plays into one of the tables on his own side; thus, if **Black** plays into his left-hand table, White plays into his right (*i. e.*, that which is exactly opposite), and *vice versâ*, their **men** advancing in contra-position to each other, as in the annexed diagram.

For right of first play each party throws a single die; **he** who throws the highest number wins, and may, if he **chooses,** adopt and play the joint number of the preliminary throw. If he reject, then the first step is made by his throwing **both** the dice, and moving any one of his men to an open point **at** the distance indicated by one of the dice, and then **moving** another man (or the same man farther on, if he think **proper),** to another open point indicated by the number of the **second** die. This completes his move, his adversary then follows **in** a similar manner, and so on alternately to the end of **the** game. Thus, double aces (which count as 4) would **entitle** you (say White) to move two men from 8 w. to 7 w., **and** two from 6 w. to 5 w., which covers the bar point (No. **7),** and also covers the cinque point in your inner table, and **then,** should your next throw be 5 and 6, you would play the **five** from 12 b. to 8 w., and so cover the blot before left; **and** you would play the six from 12 b. to your bar point. **Pairs** count double; thus, sixes entitle you to move four men, **each** six points forward, and you may either move four **together,**

say, from 12 B. to 7 w., or two together, as, say, two from
1 B. to your adversary's bar point (No. 7), and two from 12 B.
to 7 w. (your own bar point), or singly,—as, say, a single man
from 1 B. to 1 w. in your own inner table, presuming that your
adversary had ceased to occupy it.

The direction in which your men move is from the adverse
inner table over the bar, through the adversary's outer table
round into your own outer table, and then over your bar,
home.

When during the progress of the game only a single man
is left on a point, it is called "a blot," and is exposed to be
taken by the adversary, who generally endeavours to "hit"
the blot by bringing one of his own men to that point. When
a man is thus captured it must be removed, and placed upon
the bar (*i. e.*, the division joint of the table), and the player to
whom it belongs cannot move again, until he has "entered
his man." This can only be effected by throwing a number
which is vacant, or is left a "blot" on the adversary's inner
table, playing it as from a point off the board, adjoining to
the adversary's ace point. Towards the end of the game,
when most of the points in your adversary's inner table are
covered (*i. e.*, have two or more men on each), it becomes
difficult to enter, and you must remain on the bar, till you
have either thrown the exact number required to suit perhaps a single open point, or till more points are exposed,
by your adversary having played some of his men off the
table. When all the six points are blocked, it is of course
useless your throwing, and your adversary throws alone.
"Hitting" a blot frequently adds extreme variety and interest
to the game.

When doublets are thrown, four moves are played of the
distance indicated by the dice, instead of two, as usual in
ordinary throws. For instance, should two quatres be thrown,
any of the following moves may be played, either one man
may be moved sixteen points; two men each eight points;
one man eight, and two men four points; or four men four
points each. Should, however, the points indicated by the
throw of the dice be covered, the moves are lost. For instance, if double quatres be cast, and the first fourth point
from all the player's men be covered by the adversary, the
move is lost, although the eighth, twelfth, and sixteenth points

be uncovered, as the first fourth point, if occupied, cannot be passed over.

If, during the course of the game, every point upon which a man could be moved is covered by the adversary's men, your men are compelled to remain in *statu quo*, and the adversary takes his turn. If one man only can be played, it must be played.

When a player has brought all his men home, he must begin to " bear them," *i. e.*, to take them off the board. For every number thrown a man is removed from the corresponding point, until the whole are borne off. In doing this, should the adversary be waiting to " enter" any of his men which have been "hit," care should be taken to leave no " blots" or uncovered points. In " bearing off" doublets have the same power as in the moves, four men are removed; if higher numbers are on the dice than on the points, men may be taken from any lower point, thus if double sixes are thrown, and the point has been already stripped, four men may be removed from the cinque point of any lower number. If a low number is thrown, and the corresponding point hold no men, they must be played up from a higher point. Thus, if double aces be thrown, and there are no men upon the ace point two or more men must be played up from the higher points, or a fewer number played up and taken off.

If one player has not borne off his first man before the the other has borne off his last, he loses a " gammon," which is equivalent to two games, or " hits." If each player has borne off it is reduced to a " hit," or game of one. If the winner has borne off all his men before the loser has carried his men out of his adversary's table, it is a " back-gammon," and usually held equivalent to three hits or games.

Calculation of the Chances.

As it is necessary for a learner to know how many points he ought to throw upon the two dice, one throw with another; we will take the following method to demonstrate it

There are thirty-six chances upon two dice, the points of which are as follows :

	Points.
2 aces	4
2 deuces	8
2 trois	12
2 fours	16
2 fives	20
2 sixes	24
6 and 5 twice	22
6 and 4 twice	20
6 and 3 twice	18
6 and 2 twice	16
6 and 1 twice	14
5 and 4 twice	18
5 and 3 twice	16
5 and 2 twice	14
5 and 1 twice	12
4 and 3 twice	14
4 and 2 twice	12
4 and 1 twice	10
3 and 2 twice	10
3 and 1 twice	8
2 and 1 twice	6

$$\text{Divided by 36 .} \quad \left\{ \begin{array}{c} 294 \\ 288 \end{array} \right\} 8$$

$$6$$

294 divided by 36, shews that one throw with another you may expect to throw 8 upon two dice.

The chances upon two dice are as follows:

	Points.
2 sixes	1
2 fives	1
2 fours	1
2 trois	1
2 deuces	1
* 2 aces	1
6 and 5 twice	2
6 and 4 twice	2

Carried over .	10

2 c

		Points.
	Brought forward	10
6 and 3 twice	. . . . .	2
6 and 2 twice	. . . . .	2
* 6 and 1 twice	. . . . .	2
5 and 4 twice	. . . . .	2
5 and 3 twice	. . . . .	2
5 and 2 twice	. . . . .	2
* 5 and 1 twice	. . . . .	2
4 and 3 twice	. . . . .	2
4 and 2 twice	. . . . .	2
* 4 and 1 twice	. . . . .	2
3 and 2 twice	. . . . .	2
* 3 and 1 twice	. . . . .	2
* 2 and 1 twice	. . . . .	2
		‐‐
		36

To find out by this table, what are the odds of being hit, upon a certain, or flat die, look in the table, where thus* marked,

		Points.
* 2 aces	. . . . . .	1
* 6 and 1 twice	. . . . .	2
* 5 and 1 twice .	. . . . .	2
* 4 and 1 twice	. . . . .	2
* 3 and 1 twice .	. . . . .	2
* 2 and 1 twice	. . . . .	2
		‐‐
	Total	11
		‐‐
	Which deducted from .	36
	The remainder is . .	25

By this it appears, that it is twenty-five to eleven against hitting an ace, upon a certain, or flat die.

The like method may be taken with any other flat die, as with the ace.

What are the odds of entering a man upon one, two, three. four, or five points?

		for.	against.		Reduced. for.	against.
A. To enter it upon 1 point is		11	to 25,	or about	4	to 9
upon 2 points		20	„ 16,	„	5	„ 4
upon 3 points		27	„ 9,	„	3	„ 1
upon 4 points		32	„ 4,	„	8	„ 1
upon 5 points		35	„ 1,	„	35	„ 1

What are the odds of hitting, with any chance, in the reach of a single die?

		for.	against.		Reduced. for.	against.
A. To hit upon 1 is		11	to 25,	or about	4	to 9
upon 2	„	12	„ 24,	„	1	„ 2
upon 3	„	14	„ 22,	„	2	„ 3
upon 4	„	15	„ 21,	„	5	„ 7
upon 5	„	15	„ 21,	„	5	„ 7
upon 6	„	17	„ 19,	„	$8\frac{1}{2}$	„ $9\frac{1}{2}$

What are the odds of hitting with double dice?

		for.	against.		Reduced. for.	against.
A. To hit upon 7	is	6	to 30,	or about	1	to 5
upon 8	„	6	„ 30,	„	1	„ 5
upon 9	„	5	„ 31,	„	1	„ 6
upon 10	„	3	„ 33,	„	1	„ 11
upon 11	„	2	„ 34,	„	1	„ 17
upon 12 (or 2 sixes)		1	„ 36,	„	1	„ 36

To explain farther how to use the table of thirty-six chances, to find the odds of being hit upon any certain or flat die, this second example is added to shew how to find by that table the odds of being hit upon a 6.

2 sixes	1
2 trois	1
2 deuces	1
6 and 5 twice	2
6 and 4 twice	2
6 and 3 twice	2
6 and 2 twice	2
	—
Carried over . .	11

2 c 2

Brought forward   .   11

6 and 1 twice   2
5 and 1 twice   2
4 and 2 twice   2

                 17

Which deducted from   .   36
The remainder is   . .   19

So that it is nineteen to seventeen against being hit upon a 6.

The odds of 2 love are about 5 to 2,
and of 2 to 1   are 2 ,, 1,
and of 1 love   is 3 ,, 2.

General Instructions.

I. If you play three up at Backgammon, your principal view, in the first place, is to secure your own, or your adversary's cinque point, or both; when that is effected, you may play a pushing game, and endeavour to gammon your adversary.

II. The next best point (after you have gained your cinque point) is to make your bar point, thereby preventing your adversary's running out with doublet sixes.

III. After you have proceeded thus far, prefer the making your quatre point in your own table, rather than the quatre point out of it.

IV. Having gained these points, you have a fair chance to gammon your adversary, if he is very forward: For, suppose his tables are broke at home, it will be then your interest to open your bar point, and to oblige him to come out of your tables with a six; and having your men spread, you not only may catch that man which your adversary brings out of your tables, but you will also have a probability of taking up the man left in your tables (upon supposition that he has two men there). If he should have a blot at home, it will then be your interest not to make up your tables; because, if he should enter upon a blot, which you are to make for the purpose, you will have a probability of getting a third man; which, if accomplished, will give you, at least, 4 to 1 of the gammon; whereas, if you have only two of his men up, the odds are that you do not gammon him.

V. If you play for a hit only, 1 or 2 men taken up of your adversary's, makes it surer than a greater number, provided your tables are made up.

Directions how to carry your Men home.

VI. When you carry your men home, in order to lose no point, you are to carry the most distant man to your adversary's bar point, that being the first stage you are to place it on; the next stage is six points further, viz., the place where your adversary's five men are first placed out of his tables; the next stage is upon the six point in your tables. This method is to be pursued till all your men are brought home, except two, when, by losing a point, you may often save your gammon, by putting it in the power of two fives, or two fours to save it.

VII. If you play to win a hit only, endeavour to gain either your own or your adversary's cinque point; and if that fails, by your being hit by your adversary, and you find that he is forwarder than you, you must throw more men into his table. Thus: put a man upon your cinque or bar point, and if your adversary neglects to hit it, you may then gain a forward instead of a back game; but if he hits you, you must play a back game, and then the greater number of men which are taken up, the better it makes your game, because you by that means preserve your game at home; and you must then always endeavour to gain both your adversary's ace and trois points, or his ace and deuce points, and take care to keep three men upon his ace point, that if you chance to hit him from thence, that point may remain still secure to you.

VIII. At the beginning of a set do not play for a back game, because by so doing you would play to a great disadvantage, running the risk of a gammon to win a single hit.

Directions for Playing at setting out the Thirty-six Chances of Dice, for a Gammon, or for a Single Hit.

I. Two aces (the best of all first throws), to be played two on your cinque point, and two on the bar point for a gammon, or for a hit.

II. Two sixes (the second best throw), should be played two on your adversary's bar point, and two on your own bar point, for a gammon, or a hit.

III. Two trois, two to be played on your cinque point, and the other two on your trois point in your own tables, for a gammon only.

IV. Two deuces, to be played on the quatre point in your own tables, and two to be brought over from the five men placed in your adversary's outer tables, for a gammon only.

V. * Two fours, to be brought over from the five men placed in your adversary's outer tables, and to be put upon the cinque point in your own tables, for a gammon only.

VI. Two fives, to be brought over from the five men placed in your adversary's outer tables, and to be put on the trois point in your own tables for a gammon, or a hit.

VII. Size ace, you are to make your bar point, for a gammon, or for a hit.

VIII. Size deuce, a man to be brought from the five men placed in your adversary's outer tables, and to be placed on the cinque point in your own tables, for a gammon, or a hit.

IX. Six and three, a man to be brought from your adversary's ace point, as far as he will go, for a gammon, or a hit.

X. Six and four, a man to be brought from your adversary's ace point, as far as he will go, for a gammon, or a hit.

XI. Six and five, a man to be carried from your adversary's ace point, as far as he can go, for a gammon, or a hit.

XII. Cinque and quatre, a man to be carried from your adversary's ace point, as far as he can go, for a gammon, or a hit.

XIII. Cinque-trois, to make the trois point in your table, for a gammon, or a hit.

XIV. Cinque-deuce, to play two men from the five placed in your adversary's outer tables, for a gammon, or a hit.

XV. Cinque-ace, to bring one man from the five placed in your adversary's outer tables for the cinque, and to play one man down on the cinque point in your own tables for the ace, for a gammon only.

XVI. Quatre-trois, two men to be brought from the five placed in your adversary's outer tables, for a gammon, or a hit.

XVII. Quatre-deuce to make the quatre point in your own tables, for a gammon, or a hit.

XVIII. Quatre-ace, to play a man from the five placed in your adversary's outer tables for the quatre, and for the ace, to play a man down upon the cinque point in your own tables, for a gammon only.

XIX. Trois-deuce, two men to be brought from the five placed in your adversary's tables, for a gammon only.

XX. Trois-ace, to make the cinque point in your own tables, for a gammon, or a hit.

XXI. Deuce-ace, to play one man from the five placed in your adversary's tables for the deuce; and for the ace, to play a man down upon the cinque point in your own tables, for a gammon only.

Directions how to Play the Chances that are marked thus (*) when you are only to Play for a Hit.

I. * Two trois, two of them are to be played on your cinque point in your own tables, and with the other two take the quatre point in your adversary's tables.

II. *Two deuces, two of them are to be played on your quatre point in your own tables, and with the other two take the trois point in your adversary's tables.

The two foregoing cases are to be played in this manner, for this reason, viz. That thereby you avoid being shut up in your adversary's tables, and have the chance of throwing high doublets to win the hit.

III. * Two fours, two of them are to take your adversary's cinque point in his tables; and for the other two, two men are to be brought from the five placed in your adversary's tables.

IV. 1. * Cinque-ace, play the cinque from the five men placed in your adversary's tables, and play the ace from your adversary's ace point.

V. 2. * Quatre-ace, play the quatre from the five men placed in your adversary's tables, and the ace from the men on your adversary's ace point.

VI. 3 * Deuce-ace, play the deuce from the five men placed in your adversary's tables, and the ace from your adversary's ace point.

The three last chances are played in this manner, for, by

laying an ace down in your adversary's tables, you have a probability of throwing deuce ace, trois deuce, quatre trois, or size cinque, in two or three throws; in any of which cases you are to make a point, which gives you the better of the hit.

You may observe, by the directions given in this chapter, that you are to play nine chances out of the thirty-six in a different manner for a single hit, to what you would do when playing for a gammon.

Some Observations, Hints, and Cautions, which are to be attended to.

I. By the directions given to play for a gammon, you are voluntarily to make some blots, the odds being in your favor, that they are not hit; but should it so happen, that any blot is hit, as in this case, you will have three men in your adversary's tables, you must then endeavour to secure your adversary's cinque, quatre, or trois point, to prevent a gammon, and must be very cautious how you suffer your adversary to take up a fourth man.

II. Take care not to crowd your game at any time, if possible. What is meant by crowding a game, is the putting many men either upon your trois or deuce point in your own tables; which is, in effect, losing those men, by not having them in play.

Besides, by crowding your game, to attempt to save a gammon, you are often gammoned; because when your adversary finds your game open, by being crowded in your own tables, he may then play his game as he thinks fit.

III. By recourse had to the calculations, you may know what are the Odds of your entering a single man upon any certain number of points, and by that means you may play your game accordingly.

IV. If you are obliged to leave a blot, by recourse to the calculation for hitting it, you will find the chances for and against; and consequently you will be enabled to judge how to play your game to the greatest advantage.

V. You will also find by the calculations, the odds for and

against you, upon being hit by double dice, and consequently you will choose such a method of play as is most to your advantage.

VI. If it is necessary to make a run, in order to win a hit, and you would know to a point which is the forwarder, take the following method :

Begin with reckoning how many points you must have, to bring home to your size point in your own tables, the man that is at the greatest distance from it, and do the like by every other man that is abroad ; when the numbers of those absentees are summed up, add to them the following numbers for those already in your own tables, (supposing the men that were abroad as on your size point for bearing) namely, six for every man on the size point, five for every man on the cinque point, four for every man on the quatre point, three for every man on the trois point, two for every man on the deuce point, and one for every man on your ace point. Do the like to your adversary's game, and then you will know which of you is forwardest, and likeliest to win the hit.

Observations and Directions for a Learner who has made some Progress at Back-gammon ; particularly Directions for bearing his men.

I. If your adversary be greatly before you, never play a man from your quatre, trois, or deuce points, in order to bear that man from the point where you put it, because nothing but high doublets can give you any chance for the hit ; therefore, instead of playing an ace or a deuce from any of the afore-said points, always play them on from your size or highest point ; by which means you will find, that throwing two fives, or two fours, will, upon having eased your size and cinque points, be of great advantage to you : Whereas, had your size point remained loaded, you must, perhaps, be obliged to play at length those fives and fours.

II. Whenever you have taken up two of your adversary's men, and happen to have two, three, or more points made in your own tables, never fail spreading your men, in order either to take a new point in your tables, or to be ready to hit the man your adversary may happen to enter. As soon as he enters one of his men, you are to compare his game with your's ; and if you find your game equal to his, or better, never fail taking his man up, if you can, because it is 25 to 11 against his hitting you ; which chance being so much in your favor, you ought always to run that risk, when you have already two of his men up.

There is this exception to this rule, that if you play for a single hit only, and your playing that throw otherwise gives you a better chance for the hit, you ought not to take up that man.

III. Never be deterred from taking up any one man of your adversary's, by the apprehension of his hitting you with double dice, because the fairest probability your adversary has of hitting you, is 5 to 1 against him.

IV. If you should happen to have five points covered in your tables, and to have taken up one of your adversary's men, and are obliged to leave a blot out of your tables, rather leave it upon doublets, than any other chance, because doublets are 35 to 1 against his hitting you, and any other chance is but 17 to 1 against him.

V. Two of your adversary's men in your tables, are better for a hit, than any greater number, provided your game be forwardest, because his having three or more men in your tables, gives him more chance to hit you, than if he had only two men there.

VI. If you are to leave a blot, upon entering a man in your adversary's tables, or otherwise, and have it in your choice to leave it upon what point you please, always choose that which is the most disadvantageous to him.   To illustrate this by an example, let us suppose it his interest to hit you or take you up as soon as you enter, in that case leave the blot upon his lowest point ; that is to say, upon his deuce, rather than upon his trois point, or upon his trois, preferable to his quatre point ; or upon his quatre, preferable to his cinque point ; because, (as has been mentioned before) all the men your adversary plays upon his trois, or his deuce points, are deemed as lost, being in a great measure out of play, those men not having it in their power to make his cinque point, and consequently his game will be crowded there, and open elsewhere, whereby you will be able also much to annoy him.

VII. To prevent your adversary from bearing his men to the greatest advantage, when you are running to save your gammon; as, for instance, suppose you should have two men upon his ace point, and several other men abroad, though you should lose one point or two in putting your men into your tables, yet it is your interest to leave a man upon your adversary's ace point, which will have this consequence; that it will prevent his bearing his men to the greatest advantage, and will also give you the chance of his making a bolt, which you may chance to hit. But if, upon a calculation, you find that you have a throw, or a probability of saving your gammon, never wait for a blot, because the odds are greatly against hitting it.

Cases, shewing how to calculate the odds of saving or winning a Gammon.

I. Suppose your tables are made up, and that you have taken up one of your adversary's men; and suppose your adversary has so many men abroad as require three throws to put them in his tables:

It is then about an equal wager that you gammon him.

Because, in all probability, you will bear two men before you open your table, and when you bear the third man, you will be obliged to open your size or cinque point; in that case it is probable, that your adversary must take two throws before he enters his man in your tables, and two throws more before he puts that man into his own tables, and three throws more to put into his own tables the men which were abroad, which in all, make seven throws; and as you have twelve men to bear, these probably will take seven throws in bearing, because you may twice be obliged to make an ace, or a deuce, before you can bear all your men.

No mention is made of doublets on either side, that event being equal to each party.

The foregoing case shows it is in your power to calculate very nearly the odds of saving or winning a gammon upon most occasions.

II. Suppose I have three men upon my adversary's ace point, and five points in my tables, and that my adversary has all his men in his tables, three upon each of his five highest points :

What is the probability for his gammoning me, or not?

For	his	bearing	3	men	from his 6 point,	is	18
					from his 5 point,		15
					from his 4 point,		12
					from his 3 point,		9
					from his 2 point,		6
					Total,	——	60

To bring my three men from my adversary's ace point, to my size point in my tables, being for each 18 points, makes in all   —— 54

The remainder is   6

And besides the six points in your favor, there is a further consideration to be added for you, which is, that your adversary may make one or two blots in bearing, as is frequently the case. You see by this calculation, that you have greatly the better of the probability of saving your gammon.

This case is supposed upon an equality of throwing.

III. Suppose I leave two blots, neither of which can be hit but by double dice; to hit the one, that cast must be eight, and to hit the other it must be nine ; by which means my adversary has only one die to hit either of them.

What are the odds of his hitting either of these bolts?

The chances on two dice are in all, 36.

The chances to hit 8 are,	6 and 2 twice, . .	2
	5 and 3 twice, . . .	2
	2 deuces . . .	1
	2 fours, ...	1
The chances to hit 9 are,	6 and 3 twice, . .	2
	5 and 4 twice, . . .	2
	2 trois, . . .	1

Total chances for hitting, . . 11

Remaining chances for not hitting, . 25

So that it is 25 to 11 that he will not hit either of those blots.

IV. To give another example, let us suppose that I leave two other blots than the former, which cannot be hit but by double dice, the one must be hit by eight, and the other by seven.

What are the odds of my adversary's hitting either of these blots?

The chances on two dice are in all, 36.

The chances to hit 8 are,	6 and 2 twice,	.	.	2
	5 and 3 twice,		.	2
	two fours,	.	.	1
	two deuces,	.	.	1
The chances to hit 7 are,	6 and 1 twice,	.	.	2
	5 and 2 twice, .	.		2
	4 and 3 twice,	.	.	2

Total chances for hitting, . .   12

Remain chances for not hitting, .   24

Therefore it is two to one that I am not hit.

The like method is to be taken with three, four, or five blots upon double dice; or with blots made upon double and single dice at the same time; you are then only to find out (by the table of 36 chances) how many there are to hit any of those blots, and add all together in one sum, which subtract from the number of 36, which is the whole of the chances upon two dice: so doing resolves any question required.

V. The following cases are to show a way of calculating which may be called a mechanical way of solving questions of the like nature.

What are the odds of throwing 7 twice, before 10 once?

It is 5 to 4 that 10 is thrown once before 7 is thrown twice, which is demonstrated as follows:

Suppose the stake depending is nine pounds, my first throw entitles me to have one-third part of that money, because 7 has 6 chances for it, and 10 has but 3 chances, and therefore it is two to one.

	£	s.	d.

For the first throw, ...   3   0   0

Having taken 3*l.* out of the 9*l.* for the first throw,
the remainder is 6*l.* out of which a third part is
to be taken for the second throw   2   0   0

The total is,   5   0   0
Remains,   4   0   0
The whole stake is,   £9   0   0

VI. What are the odds of entering a man upon any certain point in two throws?

Suppose 36 shillings is the whole stake depending, what is my share of that stake, having laid 18 shillings that I enter in two throws? By the calculations in the table of 36 chances, it is found that I have 11 chances out of the 36 for entering the first throw, for which therefore I am entitled to 11 out of the 36 shillings.

The stake is,   0 36   0

For the first throw,   0 11   0

Remains,   £ 0 25   0

The remainder, being 25 shillings, is to be divided into 36 equal parts, of which I am entitled to eleven of those parts, which makes 7*s.* 7½*d.*, for the second throw   .   .   0   7 7½

Adding this to the other 11 shillings, makes my
share of the stake to be   .   .   .   0 18 7½
Then my adversary's share will be   .   .   0 17 4½
Total of the stake,   £ 0 36   0

Therefore it is very nearly 15 to 14 in favor of entering a man upon any certain point in two throws.

CHAPTER VIII.—*Critical case for a Back-game.*

I. Let us suppose A plays the fore-game, and that all his men are placed in the usual manner:

For B's game suppose, that fourteen of his men are placed upon his adversary's ace point, and one man upon his adversary's deuce point, and that B is to throw:

Which game is likeliest to win the hit?

A's is the best by 21 for, to 20 against; because, if B misses an ace to take his adversary's deuce point, which is 25 to 11 against him, A is, in that case, to take up B's men in his tables, either singly, or to make points; and if B secures either A's deuce or trois point, in that case, A is to lay as many men down as possible, in order to be hit, that thereby he may get a back-game.

When you are pretty well versed in the game of Backgammon, by practising this back-game, you will become a greater proficient in the game than by any other method, because it clearly demonstrates the whole power of the backgame.

Back-game.

II. Let us suppose A to have five men placed upon his size point, five men upon his quatre point, and five men upon his deuce point, all in his own tables:

And suppose B to have three men placed upon A's ace point, three men upon A's trois point, and three men upon A's cinque point; let B also have three men upon his size point in his own tables, and three men placed out of his tables, in the usual manner:

Who has the better of the hit?

It is an equal game; but to play it critically, the difficulty lies upon B, who is in the first place to endeavour to gain his cinque and quatre points in his own tables; and when that is effected, he is to lay two men from A's cinque point, in order to oblige his adversary to blot, by throwing an ace, which, if B hits, he will have the fairest probability of winning the hit.

Back-game.

III. Suppose A has three men upon B's ace point, and three men upon B's deuce point, also three men upon his size point in his own tables, and three men upon his usual point out of his tables, and three men where his five men are usually placed in his adversary's tables:

And let us suppose B has his men placed in the same manner, both in his own and his adversary's tables, with this difference only, viz. instead of having three men put upon A's deuce point, let him have three men upon A's trois point:

Q. Who has the best of the hit?

A. A, because the ace and trois points are not so good for a hit, as the ace and deuce points in your adversary's tables, for when you are bearing your men, you have the deuce point in your own tables to play your men upon, which often prevents your making a blot, which must happen otherwise to your adversary; and take care to lay down men to be hit as often as you can, in order to keep your game backward, and for the same reason avoid hitting any blots which your adversary makes.

A Case of Curiosity and Instruction.

IV. Let us suppose A has his fifteen men upon B's ace point, B is supposed to have his bar point, also his size, cinque, quatre, and trois points in his own tables:

How many throws is A likely to take to bring his fifteen men into his own tables, and to bear them?

A. You may undertake to do it in seventy-five throws.

It is odds in A's favor that he throws an ace in two throws; it is also odds in A's favor that he throws a six in two throws; when these events happen, A has a probability of not wanting above two or three throws to play till he has got all his fifteen men into his own tables: therefore, by a former rule laid down to bring your men home, and also for bearing your men, you may be able to find out the probability of the number of throws required. Note, B stands still, and does not play.

A Case of Curiosity and Instruction.

V. Where A and B shall play as fast as usual, and yet A shall make the hit last, probably, for many hours.

We will suppose B to have borne thirteen men, and that A has taken up the two remaining men:

And let us suppose that A has fifteen men in B's tables, viz. three men upon his size point, three men upon his cinque point, three upon his quatre point, three upon his trois point, two upon his deuce point, and one upon his ace point:

The method, which A is to take, is this : let him bring his fifteen men home, by always securing six close points, till B has entered his two men, and brought them upon any certain point; as soon as B has gained that point, A must open an ace, deuce, or trois, or all three ; which effected, B hits one of them, and A, taking care to have two or three men in B's tables, is ready to hit that man ; and also, he being assured of taking up the other man, has it in his power to prolong the hit to almost any length, provided he takes care not to open such points, as two fours, two fives, or two sixes, but always to open the ace, deuce, or trois points, for B to hit him.

VI. To know what are the odds upon two dice, for throwing two sixes, two fives, or two fours, in three throws ; by mechanical calculation, it may be found thus :

A. Supposing 36 shillings to be the stake depending, the thrower will be entitled to have for his first throw, which deducted out of 36, remains 33; which divided again into 36 parts, make so many eleven pences, out of which the thrower is to have 3 for his second throw,

	s.	d.
A. Supposing 36 shillings to be the stake depending, the thrower will be entitled to have for his first throw,	3	0
which deducted out of 36, remains 33; which divided again into 36 parts, make so many eleven pences, out of which the thrower is to have 3 for his second throw,	2	9

The remainder, 30 shillings and three pence, is again to be divided into 36 parts ; dividing the 30 shillings so, make so many ten pences, and the three pence divided into so many parts, make so many thirds of farthings, of which the thrower is to have three parts for his share for his third throw   .   .   .   .   .   .   2 $6\frac{1}{4}$

Total for the thrower   .   8 $3\frac{1}{4}$

So that it is 27s. $8\frac{3}{4}d.$ to 8s. $3\frac{1}{4}d.$ against the thrower; which reduced into the smallest number, is very nearly as 10 to 3, that two sixes, or two fives, or two fours, are not thrown in two throws.

Back-game.

VII. Suppose A to have two men upon his size point in his own tables, three men upon his usual point in his outer table, two men upon the point where his five men are usually placed in his adversary's tables, five men upon his adversary's ace point, and three men upon his adversary's quatre point :

And suppose B to have two men upon his size point in his own tables, three men upon his usual point in his outer table, two men upon the point where his five men are usually placed in his adversary's tables, five men upon his adversary's ace point, and three men upon his adversary's trois point:

Who has the fairest chance to win the hit?

A has, because he is to play either an ace, or a deuce, from his adversary's ace point, in order to make both these points as occasion offers; and having the quatre point in his adversary's tables, he may more easily bring those men away, if he finds it necessary, and he will also have a resting place by the conveniency of that point, which at all times in the game will give him an opportunity of running for the hit, or staying, if he thinks proper. Whereas B cannot so readily come from the trois point in his adversary's tables.

A Case of Curiosity.

I. Let us suppose A and B place their men in the following manner for a hit:

Suppose A to have three men upon his size point in his own tables, three men upon the usual point in his outer table, and nine men upon his adversary's ace, deuce, and trois points, three men to be placed upon each point; and suppose B's men to be placed in his own, and in his adverary's tables, in the same order and manner.

The result is, that the best player ought to win the hit; and the dice are to be thrown for, the situation being perfectly equal in A's and B's game.

If A throws first, let him endeavour to gain his adversary's cinque point; when that is effected, let him lay as many blots as possible, to tempt B to hit him; for every time that B hits them will be in A's favor, because it puts B backward; and let A take up none of B's men for the same reason.

A is always to endeavour to have three men upon each of his adversary's ace and deuce points; because when B makes a blot, these points will remain secure, and by recourse had to a former case (No. V. in the former chapter) when A has borne five, six, or more men, yet A may secure six close points out of his tables, in order to prevent B from getting his man home; and by recourse had to the calculations, he may easily find out (in case he makes up his tables) who has the better of the hit; and if he finds that B is forwarder, he is then to endeavour to lay such blots to be taken up by his adversary, as may give him a chance for taking up another man, in case B should happen to have a blot at home.

Those who play the foregoing game well, may be ranked in the first form.

A Case of Curiosity.

II. A and B play at Backgammon. A has borne thirteen men, and has two men to bear upon his deuce point, B has thirteen men in his own tables, with two men to enter. B is to throw, and to name the throws both for himself and A, but not to hit a blot on either side :

What throws is B to name for both parties, in order to save his gammon ?

B calls for himself two aces, which enter his two men upon A's ace point. B also calls two aces for A, and consequently A cannot either bear a man, nor play one ; then B calls for two sixes for himself and carries one man home upon his size point in his own tables, and the other he places upon his adversary's bar point : B also calls size-ace for A, so that A has one man left to bear, and then B calls for himself either two sixes, two fives, or two fours, any of which bear a man, in case he has men in his own tables upon those points, and to save his gammon.

II. The following question is to be attended to, as being critical and instructive :—

Suppose that all the points both on yours and your adversary's tables are covered :

Also that you have one man to carry home, but that he has two men on your barr point to carry home, which lie in wait to catch your man, and that if you pass him you are to win the hit : suppose also that you have it in your choice to run the risk of being hit, by 7, or by 8, both of which are chances upon double dice :—

Which of these chances is it best for you to venture ?

That of 7, for the following reasons: First, because that the chances of being hit by 7, or by 8, are equal.

Secondly, If he does not hit 7, you will then have in your favor 23 chances to 13, that by your next throw you either hit him or pass beyond him.

Thirdly, In case your second throw should happen to be

under 7, and that consequently you cannot hit him, yet you may play that cast at home, and consequently leave the blot upon double dice.

Whereas if, on the contrary, you had left the blot upon 8, you would have made a bad choice, for the reasons following:—

First. Because the chances of being hit by 7, or by 8, are only equal.

Secondly. Because if you should escape the being hit by 8, yet you would then have but 17 chances in your favor, against 19 for either hitting him, or passing beyond him by your next throw.

Thirdly. In case your second throw should happen to be size-ace, which is short of him, you would then be obliged to play the man that is out of your tables, not being able to play the 6 at home, and consequently to leave a blot to be hit by a single (or flat) die; which event, upon supposition that you play for 18 shillings a game, would entitle him to 11 shillings of the whole stake depending

THE LAWS OF BACKGAMMON.

I. If you take a man from any point, that man must be played; the same must be done if two men are taken from it.

II. You are not understood to have played any man, till you have placed him upon a point, and quitted him.

III. If you play with fourteen men only, there is no penalty attending it, because by playing with a lesser number than you are entitled to, you play to a disadvantage, by not having the additional man to make up your tables.

IV. If you bear any number of men, before you have entered a man taken up, and which consequently you were obliged to enter, such men, so borne, must be entered again in your adversary's tables, as well as the man taken up.

V. If you have mistaken your throw, and played, and if your adversary has thrown, it is not in your or his choice to alter it, unless both parties agree.

DRAUGHTS.

THIS interesting and highly scientific game has, by several of the writers upon it, been held to have preceded chess, of which it is supposed to be the root or source. Whether it may claim descent from the Greeks or Scandinavians is a point that may be left to the antiquarian without any great social loss should he never succeed in settling it. In like manner the attempt to confer upon it any higher character than that of a rational means for the employment of a leisure hour may as conveniently be spared. The utility—in a general sense—of any mere game of science or skill, may be a question for philosophy—but it is one with which those who treat of its practical details have nothing to do—and of which most probably they could make nothing, if they had. Chess, according to Sir William Jones, dates some four thousand years back: if Draughts anticipated it, then, upon the principle that "age is honorable" the recreation we are about to treat of is one of no mean pretensions.*

We do not discover from any written record, that Draughts was much practised in Europe till the middle of the sixteenth century. In 1668, an elaborate treatise upon it was published in Paris, written by a celebrated professor of mathematics, M. Mallet. Nearly a century later Mr. William Payne, teacher of mathematics, published his celebrated Introduction to the Game of Draughts, London, 1756. Subsequently, in 1767, appeared "a Companion for the Draught-player," by W. Painter, and there are other essays in type, but none that bear any comparison with "The Guide to the Game of Draughts, by Joshua Sturges, printed for the author, in London, 1800." Sturges worked up the whole of his predecessor's treatise in his more extended work, and with so much care and diligence, that half a century has elapsed without disturbing the authority of his book. Mr. Walker re-edited Sturges in 1835, and this improved edition is here given entire, with

---

* In Mr. Angas's "Savage Life and Scenes," it is stated that draughts is played by the savage tribes of the interior of New Zealand, under the name of E'mu, and that it does not seem possible they could have derived their knowledge of it from any other people.

some additions by a skilful player of our metropolis, Mr.
Martin.

Draughts it should always be remembered is purely a
game of calculation, and as such craves wary policy. It
is played by two persons upon a board of sixty-four squares,
colored alternately Black and White, or any other two
opposite colors. The board is placed with an upper white
corner on the right hand, which brings the double white
square to the lower right-hand corner.

Each player has twelve men; which on beginning the game,
are placed on their respective sides, on the first three lines of
white squares. The following diagrams represent the board
and men in their original position; and also the mode in which
the squares are conventionally numbered for the sake of
reference.* It will be seen that, throughout this work, the
upper half of the board is occupied by the twelve Black men,
and the lower half by their antagonists, the White.

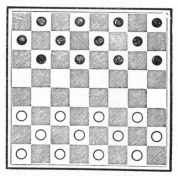

The men being placed, the game is begun by each player
moving alternately one of his men, along the white diagonal
on which they are first posted. The men can only move forward, either to the right or left, one square at a time, unless
they have attained one of the four squares on the extreme line
of the board, on which they become kings, and can move
either forward or backward, but still only one square at a
time. The men take in the direction they move, by leaping

* Practised players who have studied printed games are generally so
familiar with the numerical position of the square that they can read and
comprehend a series of intricate moves without even referring to the
board.

over any hostile piece or pieces that may be immediately contiguous, provided there be a vacant white square behind them. The piece or pieces so taken are then removed from off the board, and the man taking them is placed on the square beyond. If several pieces, on forward diagonals, should be exposed by alternately having open squares behind them, they may all be taken at one capture, and the taking piece is then placed on the square beyond the last piece. To explain the mode of taking by practical illustration, let us begin by placing the draughts in their origional position. You will perceive that if Black should move first he can only move one of the men placed on 9, 10, 11, or 12.—Supposing him then to play the man from 11 to 15, and White answering this move by playing his piece from 22 to 18, Black can take White by leaping his man from 15 to 22 and removing the captured piece off the board. Should Black not take in the above position, but move in another direction,—for instance, from 12 to 16, he is liable to be huffed; that is, White may remove the man with which Black should have taken, from the board, as a penalty for not taking; for, at Draughts, you have not the option of refusing to take, as at Chess, but must always take when you can, whatever be the consequence. The player who is in a position to huff his adversary has also the option of insisting on his taking, instead of standing the huff. When one party huffs the other, in preference to compelling the take, he does not replace the piece his adversary moved; but simply removes the man huffed, from off the board, and then plays his own move. Should he, however, insist upon his adversary taking the piece, instead of standing the huff, then the pawn improperly moved must first be replaced.

To give another example of huffing. Suppose a white man to be placed at 28, and three black men, at 24, 15, and 6, or 24, 16, and 8, with unoccupied intervals he would capture all three men, and make a king, or be huffed for omitting to take them all, and it is not uncommon with novices to take one man, and overlook a second or third, " *en prise*" (*i.e.*, liable to be taken).

When either of the men reaches one of the extreme squares of the board, he is, as already indicated, made a king, by having another piece put on, which is called crowning him. The king can move or take both forward or backward; keeping, of course, on the white diagonals. Both the king and common man can take any number of pieces at once which may be " *en prise* " at one move, and both are equally liable to be huffed. For instance: if White by reaching one of the back squares on his antagonist's side, say No. 2, had gained a king, he might upon having the move, and the Black pieces (either kings or men) being conveniently posted at No. 7, 16, 24, 23, and 14, with intermediate blanks, take them all at one fell swoop, remaining at square 9. But such a coup could hardly happen in English draughts. One of the great objects of the game, even at its very opening, is to push on for a king; but it is unnecessary to dwell much on the elementary part of the science, as the playing through one of the many games annexed, from the numbers, will do more in the way of teaching the rudiments of Draughts, than the most elaborate theoretical explanation.

The game is won by him who can first succeed in capturing, or blocking up, all his adversary's men, so that he has nothing left to move; but when the pieces are so reduced that each player has but a very small degree of force remaining; and, being equal in numbers, neither can hope to make any decided impression on his antagonist, the game is relinquished as drawn. It is obvious that were this not the case, and both parties had one or two kings, the game might be prolonged day and night, with the same hopeless chance of natural termination, as at the first moment of the pieces being resolved into the position in question. It has already been shewn that when a man reaches one of the squares on the extreme line of the board, he is crowned and becomes a king; but there is another point relative to this, which it is necessary to understand. The man, thus reaching one of the extreme squares, finishes the move on being made a king, and cannot take any piece which may be " *en prise.*" He must first await his antagonist's move, and should he omit to remove or fortify an exposed piece it may then be taken. To exemplify this, place a White man on 11, and Black men on 7 and 6 :—White, having the move, takes the man and demands that his own man should be crowned; but, he cannot take the man on 6 at the same move; which he could do were his piece a king when it made the first capture. But if the piece be left there after the next move he must take it.

In particular situations, to have the move on your side, is a decisive advantage. This is a matter little understood by ordinary players, but its importance will fully appear by studying the critical situations. To have the move, signifies your occupying that position on the board which will eventually enable you to force your adversary into a confined situation, and which at the end of the game, secures to yourself the last move. It must, however, be observed, that where your men are in a confined state, the move is not only of no use to you, but, for that very reason, may occasion the loss of the game. To know in any particular situation whether you have the move, you must number the men and the squares, and if the men are even and the squares odd, or the squares even and the men odd, you have the move. With even men and even squares, or odd men and odd squares, you have not the move.—This will be best explained by an example: Look, then, at the 8th critical situation, where White plays first; there the adverse men are even, two to two: but the White squares, being five in number, are odd. The squares may be thus reckoned—from 26, a White king, to 28, a Black king, are three, viz. 31, 27, and 24—The White squares between 32, a White man, and 19, a Black man, are two, viz. 27 and 23. You may reckon more ways than one, but reckon which way you will, the squares will still be found odd, and therefore, White, so situated, has the move. When you have not the move, you must endeavour to procure it by giving man for man, a mode of play fully and successfully exemplified in this treatise.

There is another mode which will, in less time than reckoning the squares, enable you to see who has the move. For instance, if you wish to know, whether any one man of your's has the move of any one man of your adversary's, examine the situation of both, and if you find a Black square on the right angle, under his man, you have the move :—For example, you are to play first, and your White man is on 30, when your adversay's Black man is on 3—In this situation, you will find the right angle in a black square between 31 and 32, immediately under 3, and therefore you have the move. This Rule will apply to any number of men, and holds true in every case.

There is a third mode, more ingenious still, communicated

by Mr. Martin, and now published for the first time. Count
all the pieces (of both colors) standing on those columns
(not diagonals) which have a white square at the bottom, and
if the number be odd, and White has to play, he has the
move; if the number be even, the move is with Black.

It is a mistake to suppose that any advantage is derived from
playing first. It is admitted, that he who plays first has not
the move, the men and squares being then both even; but,
though he who plays second has the move, it can be of no
service to him in that stage of the game. The truth is, that
when the combatants continue giving man for man, the move
will alternately belong to one and the other. The first player
will have it at odd men, at 11, 9, 7, 5, 3, and 1 ; the second
player will have it at even men, at 12, 10, 8, 6, 4, and 2 ;
and therefore some error must be committed, on one side
or the other, before the move can be forced out of that
direction.

To play over the games in this work, number the White
squares on your draught-board from 1 to 32, and remember
that in our diagram the Black pieces always occupy the first
twelve squares. The abbreviations are so obvious, that they
cannot need explanation ;—as B. for Black, W. for White, Var.
for Variation, &c. Occasionally, stars (asterisks) are introduced, to point out the move causing the loss of the game. The
learner begins with the first game, and finding the leading
move to be 11. 15 (that is, from 11 to 15), knows that Black
begins the game. The second move 22. 18 belongs to White,
and the game is thus played out; each party moving alternately.
After finishing the game, the player proceeds to examine the
variations to which he is referred by the letters and other
directions. The numerous variations on some particular
games, and the consequent necessity each time of going
through the leading moves up to the point at which the
variation arises, will, probably, at first, occasion some little
fatigue ; but this will be soon forgotten in the speedy and
decided improvement found to be derived from this course of
study. One of the minor advantages resulting from a
numerous body of variations is, that, in tracing them out, the
leading moves are so frequently repeated that they become
indelibly fixed in the mind of the player ; who thus remembers
which moves are to be shunned as dangerous if not ruinous,

and which moves are to be adopted as equally sound and scientific.

As to general advice relative to draught-playing, next to nothing can be learnt from a volume of such instruction. The various modes of opening will be seen by reference to the accompanying examples. Among the few general rules that can be given you should bear in mind, that it is generally better to keep your men in the middle of the board, than to play them to the side squares,—as, in the latter case, one-half of their power is curtailed. And when you have once gained an advantage in the number of your pieces you increase the proportion by exchanges; but in forcing them you must take care not to damage your position. If you are a chess-player, you will do well to compare the draughts in their march and mode of manœuvring with the Pawns at Chess; which, as well as the Bishops, or other pieces, are seldom so strong on the side squares as in the centre of the board. Accustom yourself to play slow at first, and, if a beginner, prefer playing with those who will agree to allow an unconditional time for the consideration of a difficult position, to those who rigidly exact the observance of the strict law. Never touch a man without moving it, and do not permit the loss of a few games to ruffle your temper, but rather let continued defeat act as an incentive to greater efforts both of study and practice. When one player is decidedly stronger than another, he should give odds to make the game equally interesting to both parties. There must be a great disparity indeed if he can give a man, but it is very common to give one man in a rubber of three games; that is, in one of the three games, the superior player engages to play with only 11 men instead of 12. Another description of odds consists in giving the drawn games; that is, the superior player allows the weaker party to reckon as won, all games he draws. Never play with a better player without offering to take such odds as he may choose to give. If you find yourself, on the other hand, so superior to your adversary, that you feel no amusement in playing even—offer him odds, and should he refuse, cease playing with him unless he will play for a stake; the losing which, for a few games in succession, will soon bring him to his senses, and make him willing to receive the odds you offer. Follow the rules of the game most rigorously, and compel your antagonist to do the same ; without which, Draughts are mere child's play.   If you wish to improve, play with better players, in preference to such as you can beat ; and take every opportunity of looking on when fine players are engaged. Never touch the squares of the board with your finger, as some do, from the supposition that it assists their powers of calculation, and accustom yourself to play your move off-hand when you have once made up your mind : without hovering with your fingers over the board for a couple of minutes, to the great anoyance of the lookers-on.   While you play, do not fall into the vulgar habit of incessantly chattering nonsense ; and shew no impatience at your adversary, should he be a little slow.   Finally, bear in mind what may well be termed the three golden rules to be observed in playing games of calculation :—Firstly, to avoid all boasting and loud talking about your skill—Secondly, to lose with good temper— and, Thirdly, to win with silence and modesty.

LAWS OF THE GAME.

1. The first move of each game is to be taken by the players in turn, whether the game be won or drawn. For the move in the first game at each sitting, the players must cast or draw lots, as they must for the men, which are, however, to be changed every game, so that each player shall use the black and white alternately.   Whoever gains the choice may either play first, or call upon his adversary to do so.

2. You must not point over the board with your finger, nor do any thing which may interrupt your adversary's full and continued view of the game.

3. At any part of the game you may adjust the men properly on the squares, by previously intimating your intention to your adversary.   This in polite society is usually done by saying "J'adoube."   But after they are so adjusted, if you touch a man, it being your turn to play, you must play him in one direction or other if practicable; and if you move a man so far as to be in any part visible over the angle of an open square, that move must be completed, although by moving it to a different square you might have taken a piece, for the omission of which you incur huffing. The rule is "touch and move." No penalty, however, is attached to your touching any man which cannot be played.

4. In the case of your standing the huff, it is optional on the part of your adversary, to take your capturing piece, whether man or king, or to compel you to take the piece or pieces of his, which you omitted by the huff. The necessity of this law is evident, when the young player is shewn that it is not unusual to sacrifice two or three men in succession, for the power of making some decisive " *coup.*" Were this law different, the players might take the first man so offered, and on the second's being placed " *en prise,*" might refuse to capture, and thus spoil the beauty of the game, (which consists in the brilliant results arising from scientific calculation,) by quietly standing the huff. It should be observed, however, that on the principle of " touch and move," the option ceases the moment the huffing party has so far made his election as to touch the piece he is entitled to remove.— After a player entitled to huff has moved without taking his adversary, he cannot remedy the omission, unless his adversary should still neglect to take or to change the position of the piece concerned, and so leave the opportunity. It does not matter how long a piece has remained " *en prise,*" it may at any time either be huffed or the adversary be compelled to take it.— When several pieces are taken at one move, they must not be removed from the board until the capturing piece has arrived at its destination ; the opposite course may lead to disputes, especially in Polish draughts.—The act of huffing is not reckoned as a move, a " huff and a move" go together.

5, If, when it is your turn to play, you delay moving above three minutes, your adversary may require you to play ; and should you not move within five minutes after being so called upon, you lose the game ; which your adversary is adjudged to have won, through your improper delay.

6. When you are in a situation to take on either of two forward diagonals, you may take which way you please ; without regard (as in Polish Draughts) to the one capture comprising greater force than the other. For example, if one man is " *en prise*" one way and two another, you may take either the one or the two, at your option.

7. During the game, neither party can leave the room without mutual agreement ; or the party so leaving forfeits the game. Such a rule, however, could only be carried out with certain limitations.

8. When, at the end of the game, a small degree of force alone remains, the player appearing the stronger, may be required to win the game in a certain number of moves; and, if he cannot do this, the game must be abandoned as drawn. Suppose that three Black kings and two White kings were the only pieces remaining on the board; the White insists that his adversary shall win or relinquish the game as drawn, after forty* moves (at most) have been played by each player.—The moves to be computed from that point at which notice was given. If two kings remain opposed to one king only, the moves must not exceed twenty on each side. The number of moves once claimed they are not to be exceeded even if one more would win the game. A move, it should be observed, is not complete until both sides have played; therefore, twenty moves, so called, consist of twenty on each side. In giving the odds of "the draw," the game must, however, be played to a more advanced state than is required in any other case. When in such a game the situations become so equal that no advantage can be taken, he who gives the draw shall not occasion any unnecessary delay by uselessly repeating the same manœuvres; but shall force his adversary out of his strong position, or, after at most 20 moves, lose the game through its being declared drawn.

9. By-standers are forbidden to make any remarks whatever, relative to the game, until that game shall be played out. Should the players be contending for a bet or stake, and the spectator say anything that can be construed into the slightest approach to warning or intimation, that spectator shall pay all bets pending on the losing side, should that side win which has received the intimation.

10. Should any dispute occur between the players, not satisfactorily determined by the printed rules, the question must be mutually referred to a third party, whose decision shall be considered final. Of course, should a player commit any breach of the laws, and refuse to submit to the penalty, his adversary is justified in claiming the game without playing it out.

11. Respecting a false move, such as giving a common man the move of a king, or any other impropriety of the same sort, the law varies in different countries as to the penalty to be exacted by the opposite party. We cannot but suppose that

* We think half the number would be better.

such mistakes are unintentional, and consider it sufficient penalty that in all such cases the piece touched must be moved to whichever square the adversary chooses; or, he has the option of allowing the false move to stand, if more to his advantage. Should the piece be unable to move at all, that part of the penalty cannot be inflicted.

12. The rule (almost universal with English Draughts) is to play on the white squares. The exception (limited we believe to Scotland) is to play on the *black*. When, therefore, players are pledged to a match without any previous agreement as to which squares are to be played on, white must be taken as the law. The color of the squares, excepting so far as habit is concerned, makes no difference in their relative position on the board.

In all cases, a player refusing to take, to play, or to comply with any of the rules, loses the game. Hence the saying "whoever leaves the game loses it."

EXAMPLES OF GAMES, FROM STURGES,

(See Explanations at page 410.)

GAME 1.	5.14	23.27	7.10	15.24	32.28
	27.23	8. 4	17.14	23.19	3. 7
11.15	6.10	27.31	10.17	10.14	28.24
22.18	16.12	*4. 8	22.13	26.22	10.14
15.22	8.11	31.27	15.22	6. 9	31.26
25.18	28.24	24.20	26.17	25.21	14.18
8.11 var.	25.29	27.23	8.12 A.	9.13	Drawn.
29.25	30.25	8.11	27.24	11. 7	
4. 8	29.22	23.18	3. 7	W. wins.	B.
25.22	26.17	11. 8	30.25		25.21
12.16	11.15	18.15	7.10	A.	10.14
24.20	20.16	B. wins.	24.19 B.	9.14	17.10
10.15	15.18		10.14	17.10	6.15
27.24*	24.20	Var.	17.10	6.15	13. 6
16.19	18.27	12.16	6.24	27.24	2. 9
23.16	31.24	29.25	13. 6 D.	8.12	24.19
15.19	14.18	8.11	1.10 E.	24.19	15.24
24.15	16.11	24.20	28.19	15.24	28.19
9.14	7.16	10.15	2. 6	28.19	9.14
18. 9	20.11	25.22	31.26 G.	5. 9	19.15
11.25	18.23	4. 8	11.15	13. 6	11.27
32.27	11. 8	21.17	20.11	1.10	20.11

* These asterisks, wherever they occur, denote the moves which cause the loss of the game.

416 — DRAUGHTS.

1. 6	20.11	24. 8	2. 7	**GAME** 3.	14.10
32.23	Drawn.	17.14	30.25	11.15	17.14
6. 9		12.19	7.11	22.18	10. 7
23.19	E.	14.16	25.21	15.22	18.23
14.17	2. 9	8.12	18.22	25.18	7. 3
21.14	28.19	W. wins.	26.17	8.11	23.27
9.18	9.14		11.15	29.25	3. 7
11. 7	25.22	G.	20.16	4. 8	14.18
18.22	1. 6	25.22	15.18	25.22	7.11
7. 3	32.28	6. 9	24.20	12.16	27.31
5. 9	6. 9 F.	32.28	18.22	24.19	11.16
3. 7	31.27	9.13	27.24	16.20	31.27
9.13	9.13	28.24	22.26	28.24 var 1	16.20
7.10	27.24	10.14	19.15	8.12	18.22
22.25 C.	13.17	31.26	12.19	32.28	B. wins.
10.14	22.18	13.17	13. 9	10.15	
25.29	14.17	22.13	6.22	19.10	Var. 1.
31.27	23.18	14.17	15. 6	7.14	19.15
29.25	16.23	19.15	1.10	30.25	10.19
Drawn.	24.19	11.27	24. 6	11.16	23.16
	W. wins.	B. wins.	Drawn.	18.15	9.14
C.			Var.	3. 8	18. 9
13.17	F.	**GAME** 2.	9.13	22.17	5.14
10.14	6.10	11.15	17.14	14.18	16.12
17.21	28.24	24.20	16.19	23.14	11.15
14.17	5. 9	8.11	23.16	9.18	27.23
22.25	31.27	22.18	8.12	26.23	6.10
17.22	9.13	15.22	14.10	6. 9	31.27
25.29	22.18	25.18	7.23 A.	23.14	8.11
22.26	13.17	4. 8	16. 7	9.18	22.17
29.25	18. 9	29.25	2.11	15.10	15.18
31.27	17.22	10.15	26.10	8.11	30.25
W. wins.	9. 6	25.22	6.15	10. 7 var 2	2. 6 A.
	22.26	12.16	28.24	11.15	23.19 B.
D.	6. 2	21.17	5. 9	7. 3	11.15
28.19	26.31	7.10 var	27.23	2. 7	28.24
9.14	2. 7	17.13	1. 6	3.19	6. 9
25.22	10.14	8.12	31.26	16.32	17.13
2. 6	19.15	28.24	6.10	24.19	1. 6
22.18	11.18	9.14	32.28	32.27	26.22
6.10	20.11	18. 9	3. 7	31.24	7.11
18. 9	31.26	5.14	23.19	20.27	19.16
5.14	23.19	23.19	W. wins.	17.14	3. 7
13. 9	26.23	16.23		27.31	24.19
14.17	24.20	26.19	A.	21.17	15.31
9. 6	23.32	3. 8	12.19	31.26	22. 8
10.14	7.10	31.26	27.23	25.21	W. wins.
6. 2	32.27	15.18	7.14	26.22	
17.22	10.17	22.15	23. 7	17.13	A.
19.15	27.24	11.18	W. wins.	22.17	1. 6
11.27	20.16	32.28			17.13

11.15	24.19	17.21	23.19		2. 6
28.24	7.10	B. wins.	16.12	**GAME** 5.	10.14
7.11	32.27		19.15	11.15	6. 9
23.19	9.13	A.	5. 1	22.18	25.21
11.16	18. 9	27.24	15.10	15.22	31.26
26.23	5.14	3. 7	1. 5	25.18	14.17
6. 9	22.18	26.22	10. 6	8.11	Drawn.
13. 6	1. 5	14.17	B. wins.	29.25	
2. 9	18. 9	21.14		4. 8	Var. 1.
21.17	5.14	10.26	C.	25.22	23.19
Drawn.	19.15 A.	31.22	30.26	12.16	16.23
B.	11.18	7.10	9.14	24.20	26.19
17.13	20.11	30.25	10. 6	10.15	3. 7
11.16	18.22	10.14	3. 8	21.17	31.27
28.24	26.17	25.21	24.20	7.10	14.18
1. 5	13.22	13.17	8.11	27.24	30.25
32.28	11. 8	22.13	6. 1	8.12	11.16
7.11	22.25	6. 9	11.15	17.13	20.11
26.22	8. 4	Drawn.	1. 6	9.14	7.23
11.15	25.29	B.	15.19	18. 9	25.21
B. wins.	4. 8	11. 7	20.16	5.14 ⌈var.	18.25
	2. 7	6. 9	18.23	24.19 ⎱1, 2,	27.11
Var. 2.	23.19	13. 6	26.22	15.24 ⎰& 3.	25.30
17.14	29.25	23.27	23.26	28.19	11. 8
11.15	27.24	31.24	16.11	14.17	30.26
21.17	14.18	10.15	26.30	32.27	8. 3
16.19	21.17	19.10	11. 7	10.14	26.23
31.26	25.22	12.19	30.26	27.24 var 4	3. 8
2. 6	17.13	24.15	B. wins.	3. 7	23.18
17.13	18.23	18. 9		30.25 var 5	8.11
12.16	8. 4	28.24	D.	6. 9	10.14
25.21	10.14	14.18	16.12	13. 6	24.19
18.23	24.20	24.19 C.	10.14	1.10	18.23
Drawn.	22.18	18.23	1. 5	22.13	11.16
	4. 8	19.16	26.23	14.18	14.17
GAME 4.	18.22	9.14	5. 1	23.14	21.14
11.15	20.16	10. 6	23.19	16.30	6.10
22.18	22.18	23.27	1. 6	25.21	14. 7
15.22	8.11	6. 1	19.15	10.17	2.20
25.18	7.10	14.10	6. 2	21.14	19.15
8.11	28.24 B.	30.25	15.11	30.25	1. 6
29.25	14.17	27.31	2. 6	14. 9	B. wins.
4. 8	24.20	25.21	3. 7	11.15 var 6	
25.22	10.14	31.26	6.10	9. 6	Var. 2.
12.16	11. 8	21.17 D.	14.18	2. 9	30.25
24.20	17.22	26.23	10. 3	13. 6	14.17
10.14	8.11	17.13	18.14	15.18	25.21
27.24	14.17	10.14	12. 8	6. 2	3. 7
8.12	11. 8	1. 5	B wins.	7.10	21.14

2 E

10.17	14.17	**Var. 4.**	19.28	E.	**1.10**
24.19	24.19	22.18	18.14	9. 5	**31.26**
15.24	15.24	1. 5	28.32	22.18	**5. 9**
28.19	28.12	18. 9	8. 3	31.26	26.23
7.10	17.26	5.14	7.11	11.15	9.13
32.27	23.18	19.15	23.19	5. 1	23.19
17.21	6.10	11.18	32.27	7.11	13.17
22.18	B. wins.	20.11	3. 8	1. 5	22.13
21.25		12.16	2. 7	12.16	15.22
18.15	B.	27.24	8.15	13. 9	32.28
11.18	27.18	18.27	7.10	16.19	10.14
20.11	16.19	24.20	14. 7	B. wins.	19.16
25.30	32.27 C	27.32	6. 9		12.19
23. 7	5. 9	31.27	B. wins.	F.	24. 8
B. wins.	20.16	32.23		31.26	3.12
	11.20	26.12	**Var. 6.**	11.15	13. 9
Var. 3.	18.11	17.22	25.22†	6. 2	14.18
31.27	10.15	11. 8	9. 6 E.	7.11	28.24
1. 5	22.17	14.18	2. 9	2. 6	18.23
23.19 A.	3. 7	8. 4	13. 6	18.14	24.19
16.23	11. 8	18.23	22.18	26.23	23.27
27. 9	7.10	4. 8	6. 2 F.	12.16	19.15
5.14	8. 3	22.26	18.23	B. wins.	27.32
24.19	9.14	30.25	2. 6		15.11
15.24	3. 8	26.30	11.15	**GAME 6.**	32.27
28.19	14.21	25.22	6. 2	11.15	9. 5
11.15	8.11	30.25	7.11	22.18	27.23
32.28	6. 9	22.17	2. 6	15.22	5. 1
15.24	B. wins.	25.21	15.18	25.18	22.26
28.19		17.14	6.10	8.11	Drawn.
3. 8	C.	21.17	18.22	29.25	
26.23	22.17 D.	14. 9	10.14	4. 8	**Var.**
14.17	15.31	17.14	22.25	25.22	9.14
22.18	24. 8	Drawn.	14.17	12.16	18. 9
17.22	5. 9		25.29	24.20	5.14
B wins.	30.25	**Var. 5.**	17.14	10.15	23.18 C.
	31.26	22.18	29.25	21.17	14.23
A.	B wins.	1. 5	14.10	7.10	27.18 A.
23.18		18. 9	25.22	17.13	16.19
14.23	D.	5.14	10.14	8.12	32.28
26.19 B.	26.23	26.22	23.27	28.24	10.14
16.23	19.26	17.26	14.10	10.14 var	18. 9
27.18	30.23	31.22	22.17	23.19	1. 5
10.14	10.14	14.17	31.26	16.23	26.23
18. 9	18. 9	22.18	27.32	26.10	19.26
5.14	5.14	17.22	26.23	14.23	30.23
30.26	23.19	19.15	32.28	27.18	5.14
12.16	6.10	16.19	23.19	6.15	24.19
26.23	32.27	15. 8	28.32	13. 6	15.24
	B. wins.		B. wins.		

28.19	14.23	1. 5	F.	6.22	2.27
14.17	27.18	6. 1	26.19	15. 6	17.14
22.18	12.16	5. 9	3. 8	1.10	27.32
17.22	32.27 D.	10.15	31.26 H.	24. 6	19.15
18.14	16.19	9. 5	15.18	8.12	32.27
6.10	18.14	15.18	22.15	Drawn.	B. wins.
14. 7	19.28	21.17	11.18		
3.10	14. 7	18.22	32.28 I.	H.	L.
23.18	15.18	17.14	2. 7	27.23	19.16
2. 6	22.15	1. 6	30.25	15.18	12.19
B. wins.	11.18	5. 1	14.17 G.	22.15	11.15
	7. 3	6. 2	25.21	11.27	Drawn.
A.	8.12	14. 9	18.22	32.23	
26.19	27.24	B. wins.	21.14	8.11	GAME 7.
16.23	28.32		10.17	30.26	22.18
27.18	24.19	D.	26.23	14.17	11.15
12.16	6.10	30.26	17.21	26.22	18.11
32.28	3. 8	16.19	23.18	17.26	8.15
16.19	32.28	32.28	22.26	31.22	21.17
30.26 B.	8.11	8.12	18.14	10.14	4. 8
1. 5	28.24	22.17	1. 5	22.18	23.19
31.27	11.15 L.	15.31	19.15	1. 5	8.11 var 1
5. 9	18.23	24. 8	26.31	18. 9	17.13
20.16	15. 6	31.26	27.23	5.14	9.14
11.20	2. 9	B. wins.	7.11	B. wins.	27.23
18.11	13. 6		23.19		5. 9
10.15	24.15	E.	11.18	I.	25.22
22.17	30.25	32.28	19.15	26.22	14.17
3. 7	15.10	5.14	18.22	18.25	29.25
11. 8	6. 1	26.23	24.19	30.21	17.21
7.10	10.14	3. 8	31.27	14.18	22.17
B wins.	1. 6	23.19	28.24	32.28 K.	11.16
	23.26	15.18	Drawn.	10.15	25.22
B.	25.21	22.15		19.10	16.20
18.14	26.30	11.18	G.	6.15	19.16
10.26	6. 1	31.26	7.11	21.17	20.27
30. 7	30.26	18.22	25.21	8.11	31.24
B. wins.	1. 5	26.17	18.22	B. wins.	12.19
	26.22	14.21	26.17		23.16
C.	5. 1	30.26	11.15	K.	10.14
23.19	22.17	21.25	20.16	21.17	17.10
16.23	1. 5	26.23	15.18	8.11	7.14
27. 9 F.	17.13	25.30	24.20	27.23	24.19
1. 5	5. 1	23.18	18.22	18.27	15.24
26.23 E.	13. 9	30.26	27.24	32.23	28.19
5.14	1. 5	18.15	22.26	11.15	1. 5
31.27	9. 6	26.31	19.15	20.16	22.17
3. 8	5. 1	B. wins.	12.19	15.18	14.18
23.18	14.10		13. 9	23. 7	26.23

18.27	24.15	19.16	23.14	22.26	20.11
32.23	17.22	24.27	19.23	29.25	7.23
6.10	26.17	16.12	26.19	26.31	5. 9
13. 6	13.29	27.31	17.26	25.22	21.25
2. 9	15.10	12. 8	30.23	2. 6	30.21
17.13	29.25	1. 6	6. 9	22.18 F.	22.26
9.14	7. 2	8. 3	13. 6	16.20	21.17
Drawn.	25.22	14.18	2.27	18.14	26.31
	Drawn.	22.15	B. wins.	10.17	9.13
Var. 1.		31.22		23.18	10.15
15.18	**Var. 2.**	11.16	**C.**	17.22	13. 9
17.13	31.26	10.19	29.25	30.26	15.19
9.14	10.17	16.23	3. 8	22.25	24.15
26.23	25.22	6.10	27.23	26.22	31.24
14.17	8.11 D.	3. 7	8.12	25.30	9.14
23.14	27.23	10.14	16.11	22.17	12.16
17.21	7.10	7.10	5. 9	30.26	Drawn.
27.23 var 2	29.25 A.	22.26	23.16	18.14	
10.17	11.15	23.19	12.19	26.22	**F.**
31.26	32.27	26.22	11. 8	14. 9	22.17
5. 9	3. 7	10.15	19.23	6.10	31.26
25.22	19.16	W. wins.	26.19	9. 6	23.18
9.14	12.19		17.26	22.18	16.32
29.25	23.16	**A.**	30.23	6. 2	30.23
8.11	7.11	24.20	21.30	31.26	32.27
24.20	16. 7	11.15	19.16	2. 7	24.20
11.16	2.11	19.16	30.26	10.14	21.25
20.11	27.23	12.19	23.19	17.10	23.19
7.16	5. 9	23.16	Drawn.	26.23	25.30
32.27	24.20	15.19		7. 2	18.14
3. 8	9.14	32.27	**D.**	23.16	27.24
19.15	28.24	10.14	5. 9	2. 6	10. 7
16.19	11.16	16.11 B.C.	22.18	21.25	24.15
23.16	20.11	19.24	8.11	6. 9	7. 2
12.19	15.18	28.19	26.23	18.15	6.10
15.10	22.15	21.25	17.22	10. 7	2. 6
6.15	10.28	30.21	18.15	B. wins.	30.25
13. 9	11. 7	14.18	11.18		6. 9
15.18	6.10	21.14	23. 5	**E.**	25.21
22.15	7. 2	18.25	7.11	28.24	9.14
14.18	28.32	29.22	24.20	6.10	12.16
15.10	2. 7	6. 9	3. 7	13. 9	14. 7
8.12	32.27	13. 6	27.23 E.	10.14	21.14
9. 5	23.19	2.25	6.10	9. 6	20.11
2. 6	27.31	Drawn.	32.27	1.10	B. wins.
10. 7	25.22		11.16	5. 1	
6. 9	31.27	**B.**	20.11	14.18	**GAME 8.**
27.24	7.11	27.23	7.16	1. 5	22.18
9.13	27.24	14.18	28.24	11.16	11.15

18.11	12.19	**B.**	**D.**	20.11	12.19
8.15	23. 7	5.14	30.26	7.16	24.20
21.17	14.18	22.13	13.17	19.15	14.18
4. 8	21.14	14.17	25.21	9.14	20.16
23.19	18.25	13. 9	19.23	22.18	18.25
8.11	30.21	6.13	21. 5	1. 5	30.14
17.13	10.17	25.21	23.32	18. 9	6. 9
9.14	21.14	15.18	26.22	5.14	13. 6
27.23	3.17	23.14	32.27	15.11	2.18
6. 9 var 1	24.19	17.22	Drawn.	16.20	31.27
13. 6	15.24	26.17		11. 8	8.12
2. 9	28.19	13.22	**Var. 2.**	2. 7	15.10
24.20	17.21	28.24	32.27	29.25	5. 9
15.24	Drawn.	1. 6	14.17 G.	7.11	10. 7
28.19		27.23	23.14	25.22	9.14
14.17	**Var. 1.**	22.25	17.21	6.10	7. 2
25.22	15.18	21.17	24.20 H.	W. wins.	14.17
9.13	19.15 var 2	25.29	10.17		Drawn.
29.25	18.27	24.19	27.23	**F.**	
5. 9	15. 8	W. wins.	7.10 E.F.	11.16	**H.**
32.28	12.16		25.22	20.11	25.22
9.14	32.23	**C.**	11.15	7.16	10.17
31.27	3.12	10.15	19.16	19.15	29.25
1. 5	24.20	20.11	12.19	3. 8	11.16
25.21	7.11 C.	7.16	23.16	25.22	27.23
11.15	25.22	13. 9	10.14	2. 7	16.20
27.24	14.17	6.13	29.25	31.27	31.27
7.11	29.25	23.18	15.19	5. 9	3. 8
30.25 A.	10.15	15.22	31.27	15.10	23.18
3. 7	31.27	26.10	3. 8	7.14	5. 9
19.16	2. 7	16.19	27.23	28.24	19.16
12.19	13. 9	31.27	8.12	8.11	12.19
23.16	6.13 B.	5. 9	16.11	Drawn.	24.15
14.18	25.21	25.22 D.	5. 9		8.12
21.14	1. 6	9.14	23.16	**G.**	27.23
10.17	21.14	29.25	12.19	11.16	7.10
24.19	6. 9	12.16	11. 8	25.22	15.11
15.24	23.18	25.21	19.23	18.25	20.24
22. 8	13.17	16.20	26.19	29.22	28.19
17.21	22. 6	27.23	17.26	14.17	B. wins.
28.19	15.30	19.26	30.23	24.20	
21.30	27.24	30.23	21.30	10.14	**GAME 9.**
16.12	31.27	1. 5	19.16	20.11	22.18
30.16	6. 1	22.18	Drawn.	7.16	11.15
20. 2	27.23	13.17		19.15	18.11
W. wins.	1. 6	18. 9	**E.**	3. 8	8.15
	23.18	5.14	5. 9	27.24	21.17
A.	6.10	Drawn.	25.22	16.19	4. 8
19.16	W. wins.		11.16	23.16	23.19

8. 11
17. 13
9. 14
27. 23
5. 9
25. 22
14. 17
29. 25
11. 16
32. 27 var 1
16. 20
19. 16
12. 19
23. 16
17. 21
22. 17
15. 18
26. 23
18. 22
25. 18
10. 14
17. 10
6. 22
13. 6
1. 10
23. 18
22. 25
18. 15
10. 19
24. 15
7. 10
15. 6
2. 9
27. 23
25. 29
23. 18
29. 25
31. 26
9. 13
18. 14
13. 17
14. 10
25. 22
26. 23
22. 26
23. 19
26. 23
10. 6
17. 22
6. 2
22. 26
16. 12
23. 16
30. 23
21. 25
2. 6
25. 30
6. 10
30. 26
23. 18
20. 24
B. wins.

Var. 1.

24. 20
15. 24
20. 11
7. 16
28. 19
17. 21
22. 18 var 2
2. 7
31. 27 B.C.
10. 14
18. 15
3. 8
26. 22
7. 11
22. 18
1. 5
25. 22
14. 17
30. 26
21. 25
27. 24
25. 30
15. 10
6. 15
13. 6
16. 20
19. 10
20. 27
22. 13
27. 31
26. 22
31. 26
22. 17
26. 19
Drawn.

Var. 2.

32. 28
2. 7
28. 24
7. 11
24. 20
11. 15 A.
20. 11
15. 24
23. 19
10. 14
11. 8
24. 28
8. 4
28. 32
4. 8
32. 28
8. 11
28. 24
19. 15
14. 18
22. 17
24. 19
17. 14
19. 17
26. 22
17. 26
31. 15
12. 16
11. 20
Drawn.

A.

3. 8
23. 18
16. 23
26. 19
10. 15
19. 10
6. 15
13. 6
1. 10
31. 26
Drawn.

B.

25. 22
7. 11
32. 28 D.
10. 14
28. 24
16. 20
19. 15
20. 27
31. 24
11. 16
15. 10
6. 15
13. 6
1. 10
18. 11
16. 20
Drawn.

D.

31. 27
3. 8 E.
19. 15
10. 19
22. 17
1. 5
17. 14
W. wins.

E.

10. 14
19. 15
3. 7
15. 8
21. 25
30. 21
16. 19
23. 16
14. 30
16. 11
Drawn.

C.

18. 15
3. 8 var 3
32. 27
16. 20
25. 22
7. 11
22. 18
10. 14
27. 24
Drawn.

Var. 3.

16. 20
25. 22 F.
20. 24
32. 28 G.H.
3. 8
23. 18
7. 11
26. 23
1. 5
22. 17
11. 16
31. 26
16. 20
19. 16
10. 19
18. 15
24. 27
23. 18
27. 31
26. 22
31. 26
30. 23
19. 26
16. 11
26. 30
11. 4
Drawn.

F.

31. 27
9. 14
25. 22
21. 25
30. 21
14. 17
21. 14
10. 17
19. 16
12. 19
23. 16
7. 11
16. 7
3. 19
32. 28
17. 21
27. 23
Drawn.

G.

22. 18
3. 8
26. 22
7. 11
32. 28
11. 16
15. 11
8. 15
18. 11
24. 27
31. 24
16. 20
11. 7
Drawn.

H.

23. 18
3. 8
32. 28
7. 11
26. 23
1. 5
22. 17
11. 16
31. 26
16. 20
19. 16
12. 19
23. 16
10. 19
26. 23
19. 26
Drawn.

GAME 10.

22. 18
11. 15
18. 11
8. 15
21. 17
4. 8
23. 19
8. 11
17. 13
9. 14
27. 23
5. 9
25. 22

14.17	**Var. 1.**	19.15	**E.**	31.27	27.31
29.25	7.11	31.26	1. 5	2. 7 I.	17.14
17.21	16. 7	2. 7	26.22	30.25	15.19
22.17 F.	2.11	26.23	30.26	21.30	14. 5
11.16 C.	26.23	W. wins.	15.11	20.16	3. 8
25.22	3. 8		8.15	W. wins.	Drawn.
16.20	23.18	**C.**	23.19		
19.16	15.19 B.	9.14	26.17	**I.**	**M.**
20.27	24.15	25.22	W. wins.	3. 7	22.18
31.24	10.19	3. 8 D.		30.25	14.17
12.19	17.14	23.18	**F.**	21.30	19.16
23.16	1. 5	14.23	24.20	20.16	12.19
10.14	14.10	17.14	15.24	12.19	23.16
9.14 var 1	6.15	10.17	28.19	23.16	1. 5
24.19	13. 6	19. 3	9.14 K.	30.23	25.22
15.24	19.23	11.16	22.17	27.11	5. 9
28.19	28.24	26.19	11.15	Drawn.	26.23
10.15	5. 9	17.26	25.22		17.26
19.10	6. 2	30.23	15.24	**K.**	31.22
6.15	15.19	16.20	22.18	11.15	7.11
17.10	24.15	32.27	7.11	32.28 L.	16. 7
7.14	9.14	21.25	18. 9	15.24	2.11
22.17	18. 9	31.26	11.15	28.19	22.17
2. 7	11.25	25.30	9. 5	9.14	3. 8
17.10	2. 7	19.15	3. 7 G.H.	22.17 M.	23.19
7.14	25.29	30.25 E.	20.16	10.15	8.12
13. 9	7.10	23.19	12.19	19.10	17.14
14.17 A	29.25	25.30	23.16	6.15	Drawn.
16.11	10.15	26.23	7.11	17.10	
15.18	25.22	30.25	16. 7	7.14	**GAME** 11.
26.23	15.19	15.10	2.11	25.22	22.18
18.27	W. wins.	6.15	26.23	Drawn.	11.15
Drawn.		19.10	11.16		18.11
	B.	2. 7	31.26	**L.**	8.15
A.	8.12	10. 6	24.27	19.16	21.17
15.19	24.20	1.10	26.22	12.19	4. 8
16.11	12.16	23.19	15.19	23.16	23.19
19.24	28.24	W. wins.	23.18	7.11	8.11
26.22	1. 5		19.23	16. 7	17.13
24.28	32.28	**D.**	18.14	2.11	9.14
9. 5	16.19	14.18	Drawn.	22.17	27.23
1. 6	17.14	23.14		15.19	5. 9
5. 1	10.26	1. 5	**G.**	25.22	25.22
6. 9	30. 7	14. 9	2. 7	10.15	14.17
1. 6	15.22	5.14	30.25	31.27	29.25
9.13	7. 2	26.23	W. wins.	19.24	17.21
W. wins.	22.26	W. wins.		27.23	22.17
	24.19		**H.**	24.27	11.16
	26.31		24.28	23.18	25.22

7.11 }var.	25.30	**C.**	28.19	**Var.**	14.17
24.20 }1, 2,	4. 8	23.18	6.10 A.	12.16	9. 5
15.24 }& 3.	30.25	10.15	22.17	18.14 C.	17.21
28.19	8.11	18.14	13.22	10.17	5. 1
10.14	22.26	15.19	26.17	22.13	22.25
17.10	31.22	32.28	11.15	16.20 B.	31.26
6.24	25.18	3. 7	32.28	21.17	Drawn.
13. 6	B. wins.	22.18	15.24	7.10	
1.10		19.23	28.19	26.23	**C.**
22.17 C.	**Var. 2.**	28.19	1. 6	9.14	24.20
24.28	31.27	21.25	30.26	25.21	16.19
17.13	21.25	30.21	3. 8	15.18	27.23 D.
3. 7	30.21	23.30	26.23	30.25	9.13
13. 9	9.14	19.15	8.11	10.15	B. wins.
16.19	B. wins.	30.25	23.18	17.10	
23.16		15. 8	11.16	18.22	**D.**
12.19	**Var. 3.**	25.22	27.23	25.18	27.24
9. 5	32.27	20.11	16.20	15.22	10.14
19.24	3. 8	22.15	31.27	23.19	20.16 E.
5. 1	22.18 B.	8. 3	6. 9	6.15	14.23
11.16	15.22	7.16	18.15	19.10	31.27
20.11	19.15 A.	3. 8	9.18	22.25	11.20
7.16	11.18	16.19	23.14	24.19	27.11
1. 5	23. 5	14. 9	12.16	2. 7	7.16
16.20	22.25	19.24	19.12	Drawn.	24.15
5. 9	B. wins.	21.17	10.19		Drawn.
24.27		Drawn.	12. 8	**B.**	
Drawn.	**A.**		Drawn.	9.14	**E.**
	24.20	**GAME** 12.		24.20	22.17
Var. 1.	22.25	22.18	**A.**	6.10	14.23
23.18	27.24	11.15	11.16	27.24	25.22
16.23	25.29	18.11	27.23	16.19	9.13
26.19	19.15	8.15	6. 9	25.22	17.14
11.16	11.27	25.22	22.18	14.18	11.16
18.11	20. 4	4. 8	1. 6	22.17	20.11
16.23	29.25	29.25	30.25	1. 6	7.16
22.18	B. wins.	8.11	6.10	32.27	14.10 F.
10.14		23.18	25.21	19.23	16.20
17.10	**B.**	9.13 var	10.17	26.19	31.27
6.22	24.20	18.14	21.14	18.23	15.18
13. 6	15.24	10.17	7.10	27.18	B. wins.
1.10	28.19	21.14	14. 7	15.22	
11. 8	10.14	6.10	3.10	17.14	**F.**
23.26	17.10	25.21	32.28	10.17	14. 9
30.23	6.24	10.17	10.14	21.14	5.14
21.25	13. 6	21.14	26.22	6.10	22.18
23.19	1.10	2. 6	14.17	14. 9	15.22
10.14	B. wins.	24.19	19.15	5.14	24.15
8. 4		15.24	Drawn.	13. 9	6.10

15. 6	24.19	23.18	31.27	9.14	31.26
1.10	3. 7	2. 7	22.18	25.21	22.31
26.12	28.24	11. 2	27.24	14.18	25.22
22.25	22.25	27.31	14. 9	26.23	18.25
28.24	29.22	2. 9	24.20	18.22	29.22
25.29	14.18	5.23	18.14	23.18 var.	31.24
24.20	23.14	17.14 B.	20.16	11.16	28.10
29.25	6.10	10.17	15.11	18.11	16.19
31.26	15. 6	21.14	16.23	16.23	22.18
13.17	2.25	31.26	11. 8	27.18	19.23
26.23	19.15	14.10	23.19	7.16	10. 6
25.22	25.30	22.25	B. wins.	24.20	23.26
20.16	27.23	29.22		16.19	6. 2
2. 7	20.27	26.17	D.	18.15	26.31
B. wins.	31.24	B. wins.	31.26	19.23	2. 6
	30.26		22.31	15.11	31.27
GAME 13	23.18	B.	29.25	10.14	6.10
22.18	26.22	13. 9	11.18	11. 8	27.23
11.15	18.14	31.27	23. 7	22.26	18.14
18.11	12.16	17.14	2.11	31.22	23.19
8.15	15.11	10.17	17.14	14.17	14. 9
21.17	Drawn.	21.14	6. 9	21.14	11.15
4. 8		23.26	13. 6	6. 9	20.16
23.19	A.	19.15	1.17	13. 6	19.12
8.11	18.14	27.23	21.14	1.26	10.19
17.13	16.23	15.10	31.26	8. 4	12. 8
9.14	27.18	23.18	14.10	Drawn.	9. 6
25.21	10.15	10. 7	26.30		8.11
14.18	18.11	18.15	25.21	**Var.**	6. 2
26.23	7.16	B. wins.	30.25	21.17	11. 8
18.22	13. 9		10. 7	5. 9	19.23
30.26	6.13	C.	25.22	23.18	8.11
15.18	32.27	18.14	7. 3	10.14 A.	23.18
26.17	Drawn.	8.11	11.16	17.10	11.16
18.22		14. 9	19.15	7.23	Drawn.
23.18	**Var.**	5.14	16.19	19.10	
11.16	3. 8†	19.15	3. 7	6.15	A.
27.23 A.	18.15 C.	11.18	B. wins.	13. 6	11.16
16.20	7.11	23.19		2. 9	18.11
32.27	23.18 D.	22.26	**GAME** 14.	27.18	16.23
10.14 Var.	11.16	31.15	22.18	1. 5 D.	27.18
17.10	27.23	14.18	11.15	24.20	7.16
7.14	20.27	29.25	18.11	9.14	18.15
18. 9	31.24	18.23	8.15	18. 9	10.19
5.14	16.20	27.18	21.17	5.14	24.15
13. 9	15.11	20.27	4. 8	32.27	16.19
6.13	8.15	18.14	23.19	14.18 B.	30.26
19.15	18.11	27.31	8.11	30.25	3. 7
1. 6	20.27	25.22	17.13	12.16 C.	**32.27**

1. 5	6.10	Var. 1.	18. 9	13.22	6.13
27.24	27.23	6. 9	10. 6	26.10	25.18
7.10	10.14	25.21	9.14	19.26	3. 8
15.11	29.25	1. 6	6. 1	31.22	18.14
Drawn.	22.29	30.26	14.18	16.19	10.17
	30.26	12.16	28.24	32.28	21.14
B.	15.22	19.12	Drawn.	9.14	11.16
14.17	26.10	8.11		8. 4	14. 9
27.23	29.25	22.17	Var. 2.	5. 9	2. 7
12.16	28.24	13.22	12.16	4. 8	9. 6
30.26	3. 8	26.17	15. 8	19.23	7.10
W. wins.	Drawn.	9.13	3.12	27.18	Drawn.
		23.19	18.15	14.23	
C.	GAME 15.	13.22	9.18	10. 7	A.
15.19	22.17	19.15	23.14	2.11	12.16
27.24	11.15	11.16	1. 6	8.15	17.14
11.15	25.22	15.10	15.11	23.26	10.17
20.16	8.11	6.15	6. 9	15.18	21.14
19.23	29.25	18.11	11. 8	26.30	16.19
16.11	9.13	22.25	9.18	22.17	24.20
23.26	17.14	11. 8	22.15	9.13	6.10
24.19	10.17	25.29 A.	7.11	17.14	29.25
15.24	21.14	8. 4	15.10	W. wins.	10.17
28.19	4. 8	29.25	11.15		25.21
26.30	24.19	4. 8	8. 4	GAME 16.	1. 6
25.21	15.24	25.22	5. 9	11.15	21.14
18.23	28.19	8.11	4. 8	22.17	6.10
11. 8	11.16	16.19	9.14	8.11	30.25 B.
30.25	22.18	11.15	8.11	25.22	10.17
8. 4	16.20	19.23	14.17	9.13	25.21
23.26	26.22	27.18	11.18	23.18	19.23
4. 8	8.11 var 1	7.10	17.22	6. 9 A.	26.10
26.30	30.26	15. 6	26.17	27.23	17.26
8.11	6. 9	2. 9	13.29	9.14 C.	31.22
30.26	19.15	Drawn.	18.22	18. 9	7.33
19.15	11.16 var 2		16.19	5.14	27.18
26.23	25.21	A.	W. wins.	30.25	3. 7
15.10	16.19 var 3	16.19		1. 6	28.24
25.30	23.16	8. 4	Var. 3.	24.19	7.10
10. 6	12.19	25.29	7.10	15.24	24.19
23.18	32.28	4. 8	14. 7	28.19	4. 8
6. 1	1. 6	29.25	3.19	11.15	19.16
W. wins.	15.11	32.28	18.15	32.28	10.14
	7.16	25.22	1. 6	15.24	16. 7
D.	14.10	27.24	15.11	28.19	2.11
12.16	6.15	20.27	6.10	7.11	18. 9
24.20	18.11	31.15	11. 8	22.18	5.14
1. 6	2. 6	22.18	10.14	13.22	32.27
32.27	22.18	15.10	22.17	18. 9	8.12
	W. wins.				

27.23	17.14	8.11	14.10	29.25	30.25
11.15	7.11	25.22	12.16	27.31	15.24
B. wins.	14.10	11.16	26.23	18.22	25.18
	13.17	23.18	20.24	32.27	1. 6
B.	10. 7	3. 8 var 1	27.20	23.19	5. 1
27.23	3.10	18.11	9.14	Drawn.	6.13
10.17	15. 6	8.15	18. 9		Drawn.
23.16	17.22	24.19	11.27	**GAME** 18.	
2. 6	6.10	15.24	32.23	11.15	**Var.**
32.27	22.26	27.11	5.14	22.17	18.15
17.21	10.14	7.16	20.11	8.11	4. 8
27.23	26.31	22.18	8.15	25.22	27.24
6. 9	29.25	9.14	31.26	11.16	16.20
28.24	31.26	18. 9	4. 8	23.18	32.27
4. 8	14.17	5.14	10. 7	15.19	7.10
16.12	26.31	28.24	2.11	24.15	17.13
9.14	25.21	4. 8	23.18	10.19	10.14
18. 9	31.27	24.19	14.23	17.13 var.	22.17
5.14	17.14	16.23	26.10	9.14	14.18
W. wins.	27.24	26.19	Drawn.	18. 9	17.14 A.
	19.15	8.11		5.14	18.22
C.	24.19	31.26	**Var 2.**	22.17	26.17
4. 8	15.10	2. 7 var 2.	11.15	7.10	9.18
23.19	19.26	26.23	32.28	27.24	30.26
9.14	18.15	11.15	15.24	19.23	18.22
18. 9	11.18	32.28	28.19	26.19	13. 9
5.14	Drawn.	15.24	14.18	16.23	6.13
26.23		28.19	17.14	31.26	15.10
2. 6	D.	7.11	10.17	14.18	12.16
22.18	10.15	30.26	21.14	26.19	24.15
15.22	19.10	11.15	18.23	18.22	2. 6
31.26	7.14	19.16	19.15	17.14	26.23
22.31	32.27	12.19	23.27	10.17	8.12
30.25	31.26	Drawn.	15.11	21.14	23.18
13.22	23.19		27.32	3. 7	16.19
25. 2	11.16	**Var. 1.**	11. 8	14. 9	18.14
31.27 D.	19.15	7.11	32.27	4. 8	6. 9
23.18	16.20	17.14	8. 4	9. 5	10. 7
27.20	24.19	10.17	12.16	8.11	9.18
28.24	14.18	21.14	4. 8	32.27	27.24
20.27	15.10	16.20	16.20	6.10	20.27
32.23	26.23	29.25	8.11	27.23	31.24
1. 5	10. 7	9.13	20.24	11.15	3.10
2. 6	23.32	24.19	14.10	13. 9	15. 6
11.16	B. wins.	15.24	6.15	7.11	1.10
6.15		28.19	11.18	24.20	24. 6
5. 9	**GAME** 17.	3. 8	24.28	15.24	18.23
21.17	11.15	19.15	26.23	28.19	17.14
9.13	22.17	6. 9	28.32	11.15	Drawn.

A.	14.18	26.22	9.13	15.24	27.23
29.25	23. 7	25.18	32.28*	28.19	18.27
12.16	Drawn.	15.22	1. 6	11.15	17.14
17.14		11.16	21.17	19.16	16.23
8.12	**Var. 1.**	20.11	14.21	12.19	31.26
26.23	17.14	8.24	23.14	23.16	10.17
19.26	10.17	22.26	10.26	8.11	26. 1
20.26	21.14	12.16	19. 1	16. 7	17.22
16.19	6.10	26.31	13.17	2.11	Drawn.
23.16	29.25	16.20	30.23	26.23 A.	
12.19	10.17	Drawn.	21.30	11.16	C.
31.26	25.21		1. 6	20.11	6. 9
18.23	1. 6	**Var. 2.**	3. 8	15.18	13. 6
B wins.	21.14	5. 9	6. 2	22.15	2. 9
	6.10	15.11	7.10	10.26	25.22
GAME 19.	22.17	8.15	23.19	30.23	14.18 D.
22.17	13.22	27.23	10.14	21.30	23.14
11.15	26.17	15.19	Drawn.	Drawn.	9.25
25.22	15.18	24.15			29.22
9.13	17.13	10.19	**Var. 1.**	A.	10.14
23.18 var 1	10.17	23.16	9.14	22.17	19.10
5. 9 var 2	23.14	12.19	27.23	15.19	14.18
18.11	17.22	29.25	15.18 B.C.	25.22	22.15
8.15	24.19	7.10	32.27	1. 5	11.18
27.23	8.11	17.14	11.15	26.23	24.19
9.14	27.24	9.18	26.22	19.26	7.14
30.25	2. 6	22.15	7.11	30.23	19.15
5. 9	24.20	4. 8	21.17	11.15	1. 6
24.19	6.10	Drawn.	14.21	20.16	28.24
15.24	14. 9		23. 7	21.25	3. 7
28.19	5.14	**GAME 20.**	3.10	16.11	24.20
7.11	13.19	11.15	27.23	14.21	5. 9
22.18	14.17	22.17	5. 9	22.17	31.27
13.22	9. 6	8.11	31.26	25.30	7.10
26.17	17.21	17.13	9.14	11. 7	21.17
3. 8	6. 1	4. 8	24.20	30.26	14.21
32.28	22.25	23.19	* White ought	7. 3	26.23
11.15	1. 5	15.18 var 1	to win thus—	26.19	10.26
18.11	25.29	24.20	20 . 16	B. wins.	30. 5
8.24	5. 9	11.15 var 2	11 . 20		6. 9
28.19	29.25	28.24	22 . 17	B.	5. 1
4. 8	31.26	8.11	13 . 22	5. 9	9.13
17.13	11.15	26.23	21 . 17	32.27	1. 6
2. 6	9. 6	9.14	14 . 21	1. 5	8.11
25.22	15.24	31.26	23 . 14	26.22	6.10
8.11	6.15	6. 9	10 . 17	14.18	21.25
31.26	3. 8	13. 6	25 . 2	23.14	27.23
11.16	28.19	2. 9	1 . 6	9.18	25.30
22.17	7.11	26.22	2 . 9	22.17	23.18
			5 . 14	11.16	
			19 . 15		
			3 . 8		
			24 . 19		

30.25	20.27	15.18	6.15	8.11	17.13
18.14	18.15	17.10	13. 6	26.23	7.11
25.22	27.31	7.14	1.10 L.	18.22 B.	4. 8
14. 9	15. 6	30.26	28.24	25.18	10.15
22.17	Drawn.	8.12	8.11	15.22	13. 9
10. 6		26.22	30.26	30.26	19.24
Drawn.	**Var. 2.**	18.25	2. 6	11.15	9. 6
	10.14	29.22	26.22	26.17	24.28
D.	26.23	9.13	3. 8	15.18	6. 2
9.13	6.10 K.	22.18	22.17	23.14	28.32
32.27	13. 6	14.23	5. 9	9.18	2. 6
1. 6	2. 9	27.18	24.19	27.23	32.28
22.17	31.26 H.	3. 7	15 24	18.27	21.17
13.22	11.15 G.	28.24	25.22	32.23	28.32
26.17	28.24	7.10	18 25	7.11 D.	17.14
14.18	1. 6	24.19	29.22	29.25	32.28
23.14	26.22	10.14	24.28	5. 9 A.	14.10
6. 9	8.11	18. 9	22.18	25.22	28.24
30.26	32.28	5.14	12.16	11.15	6. 2
9.18	9.13	32.27	W. wins.	20.16	Drawn.
26.22	20.16	13.17		9.14	
18.25	Drawn.	27.23	**L.**	16.11	**A.**
29.22		17.22	2. 9	12.16	11.15
5. 9	**G.**	21.17	28.24	19.12	17.14
27.23	9.13	14.21	8.11	15.18	10.17
9.13	28.24	23.18	30.26	22.15	19.10
23.18 E.	1. 6	11.16	9.13	10.28	6.15
10.14	26.22	20.11	26.22	17.10	21.14
18. 9	5. 9	22.26	3. 8	6.15	15.18
15.18	22.15	Drawn.	23.19	8.11	31.27
22.15	11.18		7.10	28.32	1. 6
13.22	25.22	**I.**	27.23	8. 4	24.19
Drawn.	18.25	9.13	18.27	32.28	2. 7
	29.22	22.18	32.23	4. 8	25.21
E.	8.11	14.23	5. 9	2. 7	18.22
31.26	22.18	27.18	31.27	31.26	23.18
15.18	13.17	5. 9	W. wins.	28.24	22.26
23.14	32.28	30.26		26.22	27.23
11.16	17.22	10.14	**GAME** 21.	24.27	W. wins
19.15 F.	Drawn.	26.23	11.15	23.18	
10.19		7.10	22.17	15.19	**B.**
24.15	**H.**	29.25	8.11	22.17	3. 8
7.11	19.16	10.15	17.13	27.23	23.14
Drawn.	12.26	25.22	4. 8	18.14	9.18
	31. 6	Drawn.	23.19	23.18	30.26
F.	1.10		15.18	8. 4	6. 9 C.
26.23	25.22	**K.**	24.20	18. 9	13. 6
16.20	10.15 I.	11.15	11.15	13. 6	2. 9
23.18	22.17	19.10	28.24 var	1.10	26.22

9.14	26.22	31.22	15.24	3. 8	8. 3
27.23	9.14	29.25	28.19	B. wins.	W. wins.
18.27	22.17	22.17	9.14		
32·23	6. 9	25.22	22.15	**GAME 22.**	**Var. 1.**
5. 9	13. 6	17.13	7.11	11.15	5. 9
31.27	2. 9	22.18	30.26	22.17	21.17
1. 5	17.13	10. 6	11.18	8.11	14.21
22.17	1. 6	2. 9	26.22	17.13	23. 5
9.13	27.23	13. 6	2. 7	4. 8	15.18
25.22	18.27	Drawn.	22.15	23.19	26.23
5. 9	32.23		7.11	15.18	18.22
29.25	15.18	**Var.**	31.26	24.20	25.18
15.18	31.27	27.24 F.	11.13	11.15	10.15
22. 6	11.15	8.11	26.22	28.24	19.10
13.29	25.22	25.22 E.	3. 7	8.11	6.22
6. 1	18.25	18.25	22.15	26.23	23.18
7.10	29.22	29.22	7.11	9.14 B.	7.10
1. 5	7.11	9.14	25.22	31.26 (var1	32.28
9.13	22.17	22.17	11.25	14.17 (var2	10.15
5. 9	Drawn.	11.16	29.22	21.14	27.23
13.17		20.11	8.11	10.17	22.26
9.18	**D.**	7.23	27.23	23.14	18.14
17.22	10.14	26.19	11.15	6.10	15.18
18.25	17.10	2. 7	32.28	25.22	23.19
29.22	7.14	31.26	15.24	17.21	26.31
23.18	13. 9	7.11	28.19	22.17	14. 9
22.15	6.13	26.23	10.15	15.18	W. wins.
27.23	19.15	15.18	19.10	26.22	
10.14	1. 6	24.20	6.15	18.25	**Var. 2.**
19.10	23.19	18.27	Drawn.	29.22	11.16
11.15	6. 9	32.23		11.15	20.11
10. 7	15.10	11.15	**E.**	13. 9	7.16
15.18	14.17	30.26	26.22	7.11	21.17
21.17	21.14	15.24	9.14	14. 7	14.21
18.27	9.18	28.19	31.27	3.10	23. 7
17.10	19.15	3. 8	6. 9	9. 6	2.11
27.32	18.22	20.16	13. 6	2. 9	19.10
24.19	15.11	5. 9	2. 9	17.13	6.15
8.11	13.17	26.22	27.23	9.14	25.22 A.
10. 6	11. 8	10.15	18.27	22.17	16.19
32.28	17.21	17.10	32.23	1. 6	32.28
7. 3	8. 4	15.24	14.18	32.28	5. 9
28.24	21.25	23.19	23.14	5. 9	13. 6
3. 8	4. 8	6.15	10.26	27.23	1.10
24.15	25.30	19.10	30.23	15.18	29.25
W. wins.	8.11	Drawn.	7.10	19.15	10.14
	30.26		23.18	18.27	24.20
C.	29.25	**F.**	15.22	15. 8	Drawn.
5. 9	22.29	26.22	25.18	14.18	

A.					16.19
24.20	30.23	9.13	15. 6		24.15
16.19	31.26	10. 7	1.10	**GAME 23.**	31.24
27.23	Drawn.	11.15	32.27	11.15	15.11
3. 7		2. 6	25.22	22.17	24.19
23.16	B.	15.18	27.23	8.11	11. 7
12.19	18.22	6.10	2. 7	17.13	19.15
25.22	25.18	18.22	31.27	4. 8	2. 6
7.10	15.22	10.14	7.11	23.19	15.11
22.17	30.26	22.25	27.24	15.18	7. 2
19.24	11.15	7. 2	22.26	24.20	20.24
29.25	26.17	25.29	23.18	11.15	22.18
1. 6	15.18	2. 7	26.22	28.24	11.16
25.22	23.14	29.25	18.14	8.11	21.17
5. 9	9.18	7.10	3. 7	26.23	W. wins.
26.23	29.25	25.21	19.15	9.14	
24.27	7.11 D.	10.15	Drawn.	31.26	B.
20.16	17.14	13.17		6. 9	1. 6
11.20	10.17	15.19	E.	13. 6	30.26 C.D.
23.18	21.14	17.22	20.16	2. 9	9.13
27.31	6. 9	19.23	3. 8	26.22	32.28
18.11	13. 6	W. wins.	17.14	9.13 B.	6. 9
9.14	1.17		10.17	20.16†	B. wins.
11. 7	25.21	C.	21.14	11.20	
14.18	17.22	30.26	2. 6	22.17	C.
22.15	19.15	6. 2	31.27	13.22	32.28
10.19	3. 8	5. 9	23.26	21.17	9.13 E.
7. 2	15.10	2. 6	25.21	14.21	20.16
6.10	11.15	9.13	26.31	23.14	11.20
2. 7	21.17	6.10	27.23	10.17	Drawn.
10.15	22.26	15.18	31.27	25. 2	
7.11	31.22	10.14	23.18	1. 6 A.	E.
15.18	18.25	18.22	27.23	2. 9	3. 8
11.15	17.13	32.28	14. 9	5.14	30.26
18.23	25.30	Drawn.	23.14	19.15	9.13
15.24	10. 6		9. 2	3. 8	19.16
20.27	2. 9	D.	14.10	24.19	12.19
17.14	13. 6	18.23	13. 9	W. wins.	23.16
31.26	30.25 C.	27.18	5.14		8.12 F.
14. 9	27.23	10.15	2. 6	A.	24.19
26.22	25.22	18.11	10. 7	17.22	15.31
9. 6	23.18	7.23	6.10	19.15	22. 8
27.31	8.11	24.19	8.11	21.25	12.16
6. 2	24.19	6.10	10. 3	30.21	8. 3
22.18	15.24	25.22 E.	11.20	22.26	W. wins.
2. 6	32.28	23.26	3. 7	15.10	
18.15	22.15	22.18	14.18	26.31	F.
13. 9	28.10	26.30	Drawn.	29.25	13.17
23.26	5. 9	18.15		12.16	22.13
	6. 2	30.25		25.22	

8.12	8. 4	14.17	Var.	19.16	17.13
25.22	17.22	7.10	17.13	12.19	3. 7
12.19	4. 8	17.21	8.11	23.16	28.24
22.17	22.26	10.14	26.23	14.17 B.	12.16
5. 9	19.15	13.17	10.14	21.14	26.23
26.22	26.30	19.15	24.20	10.17	8.12
18.25	15.10	17.22	11.15	16.12	23.19
29.22	Drawn.	14.17	28.24	11.15	16.23
14.18		22.26	4. 8	12. 8	31.26
27.23	G.	15.10	30.26	17.21	7.10
19.26	9.13	Drawn.	8.11	25.22	26.19
17.14	25.22		26.22	18.25	11.16
18.25	18.25	**GAME** 24.	3. 8	Drawn.	18.11
14. 5	29.22	11.15	32.28		16.23
15.18	14.18	22.17	7.10	B.	27.18
21.17	23.14	15.18	24.19	10.15	W. wins.
11.15	6. 9	23.14	15.24	27.24	
5. 1	22.18	9.18	28.19	6.10	A.
Drawn.	15.22	17.14 var	11.15 A.	16.12	28.24
	32.28	10.17	27.24	14.17	7.10
D.	9.18	21.14	18.27	21.14	24.19
22.17	17.14	8.11	13. 9	10.17	3. 7
18.22 G.	10.17	24.20	6.13	25.21	19.16
25.18	21.14	6. 9	22.17	18.22	10.19
15.22	13.17	26.23	13.22	21.14	32.28
23.18	19.15	3. 8	25. 4	22.31	7.10
14.23	17.21	23.19	27.32	W. wins.	16. 7
27.18	15. 8	18.22	4. 8		2.11
9.13	22.25	25.18	32.27	**GAME** 25.	23. 7
17.14	24.19	11.16	29.25	22.18	14.32
10.17	25.29	20.11	5. 9	11.16	7. 3
21.14	19.15	8.22	25.22	25.22	32.27
6.10	29.25	30.25	9.13	10.14	31.24
30.25	15.10	9.18	8.11	29.25	20.27
10.17	25.22	27.23	1. 5	16.20	22.18
25.21	10. 6	18.27	11. 8	24.19	27.31
22.26	22.17	25.18	2. 7	8.11	26.22
21.14	6. 2	5. 9	8. 3	19.15	10.14
26.30	17.10	32.23	7.11	4. 8	18.15
19.15	2.11	4. 8	3. 7	22.17 A.	14.18
30.26	Drawn.	29.25	27.23	*7.10 var	B. wins.
15. 8		12.16	Drawn.	25.22	
26.22	H.	19. 3		10.19	Var.
32.28	7.10	2. 6	A.	17.10	9.13
22.15	14. 7	3.10	2. 7	6.15	17.10
24.19	3.10	6.29	22.15	23. 7	7.14
15.24	8. 3	Drawn.	11.18	2.11	18. 9
28.19	10.14		31.26	21.17	5.14
13.17 H.	3. 7		8.11	1. 6	26.22

11.18	16.20	A.	27.31	9.13	3. 7
22.15	24.19	23.26†	10. 7	11.16	11. 2
2. 7	8.11	30.23	20.24	5. 9	9.13
30.26	19.15	21.30	7. 3	16.20	2. 9
7.10	4. 8	18.15	24.28	9.14	5.14
23.19	22.17	30.26	3. 7	22.18	23.19
3. 7 B.	12.16	23.18	28.32	14.17	15.24
19.16	17.10	26.22	7.10	18.14	26.23
12.19	7.14	14.10	32.27	17.21	24.27
28.24	26.22	13.17	18.15	25.22	22.18
19.28	2. 7	10. 7	27.24	23.19	1. 5
25.22	28.24	17.21	15.11	14. 9	18. 9
10.19	16.19	7. 2	31.27	19.15	5.14
22.17	23.16	21.25	10.15	Drawn.	B. wins.
13.22	14.23	2. 7	9.14		
26. 3	27.18	25.30	15.10	C.	F.
8.12	20.27	7.11	5. 9	30.26	23.19
27.24	31.24	30.26	10.17	10.19	27.31
20.27	11.27	18.14	27.23	23.16	19.15
31.15	32.23	26.23	26.19	8.12	31.26
6.10	7.10 var	14.10	24. 8	B. wins.	B. wins.
15. 6	15.11 C.	22.18	16.19		
1.10	8.15	B. wins.	8.11	D.	GAME 27
W. wins.	18.11		19.23	23.18	11.15
	10.15	Var.	11.16	15.19	22.17
B.	21.17D.E.	8.12	23.27	22.17	9.13
1. 5	3. 7	23.19	16.19	3. 7	17.14
19.16	11. 2	7.10	27.32	11. 2	10.17
12.19	9.13	21.17	19.23	9.13	21.14
28.24	2. 9	9.13 B.	32.28	2. 9	8.11
19.28	5.21	25.21	Drawn.	5.23	24.19
25.22	23.18	3. 7		17.14	15.24
10.19	15.19	30.26	B.	23.27	28.19
22.17	18.14	12.16	12.16	14.10	11.16
13.22	19.23	19.12	19.12	27.31	25.21
26. 1	22.18	10.19	10.19	10. 7	6. 9
19.24	13.17 A.	12. 8	17.14	31.27	29.25
1. 6	18.15	7.11	19.23	25.22	9.18
8.11	23.26	8. 3	14.10	27.23	23.14
21.17	30.23	11.16	6.15	21.17	16.23
11.15	21.30	3. 7	18.11	19.24	26.19
Drawn.	14.10	16.20	23.27	17.14	4. 8
	30.26	7.11	11. 8	24.27	25.22
GAME 26.	23.19	19.24	27.31	14.10	8.11
22.18	26.23	11.16	8. 4	27.31	22.18
11.16	19.16	24.27	31.27	Drawn.	11.16
25.22	23.18	17.14	4. 8		27.23
10.14	16.11	6. 9	27.23	E.	16.20
29.25	Drawn.	14.10	8.11	30.26	31.27

2 F

13.17	25.22	8.11 B.	11.18	5. 9	10.15
30.26	8.11	22.18	23.14	Drawn.	20.11
1. 6	22.18	16.20	16.23		3.10
19.16	11.16	30.26	26.19	D.	31.27 H.
12.19	27.23	6. 9	1. 6	14.10	10.15
23.16	16.20	29.25	25.22	18.22	B. wins.
6. 9	31.27	1. 6	8.11	30.25	
18.15	13.17	19.15	22.18	11.18	H.
9.18	30.26	11.16	6. 9	23.14	11. 7
21.14	25.22	25.22	19.15	16.23	19.23
7.11	18.15*A.	7.10 E.	12.16	27.18	26.19
15. 8	20.24	14. 7	15. 8	8.11	15.24
3.19	27.20	3.19	3.12	32.27	28.19
27.23	7.10	18.15	30.26	2. 6	10.14
18.27	14. 7	2. 7	2. 7	18.15	Drawn.
32.16	2.27	15.11	27.24	11.18	
20.24	21.14	7.10	16.20	27.23	Var. 2.
14.10	6. 9	11. 7	32.27	6.15	27.23
24.27	32.23	9.14	7.11	B. wins.	7.10
23.19	B. wins.	7. 3	14.10		23.16 I.
27.31		6. 9	9.14	E.	10.19
19.15	A.	3. 8	18. 9	16.19	14.10
31.27	14. 9	10.15	5.14	23.16	6.15
15.11	6.13	22.18	26.23	12.19	18.11
27.24	21.14	15.22	14.18	15.11 var 2	2. 6
16.12	13.17	26.10	23.14	7.16	32.28 K.
24.19	14. 9	19.26	11.15	14.10	6.10
Drawn.	5.14	31.22	Drawn.	6.15	7.11
	18. 9	16.19		18.11	10.14
GAME 28.	17.21	32.28	C.	2. 6	16.11
11.15	26.22	9.14	22.18	22.18 F.	3.10
22.17	21.25	10. 6	13.17	19.24	11. 8
9.13	22.17	5. 9	18.15	Drawn.	19.23
17.14	25.30	6. 1	9.18		26.19
10.17	17.13	19.23	21.14	F.	10.15
21.14	30.26	27.18	7.11	32.28	Drawn.
8.11	9. 6	14.23	29.25 D.	20.24	
24.19	2. 9	1. 5	1. 6	27.20	I.
15.24	13. 6	9.14	25.22	6.10	14. 7
28.19	7.11	5. 9	18.25	11. 8 G.	3.10
11.16	6. 2	W. wins.	30.21	3.12	23.16
25.21	11.16		11.15	20.11	10.19
6. 9 var	2. 6	B.	14.10	19.23	18.15
29.25	26.31	6. 9	6.24	26.19	2. 7
9.18	B. wins.	29.25 C.	27. 4	10.14	15.11
23.14		9.18	18.27	Drawn.	7.10
16.23	Var.	22.15	31.24		11. 7
26.19	4. 8	7.11	12.16	G.	19.23
4. 8	26.22	31.26	21.17	11. 7	26.19

10.14	10.15	31.27	22.26	8.11	29.25
19.15	22.17 A.	30.26	15.18	25.22	12.16
14.17	15.18	27.23	13.22	4. 8	18.15
Drawn.	Drawn.	19.15	18.25	29.25	8.12
		23.30	Drawn.	10.14	15.11
K.	A.	15.19		24.19	7.10
16.12	21.17†	W. wins.	B.	7.10	22.18
6.10	14.21		18.23	27.24	10.15
11. 8	23.18	Var.	22.17	16.20	25.22
19.23	16.20	7.11	14.18	19.16	6.10 A.
26.19	18.11	24.15	17.14	20.27	24.19
10.14	20.24	11.18	1. 5	16. 7	15.24
22.18	11. 7	28.24	19.15	2.11	28.19
14.23	24.27	8.11	9.13	31.24	9.13 B.
Drawn.	7. 3	29.25	14.10	12.16	18. 9
	27.31	4. 8	22.27 C.	24.19	5.14
GAME 29.	3. 7	24.19	31.24	8.12	19.15
11.16	31.27	6. 9	18.23	32.27	10.19
22.18	7.11	26.22	10. 7	16.20	22.17
16.19	1. 5	1. 5 B.	15.18	21.17	13.22
23.16	11.16	22.15	7. 3	14.21	26.10
12.19	27.23	11.18	8.12	19.16	19.26
24.15	28.24	19.16	3. 8	12.19	30.23
10.19	19.28	18.22	23.27	23. 7	3. 8 C.
25.22	26.19	25.18	8.11	10.14	11. 7
9.14	28.32	14.23	27.32	26.23	2.11
18. 9	19.15	21.17	24.20	3.10	10. 7
5.14	32.27	8.12	18.23	28.24	11.15
22.17	16.19	16.11	11.15	10.15	7. 3
7.10	5. 9	9.13	32.28	18.11	15.19
27.24	15.11	17.14	25.22	9.13	23.18
2. 7	9.13	12.16	Drawn.	22.18	19.23
24.15	11. 7	11. 7		6. 9	18.15
10.19	4. 8	16.20	C.	11. 7	23.26
17.10	7. 3	7. 2	11.16	13.17	31.22
7.14	8.12	23.27	10. 7	18.15	16.19
32.27	3. 7	31.24	8.12	14.18	15.10
3. 7	27.32	20.27	7. 3	23.14	19.24
27.24	7.10	2. 6	5. 9	9.18	27.23
7.10 var	23.27	27.31	3. 8	24.19	24.27
24.15	10.14	6.10	9.14	17.22	23.18
10.19	27.32	31.27	8.11	Drawn.	27.31
31.27	14.18	10.15	16.20		18.14
8.11	32.27	27.23	31.26	GAME 31.	8.11
29.25	22.17	30.25	W. wins.	11.16	10. 7
6.10	13.22	23.26		22.18	Drawn.
27.23	18.25	25.21	GAME 30.	10.14	
11.16	27.31	26.22	11.16	25.22	A.
25.22	25.22	21.17	22.18	16.20	3. 8

11. 7	2. 6	14.10	17.14	19.26	30.26
2.11	10. 7	20.24	26.17	31.13	9.13
24.19	3.10	18.14	14. 7	8.12	26.22
15.24	11. 8	11.16	15.29	13. 9	Drawn.
28.19	4.11	30.26	21. 5	7.10	
6.10	27.24	16.20	11.16	14. 7	**E.**
19.15	20.27	22.17	27.23	5.14	9.13
10.19	31. 8	13.32	16.20	7. 2	19.15
22.17	Drawn.	26.17	7. 2	Drawn.	11.18
19.24		Drawn.	20.27		22.15
17.10	**GAME 32.**		2. 9	**B.**	12.16
24.28	22.18	**Var. 1.**	29.25	9.13	15.10
10. 7	10.15	22.17	19.15	17. 14	14.18
11.15	25.22	15.22	25.22	13.17	31.26
18.11	6.10	17.13	9.14	31.26	2. 6
8.15	29.25 var 1	9.14	12.16	8.11	26.23
7. 3	10.14	26.17	15.10	24.20	6.15
15.18	24.19 var 2	11.15	B. wins.	3. 7	23.14
23.14	15.24	29.25		27.23	16.20
9.18	28.19	8.11	**Var. 2.**	18.27	25.22
3. 7	11.16	25.22	23.19	32.23	8.11
W. wins.	18.15	4. 8	14.23	1. 6	27.23
	7.11	23.19	19.10	23.18	20.27
B.	22.18	14.18	7.14	17.22	23.18
3. 8	16.20	30.25	26.19	26.17	13.17
11. 7	26.22	11.16 A.	14.18 E.F.	11.16	22.13
2.11	11.16	13. 9	22.15	20.11	15.22
19.15	15.10	16.23	11.18	7. 23	32.23
10.19	9.13	17.13	21.17	25.22	22.26
22.17	18. 9	W. wins.	8.11 B.	2. 7	23.18
19.24	5.14		24.20 C.	17.13	26.31
17.10	19.15	**A.**	9.13	23.27	14.10
24.28	16.19	2. 6	17.14	18.15	31.27
10. 7	23.16	31.26	2. 7	Drawn.	30.26
11.15	12.19	11.16	28.24		Drawn.
18.11	22.18	26.23	4. 8	**C.**	
8.15	14.23	16.20	19.15	17.14	**F.**
7. 3	27.18	23.14	7.10	2. 7	11.16
15.18	2. 6	7.11	15. 6	19.15	19.15
23.14	25.22	14. 7	1.17	4. 8	16.19
9.18	19.24	3.10	25.22	24.19 D	15.10 H.
3. 7	18.14	27.23	17.26	9.13	19.23
W. wins.	24.27	20.27	30.14	31.26	27.18
	32.23	28.24	3. 7	11.16	14.23
C.	8.11	27.31	24.19	Drawn.	22.18
16.19	15. 8	23.18	13.17		8.11
23.16	4.11	5. 9	19.16	**D.**	25.22
12.19	23.18	32.27	12.19	24.20	4. 8
32.28	6.15	31.26	27.23	1. 6	22.17 G.

9.13	3. 7		23.16	B.	6.15
17.14	17.14	**GAME 33.**	12.28	7.10	19.10
2. 6	9.13	22.18	17.10	32.28	12.16
10. 7	24.20	10.15	15.19	1. 6	10. 7
3.17	13.17	25.22	27.23	19.15	8.12
21.14	31.26	6.10	19.24	10.19	7. 3
13.17	17.21	29.25	Drawn.	24.15	Drawn.
24.20	32.27	10.14		12.16	
17.22	6. 9	24.19	Var. 1.	22.17	D.
28.24	27.24	15.24	27.24	6.10	2. 6
23.26	7.11	28.19	16.20	15. 6	30.26
30.23	25.22	11.16	31.27	16.19	7.10
22.25	9.13	18.15 var 1	8.11 B.	17.10	17.14
24.19	15.10	7.11	19.15 C.	2. 7	10.17
25.30	11.15	22.18	4. 8	23.16	22.13
31.26	18.11	16.20	22.17	7.32	12.16
6. 9	8.15	26.22	7.10	6. 1	19.12
14.10	20.16	11.16 var 2	15. 6	32.27	6. 9
9.14	4. 8	31.26	1.10	25.22	13. 6
Drawn.	Drawn.	2. 6	23.19	Drawn.	1.28
		32.28	14.23		26.22
G.	I.	3. 7	27.18	C.	20.24
24.19	25.22	28.24 var 3	20.27	18.15	Drawn.
11.16	9.14	7.10 var 4	32.23	11.18	
19.15	18. 9	15.11	11.16	22.15	Var. 2.
2. 6	5.14	8.15	17.13	4. 8	2. 6 E.
31.27	22.17	18.11	2. 6	26.22	27.24
9.13	14.18	10.15	21.17	14.18	20.27
15.11	17.14	19.10	16.20	23.14	31.24
8.15	3. 7	6.15	25.21	9.18	6.10
18.11	21.17	22.17	20.24	21.17	15. 6
6.15	18.22	14.18 A.	17.14	1. 6 D.	1.10
27.18	17.13	23.14	10.17	30.26	32.28
15.19	7.10	9.18	21.14	7.10	9.13
18.14	14. 7	26.23	24.27	17.14	18. 9
19.23	2.18	16.19	19.15	10.17	5.14
21.17	24.15	23.14	27.31	22.13	30.26
16.19	8.11	19.28	26.22	3. 7	11.15
11. 7	15. 8	25.22	3. 7	26.22	19.16
3.10	4.11	28.32	14.10	7.10	12.19
14. 7	28.24	27.23	7.14	22.17	23.16
Drawn.	11.15	32.27	15.10	2. 7	8.12
	31.27	23.18	6.15	25.21	16.11
H.	6.10	27.24	18. 4	18.22	12.16
22.18	13. 9	11. 7	14.18	17.14	24.20
14.23	10.14	Drawn.	13. 6	10.17	16.19
27.18	9. 6		18.27	21.14	11. 7
1. 6	12.16	A.	Drawn.	7.11	19.23
21.17 I.	Drawn.	16.19		15.10	Drawn.

E.
2. 7
15.10
W. wins.

Var. 3.
22.17
6.10
15. 6
1.10
19.15
10.19
17. 3
20.24
27.11
8.31
23.16
Drawn.

Var. 4.
8.11 H.I.
15. 8
4.11
22.17
7.10 F.
26.22
9.13
18. 2
1. 6
2. 9
5.14
19.15
11.18
22. 6
13.29
6. 2
29.22
2. 6
25.22
30.25
22.29
6.10
14.17
21.14
29.25
10. 7
25.22
7.10
Drawn.

F,
6.10
17.13
1. 6
18.15
11.18
26.22
14.17
22.15
9.14
15.11 G.
14.18
11. 2
17.22
23. 7
22.29
Drawn.

G.
13. 9
6.13
15. 6
14.18
21.14
5. 9
14. 5
7.11
Drawn.

H.
6.10
15. 6
1.10
21.17
14.21
18.15
W. wins.

I.
7.11
22.17
6.10
15. 6
1.10
18.15
11.18
17.13
8.11
13. 6
Drawn.

GAME 34.
22.18
10.15
25.22
6.10
29.25
10.14
24.19
15 24
28.19
11.16
18.15
7.11
22.18
16.20
26.22
11.16
15.10 var
20.24
27.11
8.24
18.15
4. 8
32.28
2. 6
28.19
8.11
15. 8
6.24
23.19
24.28
8. 4
28.32
4. 8
32.28
8.11
28.24
19.15
14.17
22. 6
1.19
21.17
19.23
17.14
23.27
25.21
Drawn.

A.
32.28
9.13 B.
18. 9
5.14
22.18
6. 9

Var.
31.26
1. 6
22.17 A.
6.10
15. 6
20.24
17.10
24.31
26.22
9.13
6. 1
2. 6
32.28
6.24
28.19
31.27
19.15
8.15
15. 8
4.11
1. 6
3. 8
6.10
16.20
30.26
20.24
21.17
24.28
25.21
28.32
17.14
27.31
21.17
32.27
10.15
27.24
14.10
24.27
10. 7
Drawn.

B.
3. 7
22.17 C.
6.10
15. 6
7.11
17.10
11.15
18.11
8.31
26.22
9.13
6. 1
31.27
23.18
27.23
18.15
4. 8
B. wins.

C.
28.24
7.10 D.
15.11
8.15
18.11
14.18
22.15
9.14
21.17
14.21
25.22
5. 9
22.18
9.14
18. 9
6.13
15. 6

26.22
2. 6
28.24
8.11
15. 8
4.11
18.15
11.18
22.15
Drawn.

2. 9
W. wins.

D.
7.11
22.17 F.
6.10
15. 6
11.15 E.
18.11
8.15
19.10
9.13
25.22
2. 9
10. 7
14.18
23.14
9.25
Drawn.

E.
9.13
17.14
2. 9
25.22
11.15
18.11
8.15
10. 7
15.18
22.15
13.17
21.14
9.18
23.14
16.32
24.19
W. wins.

F.
21.17
14.21
22.17
9.13 H.
26.22
6. 9 K.
17.14
13.17 G.

22. 6	H.	27.23	18.14	9.14	32.27
2. 9	6.10	28.32	11.15	17.10	2. 7
25.22	15. 6	23.18	14. 9	7.23	17.14
9.13	9.14 I.	15.19	7.10	27.18	7.11
15.10	18. 9	22.17	12. 8	11.16	27.24
11.15	5.14	19.23	10.14	18.15	11.15
18.11	17.10	Drawn.	8.11	6. 9	18.11
8.15	2. 9		14.18	22.17	8.15
10. 7	19.15	**GAME** 35.	24.20	1. 6	14.10
5. 9	11.18	22.18	18.25	26.22	6. 9
14. 5	23. 5	11.16	11.18	3. 7	10. 7
13.17	8.11	25.22	25.29	22.18	9.14
19.10	Drawn.	8.11	9. 5	7.10	W. wins.
17.26		29.25	W. wins.	17.13	
23.18	I.	4. 8		16.20	A.
26.31	9.13	18.14	**GAME** 36.	25.22	9.13
7. 3	26.22	10.17	11.16	9.14	26.23
16.19	2. 9	21.14	22.18	18. 9	8.11
24.15	17.14	9.18	8.11	5.14	15. 8
W. wins.	11.15	23.14	25.22	22.18	4.11
	19.10	6.10	4. 8	14.23	28.24
G.	8.11	22.18	29.25	31.27	3. 7
2. 6	10. 7	10.17	16.19	8.12	24.19
14.10	11.15	25.21	24.15	Drawn.	6.10
9.14	18.11	1. 6	10.19		17.14
18. 2	9.18	21.14	23.16	**GAME** 37.	10.17
11.18	23.14	6.10	12.19	11.15	21.14
22.15	W. wins.	24.20	27.24 A.	22.17	1. 6
5. 9		10.17	9.14	15.19	30.25
10. 6	K.	18.15	18. 9	24.15	6.10
9.14	2. 7	11.18	5.14	10.19	25.18
15.11	15.10	20. 4	24.15	23.16	10.17
8.15	6.15	17.21	11.18	12.19	19.15
19.10	19. 3	4. 8	22.15	25.22	11.16
4. 8	11.15	5. 9	7.10	7.10	15.11
2. 7	18.11	28.24	32.27	27.24	7.10
8.11	8.15	9.13	10.19	10.15	Drawn.
6. 1	3. 8	27.23	27.23	22.18	
14.17	4.11	18.27	8.12	15.22	**GAME** 38.
10. 6	17.14	32.23	23.16	24.15	22.18
11.15	13.17	12.16	12.19	*3. 7 A.	11.16
7.10	22.13	8.12	31.27	30.25	18.14
16.19	15.18	16.20	3. 8	9.13	10.17
23.16	14.10	26.22	27.24	25.18	21.14
12.28	11.15	20.27	2. 7	13.22	9.18
10.19	23.14	31.24	Drawn.	26.17	23.14
W. wins.	16.19	7.11		7.10	8.11
	25.22	23.18	A.	31.26	25.22
	19.24	3. 7	21.17	10.19	6.10 **var 1**

29.25 var 2	15.11	2. 7	C.	15.22	E.
10.17	14.18	27.31	25.19	30.23	1. 6
22.13	11. 7	7.11	6.10	22.26	30.25
4. 8	Drawn.	31.27	25.21	23.19	6. 9
26.23		11.15	10.17	11.15	25.21
2. 6	Var. 1.	3. 8	21.14	17.14	12.16
23.18	11.15	15.18	7.10	10.17	32.28
16.20	24.19	8.12	14. 7	19.10	16.20
24.19	15.24	10. 6	3.10	26.31	24.19
11.16	27.11	12.16	31.26	10. 7	15.24
27.23	7.16	14.10	10.14	Drawn.	28.19
8.11	22.18	W. wins.	18. 9		20.24
31.27	4. 8 B.		5.14	D.	19.15
7.10	29.25	B.	26.22	16.20	10.19
18.15	8.11	16.20	1. 5	24.19	17.13
11.18	28.24	26.23	30.25	11.15 F.	11.16
23. 7	16.20	12.16	5. 9	28.24	13. 5
3.10	31.27	32.27	25.21	8.11	Drawn.
25.22 A.	11.16	4. 8	9.13	25.22	
16.23	26.23	28.24	Drawn.	11.16	F.
27.18	2. 7	8.12		26.23	11.16
5. 9	25.21	29.25	Var. 2.	7.11	25.22
32.27	6. 9	2. 7	22.17	14. 7	16.23
12.16	24.19	25.21 C.	4. 8	3.10	26.19
27.23	1. 6	16.19	29.25	23.18	8.11 G.
10.14	21.17	24.15	2. 6 D.	16.23	19.16
18.15	9.13	7.10	24.20	18.14	12.19
14.17	19.15	14. 7	16.19	2. 7	27.24
23.18	13.22	3.26	27.24	27.18	20.27
17.26	14.10	30.23	11.15	20.27	31. 8
30.23	7.14	6.10	25.22	31.24	3.12
1. 5	18. 2	21.17	6. 9	12.16 E.	28.24
15.11	22.26	12.16	22.18	24.20	10.15
6.10	23.19	31.26	15.22	1. 6	32.28
13. 6	16.23	1. 6	24. 6	30.25	12.16
10.15	27.18	26.22	1.10	6. 9	24.20
Drawn.	26.31	5. 9	17.13	25.21	16.19
	2. 6	17.13	9.18	16.19	30.25
A.	12.16	10.14	26.17	32.27	1. 6
25.21	15.11	18.15	18.22	19.23	25.21
16.23	16.19	14.17	32.27	27.24	6.10
27.18	18.14	22.18	8.11	23.27	20.16
12.16	19.23	17.22	27.24	20.16	19.23
30.26	6.10	18.14	11.15	11.20	16.12
16.19	31.26	9.18	31.27	18. 2	23.27
32.27	11. 7	23.14	7.11	9. 25	12. 8
5. 9	20.24	16.19	27.23	24.19	27.31
18.15	7. 2	Drawn.	22.26	Drawn.	8. 3
9.14	24.27		23.18		30.26

28.24	24.19	18. 9	Var. 1.	25.30	7. 2
26.23	2. 7	13. 6	6.10	6. 1	6. 9
24.20	30.26	2. 9	25.22	30.26	16.11
23.18	14.18	11. 7	11.15	1. 6	1. 6
Drawn.	26.23	9.14	18.11	26.23	23.19
	18.25	25.22	8.24	21.17	22.26
G.	29.22	5. 9	28.19	Drawn.	11. 7
10.15	7.10	7. 2	4. 8		3.10
19.10	23.18	9.13	27.24	C.	2. 7
2. 6	5. 9	2. 6	8.11	31.27	9.13
17.13	27.24	14.17	24.20	6.10	27.23
6.15	20.27	22.18	11.15	27.23	14.18
13. 9	32.23	17.22	19.16	19.24	7.14
8.11	W. wins.	6. 9	12.19	Drawn.	18.27
30.26		22.26	23.16		19.15
11.16	A.	9.14	14.18	Var. 2.	26.30
27.23	29.25	26.31	29.25	16.20	14. 9
16.19	7.10	18.15	1. 6	31.27	27.31
23.16	19.15	31.26	16.11	8.11	9. 2
12.19	10.19	Drawn.	7.16	19.16	13.17
32.27	24.15		20.11	12.19	Drawn.
7.10	16.19	B.	18.23	24. 8	
14. 7	23.16	1. 6	26.19	4.11	D.
3.10	12.19	19.16	15.24	28.24	16.12
Drawn.	27.23	3. 7	22.17	6.10	19.24
	19.24	21.17	10.15	24.19	28.19
GAME 39.	24.19	7.10	25.22	9.13	3. 8
22.18	20.24	16.12	24.28	18. 9	12. 3
10.14	15.10	10.19	30.26	5.14	14.17
24.19	6.15	11. 8	15.19	25.22	21.14
11.16 var 1	18.11	4.11	17.13 C.	11.16	10.17
27.24	24.27	17.14	9.14	19.16	3.10
8.11 var 2	19.15	9.18	22.17	15.19	6.31
25.22	27.31	22. 8	6.10	32.28	23.19
16.20	23.18	19.23	13. 9	2. 6	17.21
31.27	14.23	8. 3	10.15	22.18 D.E.	19.15
11.16	26.19	6.10	17.10	14.17	20.24
19.15 A.	9.14 B.	3. 8	5 14	21.14	B. wins.
16.19	22.17	10.14	26.22	10.17	
23.16	14.18	8.11	14.18	18.15 G.	E.
12.19	15.10	14.17	22.17	17.22	29.25
15.11	18.23	25.21	19.23	26.17	19.24
14.23	17.13	17.22	17.13	19.26	28.19
24.15	23.26	21.17	23.26	30.23	10.15
7.16	30.23	31.27	31.22	13.22	19.10
26.12	31.27	11.15	18.25	15.11	6.15
4. 8	21.17	22.26	10. 6	7.10	27.24 F.
28.24	27.18	15.18	2. 9	11. 7	20.27
9.14	17.14	W. wins.	3. 6	10.14	16.11

7.16		20.27	**C.**	12.19	7.11
23.18	**GAME 40.**	23. 7	2.18	24.15	22.15
14.23	22.18	3.19	22.15	18.23 G.	11.18
26.10	10.14	32.16	3. 7	27.18	10. 7
27.31	24.19	6.10	25.22	14.23	5. 9
22.18	11.16	16.12	9.13	15.10	7. 3
31.27	27.24	W. wins.	30.26	8.11	8.12
18.15	16.20		5. 9	10. 6	27.23
27.23	31.27	**Var.**	26.23	11.15	18.27
15.11	8.11	16.19	7.10	6. 2	32.23
23.18	25.22	23.16	15.11	9.13	1. 5
11. 7	4. 8	14.23	8.15	2. 6	25.22
16.19	29.25	26.19	23.18	3. 7	W. wins.
7. 2	11.16	7.11 D.E.F.	W. wins.	W. wins.	
19.23	19.15	16. 7			**H.**
2. 7	7.11 var	3.10 C.	**D.**	**G.**	7.11
1. 6	24.19 A.	22.17	9.13	8.11	30.26
B. wins.	9.13	9.13 B.	22.18	15. 8	11.18
	18. 9	17.14	6. 9	3.12	22.15
F.	5.14	10.17	25.22	30.26	5. 9
16.12	22.18*	21.14	9.14	12.16	26.23
7.10	1. 5	6. 9	18. 9	28.24	2. 6
21.17	18. 9	19.16	5.14	9.13	28.24
14.21	5.14	12.19	15.11	26.22	9.13
23.18	26.22	15.10	8.15	5. 9	25.22
15.19	11.18	9.18	19.10	22.15	8.12
27.23	22.15	24.15	12.19	16.19	22.18
19.24	3. 7	2. 6	24.15	25.22	6. 9
18.15	28.24	10. 7	14.18	19.28	23.19
10.19	7.10	W. wins.	30.25	15.10	W. wins.
23.16	30.26		7.14	W. wins.	
24.27	14.17	**B.**	15.11		**GAME 41.**
26.23	21. 7	2. 7	3. 7	**F.**	22.18
27.31	2.18	17.13	22.15	9.14	10.14
23.19	23.14	7.11	7.16	15.10	24.19
31.26	16.30	21.17	15.11	6.15	11.16
30.23	14. 9	11.18	W. wins.	19.10	27.24
B. wins.	B. wins.	19.15		12.19	16.20
		10.19	**E.**	24.15	31.27
G.	**A.**	24.15	6.10	14.18 H.	8.11
16.12	22.17†	9.14	15. 6	22.17	25.22
19.24	16.19	17.10	1.10	7.14	4. 8
28.19	17.10	18.23	22.18	17.10	29.25
3. 8	2. 6	27.18	10.14	2. 7	11.16
12. 3	23.16	8.11	18.15	20.26	19.15
17.21	12.19	15. 8	7.11	7.14	7.11
B. wins.	21.17	6.29	16. 7	26.22	24.19 A.
	7.21	8. 3	2.18	3. 7	9.13
	27.23	W. wins.	19.16	15.10	18. 9

5.14	24.15	24.19	19.15 A.	16.19	25.22
28.24	2.11	11.16	10.19	B. wins.	1. 6
11.18	21.17	27.24	24.15		22.18
22.15	6. 9	8.11	2. 6	D.	7.11
6.10	17.14	31.27	28.24	26.22	30.26
15. 6	9.13	16.20	Drawn.	2. 6	11.16
1.10	14.10	25.22		18.15	26.23
26.22	13.17	4. 8	A.	11.18	5. 9
3. 7	10. 7	29.25	22.18	22.15	B. wins.
22.18	1. 6	11.16 var	7.11	13.17	
14.17	7. 3	19.15	19.15 C.D.	B. wins.	F.
21.14	8.12	7.11	10.19		27.24
10.17	15. 8	22.17	24.15	Var. 2.	20.27
18.14	W. wins.	16.19	16.19	19.15	32.14
8.11		17.10	23. 7	11.18	7.10
14. 9	B.	2. 7	14.30	22.15	14. 7
7.14	10.17	23.16	7. 3	7.10	3.19
9. 5	21.14	12.19	9.14	25.22 E.	22.18
10.14	9.18 C.	25.22	25.22 B.	10.19	8.11
25.21	23.14	7.23	30.26	23.16	18.14 G.
17.22	11.18	27.18	22.18	12.19	1. 5
5. 1	24.15	20.27	14.23	24.15	25.22 H.
22.25	2. 7	32. 7	27.18	14.18	11.15
1. 5	26.23	3.19	26.23	30.25	14.10
25.29	6.10	21.17	15.10	2. 7	6. 9
5. 9	15. 6	6.10	23. 7	15.10 F.I.	10. 7
13.17	1.17	17.14	3.10	7.14	9.14
9.18	23.14	10.17	12.16	22.15	7. 3
17.22	8.11	22. 6	B. wins.	3. 7	14.18
18.25	28.24	1.10		28.24	3. 7
29.22	W. wins.	18.15	B.	14.17	18.25
19.15		10.14	27.23	21.14	26.22
11.18	C.	15.10	30.26	6.10	19.23
23.14	11.18	Drawn.	23.19	15. 6	Drawn.
2. 7	24.15		2. 7	1.17	
21.17	9.13	Var.	3.17	25.21	G.
Drawn.	28.24	9.13	13.29	17.22	26.22
	8.12	18. 9	15.10	26.17	6.10
A.	15.11	5.14	26.23	13.22	21.17
22.17†	6. 9	22.18 var 2	19.15	24.19	B. wins.
16.19	14.10	6. 9 R.	23.19	22.26	
17.10	9.14	26.22 U.	B. wins.	19.15	H.
12.16	10. 7	11.16 Q.		Drawn.	26.22
10. 7	13.17	18.15 N.	C.		19.23
3.10	W. wins.	7.10	25.22	E.	28.24
18.14		15. 6	2. 7	23.18	23.26
9.18 B.	GAME 42.	1.10	19.15	14.23	24.19
23. 7	22.18	30.26	10.19	26.19	26.30
11.18	10.14	3. 7	24.15	2. 7	19.15

11.18	20.27	**T.**	4. 8	15.19	**A.**
22.15	32.16	6.10	29.25	24.27	19.16
6. 9	8.11	19.16	9.13	19.23	11.20
B. wins.	15. 8	12.19	18. 9	27.31	28.19
	3.19	24. 6	5.14	22.18	20.24 C.
I.	B. wins.	W. wins.	22.18	31.26	18.15
28.24			6. 9	18. 9	2. 6
7.11	**O.**	**U.**	19.16	26.19	25.22
24.19 K.	30.26	25.22	12.19	9. 5	3. 7
20.24	20.27	1. 6	24.15	19.15	22.18
27.20	32.16	19.15V.Y.	7.10 var	5. 1	7.11 D.
18.23	8.11	7.10	15. 6	15.18	26.22
B. wins.	B. wins.	24.19	1.10	1. 5	10.14
		2. 7	23.19 E.	18.14	19.16
K.	**P.**	19.16	14.23	5. 1	11.20
26.23	15.11	12.19	27.18	30.26	15.10
11.16	8.15	23.16	20.24	1. 6	14.23
23.14	18.11	B. wins.	18.14 A.	26.23	10. 1
6.10	B. wins.		9.18	6. 1	24.27
B. wins.		**V.**	19.15	23.18	1. 5
	Q.	19.16	10.19	1. 5	27.31
L.	1. 5	12.19	26.23	13.17	5.14
27.23	19.15	24.15	18.27	5. 1	23.27
18.27	2. 6	7.10	32. 7	B. wins.	32.23
32.23	24.19	23.19	3.10		31.26
7.10	7.10	14.23	28.19	**B.**	14.18
22.18 M.	28.24	27.18	8.11	30.26	26.19
10.19	12.16	9.14	25.22 B.	11.15	21.17
23.16	19.12	B. wins.	11.15	19.16	20.24
8.12	10.28		19.16	15.18	17.14
B. wins.	18.15	**Y.**	10.14	16.11	Drawn
	11.18	30.25	16.11	10.15	
M.	22.15	11.16	14.18	11. 8	**C.**
23.19	Drawn.	18.15	30.25	15.19	8.11
1. 5		7.10	18.23	26.22	32.27
22.18	**R.**	22.18	11. 8	18.23	10.14
5. 9	1. 5	3. 7	23.26	22.18	26.23
25.22	18. 9	B. wins.	8. 3	23.26	3. 8
3. 7	5.14		26.30	18.15	30.26
B. wins.	25.22	**GAME 43.**	3. 8	26.30	8.12
	6. 9 S.T.	22.18	2. 7	15.10	26.22
N.	22.18	10.14	8. 3	19.24	11.16
19.15	W. wins.	24.19	7.10	8. 4	18.15
16.19		11.16	3. 8	24.27	14.18
23.16	**S.**	27.24	10.14	4. 8	23. 5
14.23	11.16	8.11	8.11	27.31	16.32
27.18	22.18	25.22	15.19	Drawn.	5. 1
12.19	6. 9	16.20	11.15		32.27
21.17 O.P.	18.15	31.27	19.24		Drawn.
	W. wins.				

D.	18. 23 G.	I.	14. 23	21. 17	Var.
24. 28	27. 18	2. 7	27. 18	7. 21	9. 13
26. 23	20. 27	30. 26	20. 27	27. 23	18. 9
10. 14	32. 23	15. 19 K.	32. 23	20. 27	5. 14
30. 26	22. 26	23. 16	W. wins.	23. 7	22. 18
13. 17	15. 10	14. 30	GAME 44.	3. 19	6. 9
19. 16	W. wins.	22. 18	22. 18	32. 16	19. 16
8. 12		W. wins.	22. 18	6. 10	12. 19
15. 11	G.		10. 14	25. 22	24. 15
12. 19	11. 16	K.	24. 19	9. 14	7. 10
23. 16	5. 9	13. 17	11. 16	18. 9	15. 6
14. 30	18. 23	22. 6	27. 24	W. wins.	1. 10
21. 5	27. 18	18. 31	8. 11		23. 19
7. 10	20. 27	32. 28	25. 22	GAME 45.	14. 23
5. 1	32. 23	W. wins.	16. 20	22. 18	27. 18
30. 26	22. 26		31. 27	10. 14	20. 24
11. 7	Drawn.	L.	4. 8	24. 19	26. 22
26. 23		16. 19	29. 25	11. 16	10. 15 A.
W. wins.	Var.	23. 16	11. 16	27. 24	19. 10
	2. 6 H.	14. 23	19. 15	8. 11	2. 7
E.	28. 24	26. 19	7. 11	25. 22	28. 19
28. 24	7. 10	7. 11 M.N.	22. 17	16. 20	7. 23
10. 15	24. 19	16. 7	16. 19	31. 27	19. 15
25. 22	1. 5	2. 18	23. 7 var	4. 8	11. 18
2. 7 F.	25. 22	30. 26	14. 23	29. 25	22. 15
23. 19	3. 7	8. 11	26. 19	11. 16 var	8. 11
14. 23	30. 25	19. 15	2. 18	19. 15	15. 8
19. 10	14. 17	11. 16	17. 14	7. 11	3. 12
7. 14	21. 14	15. 10	9. 13	22. 17	25. 22
26. 19	10. 17	W. wins.	14. 10	16. 19	12. 16
14. 18	25. 21		6. 15	17. 10	22. 18
22. 15	W. wins.	M.	19. 10	2. 7	Drawn.
11. 18		9. 14	12. 16	23. 16	
19. 15	H.	16. 11	30. 26	12. 19	A.
8. 11	11. 16	7. 23	8. 11	21. 17†	10. 14
15. 8	28. 24	27. 9	26. 23	7. 23	18. 15
Drawn.	7. 10 L.	20. 27	11. 15	27. 18	11. 18
	15. 6	32. 23	23. 14	20. 27	22. 15
F.	1. 10	1. 5	15. 18	32. 7	14. 18 F.G.H.
13. 17	24. 19	25. 22	10. 7	3. 19	15. 11 B.
22. 6	8. 11	W. wins.	3. 17	17. 13	8. 15
15. 31	19. 12		21. 14	8. 11	19. 10
6. 1	10. 15	N.	Drawn.	25. 22	2. 7
31. 26	26. 22	8. 12		11. 16	28. 19
23. 19	2. 6 I.	15. 11	Var.	22. 17	7. 14
26. 22	30. 26	9. 14	17. 10†	16. 20	19. 15
1. 5	W. wins.	25. 22	2. 7	26. 23	18. 22 D.E.
14. 18		1. 6	23. 16	19. 26	25. 18
19. 15		22. 18	12. 19	W. wins.	14. 23

15.10	30.25	**G.**	13.29	21.14	**8.12**
9.14	10. 6	2. 7	6. 1	3. 7	31.27
10. 6	25.22	15.10	29.25	29.25	1. 6
14.18	6. 1	7.11	1. 6	6.10	17.14
6. 2	22.17	25.22	18.22	25.21	16.20
18.22	27.23	8.12	6. 9	10.17	27.23
21.17	17.14	W. wins.	25.29	21.14	15.18
22.25	1. 5		9.35	1. 6	22.15
Drawn.	20.24	**H.**	29.22	19.15	6.10
	23.19	8.12	32.27	8.11	23.16
B.	24.27	15.10	3. 7	15. 8	12.19
19.16	19.16	14.18	27.24	4.11	14. 7
8.11	27.31	19.15	7.11	23.19	2.18
28.19	16.11	2. 7	B. wins.	6. 9	Drawn.
11.20	B. wins.	28.19		14.10	
32.27		7.14	**K.**	7.14	**GAME 48.**
9.14	**D.**	15.11 I.	10. 6	19.16	11.15
30.26	13.17	18.22	17.22	Drawn.	23.19
13.17	30.26	25.18	6. 1		9.13
19.16 C.	3. 8	14.23	22.29	**GAME 47.**	26.23 A.
2. 6	26.23	19.15	1. 6	22.17	8.11 var
16.12	18.27	9.14	9.13	11.15	23.18
6. 9	32.23	15.10	6. 9	23.19	4. 8
15.11	W. wins.	14.18	18.22	8.11	27.23
9.13		10. 6	9.25	25.22	6. 9
11. 8	**E.**	18.22	29.22	11.16	30.26
3. 7	18.23	6. 1	19.15	24.20	9.14
8. 3	15.10	22.26	3. 7	16.23	18. 9
7.11	14.18	1. 6	B. wins.	27.11	5.14
3. 7	10. 6	26.31		7.16	32.27
11.16	9.14	11. 7	**GAME 46.**	20.11	1. 5
7.11	6. 2	3.10	22.18	3. 8	19.16
16.19	23.27	6.15	11.16	26.23	12.19
11.15	32.23	12.16	25.22	8.15	23.16
19.24	18.27	15.11	10.14	23.18	11.20
15.22	25.22	16.20	24.19	15.19	22.17
24.31	27.31	11.15	16.20	30.26	13.22
12. 8	2. 6	20.24	22.17	9.14	25. 4
20.24	W. wins.	15.10	9.13	18. 9	5. 9
Drawn.		Drawn.	17.10	5.14	29.25
	F.		6.22	32.27	9.13
C.	3. 7	**I.**	26.17	4. 8	25.22
15.11	15.10	15.10	13.22	27.24	14.17
18.22	7.11	13.17	30.26	12.16	21.14
25. 9	10. 7	30.26	2. 6	24.15	10.17
3. 7	8.12	17.22	26.17	10.19	26.23
21.14	7. 3	26.17	7.10	17.10	17.26
7.30	11.16	9.13	17.14	6.15	31.22
14.10	3. 8	10. 6	10.17	21.17	7.11
	W. wins.				

24.19	19.16	C.	30.26	23.18	19.12
2. 7	12.19	4. 8	10.15 G.	4. 8 C. D.	2. 7
W. wins.	23. 7	24.20	19.10	27.23	12.16
	2.11	10.15	6.15	6. 9	31.27
A.	27.23	19.10	21.17	30.26	W. wins.
21.17	W. wins.	6.15	14.21	9.14	
5. 9		27.24	20.16	18. 9	A.
25.21	B.	2. 7	12.19	5.14	24.20
9.14	1. 5	24.19	23.16	32.27	16.11
27.23	29.25	15.24	11.20	14.17	20.24
8.11	13.17	28.19	18. 2	21.14	6. 2
24.20	21.14	7.10	21.25	10.17	24.19
15.24	10.17	22.17	22.18	19.10	2. 7
28.19	31.26	13.22	Drawn.	7.14	W. wins.
4. 8	9.13	26.17		25.21	
30.25	25.22	9.13	F.	11.15	B.
11.15	8.11	18. 9	31.26	24.19	25.22
32.28	24.20	13.22	4. 8	15.24	14.18
15.24	4. 8	21.17	19.15	28.19	22.15
28.19	27.24	11.15	10.19	8.11	3. 7
8.11	6. 9	32.28	24.15	22.18	21.14
22.18	32.27	15.24	12.16	1. 5	7.10
13.22	17.21	28.19	28.24	18. 9	15. 6
26.17	19.16	8.11	16.20	5.14	2.18
1. 5	12.19	23.18	24.19	29.25	23.14
18. 9	23.16	22.25	2. 6	11.16	16.30
5.14	2. 6	9. 6	19.16	19.15 B.	14.10
B. wins.	16.12	25.29	8.12	2. 6	30.25
	6.10	6. 2	15. 8	15.11	10. 6
Var.	27.23	29.25	12.19	16.19	25.22
5. 9	9.14	Drawn.	23.16	23.16	6. 2
22.18	18. 9		B. wins.	12.19	Drawn.
15.22	5.14	D.		27.23	
25.18	22.18	10.15	G.	19.24	C.
10.14 B.	14.17	19.10	4. 8	25.22	5. 9
29.25	18.14	6.15	27.24	24.28	27.23
8.11	17.22	24.19	10.15	22.18	10.14
25.22	26.17	15.24	19.10	6. 9	19.10
7.10 E.	13.22	28.19	6.15	18.15	6.15
30.26	14. 9	2. 6	21.17	28.32	30.26
3. 8 C.D.	22.26	27.24	14.21	23.19	7.10
24.20	9. 6	11.16	Drawn.	32.28	32.27
11.15	26.31	32.27		11. 7	1. 5
18.11	6. 2	Drawn.	GAME 49.	3.10	24.19
8.24	31.26		11.15	15. 6	15.24
28.19	23.19	E.	23.19	28.24	28.19
4. 8	27.23	6.10	9.13	19.16	11.16
32.28	2. 6	24.20 F.	26.23	24.19 A.	22.17
8.11	W. wins.	2. 6	8.11	6. 2	13.22

26.17	8.11	11. 8	1. 6	19.15	**A.**
4. 8	18.14	4.11	21.17	14. 9	27.23
17.13	10.17	27.24	4. 8	23.19	2. 6
3. 7	21.14	11.15	11. 4	9. 5	23.16
13. 6	1. 6	22.17	6.10	15.10	12.19
2. 9	32.27	13.22	Drawn.	5. 1	26.22
25.22	6.10	25.11		19.15	7.10 B.
8.11	14. 7	10.15	**H.**	17.13	18.15
29.25	3.10	24.20	32.27	15.11	11.18
9.13	27.24	W. wins.	8.11	1. 5	22.15
18. 9	10.15		27.24	11. 7	6. 9
5.14	24.20	**F.**	19.23	B. wins.	15. 6
22.18	19.23	6.10	24.19		1.10
14.17	31.26	11. 8 G.	3. 8	**GAME 50.**	20.16
21.14	23.27	4.11	28.24	11.15	9.14
10.17	26.23	27.24	23.27	23.19	16.11
19.15	27.32	11.15	24.20	9.13	Drawn.
16.19	23.19	22.17	1. 5	26.23	
23.16	15.24	13.22	31.24	6. 9	**B.**
11.20	28.19	25.11	8.12	22.18	19.23
25.22	32.27	16.20	22.18	15.22	18.15 C.
17.26	19.16	24. 6	10.14	25.18	11.18
31.22	11.15	7.16	18. 9	8.11	22.15
12.16	16.12	29.25	5.14	29.25	6.10
27.23	27.24	1.10	19.15	9.14	15.16
20.24	12. 8	21.17	11.18	18. 9	1.10
18.14	24.19	5. 9	24.19	5.14	20.16
24.27	8. 4	17.13	30.26	23.18	23.26
Drawn.	15.18	2. 6	19.15	14.23	16.12
	4. 8	25.22	18.23	27.18	26.31
D.	18.22	9.14	15.10	10.15 E.	12. 8
11.16	8.12	26.23	23.27	19.10	31.27
18.11	30.26	10.15	10. 6	7.23	8. 3
16.23	20.16	31.26	27.31	31.27	Drawn.
27.18	19.15	15.19	6. 1	12.16 G.	
7.16	12. 8	22.18	31.27	27.18	**C.**
24.20 E.	Drawn.	14.17	1. 6	4. 8	28.24
16.19		18.14	26.23	24.20	6.10
30.26	**E.**	20.24	25.22	16.19	24.19
12.16	18.15	23.18	23.19	30.26	23.27
20.11	10.19	24.27	6.10	3. 7	19.16
2. 7	24.15	18.15	27.23	32.27	27.31
11. 2	16.19	27.31	10.17	8.12	16.12
4. 8	30.26	Drawn.	23.26	27.24 A.	31.26 D.
2. 9	12.16		22.18	19.23	12. 8
5.30	32.27	**G.**	13.22	26.19	26.17
22.17 H.	3. 7	27.23	21.17	11.16	21.14
13.22	15.11	10.15	26.23	20.11	10.17
25.18	7.10 F.	23.18	18.14	7.23	25.21
				Drawn.	

17.22	27.31	13.17	2. 7	21.17	9.14
8. 3	24.20	18. 9	28.24 M.	1. 6	25.30
7.10	31.27	5.14	7.11	17.14	Drawn.
3. 7	18.15	23.18	18.14	10.26	
10.14	27.24	16.23	3. 7	19. 1	**GAME** 51.
Drawn.	20.16	18. 9	14. 9 N.	26.31	11.15
	24.27	17.22	7.10	23.18	22.17
D.	16.11	21.17	21.17 I.K.L.	31.26	8.11
31.27	27.23	23.26	1. 5	B. wins.	25.22
21.17	8. 4	17.14	9. 6		9.13
27.23	23.16	26.31	5. 9	**L.**	29.25 var
18.14	4. 8	14.10	6. 2	22.18	15.18
23.26	16.11	31.27	11.15	1. 5	23.14
12. 8	8. 4	10. 7	2. 7	18.14	11.15
26.30	Drawn.	27.23	9.14	10.17	24.19
25.21		7. 3	7.11	21.14	15.24
30.25	**F.**	23.18	14.21	13.17	28.19
22.18	30.26	9. 5	11.18	9. 6	4. 8
13.22	16.19	11.15	21.25	17.22	26.23
8. 3	15.11	24.19	18.15	6. 2	8.11
10.17	19.23	15.24	10.14	22.26	23.18
21.14	26.19	28.19	22.18	B. wins.	6. 9
Drawn.	3. 7	22.26	14.17		27.24
	19.15	3. 8	18.14	**M.**	1. 6
E.	7.11	26.31	25.80	21.17	32.28
11.16	15.11	8.11	14.10	1. 6	11.15
18.15	2. 6	31.27	30.26	B. wins.	18.11
16.23	11. 7	19.15	10. 7		9.18
15. 6	6.10	27.23	17.22	**N.**	22.15
1.10	7. 2	15.10	7. 2	22.18	13.29
31.26	Drawn.	23.19	13.17	13.17	11. 8
10.14		1. 5	B. wins.	14.10	29.25
26.19	**G.**	19.24		7.14	31.26
14.18	23.26	10. 7	**I.**	18. 9	5. 9
32.27	30.23	18.23	9. 6	17.22	B. wins.
7.11	12.16	7. 3	10.14	19.15	
19.15	24.20 H.	12.16	6. 2	11.18	**Var.**
11.16	4. 8	Drawn.	13.17	23.14	23.19
15.10 F.	28.24		22.13	22.25	4. 8
4. 8	8.12	**H.**	14.18	14.10	27.23
30.26	24.19	23.18	23.14	1. 5	6. 9
18.23	3. 7	4. 8	16.32	9. 6	23.18
27.18	25.22	27.23	24.19	5. 9	9.14
16.20	7.10	16.20	32.27	6. 2	18. 9
24.19	27.24	31.27	B. wins.	9.14	5.14
20.24	1. 5	8.12		2. 6	26.23
26.22	32.28	24.19	**K.**	14.18	2. 6
24.27	10.14	11.16	9. 5	6. 9	24.20
28.24	22.18	25.22	11.15	18.22	15.24

28.19	23.14	22.17	21.14	30.23	16.19
10.15	9.18	W. wins.	10.17	5. 9	17.14
19.10	22. 6		18.14	24.19	9.18
6.15	13.29	C.	17.21	15.24	22.15
17.10	6. 2	3. 8	19.15	28.19	6. 9
7.14	7.10	26.23	Drawn.	11.15	15. 6
31.27	16.11	5. 9		20.16	1.10
3. 7	10.14	17.13	C.	15.24	20.16
23.18	2. 6	11.16	4. 8	16.11	2. 7
Drawn.	29.25	24.20	26.23	24.27	32.27
	Drawn.	15.24	9.14	11. 7	9.14
GAME 52.		28.19	24.19	27.31	8.12
11.15	A.	1. 5	8.11	7. 3	5. 9
23.19	6. 9	20.11	30.26	31.27	25.22
8.11	27.24	8.24	16.20	23.19	9.13
22.15	2. 7	27.20	17.13	27.23	27.23
9.14 var	19.15	14.17	20.24	19.15	19.24
25.22	10.26	Drawn.	22.17	10.19	22.18
11.16 C.	17. 3		11.16	17.10	14.17
24.20	9.14	Var.	26.22	19.24	21.14
16.23	3. 7	11.16	16.20	10. 6	10.17
27.11	26.31	24.20	31.27	B. wins.	18.15
7.16	24.19	16.23	24.28		24.27
20.11	31.27	27.11	29.25	E.	23.18
3. 7	7.10	7.16	20.24	30.25	27.31
28.24	27.24	20.11	W. wins.	2. 7	26.23
7.16	10.17	3. 7		22.18	31.26
24.19	24.15	28.24	D.	15.22	23.19
16.23	17.14	7.16	10.15	25.18	26.23
26.19	1. 5	25.22	24.20	7.10	18.14
4. 8	21.17	16.20 C.D.	16.19	29.25	23.16
30.26	Drawn.	29.25	17.13	10.14	15.11
8.11		20.27	4. 8	18.15	17.22
26.23	B.	31.24	31.27 E.	14.17	11. 2
11.15 B.	6. 9	9.14 F.	8.11	21.14	13.17
32.28	17.13	26.23	32.28	9.18	14.10
15.24	1. 6	4. 8	9.14	20.16	16.19
28.19	22.18	24.19	29.25	18.23	2. 7
5. 9	2. 7	8.11	6.10	26.22	19.23
29.25	29.25	30.26	27.24	19.24	7. 3
9.13	11.16	11.16	5. 9	16.11	Drawn.
31.27	32.27	17.13	13. 6	12.16	
1. 5 A.	14.17	2. 7	2. 9	11. 4	GAME 53.
27.24	21.14	22.18	22.17	23.27	11.15
6. 9	10.17	14.17	9.13	Drawn.	22.17
24.20	25.22	21.14	25.22		8.11
2. 7	17.26	10.17	1. 5	F.	23.19
20.16	31.22	25.21	26.23	12.16	4. 8
14.18	16.20	6.10	19.26	24.20	25.22

15.18	10.17	C.	7.10	26.22	32.27
22.15	27.23	6.10	31.26	17.26	10.14
11.18	8.11	25.22	3. 7 F	31.15	27.23
17.13	31.26 E.	11.15 D.	25.22	7.10 K.	14.17
9.14	1. 6	32.27	1. 6	24.20	25.21
29.25	28.24	7.11	22.18	2. 7 H.	9.14
14.17 var	7.10 C.	23.18	10.14	27.23	18. 9
21.14	32.28	5. 9	18. 9	10.14	11.27
10.17	11.15	13. 6	5.14	28.24	21.14
26.22 A.	25.22	2. 9	32.28	14.17	8.11
17.26	3. 7	22. 6	14.18	15.11	9. 5
31.15	20.16	15.31	Drawn.	W. wins.	6. 9
7.11	7.11	6. 1			13. 6
30.26	16. 7	10.14	F.	L.	W. wins.
11.18	2.11	1. 6	11.15	7.11	
26.22	23.18 B.	14.17	25.22	19.15	K.
5. 9	6. 9	6.10	1. 6 G.	10.19	5. 9
22.15	13. 6	17.22	20.16	24.15	27.23
9.14	5. 9	10.14	3. 7	3. 7	7.10
24.20	22.13	22.25	22.18	26.22	24.20
14.17	15.31	14.18	W. wins.	W. wins.	9.14
27.24	24.20	25.29			25.21
2. 7	31.27	19.15	G.	H.	3. 7
25.21	6. 2	3. 8	3. 7	3. 7	13. 9
17.22	27.24	15.10	20.16	27.23	6.13
20.16	13. 6	W. wins.	7.11	5. 9	15. 6
22.26	24.15		16. 7	25.21 I.	2. 9
32.27	6. 1	D.	2.11	9.14	19.15
26.31	10.14	2. 6	32.28	13. 9	7.11
15.10	1. 6	22.18	1. 6	6.13	15.10
7.14	14.18	5. 9	24.20	15. 6	11.15
16.11	Drawn.	32.27	15.24	2. 9	28.24
8.15		10.14	28.19	19.15	8.11
19.10	B.	19.15	11.15	7.11	10. 6
6.15	24.20	3. 8	19.16	15.10	11.15
24.20	15.24	24.19	12.19	11.15	24.19
31.24	28.19	7.10	23.16	28.24	W. wins.
28.10	11.15	27.24	Drawn.	13.17	
14.18	23.18	12.16		10. 6	M.
13. 9	15.24	19. 3	Var.	9.13	7.11
18.23	18.14	10.28	5. 9 M.	6. 2	24.20
Drawn.	10.15	3. 7	26.23	17.22	11.15
	14.10	28.32	1. 5	2. 6	26.22
A.	24.27	7.16	30.26	22.26	15.24
24.20	10. 1	32.28	14.17 L.	W. wins.	28.19
17.21	27.31	W. wins.	21.14		10.15
26.23	1. 6		10.17	I.	19.10
6.10	15.18	E.	23.14	23.18	6.15
23.14	Drawn.	28.24	9.18	7.11	30.26

8.11	12.16	19.16	1.17	28.24	19.10
26.23	27.23	12.12	28.14	17.21	8.11
12.16	2. 6	32.28	11.15	26.23	25.22
22.17	32.27	13.22	19.10	13.17	18.25
2. 6 N.	16.20	Drawn.	17.22	31.26	29.22
17.10	23.19		25.18	6. 9	11.15
18.22	15.24	Var.	5. 9	20.16	23.19
25.18	28.19	9.13	14. 5	11.20	2. 6
15.22	6.10	17.14	7.32	25.22	26.23
10. 7	22.17	10.17	31.27	18.25	6. 9
3.10	13.22	21.14	32.23	29. 6	22.17
27.24	26.17	15.18	24.19	2.18	Drawn.
W. wins.	1. 6	19.15	Drawn.	23.14	
	31.26	4. 8		7.11	G.
N.	20.24	24.19	B.	15.10	6.10
2. 7	Drawn.	6. 9 F.G.	13.17	11.16	15. 6
17.10		13.17 E.	31.26	26.23	1.17
7.14	GAME 55.	24.20	6. 9	8.11	25.22
31.26	11.15	9.13	14.10	10. 6	18.25
1. 6	22.17	32.28	7.14	W. wins.	30.14
32.28	8.11	2. 6 D.	25.22		13.17 I.
5. 9	23.19	28.24	18.25	E.	27.23
26.22	4. 8 var	17.21	29. 6	11.16	2. 6 H.
3. 7	25.22	26.23	11.18	15.11	23.18
28.24	9.13	18.22 A.B.	6. 2	8.15	17.21
7.10	27.23	25.18	5. 9	19.10	26.23
W. wins.	6. 9	6.10	19.15	16.20	11.16
	23.18	15. 6	9.13	24.19	28.24
GAME 54.	9.14	1.17	23.19	13.17	6. 9
11.15	18. 9	18.15	13.17	25.22	32.27
22.17	5.14	11.18	26.23	18.25	Drawn.
8.11	26.23	23.14	18.22 C.	29. 6	
23.19	2. 6	8.11	20.16	2.18	H.
4. 8	30.25	29.25	22.26	10. 6	11.16
25.22	6. 9	11.15	16.11	1.10	26.22
9.13	31.27	19.10	26.31	19.16	17.26
17.14	1. 5	17.22	11. 4	12.19	31.22
10.17	23.18	25.18	31.26	W. wins.	16.20
19.10	14.23	5. 9	W. wins.		32.27
6.15	27.18	14. 5		F.	8.11
21.14	9.14	7.32	C.	13.17	22.18
15.19	18. 9	24.19	17.22	28.24	7.10
24.15	5.14	13.17	15.10	11.16	14. 7
11.25	24.20	Drawn.	22.26	26.23	3.10
30.21	15.24		19.15	16.20	18.15
8.11	28.19	A.	W. wins.	31.26	11.18
29.25	11.15	6.10	D.	17.21	23. 7
11.15	22.18	15. 6	1. 6	15.10	2.11
25.22	14.23			6.15	Drawn.

I.	ı2. 19	9. 6	27. 23	F.	23. 19
2. 6	20. 16	10. 15	W. wins.	8. 11	11. 15
29. 25	3. 8	18. 14		26. 23	19. 16
13. 17	W. wins.	15. 19	C.	11. 15	15. 19
25. 21		6. 2	6. 9	16. 11	16. 11
11. 16 K.	GAME 56.	19. 23	30. 26	7. 16	3. 8
14. 10	11. 15	26. 19	11. 15 E.	20. 11	11. 7
16. 30	22. 17	16. 23	32. 28	W. wins.	8. 11
21. 14	8. 11	22. 18	15. 24		7. 2
6. 15	23. 19	24. 27	28. 19	Var.	1. 6
31. 26	4. 8 var	14. 10	8. 11	9. 13	22. 18
30. 23	25. 22	27. 31	19. 16	25. 22	13. 22
27. 2	9. 13	10. 7	12. 19	6. 9	2. 7
8. 11	27. 23	31. 26	23. 16	27. 23	14. 23
2. 6	6. 9	7. 3	1. 6 D.	9. 14	7. 5
11. 15	23. 18	26. 22	26. 23	24. 20	W. wins.
6. 10	9. 14	18. 14	11. 15	15. 24	
15. 18	18. 9	11. 15	22. 18	28. 19	H.
W. wins.	5. 14	3. 7	15. 22	11. 15	4. 8
	26. 23	Drawn.	16. 11	32. 28	22. 18
L.	2. 6		7. 16	15. 24	13. 22
6. 10	24. 20	A.	20. 11	28. 19	18. 9
27. 23 M.	15. 24	1. 6	W. wins.	7. 11 I.	5. 14
11. 16	28. 19	22. 17		19. 16	30. 25
28. 24	10. 15 C.	18. 22	D.	12. 19	22. 26
16. 20	19. 10	30. 26	11. 15	23. 7	31. 22
32. 28	6. 15	22. 31	16. 11	2. 11	3. 7
20. 27	17. 10	32. 28	7. 16	26. 23	22. 18
31. 24	7. 14	31. 24	20. 11	11. 15 G.H.	14. 17
8. 11	31. 27	28. 1	15. 19	20. 16	21. 14
24. 20	3. 7 A.B.	11. 15	11. 7	3. 7	10. 17
W. wins.	23. 18	1. 6	19. 24	22. 18	25. 21
	14. 23	8. 11	7. 2	15. 22	17. 22
M.	27. 18	29. 25	W. wins.	23. 19	23. 19
27. 24	15. 19	12. 16		14. 18	22. 26
11. 15	30. 26	6. 10	E.	17. 14	21. 17
24. 20	19. 24	15. 18	1. 5	10. 17	1. 6
15. 24	29. 25	W. wins.	32. 27	21. 14	18. 14
28. 19	1. 6		11. 15	1. 6	6. 10
8. 11	21. 17	B.	20. 16	19. 15	14. 9
32. 27	7. 10	15. 18	15. 24	18. 23	8. 12
3. 8 N.	17. 14	22. 15	27. 20	30. 25	9. 6
27. 23	10. 17	11. 18	12. 19	23. 26	Drawn.
17. 22	25. 21	29. 25	23. 16	25. 18	
Drawn.	12. 16	1. 6	8. 12 F.	26. 30	I.
	21. 14	30. 26	16. 11	Drawn.	4. 8
N.	8. 12	3. 7	7. 16		30. 25
11. 15	14. 9	23. 19	20. 11	G.	8. 11 K.
19. 16	6. 10	13. 17	W. wins.	5. 9	22. 18

13.22	1. 5	27.24	20.11	32.14	26.23
18. 9	16.11	19.23	7.32	11.18	2. 6 B.
5.14	7.16	26.19	B. wins.	22.15	30.25
25. 9	20.11	6.10		6.10	6. 9
1. 5 L.	5.14	30.26	A.	14. 7	31.27
26.22	26.23	10.17	27.23	2.18	1. 5
5.14	15.18	26.22	8.12	28.24	23.18
22.18	29.25	17.26	23.16	3. 7	14.23
14.17	18.27	31.22	12.19	21.17	27.18
21.14	31.24	2. 6	31.27	7.10	12.16†
10.17	14.18	18.15	6.10	17.14	19.12
19.15	21.17	7.10	27.23	10.17	10.14
Drawn.	18.23	20.16	3. 8	25.22	17.10
	24.19	10.14	23.17	18.25	7.23
K.	23.26	15.11	8.12	30.14	24.19
7.11	25.21	8.15	26.23	8.11	15.24
22.18	26.31	19. 1	12.26	Drawn.	28.19
13.22	17.14	12.19	30.23		23.26
18. 9	10.17	24.15	10.15	A.	19.15 A.
5.14	21.14	14.18	22.17	24.19	11.18
25. 9	Drawn.	1. 6	7.10	7.10	22.15
11.15		Drawn.	25.22	19.16	26.30
19.16	GAME 57.		3. 7	10.19	32.23
12.19	22.17	GAME 58.	28.24	25.22	13.17
23.16	11.15	11.16	1. 5	2. 7	21.14
8.12	23.19	22.18	23.19	22.18	9.18
16.11	8.11	10.14	14.18	7.10	25.21
1. 5	25.22	25.22	Drawn.	18.15	30.26
9. 6	4. 8	8.11		3. 7	28.24 D.
2. 9	29.25	29.25	GAME 59.	27.24	26.23
11. 7	9.13	4. 8	11.16	20.27	15.10
10.14	17.14	24.20	22.18	31.24	8.11
7. 2	10.17	16.19	10.14	14.17	10. 6
3. 7	19.10	23.16	25.22	Drawn.	18.22
2.18	7.14	14.23	8.11		21.17 E.
14.30	22.18	27.18	29.25	GAME 60.	23.18
21.17	14.23	12.19	4. 8	11.15	6. 1
9.13	21.14	32.27	18.15	22.17	11.16
10.14	11.16	9.14	11.18	8.11	24.20
13.17	27.18	18. 9	22.15	23.19	16.19
14.10	3. 7	5.14	16.20	4. 8	1. 6
17.22	24.20	22.17 A.	26.22 A.	25.22	18.15
Drawn.	16.19	19.23	14.18	9.13	17.14
	32.27	26.19	23.14	27.23	19.23
L.	6.10	8.12	9.18	6. 9	6. 1
11.15	25.21	17.10	24.19	23.18	15.11
19.16	10.17	6.24	7.11	9.14	1. 6
12.19	21.14	28.19	27.24	18. 9	23.26
23.16	1. 6	11.16	20.27	5.14	6. 1

26.30	26.23	19.10	25.21	27.23	6. 9
1. 6	15.10	7.14	6.10	8.12 E.	15.10
30.26	8.11	29.25	21.17	28.24	9.13
B. wins.	10. 6	2. 7	7.11	5. 9	10. 6
	18.22	27.23	14. 7	23.19	13.17
A.	6. 1	6.10 A.	3.10	16.23	6. 2
32.28	23.18	31.27	19.16	26.10	8.11
26.31	1. 6	4. 8	12.19	17.26	2. 6
28.24	18.15	24.20	17.14	30.23	11.15
31.27	17.14	12.16 D.	10.26	13.17	6.10
24.20	11.16	27.24	Drawn.	23.19	15.19
3. 7	6. 9	8.12		17.22	Drawn.
12. 3	16.19	24.19	B.	25.21	
27.24	9.13	5. 9 B.	3. 8	22.26	G.
3.10	19.23	19.15	32.27	21.17	3. 7
24. 6	13. 9	10.19	5. 9 C.	9.13	25.21
21.17	23.26	23.18	22.18	17.14	1. 6
6.10	9. 6	14.23	17.22	26.30	21.14
25.21	26.30	21. 5	26.17	19.15	13.17
10. 6	14.10	7.10	13.29	30.26	22.13
29.25	5. 9	25.21	18.15	15. 8	15.31
B. wins.	B. wins.	10.15	11.18	26.22	30.25
		28.24	20. 2	14. 9	31.24
B.	E.	19.28	8.11	22. 6	28.19
1. 5	24.20	26.10	21.17	9. 2	5. 9
30.25	23.18	16.19	14.21	Drawn.	Drawn.
5. 9	6. 1	21.17	23. 7		
32.27	5. 9	Drawn.	11.16	E.	H.
2. 6	1. 5		Drawn.	15.19	17.21
22.18	18.14	A.		25.21	20.16
15.22 C.	21.17	11.16	C.	1. 6	12.19
25.18	14.21	31.27	11.15	21.14	27.23
13.22	5.14	16.20	20. 4	6.10	19.24
24.20	22.26	23.18	15.31	14. 7	28.10
12.16	14.18	14.23	4. 8	3.10	11.16
19.12	26.31	21.14	1. 6	30.25	23.19
W. wins.	18.23	6. 9	8. 3	Drawn.	16.23
	11.15	27.18	Drawn.		26.19
C.	B. wins.	20.27		F.	8.12
13.22		32.23	D.	15.18	18.14
24.20	GAME 61.	4. 8	10.15	26.19	3. 8
15.24	22.17	23.19	23.18	1. 6	10. 7
28.19	11.15	8.11	14.23	22.15	8.11
12.16	23.19	28.24	21.14	11.18	19.15
19.12	8.11	11.16	7.10 F.	27.24	W. wins.
W. wins.	25.22	24.20	27.18	13.17	
	9.13	16.23	10.17	32.27	GAME 62.
D.	17.14	26.19	32.27	17.21	11.15
21.17	10.17	1. 6	12.16G.H.	19.15	22.17

8.11	21. 7	7.11	24.20	10.17	28.24
23.19	3.10	26.23	11.15	19.10	10.15 C.
4. 8	26.19	15.18	20.11	7.14	23.18
25.22	24.27	31.26	7.16	29.25	14.23
9.13	12. 8	18.27	25.22	2. 7	26.12
17.14	15.24	32.23	16.19	27.23	17.26
10.17	22.18	11.15	23.16	6.10	30.23
19.10	27.31	25.22	12.19	24.20	5. 9
7.14	8. 3	W. wins.	27.23	11.15 B.	32.28
29.25	31.27		1. 6	28.24	1. 5
2. 7	3. 7	**GAME** 63	23.16	8.11	24.19
27.23	27.23	11.15	14.18	31.27 E.	15.24
11.16 B.	7.14	22.17	21. 7	12.16	28.19
22.18	13.17	8.11	18.25	23.18	13.17
6.10	14.21	23.19	30.21	14.23	21.14
18. 9	23.14	4. 8	2.20	26.12	9.27
5.14	Drawn.	25.22	Drawn.	17.26	31.24
24.20		9.13		30.23	Drawn.
16.19 C.	**B.**	17.14	**B.**	5. 9 A.	
23.16	11.15	10.17	6.10	25.22	**C.**
12.19	31.27	19.10	24.20	1. 5	8.12
32.27	8.11	7.14	1. 6	21.17	24.19
1. 6	24.20	29.25	28.24	9.14	10.15
27.23	15.19	3. 7	6. 9	20.16	19.10
8.12	23.16	27.23	24.19	14.21	16.19
23.16	12.19	11.16 B.	2. 6	23.18	23.16
12.19	27.23	31.27	32.28	11.20	12.19
31.27	3. 8	8.11 A.	14.18	Drawn.	22.18
14.18	23.16	22.18	22.15		14.23
21.14 A.	8.12	16.20	11.27	**A.**	21.14
10.17	32.27	18. 9	31.24	13.17	13.17 D.
25.22	12.19	5.14	10.14	21.14	25.21
18.25	27.23	23.19	25.22	10.17	11.15
Drawn.	11.15	11.16	7.11	32.28	20.16
	23.16	19.15	30.25	17.22	5. 9
A.	15.19	7.10	14.18	25.18	14. 5
10.15	16.11	25.22	22.15	15.22	7.14
25·22	7.16	10.19	11.18	12. 8	16.11
6.10	Drawn.	24.15	Drawn.	3.12	15.18
27.23		14.18		23.19	31.27
19.24	**C.**	21.14	**GAME** 64.	7.10	W. wins.
28.19	8.11	Drawn.	11.15	19.16	
15.24	28.24		22.17	12.19	**D.**
20.16	10.15	**A.**	8.11	24. 8	5. 9
10.15	23.19	6.10	23.19	10.14	14. 5
16.12	16.23	22.18	4. 8	Drawn.	7.14
.7.10	26.10	8.11	25.22		25.22
23.18	11.15	18. 9	9.13	**B.**	3. 7
14.23	30.26	5.14	17.14	12.16	31.27

14.17	7. 2	24.19	20.27	20.11	32.27
27.18	15.10	18.14	32. 7	7.16	16.20
19.24	12. 8	19.15	2.11	28.19	24.19
18.14	13.17	8. 3	17.14	10.15	15.24
W. wins.	8. 3	7.11	11.16	19.10	28.19
	17.22	3. 8	28.24	2. 6	8.11
E.	2. 7	17.22	16.23	Drawn.	17.14
32.28	25.22	14.10	26.19		10.17
5. 9 E.	9.13	15. 6	Drawn.	A.	21.14
24.19	18.23	8.15		2. 6	4. 8
15.24	13. 9	22.25	A.	30.26	29.25
28.19	Drawn.	31.27	1. 5	6. 9 B.	8.12
1. 5 G.		25.30	18.15	26.22	26.23
19.16	F.	27.24	8.11	9.14	1. 6
12.19	14.18	30.26	15. 8	31.26	14. 9
23.16	23.14	24.19	4.11	4. 8	6.10
10.15	1. 6	26.30	22.18	17.13	22.18
31.27	24.19	19.16	9.13	1. 6	11.15
15.18	15.24	Drawn.	18. 9	24.20	18.11
22. 8	28.19		5.14	15.24	7.16
3.19	11.15	GAME 65.	25.22	28.19	25.22
26.22	20.16	9.14	11.15	Drawn.	10.14
13.26	15.24	22.18	22.17		19.15
30.16	16.11	5. 9	15.24	B.	16.19
7.10	Drawn.	25.22	28.19	4. 8	23.16
16.11		11.16	Drawn.	25.22	12.19
10.15	G.	29.25		6. 9	Drawn.
27.24	3. 8	16.20	GAME 66.	17.13	
15.18	23.18	24.19	9.14	1. 6	D.
11. 7	14.23	8.11 A.	22.18	22.17	8.11
13.17	21. 5	21.17	18. 9	9.14	17.14
7. 2	11.15	14.21	5.14	24.20	10.17
9.13	25.21	18.15	23.19	15.24	21.14
2. 6	15.24	11.18	6. 9 C.	28.19	4. 8
17.22	26.19	23. 5	25.22	11.15	24.19
6. 9	8.11	4. 8	9.13	W. wins.	15.24
22.29	22.18	22.18	22.17		28.19
24.19	24.28	7.11	13.22	C.	11.16
29.25	30.26	25.22	26.17	8.11	26.23
19.15	28.32	11.16	8.11	25.22	16.20
25.22	21.17	18.15	29.25	3. 8	32.27
15.10	13.22	16.23	14.18	22.17	8.11
22.26	26.17	26.19	27.23	11.16	29.25
20.16	32.28	3. 7	18.27	26.22	Drawn.
26.23	17.14	22.17	32.23	16.23	
16.12	10.17	7.11	11.16 A.	27. 9	GAME 67.
23.19	19.15	31.26	24.20	6.13	22.18
10. 7	28.24	11.18	15.24	30.26	9.13
19.15	15. 8	27.24		12.16 D.	25.22

5. 9 A.	A.	9.14	23.19	8.12	8.11
29.25	11.16	11. 4	4. 8 G.	16.11	27.23
10.15	29.25	17.21	32.28	12.16	10.14
21.17	16.19	25.22	11.15	11. 7 A.	24.19
7.10	23.16	14.18	28.24	2.11	15.24
25.21	12.19	22.17	14.18	32.28	28.19
1. 5	24.15	W. wins.	Drawn.	24.27	7.10
23.19	10.19			31.24	32.27
9.14	27.24	C.	G.	16.20	3. 7
18. 9	7.10	2. 6	11.15	24.19	29.25
5.14	24.15	24.19	32.28	15.24	11.16
26.23	10.19	15.24	15.24	28.19	18.15 C.
6. 9 B.	81.27	28.19	28.19	11.15	1. 5
30.26	2. 7	Drawn.	4. 8	19.16	15. 6
11.16 C.D.	27.24		19.15	4. 8	13.17
24.20	7.10	D.	Drawn.	16.11	22.13
15.24	24.15	3. 7		15.19	14.18
28.19	10.19	24.20	GAME 68.	23.16	23.14
3. 7 E.	82.27	15.24	22.18	8.15	16.32
20.11	3. 7	28.19	9.14	16.11	14.10
8.24	18.14	11.15	18. 9	14.18	7.14
27.20	7.11	20.16	5.14 B.	Drawn.	6. 1
12.16 F.	27.24	15.24	25.22		14.17
20.11	6. 9	27.20	11.15	A.	13. 6
7.16	24.15	12.19	23.19	32.28	2. 9
32.28	11.18	23.16	8.11	16.19	21.14
4. 8	22.15	Drawn.	22.17	23.16	9.18
28.24	9.18		3. 8 D.	14.18	Drawn.
16.20	15.10	E.	29.25	28.19	
24.19	5. 9	8.11	11.16	18.25	C.
8.11	10. 7	27.24	17.13	17.14	30.26
19.16	8.12	3. 7	16.23	15.24	16.20
20.24	7. 3	32.28	27. 9	14. 7	18.15
16. 7	4. 8	4. 8	1. 5	24.27	2. 6
2.11	26.22	22.18	25.22	31.24	15.11
22.18	18.23	13.22	5.14	4. 8	7.16
13.22	21.17	26.17	22.17	Drawn.	22.18
26.17	23.27	9.13	12.16 E.		10.15
10.15	17.14	18. 9	26.23	B.	18.11
Drawn.	9.18	13.22	16.20	6.13	14.18
	22.15	21.17	24.19 F.	25.22	23. 5
B.	27.31	22.25	15.24	11.15	16.30
15.18	3. 7	17.13	28.19	23.18	11. 7
22.15	1. 6	10.14	7.11	5. 9	Drawn.
13.22	7. 2	9. 6	30.25 G.	18.11	
30.26	6. 9	W. wins.	20.24	8.15	D.
11.18	2. 7		25.22	26.23	6. 9
Drawn.	13.17	F.	11.15	4. 8	17.13
	7.11	7.11	19.16	23.18	

1. 5	F.	19.15	11.15	31. 6	B.
13. 6	32.27	Drawn.	25.22	Drawn.	11.16
2. 9	8.11	H.	4. 8		20. 4
29.25	24.19	23.19	23.18	A.	3. 8
4. 8	15.24	4. 8	8.11	15.18	4.11
27.23	28.19	30.25	28.24	22.15	7.32
14.17	11.15	20.24	12.16	11.18	14.10
21.14	19.16	32.28	24.20	29.25	17.21
9.27	7.11	11.25	16.19	8.11	25.22
32.23	16. 7	25.22	27.23	24.19	5. 9
5. 9	2.11	8.11	19.24	4. 8	10. 6
25.22	30.26	22.18	14. 9	28.24	9.14
9.14	4. 8	15.22	5.14	1. 6	6. 1
30.25	26.22	19.15	18. 9	24.20	W. wins.
14.18	8.12	Drawn.	24.28	6.10	
23.14	27.24	GAME 69.	9. 5	32.28	C.
10.17	Drawn.	9.13	7.10	10.17	6.10
22.13		22.18	23.18	23.14	22.17
W. wins.	G.	10.15	15.19	2. 6 B.	13.22
	19.16	25.22	18.14	27.24	26.17
E.	8.12	6.10	10.17	17.21	11.15
7.11	16. 7	18.14	21.14	25.22	31.26
26.23	2.11	10.17	2. 7	6. 9 C.	8.11
15.18	31.26 H.	21.14	22.18	22.18	26.22
23.19	11.15	15.19 A.	7.10	13.17	3. 8
18.22	32.28	24.15	14. 7	26.22	19.16
19.15	15.18	11.25	3.10	17.26	12.19
11.18	23.19	30.21	18.15	31.22	22.18
24.19	18.22	8.11	11.18	9.13	15.22
6. 9	26.23	29.25	26.23	19.15	24. 6
W. wins.	4. 8		18.27	W. wins.	W. wins.

STURGES' CELEBRATED COLLECTION OF 150 CRITICAL POSITIONS, TO BE WON OR DRAWN BY SCIENTIFIC PLAY.

** Throughout these Critical Situations the White are supposed to have occupied the lower half of the board: their men are, consequently, moving upwards.

No. 1. *White to move and win.**   No. 2. *White to move and win.*

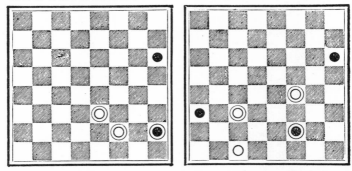

No. 3. *White to move and draw.†*   No. 4. *Either to move, W. win.*

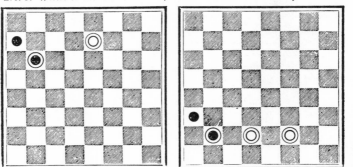

* This situation occurs in a great number of games, and ought to be well understood.

† This situation often occurs when each player has equal men on different parts of the board; Black, however, not being able to extricate those men, it becomes a draw.

No. 5. *White to move and win.* No. 6. *White to move and draw.**

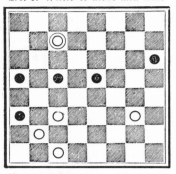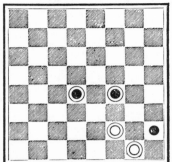

No. 7. *Either to move, B. win.†* No. 8. *White to move and win.*

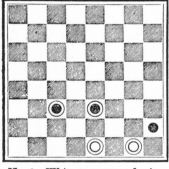

No. 9. *White to move and win.* No. 10. *Black to move and win.*

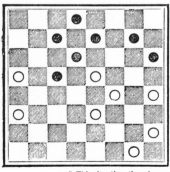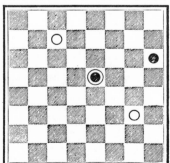

* This situation, though apparently simple, should be noted.
† White loses through being unable to keep the command of square 20.

No. 11. *White to move and win.*   No. 12. *White to move and draw.*

 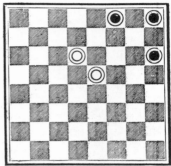

No. 13. *White to move and win.*   No. 14. *White to move and win.*

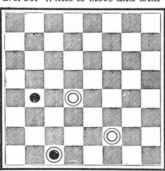 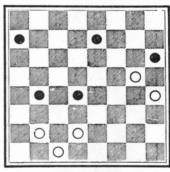

No. 15. *B. to move, W. to win.**   No. 16. *White to move and win.*

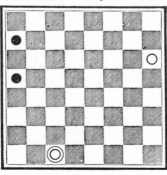 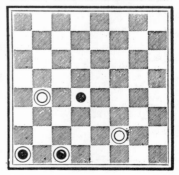

* Similar endings often occur.

No. 17. *B. to move, W. to draw.**   No. 18. *White to move and win.*†

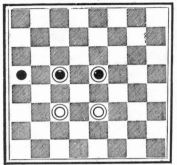

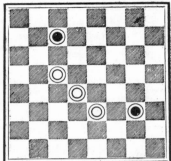

No. 19. *B. to move, W. to win.*‡   No. 20. *White to move and win.*

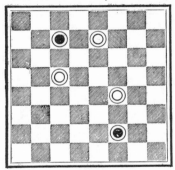

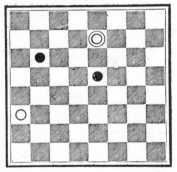

No. 21. *White to move and win.*   No. 22. *White to move and win.*

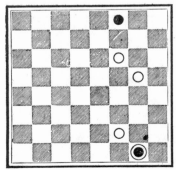

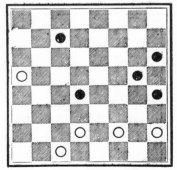

* An instructive position.   ‡ A very neat piece of play.
† White can force the game in a few moves. Three kings win against two, whenever the Black
are in the double corners, as above.

No. 23. *White to move and draw.*   No. 24. *White to move and win.*

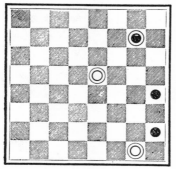

No. 25. *White to move and win.*   No. 26. *Black to move and draw.*

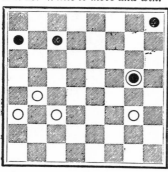
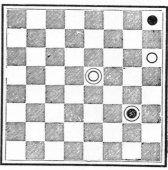

No. 27. *White to move and win.*   No. 28. *White to move and win.*

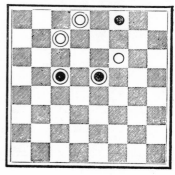

No. 29. *White to move and win.*   No. 30. *White to move and win.*

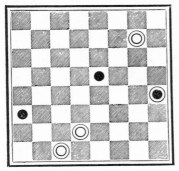
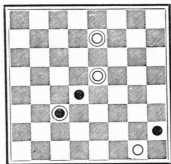

No. 31. *White to move and win.*   No. 32. *White to move and win.*

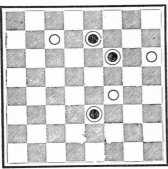
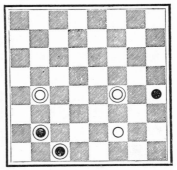

No. 33. *Black to move and win.*   No. 34. *White to move and win.*

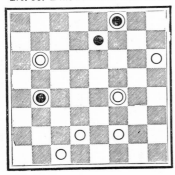
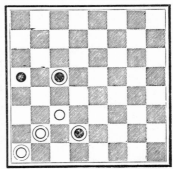

No. 35. *White to move and win.*   No. 36. *B. to move, W. to draw.*

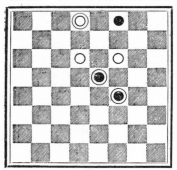   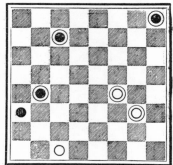

No. 37. *White to move and win.*   No. 38. *White to move and win.*

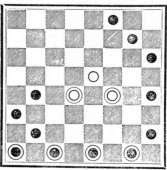   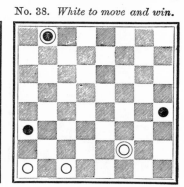

No. 39. *White to move and win.**   No. 40. *B. to move, W. to win.*

* This position, though it could never occur in play, is not the less curious.

No. 41. *B. to move, W. to draw.* No. 42. *White to move, B. wins.**

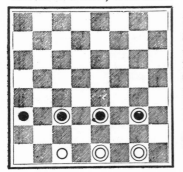 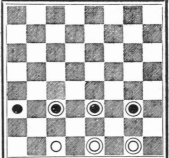

No. 43. *White to move and win.* No. 44. *Black to move and win.*

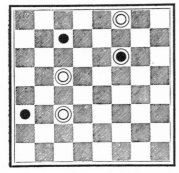 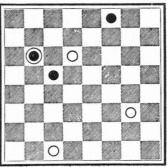

No. 45. *White to move and win.* No. 46. *White to move and win.*

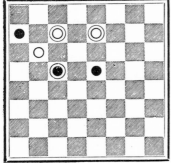 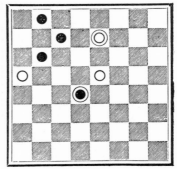

† The same as No. 41, with the difference of the move.

2 H 2

No. 47. *White to move and win.*   No. 48. *White to move and **win.***

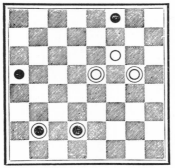

No. 49. *White to move and win.*   No. 50. *Black to move and win.*

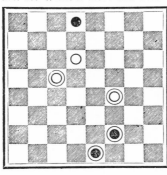
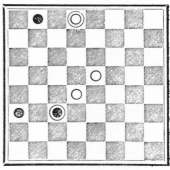

No. 51. *White to move and win.*   No. 52. *White to move and win.*

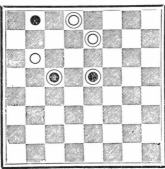
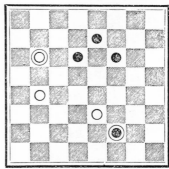

No. 53. *White to move and win.*   No. 54. *White to move and win.*

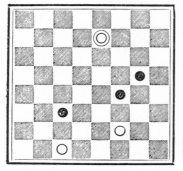 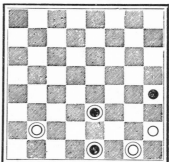

No. 55. *White to move and win.*   No. 56. *White to move and win.*

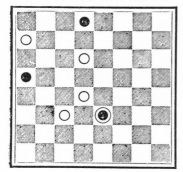 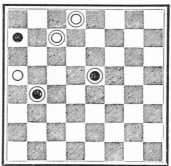

No. 57. *B. to move, W. to win.*   No. 58. *White to move and win.*

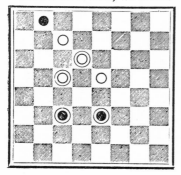 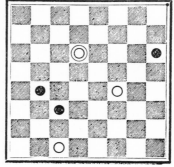

No. 59. *White to move and win.*   No. 60. *White to move and win.*

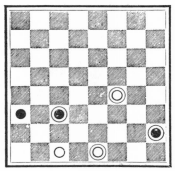

No. 61. *White to move and win.*   No. 62. *White to move, B. wins.*

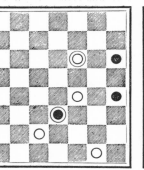

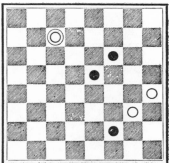

No. 63. *White to move and win.*   No. 64. *White to move and win.*

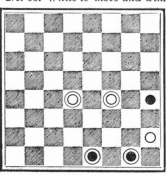

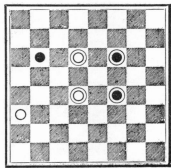

No. 65. *White to move and win.*   No. 66. *White to move and win.*

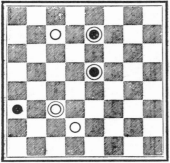   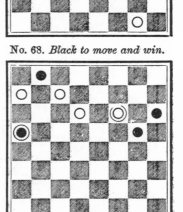

No. 67. *White to move and win.*   No. 68. *Black to move and win.*

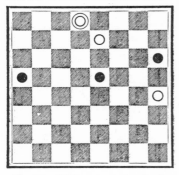

No. 69. *White to move and win.*   No. 70. *White to move and win.*

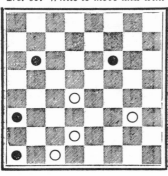   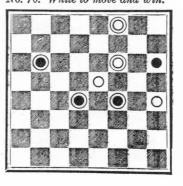

No. 71. *White to move and win.*   No. 72. *White to move and win.*

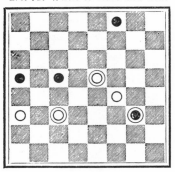

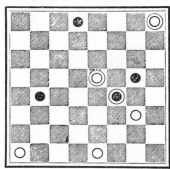

No. 73. *White to move and win.*   No. 74. *White to move and win.*

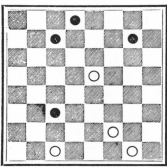

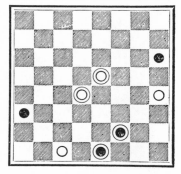

No. 75. *White to move and win.*   No. 76. *White to move and win.*

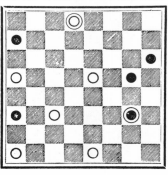

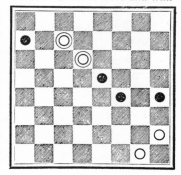

No. 77. *White to move and win.*　　No. 78. *Black to move and win.*

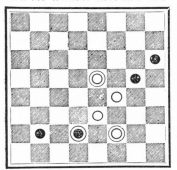　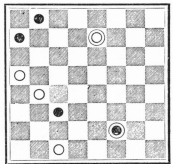

No. 79. *Black to move and draw.*　　No. 80. *White to move and win.*

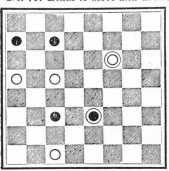　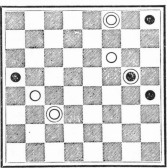

No. 81. *White to move and win.*　　No. 82. *White to move and win.*

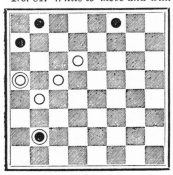　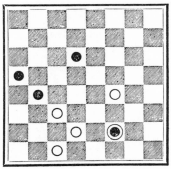

No. 83. *White to move and win.*   No. 84. *White to move and win.*

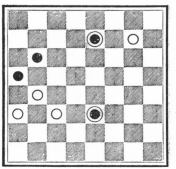 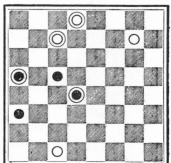

No. 85. *White to move and win.*   No. 86. *White to move and win.*

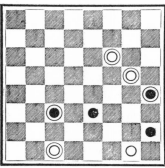 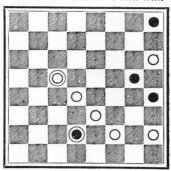

No. 87. *White to move and win.*   No. 88. *White to move and win.*

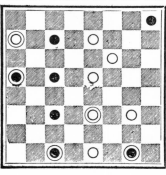 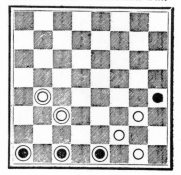

No. 89. *Black to move and win.*

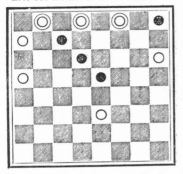

No. 90. *White to move and win.*

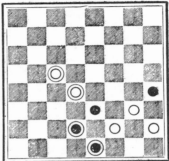

No. 91. *Black to move and win.*

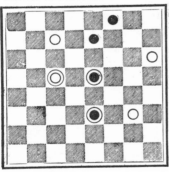

No. 92. *White to move and win.*

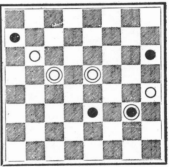

No. 93. *White to move and win.*

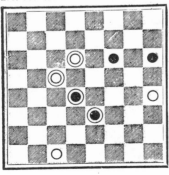

No. 94. *White to move and win.*

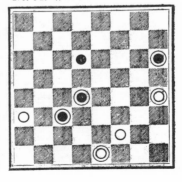

No. 95. *Black to move and win.*   No. 96. *Black to move and win.*

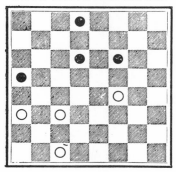 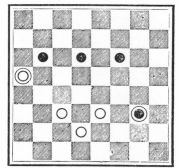

No. 97. *White to move and win.*   No. 98. *Black to move, W. to win.*

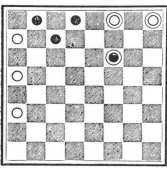 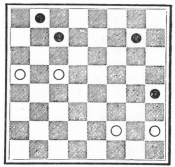

No. 99. *White to move and win.*   No. 100. *Black to move and win.*

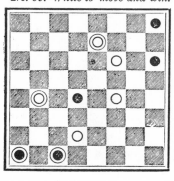 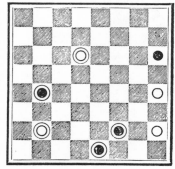

No. 101. *Black to move and win.*   No. 102. *White to move and win.*

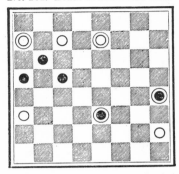   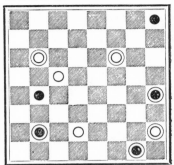

No. 103. *White to move and win.*   No. 104. *White to move and win.*

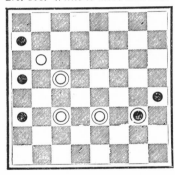   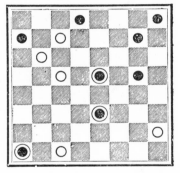

No. 105. *White to move and win.*   No. 106. *Black to move and win.*

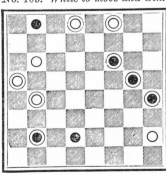   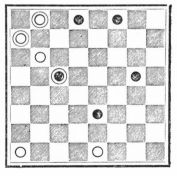

No. 107. *White to move and win.*   No. 108. *White to move and win.*

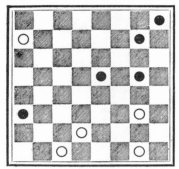

No. 109. *White to move and win.*   No. 110. *White to move and win.*

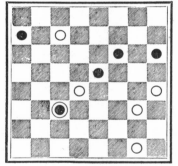
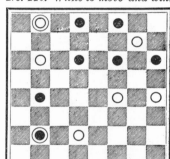

No. 111. *White to move and win.*   No. 112. *White to move and win.*

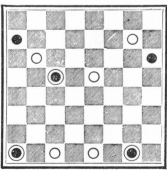
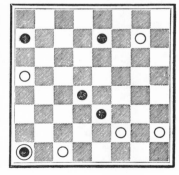

No. 113. *White to move and win.*   No. 114. *White to move and win.*

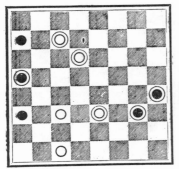
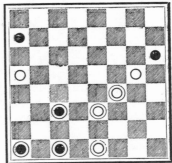

No. 115. *White to move and win.*   No. 116. *White to move and win.*

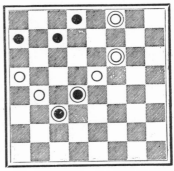

No. 117. *White to move and win.*   No. 118. *White to move and win.*

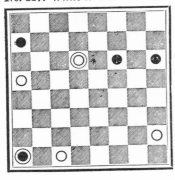
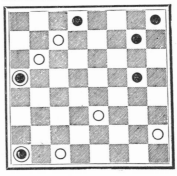

No. 119. *White to move and win.*   No. 120. *Black to move and win.*

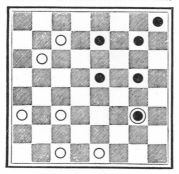 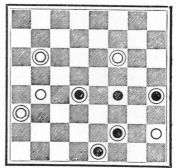

No. 121. *White to move and win.*   No. 122. *White to move and win.*

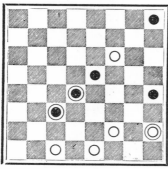 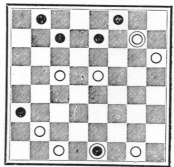

No. 123. *Black to move and win.*   No. 124. *White to move and win.*

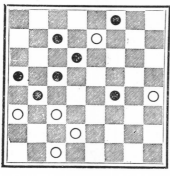 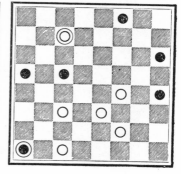

No. 125. *White to move and win.* No. 126. *White to move and win.*

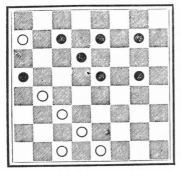 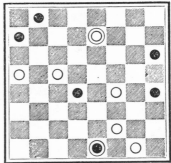

No. 127. *White to move and win.* No. 128. *White to move and win.*

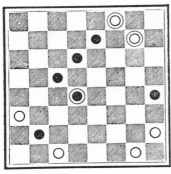 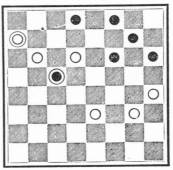

No. 129. *White to move and win.* No. 130. *White to move and win.*

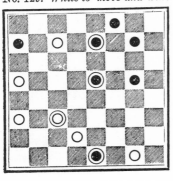 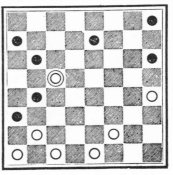

2 I

No. 131. *White to move and win.*   No. 132. *White to move and win.*

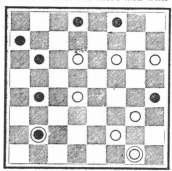

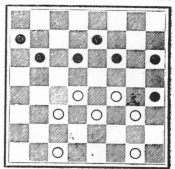

No. 133. *White to move and win.*   No. 134. *Black to move and win.*

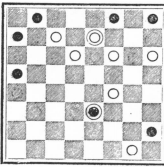

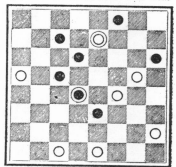

No. 135. *White to move and win.*   No. 136. *White to move and win.*

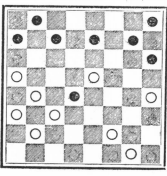

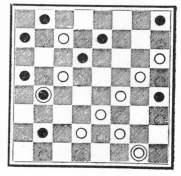

No. 137. *White to move and win.*   No. 138. *White to move and win.*

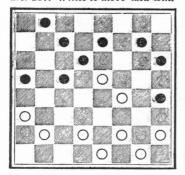

No. 139. *Black to move and win.*   No. 140. *White to move and win.*

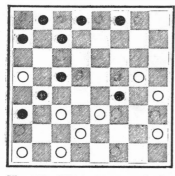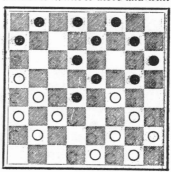

No. 141. *White to move and win.*   No. 142. *White to move and win.*

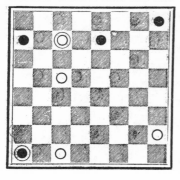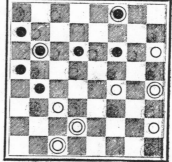

No. 143. *White to move and win.*   No. 144. *White to move and win.*

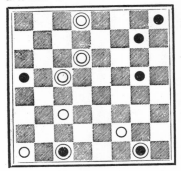
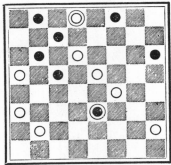

No. 145. *White to move and draw.*   No. 146. *White to move and draw.*

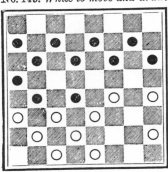
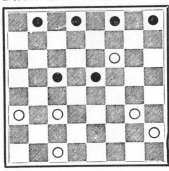

No. 147. *White to move and win.*   No. 148. *White to move and win.*

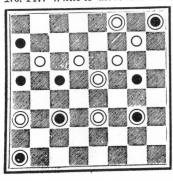
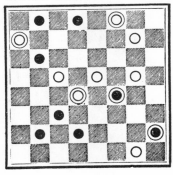

No. 149. *White to move and win.*   No. 150. *White to move and win.*

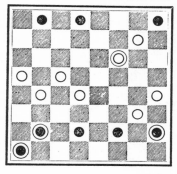 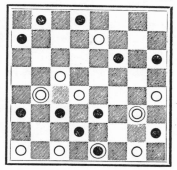

SOLUTIONS OF THE
FOREGOING HUNDRED AND FIFTY POSITIONS.

No. 1.	18.15	22.29	29.25	19.16	7.11
27.32	16.20	30.26	26.30	24.20	15.10
28.24	15.18	29.25		15.11	11.15
23.18	24.19	26.31	No. 5.	20.24	28.24
24.28 A.	32.28	25.22	24.19	16.20	8.11
18.15	19.16	31.27	15.24	24.27	10. 6
28.24	18.23	22.18	30.26	11.15	15.18
32.28	16.11	27.32	21.30	27.31	24.19
24.27	23.19	18.23	6. 9	20.24	
15.18	11. 8	32.28		32.27	No. 10.
12.16	28.32	23.27	No. 6.	15.19	12.16
28.32	8.11	28.32	27.24	27.20	24.20
27.24	32.27	19.23	18.15	28.32	15.10
18.15	11. 8	32.28	24.20		20.11
24.28	27.23	See No. 1.	15.11	No. 8.	10. 1
15.11	8. 3		20.24	32.27	11. 7
16.19	23.18	No. 3.	19.23	28.32	
32.27	3. 8	7.10	24.20	27.24	No. 11.
28.32	18.15	9.13		19.28	26.23
27.31		10.14	No. 7.	26.23	32.28
19.23	No. 2.	13. 9	31.27		27.32
11.15	30.26	14.10	22.18	No. 9.	28.24
32.28	27.23		27.24	13. 9	32.28
15.19	19.15	No. 4.	18.15	6.13	24.20
	23.30	27.23	24.27	15. 6	23.19
A.	15.19	25.29	23.19	2. 9	20.24
12.16	21.25	23.18	27.24	19.15	19.15

24. 27	21. 17	1. 5	No. 24.	11. 4	22. 17
15. 18	27. 32	9. 6	18. 15	6. 2	9. 6
3. 8	17. 14	28. 32	9. 14		17. 14
18. 15	32. 27	19. 24	26. 22	No. 32.	6. 1
8. 12	15. 11	5. 1	14. 18	19. 23	14. 9
28. 32		24. 19	15. 11	25. 29	1. 5
27. 24	No. 15.			17. 21	9. 6
15. 11	13. 17	No. 19.	No. 25.		5. 1
24. 28	30. 26	6. 10	24. 19	No. 33.	6. 2
32. 27	5. 9	19. 23	16. 23	3. 8	1. 5
28. 32	12. 8	No. 20.	22. 18	12. 3	2. 6
27. 24	9. 13	7. 10		17. 13	5. 1
32. 28	26. 30	15. 19	No. 26.		6. 9
24. 19	17. 22	21. 17	24. 27	No. 34.	1. 5
28. 32	8. 4	9. 14	15. 11	25. 21	9. 14
11. 15	13. 17	10. 15	27. 23	26. 17	5. 1
32. 28	4. 8		11. 15	29. 25	14. 18
15. 18	17. 21	No. 21.	23. 27		1. 5
28. 32	8. 11	27. 23	15. 19	No. 35.	18. 22
18. 23	22. 25	32. 27	27. 32	10. 7	5. 9
32. 28	11. 15	23. 18		15. 8	30. 26
23. 27	25. 29	27. 23	No. 27.	2. 6	9. 14
28. 32	15. 18	18. 15	22. 18		26. 23
19. 23	29. 25	23. 19	15. 22	No. 36.	14. 9
32. 28	30. 26	15. 10	17. 26	4. 8	23. 18
See No. 1.		19. 12	28. 32	19. 23	9. 5
	No. 16.	10. 6	27. 24	8. 11	18. 14
No. 12.	17. 22	12. 16	19. 28	24. 28	5. 1
15. 11	18. 25		26. 23	11. 16	14. 9
3. 8	27. 23	No. 22.		23. 27	1. 5
10. 15		26. 23	No. 28.	6. 10	22. 17
8. 3	No. 17.	18. 22	11. 7	28. 32	5. 14
15. 19	14. 17	23. 18	3. 10	16. 20	17. 10
12. 8	23. 26	16. 19	2. 7	32. 28	
	15. 10	18. 15			No. 39.
No. 13.	22. 25	22. 26	No. 29.	No. 37.	18. 22
18. 22	17. 21	30. 16	30. 25	10. 6	17. 26
17. 26	25. 22	12. 19	21. 30	1. 10	19. 24
27. 31	10. 14	13. 9	8. 11	23. 19	20. 27
	26. 30	6. 13		8. 11	
No. 14.	14. 17	15. 11	No. 30.	31. 27	No. 40
26. 22	22. 18	13. 17	32. 27	5. 9	28. 24
12. 19			28. 32	27. 23	20. 16
22. 15	No. 18.	No. 23.	7. 10		24. 8
19. 23	18. 15	15. 19	32. 23	No. 38.	17. 14
20. 16	6. 1	8. 11	10. 14	29. 25	
23. 27	14. 9	19. 23		1. 6	No. 41.
25. 21	24. 28	11. 15	No. 31.	25. 22	24. 28
17. 22	23. 19	23. 27	12. 8	6. 9	31. 27

23.19	15.19	5. 1	No. 54.	No. 62.	19.23
27.31	20.16	15.10	28.24	6.10	
19.24	18.23	1. 5	20.27	27.32	No. 68.
32.27	26.22	10. 6	25.22	10.19	13. 9
24.20	23.26			32.28	11.20
27.32	16.11	No. 45.	No. 55.		9. 2
22.18	26.30	7.10	10. 6	No. 63.	20.24
31.27	11. 7	14. 7	23.14	19.24	12.16
	30.26	6. 2	5. 1	20.27	24.28
No. 42.			2. 9	18.22	16.19
32.28	A.	No. 46.	1. 5		28.32
24.20	24.19	15.10		No. 64.	19.24
28.32	18.23		No. 56.	21.17	
22.18	19.16	No. 47.	13. 9	9.13	No. 69.
31.27	9.14	11. 7	5.14	10.15	18.14
23.19	10. 6		6.10	19.10	9.18
27.31	23.27	No. 48.		18.14	26.22
19.24	6. 1	11. 8	No. 57.	13.22	18.25
32.27	14.10		22.18	14.16	24.19
24.28	30.25	No. 49.	14.17		
27.32	27.31	10. 7	18.11	No. 65.	No. 70.
18.22	25.21	2.11	10.14	22.25	20.16
31.27	31.26	19.15		21.30	19.10
22.26	16.12 B.		No. 58.	6. 2	11. 7
30.23	10.14	No. 50.	10.15		
28.24	1. 5	21.25	17.21	No. 66.	No. 71.
	26.23	2. 7	19.16	22.18	21.17
No. 43.	5. 1	25.30	12.19	13.17	14.21
22.17	23.19	7.11	15.24	10. 6	15.18
21.25	1. 6	30.26	22.25	2. 9	
17.13	19.15	18.14	24.19	18.14	No. 72.
25.30	6. 2	26.23			24.20
14. 9	15.11	14.10	No. 59.	No. 67.	19.10
6.10	2. 6	22.18	30.26	2. 6	20.11
3. 7	3. 7		22.18	15.18	10. 7
11. 2	6.10	No. 51.	19.24	6.10	29.25
9. 6	14.18	9. 6	28.19	18.22	7.16
	10. 3	1.10	26.23	10.14	31.26
No. 44.	18.14	2. 6		22.25	17.21
14.18			No. 60.	7. 2	4. 8
30.26 A.	B.	No. 52.	32.27	25.29	No. 73.
9.14	21.17	17.14	23.32	2. 7	15.11
10. 6	26.23	10.17	26.23	29.25	8.15
3. 8	17.13	9.13		7.10	30.26
24.20	10.14		No. 61.	25.21	22.31
8.11	1. 5	No. 53.	11.15	10.15	32.28
6. 1	23.19	30.26	23.30	13.17	
11.15	16.12	22.31	32.27	15.19	No. 74.
1. 6	19.15	7.11		17.22	30.26

31.22	No. 82.	20.27	No. 96.	26.22	14.18
18.25	26.23	17.21	11.15	14.10	16.19
21.30	17.26	30.26	13. 6	5. 9	6.10
20.16	19.16	21.17	15. 19	10. 7	5. 9
			6.15	9.14	10. 6
No. 75.	No. 83.	No. 89.	24.20	7.11	9.13
29.25	22.18	6. 9		14.17	6.10
21.30	13.22	13. 6	No. 97.	11. 8	11. 8
31.26	8. 3	15.18	3. 7		10.15
30.23			11.16	B.	
22.18	No. 84.	No. 90.	13. 9	8.12	C.
23.14	6. 9	14. 9	6.13	14. 9	11.15
15.10	13. 6	23.32	4. 8	6.10	14.10
	2. 9	9.13		9. 6	15.11
No. 76.	14.17	20.27	No. 98.	10.14	6. 9
28.24	9.13	18.22	8.11 B	6. 2	5.14
19.28	17.22		14. 9	14.18	10.17
10.19	13.17	No. 91.	6.10	2. 7	12.16
20.24	22.25	3. 8	9. 6	18.22	17.22
19.15	17.22	12. 3	10.14	13. 9	16.19
		15.18	6. 2	22.26	22.18
No. 77.	No. 85.		14.17	7.10	11. 7
27.24	16.19	No. 92.	2. 7	1. 5	18.15
16.20	22.26	20.16	11.16	10.14	19.23
23.18	11.16	12.19	7.10	26.30	
	20.11	14.18	17.22	9. 6	No. 99.
No. 78.	32.27		13. 9	30.26	26.22
5. 9		No. 93.	22.26	6. 2	18.25
13. 6	No. 86.	30.26	9. 6	26.31	19.16
1.10	12. 8	18. 9	26.30 A.	2. 7	12.19
7.14	26.19	26.19	6. 2	31.24	
22.26	14.10	11.15	30.26	28.19	No. 100.
	4.11	10. 6	2. 7	20.24	31.26
No. 79.	18.14		26.22	7.11	25.22
23.18		No. 94.	10.15	24.28	26.23
11. 7	No. 87.	19.16	1. 6	11.16	22.13
18. 9	23.26	12.19	7.11	28.32	12.16
7. 2	30.23	21.17		16.20	
	24.19	22.13	A.	32.27	No. 101.
	23.16	27.23	1. 5	19.15	14.18
No. 80.	31.27		10.14	27.23	5.14
22.18	32.23	No. 95.	26.30	15.10	23.19
13.22	15.10	11.15	6. 2	23.19	
	6.15	19.16	30.26	10. 6	No. 102.
No. 81.	5. 9	10.14	2. 6	19.15	28.24
10. 6	13. 6	16.11	26.22	6. 2	20.27
1.10	7. 3	14.18	6.10	15.11	26.23
14. 7		30.25	22.26	2. 6	27.18
3.10	No. 88.	18.23	10.15	12.16 C.	9. 5
17.14	27.23				

No. 103.	28.10	No. 113.	14.17	31.24	24.19
23.19	5. 9	30.25	22.25	15.11	23.16
24.15	6. 2	21.30		7.16	9. 6
14.17	9.13	23.26	No. 117.	30.26	
	10. 7	30.23	28.24	21.30	No. 129.
No. 104.	11.15	22.17	12.16	8.11	32.27
30.25	2. 6	13.22	24.19		31.24
29.22	15.18	6. 9	16.23	No. 123.	13. 9
14.10	6.10		20.25	19.23	5.14
5.14	18.22	No. 114.	29.22	26.19	21.17
6. 1	10.14	13. 9	13. 9	17.26	14.21
	22.25	5.14		30.23	22.25
No. 105.	7. 2	23.26	No. 118.	14.18	21.30
17.22	25.29	30.23	30.25		6. 2
25.18	2. 7	19.10	29.22	No. 124.	
28.24	29.25	12.19	23.18	6.10	No. 130.
20.27	7.10	31.27	22.15	14.17	14.10
2. 6	25.21		6. 1	10.15	7.14
1.10	10.15	No. 115.		17.26	20.16
3. 7	13.17	30.25	No. 119.	27.24	12.19
11. 2	15.19	29.22	22.18	20.27	27.23
9. 6	17.22	14. 9	15.22	19.16	
	19.23	5.14	31.26		No.131.
No. 106.		10.19	22.31	No. 125.	11. 7
23.27	No. 110.	3.10	30.26	17.14	3.11
31.24	26.22	19.23	31.22	10.17	27.23
16.19	25.18	10.14	21.17	22.18	20.27
23.15	9. 6	4. 8	22.13	15.22	18.15
14.10	2. 9	14.17	6. 1	31.27	
	19.16	8.11		22.31	No.132.
No. 107.	12.19	17.21	No. 120.	5. 1	22.17
24.19	1. 5	11.15	20.16		20.27
15.24		21.25	11.20	No. 126.	18.15
30.25	No. 111.	15.18	19.24	19.16	
21.30	30.25		28.19	12.19	No.133.
32.28	29.22	No. 116.	18.14	14.10	12. 8
	31.27	17.14	17.10	31.24	3.12
No. 108.	32.23	18. 9	27.24	10. 6	6. 2
23.19	15.10	15.10			23.16
16.23	14. 7	6.15	No. 121.	No. 127.	10. 6
22.18	8. 3	13. 6	27.23	21.17	1.10
13.22		2. 9	18.27	14.21	7.14
14. 9	No. 112.	11.25	31.24	28.24	16. 7
	13. 9	9.13	20.27		2.11
No. 109.	23.32	25.22	30.26	No.128.	5. 9
24.19	30.25	5. 9	22.31	10. 7	14. 5
15.24	29.22	3. 7		3.10	13.17
32.28	8. 3	9.14	No. 122.	23.18	5. 9
22.15		7.10	32.27	14.23	17.22

9.14	7.16	2. 9	No.144.	No.146.	21.14
22.26	12. 8	13. 6	25.22	24.19	29.25
14.18	4.11	1.10	23.16	15.24	14.18
26.31	19.12	27. 9	15.11	28.1)	
18.22	26.19		6.15	1. 6	No.148.
4. 8	32.30	No.141.	13. 6	30.26	15.10
11. 4		28.24	1.10	6.10	19.12
12.16	No.137.	7.11	28.24	26.23	3. 7
4. 8	19.16	24.19		3. 8	2.11
16.19	12.19	4. 8	No.145.	19.16	32.27
8.11	28.24	6. 2	22.15	8.15	12. 3
19.23	19.28	8.12	11.27	16.11	27.24
22.25	25.22	2. 7	31.24	2. 6	
31.26	10.19	11.16	10.14	22.17	No.149.
25.30	22.17	7.10	25.22	6. 9	14. 9
		16.23	7.11	17.13	28.19
No.134.	No.138.	30.25	30.25	15.18	18.15
6. 9	22.18	29.22	14.18	13. 6	19.10
13. 6	15.22	14. 9	22.15	18.27	17.14
23.27	13. 9		11.18	6. 2	10.17
31.24	6.13	No.142.	21.14	10.15	9. 6
10.15	27.24	12. 8	13.17	2. 6	1.10
		3.12	14.10	15.19	11.16
No.135.	No.139.	19.16	6.15	6.10	
13. 9	14.18	12.19	19.10		No.150.
6.13	22.15	28.24	9.18	No.147.	18.15
15.10	17.22	19.28	25.21	23.18	11.18
7.14	26.17	26.23	18.22	14.23	24.19
17.10	19.26	17.26	21.14	3. 7	2.11
	30.23	20.24	22.31	5.14	20.16
No.136.	6. 9		10. 6	15.19	11.20
26.22		No.143.	13.17	24. 6	29.25
17.26	No.140.	29.25	6. 2	7.10	22.29
32.28	13. 9	32.23	31.27	6.15	17.22
10.17	16.23	2. 7	2. 6	8. 3	18.25
28.32	17.13	30.21	8.11	15. 8	19.24
1.10	5.14	22.17	6.10	3.10	20.27
27.24	24.19	13.22	11.16	4. 8	14.10
20.27	15.24	14.17		10.15	
16.11	22. 6			13.17	

A SERIES OF ORIGINAL GAMES, BY MR. R. MARTIN.

GAME 1.	23. 16	23. 19	26. 22	**G.**	26. 17
11. 15	12. 19	16. 23	7. 10	10. 15	13. 22
22. 18	2. 7	26. 19	9. 6	19. 10	9. 6
15. 22	19. 23	W. wins.	10. 15	7. 14	10. 14
25. 18	7. 11		6. 2	18. 9	6. 2
8. 11	23. 27	**C.**	W. wins.	17. 22 H	14. 18 K
29. 25	11. 15	2. 7		26. 17	23. 14
4. 8	27. 32	24. 19	**E.**	13. 22	16. 23
24. 20	17. 13	15. 24	14. 17	27. 24	24. 19
10. 15	W. wins.	28. 19	13. 9	3. 7	3. 7
25. 22		10. 15 E	6. 13	24. 19	19. 15
12. 16	**A.**	19. 10	22. 18	7. 10	11. 18
21. 17	32. 28	6. 15	10. 14 G	9. 6	2. 11
8. 12	18. 14	22. 18	18. 9	11. 15	W. wins.
17. 13	3. 7	15. 22	7. 10	20. 11	
7. 10	13. 9	26. 10	27. 24	15. 24	**K.**
27. 24	6. 13	7. 14	10. 14 I	6. 2	14. 17 L
9. 14	27. 23	13. 9	9. 5	10. 14	31. 27
18. 9	17. 21	14. 17 D	17. 21 F	2. 7	17. 26
5. 14	23. 19	23. 18	26. 22	14. 17	19. 15
32. 27	16. 23	16. 19	14. 17	7. 10	11. 18
*14. 17 C	26. 19	9. 6	31. 26	17. 21	23. 14
23. 18	10. 26	1. 10	3. 7	10. 14	16. 19
17. 21 A	19. 3	18. 15	22. 18	21. 25	24. 15
27. 23	11. 15	11. 18	17. 22	14. 18	26. 31
6. 9 B	31. 22	27. 23	26. 17	25. 29	27. 24
13. 6	5. 9	19. 26	13. 22	18. 22	31. 27
2. 9	3. 8	31. 6	19. 15	12. 16	15. 11
24. 19	9. 14	3. 8	16. 19	11. 7	17. 22
15. 24	24. 19	6. 2	15. 8	16. 20	14. 10
28. 19	15. 24	8. 11	19. 28	7. 2	27. 23
1. 5	28. 19	2. 6	8. 3	24. 27	11. 8
22. 17	14. 17	11. 15	7. 10	31. 24	23. 27
9. 13	22. 18	6. 10	3. 7	20. 27	8. 4
18. 14	17. 22	15. 19	W. wins.	23. 18	12. 16
13. 22	18. 14	10. 14		W. wins.	20. 11
26. 17	22. 25	17. 21	**F.**		27. 20
11. 15	8. 11	14. 18	3. 7	**H.**	2. 7
14. 7	25. 29	W. wins.†	26. 22	3. 7	20. 16
15. 24	11. 15		17. 26	27. 24	11. 8
20. 11	29. 25	**D.**	31. 22	17. 21	3. 12
3. 10	15. 18	3. 7	14. 17	26. 22	10. 6
11. 7	W. wins.	27. 24	22. 18	W. wins.	1. 10
10. 15		14. 17	17. 22		7. 14
7. 2	**B.**	31. 26	19. 15	**I.**	W. wins.
15. 19	2. 7	17. 21	W. wins.	17. 22	

* This move loses the game.   † See Sturges' 38th critical situation

L.				27.32	11.15
3. 7	19.15	19.23	19.24	B. wins.	20.16
23.18	24.19	27.24	B. wins.		12.19
16.23 N	15.10	10.15		F.	3.12
18. 9	19.15	18.14	D.	23.19	19.24
23.27 M	10. 6	23.27	27.24	30.23	13. 9
24.19	15. 8	31.26	10.15	19.10	1. 5
27.32	30.26	27.32	19.10	23.18	12.16
19.15	1.10	26.23	6.15	6. 2	Draw.
11.18	7.23	15.18	22.18 G	16.19	
2.11	Draw.	23.19	15.22	24.15	I.
32.28		32.28	13. 9	14.17	1. 5
11. 7	**GAME** 2.	B. wins.	3. 8	21.14	24.19
18.23	11.15		24.19 E	18. 9	15.24
9. 6	22.18	A.	7.10	B. wins.	28.19
1.10	15.22	31.22	9. 6		3. 7
W. wins.	25.18	16.19	10.14	G.	22.18
	8.11	18.14 B	6. 2	23.19	14.17
M.	29.25	6.10	22.25	16.23	26.22 S
7.10	4. 8	13. 9	30.21	26.10	17.26
24.19	24.20	10.15	14.18	7.14	31.22
11.15	10.15	30.25	23.14	24.19	10.14 R
2. 6	25.22	19.24	16.30	17.26	18. 9
15.24	12.16	27.23	B. wins.	30.23	5.14
6.15	21.17	24.27		14.17	22.18 K
W. wins.	8.12	25.21	E.	23.18	6.10
	17.13	27.31	23.18	1. 6 H	18. 9
N.	7.10	23.18	7.10	19.15	11.15
14.23	27.24	31.26	18.14	3. 8	20.11
19.15	9.14	9. 5	10.15	31.26	15.31
11.18	18. 9	B. wins.	26.23	17.21	11. 8
2.11	5.14		17.21	26.22	31.27
23.27	32.27	B.	9. 5 T	21.25	8. 3
11. 7	2. 7 I	27.23 C	22.25	18.14	27.18
27.32	24.19	19.26	14. 9	W. wins.	9. 6
20.11	15.24	30.23	25.29		2. 9
32.28	28.19	6.10	31.26	H.	13. 6
24.20 O	14.17	13. 9	21.25	17.22	7.11
18.23	19.15 D	10.15	30.21	19.15	B. wins.
7.10	10.19	B. wins.	29.25	3. 8	
23.27	22.18		9. 6	15.10	K.
31.24	17.22	C.	1.10	22.25	27.24
28.19	26.17	30.25	5. 1	10. 7	7.10 Q
10.14	19.26	11.16	10.14	25.30	22.18
19.23	30.23 A	20. 2	1. 6	7. 3	6. 9
Draw.	16.19	1. 5	25.30	30.25	13. 6
	23.16	2. 9	6.10 F	18.14	2. 9
O.	12.19	5.30	15.18	25.22	30.25
24.19	17.14	22.17	10.17	14.10	14.17
28.24	6.10	30.26	18.27	22.18	25.21
	14. 9	27.23	26.23	10. 7	

17.22	21.17	15.24	R.	22.17	22.17
21.17	11.15	16.20	5. 9	9.13	14.18
9.13	17.21	24.28	22.17	17.22	26.23
17.14	19.16	5. 9	9.14	Draw.	4. 8
10.17	W. wins.	W. wins.	18. 9		23.14
19.15	L.	O.	11.15	U.	9.18
22.26	17.14	9.14	20.11	1. 5	27.23
15. 8	10.17	23.18	15.31	9. 6	18.27
26.31	22.13	14.23	23.18	5. 9	32.23
20.11	24.20	16.20	7.16	6. 2	10.14 E
31.26 P	13. 9	W. wins.	Draw.	9.14	17.10
24.19	11.15			2. 6	7.14
17.21	9.14	P.	S.	22.25	19.10
18.14	15.18	31.27	27.24	6. 9	6.15
21.25	14.10	24.20	5. 9	14.18	24.19
14. 9	19.15	17.22	26.22	23.14	15.24
25.30	W. wins.	7.11	17.26	16.19	28.19
9. 6		22.25	31.22	10. 7	11.16
30.25	M.	23.19	10.14	19.28	31.26 D
6. 1	17.14	W. wins.	19.15	7. 3	16.20
25.22	10.17		16.19	28.32	26.22
8. 3	22.13	Q.	15. 8	14.10	20.24
13.17	15.18	14.17	19.28	15.19	22.17
1. 6	13. 9	22.18	8. 3	9.14	24.27
17.21	11.16	17.22	7.10	32.28	17.10
6.10	9.13 N	19.15	3. 8	10. 6	27.31
21.25	18.14	16.19	28.32	19.23	30.25
11. 7	26.22	15.11	8.11	6. 2	8.11
25.30	14.17	19.28	32.27	11.15	23.18
7. 2	22.26	18.14	11. 8	20.16	31.27
30.25	17.21	28.32	14.17	12.19	10. 7 B
2. 7	26.22	8. 3	8.11	3.12	3.10
25.21	16.20	6.10	17.26	19.24	21.17
7.11	13. 9	23.18	18.15	14.10	27.24
21.25	19.15	10.17	10.19	15.18	18.14
11.15	9.14	3.10	23.16	10.15	24.15
25.21	15.11	32.27	12.19	18.22	14. 7
3. 8	14.10	13. 9	30.16	15.19	11.16
21.17	11. 8	27.23	Draw.	Draw.	25.21
8.11	W. wins.	18.15			16.19
17.21 M	N.	23.18	T.	GAME 3.	7. 2
11.16	26.31	10.14	14.10	11.15	1. 6
21.17	18.22	18.11	22.25 U	23.19	2. 9
16.20	31.27 O	14.21	9. 6	9.14	5.14
17.21	22.17	22.25	25.29	22.17	17.10
15.11	27.18	21.17	6. 2	6. 9	15. 6
21.17	17.14	25.29	29.25	17.13	29.25
20.24	18.15	9. 5	2. 6	2. 6	19.23
17.21 L	14. 9	12.16	25.22	25.22	25.22
24.28		Draw.	6. 9	8.11	23.26

22.18	21.17	28.19	14. 7	19.10	26.22
26.30	11.15	11.15 F	3.10	7.30	23.26
18.15	17.14	25.22	24.20	6. 2	22.18 N.
30.26	15.18	15.24	15.24	12.16	8.11
15.11 A	14. 9	22.18	20.11	24.20	15. 8
26.22	6. 1	6. 9	W. wins.	16.19	26.30
11. 7	29.25	13. 6	**H.**	17.14	24.15
6.10	Draw.	1. 5	18.23	30.25	30.23
7. 2	**C.**	18. 9	26.22	14.10	15.11
10.14	11.15	5.14	23.26	25.22	9.14
B. wins.	25.21	6. 1	14. 9	2. 7	11. 7
	16.11	25.22	5.14	19.23	10.15
A.	7. 2	1. 6	19.15	7.16	7. 2
21.17	15.18	22.18	10.28	23.32	6.10
26.23	13. 9	17.13	17. 1	16.19	2. 6
17.14	5.14	7.11	8.11	Draw.	14.17
6. 1	17.10	13. 9	1. 6		8. 3
13. 9	18.22	12.16	11.15	**L.**	10.14
23.18	10. 7	9. 5	13. 9	11.16	3. 7
15.11	Draw.	24.28	15.19	19.15	15.19
18.15	**D.**	5. 1	9. 5	10.19	B. wins.
11. 8	29.25	28.32	19.24	24.15	
15.11	14.18	1. 5	5. 1	16.19	**N.**
8. 4	23.14	32.28	24.27	17.14	25.21
11. 7	16.23	5. 9	6. 2	7.10	9.14
4. 8	14.10	W. wins.	7.11	14. 7	22.18
7. 2	12.16		1. 6	3.10	14.23
8.11	21.17	**F.**	Draw.	21.17	17.14
1. 5	16.20	14.18		5. 9	Draw.
11.15	17.14	23.14	**I.**	27.24	
12.16	23.27	1. 5	1. 5	9.14 M.	**GAME 4.**
B. wins.	31.24	31.27	31.26 K.	25.21	11.15
	20.27	11.15	12.16	18.23	23.19
B.	25.21	27.24	19.12	26.22	9.14
21.17	8.12	15.18	15.19	23.26	22.17
27.23	21.17	30.26	24.15	22.18	6. 9
18.14	27.31	8.11 H	11.27	14.23	17.13
23.16	10. 7	26.22	B. wins.	17.14	2. 6
10. 7	3.10	18.23 G		10.17	25.22
3.10	14. 7	14. 9	**K.**	21.14	8.11
14. 7	5. 9	5.14	30.26	26.30	29.25
16.19 C	Draw.	22.18	15.18	24.20	4. 8
25.21		W. wins.	23.14	30.26	24.20
19.15	**E.**		9.18	14. 9	15.24
7. 2	5. 9	**G.**	31.27	6.10	28.19
1. 6	29.25	11.15	6. 9 L.	15. 6	11.15
2. 9	9.14 I	20.16	13. 6	Draw.	27.24
5.14	24.20	18.23	18.22		14.17
17.10	15.24	16.11	25.18	**M.**	21.14
15. 6		7.16	10.15	18.23	9.18

26.23	11. 7	5.14	27.31	14.18 I.	10. 7
18.27	14. 9	26.19	20.16	23.14	32.27
32.23	7. 2	14.18	31.27	16.19	7. 2
10.14	26.30	15.10 F.	10. 6	21.17	11.15
19.10	21.17	18.23	3.10	19.28	16.11
6.15	9.13	30.25 E.	15. 6	10. 7	27.20
13. 9	17.14	23.26	27.24	3.10	Draw.
7.11	30.26	25.22	16.11	14. 7	
23.19 G.	B. wins.	26.31	24.15	15.19	M.
15.18		22.18	11. 4	22.18	24.19
22.15	A.	31.26	12.16	28.32	15.24
11.18	25.21	18.15	6. 2	7. 3	10. 7
31.26 B.	18.22	26.22	15.18	32.27	24.27
18.23	21.17	20.16 D.	2. 6	17.14	7. 3
19.15	16.19	22.18	18.14	W. wins.	8.12
23.27	15.10	24.20 C.	B. wins.		22.17
24.19	19.15	18.11		I.	11.15
27.31	17.13	16. 7	F.	3. 8	17.10
26.22	15. 6	8.11	20.16	10. 7 K.	27.31
14.17	9. 2	B. wins.	3. 7	16.19	20.11
22.13	12.16		30.25	23.16	31.26
5.14	2. 7	C.	7.10	8.12	Draw.
20.16	3.10	16.11	15. 6	24.19	
31.27	4. 8	1. 5	1.10	15.24	N.
16.11	16.19	11. 4	24.20	22.17	14.18
27.23	8.11	18.11	10.14	12.19	22.15
11. 4	19.23	B. wins.	B. wins.	17.10	11.18
23.16	11. 7			11.15	25.22
13. 9	10.14	D.	G.	Draw.	18.25
14.18	7.10	10. 6	31.27 H.		30.21
30.26 A.	14.18	1.10	12.16	K.	8.11
18.23	10.14	15. 6	25.21	22.17 M.	21.17
26.19	22.26	8.11	14.18	8.12	11.15
16.23	14.10	6. 1	23.14	10.7	17.14
15.10	26.31	22.17	16.19	1. 5 L.	15.18
23.18	10.15	1. 6	27.23	17.10	14. 9
10. 6	18.22	17.14	19.28	16.19	18.23
12.16	15.18	6. 1	B. wins.	23.16	9. 6
6. 2	22.25	14. 9		12.28	23.27
16.19	30.21	1. 5	H.	7. 3	6. 2
2. 7	1. 5	9. 6	23.18	15.19	27.32
19.23	18.27	5. 1	14.23	3. 8	24.19
25.21	31.24	6. 2	31.26	W. wins.	32.27
18.22	B. wins.	1. 5	5.14		19.15
7.11		3. 7	26.10	L.	27.23
23.26	B.	B. wins.	11.15 N.	15.18	15.11
11.16	19.15		30.26	17.10	23.19
22.18	18.22	E.	8.11 O	18.27	11. 8
16.11	25.18	19.15	26.23	7. 3	12.16
18.14	31.26	23.27	12.16	27.32	Draw.
		24.19	25.21		

O.	A.				H.
14.18	3. 7	28.32	23.19	10.15	7.10
10. 6	22.17	9. 6	14.17	Draw.	14. 7
1.10	12.16	1.10	5. 9		3.10
24.19	24.19	14. 7	15.11	E.	30.26
Draw.	15.24	32.27	9.13	31.26	5.14
	14.10	10. 3	17.22	7.10 F.	26.23
GAME 5.	7.21	27.23	19.23	23.18	1. 6
11.15	25.22	17.13	10.14	14.23	23.19
23.19	5.14	15.19	23.19	26.19	8.11
9.14	22.18	3. 8	22.26	3. 7	25.21
22.17	14.23	11.15	19.16	30.26	6. 9
6. 9	26. 3	8.11	11.15	15.18	31.27
17.13	11.15	23.18	16.19	22.15	14.18
2. 6	3. 7	22.17	15.10	7.11	22.17
25.22	24.28	19.24	24.27	13. 9	18.22
8.11	B. wins.	17.14	14.18	B. wins.	17.13
29.25		18. 9	27.31		9.14
4. 8	B.	13. 6	26.30	F.	13. 9
24.20	30.26	15.18	31.27	14.17	22.26
15.24	3. 7	11.15	Draw.	30.25	9. 6
28.19	31.27	18.22		17.21 G.	26.31
11.15	12.16	15.18	D.	23.19	6. 2
27.24	26.23 C.	22.26	14.17	21.30	31.26
14.17	8.12	21.17	22.13	19. 1	27.23*
21.14	14.10	26.31	5.14	30.23	26.22
9.18	7.14	6. 2	25.22	24.19	2. 7
26.23	25.21	31.27	1. 6	W. wins.	11 16 I.
18.27	14.18	2. 6	23.19 E.		20.11
32.23	23.14	24.28	7.10	G.	22.18
10.14	16.19	6.10	30.25	7.11	24.20
19.10	21.17	28.32	14.17	25.21	18.27
6.15	19.28	10.15	25.21	3. 7	7. 2
13. 9	9. 6	27.24	17.26	21.14	15.24
14.18 D.	1.10	17.13	31.22	15.18	2. 6
23.14	14. 7	32.27	8.11	22.15	Draw.
7.11 H.	28.32	18.14	22.17	11.27	
31.26 B.	B. wins.	27.23	15.18	14. 9	I.
12.16 A.		13. 9	17.14	6.10	15.18
24.19	C.	23.19	10.17	9. 6	7.16
15.24	27.23	15.10	21.14	27.32	18.27
14.10	8.12	19.23	6.10	6. 2	16.11
5.14	14.10	9. 6	14. 6	8.11	22.18
10. 7	7.14	23.19	3.10	26.23	11. 7
3.10	25.21	6. 2	13. 9	32.28	18.15
22.18	14.18	19.23	18.23	23.19	21.17
14.23	23.14	2. 7	9. 6	11.16	14.21
26. 3	16.19	23.19	23.27	20.11	7.14
W. wins.	22.17	7.11	6. 2	7.23	15.11
	19.28	19.23	27.32	2. 6	14.18
	26.22	11.15	2. 7	28.19	
				6.24	
				Draw.	

* If White plays 2.7, Black should win in two moves.

27.32	9.14	25.30	14.21	22.17	7.11
19.15	26.22	26.23	22.17	15.18	B. wins.
11. 8	14.21	30.26	12.16	32.28	**K.**
15.10	23.18	23.19	19.12	3. 7	27.24
Draw.	21.25	26.23	21 25	17.14	3. 8
GAME 6.	27.23	19.16	23.19	10.17	26.22
11.15	15.19	23.14	15.18	21.14	7.10
23.19	23.16	16. 7	20.16	6.10	22.18
9.14	11.27	10.15	11.27	14. 9	5. 9
22.17	32.23	7. 2	32.14	10.14	B. wins.
5. 9	25.30	15.18	7.11	9. 6	**L.**
26.23	22.17	2. 9	14. 7	18.22	31.26
9.13	30.25	14. 5	3.10	6. 2	11.16
30.26	28.24	B. wins.	Draw.	14.18	26.22
13.22	8.11	**D.**	**F.**	19.16	8.11
25. 9	18.14	24.19 Y	5. 9	12.19	22.17
6.13	25.21	15.24	31.26	24.15	5. 9
29.25	B. wins.	28.19	9.14	Draw.	17.14
8.11	**B.**	9.14	26.22	**H.**	9.18
25.22	17.14 D.	23.18	7.11	32.28	23.14
4. 8	9.18	14.21	21.17 G.	15.24	16.23
22.17	23.14	27.23	14.21	28.19	27.18
13.22	10.17	21.25	22.17	8.11	10.17
26.17	24.19 C.	31.26	15.18	31.26	21.14
1. 5	15.24	25.29	23. 7	10.14	15.22
17.13 M.	28.19	26.22	3.10	19.16 I.	B. wins.
2. 6	11.16	29.25	32.27	12.19	**M.**
21.17 E.	27.23	22.17	21.25	23.16	17.14 U.
12.16	17.22	11.16	27.23	14.18 `	10.17
19.12	31.27	32.27	25.30	27.24	21.14
5. 9	7.10	16.20	23.18	6.10	15.18
23.19 A.	27.24	18.14	30.25	B. wins.	31.26
9.14	8.11	25.21	18.14	**I.**	2. 6
27.23	31.27	19.16	25.21	26.22 K.	19.15 O.
14.21	22.26	8.11	14. 7	3. 8	18.22
2. 7	B. wins.	23.18	21.14	22.18	26.17
21.25	**C.**	10.15	7. 2	6.10	11.18
7.11	27.23	B wins.	14. 9	18. 9	23.19 N.
15.18	15.19	**E.**	2. 7	5.14	18.22
22.15	24.15	24.20 L	9.14	13. 9	27.23
11.27	11.27	15.24	7.16	11.15	22.26
32.23	32.23	28.19	14.10	27.24	23.18
25.30	17.22	11.15	16.11	15.18	26.31
23.18	23.18	27 24 H.	8.15	9. 6	32.27
30.26	7.10	8.11 F.	20.16	18.27	31.26
24.20	28.24	31.26	6. 9	6. 1	27.23
8.11	8.11	5. 9	B. wins.	8.11	26.31
B. wins.	24.20	26.22	**G.**	1. 6	17.13
A.	22.25	9.14	23.18	11.15	6.10
31.26 B.	31.26	21.17	14.23	6. 2	

2 K

14. 9	6. 2	18. 14	6. 2	**T.**	26. 23
5. 14	17. 10	22. 26	8. 11	22. 18	18. 22
18. 9	20. 16	15. 10	2. 6	25. 30	23. 19
31. 27	11. 20	7. 2	22. 18	27. 23	22. 26
9. 6	2. 4	14. 9	6. 9	30. 26	28. 24
27. 20	5. 9	26. 31	7. 10	32. 28	26. 31
B. wins.	32. 28 Q.	10. 6	14. 7	26. 22	20. 16
N.	10. 7	31. 26	5. 14	19. 15	2. 7
24. 20	4. 8 P.	6. 1	7. 2	22. 26	32. 28
18. 22	9. 14	26. 23	18. 22	23. 19	W. wins.
23. 18	8. 4	1. 5	24. 19	26. 22	**X.**
22. 26	14. 18	23. 19	14. 17	B. wins.	7. 10
27. 23	4. 8	5. 1	32. 28	**U.**	14. 7
26. 30	18. 22	20. 24	17. 21	3. 7	3. 10
32. 27	8. 4	1. 5	27. 24	11. 16	26. 22
30. 26	22. 26	24. 27	3. 8	17. 14	8. 11
23. 19	4. 8	5. 1	2. 7 S.	10. 17	22. 17
26. 30	26. 31	27. 31	22. 26	21. 14	16. 20
27. 23	8. 4	1. 5	7. 16	15. 18 X.	23. 18
30. 26	31. 26	31. 27	26. 23	24. 20	15. 22
17. 13	4. 8	5. 1	19. 15	7. 11	19. 16
7. 10	26. 22	27. 24	12. 19	19. 15	12. 19
14. 7	8. 4	1. 6	15. 10	2. 7 W.	24. 8
3. 10	22. 18	3. 8	23. 18	15. 10	22. 26
20. 16	4. 8	4. 11	24. 15	18. 22 V.	27. 24
26. 31	7. 2	19. 23	18. 11	26. 17	20. 27
28. 24	8. 11	28. 19	B. wins.	5. 9	32. 23
31. 27	2. 6	23. 7		14. 5	Draw.
24. 20	11. 8	B. wins.	**S.**	7. 21	**Y.**
27. 24	6. 9		2. 6	27. 24	24. 20
18. 15	8. 11	**Q.**	21. 25	3. 7	9. 14
24. 27	9. 14	4. 8	6. 9	23. 18	13. 9
B. wins.	11. 8	10. 7	25. 30	W. wins.	6. 22
O.	14. 17	8. 4	9. 14	**V.**	20. 16
24. 20	8. 11	9. 14	22. 26	16. 19	11. 20
6. 10	17. 22	32. 28	14. 10	23. 16	23. 18
28. 24	19. 16	14. 18	26. 31	12. 19	14. 23
10. 17	12. 19	19. 15	10. 14	27. 23	27. 2
23. 14	24. 15	7. 11	30. 25	18. 27	10. 14
17. 21	22. 26	15. 8	19. 15	32. 16	2. 6
26. 22	B. wins.	12. 16	11. 18	8. 12	14. 17
21. 25		B. wins.	14. 23	10. 6	6. 10
22. 17 R.	**P.**	**R.**	25. 30	12. 19	17. 21
25. 30	19. 16	19. 15 T.	24. 19	6. 2	10. 15
17. 13	12. 19	11. 18	31. 26	W. wins.	21. 25
30. 26	24. 15	22. 15	20. 16		31. 27
13. 9	9. 13	25. 30	26. 22	**W.**	25. 30
26. 22	27. 23	15. 10	28. 24	16. 19	27. 23
9. 6	13. 17	30. 26	22. 26	23. 7	30. 26
22. 17	23. 18	10. 6	23. 27	3. 17	Draw.
	17. 22	26. 22	Draw.		

TWELVE ORIGINAL CRITICAL POSITIONS, BY R. MARTIN.

No. 1. *White to move and win.*   No. 2. *White to move and win.*

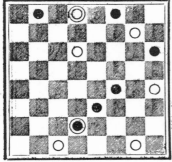

No. 3. *White to move and win.*   No. 4. *White to move and win.*

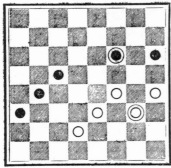

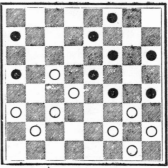

No. 5. *White to move and win.*   No. 6. *White to move and draw.*

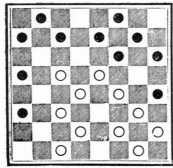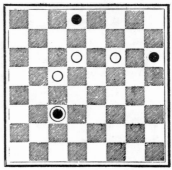

2 K 2

No. 7. *White to move and win.*   No. 8. *White to move and win.*

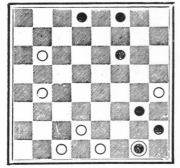
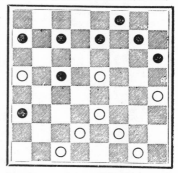

No. 9. *White to move and win.*   No. 10. *White to move and win.*

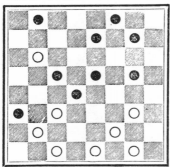
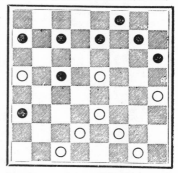

No. 11. *White to move and win.*   No. 12. *White to move and win.*

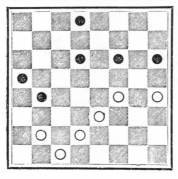
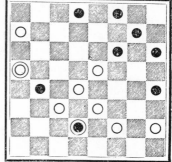

SOLUTIONS OF MR. MARTIN'S 12 CRITICAL POSITIONS.

No. 1.	6.10	No. 5.	No. 7.	21.30	15.19
10. 6	13.17	19.16	24.27	24.20	23.16
1.10	18.23	12.19	31.24	30.23	12.19
32.27	17.22	15.10	13.17	20. 4	8. 4
23.32	10.14	6.15	22.13	18.25	19.24
30.16	22.25	14.10	16.19	27. 2	W. wins.
12.19	23.26	7.23	24.15	W. wins.	
2. 6	25.29	27.18	7.10		No. 12.
W. wins.	26.30	20.27	15. 6	No. 10.	15.10
	W. wins.	32. 7	W. wins.	15.11	26.19
No. 2.		3.10		8.15	5. 1
15.11	No. 3.	18. 4	No. 8.	30.25	17.26
8.15	26.22	W. wins.	2. 7	21.30	27.24
24.20	17.26		3.10	20.16	20.27
15.24	19.15		19.24	12.19	10. 7
20.18	11.27	No. 6.	20.27	23.16	3.10
17.21	24.22	19.24	11.16	30.23	18.15
18.22	W. wins.	11.15	12.19	27. 2	11.18
1. 5		24.28	17.13	W. wins.	1. 6
10. 6	No. 4.	15.18	10.17		2. 9
5. 9	19.23	22.26	13.15	No. 11.	13.15
6. 1	26.10	31.22	W. wins.	8.12	W. wins.
9.13	6.15	28.32		16.11	
1. 6	13. 6	18.27	No. 9.	7.16	
21.17	1.26	32.23	9. 6	20.11	
22.18	30.23	Draw.	1.10	10.15	
17.21	15.22		30.26	11. 8	
	W. wins.				

POLISH DRAUGHTS.

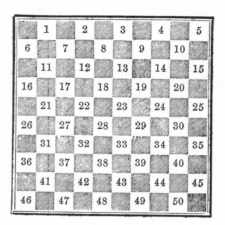

THIS variety is played with a table divided into one hundred squares, fifty of each colour, and with forty counters, (called indifferently either pieces, pawns, or men), one-half black and the other white, each player having twenty of one colour. (In Germany, however, Polish Draughts is now frequently played on the ordinary board, with the usual complement of twenty-four pieces.) The counters are moved forwards, as in the English game, and upon the same system, namely, obliquely from square to square; but in taking, they move in the Polish game either backwards or forwards. The Kings*, too, have the privilege of passing over several squares, and even the whole length of the diagonal, when the passage is free, at one move, which vastly adds to the amount of combinations.

It is usual both in France and England to arrange the counters on the white squares; but they may by consent

---

* In the Polish game, almost the only one played on the Continent, the crowned piece is called a Queen, instead of King. Indeed the common name for Draughts is Damen (women), it follows therefore naturally that the principal piece should be a queen.

be placed on the black. The colour adopted is a matter of indifference, excepting that the black pieces are not seen quite so well on their own colour as the white on theirs.

The table is so placed, that each of the players has a double corner of the colour played on, to his right, viz., the squares numbered 45 and 50. The board, in first placing the pieces, is divided into two portions: that occupied by the black counters, comprising the twenty squares, from 1 to 20, and that occupied by the white, comprising those numbered from 31 to 50, leaving between them two rows of squares unoccupied, upon which the first moves take place.

The laws which regulate the English game are with a few additions equally applicable to the Polish. We have therefore merely to give the directions for playing, and the two or three additional rules which belong peculiarly to this variety.

The march of the Pawn, as already observed, is the same as in the English game, with this addition, that when there are pieces *en prise* (but not else) the taking Pawn may move backwards. Thus, White having a pawn at 25, and Black unsupported Pawns at 20, 9, 8, 17, 27, 38 and 39, White having the move would take them all, and finish at square 34. It will be observed that in this *coup* White passes a crowning square at 3, but he does not therefore become entitled to be made a King, nor has he the option of stopping *en route*, but must go on to the termination of his move at 34 or be huffed.

The piece which captures, whether Pawn or King, cannot in the course of one *coup* repass any covered square which it has leaped over, but must halt behind that piece which, but for this restriction, would be *en prise*. For example, suppose *White* to have a Pawn upon 22, 32, 33, and 37, with a King at 43, and *Black* a Pawn at 3, 4, 9, and 19, with Kings at 10 and 13. The black Queen at 13 takes the four Pawns' 22, 37, 43 and 33, and must stop at 28, which he would have to touch in preparing to take 32, but is prohibited from going to square 37 in consequence of having passed over it before. A square which is vacant may be passed or repassed several times in the course of one *coup*, provided no piece is passed over a second time. It is the intricacy of such moves which renders the rule imperative that the pieces taken be not removed till the capturing Pawn is at its destination or "en repos." The White Pawn at 32, then takes the Black Pawn jeopardized at 28, as well as the pieces at 19 and 10, making a King.

As regards huffing at this game the player is bound to take the greatest number of pieces where he has the choice, notwithstanding the smaller number may be most to his advantage, and failing to do so he may be huffed or compelled to take at the option of his adversary. Thus if on the one hand there are three Pawns *en prise*, and on the other two Kings, you are compelled to take the Pawns, but were there only two Pawns instead of three, vou must take the Kings, as being of greatest value. When pieces, at the option of taking, are numerically and intrinsically the same, you may take which you please. The rule resolves itself into this, that you are controlled by numerical value, excepting when the numbers are equal, and then by the actual value of the pieces.

Kings are made in the same manner as in the English game. It has already been said that you cannot claim to have your Pawn crowned if it touches a King's square merely in its passage over it *en coup*. Good players, when they cannot prevent the adversary from reaching a King's square, commonly endeavour to lead him out again by placing a man or two in take, so as to disentitle him from being crowned. Indeed, it is sometimes good play to sacrifice three men, either for the object of gaining or capturing a King, especially towards the end of the game, when he is of the greatest importance, much greater in proportion than at the English game.

The movement of the King is the great feature in this game, and in *coup* he may accomplish more angles on the draught-board than a billiard ball can be made to perform, even in the hands of a Kentfield. He has the privilege of traversing the board from one extremity to the other (if the line be unoccupied) or of halting on any of the intermediate squares, like the Bishop at chess. Thus, if he stand at 28, he may move anywhere on the line between 5 and 46, or between 6 and 50, but he can only move on one line at a time, unless there are pieces *en prise*, and then he may move diagonally all over the board, in which respect he has an advantage over the Bishop at chess. For example, place isolated black Pawns or Kings at 37, 17, 20, 30, 40, and a white King at 48. He will take all the pieces, by touching at the following squares, viz., 26, 3, 25, 34, and 45, where he rests, which squares, it will be perceived, though not close to the pieces, are within the angles. Indeed, it is possible so to place the pieces that a single King might capture a dozen in rotation. The following example is a case in which 19 may be taken at one *coup*. Place a white King at 45, and he may take all the intervening pieces, by touching at the following squares, viz., 29, 18, 4, 15, 29, 38, 27, 18, 7, 16, 27, 36, 47, 28, 49, 35, 24, 13, and 2, where he rests. The player who may wish to try this experiment, will have to place the pieces on squares 8, 9, 10, 11, 12, 19, 20, 21, 22, 23, 30, 31, 32, 33, 34, 41, 42, 43, 44.

Between equal and skilful players the game would of necessity be "drawn" in many positions, when the uninitiated would lose; it is difficult therefore to define what are drawn games, but one or two of the simplest may be instanced. Suppose that at the end of the game one party, say White, has a King on the great central line, between Nos. 5 and 46, and Black has two or even three Kings, the game is drawn, as White cannot be driven from his hold, or captured, if he play correctly, and takes care to keep on the other side of a trap; thus, if he finds White preparing to get his pieces at 37, 38, and 49, he must be between 5 and 28, and *vice versâ*, that is, always on the adversary's unfortified or weak side. But when the single King does not occupy the central line, there are many ways of winning, especially against an inferior player, but as these cannot be forced, the game must be considered drawn after 15 moves, and this rule holds good although the stronger party may have given odds. Should the odds, however, consist in ceding the draw as a game won, then twenty moves may be claimed by the party giving such odds.

When at the conclusion of a game, a player, who has only one King, offers to his adversary, who has a King and two men, or two Kings and a man, to crown his two men, or the man, for the purpose of counting the limited moves, the latter is obliged to accept the offer, otherwise the former can leave the game as a draw.

When one party at the end of a game has a King and a man against three Kings, the best way is to sacrifice the man as soon as possible, because the game is more easily defended with the King alone.

In Polish Draughts especially it is by exchanges that good players parry strokes and prepare them; if the game is embarrassed, they open it by giving man for man, or two for two. If a dangerous stroke is in preparation, they avoid it by exchanging man for man. If it is requisite to strengthen the weak side of your game, it may be managed by exchanging. If you wish to acquire the move, or an advantageous position, a well managed exchange will produce it. Finally, it is by exchanges that one man frequently keeps many confined, and that the game is eventually won.

When two men of one colour are so placed that there is an empty square behind each and a vacant square between them, where his adversary can place himself, it is called a *lunette*, and this is much more likely to occur in the Polish than the English game. In this position one of the men must necessarily be taken, because they cannot both be played, nor escape at the same time. The lunette frequently offers several men to be taken on both sides. As it is most frequently a snare laid by a skilful player, it must be regarded with suspicion; for it is not to be supposed that the adversary, if he be a practised player, would expose himself to lose one or more men for nothing. Therefore, before entering the lunette look at your adversary's position, and then calculate what you yourself would do in a similar game.

Towards the end of a game when there are but few Pawns left on the board, concentrate them as soon as possible. At that period of the game the slightest error is fatal.

The King is so powerful a piece, that one, two, or three Pawns may be advantageously sacrificed to obtain him. But in doing so it is necessary to note the future prospects of his reign. Be certain that he will be in safety, and occupy a position that may enable him to retake an equivalent for the Pawns sacrificed, without danger to himself. An expert player will endeavour to snare the King as soon as he is made, by placing a Pawn in his way, so as to cause his being retaken.

GAME I.

WHITE.	BLACK.	WHITE.	BLACK.
32 to 28	20 to 25	46 to 41	17 to 28
37 to 32	14 to 20		(taking 22)
41 to 37	10 to 14	34 to 29	23 to 34
31 to 27	17 to 21		(taking 29)
37 to 31	21 to 26	32 to 14	8 to 12
42 to 37	4 to 10	(tak. 28 & 19)	
47 to 42	20 to 24	39 to 30	25 to 34
28 to 22	14 to 20	(taking 34)	(taking 30)
33 to 28	10 to 14	27 to 22	18 to 27
34 to 30	25 to 34		(taking 22)
	(taking 30)	31 to 22	3 to 9
39 to 30	20 to 25	(taking 27)	
(taking 34)		14 to 3	12 to 17
44 to 39	25 to 34	(crn'd, tak. 9)	
	(taking 30)	3 to 21	26 to 28
40 to 20	14 to 25	(taking 17)	(tak. 21 & 22)
(tak. 34 & 24)	(taking 20)	36 to 31	7 to 12
35 to 30	25 to 34	31 to 27	12 to 18
	(taking 30)	41 to 36	11 to 17
39 to 30	18 to 23	27 to 22	18 to 27
(taking 34)			(taking 22)
45 to 40	15 to 20	37 to 32	28 to 37
40 to 35	12 to 18		(taking 32)
43 to 39	7 to 12	42 to 11	6 to 17
39 to 33	20 to 24	(taking 37, 27,	(taking 11)
49 to 43	5 to 10	& 17)	
50 to 45	10 to 15	38 to 33	17 to 22
45 to 40	15 to 20	43 to 39	34 to 43
30 to 25	2 to 7		(taking 39)
25 to 14	9 to 20	48 to 39	16 to 21
(taking 20)	(taking 14)	(taking 43)	
40 to 34	20 to 25	39 to 34	21 to 27
33 to 29	24 to 33	34 to 29	13 to 18
	(taking 29)	29 to 24	27 to 31
28 to 39	12 to 17	36 to 27	22 to 31
(taking 33)		(taking 31)	(taking 27)

24 to 20	31 to 37	9 to 4	47 to 15
20 to 14	37 to 41	(a King)	(taking 33)
14 to 9	41 to 47	4 to 36	
	(a King)	(taking 18)	

Drawn, each player remaining with a King and Pawn.

GAME II.

** *The variations are given as notes at the foot of the page.*

WHITE.	BLACK.	WHITE.	BLACK.
34 to 30	20 to 25	31 to 26	24 to 29 (a)
40 to 34	14 to 20	33 to 24	20 to 29
45 to 40	10 to 14	(taking 29)	(taking 24)
50 to 45	5 to 10	39 to 33	17 to 22 (b)
33 to 28	20 to 24	33 to 24	22 to 33
39 to 33	15 to 20	(taking 29)	(taking 28)
44 to 39	18 to 23	38 to 29	11 to 17
49 to 44	12 to 18	(taking 33)	
31 to 27	7 to 12	37 to 31	7 to 11
37 to 31	2 to 7	42 to 37	17 to 21
41 to 37	10 to 15	26 to 17	11 to 22
47 to 41	4 to 10	(taking 21)	(taking 17)

(a) Here Black in playing from 24 to 29 commits a false move, which causes the loss of a pawn. It might have been avoided by playing

	17 to 21	36 to 27
26 to 17	11 to 31	(taking 31)
(taking 21)	(taking 17 & 27)	

This would have caused a mutual exchange of two pieces.

(b) The pawn at 29 is necessarily lost, as the sequel of the game will shew, and if to save it Black had played 14 to 20, he would have lost *a coup*, thus:

	14 to 20	31 to 22	17 to 28
33 to 24	20 to 29	(taking 27)	(taking 22)
(taking 29)	(taking 24)	38 to 27	
27 to 22	18 to 27	(taking 32)	
	(taking 22)	5 to 32	It is immaterial
32 to 21	16 to 27	(taking 28)	how these moves
(taking 27)	(taking 21)	40 to 29	are played.
37 to 31	23 to 32	(taking 34)	
	(taking 28)	White having	
34 to 5	25 to 34	gained a King	
(tak. 29, 19, & 10,	(taking 30)	and three	
and crowned)		pawns.	

WHITE.	BLACK.
43 to 38	14 to 20 (c)

(c) Black, in playing 14 to 20, makes a false move, which causes him to lose the game, through a skilful *coup*, and he would not the less have lost, if White, in lieu of making the *coup*, had played as follows:

48 to 42	10 to 14	23 to 18	22 to 17
31 to 26	22 to 31	(in the lunette)	
	(taking 27)	18 to 20	27 to 38
36 to 27	12 to 17	(taking 13 & 14)	(taking 32)
(taking 31)		20 to 14	38 to 43
44 to 39	6 to 11	14 to 9	43 to 49
39 to 33	1 to 6		(a King)
26 to 21	17 to 26	9 to 3	49 to 27
	(taking 21)	(a King)	
27 to 22	18 to 27	45 to 40	6 to 11
	(taking 22)	40 to 35	11 to 16
29 to 18	20 to 29	41 to 36	27 to 43
(taking 23)	(taking 24)	24 to 19	43 to 27
33 to 24	13 to 22	35 to 30	27 to 49
(taking 29)	(taking 18)	Or	
24 to 4	8 to 13	19 to 13	15 to 20
(taking 19 & 9,		3 to 15	49 to 35
& crowned)		(taking 20)	
4 to 18	22 to 13	Immaterial where	35 takes 2
(taking 13)	(taking the King)		Drawn.
32 to 21	26 to 17	Or 30 to 24	49 to 44
(taking 27)	(taking 21)	19 to 13	44 to 22
30 to 24	14 to 20	13 to 9	22 to 4
37 to 32	20 to 29		(taking 9)
	(taking 24)	36 to 31	4 to 36
34 to 23	3 to 9		(taking 31)
(taking 29)		46 to 41	36 to 20
35 to 30	25 to 34		(taking 41 & 24)
	(taking 30)	3 to 25	16 to 21 (d)
40 to 29	9 to 14	(taking the King)	
(taking 34)		25 to 43	21 to 26
29 to 24	16 to 21	43 to 48	15 to 20
38 to 33	17 to 22	48 to 42	20 to 25
42 to 38	22 to 27	42 to 48	25 to 30
33 to 28	21 to 26	48 to 25	26 to 31
32 to 21	26 to 17	(taking 30)	
(taking 27)	(taking 21)	25 to 14	31 to 36
38 to 32	17 to 22	14 to 46	36 to 41
28 to 17	11 to 22	46 to 37	Lost.
(taking 22)	(taking 17)	(taking 41)	

(d) Here commence a series of moves necessary, in order with a single King, to arrest the two pawns which are advancing from the right and left of the board to the crowning line.

WHITE.	BLACK.	WHITE.	BLACK.
31 to 26	22 to 33	34 to 5	25 to 34
	(tak. 27, 37, & 38)	(a King, taking	(taking 30)
29 to 38	20 to 29	29, 19, & 10)	
(taking 33)	(taking 24)	48 to 30	Lost.
32 to 28	23 to 43	(tak. 43 & 34)	
	(tak. 28 & 38)		

We nevertheless continue the game to its conclusion, that nothing may be omitted which the learner could desire.

WHITE	BLACK	WHITE	BLACK
	12 to 17	25 to 23	17 to 22
5 to 37	9 to 14	(taking 20, 9,	
37 to 5	18 to 23	8, & 18)	
(taking 14)		26 to 21	15 to 20
5 to 11	6 to 17	35 to 30	13 to 18
(tak. 23 & 17)	(tak. the King)	23 to 12	22 to 28
30 to 24	16 to 21	(taking 18)	
35 to 30	3 to 9	45 to 40	28 to 33
40 to 35	1 to 7	40 to 34	33 to 38
44 to 39	7 to 12	37 to 28	38 to 16
39 to 33	12 to 18		(tak. 32 & 21)
41 to 37	21 to 27	12 to 8	16 to 21
36 to 31	27 to 36	8 to 3	21 to 27
	(taking 31)	3 to 25	27 to 32
46 to 41	36 to 47	(taking 20)	
	(crn'd, tak. 41)	25 to 20	32 to 37
30 to 25	47 to 20	20 to 47	Lost.
	(tak. 33 & 24)		

LOSING GAME.

THIS game, which is lively and amusing, may for variety's sake be occasionally played. Although not ranked as scientific, it has its niceties, and requires considerable attention and management.

The player who first gets rid of all his men wins the game. Your constant object therefore is to force your adversary to take as many pieces as possible, and to compel him to make Kings, which is accomplished by opening your game freely, especially the back squares. Huffing, and the other rules, apply equally to this game.

Fig. 1.

BILLIARDS.

CHAPTER I.—OF BILLIARDS IN GENERAL—OF THE BIL-
LIARD TABLE—OF THE INSTRUMENTS EMPLOYED IN
THE GAME—AND OF THE MANNER OF USING THEM.

BILLIARDS, like the greater number of games which are
prevalent in modern Europe, is of French invention. Soon
after the French, the Germans, the Dutch, and the Italians
brought it into vogue throughout the Continent; and in a
few years afterwards it became a favourite diversion in
England, particularly among persons of rank. The precise period of its introduction into this country is not
known, but, as it is mentioned by Shakspeare, the game must
at least have been somewhat familiar to us in the sixteenth
century. As it is replete with entertainment, and attended
with that kind of moderate exercise, which renders it at the
same time both agreeable and conducive to health, it will, in
all probability, long remain in fashion.

The game of billiards is played by two or more persons, with
ivory balls, upon a table, which in different countries is made
of different shapes. In some parts of the Continent, a round
or an oval form is most in use, in others, nearly a square

one; in this country the shape universally employed is the oblong, varying in size from six to twelve feet long, the width being always half its length. But the established table is twelve feet long by six wide, (supported on eight legs), the height three feet from the ground to the top of the cushion; and this is the size adopted in all our public rooms. The frame should be made of old oak or mahogany, or some well seasoned wood, not given to warp, and the bed be of metal or slate, (in preference to either marble or oak), covered with fine green cloth, tightly fitted and perfectly smooth. The table should not be liable to the least vibration, and the bed be perfectly horizontal, the accuracy of which may be tested by a spirit-level. The cushion, as it is called, is a raised edge or border, (generally two inches or a little less in depth), lined with a stuffed elastic pad*, and intersected by six netted pockets, (usually three inches and one-eighth in the opening) four of which are situated at the four corners, and the other two midway in the sides. At the lower end of the table, two feet six inches from the end cushion, is a line technically termed the *baulk line*, in the middle of which is a semicircle of ten inches radius, termed the striking point. From any part of this striking point the player is at liberty to commence the game, but he is not allowed to place his ball beyond the area of the semi-circle. At the opposite or upper end of the table, and in its centre, at a distance of two feet six from the end cushion, is a point called the *spot*, on which is placed the red ball, for the *winning* game; and seventeen inches further on *i.e.*, within thirteen inches of the cushion, is a second spot for the red ball, in the *winning and losing game*, (the game now commonly played.)

Two or three ivory balls are the usual number employed,

---

* The old mode of stuffing the cushion was with list or layers of fine cloth, the present is with India rubber, by means of which the elasticity is considerably increased. Both modes have their respective advocates, but the India rubber is generally preferred; and now that what are called vulcanized India rubber cushions have been patented by Mr. Thurston, the former objection, that of their being sensibly affected by variations in the atmosphere, is removed. It appears, however, that scientific players are by no means unanimous as to the advantages of highly elastic cushions, or what are technically termed very fast tables. Mr. Mardon says, that the more elastic the cushion the more incorrect will be the angle, while Mr. Kentfield maintains that a little study of the variations occasioned by extra elasticity, is all that is required.

(according to the game played) one red, the others white, and one of the latter marked with a small black spot by way of distinction. They vary in diameter from one inch and seven-eighths to two inches, (in proportion to the size of the pockets and height of the cushion), and weigh from four ounces to four and a quarter, but those used together must be exactly uniform both in size and weight, and constructed with the utmost accuracy*.

The instruments employed for the purpose of striking the balls are two; the cue and the mace. The former of these is a long round stick, which should be made of fine, close-grained, well-seasoned ash, slightly conical in shape, being broad at one end, and at the other converging to a narrow, flattened or rounded point. The mace consists of a long slender rod, with a thick piece of mahogany or other wood affixed to its extremity, and adapted to it in such an angle, as to rest flat upon the table while the stick is held up to the shoulder in the act of striking. The under side of this is flat and smooth, in order that it may move with facility over the cloth, the upper side is concave, and the end to be opposed to the ball is plain and broad.

Of these instruments, the cue is by far the most universally used. It possesses various advantages over the mace, and is invariably preferred by all good players, indeed the mace is now scarcely ever used except by ladies. There is also a long cue, and a rest or jigger for strokes which are out of reach with the ordinary cue†. "In the choice of a cue,"

---

* Great nicety is required in making billiard-balls, as the centre of the ball must be the centre of gravity, and this it would not be unless the portion of the tooth from which it is made contained the common centre (the heaviest part of the ivory). The modes of testing the sphericity of a ball are by a steel gage, a hollow cone, or calliper-compasses. There are modes of testing its gravity besides propelling it on a straight line, such as dropping a marked ball through a transparent fluid, in descending through which, if perfectly true, it will retain its position, but the success of the experiment depends on very nice management. After all, it is best to rely on some maker of talent and integrity, such as Messrs. Holzapfel, Mr. Thurston, and, we are happy to say, many others in this metropolis.

† The advantages which the cue possesses over the mace, are undoubted. The cue is the only instrument in vogue abroad, and it is astonishing to what a degree of skill its management has in many instances been carried. Examples of this will daily present themselves to those who are much in the habit of frequenting the billiard rooms of

says Mr. Kentfield, "much will depend on the fancy of the player; some prefer light, others heavy, cues; some small, others those which are large at the point, and so on; but the cue to be recommended should be four feet eight inches long,* of moderate weight, say from fourteen to sixteen ounces; half an inch in diameter at the small end, and about one inch and a half at the butt. It should be formed of fine, straight, close-grained, well-seasoned ash, rather stiff, or with very little spring in it. [Mr. Mardon says, that a cue which has any spring in it should not be used.] The point is covered with leather to prevent its slipping from the ball in striking. Some players prefer double leathers, others single ones, the best players have generally decided in favour of the latter. Should, however, the former be selected, the under one should be very hard, and the top one soft. For preserving the cue such an arrangement is perhaps the best; it

our own country; but I think I have upon the whole seen more instances of superior address among foreigners. [This is Mr. White's note, written before the time of Mr. Kentfield, whose prodigious achievements in this game surpass everything on record.] The keeper of a billiard room in Hamburgh, where perhaps the game is played as much as in any other town in Europe, will at any time engage to make the straight hazard across two contiguous tables: that is, that he will strike the object ball from one table to the other, and hole it in any specified pocket of the latter. But the most remarkable instance of this unusual dexterity, that has hitherto come within my observation, occurred in an Italian, who frequented the billiard rooms at Paris, about the period of the revolution in 1789. I have frequently seen him place two balls in the middle of the table, parallel to each other, and venture an even bet that he would make either the winning or the losing hazard, in any one of the six pockets; and this he usually performed with facility, upon the nature of the hazard, and the particular pocket being determined upon by the spectators. He had so great a facility of making what are called doublet hazards, (i. e. hazards made after a reverberation of the ball from an opposite cushion,) that he has been known to hole the red ball in one of the upper holes, by playing at it from the striking point, thirty times, without an intervening failure.

* The length of the cue should in some degree be proportioned to the height of the player; if too short it will cramp the movement of his arm, if too long, it will give a fatiguing counterpoise, and so affect the stroke. Mr. Mardon prefers a cue four feet seven inches, but observes that the standard is considered four feet ten inches. Mr. Bedford, who exceeds the average stature, plays with a very short cue, viz., four feet five. Mr. Thurston, on the other hand, is sometimes called upon to make them even of the length of five feet.

is also well adapted for certain strokes, but cannot be de-
pended upon when the ball is to be struck at a distance.
Soft sole leather or saddle flap is an excellent material for
points, but for single points nothing perhaps is better than
old harness or strap, provided the leather be not too old,
which would render it hard and useless. It may be affixed
with common glue, Indian glue, shell lac, or any other kinds
of cement, taking care to avoid anything greasy."

The first thing to be attended to, is THE BRIDGE, or support
upon which the cue is to act. This is formed by the left hand
of the player being placed firmly upon the table, about six
inches from the ball to be struck, and drawn up until the hand
rests only upon the wrist and points of the fingers; the latter
being bent up to such an angle, as to leave the palm considerably hollowed, at the same time that the thumb is elevated above the level of the knuckles, so as to form a furrow
between it and the forefinger, for the cue to slide in. "Some
make their bridge much too long, that is, lay their hand

Fig. 2.

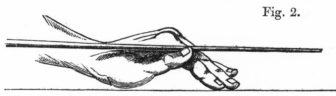

nearly flat, and so are apt to lose hazards which require force
and others spread their fingers too much, and thus are deficient
in firmness. "And many players," says Mr. Mardon, "press
the thumb closely against the forefinger; but a bridge thus
formed is contracted and imperfect. The thumb, well raised,
should be separated from the forefinger by half an inch, the
thumb can then be lowered, should it be necessary to strike
much below the centre." The next thing is to handle and
adapt the cue in such a manner, as to render it perfectly free
and easy in its motion. This consists in grasping it about four
or five inches from the broad extremity with the right hand,
with sufficient force to enable the striker to use an adequate
strength in his stroke, and yet free enough to allow of a
considerable extent of motion; and in applying the other
extremity to the bridge, about six or eight inches from its

point. The bridge being made, and the cue thus adapted to
it, it only remains to strike the ball, which is to be done in
the following manner. The point of the cue, [which should
be rubbed over with a little chalk, or made rough with glass-
paper, to prevent its slipping,] ought, in the first place, to
be made accurately to approach the centre of the ball, which,
as was before observed, should be rather more than half a
foot from the hand. The cue should then be drawn four or
more inches (Mr. K. says six, and a German writer says from
six to ten) backwards, according to the strength required,
slightly depressed towards the cloth, then gradually elevated
till perfectly horizontal, and lastly forced against the ball, so
as to drive it onwards with more or less velocity, as occasion
may require.*   The stroke should be made freely from the
shoulder, and not in a cramped manner from the elbow, and
the arm should be parallel to the side, not at an angle.   In very
gentle and pushing strokes the cue may be close to the ball.
If the right hand be at all elevated the ball will have a ten-

* Almost every cue player has a mode of striking peculiar to himself.
Some in making the bridge have accustomed themselves to lay the hand
quite flat upon the cloth ; others hollow it to the utmost and expand it by
separating the fingers widely from each other; while some again suffer the
fingers to remain close, and only give the palm a moderate degree of concavity. Some press the thumb close to the forefinger, others keep it wide
asunder. In holding the cue, many players grasp it firmly in the hollow of
the hand ; a great number retain it between the thumb and fingers only,
while these are held perpendicular to the table ; and some use the thumb
and fingers only, but at the same time turn the wrist inwards, so that the
fingers and back of the hand shall be horizontal instead of perpendicular.
Lastly, in striking the ball some use a simple push, others a sudden impulsive jerk. It is habit only that has made these different modes of using the
instrument familiar and indispensable to the individuals who employ them ;
but the young player who has not yet formed any particular habit, will,
I am convinced, find it preferable to accustom himself to the mode here
recommended, as it is not only the most elegant, but infinitely the most
commodious. This briefly is, with regard to the bridge, to turn the fingers
outwards, but to retain them close to each other, and to give the palm
such a degree of concavity, that the cue when held level with the cloth,
may approach the ball about the eighth of an inch above its centre: in
holding the broad end of the cue with the striking hand, to employ either
the thumb and fingers alone, or the palm with a moderate firmness, and
at the same time to turn the wrist inwards, so that the phalanges of the
fingers, and back of the hand may correspond, or be level with the
surface of the table.

dency to jump.   Before making the stroke the learner should
not only know where the balls will strike, but he should endeavour to calculate where they will be left.

Mr. Kentfield's directions for striking the ball may be
advantageously subjoined, although in part a repetition of
what is given by Mr. White in the preceding and succeeding
chapter.   He says, "It is scarcely necessary to observe how
much importance attaches to this circumstance.   A player
may take the right position, hold the cue correctly, and thus
far perform all that is required, and yet he may be unable to
strike a ball with firmness and with truth; and for this
simple reason, that in the act of striking he draws his cue
back perhaps one inch instead of six, so as rather to make
a sort of *push* at the ball instead of a firm and distinct stroke.
His first endeavour should be to place the point of his cue to
that part of the ball he intends to strike, then to draw it back
about six inches, keeping it at the same time as horizontal as

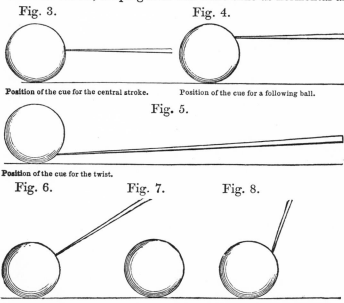

Fig. 3.   Fig. 4.

Position of the cue for the central stroke.   Position of the cue for a following ball.

Fig. 5.

Position of the cue for the twist.

Fig. 6.   Fig. 7.   Fig. 8.

Position of the cue   Perpendicular position of the cue for a twist when one ball
for jumping the ball.   is near another.

possible, and with a rectilinear motion to force it forwards with a kind of jerk,* taking care also to strike the ball when he takes aim, or he will fail in his object. This is perhaps one of the most difficult things for the learner to overcome, and even old players who have acquired considerable knowledge of the game, have fallen into an error of this kind, and felt surprised that the ball did not return from the cushion in the direction they had expected, and probably condemned the cushion for a fault which was entirely their own. The necessity of keeping the cue in a horizontal line cannot be urged too forcibly, for if the right hand is too much elevated the ball will jump and the stroke fail." In the diagrams No. 1, 2, and 3, the proper position of the cue in striking is represented.

The action of the mace is much more simple. Previous to the act of striking, its broad extremity is to be adapted very accurately to the centre of the ball; and the stick being then carried up even with the right shoulder, the instrument and the ball are to be, at once, pushed onwards, by the same effort, and without any sudden impulsive force. *To strike* the ball with the mace, instead of to *push* it forward, is deemed a foul stroke, as will be seen in the rules.

CHAPTER II.

Section I.—General Principles of the Game.

In the game of Billiards, the general object of the player is, briefly, by striking one ball against another, either to propel one or both of them into a pocket, or with one ball to strike two others successively. Two balls lying in such a situation as to admit of one or both of them being pocketed, presents to the striker what is termed a hazard. If the red ball be one of these, it is then called a red hazard; if it consist of the two white balls only, it is called a white hazard. When after the contact of the balls, the white or striking one is pocketed, the striker is said to have made a losing hazard; on the contrary, when the ball struck at, whether red or

* Mr. Mardon, in reference to this "jerk," says, that more dangerous advice could scarcely be given, and recommends that the cue should be delivered as smoothly as possible, after drawing it back four inches rather than six.

white, is made to enter a hole, he makes what is termed the winning hazard. If with his own ball he strike two others successively, the stroke is called a canon (formerly *carom* or *carambole*, which is the French term).

It will be the object of the present chapter to lay down those established principles, which are applicable to Billiards in general, without having an immediate reference to any particular game, the consideration of which will form the subject of a subsequent chapter.

Attention to various circumstances is necessary, in order to play the game of Billiards with delicacy and correctness; namely, the particular modification of the action of the instrument, with which the impulse is given to the ball; the proper regulation of the eye of the striker; the position he assumes in striking, and the mode in which he accommodates the instrument to his hand; the precise point of the distant or object ball*, or of the cushion which is made to receive the stroke; and lastly, the degree of strength necessary to be employed, in order to obtain the desired end.

The accuracy of every stroke will very materially depend upon the proper regulation of the eye of the striker; and this requires a great degree of nicety. There are two objects to be attentively regarded, nearly in the same instant; namely, the cue ball, or that to be struck with the instrument, and the object ball, or that to be struck at, in order to effect the desired hazard, or canon. The position of the object ball should first be attentively marked; the cue is then to be adapted to the bridge formed by the hand, as before directed, and upon this the eye should be suffered to rest until the instant of striking; previous to the act of which, it should be again carried to the object ball, and remain intently fixed on it until the stroke is completed: for the less frequently the eye wanders from ball to ball, the more correct will be the stroke. Two glances alone are sufficient, and the last of these, namely, from the first to the second ball, should be extremely rapid, at the same time that it is accurately distinct; for if the least hesitation take place after the eye has

---

* For the sake of perspicuity throughout the following pages, the ball with which the striker plays is termed (in some instances, however, improperly) the striking, or CUE BALL, and that which he strikes at, whether red or white, is designated by the term OBJECT BALL.

left the striking ball, either a miss of the cue, or an imperfect stroke will very generally be the consequence. " The eye," says Mr. Mardon, " will direct the hand. If in the act of throwing a stone at a bird, which do you look at, certainly not the stone? If a bowler kept his eye upon the ball in his hand, and not on the wicket, he would seldom or never hit it. Mr. Bedford, one of our best winning hazard strikers, invariably directs his attention to the ball played upon, and considers any deviation from that course to be a certain indication of nervousness or want of confidence."

THE REST.—When your ball is at such a distance that you have occasion to use the rest, do not place it too near, lest it prevent your seeing the precise spot where you ought to strike. If ten or twelve inches be left between the ball and the rest, the cue can be kept in a position nearly horizontal. The generality of players raise their hand too high.

THE POSITION in which the striker stands, whilst in the act of playing, is also of essential importance, beyond what regards the elegance of his appearance. I have for many years repeatedly had occasion to observe, that a player whose posture is elegant, who strikes with ease and grace, and who is calm and collected in his game, will uniformly attain a degree of skill, superior to him who stands inelegantly, delivers his ball ungracefully, and in his play is bustling and impatient. These are circumstances, however, which are much more easily to be acquired by observation, and by the direction of a good player, than by written rules. But thus much may be observed; the body should be bent just enough to allow of the eye being directed along the cue with ease, and one foot should be extended foremost: a person who plays with his right hand, should stand with his left foot foremost, and, on the contrary, he who is left-handed, should stand with his right foot foremost; by which he will be more steady and firm. Mr. Kentfield says, " The player should stand firmly on the right leg (if a right-handed player) with the left slightly advanced and a little bent, and the trunk nearly erect, or not more inclined forward than may be necessary for the left hand to rest with ease upon the table. This position should be steadily preserved until the stroke has been completed, and the arm be the only part moved during the act of striking.

" Every inordinate affection of the mind, immoderate bursts of passion and even the fretting at trifling disappointments in his game, are usually found prejudicial to the player: his nerves being affected, it becomes impossible for him to make his stroke with that steadiness and nicety the game requires."

The direction of the motion produced in a moveable elastic body, projected against a body that is fixed and at rest, is simple and determinate ; and is alike under all the varieties of velocity and modes of projection ; the reaction will invariably equal the action and be the counterpart thereof, or, in other words, the course of the body, after contact, will be the counterpart of the motion originally imparted to it ; hence THE ANGLE of REFLEXION MUST UNIFORMLY BE EQUAL TO THE ANGLE OF INCIDENCE*.

Fig. 9.

Thus the ball a, propelled against the cushion at D, forming with the line e drawn through the point of contact, the angle a, e, D, will be returned in the direction D, f, forming the corresponding angle D, e, f.

This, however, is by no means the case with regard to bodies, both of which are equally moveable and elastic; the motion resulting from the contact of these being compound, or modified by the peculiarity in the action of and the intensity of the moving powers; and arising from the joint effect of different causes concurring at the same instant in their operation.

It has been found expedient, for the better explanation of the varieties of motion resulting from a difference in the degree and mode of contact of the balls employed in the game of Billiards, to divide the object ball, or that against which the player directs his stroke, into four or more parts, representing the precise points upon which the centre of the striking

* This is an axiom of long standing in Billiards, and has been repeated by all writers on the subject. It must, however, be borne in mind, that angles will vary in proportion to the force applied, and that " *the stronger the stroke, the more acute will be the angle.*" On highly elastic cushions, the angles become altogether a new study, and it will be found that a ball cannot be driven up the table by angles across it, with the same uniformity as on the old fashioned list cushions.

ball is to be received for different ends. This has given rise to the denominations, a full ball, a three-quarter ball, a half ball, a third ball, a quarter ball, an eighth ball, &c.

These terms, however, employed in this sense, are liable to convey a wrong idea to persons unacquainted with the game, as they by no means coincide with what is usually understood by similar expressions in the common language of Billiards. Whenever they occur, therefore, in the progress of the present book, it is of importance that they be understood to apply to the following explanation of them only.

The term a full ball, or a full stroke, is meant to imply that the contact of the balls is full and complete; or that the central point of one ball becomes exactly opposed to the centre of the other, as in Figs. 10 and 15. By the term a three-quarter ball is understood that at the time of contact, the striking ball is made to cover three-quarters of the object ball; and in consequence that three parts of the former are

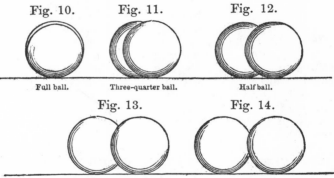

Fig. 10.   Fig. 11.   Fig. 12.

Full ball.   Three-quarter ball.   Half ball.

Fig. 13.   Fig. 14.

Quarter ball.   Fine ball.

opposed to, or come in contact with, a corresponding three parts of the latter, as described in Figs. 11 and 16. A half ball denotes that only half of each ball partakes of the stroke; or, in other words, that the centre of each is the extreme point of contact, vide Figs. 12 and 17; and a quarter ball denotes that merely one-fourth of each comes in contact as a half ball, vide Figs. 13 and 18; and in the eighth (or fine) ball, (Figs. 14 and 20;) the edges of the balls only are made to touch each other. And so for third and sixth balls.

We shall now proceed to represent the motions created by each particular mode of contact above described, in the form of diagrams, as most likely to impress a clear idea upon the mind of the reader.

Fig. 10. THE FULL BALL. Whenever the contact of the balls is accurately centrical, it follows of necessity, that the course which the object ball obtains, in consequence of the impulse of the striking one, must be precisely the original direction of the course of the latter; or that the direction acquired by the first ball, from the action of the instrument, and that obtained by the second, in consequence of its contact with the first, must, united, form a straight line. This is what is usually called a straight stroke. Vide Fig. 15, in which *a a* represents the striker's ball, *b*, the object ball, *c d*, a line drawn through the centre of each, and signifying the direction of the stroke before and after contact.

Fig. 15.   Fig. 16. Fig. 17. Fig. 18. Fig. 19. Fig. 20.

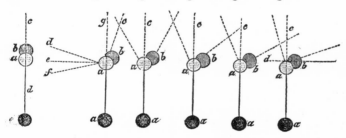

Full ball.   Three-quarter Half ball. Third ball. Quarter ball. Fine ball.
ball.

Fig. 11 and 16. THE THREE-QUARTER BALL. When a ball is propelled against three-quarters of another, the direction of the motion obtained by the one ball, will differ materially from that acquired by the other. Supposing *a*, Fig. 16, be the striker's ball, the greater part of the velocity imparted to it by the instrument with which it is projected, will be communicated to *b*, which will in consequence be propelled in the direction *b c*, whilst *a* will be reflected from its original course to *d*, if a moderate degree of strength only be employed in the stroke, and to *e*, if the ball be propelled forcibly; and by a particular modification of the action of the cue, afterwards to be spoken of, to *f.* Vide p. 525, (the low stroke.)

Fig. 12 and 17. THE HALF BALL. A half ball, or a contact, in which the half of one ball is covered by half of the other, produces in each an equal motion, both with regard to direction, strength, and velocity. Thus in figure 17, *a* and *b* separate from each other at equal distances from *c*, a line drawn through the point of contact.

Fig. 18. THE THIRD BALL. In the case of the third ball, the course described by *a*, the striker's ball, approaches nearer to the straight line, whilst that of *b*, the object ball, deviates more considerably from it.

Fig. 13 and 19. THE QUARTER BALL. In the quarter stroke represented in this figure, it will be seen, that the striking ball, *a*, obtains a nearer approximation to the perpendicular, drawn through the point of contact, and that the ball *b* is more widely reflected from it. And in proportion as the stroke is more fine, or the less the degree of contact, so will the angle formed by the acquired course of the object ball, with the original direction of the striking ball, on the line *c*, be more considerable, and the angle formed by the course of the striking ball, previous to contact, with the direction it obtains subsequently, will be smaller.

Fig. 14 and 20. THE EIGHTH OR FINE BALL. The relative directions obtained by the balls, when their extreme points only come in contact, is precisely the reverse of that produced by the three-quarter ball, above described: the object ball approaching more or less nearly to the parallel *d*, and the striking ball to the perpendicular *c*, in proportion as the stroke is more or less fine.

The motion which the striking ball obtains after contact with that against which it is struck, will in every case be modified by the particular action of the instrument with which the stroke is given; and more especially by the particular action of the cue. There are four principal points in the ball to which the cue is occasionally applied for different purposes; namely, 1. The centre. 2. Below the centre. 3. Above the centre, and level with the table. 4. Above the centre, and oblique with regard to the level of the table. The more minute divisions shown in the seventeen points of the striking or cue ball, at page 527, are all more or less modifications of this force.

1. THE CENTRAL STROKE, (see Figs. 1 and 3). This is the usual and common mode of striking. The cue ought always to be applied to the centre of the ball, unless there are any of the objects in view to be presently mentioned. The stroke is not only more sure with regard to the action of the instrument, but a more accurate and even motion is imparted to the distant ball. This mode of striking is universally employed in all common hazards; in the making of common canons; in playing at the cushion to obtain an even reverberation of the ball; and in those particular cases where it is designed that all the motion acquired by the first or cue ball should be imparted to the second or object ball, in such a manner, that the former shall lie dead, or remove little after contact*.

2. THE LOW STROKE. When a ball is struck a little below the centre, its progress will be retarded, a little lower it will be arrested, and by hitting it lower still, that is, making what is designated the *low stroke*, (No. 7, Fig. 24,) it will recoil from that against which it is propelled, with a slow whirling motion; a circumstance which affords an advantage peculiar to the cue-player, and which often enables him to score under the most adverse circumstances. This latter stroke is usually employed in making canons, where the three balls form either a right angle or less than a right angle; in effecting the losing hazard, when the object ball is too far beyond the pocket to allow of its being made in the common mode of striking; and in playing three-quarter balls,

---

* Although this observation is theoretically correct, yet it is necessary to observe, that it is by no means generally so, in a practical point of view. When the balls are near to each other, the central stroke, it is true, will produce the effect here described, or the one ball will impart to the other the whole of the velocity or quantity of motion communicated to it by the action of the original moving power; but when the balls are farther separated from each other, it will be necessary, in order to produce this effect, to play the low stroke for a recoil, otherwise unavoidable inaccuracies, either in the table or mode of projection of the ball, will frustrate the design of the striker. In the examples therefore under particular games, in the succeeding part of the work, whenever it is intended that the striker's ball shall remain dead, it is prescribed to him to play the low stroke.

when it is expedient to use only a very moderate degree of strength.

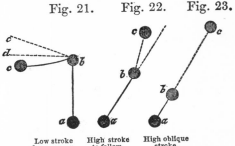

Fig. 21.　　Fig. 22.　　Fig. 23.

Low stroke
for a canon.　High stroke
to follow.　High oblique
stroke.

A diagram will render the utility of this mode of striking more obvious than a verbal description. Let *a*, fig. 21, be the striker's ball, and the object of the stroke a canon. Now it will be evident in the position of the three balls delineated, that this purpose can by no means be effected in the common way of striking; for if the ball *a* be made to receive the stroke of the cue ever so strongly in its centre, it will only recede from *b*, after contact, in the direction *b d*; if less forcibly, it will fly off to *e*; but if it be struck beneath its centre it will roll backwards to the ball at *c*.

3. THE HIGH STROKE. Above the centre, and parallel with the table. A ball, when struck above its centre, imparts only a portion of its velocity to the ball against which it is propelled, and continues its motion onwards in a direction more or less straight, in proportion to the degree of fulness of the stroke. It is technically said to walk or follow. This mode of play is advantageously used to make the balls follow each other into a pocket, when they are in a line with each other, and in making canons, when the third ball is partly masked by the second: as an instance, let *a*, Fig. 22, be the striker's ball, and his design is to canon. Now if he strike his ball in the centre, the greater part of the motion he gives it will be communicated to *b*, and in consequence it will remain in nearly the position which *b* occupied; if it be struck under the centre it will recoil; but if it be made to receive the impression of the cue above its centre, it will continue to roll onwards to *c*.

4. THE HIGH OBLIQUE STROKE. Above the centre, and oblique with regard to the table. In this stroke the cue, instead of being held in the usual way, upon a level with the table, is applied to the ball with considerable obliquity, in some instances nearly perpendicularly, or in a very considerable angle with the cloth, so that the ball is forced against the table, rather than pushed smoothly over its surface, in consequence of which it obtains a leaping, instead of a continued motion; and the striker is thus enabled to force it over a contiguous ball, either after contact with it, or without touching it at all. (See fig. 8.) This mode of play is chiefly practised in order to strike the third ball when masked by the second, and in making canons when the balls are in a line with each other, and the third is at a considerable distance from the second, as in Fig. 23 : in this position of the balls, the striker, at *a*, will, by playing in this manner, be enabled either to strike the ball *c* without touching *b*, or to strike both *b* and *c* in succession.

THE PRINCIPAL SECTIONS OF THE BALL may be subdivided into a considerable number of points from which it may be struck by the cue, and each point when struck will give rise to a different motion. The student can only acquire a knowledge of these by practice, or the instruction of an expert teacher. Annexed is a diagram of the ball divided, according to Mr. Kentfield, into seventeen points, from any of which it may be struck so as to alter its direction.

Fig. 24.

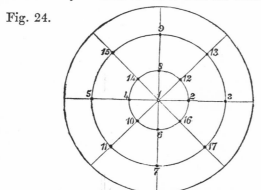

The different points for striking the ball.

The motion which the striking ball obtains after contact, will be materially modified by the degree of strength employed in the stroke, the proper regulation of which is of the utmost importance. Thus, in the case represented by the diagram 21, the ball *a*, projected forcibly, will recede after striking *b*, to *d*, but if projected with gentle strength, it will arrive at *e*.—The parts to be struck, as well as the strength to be employed in each stroke, must differ with the design in view, and will be the subject of future consideration.

We may here introduce Mr. Mardon's directions for the " side stroke," a perfect knowledge of which he deems the most important accomplishment that a billiard-player can possibly acquire. " The ball must be struck on the side it is intended to go. If it is the wish of the player that the ball should incline to the right, it must be hit on the right side, if to the left, the left side must be struck. There are several parts of the side of the ball that can be struck, and some strokes require one part to be hit, and some another, but all have greater effect when the ball is gently struck*. A very little instruction from a professor in the use of the side stroke would greatly improve the game of any amateur."

SECTION II.—OF THE ANGLES OF THE TABLE *and of the Common Hazards.*

The first thing in the game of billiards to which the attention of the novice should be directed, is what is commonly called the angles of the table, or in other words, the course which the balls obtain by reverberation from the elastic cushion. For this purpose he should at first employ one ball only; he should strike it against various parts of the pad or cushion surrounding the table, and attentively mark the course which it takes under every different relative position, and he will soon perceive what we have already stated at page 521, that "the angle of reflection will be, in every case, equal to the angle of incidence," or in other words, he will see that the direction the ball acquires after contact, will be

---

* Formerly there were *cues* made with a bevilled point for *twists* (or *screws,* as they are sometimes called), and *side-strokes.*

Fig. 25.

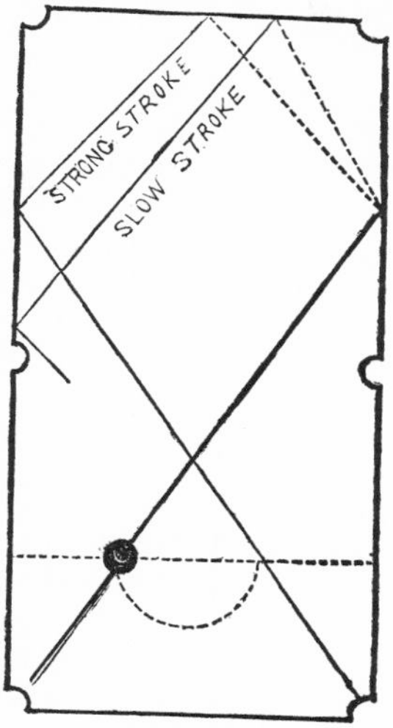

Fig. 26.

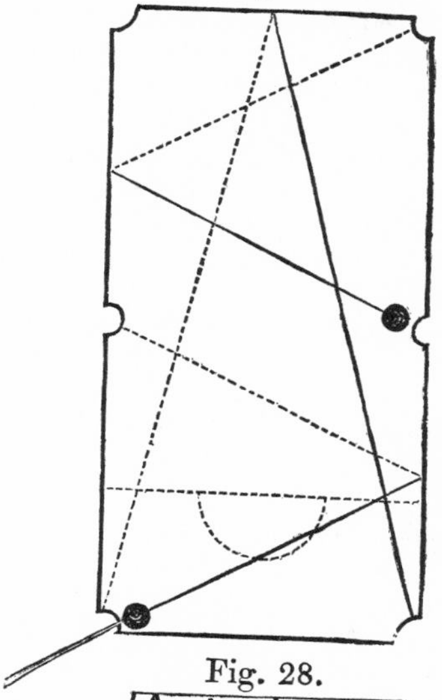

Fig. 27.

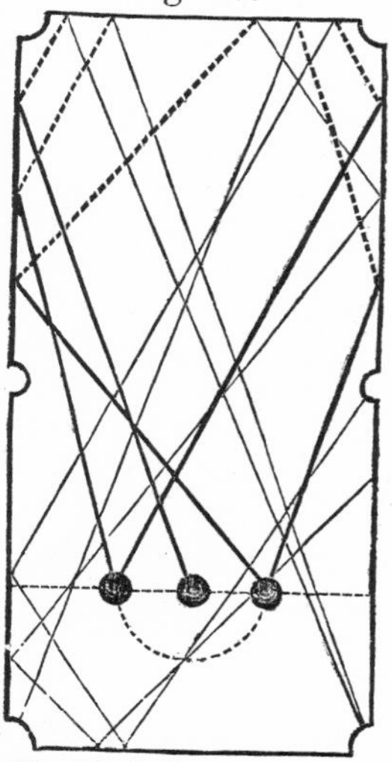

Fig. 28.

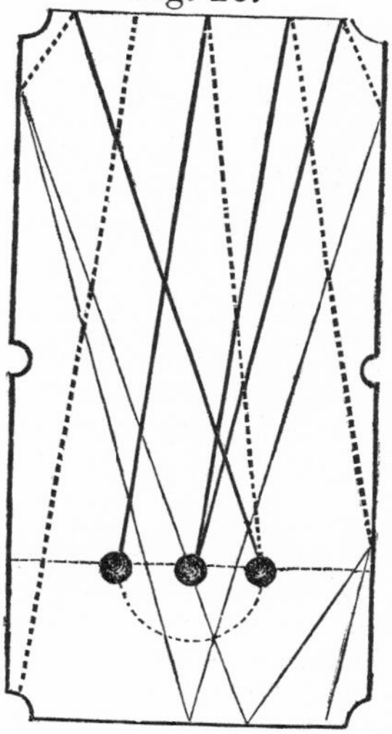

* The black lines in these, and all the following diagrams, represent the course of the ball before reverberation; the dotted lines its course after the first reflexion; the faint lines its course after the second reflexion.

2 M

precisely the reverse of, and form a counterpart to, its original course; so that before he strikes, he has only to draw a line with the cue from his ball to the particular part of the cushion he intends to strike, and then complete the angle by a corresponding one in the contrary direction, in order to ascertain with precision (provided, at least, the cloth be smooth, the cushion accurate, and the ball be propelled evenly) the event of his stroke*.

Different strengths however, as already said, will be productive of different angles, for a ball may run in the same direction to a given point in the cushion, but return from it at an angle varying with the force of the stroke. It is therefore of the utmost importance to the learner that he pay especial attention to the strengths, always keeping in mind that judicious and delicate hitting is superior to force.

We annex four diagrams of angles, two simple ones (Fig. 25 and 26) from Mr. Kentfield's work, and two somewhat elaborate (27 and 28) from White. Such examples might be multiplied ad infinitum, but the learner by practice and observation will easily form these for himself, and in so doing will the better imprint them on his memory. After a little practice with one ball, he should proceed to employ two, combining his observation of the motion acquired by the contact of

---

* In playing bricole, (*i.e.* from the cushion) one caution is absolutely necessary to be observed by the young player. He will find himself very seldom able to give an even motion to his ball after its contact with the cushion, if he strike it with the point of his cue. This arises from no defect either in the cloth, the cushion, or the rotundity of the ball; but it is the effect of the particular manner in which the point of the instrument is applied to the ball, which must be struck in the exact centre, to accomplish which requires some skill. When, therefore, the cushion is played at designedly, the striker, if he seek to obtain an accurate reverberation of his ball, will find it expedient to use the butt end of the instrument, or rather another butt, which he should keep in readiness for the purpose; for to have the handle of the cue with which he plays sufficiently flattened, would prove an obstacle to the action of his hand. The flattened portion of the cue I am myself (E. White) in the habit of using is made differently from what is usual, and I find it infinitely more commodious, and to obtain more of the action of the mace. Instead of being flattened for a considerable part of its length, as cues are generally made, it is cut off only for about two inches from its extremity, and that so obliquely as to form with the parallel nearly an angle of 45 degrees; at the same time that the end to be applied to the ball is also slanted·in the opposite direction.

these, with that obtained by their subsequent percussion against the cushion. Nothing is so essentially requisite to constitute a good player, as a perfect knowledge of the angles of the table. By an intimate acquaintance with these, the striker will often be enabled not only effectually to baffle the skill of his adversary by effecting adverse dispositions of the balls, but also to score himself under what appear to be the most unfavourable circumstances.

Having made these introductory observations on the general principles, I shall now proceed to speak of the several common strokes and hazards, which form a part of the different games, the particular laws and rules of which are afterwards to be laid down. They are introduced chiefly as lessons, which it is essentially important the learner should practise well before he attempts to play a regular game.

Fig. 29.

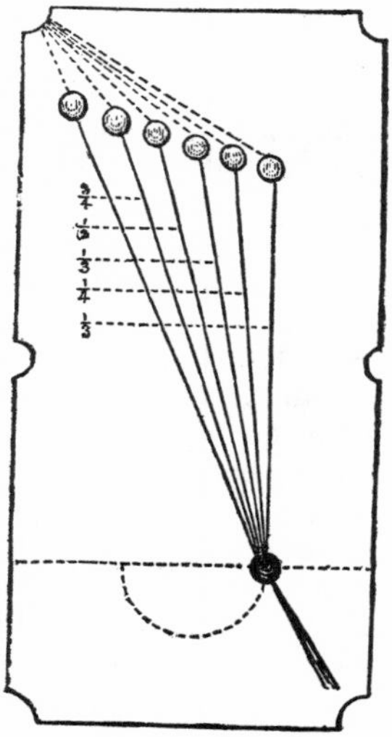

Fig. 30.

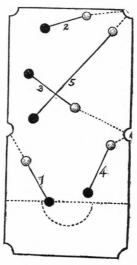

Winning hazards.
1 full ball, 2 three-quarter ball, 3 half ball, 4 third, 5 quarter ball, 6 eighth ball.

Winning hazard, explained at pages 532 and 533.

Fig. 29. WINNING HAZARDS. After the learner has acquired some intimacy with the angles of the table, his

2 M 2

next preparatory step should be to make himself master of the several common winning and losing hazards. For this purpose he will find it expedient to begin with the winning, which may be considered as a key to billiards in general, for whoever can make a good winning hazard, will find little difficulty in effecting every other which the table may present to him. The full (or straight) winning hazard should first be practised; beginning by placing the two balls near to each other, precisely in a line, and in the direction of a pocket, or what is still better, by marking a particular spot in one of the end cushions with chalk, and upon that precise point directing the stroke of the ball. After a little practice has enabled him to strike this with ease at a short distance, he is to remove the balls farther asunder, and in the end make the extent of his stroke the whole length of the table: and if his eye and hand be steady enough to enable him to strike the mark at pleasure, at this distance, he may consider himself possessing all the requisites of a good player, as the full stroke for a winning hazard requires a far greater degree of skill and delicacy than any other; for in order to produce a straight and equal motion in the distant ball, it is necessary that its centre receive the stroke with the utmost degree of precision.   The learner should next proceed to practise the other winning hazards, namely the three-quarter ball, half ball, third ball, quarter ball, and eighth ball winning hazards.

Fig. 30.   WINNING AND LOSING HAZARDS.   No. 1 illustrates a winning hazard from the baulk, into the centre pocket.   In this case, the ball should be played slow, or at least with moderate strength; for if it be played strong, however correctly, it may jump out of the pocket.   No. 2 also represents a winning hazard, which should be slowly played, since the space of entrance for the ball is confined. No. 3 this space is less narrow, and, consequently it may be more boldly played.   No. 4. is a winning hazard to be made by a moderate stroke.   No. 5 a straight hazard, which is easier in this position of the balls than if the object ball were at the point of figure 5.

With regard to winning hazards, the striker should observe one general caution, namely, if he play at the adversary's ball, to use only just strength enough to carry it to the pocket, and *if* he play at the red ball, to play strong enough to bring it away from the pocket, in the event of his failing to pocket it.* Mr. Mardon adds that if the hazard presented appears to be two to one against accomplishment, it should never be undertaken when the player has the best of the game. The ball of the adversary should be dropped close to a cushion, or the red ball doubled to a situation of equal security.

Fig. 31.   Fig. 32.

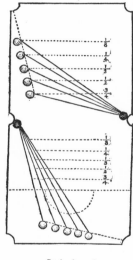

Losing hazards.   Losing hazards.

Fig. 31, 32. LOSING HAZARDS. In these figures are represented some of the most common losing hazards. They must occur, more or less frequently, in every game; and after the different degrees of strength and fulness requisite for each stroke have been once acquired, they are, of all other hazards, the most easily played, requiring only a little practice and attention to enable the striker, in every instance, to ensure suc-

* This, as a general rule, is liable to various exceptions, which will be hereafter pointed out.

cess. In playing for winning hazards, it should be observed, that the more the balls recede from a parallel with the pocket, or the more acute the angle formed by the pocket and the two balls, the more fine must be the stroke, and vice versâ. It is, however, precisely the reverse with regard to losing hazards; in playing these, the further the pocket in which the hazard is to be made, and the two balls recede from the parallel, the more full and strong will it be necessary to strike; and on the contrary, the more they approach to the straight line, the more fine and softly must the ball be played. Thus the hazard $\frac{3}{4}$ is denominated a three-quarter ball losing hazard, and requires the striking ball to be played upon three-quarters of the object ball with considerable strength; (see figures in the diagrams 31 and 32,) $\frac{1}{2}$ is a half ball losing hazard, $\frac{1}{3}$ a third ball losing hazard, $\frac{1}{4}$ a quarter ball losing hazard, and to make the hazard $\frac{1}{8}$, the object ball must be only lightly touched upon the side opposed to the pocket, into which it is designed the striker's ball shall enter. In some particular instances, however, where there are other objects in view besides the simple hazard, as also where the balls are so nearly in a line with the pocket, as to expose the striker to the danger of missing, in consequence of the fineness with which his ball must be played, and it is, at the same time, of importance to make the losing instead of the winning hazard, it becomes expedient to play nearly full instead of fine; at the same time adapting the cue to the ball above its centre, in order that the latter may continue its motion onwards, after contact, and ultimately enter the desired pocket (ff, fig. 31). The losing hazard, under a variety of circumstances, may be made to much greater advantage, by playing thus full, than in the common way, as the striker will be enabled to use a greater degree of strength in his stroke: the event, however, except to an experienced player, will be by no means so certain. In three-quarter ball losing hazards, also, it is sometimes of consequence to employ a less degree of strength than would be required in the usual manner of playing them. When this is the case, it becomes necessary to play under the centre of the ball, with gentle force; for, as has been already observed, a ball struck thus softly under its centre, will obtain the same course after contact with the distant one, as when played forbly in the usual way.

With regard to the hazards represented, in the preceding figures, the young player should invariably have in view the following rules; first, when all of the balls are out of the baulk, so to dispose of that which forms the hazard in question, that a canon, or another hazard in one of the top or middle pockets, shall remain for his next stroke: this he will in every instance be able to accomplish, by varying the action of the cue, and using more or less strength and fulness as occasion may require. And, secondly, when the third ball is within the striking line, rather to sacrifice the hazard altogether, than to play at it, when by so doing he must leave his adversary the baulk.

Fig. 33.

Fig. 34.

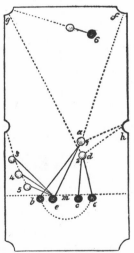

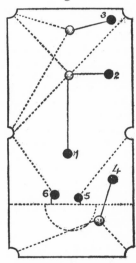

Winning and losing hazards. A Jenny.

Winning and losing hazards, explained at page 537.

Fig. 33. WINNING AND LOSING HAZARDS. Cases 1, and 2. These cases represent two hazards which, from the frequency of their occurrence, are particularly interesting to the learner, who will find his advantage in practising them frequently on the table. In these, and in similar positions of the balls, with regard to the middle pockets, the striker has the choice of three modes of playing; namely, either to try for a losing hazard in the middle pocket, and a winning hazard in a bottom pocket, by playing a three-quarter ball from the point *b*, in Case *a*, and a half ball from *c*, in Case *d*; or secondly, to attempt the losing hazard only, from *e e*, and at the same time to strike with sufficient strength, to bring the ball up again to the middle of the table, for a repetition of the stroke; or thirdly, to play for the winning hazard instead of the losing. The first of these I affirm to be invariably ill-judged play; the second is what ought generally to be attempted, at least, in the winning and losing game; and if the striker play with address, it will often be in his power to complete his game by the succession of hazards that will present themselves.* In some particular instances, however, as when the adversary's, and not the red, ball forms the hazard, and it is of importance to obtain the baulk, or when the hazard is presented by the red ball, and the adversary's ball happens to be in such a position as to afford a favourable canon, after the red ball has been holed and replaced upon the spot, it will be advisable to adopt the latter mode of play, in preference to the former. The learner will do well therefore to make each of these familiar to him, that he may employ either as occasion may require.

Cases 3, 4, 5. The hazard here delineated, constitutes what, in the language of the billiard room, is termed a JENNY; and it is one of the most common, as well as one of the most favourable cases that can present itself to the player; insomuch so, indeed, that some players who have acquired a facility of making this particular hazard, consider themselves nearly certain of obtaining the game when they are so fortunate as to have it occur to them: for by playing fine, and with a very moderate degree of strength, the ball which presents the hazard, will be propelled in a direct line against the cushion, and will return to nearly its former position; so as to admit of the same stroke being repeated, until the hazard is lost by a

---

* When the striker's ball is off the table, and he has the whole range of the ring to play from, this may be readily accomplished by every player who is tolerably well acquainted with the game. The usual source of failure among young players, is their placing their balls in an improper situation, and consequently using either too much or too little strength in their strokes. Thus in Case 1, if the striker play from the point m, (centre of the baulk line,) he will bring the object ball into the baulk; if from b, he will leave it below the middle pocket; but if he place his ball at e, such a degree of strength will become requisite, as will bring it up to nearly the same part of the table.

failure. If managed properly, it is also as generally a safe, as a successful hazard, wherever the third ball may happen to be; for the necessary gentleness of the stroke will only serve to carry the striker's ball about midway between the top and middle pockets, and near to the side cushion: but there is no hazard which requires more delicacy in playing, and consequently none which demands more practice on the part of the learner. As in the preceding cases, the success of this stroke chiefly depends upon placing the striking ball, (provided this be off the table, as is here supposed to be the case,) in the proper part of the striking ring.—It is of particular importance that the learner make these hazards familiar by frequent practice*.

Case 6. A full ball winning hazard for the pocket *g*. The red ball is here represented as occupying its proper spot, and the striker's ball is behind it in a direct line with the pocket. This is a simple and common case, but it is one, which, if managed with address, may, by a particular mode of play, be often turned to much advantage. From the balls being so near to each other, the player will be enabled to vary his manner of striking at pleasure: if therefore, he avails himself of the low stroke above described page 525), he may without difficulty make his ball return to the place which it before occupied, and thus will be able to repeat the stroke more or less frequently, proportioned to his share of dexterity. This is well deserving of practice*.

Fig. 34. WINNING AND LOSING HAZARDS. Cases 1, and 2. Each of these Cases is vulgarly termed a *Pair of Breeches*, for a half stroke will occasion the balls to separate at equal distances from the point of contact, and if the stroke be made with proper care, each will enter a pocket. Such a mode of play, however, in the generality of cases, is by no means prudent, as more advantage is usually derived from making one hazard only, and disposing the balls favourably for a succeeding; yet as, in some particular instances, the effecting the double hazard is an important advantage, the young player should endeavour to attain a facility of doing it, and this he

---

* On the present fast tables it is scarcely possible to make the *Jenny* several times in succession, as the extreme elasticity of the cushion reverberates the object ball beyond the necessary position, however fine the stroke.

will find by no means difficult. The same observations will
apply to the common Cases 3, 4. Whenever these double
hazards are attempted, one caution is absolutely necessary to
be observed by the striker, namely, always to employ such a
degree of strength, that if neither ball happen to be pocketed
by the stroke, each shall recede to some distance from the
pocket.

Cases 5, 6. The hazards represented in these Cases, although, with regard to position, nearly similar to the preceding, require a mode of play peculiar to themselves, which if
practised with address, will often ensure to the striker the most
important advantages. There are few positions of the balls
more frequent than when either the red or the adversary's ball
is before the striking ring, while the striker's ball is off the
table; and none perhaps from which a good player may score
more points. By gently touching the side of the ball he will
be able to hole himself successively in the middle pocket, and
in the end, when the ball has been so far removed, as no
longer to admit of this, he will obtain the favourable hazard
represented in Cases 1 and 2, fig. 33.—This, like the Cases 3,
4, 5, fig. 33, particularly demands the attention of the young
player, who will do well to employ a considerable time in
practising it.

Notwithstanding the particular mode of play recommended
in this case is usually so productive, it ought not to be
practised in every case; but nothing is more difficult than to
lay down fixed rules, when the propriety of certain modes of
play must almost entirely be influenced by the degree of skill
which the player may happen to possess, and by the facility
which he may have of making certain hazards in preference to
others; the young player, however, will, perhaps, find his interest in adopting the following, He will perceive that the
ball presents ten different hazards. If the adversary's ball
forms the case, and the red ball is either below the middle of
the table, or above it, and without the line; or if the case is
formed by the red ball, and the adversary's is either at the
bottom of the table, or at the top of the table, and near to a
cushion, play as above directed; but if the red ball is in the
baulk, or the adversary's ball is off the table, prefer the winning hazard and the baulk.

Fig. 35.

Fig. 36.

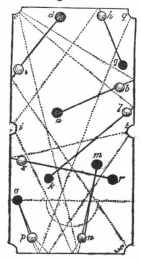

Winning Doublet Hazards.

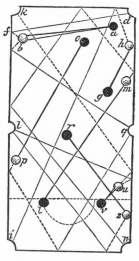

Winning Doublet Hazards.

Fig. 35.—WINNING DOUBLET (OR DOUBLE) HAZARDS.

Case a, b. A full ball winning hazard in the pocket c*.

Case d, e. A full ball winning hazard in the pocket f.

Case g, h. A full ball winning hazard in the pocket i.

Case k, l. A full ball winning hazard in the pocket c.

Case m, n. A full ball winning hazard in the pocket c.—A ¾ ball winning hazard in the pocket i.

Case o, p. A full ball winning hazard in the pocket q.—A ¾ ball winning hazard in the pocket t.

Case r, s. A full ball winning hazard in the pocket t.

Fig. 36.—WINNING DOUBLET HAZARDS.

Case a, b. A ½ ball winning hazard in the pocket d.—A ½ ball winning hazard in the pocket q.

Case g, h. A full ball winning hazard in the pocket i.

Case l, m. A full ball winning hazard in the pocket n.

Case o, p. A full ball winning hazard in the pocket q.

Case r, s. A full ball winning hazard in the pocket t.

Case v, u. A full ball winning hazard in the pocket k.—A ½ ball winning hazard in the pocket t.

* The first letter of each case distinguishes the striker's ball.

Fig. 37.   Fig. 38.

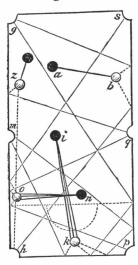

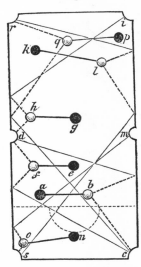

Losing Doublet Hazards.   Winning and Losing Doublet Hazards.

Fig. 37.—LOSING DOUBLET HAZARDS.

Case a, b. A $\frac{1}{2}$ ball losing hazard in the pocket g.—A $\frac{1}{4}$ ball losing hazard in the pocket h.

Case i, k. A $\frac{1}{8}$ ball losing hazard in the pocket m.—A $\frac{1}{4}$ ball losing hazard in the pocket g.—A $\frac{3}{4}$ ball losing hazard in the pocket m.

Case n, o. A $\frac{1}{8}$ ball losing hazard in the pocket q.—A $\frac{1}{8}$ ball losing hazard in the pocket p.—A $\frac{1}{4}$ ball losing hazard in the pocket s.

Fig. 38.—WINNING AND LOSING DOUBLET HAZARDS.

Case a, b. A winning hazard in the pocket d, and a losing hazard in the pocket c, by playing a $\frac{3}{4}$ ball low stroke upon the right side of b.

Case e, f. A winning hazard in the pocket d, and a losing hazard in the pocket c, by playing a third ball upon the left side of f.

Case g, h. A winning hazard in the pocket i, and a losing hazard in the pocket d, by playing a $\frac{3}{4}$ ball low stroke upon the left side of h.

Case k, l. A winning hazard in the pocket r, and a losing hazard in the pocket s, by playing a $\frac{1}{2}$ ball smart upon the right side of l.

Case n, o. A winning hazard in the pocket s, and a losing hazard in the pocket m, by playing a $\frac{1}{2}$ ball upon the right side of o.

Case p, q. A winning hazard in the pocket r, and a losing hazard in the pocket c, by playing a $\frac{3}{4}$ ball low stroke upon the left side of q.

Fig. 39.

Fig. 40.

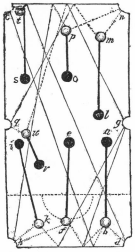

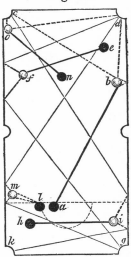

Fig. 39.—WINNING AND LOSING DOUBLET HAZARDS.

Case a, b. A winning hazard in the pocket c, and a losing hazard in the pocket d, by playing nearly full and high upon the left side of b.

Case e, f. A winning hazard in the pocket h, and a losing hazard in the pocket g, by playing a ⅛ ball upon the left side of f.

Case i, k. A winning hazard in the pocket g, and a losing hazard in the pocket h, by playing a ¾ ball upon the right side of k.

Case l, m. A winning hazard in pocket n, and a losing in q, by playing a ½ ball on the left side of m.

Case o, p. A winning hazard in the pocket h, and a losing hazard in the pocket n, by playing a ¾ ball low stroke upon the right side of p.

Case s, t. A winning hazard in the pocket c, and a losing hazard in the pocket d, by playing a ⅛ ball smart upon the right side of t.

Case v, u. A winning hazard in the pocket q, and a losing hazard in the pocket g, by playing a ½ ball smart upon the right side of u.

Fig. 40.—WINNING AND LOSING DOUBLET HAZARDS.

Case a, b. A winning hazard in the pocket d, and a losing hazard in the pocket c, by playing a ½ ball smart upon the right side of b.

Case e, f. A winning hazard in the pocket g, and a losing hazard in the pocket d, by playing a ½ ball strong up on the right side of f.

Case h, i. A winning hazard in the pocket k, and a losing hazard in the pocket c, by playing a ½ ball smart upon the left side of i.

Case l, m. A winning hazard in the pocket g, and a losing hazard in the pocket d, by playing a ⅛ ball upon the right side of m.—The reverse by playing a ⅛ ball upon its left side.

Case n, o. A winning hazard in the pocket c, and a losing hazard in the pocket d, by playing smartly upon o.

WINNING AND LOSING DOUBLET HAZARDS (made from the cushion). The hazards delineated in figures 35–40 are what are usually called doublet hazards*, and none require more judgment and dexterity, inasmuch as success in playing them entirely depends upon an intimate acquaintance with the angles of the table, and the precise degrees of strength necessary to be employed for different ends. In practising, as well as playing all hazards of this nature, it is of importance to mark well the precise point of the cushion to be struck by the ball previous to its reverberation. Use will make this familiar to the eye; but in learning hazards of this description, the learner will find it of advantage to measure the angle before he strikes his ball. This he may do either by means of his cue, or by the eye alone. Thus in Case *a b*, fig. 37, which presents a losing hazard in the top pocket, let him mark with his eye the particular point in the cushion which he designs his ball (*a*) shall strike after contact with *b*; let him suppose a line drawn through that part of the ball he purposes to strike, and then complete the angle by making a corresponding line above it; or, in other words, marking the course which the ball *a* must of necessity obtain, after striking the cushion, provided the angle of reflexion equal the angle of incidence. By this means it will be obvious to him that his stroke must, in this case, fail of success, and that it will be necessary to play fine upon the ball, so as to strike the cushion at the point marked, and enter the pocket *g*.

Nearly the same observations will apply to various winning and losing doublet hazards; the principal of which are here delineated. It has however been already observed, that it is very generally of more advantage to pocket one ball than two; and it may indeed be laid down as a general rule, to make the single in preference to the double hazard; but there are various exceptions to this, which will be pointed out in the examples applicable to the particular games. Every player therefore ought to be able to make either as circumstances may require†;

---

* Doublet. A mode of play which consists in striking the ball against one of the cushions, so as to make it rebound to the opposite side. Striking two cushions is, by some, called double double.

† What is here said should be understood with some limitation. It is not to be supposed that any player, however expert, will be able to make

and there are very few positions which a ball can occupy, in which it will not present, at the same time, a winning hazard, a losing hazard, and a double or winning and losing hazard.

CHAPTER III.

OF THE DIFFERENT GAMES OF BILLIARDS.

The following is an enumeration of the different games, but the only one now usually played in England, and recognised as " Billiards," is the Winning and Losing Carambole Game, played with three balls.

1. THE WHITE WINNING GAME. This game is played with two white balls, and is twelve up; which points are scored (independent of forfeitures) exclusively from winning hazards; the only object of this simplest of all the games being to pocket your opponent's ball and keep your own out*.   See Rules and Observations page 604, &c.

2. THE WHITE LOSING GAME, also twelve up is played with two white balls, and is the reverse of the winning.   All the losing hazards score for the striker, and all the winning hazards for his opponent.   The rules of the former game apply to this.   See page 606.

3. THE WHITE WINNING AND LOSING GAME. This is a combination of the two preceding; that is to say, all balls which are put in by striking first the adversary's ball reckon towards the game.   Eighteen up.

The three preceding games are by far the most simple that are played, and may be made introductory to those with three or more balls, which are more complicated and difficult.   For

every hazard, and more especially every doublet hazard of this description, that may present itself to him.   To accomplish this would require more dexterity than can ever, perhaps, be attained in the game of billiards; but a good player will have it in his power to make them more frequently, than it appears possible to the eye of an indifferent one; and he will often be able to manage this so adroitly, as to give his success the appearance of chance, and thereby delude his adversary, than whom he wishes to appear less skilful; and who, considering his defeat as the effect of luck, is often induced to repeat his game, to the unavoidable gain of his more skilful antagonist.

* " This is the original game of Billiards, but now very seldom played, perhaps on account of its monotony."—Kentfield.

a long while after the invention of the game, they were in almost exclusive use; but they are now superseded by the different caramboles, which have been introduced from France.

THE CARAMBOLE GAMES.

These are played with three balls; one red, whicʰ is neutral, and termed (after the French) the Carambole; the other two white, one of which is allotted to each player. The carambole, or red ball, is placed upon an appropriate spot at the upper end of the table, and in commencing is played at from the lower or baulk end, the object of the striker being either to make the winning or losing hazard, according to the particular form of the game, or (when the balls are on the table) to hit with his own ball the other two successively; which stroke is called a canon (formerly *carambole*), and for this he obtains two points.

When the carambole game was first introduced, it was sometimes made to consist exclusively of canons, which may be called the simple game (see page 603), played successively until a certain number of points (usually twelve) were gained; or in the manner of hazards, a stake depending upon each stroke. It is now, however, almost universally played in conjunction with either winning or losing hazards, or both; constituting the following games:—

1. THE WINNING AND LOSING GAME. In England this is the established and recognised game, and in the absence of any particular definition is, *par excellence*, regarded as *Billiards*. It is usually played 21 up, but sometimes 24, 30, 42 (*i. e.*, twice 21), 50, 63 (*i. e.*, three times 21), and even 100. The points are scored from canons, and winning and losing hazards, equally, both white and red. White hazards and canons each count two; red hazards three points. Misses and coups score to the adversary.

This game is, of all that are played the most replete with variety and amusement: indeed, the chances in it are so numerous that the odds are not usually calculated, but are generally laid according to fancy. For the Rules and Directions see page 559.

2. THE WINNING GAME. In this game, the points are obtained (independently of the forfeitures, which every game has peculiar to itself,) by winning hazards and canons.

Losing hazards, misses, and coups are forfeits to the adversary. The game is eighteen up*. As it is subject to fewer chances than the winning and losing game, it is sometimes preferred by good players. It is the principal game played in France. Vide Chap. V., page 597, for Rules, &c.

3. THE LOSING GAME. This is the reverse of the winning. It consists of eighteen points, which are made by canons, losing, and double hazards; counted as in the winning and losing game. Winning hazards, misses, and coups, score to the adversary. Vide Chap. VI., page 601, for Rules and Observations.

The carambole games require a considerable degree of skill and judgment, and are usually played with the cue. In these games the red ball is placed upon a spot at the further end of the table, on a line with the stringing nail (which is in the centre of the baulk line); and each antagonist, at the first stroke of a hazard, plays from the semi-circle within the baulk. After the making of canons and hazards, the grand object of the player is to obtain the baulk; that is, to pocket the white ball, and bring his own ball, and the red one, below the stringing line. By this means the opponent is obliged to play bricole from the opposite cushion, and it often happens that the game is determined by this situation. If, in commencing, the first player gives a miss, as is the common practice, this should be done from the side cushion, taking care to bring the ball into the circle.

CRAMP GAMES.

These are all played sixteen up, and generally by good players against indifferent ones, instead of giving points, in order to equalize the game. In playing them the rules of the Winning and Losing Game (page 559) are to be observed, together with some few additional ones, which are here subjoined in their respective places.

1. THE WINNING AGAINST THE WINNING AND LOSING GAME.

21 up. This is equal to giving 10 points in 24.

---

* The red winning game is played in two ways, either by the players striking alternately, or by their following their successful strokes. In the former case, the number of points are usually sixteen, in the latter, eighteen; the latter mode of play is now almost exclusively adopted.

2. CHOICE OF BALLS.

This variety consists in choosing each time which ball the player pleases. This is an incalculable advantage, and is usually played against losing and winning.

3. THE BRICOLE GAME.

Bricole is being obliged to strike a cushion, and make the ball reverbrate or recoil from it previous to hitting the adversary's ball. This is a great disadvantage; and is reckoned, between equal players, equivalent to about eight or nine points. When both players play bricole, the game is usually ten points in number, and these are scored from bricole hazards and forfeitures only*

At this game, any player striking the adversary's ball, without previously making a rebound from the cushion, forfeits one point.

Should the player, after striking his adversary's ball without a previous rebound from the cushions, pocket his own ball, or force it over the table, he forfeits three points.

And if, after playing bricole, and striking the ball of his adversary, he pocket his own ball, or force it over the table, he forfeits two points.

4. THE BAR-HOLE GAME.

This game (now quite obsolete) is so called from the hole being barred, which the ball should be played for; and the player striking for another hole. When it is played against the common game, the advantage for the latter, between equal players, is reckoned to be about six points.

5. TWO POCKETS TO FOUR.

This game is said to be equal to giving about five in sixteen, and all balls that go into the pockets score for the parties to whom they respectively belong. Canons count. Between players of equal strength the odds are very small.

* Mr. Kentfield says " A person to play this game against the 'Winning and Losing' would be giving his adversary immense advantage; for if the player of this game could give his adversary ten out of sixteen at the Winning and Losing ' game, the adversary could give him ten at this."

6. One Pocket to Five.

In this game one of the players has one pocket only, and the other player five pockets; the game is scored in the same manner as the last, and canons count. The player at it, although he seems, to those unacquainted with the game, to have the worst, has in fact the best of it*; for as all balls which go into the one pocket reckon, the player endeavours to lay his ball constantly before that pocket, and his antagonist frequently finds it very difficult to keep one or other ball out; particularly at the leads, when the one-pocket player lays his ball (which he does as often as he can) on the brink of the pocket, leading for that purpose from the opposite end of the table. This should seem to be a favourite game with Mr. Kentfield, as he states that he has played fifty thousand games with one gentleman alone.

7. Side against Side.

In playing this game, one player takes the three pockets on the one side of the table, and the other takes the three on the opposite side; and the game is scored as in the two former games. It is of course an equal game.

If the striker has made the last hazard in the game, and his adversary takes up a ball off the table, the game is over, and the striker wins it, although his ball should afterwards go into his adversary's pocket.

If the striker, after having made the last hazard in the game, should take up or move the balls when running, so as to prevent them going into his adversary's pocket, he loses the hazard.

If the striker make a hazard in the adversary's pocket, and at the same time forces his ball off the table, the hazard scores against him.

8. Hazards.

Hazards are so called because they depend entirely upon the making of hazards, there being no account kept of any

* This is Mr. White's remark, but the justice of it is not apparent. Mr. Kentfield and others consider the odds as 50 out of 100, where the players are equal; but when a practised player at this game is opposed to a novice, the odds are very much diminished, especially as canons count.

game. Any number of players may play, by having balls which are numbered; but the number seldom exceeds six, to avoid confusion. The person, whose ball is put in, pays so much to the player, according to what is agreed upon to be played for each hazard; and the person who misses pays half the price of a hazard to him whose ball he played at. The only general rule is not to lay any ball a hazard for the next player; which may be in a great measure avoided by always playing upon the next player, and either bringing him close to the cushion, or putting him at a distance from the rest of the balls. The table, when hazards are played, is usually paid for by the hour.

9. THE GO-BACK, OR PULL-DOWN GAME.

This game is said to be equal to giving about six in the sixteen, but all depends on the goodness of the play with regard to odds; the better the player the less will be the odds. The player of this game must win it at some one interval of his adversary's scoring; for every time the adversary makes a canon*, or hazard, all the points which the go-back player has made are taken off, and he has to re-commence. Against a Kentfield the odds would scarcely avail an inferior or even an ordinary player. The game is often played 21 up, sometimes even 50, giving points. In such cases the odds are of course greatly increased. Mr. Kentfield will occasionally give the long odds of the Go-back game with one pocket to five.

10. THE DOUBLET GAME.

In this game, which White says is usually played with two balls, no hazard is scored unless it is made by a reverberation from the cushion. The disadvantage compared with the white winning game, against which it is usually played, is estimated at five points. If played against the Winning and Losing Game the odds are increased. It is sometimes played as an even game, both players having to play the doublet.

The game is scored by doubles and canons (when played with three balls); the losing hazards, without a double,

* This is Mr. Kentfield's rule. In London a canon does not take off the points already scored, from the go-back player, but only a hazard.

score against the striker, and winning hazards do not score at all*.

When played with three balls as an even game, it becomes the established game of FRENCH BILLIARDS, and does not belong to the class of Cramp Games, although placed here in conformity with White's arrangement.

11. THE COMMANDING GAME.

In this game the adversary has the power of choosing at which ball the striker shall play. It is usually played by a good player against the common game of an indifferent one, and is equal to giving twelve points out of sixteen. The following rules are to be observed in addition to those of the Winning and Losing Game.

If the striker play at a different ball from that commanded, his adversary may replace the ball so played at.

If the striker should miss the ball he is commanded to play at, and strike the other, he loses one for the miss and the balls must be replaced; and, should he make a hazard or canon, it does not score.

If the striker's ball be so situated that he cannot get at the ball he is commanded to play at, so as to score, he must give a miss, or hit it in the best way he can.

If the striker's ball be touching one ball, and he is commanded to play at the other, he may, if he can do so without moving the ball in contact with his own, score all the points he makes by the stroke.

If the striker is commanded to play at the ball that is touching his own, it cannot be a fair stroke.

13. THE LIMITED GAME.

In this game the table is divided by a line or boundary beyond which the striker cannot pass his ball without a forfeiture. It is uninteresting, and rarely played

14. THE WHITE BALL AGAINST THE RED.

One plays at the white ball, and the other at the red, and neither of them is allowed, under any circumstances, to play at the other ball. As the red hazards score three points,

* Kentfield.

while the white score only two, the odds are about six or seven out of sixteen.

15. The Cushion Game.

This whimsical game consists in the striker playing his ball from off the top of the cushion (*i. e.* the frame) at the baulk end of the table, instead of following his stroke upon the table, in the customary manner. It is usually played in the winning, or the winning and losing game; and the disadvantage, among even players, is estimated at six points.

16. The Stop, or Non-cushion Game.

This game is equal to giving about half the points. The following are the peculiar rules:—

If the striker's ball touch the cushion he loses one point; but no more, even though it touch several times.

If the striker make a canon or hazard, and his ball afterwards touch the cushion, he loses one point, and does not score the canon or hazard.

In playing for a losing hazard, if the ball go into the pocket, although it may touch the edge of the cushion in going in, it scores, provided it be not by a double from a cushion.

In playing back at a ball in baulk, the striker is allowed to strike one cushion; but if he strike the second he loses one point.

FOREIGN GAMES.

The French Game.

This game is much the same as our Winning Game, except that the players are not confined to the half circle in the baulk: and when the ball is in hand, they must stand within the limits of the corner of the table. But the favourite game of the French, and the one in which they excel, is the " Doublet " game.

The Russian Game.

This game is played with five balls, and there are several ways of playing it, as pocketing the balls in the respective pockets, according as they are placed; the canon counting two, three, four, &c., according to the ball from which it is made; following the stroke after making a canon; not following the stroke after making a canon; the winning game, the losing game, &c., &c. The following is the general way of playing it in this country. The balls are two white ones, and a red, a blue. and a yellow one. The red ball is placed on the winning game spot; the blue on the centre of the baulk line, and is considered in baulk; and the yellow in the centre of the table, immediately between the two middle pockets.

The game is forty in number, and is scored by winning hazards, canons, and forfeits

The red ball may be pocketed in any pocket, and scores three; the blue may be pocketed in any pocket, and scores four; the adversary's ball may be pocketed in any pocket, and scores two; the yellow ball* must be pocketed in the middle pockets only. and scores six; a canon scores two; but there are no successive canons; that is, you cannot count more than one canon at a stroke.

The striker, in leading off, or when the ball is in hand, is not confined to the half circle, but may play his ball anywhere within the stringing line.

In leading off, the striker may play his ball out of the baulk, to any part of the table he chooses, so that it be made to pass beyond the yellow ball; and his adversary must play the first stroke at the white ball. The leader's endeavour, therefore, should be to lay his ball as close behind the yellow ball as possible.

If the striker pockets his own ball he loses according to the ball he strikes, namely, four for the blue, six for the yellow, two for the white, and three for the red.

The striker by pocketing his own ball, loses all the points that he made by the stroke: so that it would be possible for him to lose twenty-one points by one stroke; that is, if he played at the yellow ball, made a canon, and pocketed all the balls†.

If the player, in giving his lead, touch one of the three balls, he loses one point; if two, two points; if three, three points; and the balls must be replaced: and if the striker's ball occupy the place of any of the three balls, he must take it up and lead over again.

* In Germany the yellow ball is called the *Caroline* or *Carline*, and the game itself is known under this title.
† Kentfield.

If the striker force his own ball off the table after making a canon or a hazard, he loses all the points he would otherwise have gained by the stroke.

If the striker forces his adversary's ball over the table, he gains two points; if the yellow, he gains six; if the red, three; if the blue, four.

THE AMERICAN, OR FOUR-BALL GAME.

This game is played with four balls; two white ones, a red one, and a blue.

The game is thirty-one up, and is scored by winning hazards and canons.

The blue ball is placed in the centre of the baulk line, and is considered in the baulk; and the red is placed on the winning spot. Pocketing the blue ball scores four; the red ball scores three; and the white one scores two. A canon from the red to the blue, or from the blue to the red scores three points; from the red, or the blue, to the white, two points; from the white to the blue, or red, two points; from the blue to the white and afterwards to the red, four points; from the red to the white and blue, four points; from the blue to the red and white, five points; and from the red to the blue, and afterwards to the white, five points; these being double canons.

The person who leads plays his ball out of baulk to any part of the table he chooses, but without striking a ball; and the adversary plays his first stroke at the white ball.

If the striker in leading off, should strike a ball, his adversary may compel him to lead again, or have the ball so struck replaced, and the white (or striker's ball) must remain where it is.

If the striker pocket his own ball, he loses two, three, or four, according to the ball he struck first.

THE SPANISH GAME*.

This game is played with three balls, and five wooden pins, which are set up in the centre of the table between the two middle pockets, about two inches and a quarter apart, forming a diamond square.

The game is thirty-one up; and is scored by winning

* Called in Germany the *Kugel-partie*, or Skettle game.

hazards and canons (the same as in the English winning game), and by knocking down the pins.

If the striker, after striking a ball, should knock down a pin, he gains two points; if he knock down two pins, he gains four points; and so on, scoring two points for every pin he knocks down. If he knock down the middle pin alone, he gains five points; but should he knock them all down at one stroke, he wins the game.

If the striker pocket the red ball, he gains three points for that, and two for each pin he may knock down at the same stroke.

If the striker pocket the white ball, he gains two points for that, and two for each pin he may knock down.

If the striker knocks down the pins with his own ball, before striking another ball, he loses two for every pin he knocks down.

If the striker pocket his own ball from another ball, he loses all the points he would otherwise have made by the stroke; for instance, if he play at the red ball, pocket it, and make a canon, and, at the same time, knock down two pins, he loses twelve points; namely, three for the red, two for the canon, two for each pin, and three for his own ball going in from the red.

If the striker causes his own ball to fly off the table, he loses three points, and if, after making a canon or hazard, he loses as many points as he would otherwise have gained.

All the rules concerning strokes, &c., at the "Winning and Losing Game," may be observed at these games.

THE GAMES OF POOL.

In lieu of Fortification Billiards, now altogether obsolete, we have "Pool," which is played in several ways. It is sometimes played with as many balls as there are players, each ball being of a different colour; sometimes with only two balls, the player playing in turns, and with both balls alternately. Sometimes the nearest ball is played at: sometimes the player selects whichever ball he pleases—but the most popular mode is that in which the striker plays at the last player; and this is considered the fairest game.

Rules and instructions for this game will be found, at page 607.

THE GAME OF PYRAMID.

This game, which consists entirely of winning hazards, can be played with any number of balls, or players, but the usual number is sixteen, viz., fifteen coloured, and one white. Two persons generally play. It is considered excellent practice for the player desirous of improvement.

The game is scored by pocketing the coloured balls: whoever has pocketed the greatest number, at the end of the game, wins.

If the game is played with an even number of balls, the last hazard counts but one; but if with an odd number it counts two.

String for the lead.—The fifteen coloured balls are placed on the table in the form of a triangle; the first, or point, being on the winning spot.

The player plays with the white ball at the coloured ones placed as above. Should he not pocket any of the coloured balls, the next player plays with the white ball, from the place where it stopped.

In pocketing one or more of the coloured balls, the player continues until he fails.

Should the player pocket his own ball, he must replace, on the winning spot, one of the coloured balls he may have already holed. Should the spot be occupied by another ball, he must place it in a line behind the ball or balls so occupying the spot or line. Should the player not have a ball, he must place the first he may pocket on the spot; or, if the game shall have been finished before he gains one, he must pay the winner one ball extra.

Missing the balls, the player must spot a ball.

Making a foul stroke, the player must spot a ball, and the next in succession plays.

Should the player pocket his own ball, and at the same time hole one or more of the coloured balls, the balls so holed are replaced, and one more is also replaced in consequence of the striker having holed his own.

All the players play with the same ball, except when there are only two remaining on the table; in that case, the last striker plays with the white, and the other with the coloured ball.

When only two balls are on the table, should the player hole his own ball, or make a miss, he loses the games.

The *Losing Game of Pyramid*, which has been introduced, of late years, differs from the above in consisting entirely of losing hazards. The peculiarity in it is, that the player, in holing his ball, is not confined to taking the one off the table which he has struck, but may remove any ball he chooses.

THE GERMAN PYRAMID GAME. (Pyramiden-Partie.)

The Pyramid game is played in Vienna according to the following rules. Twenty-one balls are arranged in the form of a triangle, touching one another closely; this is effected by means of a triangular wooden frame in which they are placed by the marker, so as to ensure mathematical exactness. The frame is removed, and the balls stand on the part of the table of which the spot forms the centre, and with the base of the triangle about a foot distant from the cushion. The object of the game is to make a succession of winning hazards, without failing once, and without making a losing hazard till the balls are all in the pockets.

The player first breaks the mass of balls with his own ball, which at the commencement is red, to distinguish it. This may be effected either by a strong stroke on the point of the triangle, or (in cases where the player is allowed to miss once) by a bricole taking the small end of the mass angularly, after which he may drive the remainder of the mass before his cue, pocketing as many as he can, except the ball he plays with. Much depends on the manner in which the balls are broken, to ensure a succession of winning strokes into the different pockets, and for this purpose it is best for the balls to be spread well over the table. The player selects whichever ball he pleases to play at any other ball so as to make a winning stroke each time. He is not limited in his choice of balls either to play with or at, only he is bound to make a winning hazard every stroke, and never to pocket the ball he plays with. The first failure forfeits the stroke, and the game has to be placed for another player. It is also necessary that three balls should be holed in each pocket, leaving two others to be disposed of at pleasure. The last stroke of all should be with the red ball, pocketing the last white ball and at the same time losing the red, either by a following stroke or a twist, or any other mode of obtaining a losing hazard in the usual games. Should all these conditions be fulfilled and the table be cleared in twenty successive strokes, with at least three balls in each pocket, the player obtains the highest degree of success, and scores 398. Should he not succeed in losing his own ball at the last, as well as pocketing, only half, 199, is scored. If he misses a stroke, so that the game is up, before all the balls are pocketed, the score is determined by the number in the pockets, provided each pocket is found to contain at least one ball. The score then is in proportion to the number distributed; as, each ball of three in a pocket counts for more than if it were only one of two; if any pocket has only one ball, it lessens the value of each of those, however numerous, in the other pockets, and a single pocket remaining empty renders the whole void, and nothing is scored for the game, whatever number of balls may have been made in other pockets. It is usual for the marker to walk round the table during the play, and warn the striker how many balls are already placed; otherwise too many might be played in the same pocket, or some be wholly neglected till too late in the game to remedy the deficiency. The same assistance is often complaisantly given by the adversary, who is perfectly inactive during the alternate games. It is, in fact, a sort of *solitaire* for each player in turn.

When the first game is over, whether successfully, or otherwise, and the score, if any, marked up, the balls are placed in the same manner for the second player, and after he is out, the first player resumes; and so on in succession. The scores of the games on each side are added up at the end of the match, and he who has scored most, wins, the bets being generally regulated by the number of points. A very small coin, or imaginary fraction of a coin betted on each point, will make the game vary sufficiently for speculation; thus, betting a quarter of a kreutzer (viz , the 12th part of a penny) the winner of a single game 398 wins about 3 florins (6 shillings) a head of his adversary, or, betting a single kreutzer (one-third of a penny) is twenty-four shillings a head on a single game, which, unless his adversary succeeds in scoring a complete game also, is difficult to recover in scores of smaller amount, which usually run only from about 30 to 80 points.

Odds are given by allowing the inferior player to make one, two, or three faults (Fehler) in the game; *i.e.*, missing his ball, or his stroke, or losing his own ball, so many times in the game.

There is less difficulty in playing the Pyramid on a German table, than on those used in England, the pockets being cut into the table, instead of being bags which extend beyond it; so that in the case of two cushioned balls, either might pocket the other by a straight stroke, which on our tables would be next to impossible; and, indeed, very considerable skill would be required to complete the game of 398 on such a table, without some practice of the peculiar style of game required. The great art consists in varying the stroke, from one pocket to another, so as to make sure of filling all, the player usually keeping the ball he plays with nearly stationary, by a *coup sec*, (*i. e.* striking the ball very low), in order to place it for the next stroke, and also to avoid the risk of a losing hazard by too strong play. The Pyramid game is very good practice for acquiring a variety of winning strokes, difficult straight hazards, &c., and especially for placing your ball*.

SAUSAGE GAME. (𝔚urſt≈𝔓artie.)

A variety of the Pyramid game was much in vogue a few years since at Vienna, under the name of the Wurst-partie, or Sausage Game, so named from the resemblance which the mass of balls, when placed for the first stroke, had to a large sausage. In this game the balls are only fifteen, consequently two are to be placed in each pocket, instead of three, as in the other game. The marking varies accordingly. The balls at the commencement of each game are arranged in a straight line from the cushion to the red spot, by means of two cues, and the mass is then broken by a hard-played ball from the baulk, diagonally, against the first ball of the mass. The game, when complete, scores 64 points.

Handicap Sweepstakes.

Three or more persons can play, and the game may extend to any number of points agreed upon. Draw lots for the order of starting. The red ball is spotted. No. 1 plays first; No. 2 follows; and the rest in rotation. The number of points made by the player, in each inning, are marked upon the slate, and when he has ceased to score, the next player commences. If a miss be made, one point is taken from the player's score, and the others do not reap any further ad-

* The balls used in the Pyramid games are generally rather smaller than those in the Carambole games.

vantage. Should the player hole his ball without striking another, he loses three points. When the balls touch, there cannot be any score ; they must in such case be broken, the red ball spotted, and the next in succession plays. Whatever the game may be, that person is the winner whose aggregate amount of the scores made in the several innings, first completes the number specified. When there are several persons desirous of occupying the table, they will find sweepstakes very amusing; and if inferior players receive an adequate number of points each person can have a fair chance of winning. At Brighton, this method of amusing many persons at once, is very popular; and it has frequently occurred, that, in sweepstakes, handicapped by Mr. Kentfield, four or five players have been at the close within one or two hazards of winning the game. It is also very attractive to spectators, and promotes a great deal of speculation and excitement.

A Match of Four.

When four persons play this game, thirty-one is the number played for, and each player is at liberty to offer his partner advice, unless it be directly stipulated to the contrary. The pocketing of your ball, whether by your adversary's winning hazard, or your own losing hazard, or two misses without an intervening hazard, or a coup put out; but not a canon. A player must have played one stroke before he can be put out.

The Game of Three, or A la Royale.

This game is played as at the winning and losing game, by three persons, each scoring his own game.

The mode of playing it is as follows:—The three players string for the lead. The ball which is nearest to the cushion has the first choice, and the second nearest, the second. The one that has to lead off, plays; the second follows, playing with the other white ball. The third plays with the ball the first played with, the first with the ball the second played with, and so on, each taking it in turn, and changing the balls alternately. He who first completes the score wins the game; the other two losing a game each.

All forfeits, such as misses, coups, &c., score for both the adversaries. If the two adversaries are so near together at the close of the game, that the forfeiture, whatever it may be makes them both out, he whose turn it was to play next wins the game.

All the rules of the winning and losing game are to be observed at this.

CHAPTER IV.

RULES, DIRECTIONS, AND EXAMPLES

FOR PLAYING THE VARIOUS GAMES OF BILLIARDS DE-
SCRIBED IN THE PRECEDING PAGES.

OF THE WINNING AND LOSING CARAMBOLE GAME.

As the winning and losing carambole is now the established game, and all others are regarded merely as varieties, it takes precedence in this division of the work. although not in the order of its chronology. Indeed, it has been found convenient for the sake of reference to the rules and examples, to reverse the order of several of the varieties, placing them rather according to their claims than their previous numerical position.

The winning and losing carambole has been referred to at page 544. We now proceed to give the details.

SECTION I.—*Rules and Regulations.*

OF STRINGING FOR LEAD.

1. The game is to commence by stringing for the lead and the choice of balls. The player must place his ball within the striking ring; and, if his adversary require it, he must stand within the limits of the corner of the table. He whose ball rests nearest to the cushion, at the baulk end of the table, wins the lead, and chooses his ball.

2. If, after the first person has strung for the lead, his adversary who follows him should make his ball touch the other, he loses the lead.

3. If the player holes his own ball, either in stringing or leading. he loses the lead*.

4. If the leader follow his ball with either mace or cue beyond the middle pocket, it is no stroke: and if his adversary chooses, he may require him to lead again.

* The terms *to hole* and *to pocket*, are used indifferently, and mean the same thing.

POSITION OF THE BALLS.

5. The red ball is to be placed on the furthest of the two spots, at the upper end of the table (which is generally within thirteen inches of the cushion).

6. When either of the white balls is in hand, that is, has been holed, or forced off the table, it must be played from the striking ring, when it is the striker's turn to play, as at the commencement of the game. The ball, it may be observed, must be made to pass the line by a regular stroke, and not merely be laid conveniently within the baulk, on the plea of scoring a miss. When it is wished to place the ball in baulk, it must be reverberated from one of the cushions outside the line.

7. When the red ball has been holed or forced over the table, it must be replaced on the same spot where it originally stood, at the beginning of the game, and the present striker is bound to see it thus replaced, otherwise he can win no points while it is off the spot, and the stroke he may make is to be deemed foul. But it must not be replaced until the balls have done rolling, as the stroke is not finished till the balls stop.

8. After the adversary's ball is off the table, and the two remaining balls are either within the baulk line or upon it (then called line balls), they are "in baulk:" and the striker must play from the ring against a cushion outside the baulk, so as to occasion his ball in returning to hit one of the balls in the baulk (which if he does not, he loses one point; see Penalties).

9. When the red ball is pocketed, or off the table, and the spot on which it should stand is occupied by the white ball, it must be placed in a corresponding situation at the other end of the table; but if that should be occupied also by the other white ball, it must be placed in the centre of the table, immediately between the two middle pockets; and wherever it is placed, there it must remain, until it be played, or the game be over*.

10. If a ball is made to go to the brink of a pocket, and after

---

* It is the custom of some billiard rooms, if the spot be occupied by the white ball, to place the red ball in the centre of the table; but it is much more common to place it at the other end; besides, the situation is more uniform.—Kentfield.

sensibly standing still, should fall into it, the striker wins nothing, and the ball must be put on the same brink where it stood, before the adversary makes his next stroke; and should it again fall into the pocket at the instant the striker has played upon his ball, and before it touches, so as to prevent the success of his stroke, the striker's and the adversary's balls must be replaced in their original position, or as near as possible thereto, and the striker must play again.

11. If the marker, or a bystander, touch either of the balls, whether it be running or not, it must be placed as near as possible to the place it did or would apparently have occupied.

Mode of reckoning the Points.

(*The principle of calculation, it will be perceived, is, that balls pocketed off the white, without touching the red, count for two, that the red, or the balls which touch it, when pocketed, count for three, and canons, whether off white or red, invariably for two.*)

12. If the striker hits both the red and his adversary's ball with the ball he played with, he wins two points.—This stroke is called a canon.

13. If the striker with his own ball holes his adversary's ball, he wins two points. This is called a white winning hazard.

14. If the striker holes his own ball off his adversary's ball, he wins two points. This is called a white losing hazard.

15. If the striker holes the red ball, he wins three points. This called a red winning hazard.

16. If the striker holes his own ball off the red ball, he wins three points, which is called the red losing hazard.

17. If the striker holes both his adversary's and the red ball, he wins five points. If, by playing at the red ball, he holes his own and the red ball, he wins six points.

18. If the striker, by striking the white balls first, holes both his own and his adversary's ball, he wins four points. And if, by striking at the red ball first, he should hole both his own and his adversary's ball, he wins five points:—three for holing his own ball off the red, and two for holing the white ball.

19. If the striker plays at his adversary's ball first, and

2 o

should hole his own ball and the red, he wins five points:—two for holing his own ball off the white, and three for holing the red ball.

20. If the striker plays at his adversary's balls, and holes it, at the same time that he pockets his own ball, and the red, he wins seven points:—two for holing his own ball off the white; two for holing his adversary's ball; and three for holing the red ball.

21. If the striker plays at the red, and holes his own ball off the red, and the red ball, and his adversary's, by the same stroke, he wins eight points:—three for holing his own ball off the red; three for holing the red ball; and two for holing the white ball.

22. If the striker makes a canon, and pockets the red ball, he wins five points:—two for the canon, and three for the red hazard.

23. If the striker canons, and holes both the red and his adversary's ball, he gains seven points:—two for the canon; two for the white: and three for the red ball.

24. If the striker makes a canon, by striking the white ball first, and should hole either his own ball or his adversary's by the same stroke, he wins four points:—two for the canon, and two for the white losing hazard.

25. If the striker makes a canon by striking the red ball first, and by the same stroke should pocket his own ball, he wins five points:—two for the canon, and three for the red losing hazard.

26. If the striker plays at the white ball first, and should make a canon, and at the same time hole his own and his adversary's ball, he wins six points:—two for the canon, and two for each white hazard.

27. If the striker plays at the red ball first, and should canon, and by the same stroke hole his own and his adversary's ball, he gains seven points:—two for the canon; three for the red hazard; and two for the white hazard.

28. If the striker canons, by playing first at the white ball, and also hole his own and the red ball, he wins seven points:—two for the canon; two for the white losing hazard; and three for the red winning hazard.

29. If the striker canons by striking the red ball first, and at the same time should hole his own, and the red ball,

he wins eight points:—two for the canon; three for the red losing, and three for the red winning hazard.

30. If the striker makes a canon by striking the white ball first, and should hole his own ball, and his adversary's, and the red ball, he wins nine points:—two for the canon; two for each of the white hazards; and three for the red hazard.

31. If the striker makes a canon by striking the red ball first, and by the same stroke should hole his own ball, and the red, and his adversary's white ball, he gains ten points:—two for the canon; three for the red losing hazard; three for the red winning hazard; and two for the white winning hazard.

32. As long as the striker can make points, he continues game, until he ceases to count.

PENALTIES.

33. If the striker does not hit his adversary's ball, he loses one point; if by the same strokes he pockets his own ball, he loses three points (that is to say, his adversary scores so many points) and the lead*. This is called a coup.

34. If the striker happens to force either of the balls off the table, any points made by it do not count, and he loses the lead. If a ball lodges on the top of a cushion or springs from the table and strikes one of the players, or a bystander, so as to prevent its falling on the floor, it must be considered as off the table.

35. If the striker forces his own or either of the other balls over the table, after having made a canon or hazard, he gains nothing by the points he would otherwise have obtained, and loses the lead; and his adversary may, if he chooses, play on without breaking the balls.

36. If the striker wilfully forces his own ball off the table

* When the striker gives his adversary a point, by missing intentionally, it is sometimes required that he pass his ball beyond the middle pocket; or in the case of his adversary having the baulk, that he pass both the other balls by playing bricole; but these are rules now seldom enforced.

without striking another ball, he loses three points; but if the ball goes over by accident, he loses one point only for the miss*.

37. If the striker, in the act of striking, touches his ball, and make his mace-or cue go over or past it, he loses one point.

38. If the striker's ball is over the pocket, and he should, in the act of striking, miss it, but in drawing his cue back should knock it into the pocket, he loses three points, this being a coup.

39. Whoever proposes to break the balls, and his adversary agrees to it, the person who made the proposal loses the lead.

40. If the striker interrupts the course of his own ball, when it is running towards a pocket, after having made a miss, and it is the opinion of the marker that it would have been a coup, that is, have entered the pocket, had it not been interrupted, he loses three points.

41. If the striker interrupt, stop, or put his adversary's ball out of its course, when running towards or into a pocket, he is subjected to the same forfeiture.

42. If, after the striker has played, the adversary should obstruct or accelerate the running of the balls in any way, it is at the striker's option to make it a foul stroke and break the balls, or have them replaced.

43. He who blows upon a ball when running, makes the stroke foul; and if his own ball was running towards a pocket, or near a pocket, and he is seen by his adversary to blow upon it, he loses two points.

44. If after the striker has made a canon or a hazard, he takes up the ball, thinking the game is over, the adversary has the option of breaking the balls, or having them replaced.

45. If after the striker has made a miss, or a coup, he takes up a ball, supposing the game to be over, he loses the game.

46. If after the striker has made a miss or a coup, the adversary, thinking the game is over, takes up a ball, he, (the last striker) may have the balls replaced as they were, or break the balls.

* To a person conversant with the game, it is not a very difficult thing to discern whether a ball is forced over the table wilfully or not; and it would be severe upon the striker to be compelled to lose three points for what may be the fault of the table.

47. If after the striker has made a canon or hazard, the adversary thinking the game is over when it is not, takes up a ball (whether running or not) he loses the game.

Foul Strokes.

48. If the striker plays with the wrong ball, it is deemed a foul stroke.

49. If the striker, after having made a hazard or canon, should move either of the balls which remain upon the table, the stroke is deemed foul.

50. If a player, in the act of striking, touch his ball with the instrument twice, the stroke is deemed foul.

51. If the striker's ball be in hand, and the other two balls within the baulk, and should he either by accident or design, strike one or both of them, without first playing out of the baulk, the adversary has the option of letting the balls remain as they are, and scoring a miss,—of having the balls replaced in their original position, and scoring a miss,—of making the striker play the stroke over again,—or of making it a foul stroke, and breaking the balls*.

52. If the striker should accidentally touch or move his own ball, without intending at the time to make a stroke, he loses no point; but the adversary may put the ball back in the place where it stood. Should it not be replaced before the stroke is made, the adversary may claim a foul stroke.

53. If the striker's ball be in hand, and he play, at a cushion within the baulk, in order to strike a ball that is out of it, it is a foul stroke.

54. No one has a right to take up or otherwise move a ball, without permission of the adversary. And if in the course of the game, a person take up a ball, supposing it to be in hand, the adversary may break the balls, or have them replaced to his own satisfaction.

---

* Breaking the balls is to take them all off the table, place the red on its spot, and for both parties to begin again from the baulk.

At first sight this would appear a harsh rule, with a heavy penalty annexed to it; but perhaps the adverse party may have laid his plans with skill, and he must not, therefore, have them unfairly frustrated with impunity. Besides care *must* be taken that the adversary be not a sufferer by the unfair play, or blunders, of the striker.

55. If either of the players, in the act of striking, happens to move his own, the adversary's, or the red ball, from the place it occupied on the table, the stroke is deemed foul.

56. If the striker's ball be close to the ball he plays at, and he plays the stroke with the point of the cue. it is fair; but if he plays it with the butt-end, the marker must decide whether it be foul or fair*.

57. If the striker plays upon a ball which is still running, the stroke is considered foul.

58. Whoever stops a ball when running, either with the hand, the instrument with which he plays. or otherwise, loses the lead, if his adversary does not like the ball he has to play at the next stroke.

59. If the striker, after having made a hazard, or canon, interrupts or alters the course of his own ball, the stroke is foul; and he cannot score any of the points he may have thus made.

60. If the striker plays with both feet off the ground, the stroke is deemed foul.

61. Whoever strikes the table when the ball is running, makes the stroke foul.

62. If the striker throws his mace or cue upon the table, so as to baulk his adversary, he causes him to make a foul stroke.

63. If the striker, in playing a stroke, should make his mace or cue touch both balls at the same time, it is deemed a foul stroke, and if discovered by his adversary, he wins nothing for any points he may make by the stroke, and his adversary may break or part the balls.

64. All misses to be given with the point of the cue, and the ball struck only once; if otherwise given, the adversary may claim it as a foul stroke, and enforce the penalty, or may make the striker play the stroke over again, or have the ball or balls replaced where they stood.

65. Whenever a foul stroke is made, it is at the option of the adversary either to break the balls, and play from the striking ring, as at the beginning of the game, or if the balls happen to be in a favourable position for himself, to suffer

* N.B.—The principle which ought to govern the decision of the marker in such a case is this, namely, that the striker's butt must quit his ball before it comes in contact with the other ball.

the preceding striker to score the points he may have made; which the marker is obliged to do, in every case where the balls are not broken*.

Of Bystanders.

66. The adversary only, and not a bystander, is bound to see that the striker plays fair, which if he neglect to do, the striker wins all the points he may have made by that particular stroke, and the marker is obliged to score them.

67. No person has a right to proclaim whether a stroke be fair or foul until asked, unless they are playing a four match; and in that case none but the player and his partner have a right to ask it. And no person, except the adversary, has a right to inform the striker that he has played, or is about to play, with the wrong ball.

68. Should a dispute arise between the players concerning the fairness of a stroke, the marker alone is authorized to decide the question, and from his decision there is no appeal: but if, through inattention, he happen to be incompetent to make the required decision, he should inquire the particulars of the case from disinterested bystanders, and, upon demanding silence, should go round the table to each person separately, and be particularly careful to ask if he has any bet depending thereon, if he understands the game, and the nature of the dispute then in question. And the majority of the disinterested company present may decide the dispute. But no person has any right to interfere until appealed to by one or both players.

Miscellaneous.

69. If the striker plays with the wrong ball, and a canon or hazard be made thereby, the adversary may have the balls broken; but if nothing be made by the stroke, he (the adversary) may take his choice of balls the next stroke, and with the ball he chooses he must continue to play until the game is over. But the playing with the wrong ball must be discovered before the next stroke is played, otherwise, no penalty attaches to it.

* Enforcing the penalty for a foul stroke is entirely at the option of the adversary.

70. If the adversary does not see the striker play with the wrong ball, or seeing it, does not choose to enforce the penalty, the marker is bound to score all the points that may have been made by the stroke.

71. If a player, in the act of striking, is baffled or impeded in his stroke by his adversary or a spectator, he has a right to recommence his stroke.

72. If the striker, in attempting to make a stroke, does not touch his ball, it is no stroke.

73. If the striker in taking aim moves his ball, so as to strike the ball he is playing at, without intending to strike it, it is a stroke, and must pass as such, unless the adversary chooses to let him play the stroke over again.

74. If the striker, in the act of striking moves his ball ever so little, it is a stroke.

75. If the striker's ball be in hand, and he in playing from the baulk, should move his ball in the act of striking, it is a stroke, although the ball should not go out of the baulk; but the adversary may if he chooses, compel him to play the stroke over again.

76. If a ball is found to have been changed during the course of the game, and it is not known by which player, the game must be played out with the balls as they then are, even though only two strokes may have been made before the mistake is discovered.

77. He who leaves the game before it is finished, and will not play it out, loses the game, although he may only have made one stroke.

78. If a person agrees to play with the cue, he is obliged to play with it during the whole of the game or the match; but if no agreement has been previously made, he may at any time change it for the mace, and vice versâ: neither party, in such case, having any right to object to either mace or cue being played with in the said match. But when the parties agree to play mace against cue, the mace player has no right to use a cue, nor has the cue player any right to use a mace, without permission from his adversary.

79. When a person agrees to play with a cue, he must play every ball within his reach with the point thereof; and if he agrees to play with the butt of the cue, he has no right at any time to play with the point, without permission.

Also, when the parties agree to play point and point of the cue, neither of them has any right to use the butt, during the match, without permission; but every person who plays with a cue may when he thinks proper use a long one, and in some cases he may play with the point of a long cue to great advantage.

80. With regard to betting —Each person who proposes a bet, should be very cautious to name the precise sum; and also should be extremely careful not to offer a bet when the striker has taken his aim, or is going to strike, lest it may disturb or interrupt him; and no bet ought to be proposed on any stroke, that may have any tendency to influence or lessen the judgment of the player.—If A proposes a bet which is accepted by B, it must be confirmed by A, otherwise it is no bet.—If any bets are laid on the hazard, and the striker should lose the game by a miss at the stroke in question, it cannot be a hazard: the game being out by a miss. In all cases those who bet are to abide by the determination of the players, and the betters have a right to demand their money, when their game is over, to prevent disputes*.

81. Every person ought to be very attentive, and listen for the stroke, before he opens the door of a billiard-room.

82. The striker has a right to command his adversary not to stand facing him or near him, so as to annoy or molest him in his stroke.

83. Each party is to take care of his own game, and his adversary has no right to answer any questions; as—If the ball be close?—If he touch the ball? &c. &c. These and other similar circumstances the player is to discover himself.

84. The marker should be careful to make those persons who do not play, stand from the table, and give room for the players to pass freely round.

85. Those who play, ought to be particularly careful and attentive to their strokes, when any bets are depending thereon; but even should they play carelessly, the bets must in every case be decided by the event of their strokes.

---

* With regard to betting, we may here take occasion to observe that players in the least degree nervous should never back themselves for a stake which can make them feel anxious. The best players are apt to be disturbed in their play by the excitement occasioned, and inferior players have been known to be quite prostrated by it, and even to have fainted away.

86. No person has any right to chalk or otherwise mark the cushions or table, for the purpose of directing the angles.

87. No person has any right to discover to the player in what manner he may play his ball to the greatest advantage. This is often done by signs, winks, and various gestures; and when discovered by the adversary, he may prevent the striker from scoring the points he may have made by the stroke. Neither, after a stroke has been played, hath any one a right to detect any error the striker may have committed, as a stroke of the same kind may occur repeatedly in the same game.

SECTION II.

GENERAL INSTRUCTIONS*.

1. After having strung for lead, in playing first, if the match be pretty equal, and no considerable odds are given, it will be prudent to miss the red ball intentionally, and lay yourself in the baulk, about midway between the striking ring and one of the side cushions, in an advantageous position, to enable you to take advantage of any hazard your adversary may leave after the succeeding stroke: but if you give considerable odds, then bring the red ball into the baulk, in such a way, as either to double it into the corner pocket, or failing in this, to leave it at some distance from it. This is to be effected by placing your ball at one extremity of the ring, and striking a high stroke full upon the red ball, with a strength just sufficient to make it recede a little from the cushion, when brought to the bottom of the table, by which you will leave your own ball near to the side cushion at the top. Avoid placing it close to the cushion, as the adversary, taking advantage of your crippled position, might play for a score that he would not, under other circumstances, have attempted. Many make it their object to bring both balls into the baulk, by playing a half ball strong upon the red; but this is too hazardous to be generally attempted, as its failure must in every case be attended with the utmost risk. It is possible for the striker to

---

* These are, with scarcely an exception, White's directions, and inculcate the policy of leaving no chance whatever to your adversary; but they are overstrained, and a player who followed them rigidly, would be as little likely to receive pleasure in the game as to afford it to his antagonist.—H. G. B.

pocket the red ball off the spot; and Mr. Pratt can generally accomplish this feat, and has taught it to others successfully; but it is a very hazardous stroke, and failure would be very likely to leave the balls in a dangerous position.

2. If you are second player, and your adversary has previously given a miss, and brought his ball into the baulk, endeavour so to lay your own and the red ball that he may obtain no points at the succeeding stroke. This is most effectually done by striking half a ball gently on the red, so as to bring it, after recoiling from the top cushion, almost close, about midway between the middle and top pockets; and your own ball, in consequence, nearly in the same position, on the opposite side of the table: but if by his first stroke he has brought the red ball into the baulk, and left himself above the middle pocket, and in such a situation as to afford you no losing hazard, then carry his ball gently towards the corner pocket, so as to lay it close under the cushion, if you fail in your attempt to hole it.

3. In playing bricole* (from the cushion), in order to strike a ball situated in the baulk, remember the axiom that "the angle of reflexion will always equal the angle of incidence." Fig. 27, and 28, are diagrams representing the different angles, which more especially require the attention of the striker. From these, it will be seen, that, in such cases, there are two modes of playing; 1. To strike at the top cushion, in order to make the stroke by one simple reverberation; 2. To direct the ball to the corner or side cushion, in order that it may be twice reverberated, and enter the baulk obliquely: the former is the safer and easiest; the latter is the most advantageous in certain situations of the balls, as it enables the striker to canon under a greater variety of circumstances. In every case it is of importance to observe one caution, namely, to play with sufficient strength to bring your ball out of the reach of your adversary, if you fail in the object of the stroke.

4. Never make a stroke without some object in view, as by so doing, you may leave incalculable advantages to your adversary. This is a fault with most young players; they strike the balls at random, and depend more upon the chances of the

* " Playing back," as the modern phrase goes.

table than their own foresight: a fortunate hazard left after a random stroke of this description, leaves the game open, and often leads the way to a series of losses; for a skilful player will not only make the points he more immediately plays for, but will endeavour at the same time to lay the balls in such a position, as to ensure himself a hazard the next stroke.

5. Always choose that mode of play by which you have a chance of gaining most points, provided you can do so without risk; but if you are diffident of your own ability, or from the situation of the adversary, it is probable that the consequence of a failure would be a certain hazard in his favour, either decline the chance altogether, and lay the balls safe, or make that stroke which seems most sure and easy.

6. When the balls are situated so disadvantageously, as to leave no probability of your scoring off of them, let it be your object to lay your adversary in such a part of the table, that he also may make no point; namely, either close to the cushion, or out of any favourable angle.—That player will be, cæteris paribus, invariably most successful, who defends his game with the greatest address.

7. Whenever your adversary's ball is off the table, in consequence of having been just pocketed, sacrifice every doubtful hazard to the object of bringing both balls into baulk.

8. Never play at your adversary when he is close under the cushion. It is always better in this case to choose the red ball, and if you despair of scoring upon it, to lay it for a hazard in that part of the table most distant from where your adversary is situated; for if he miss in consequence of his disadvantageous position, you have, by this means, a chance of gaining four points; if he strike either ball, there are five chances to one you lose nothing by the stroke, provided the balls have been laid properly.

9. Never play at the red ball when your adversary's ball is near in, without you have a certain hazard or canon before you. Under such circumstances, if the white ball afford no favourable hazard, it is more advisable to drop it to the other extremity of the table, so as either to make it in the corner pocket, or lay it close under the cushion.

10. When you are ahead in the game, play at the white ball, in every case in which the red presents no tolerably certain hazard; and in playing at your adversary's ball, always have

two objects in view; first, to make the desired points; and, secondly, to lay your own ball safe, if you happen to fail. On the contrary, when you are backward in the game, and a tolerable red hazard presents itself, it will be right to prefer it to the white. The propriety of this caution is obvious, for the red ball being the common object of both players, it is two to one you leave a hazard, if you don't succeed in scoring; whereas, in playing with a due degree of caution at your adversary, the chances are more than equal that you leave nothing for him, if you fail to obtain the desired object.

11. Never vary your mode of striking by using the high or low strokes, without the necessity of doing so be obvious; for by frequent needless strokes of this kind, you run the risk, either of missing your cue, or striking the ball ineffectually; for a considerable degree of dexterity is required, in such cases, to prevent it acquiring an uneven motion, or assuming an unfavourable position. The cases which more especially make it requisite to strike under the centre of the ball, are, 1st, The position of the balls being such as to render the common mode of striking insufficient for obtaining the desired end: such is the case with regard to losing hazards, when the pocket and the two balls form less than a right angle; as also of canons, when the three balls are in a similar relative position: 2dly, When it is desirable to use only a gentle strength, with the design either of keeping the baulk, or retaining the balls above or below the middle pockets, at the same time that you attempt to make a losing hazard in the corner pocket; for an inconsiderable degree of strength thus employed, will be found adequate to a forcible stroke made in the common way of playing.—The chief design of striking over the centre, is to make the balls follow each other into a pocket, or to effect canons under circumstances where only an inconsiderable deviation from the straight line is required.

12. Although you may be greatly ahead in the game, never strike at the wrong ball by way of experiment, nor otherwise play carelessly; supposing it impossible for your adversary to get up with you: for by an unlucky stroke on your part, he may even win the game, although previously under the most adverse circumstances. There are so many accidental chances in the game of billiards, that it should never be considered as certain, until the whole number of points are actually made.

13. When you are close under a cushion, or otherwise situated so unfavourably as to despair of scoring, and you run the risk of leaving the balls to a disadvantage by the attempt, if there is little probability of your adversary's making the red hazard at his next stroke, it will be better, in all cases, to give an advantageous miss, than to run the chance of missing unintentionally, and thereby leaving a hazard or canon; and do not be deterred from this, by the circumstance of your adversary being ahead of the game. It is good play in many cases, thus to give him a miss, when he even wants two only of being up. Your opponent, obliged to play from a cramped position, will, in all probability, leave a good break.

14. Never be too solicitous about making canons in untoward situations of the balls, as by vain attempts, you run the risk of leaving advantages to your adversary. On the contrary a canon sometimes made happily under particular circumstances, where there are future objects in view, is followed by repeated successes, and gives a turn to the game in your favour.

15. Never play for the losing hazard when by so doing you must leave your adversary the baulk; for in this case you are likely, in the end, to lose more points than you have gained by the stroke: in the first place, a probable miss from the cushion, and afterwards, perhaps, the red hazard.

16. *Never make the white winning hazard when the balls afford any other mode of scoring*, unless you will be enabled to make a baulk by your succeeding stroke. It is always better to have three balls upon the table than two; and by pocketing the white ball when the red ball is situated unfavourably for a baulk or hazard, you give to the adversary an important advantage in his having the striking ring to play from.

17. Whenever you hole your adversary's ball, and the red ball remains upon or near the spot, and you are doubtful of making the red hazard, either give a miss, and lay your own ball in an advantageous part of the baulk; or endeavour to make a baulk by striking both balls into it; or to bring the red ball within the striking line, and leave your own at the top of the table; or to part the balls as directed in Obs. 2. The choice of one or other of these, will depend upon the position you occupy on the table.

18. Always mark well the position of the balls before you

strike, and consider the course which the ball you are striking will take after the completion of the stroke, and so regulate the strength, as to bring the latter either near a pocket, or in a favourable position for a canon. No circumstance connected with the game is so essential to success. as a judicious anticipation of the position the balls will assume after contact, and the probable consequences of every stroke.

19. Be cautious how you play for a red hazard in any pocket to which your adversary may happen to be near, and always use strength enough to bring the ball away if you fail to pocket it, otherwise he will obtain an almost certain hazard.

20. Never suffer the red ball to remain near a pocket, unless you have a dead winning hazard upon your adversary's ball; and if you are off the table in consequence of having been pocketed, and the red ball is situated near one of the baulk pockets, play at the red hazard bricole, notwithstanding you may have a tolerable losing hazard upon the white.

21. In playing white winning hazards, use a gentle strength, in order to leave the white ball near to the cushion, if you do not pocket it. In playing red winning hazards, use a strength sufficient to bring the red ball away from the pocket.

It may here be observed, as a general rule, that a thorough knowledge of strength is far more advantageous in billiard playing than the most dexterous hazard striking.

SECTION III.—*Select Examples in the Winning and Losing Carambole Game.*

Having laid down the orders to be observed in the game, and the rules and cautions necessary to be attended to by the player, we shall, in the next place, present to the reader a collection of practical diagrams, representing various positions which the balls are liable to assume; and under each, point out the most judicious mode of play : in doing which, it will be expedient, in the first place, to notice those cases which are either of most frequent occurrence, or for other reasons more particularly require the attention of the learner. and afterwards to speak of those which are more rare, or require a greater degree of skill and judgment on the part of the player.

EXPLANATION OF THE FIGURES.

In the following Diagrams, the Figures equally denote the order of the Cases, as well as the striker's ball, unless where the contrary is stated.

Fig. 41.   Fig. 42.

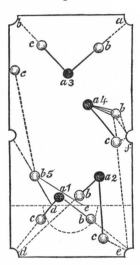

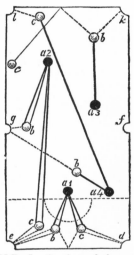

Fig. 41.   Case 1.

A full ball winning hazard upon b, in the pocket e.

A full ball winning hazard upon c, in the pocket d.

Pocket the adversary's ball and make a baulk.

Fig. 41.   Case 2.

A full ball winning hazard upon b, in the pocket d.

A losing hazard upon c, in the pocket e, by playing a ½ ball upon its left side.

Whether c be the adversary's or the red ball, make the losing hazard with sufficient strength to bring the ball to the middle of the table.

N.B. In the first of these cases it will be seen, that both balls are within the striking line; in the second, that one of them is above it. These are circumstances which should always be attentively marked by the striker, as also, in the latter case, whether the ball which is below the line be the adversary's or the red ball, and if it present a winning or a losing hazard. Whenever one of the balls is above the line, and the other which is below it, affords a losing hazard, by making which, the striker will be enabled to bring the other above also, it is invariably good play to sacrifice the baulk to the object of obtaining the advantageous hazards described in

Cases 1 & 2 of Fig. 33, and 5 & 6 of Fig. 34.

But if the ball within the line affords but an unfavourable losing hazard, or a winning one only, the prudent play is to pocket the adversary's ball and make a baulk; in doing which the striker should be cautious to play either a high or a low stroke, according to the place which the ball in the baulk happens to occupy, in order that his own may obtain such a position as will enable him either to play gently on the red ball, or reflect it from the cushion favourably for his succeeding stroke, in the event of his adversary's missing bricole.

Fig. 41. Case 3.

A full ball winning hazard upon b, in the pocket a.

A full ball winning hazard upon c, in the pocket b.

Make the red hazard by a low stroke.

N.B. This forms the reverse of Case 1.—It may be regarded as a general rule, subject, however, to exceptions, which will be pointed out hereafter, that at the bottom of the table, when each ball presents an equally good winning hazard, you ought to choose the white, and under similar circumstances at the top of the table, you ought to choose the red ball. In the latter case, after having holed the white ball, the striker would have only one ball to play at, and moreover would be in danger of leaving his game open, by affording to his adversary the advantage of the striking ring; whereas, by pocketing the red ball, he will obtain two succeeding hazards, or a canon, upon its being replaced on the contiguous spot.

Fig. 41. Case 4.

A losing hazard upon b, in the

pocket f, by playing a ⅛ ball upon its right side.

A losing hazard upon c in the pocket f, and a winning hazard in the pocket e, by playing a ¼ ball smart upon its left side.

A canon by playing a ¾ ball upon the right side of b.

Make the losing hazard upon b, with a strength just sufficient to bring it out a short distance from the cushion; and afterwards, either make the losing hazard upon c, or the winning hazard and canon, as the ball b may happen to be situated more or less favourably.

N.B. In the preceding case, if the striker were to play for the losing hazard upon c, and should even have the address to make the winning hazard in d, by the same stroke, he would, in the first place, gain less points than by adopting the mode above recommended, and in the end would leave nothing, at least no favourable hazard or canon, for his next stroke.—"In choosing one of two modes of play, provided each are equally safe, the striker should invariably prefer that which is likely to produce the most subsequent advantages."

Fig. 41. Case 5.

Striker's Ball off the Table.

A full ball winning hazard upon b, in the pocket g, by playing from the point d of the striking ring.

A canon by playing a ¼ ball upon its right side from e.

Make the canon very gently, so as to ensure a hazard in the top pocket.

In this case, by making the winning hazard upon the adversary's ball, the striker, in all probability, would be able to gain only two points, and might, more particularly if his adversary be a tolerable player, lose many subsequently; for the red ball at c, being situated unfavourably, if he fail to score upon it, he will be in danger of leaving a hazard: if he bring it into the baulk by playing a low stroke full, and leave his own ball near the cushion in the place it occupied, his adversary, it is probable, at his succeeding stroke, will either drop the latter into the corner pocket, or lay it to a disadvantage under the cushion.

Fig. 42.

Fig. 42.   Case 1.

A ¼ ball losing hazard upon b, in the pocket e.

A ½ ball losing hazard upon c in the pocket d.

A canon by playing a ¼ ball either upon the left side of b, or upon the right side of c.

Play for the canon upon the adversary's ball with gentle strength, in order to carry it near to the pocket, that you may make a baulk at your next stroke.

Fig. 42.   Case 2.

A losing hazard upon b, in the pocket g, by playing a ½ ball upon its right side.

A winning hazard upon b, in the pocket g, by playing a ⅛ ball upon its left side.

A losing hazard upon c, in the pocket e, by playing a ¼ ball upon its right side.

A winning hazard upon c, in the pocket e, by playing a ¼ ball upon its left side.

Make the losing hazard upon c, in the pocket e, with a strength that will bring it towards the opposite middle hole.

Fig. 42.   Case 3.

A losing hazard upon b, in the pocket k, by playing a ½ ball upon its right side.

A winning hazard upon b, in the pocket k, and a canon by playing a ½ ball smart upon its left side.

Whether b be the red or the adversary's ball, play for the losing hazard; and regulate the strength of your stroke in such a way as to bring it favourably for a canon afterwards.

Fig. 42.   Case 4.

A full ball winning hazard upon b, in the pocket g.

A losing hazard upon c, in the pocket l, by playing a ½ ball upon its left side.

If c be the adversary's ball, make the winning hazard upon b, by a low stroke, that your own ball may lay dead, so as to enable you afterwards to make the losing hazard or the canon.

If c be the red ball, make the losing hazard in the pocket l, smart enough to bring the ball below the middle of the table.

N.B. The four preceding cases are similar to each other, and a little consideration must render obvious the motive for the particular mode of play recommended under each.

Fig. 43.

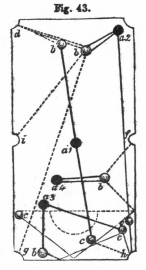

Fig. 44.

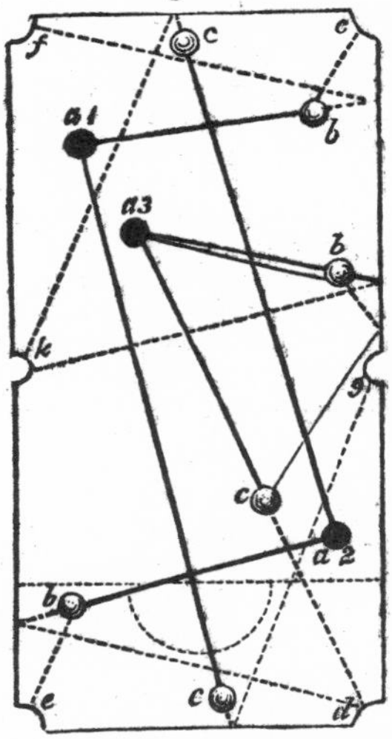

Fig. 43. Case 1.

A losing hazard upon b, in the pocket d, by playing a ¾ ball upon its left side.

A losing hazard upon c, in the pocket h, by playing a ½ ball upon its left side.

Make the hazard upon c, whichever ball it may be, with a degree of strength that will leave it below the middle of the table.

Fig. 43. Case 2.

A losing hazard upon b, in the pocket d, and a winning hazard in the pocket i, by playing a ¾ ball smart upon its right side.

A winning hazard upon b, in the pocket d, and a losing hazard in the pocket g, by playing a ¼ ball smart upon its left side.

A full ball winning hazard upon c, in the pocket h.

If c be the red ball, play for the winning hazard upon b, in the pocket d, with just sufficient strength to carry the ball the requisite distance, and that will enable you to make a good baulk if you succeed in holing it.

If c be the adversary's ball, play for the losing hazard in the pocket g, and the winning hazard in the pocket d, with considerable strength, in order to bring the balls away from the pockets if neither of them happen to be holed.

Fig. 43. Case 3.

A losing hazard upon c, in the pocket h, by playing a ¾ ball upon its left side.

A canon by playing a ½ ball smart upon the left side of b.

Fig. 43. Case 4.

A losing hazard upon b, in the

pocket f, by playing a ½ ball upon its left side.

A winning hazard upon b, in the pocket f, and a canon by playing a ¼ ball smart upon its right side.

Play a smart stroke for the canon, and the winning hazard in f.—If b be the adversary's ball, and you hole it, make a baulk.

N.B. In all of the foregoing cases it will be seen that a particular mode of play, although the most easy and obvious, is proscribed, as by adopting it the striker must almost unavoidably leave to his adversary the baulk.—The only exception to this restriction, is where the striker only wants the number of points which the hazard affords to make up his game.

Nothing is of more importance in the game of billiards than to be able to foresee the course which the balls will take after their contact The cases here represented will serve to suggest to the learner various others of a similar nature.

Fig. 44.

Fig. 44. Case 1.

A full ball winning hazard upon b, in the pocket f.

A losing hazard upon b in the pocket c, by playing a ¾ ball smart upon its left side.

A full ball winning hazard upon c, in the pocket g.

If c be the red ball, make the winning hazard upon the adversary's ball b, to obtain the baulk.

If c be the adversary's ball, make the losing hazard upon the red ball b.

Fig. 44. Case 2.

A full ball winning hazard upon b in the pocket d.

A losing hazard upon b, in the pocket e, by playing a ¼ ball upon its left side.

A full ball winning hazard upon c in the pocket k.

Make the losing hazard upon b with moderate strength.

N.B. The positions of the balls represented in these two figures, are nearly alike, but in one the losing hazard occurs at the upper end of the table, in the other at the lower end, in consequence of which the former requires a mode of play precisely the reverse of the latter.

Fig. 44. Case 3.

A full ball winning hazard upon b in the pocket k.

A full ball winning hazard upon c, in the pocket d.

A canon by playing a ¼ ball upon the right side of b.

Supposing b the adversary's ball, play for the winning hazard and the baulk.

If c be the adversary's ball, and you are ahead in the game, carry the ball c gently to the pocket d.

If c be the adversary's ball, and your game is backward, or if neither party have yet scored many points, play for the canon.

Fig. 45.

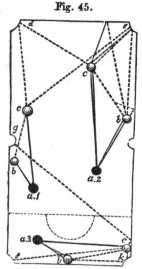

Fig. 46

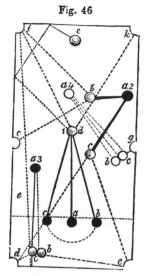

Fig. 45. Case 1.

A canon by playing a ½ ball upon the right side of the ball b.

A full ball winning hazard upon c, in the pocket d.

A ¾ ball losing hazard upon c, in the pocket e.

If c be the adversary's ball, play for the winning hazard softly.

If c be the red ball, play for the losing hazard strong.

Fig. 45. Case 2.

A canon by playing either a ¾ ball smart, or a ½ ball with moderate strength upon the left side of b.

A losing hazard upon c, in the pocket e, and a winning hazard in the pocket d, by playing a ¼ ball smart upon its right side.

A winning hazard upon c, in the pocket e, by playing a ½ ball upon its left side.

A losing hazard upon c, in the

pocket d, by playing a ¾ ball upon its left side.

A winning hazard upon b, in the pocket e, by playing a ½ ball upon its right side.

If c be the red ball, play for the losing hazard in the pocket d, strong enough to bring the ball out of the baulk.

If c be the white ball, make the losing hazard in the pocket e, just strong enough to lay the ball c over the pocket d, without pocketing it, and by your next stroke make a losing hazard, and bring the ball down for a succeeding canon.

Fig. 45. Case 3.

A canon by playing a ½ ball upon the left side of b.

A losing hazard upon b, in the pocket k, by playing a ¼ ball upon its left side.

A losing hazard upon c, in the

pocket g, by playing a ¼ ball smart upon its left side.

Play for the canon upon b, with gentle strength.

N.B. The above examples are introduced for the sake of warning the young player against a source of danger which he ought to beware of in attempting to canon or hazard (unless by a bricole or doublet stroke) when the ball to be first struck happens to be near to a cushion. In these cases the design of the striker is most frequently (and in the present instances would be unavoidably) frustrated by a kiss; the one ball returning after reflexion so as to intercept the course of the other, as will be seen by considering the figure.—This the striker should always anticipate and

guard against by an appropriate mode of play.

With regard to the last described case, it may not be amiss to observe, that when a ball is thus close under a cushion, and forms with the pocket and the striker's ball nearly right angles, as a, c, k, that the losing hazard may often be made without difficulty, through the intervention of a kiss, by playing a ¾ stroke gently upon the side of the ball opposed to the pocket. When the ball is not quite close, the hazard is made with more difficulty. It may be useful, perhaps, to know this, but it is a mode of play which ought seldom, perhaps never, to be practised in a regular game, notwithstanding the adversary's ball may happen to be near to a cushion.

Fig. 46.

Fig. 46.   Case 1.

Striker's Ball off the Table.

A losing hazard upon d, in the pocket k, by playing a ½ ball upon its right side from the point b.

A losing hazard upon d, in the pocket f, by playing a ½ ball upon its left side from the point c.

A winning hazard upon d, in either top pocket, and a canon by playing a ¾ ball upon either side, from the point a.

If d be the adversary's ball, play for the losing hazard.

If d be the red ball, play for the winning hazard and the canon.

Fig. 46.   Case 2.

A losing hazard upon b, in the pocket f, by playing a ¾ ball upon its right side.

A winning hazard upon b, in the pocket c, by playing a ¾ ball upon its right side.

A winning hazard upon b, in the

pocket f, by playing a ¼ ball upon its left side.

A full ball winning hazard upon c, in the pocket d.

A losing hazard upon c, in the pocket e, by playing a ½ ball smart upon its left side.

Supposing b the adversary's ball play for the winning hazard in the pocket f, just strong enough to carry your own ball to about e.

If c be the adversary's ball, play either for the losing hazard upon b, in the pocket f, with considerable strength, or for the winning hazard in the pocket d gently.—If you make it, bring the red ball into the baulk, as in Case 5, Fig. 54.

N.B. In the case of b being the adversary's ball, the striker must at once perceive the intention of playing for the winning hazard in the pocket f, rather than for the losing hazard in the same pocket, or the winning hazard in the pocket c. An accidental failure in attempting these last must inevitably leave the game open to the adversary, by giving him the red hazard.

Fig. 46.   Case 3.

A canon.

A losing hazard upon c, in the pocket d, by playing a ½ ball upon its right side.

Make the losing hazard strong enough to carry the ball c to the pocket f, and b to the pocket e.

N.B. In cases of this kind where the two object balls touch each other, and are near to a cushion, little advantage is usually derived from canoning. It is a mistaken opinion with young players, that they ought to canon in every case in which they can do so without difficulty. Thus, in Case 4, the striker will get most points from making the winning hazard upon c, in the pocket g, by playing very softly on the right side of the ball b.

Fig. 47*.

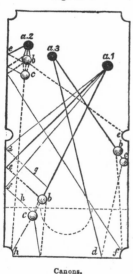

Canons.

Fig. 48.

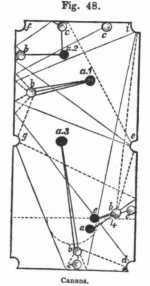

Canons.

Fig. 47.   Case 1.

A canon by playing either upon the point e of the cushion g,

h, or a ⅛ ball smart upon the left side of the ball b.

A full ball winning hazard upon c, in the pocket h.

* In this and the two following figures are represented various cases of canons, which particularly require the attention of the young player. The making of canons with address entirely depends upon an intimate knowledge of the angles of the table, and of the degrees of strength necessary to give the balls the requisite velocity, in order to obtain the ultimate desired advantage of the stroke; for in every case of canon, the judicious striker will have it in his power to create a favourable hazard.

If c be the adversary's ball, play for the canon bricole.

If c be the red ball, play either for the canon upon b, or for the winning hazard with considerable strength.

In either case of playing for the canon, employ a degree of strength that will obviate the danger of leaving your own ball near a pocket if you fail, and at the same time will afford you a subsequent hazard or canon if you succeed.

N.B. This masked situation of the balls usually proves perplexing to those whom practice has not yet rendered expert. It is also frequently a dangerous one, as in the present instance, if the upper of the two balls be the white; in this case a miss would be inevitably followed by a loss, greater or less, proportioned to the skill of the adversary.

It is expedient, therefore, in such cases of playing bricole, to mark well the precise part of the cushion to be struck with the ball. Use will make this familiar to the eye, but the novice will do well to examine accurately the relative positions of the three balls before he strikes, and to hold in mind the axiom that—the angle of reflexion equals the angle of incidence.— Thus, were he to strike the cushion at d instead of e, his ball would be reflected to g, above the ball b; if at f, it would be reverberated to h, in a line with the upper part of the ball c; but in either case it will be seen, that each returning line is equal, or answers to, the striking one. It is always easy, therefore, to measure the angle with the eye or with the cue.

Fig. 47. Case 2.

A canon either by striking the cushion at e, or by playing a $\frac{1}{2}$ ball upon the right side of b.

A full ball winning hazard upon c, in the pocket h.

A losing hazard upon b, in the pocket f, by playing a $\frac{1}{4}$ ball smart upon its right side.

A losing hazard upon b, in the pocket e, by playing a $\frac{1}{2}$ ball upon its left side.

Canon bricole smart enough to bring the balls away from the cushion, and leave hazards in the bottom and middle pockets.

N.B. It may not be improper to observe, that whenever the balls are thus close to each other, and in a direct line with a pocket, the winning hazard may always be made with the greatest ease. To do so, however, in the case here represented, would be injudicious, unless the striker could make his game by the stroke, as the canon is equally easy, and affords the greater number of chances.

Fig. 47. Case 3.

A bricole canon by playing at the cushion at d.

A losing hazard upon b, in the pocket f, by playing an $\frac{1}{8}$ ball upon its right side.

Play for the canon with a strength that will just carry the balls to the middle pocket.

Fig. 48.

Fig. 48. Case 1.

A canon by playing a $\frac{1}{2}$ ball hard upon the right side of the ball b.

A full ball winning hazard upon b, in the pocket e.

A losing hazard upon b, in the pocket i, by playing a third ball smart upon its right side.

A winning hazard upon b, in the pocket d, by playing a $\frac{1}{2}$ ball upon its right side.

If c be the adversary's ball, make the winning hazard upon b, in the pocket e, by a high stroke, that your ball may assume a position that will enable you to make the canon to advantage, upon the red ball being replaced upon its spot.

If c be the red ball, play for the canon.

Fig. 48. Case 2.

A canon by playing a ¼ ball either upon the right side of the ball b, or upon the left side of the ball c.

Canon off the red ball strong enough to carry it towards the pocket e, for a subsequent hazard.

Fig. 48. Case 3.

A winning hazard in the pocket i, and a canon by playing a high stroke full and strong upon b.

The winning and losing hazards represented in Case e, f, Fig. 38.

Canon with just enough strength to carry the ball to the pocket.

Fig. 48. Case 4.

Striker's Ball off the Table.

A winning hazard in the pocket g, and a canon by playing a high stroke full upon b, from the point a.

A losing hazard upon b, in the pocket e, by playing a ¼ ball upon its left side, from the point e.

A losing hazard upon b, in the pocket i, by playing a ¾ ball upon its left side from the point e.

If c be the adversary's ball, play for the losing hazard in the pocket e.

If b be the adversary's ball, play for the canon, and the winning hazard strong enough to bring the red ball away from the cushion. If you succeed in holing the adversary's ball, make a baulk.

N.B. Whenever the balls deviate at all from the parallel, this mode of making canons becomes easy, and may be practised although they happen to be at a considerable distance from each other. In this case, however, it is bad play to attempt it, unless the adversary is close to the cushion, as in such positions the striker may always adopt a mode of play not only more safe, but by which he may dispose the balls to a greater advantage.

Fig. 49.

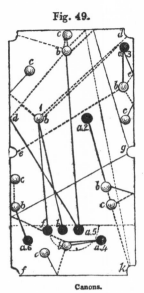

Canons.

Fig. 50.

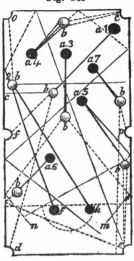

Winning and Losing Hazards.

Fig. 49.   Case 1.

Striker's Ball off the Table.

A losing hazard upon b, in the pocket d, by playing a ¾ ball hard upon its right side from the point f.

A canon and a winning hazard upon b, in the pocket d, by playing a ¼ ball smart upon its left side, from the point b.

If c be the adversary's ball, canon with very gentle strength, so as just to carry the ball b to the pocket d.

If c be the red ball, either canon smart enough to bring it away from the pocket, in the event of its not being pocketed, or play for the losing hazard in the pocket d.

N.B. Canons of this kind are by no means, generally speaking, so easy to be made, as they appear; for, as in Case 1, Fig. 47,

a considerable degree of delicacy is required, more especially where the balls are widely separated from each other, in order to strike the cushion at the necessary point. The worst consequences also are often to be apprehended from a failure, as in the case here represented, provided c be the adversary's ball. It will therefore be better, under such circumstances, if the striker is doubtful of being able to make the canon, either to lay the balls safe, or to choose the hazard, if any tolerable one present itself at the same time, as is usually the case.

Fig. 49.   Case 2.

A canon by playing a ¾ ball smart upon the left side of the ball b.

A full ball winning hazard upon c, in the pocket k.

If c be the red ball, play for the canon.

If c be the adversary's ball, play for the winning hazard in the pocket k, and the baulk.

Fig. 49. Case 3.

A bricole canon by playing upon the cushion at e.

A losing hazard upon b, in the pocket e, by playing a $\frac{3}{4}$ ball smart upon its right side.

Make the canon strong enough to carry the balls for hazards in the middle pockets.

N.B. In playing for the hazard, the striker would, in all probability, lose the baulk by a kiss. With regard to bricole canons, it should be a rule never to play for them, unless, *first*, the balls being near to each other, the striker can ensure success; or, secondly, the adversary happen to have no hazard upon the red ball, so that a miss would most likely be followed by the loss of one point only.

Fig. 49. Case 4.

A canon by playing a $\frac{3}{4}$ ball upon the left side of the ball b.

A losing hazard upon b, in the pocket g, by playing a $\frac{1}{2}$ ball smart upon its right side.

Whether c be the adversary's or the red ball, canon, and dispose b for a hazard in the pocket g: if it be the adversary's ball, endeavour to leave a winning hazard; if the red ball, a losing one.

Fig. 49. Case 5.

A bricole canon by playing upon the cushion at d.

The hazards represented by Case e, f, Fig. 39.

A $\frac{3}{4}$ ball winning hazard upon b, in either of the lower corner pockets.

If b be the adversary's ball, play for the winning hazard either in the pocket f or k, with just sufficient strength to carry it to the bottom of the table, whereby you will lay your own ball safe near to the side cushion.

If c be the adversary's ball, either part the balls by playing a $\frac{1}{2}$ ball gently upon b, or give a point and lay your ball below the middle of the table.

The same rules will hold good with regard to a similar position of the balls at the lower end of the table.

Fig. 49. Case 6.

A canon by playing a high stroke full upon b.

N.B. This is a case of by no means unfrequent occurrence, but it is one which requires a great degree of nicety in managing properly. In the hands of an expert player, the canon would be certain, but by an indifferent one, the attempt would perhaps often be dangerous. If the upper of the two balls, however, be the adversary's, the canon may always be played for with safety, but on the contrary, it will be advisable to separate the balls by playing an $\frac{1}{2}$ ball smart upon the right side of b.

Fig. 50*.

* In the game of Billiards as much judgment is required in defence as skill in execution. No stroke whatever, even though success appear certain, should be made, without maturely considering the probable consequences of a failure. It often happens that a player, much inferior to his

Fig. 50.   Case 1.
Adversary's Ball off the Table.

A full ball winning hazard upon b, in the pocket f.

A ½ ball winning hazard upon b, in the pocket d.

Play for the winning hazard in d, with gentle strength, so as to leave it within the baulk if you do not hole it, and to dispose your own ball near to the side cushion at c.

Fig. 50.   Case 2.
Both striker's and adversary's Ball off the Table.

A full ball doublet winning hazard upon b, in the pocket e, by playing from the point f.

A ¼ ball losing hazard upon b, in the pocket o, by playing from the point k.

Either play for the losing hazard in the pocket o smart, or for the doublet winning hazard in the pocket e, by a low stroke. If you fail to make the hazard in the first case, you will part the balls by laying one near to each side cushion; in the second, you will bring the red ball into the baulk, and leave your own ball nearly in the place it occupied.

Fig. 50.   Case 3.
Adversary's ball off the Table.

Make a baulk by playing a ½ ball upon b, with moderate strength, to bring the balls after reflexion to m and n.

Fig. 50.   Case 4.
Adversary's Ball off the Table.

A ¼ ball winning hazard upon b, in the pocket c.

An ⅛ ball losing hazard upon b, in the pocket c.

Play a low stroke full upon b, in order to bring it into the baulk, and leave your own ball in its place.

N.B. It would be very possible in this case to make a baulk, by playing fine and strong upon the left side of the ball b; but this is not to be ensured, and consequently ought not to be attempted, as the striker has it always in his power to lay the balls safe, as here prescribed.

Fig. 50.   Case 5.
Adversary's Ball off the Table.

A ½ ball winning hazard upon b, in the pocket e.

Make a baulk by playing upon b bricole.

N.B. In this and every case of making a baulk, the striker should, *in the first place*, be careful to regulate his strength in such a way as to leave the red ball the lowest of the two; and, *secondly*, never carry either of the balls so near a pocket, as to afford an easy bricole hazard to his adversary.

Fig. 50.   Case 6.
Adversary's Ball off the Table.

A ¾ ball winning hazard upon b, in the pocket e.

adversary in point of execution, will get the best of a match or game merely by the policy of his strokes. This is a circumstance often taken advantage of by those who are much in the habit of betting, and who almost uniformly gain, by making their bets in favour of the side which, to those not so well acquainted with the game, appears the weakest. A bold and inexperienced player will play at every ball that offers to him a probability of scoring; on the contrary, a judicious player will never attempt any point, unless, on the one hand, he is pretty certain of making it, or, on the other, is conscious the balls will be left safe in the event of his not succeeding.

Make a baulk, by playing for the winning hazard: and use a strength that will bring your own ball sufficiently away from the cushion to allow of your making the hazard subsequently, if you fail in the first attempt.

Fig. 50. Case 7.

Adversary's Ball off the Table.

A ⅛ ball losing hazard upon b, in the pocket p.

A ½ ball losing hazard upon b, in the pocket e.

Make a baulk by playing a ¾ ball upon its right side.

Fig. 51.

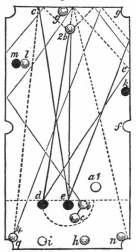

Fig. 52.

Fig. 51. Case 1.

Both adversary's and striker's Balls off the Table.

A ¼ ball losing hazard upon b, in each middle pocket.

A full ball winning hazard upon b, in each middle pocket.

A full ball doublet winning hazard upon b, in either of the lower pockets.

Play for the doublet winning hazard, and strike beneath the centre of your ball, that it may recoil and make a baulk.

Fig. 51. Case 2.

Both striker's and adversary's Balls off the Table.

Make a baulk by playing an ⅛ ball strong upon its left side from the point k.

Fig. 51. Case 3.

Adversary's Ball off the Table.

A ¼ ball losing doublet hazard upon b, in the pocket f.

Make a baulk by playing a ⅛ ball strong upon its right side.

Fig. 51. Case 4.

Adversary's Ball off the Table.

A $\frac{1}{2}$ ball doublet winning hazard upon b, in the pocket a.

An $\frac{1}{8}$ ball losing doublet hazard upon b, in the pocket a.

The same in the pocket f.

A $\frac{1}{2}$ ball losing doublet hazard upon b, in the pocket c.

Play a $\frac{1}{4}$ ball upon its right side with a strength that will carry it below the line, and bring your own ball to about g.

Fig. 51. Case 5.

Adversary's Ball off the Table.

A full ball winning hazard upon b, in the pocket c.

A $\frac{3}{4}$ ball winning doublet hazard upon b, in the pocket d.

Fig. 52. Case 1.

*Striker's Ball off the Table.—
Adversary has the baulk.*

If b (in the baulk) be the adversary's ball, play from d, upon the point e of the cushion off b and c for a canon.

If c be the adversary's ball, give a miss (if your game will admit of it,) and lay your ball at a, in a line with the other balls, and with the pocket f.

N.B. This is a very common case; the adversary has the baulk, and a dead hazard in the middle pocket, (supposing c to be his ball,) if the striker miss in playing bricole. It will be prudent, therefore, to give him a point, by disposing the balls as above recommended, so as to intercept his hazard, and obtain the chances of the table; there only remaining the choice of a canon from the cushion i, or by playing the high oblique stroke described, Chap. 2,

Play for the doublet hazard in the pocket d, with a strength that will leave b within the baulk, and carry your own ball to about f.

N.B. In all of the foregoing cases, it will be observed, that the hazard is declined for the purpose either of making a baulk, or of laying the balls safe; and it should be a rule with the striker to do so in every instance where the adversary's ball is *in hand*, unless, *in the first place*, he anticipate more important advantages from the hazard, and is able to make it with facility: or, *secondly*, when a certain number of points only, which the hazard would give him, are necessary for the completion of his game.

Fig. 52.

Sect. 1, p. 527, and a losing hazard in the pocket k. In doing this, however, the striker should be extremely cautious to dispose the balls precisely in a line with each other, otherwise he will give his adversary an easy canon.

Fig. 52. Case 2.

Both striker's and adversary's Balls off the Table; b red ball.

The hazards represented by Case e, f, Fig. 39.

A full ball doublet winning hazard in either of the lower pockets.

Either part the balls by playing a $\frac{1}{2}$ ball gently upon either side of b, or play for the doublet winning hazard, by striking either a low stroke, in order that your b ll may remain at the top of the table, or a high stroke, that it may be reflected near to the side cushion.

N.B. The case here described, must occur more or less frequently in every game: both of the white balls have been pocketed, and the red remains upon the spot. Under such circumstances the striker has the choice of three modes, by which he may lay the balls safe; either, *first*, to bring the red ball into the baulk, and leave his own ball at the top of the table by a full stroke, as above mentioned; or, *secondly*, to bring both his own and the red ball into the baulk, by playing a ½ ball hard upon the latter; or, *thirdly*, to part the balls, or lay each near a side cushion, by playing a ½ ball with gentle strength upon the red. Of these, the last is attended with least risk: in bringing the red ball into the baulk, it often happens that you leave a hazard upon your own; and the consequence of a failure in an attempt to bring both balls into the baulk, would be too destructive to admit of it being made, where the game is pending on the event of a stroke.

In disposing the balls as above directed, the striker should observe two cautions, first, never to use strength enough to produce the case b, c, Fig. 54; secondly, to avoid laying the balls quite close to the cushion.

Fig. 52. Case 3.

k, Striker's Ball; h, red Ball; g, adversary's Ball close under the cushion.

Give a point and lay your ball at i.

N.B. The intention of disposing the balls as recommended in this case, is too obvious to be insisted upon; the adversary is close under the cushion, the striker himself in a situation that renders him incapable of easily scoring upon either ball: by placing his own ball, therefore, thus advantageously, if the adversary should either miss or make an imperfect stroke, a certain hazard must be the consequence. Whenever, from an unfavourable position, you are incapable of scoring, and your adversary happen to have no hazard upon the red ball, it should be an invariable rule rather to give a point, than to run the hazard of missing unintentionally, and thereby leaving the balls to a disadvantage.

Fig. 52. Case 4.

Striker's Ball off the Table; adversary's Ball in any part of the Table in which it does not present a dead hazard; red Ball before the pocket q.

Play for the red hazard bricole, by striking with a due degree of strength upon the top cushion at c, from the point e.

N.B. In cases of this kind it is always better to play bricole by one reflexion than by two. The inevitable consequence of leaving the red ball over a pocket, unless you have a sure hazard upon your adversary's ball, must be at least a loss of three, perhaps of six points; but whenever you have at the same time a favourable winning hazard upon your adversary's ball, it is in every such case good play to prefer the latter, in order to gain the red hazard subsequently.

Fig. 52. Case 5.

m, Striker's Ball; l, adversary's Ball, n, red Ball.

Push your ball gently round to the lower side of l.

N.B. In doing this, the striker must be cautious to make the balls touch each other, and to leave them close to each other, otherwise his design will be in a great measure frustrated:

Fig. 53.

Fig. 54.

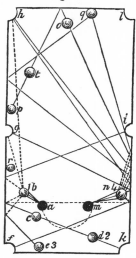

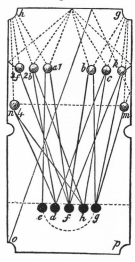

Fig. 53. Case 1.
Striker's Ball off the Table.

A full ball doublet winning hazard upon b, in the pocket i.

A canon by playing a ½ ball upon the left side of b.

A losing hazard upon b, in the pocket g, by playing a ¼ ball upon its right side.

A losing hazard upon b, in the pocket h, by playing a ¾ ball hard upon its right side.

Whether b be the adversary's or the red ball, canon with a strength that will leave b below the middle of the table, and create a hazard upon c, in the pocket k.

Fig. 53. Case 2.

Striker's Ball off the Table;—one of the Balls at b, as before, the other at d.

If b be the adversary's ball, play for the winning hazard to make a baulk.

If b be the red ball, play for the canon strong enough to bring your own ball away from the pocket k, and the red ball from l, in case you do not succeed in making it.

Fig. 53. Case 3.

Striker's Ball off the Table;—one of the Balls at b, as in the first and second cases, the other Ball at e.

The hazards as before.

A canon and a winning doublet hazard upon b, in the pocket i, by playing a ¾ ball upon its left side, from the furthest part of the striking ring.

If b be the red ball, and the adversary's ball is close under the cushion at e, play for the winning hazard and canon.

If b be the adversary's ball, play for the losing hazard in the pocket g, and bring the ball out for a subsequent winning hazard in the same pocket: if you succeed, make a baulk.

N.B. The cases here described are particularly interesting to the young player, from the frequency of their occurrence: the striker's ball being off the table, with one of the balls in the baulk, and the other at a short distance from the side cushion, and near to the striking line; the striker should be influenced in the mode of play he adopts by two circumstances, namely, by the position of the ball within the baulk, and whether it be the white or red ball. Thus, in Case 1, the ball c is so near as to render the canon certain, in consequence of which it should in all cases be played for, as being most profitable. Case 2, however, is materially different; the ball d being at a considerable distance from b, the canon may be readily missed, by playing either with more or less than the requisite degree of fullness; when, by the position the balls will obtain, if incautiously and unsuccessfully struck, an almost certain hazard or canon will remain: it will, therefore, be more expedient to play for the winning hazard to make a baulk; as it will also in Case 3, provided e be the red ball, but if e be the adversary's ball, no loss can ensue from playing for the canon, as the adversary, in his close situation, will be incapable of taking advantage of a failure. In the two last cases of canoning, a little address will enable the striker either to pocket the ball b by the same stroke, or dispose it before a pocket for the succeeding: in the former case, before the pocket 1; in the latter, before the pocket i.

Fig. 53.   Case 4.

Striker's Ball off the Table.

A full ball doublet winning hazard upon n, in the pocket g.

A winning doublet hazard upon n, in the pocket h, and a losing doublet hazard in the pocket f, by playing a $\frac{1}{4}$ ball smart upon its right side.

The reverse, by playing an $\frac{1}{8}$ ball smart upon its left side.

A canon by playing a $\frac{1}{4}$ ball, or a $\frac{3}{4}$ ball upon the left side of n, if the third ball is situated at q; if at either o or p, by playing a $\frac{1}{2}$ ball upon its left side.

If n be the adversary's ball, and the red ball be at q, play for the winning hazard to obtain the canon, upon n being replaced upon its proper spot.

If n be the adversary's ball, and the red ball be either at o or p, give a miss, if your adversary wants more than three points to complete his game, and lay your ball at a short distance from the opposite cushion.

Supposing n the adversary's ball, and the red ball to be situated at t, play to hole the latter in the pocket h, with moderate strength.

If n be the red ball, and the adversary's ball occupy the spot at o, give a point, if the adversary's game wants more than three of being up, and lay your ball at r.

If n be the red ball, and the adversary's ball is either at p or t, carry the latter gently to the pocket h, and in the event of holing it, make a baulk.

N.B. It should be a rule never to make the winning hazard upon the white ball, (if any other mode of scoring presents itself at the same time,) when you will have no hazard upon the red ball afterwards, or will be unable to make a baulk, or bring one of the balls into the baulk, and leave the other safe. By pocketing the adversary's ball,

you give him the whole range of the striking ring to play from, and consequently an opportunity of profiting by your leaving the balls to any disadvantage.

Fig. 54.

Fig. 54.   Case 1.
Striker's Ball off the Table.

A $\frac{3}{4}$ ball winning hazard upon a, in the pocket h.

A $\frac{3}{4}$ ball winning hazard upon b, in the pocket g.

A losing hazard upon a, in the pocket h, by playing either a $\frac{1}{8}$ ball, or a high stroke nearly full upon its left side, from the point e.

The same with regard to b, in the pocket g.

A canon by playing a $\frac{1}{4}$ ball either upon the right side of a, or upon the left side of h, from the point f.

Play for the canon with moderate strength upon the adversary's ball.

Fig. 54.   Case 2.
Striker's Ball off the Table.

A full ball winning hazard upon b, in the pocket h.

A full ball winning hazard upon c, in the pocket g.

A canon by playing a $\frac{1}{2}$ ball upon the right side of b, from the point d, or upon the left side of c from the point h.

Either by a low stroke carry the adversary's ball to the corner pocket, or canon upon the adversary's ball, with a strength that will bring your own rather below the middle pocket, if you happen to fail, and leave the former above the red ball.

Fig. 54.   Case 3.

A winning hazard upon f, in the

pocket h, by playing a $\frac{1}{2}$ ball upon its left side from the point f.

The same upon k, in the pocket g.

A canon by playing a $\frac{1}{4}$ ball strong upon the cushion side of either ball.

Carry the adversary's ball gently to the corner pocket, and play a low stroke, so as to leave your own near to the side cushion: if you succeed in holing it, give a point, and lay your ball in the baulk.

N.B. In the cases above described, and all similar ones, it should be a rule to play at the adversary's rather than the red ball. In the first, it will be proper to play for the canon in preference to the hazard, as a failure with regard to the latter, would almost inevitably prove the loss of two or more points, by leaving a canon for the adversary; whereas, by playing for the former you will be enabled to lay the balls safe, in the event of your stroke proving unsuccessful; but in the last, in playing at the hazard, although unsuccessfully, the striker's ball will remain out of danger, and the adversary will be laid close under the cushion, in which situation he must play to a disadvantage, and will run the risk of leaving his game open, if he attempt to score otherwise, than by gently dropping the white ball in return, to the opposite corner pocket.

Fig. 54. Case 4.
Striker's Ball off the Table.

A winning hazard upon n, in the pocket h, by playing a ½ ball upon .ts left side, from the point d.

A winning hazard upon m, in the pocket g, by playing a ½ ball upon its right side from the point h.

A winning doublet hazard upon n, in the pocket p, by playing a full ball from the point e.

A winning doublet hazard upon m, in the pocket o, by playing a full ball from the point g.

A canon by playing strong upon either ball in the nick, from the most distant part of the striking ring, as from the point h, with regard to the ball n.

Play for the doublet hazard upon the adversary's ball, by a low stroke, and use a strength that will leave it near to the lower cushion, if you do not pocket it.

Fig. 55.

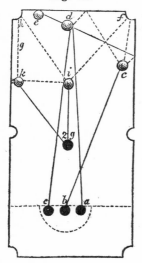

Fig. 56.

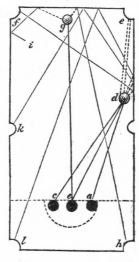

Fig. 55. Case 1.
Striker's Ball off the Table.

A canon, and a winning hazard upon, c in the pocket f, by playing a ½ ball smart upon its right side from the point b.

A canon by playing a ½ ball upon the right side of d, from the point a, or a ¼ ball upon its right side from the point e.

If c be the adversary's ball, ca-

non upon d, from the point a, strong enough to leave it a hazard for the middle pocket.

Supposing c the red ball, and the adversary's ball to be d, play for the canon upon the latter from the point e, smart enough to carry c to the middle of the table, and leave a winning hazard upon d, in the pocket h.

If c be the red ball, and the ad-

2 Q 2

versary's ball be near to the cushion as at e, play upon c for the winning hazard and the canon.

Fig. 55. Case 2.

The hazard represented in Case 1, Fig. 34.

A winning hazard in the pocket

h, and a canon by playing smart upon k in the nick.

If i be the adversary's ball, play for the winning and losing hazard upon its right side.

If i be the red ball, play upon k for the winning hazard and the canon.

Fig. 56.

Fig. 56. Case 1.

Striker's Ball off the Table;—red Ball on the spot;—d, adversary's Ball, too high for a canon, by playing as in Case 4, Fig. 53, and too low to admit of a canon being easily made, as in Case 1, Fig. 55.

A winning hazard upon d, in the pocket e, by playing a ¼ ball upon its right side from the point e, or a ¾ ball from the point a.

A losing hazard upon d, in the pocket e, by playing a ¼ ball upon its left side from the point c.

A full ball winning doublet hazard upon d, in the pocket k, by playing from the point e.

A full ball winning doublet hazard upon d, in the pocket l, by playing from the point a.

A losing doublet hazard upon d, in the pocket f, by playing a ¼ ball smart upon its right side from the point a.

Play for the doublet hazard in the pocket l, and strike low upon your ball, that it may remain nearly

in the place occupied by that of the adversary, and with such a degree of strength as will just serve to bring the latter to the bottom of the table.

Should the order of the balls be reversed, and the adversary's ball happen to occupy the neighbourhood of the spot, and the red ball be at d, while the striker is either off the table, or situated about the striking ring, he may either play fine upon the right side of g, for the canon, by which he will either hole g in f, or lay it over the pocket, or he may play for the losing hazard in the pocket e smart, by which he will part the balls, as in Case 2, Fig. 50; or he may play a ¾ ball high stroke smart upon the left side of g, in order either to hole it in the upper corner pocket h, or lay it under the cushion, while his own ball assumes the position i. Of these modes of play, the first will be most profitable if successful. the latter more safe, if the stroke prove ineffectual.

CHAPTER V.

RULES OF THE RED WINNING (CARAMBOLE) GAME.

The Red Winning Game is described at page 545. We have now to give the rules and directions

SECTION I.—*Rules for the Red Winning Game.*

1. The stroke, and the choice of balls must, in the first place, be strung for, as in the winning and losing game.

2. The red ball is to be placed on a spot made for that purpose, in the centre, between the stringing nails or spots at the bottom of the table, lower down than in the carambole winning and losing game.

3. The white or striker's ball is to be played from a spot made for that purpose, or from within the ring in the centre of the baulk.

4. After the first striker has played, his adversary is to play next, and so on alternately; or the striker is to follow his gaining stroke, as may have been previously agreed upon.

5. If the striker miss both balls, he loses one point; if by the same stroke he strike his own ball into a pocket, he loses three points.

6. If the striker hits the red ball and his adversary's ball with his own ball he wins two points; this is called a canon.

7. If the striker holes his adversary's ball, he wins two points.

8. If the striker holes the red ball, he wins three points.

9. If the striker holes his adversary's ball, and the red ball by the same stroke, he wins five points.—N.B. Two for the white, and three for the red ball.

10. If the striker makes a canon, and at the same time pockets his adversary's ball, he wins four points.—N.B. Two for the canon, and two for holing the white ball.

11. If the striker makes a canon, and at the same time holes the red ball, he wins five points.—N.B. Two for the canon, and three for pocketing the red ball.

12. If the striker makes a canon, and by the same stroke holes both his adversary's and the red ball, he wins seven points.—N.B. Two for the canon, two for the white, and three for the red hazard.

13. If the striker forces either his adversary's or the red ball over the table, and by the same stroke holes his own ball, he counts nothing, but makes no forfeit.

14. If the striker in playing a stroke should make his mace or cue touch two balls at the same time, it is deemed a foul stroke, and if discovered by the adversary, he wins nothing for any points he may have made by the stroke, and his adversary may break or part the balls, and play from the proper spot on the red ball, as at the beginning of the game. But if upon the foregoing stroke, which is deemed foul, his adversary does not break the balls, and play from the proper spot, &c., then the striker may reckon all the points he made by the stroke, and the marker is obliged to reckon them.

15. If the striker makes a foul stroke, and at the same time holes his own ball, he loses two or three points, according to which ball he struck first. Three for the red, and two for the white.

16. After a red ball has been holed or forced over the table, the striker is bound to see the ball placed on its proper spot again, before he strikes, otherwise he can win no points while the ball is out of its place, and the stroke he made is deemed foul.

17. After the striker has made either a canon or a hazard, if he should touch either of the balls with his hand, stick, or otherwise, he gains no points, and the stroke is deemed foul.

18. If the striker play with the wrong ball, the stroke is considered foul.

19. If the striker play with the wrong ball, and his error be not discovered by his adversary, he may reckon all the points he made by the stroke, and the marker is obliged to score them.

20. If the striker is about to play with the wrong ball, no one hath a right to discover his error to him, except his partner, if they are playing a four match.

21. If the striker plays with the wrong ball, and at the same time makes a losing hazard, he loses either two or three points, according to which ball he struck first, and the stroke is considered foul.

22. If the striker plays with the wrong ball, and misses both the remaining balls, he loses one point, and if the ball should

go into a pocket by the stroke, he loses three points, and it is deemed foul.

N.B. The rest of the rules and regulations are likewise to be observed as in the carambole winning and losing game.

Section II.—*General Instructions for the Red Winning (Carambole) Game.*

The carambole winning game is by no means so full of variety as the winning and losing, but it requires a greater degree of judgment, and depends more materially upon the skill of the player.

The general principles of the game however differ little from those of the preceding, and most of the observations and cautions laid down for that, are applicable to both : the canons are precisely similar, and the striker is influenced by the same grand object of making the baulk.

In the carambole winning game, the principal objects to be held in view by the striker, are, first, so to regulate his stroke, that in making the desired winning hazard, he may not at the same time make the losing, and secondly, to dispose the balls in such a manner, that his adversary may either have no hazard at all, or a hazard in playing which there will be an equal chance of holing his own and the ball he plays at.

The first of these often requires a considerable share of address, for in certain situations of the balls, it will be found extremely difficult to pocket the one without the other ; or to canon without at the same time pocketing the striking ball. The requisites in order to avoid these sources of danger, are, a perfect knowledge of the angles of the table, an ability in the striker to avail himself of the different modifications in the action of his instrument, and a studious attention to the different degrees of strength.

It is not prudent in this, as in the winning and losing game, for the first player to make a miss ; for the red ball being upon the lower mark, (about midway between the centre of the table and the top cushion) the adversary will have a good winning hazard. It is preferable to bring the red ball into the baulk, and at the same time play rather high upon the striking ball, in order that it may roll onwards towards the top cushion. In case of playing for the winning hazard, it will be prudent to use a degree of strength that will bring the red ball away from the pocket and your own in baulk, in the event of the attempt proving unsuccessful.

Much of the success of the striker in this game, will depend upon his skill in striking the full or straight hazard. Some players are extremely expert at this, inasmuch as that when they get the balls in a direct line between two pockets, they are enabled to make the game by successive winning hazards, without allowing their adversary another opportunity of playing. Thus suppose the red ball to be on the spot, and the striker's ball behind it, in an angle with one of the middle pockets, his ball after holing the red, will, if it be projected evenly by the cue, roll a little onwards, in consequence of which the striker will have to repeat his stroke for the corner pocket, after it has been replaced, and so on, backwards and forwards, until he commit a blunder, and lose the hazard. Others, on the contrary, who are, with regard to billiards in general, equally good players, make all other hazards with greater facility. The great art in making straight hazards, consists in the rapidity with which the eye surveys the pocket and the balls, and in the consequent smartness and suddenness of the stroke; for success in these cases will seldom allow of a very studied attention to the mode of striking, and "the more frequently the eye is suffered to wander from one ball to another, the more certainly will the stroke be unsuccessful,"

In this game the striker may often avail himself with great advantage, of a facility of making what are called reflected or doublet hazards; for whenever the red ball is situated unfavourably, and the white ball presents no direct hazard, it is uniformly preferable to attempt the reflected hazard with gentle strength upon the latter. Hazards of this description are more easily to be made than they appear to be; indeed there are few positions which a ball can obtain, in which it may not be doubled into one or another pocket, by a player perfectly acquainted with the angles of the table; as is exemplified in Fig. 35, 36. The same directions however will not hold good with regard to the red ball, for in playing at this, the utmost caution should be used not to bring it into any hazardous situation, for which reason when the chances of scoring are equal upon each ball, and no important advantage is in view, from playing at the red, it is uniformly deemed better play to choose the white. Whenever the reflected hazard is attempted, one caution should always be observed, namely, " in the case of the red hazard, to play strong enough to bring the ball away from the pocket, and in the case of the white hazard, to use such a moderate degree of strength as will leave it over the hole if it do not enter it.

The red winning game possessing fewer chances than the winning and losing, the striker may more frequently with impunity sacrifice an uncertain or difficult hazard, to the purpose of laying the balls safe; he ought therefore, in every case in which he despairs of scoring, to have one object only in view; to lay his own or his adversary's ball in that part of the table which affords no hazard or canon.

CHAPTER VI.

RULES OF THE RED LOSING CARAMBOLE GAME.

The Losing Carambole Game is the reverse of the Winning, as stated at page 597.

SECTION I.—*Rules for the Red or Carambole Losing Game.*

1. The game begins in the same manner as the carambole winning game.

2. If the striker misses both balls, he loses one point, and if he holes his own ball by the same stroke, he loses three points.

3. If the striker pockets the red ball, he loses three points, and the red ball must be replaced upon its proper spot.

4. If he pockets the white ball, he loses two points.

5. If the striker by the same stroke, hole both the red and the white ball, he loses five points, two for the white, and three for the red ball.

6. If the striker makes a canon, he wins two points.

7. If the striker makes a canon and holes either of the object balls, he wins nothing for the canon, and loses either two or three points, as he may have struck the red or the white ball first.

8. If the striker plays at the white ball first, makes canon, and at the same time holes his own ball, he wins four points;—two for the canon, and two for his losing hazard.

9. If the striker plays first at the red ball, makes a canon, and also holes his own ball, he wins five points:—three for the losing hazard off the red ball, and two for the canon.

N.B. The rest of the rules and regulations are likewise to be observed, as in the carambole winning, losing game, &c.

Section II.—*General Instructions of the Carambole Losing Game.*

The red or carambole losing game requires even more judgment than the winning, and the chances in it are often more various; especially if the players do not properly understand the skilful part. It depends entirely upon the defence, and the knowledge of the degree of strength with which each stroke should be played, either to defend or make a hazard. When properly understood, however, a losing game hazard is much more easy to be made than a winning game hazard is in general.

It will be unnecessary to repeat here many of the observations we have already made, which will apply to billiards in general; vide the general observations on the winning and losing game, Chap. 4, Sect. 2; precisely the reverse, however, of the rules laid down for the carambole winning game is applicable to the losing; the chief objects to be attended to by the striker, being to avoid making the winning hazard in attempting the losing. After what has been said with regard to the preceding games, the means of effecting this will readily suggest themselves to the striker.

It is of particular importance in this, as well as in the white losing game, for the striker to be able to play bricole, as it is termed; for it is very common for a player, in order to ensnare his adversary, to lay his ball in such a way before a pocket, that the latter will often find it extremely difficult to avoid holing it, if he play the direct stroke; by taking the proper angle however, and striking the cushion previously, he may always obviate this danger, and will very generally be enabled to make the desired losing hazard.

CHAPTER VII.

OF THE SIMPLE CARAMBOLE OR FRENCH GAME.

The simple carambole game (referred to at page 544) is played with three balls, and consists usually of twelve points, which are scored by canons only, and forfeitures. It possesses but few chances, and consequently requires a considerable share of skill and judgment. It is seldom played alone, but usually by an able player against the winning and losing, or the winning game of an indifferent one; and is considered equal to giving fifteen out of twenty-four points. This is the game now played in France. A variety of this game is to make it consist entirely of doublet canons, and at the present day this is almost the only mode of play recognised in France; it is therefore, *par excellence*, called FRENCH BILLIARDS.

SECTION I.—*Rules for the Simple Carambole Game.*

1. The game commences in the usual manner, the red ball being placed upon its appropriate spot, and the players stringing for lead, and choice of balls, as in the preceding games.

2. The game is played in two different ways. In the first, both kinds of hazards lose, in the second, they count for nothing; the first is the most usual mode of play, and the striker upon making either a winning or losing hazard, loses as many points as he would have gained by that particular stroke in the winning or losing game.

3. If the striker misses both balls, he loses one point; if by the same stroke he pockets his own ball, he loses three points.

4. If the striker makes a canon, he gains two points.

5. If the striker makes a canon and holes himself off the adversary's ball, he loses two points for the hazard, and gains nothing for the canon.

6. If the striker makes a canon and holes himself off the red ball, he loses three points, and gains nothing for the canon.

7. If the striker canons, and by the same stroke holes the adversary's ball, he loses two points.

8. If the striker canons, and holes the red ball by the same stroke, he loses three points.

9. If the striker canons, and hole both his own and the adversary's ball, he loses four points.

10. If the striker canons, and at the same time holes both his own and the red ball, he loses five points, if he played at the white, and six if he played at the red ball.

11. If the striker canons, and holes all three of the balls by the same stroke, he loses either seven or eight points, according to the ball which he played at.

The rules for the carambole winning and losing game, are also to be observed in the simple carambole game.

SECTION II.—*General Observations in the Simple Carambole Game.*

In the simple carambole game, as hazards are disregarded, it only remains for the striker either to endeavour to canon, as the only means of scoring, or to lay the balls safe, or in such a position that his adversary may obtain no canon. If he despairs of accomplishing the first, or deems the attempt attended with risk, the latter is more easily to be effected in this game than in any other, it having fewer chances; and yet there are few positions of the balls in which it is not possible for an expert player to canon. Whoever has been much in the habit of frequenting billiard rooms, must have observed matches in which a common walking stick, or the hand without any stick, is played by a good player against the cue or mace of a bad one, and that the stick or hand player most commonly comes off victor. If he were to pay a more minute attention to such games, he would perceive that the greater number of points gained by the latter, are scored from canons, which his adversary had thrown in his way, through ignorance of the game; and upon which he almost exclusively depends, being unable, under the disadvantage in which he is placed, to make a stroke firm enough to ensure many of the common winning and losing hazards; but to canon under a variety of circumstances, requires a very great share of judgment and dexterity.

CHAPTER VIII.

RULES OF THE WHITE WINNING GAME.

The white winning game is much more simple than any we have hitherto described. Together with the white losing game, it is considered a key to Billiards in general, and may be usefully practised by learners, before they attempt the more complex carambole games. (See the introductory account of the White Ball Games, at page 543.)

SECTION I.—*Rules for the White Winning Game.*

1. The game begins by stringing for the lead and choice of balls, as in the " Winning and Losing Game." Rules 1-6.

2. Immediately after a hazard has been won, the balls are to be broken, and the striker is to lead as at first.

3. When a hazard has been lost in either of the corner pockets, the leader is, if his adversary requires it, to lead from the end of the table where the hazard was lost; but if the hazard was lost in either of the middle pockets, it is at the leader's option to play from either end of the table he pleases.

4. If the striker misses his adversary's ball, he loses one point; if by the same stroke he holes his own ball, he loses three points, as in the carambole games.

" 5. If the striker holes his own or both balls, or forces both of them over the table, or on a cushion, he loses two points."

" 6 If the striker forces his adversary's ball over the table, or on a cushion, he scores two points."

" 7. If the striker who plays the stroke, should make his adversary's ball go so near the brink of a pocket, as to be judged to stand still, and it should afterwards fall into it, the striker wins nothing, and the ball must be put on the brink where it stood, for his adversary to play at the next stroke."

" 8. If the striker's ball should stand on the brink or edge of a pocket, and if in attempting to play it off he should make the ball go in, he loses three points."

" 9. If a ball should stand on the brink or edge of a pocket, and it should fall into the pocket, before or when the striker has delivered his ball from his mace or cue, so as to have no chance for his stroke, in that case the striker's and his adversary's balls must be placed in the same position, or as near as possible thereto, and the striker must play again."

" 10. If by a foul stroke, the striker holes his own or both balls, or forces his own or both balls over the table, or on a cushion, he loses two points."

11. He who does not play as far as his adversary's ball, loses one, or his adversary may oblige him to pass the ball,

more especially in giving a miss; or, he can, if he choose, make him replace the ball, and play until he has passed it.

12. If the striker plays with a wrong ball he loses the lead, if his adversary requires it.

13. If the ball should be changed in a hazard, or in a game, and it is not known by which party, the hazard must be played out by each party with their different balls, and then changed.

14. If the striker plays with his adversary's ball, and holes or forces the ball he played at over the table, it is deemed a foul stroke.

"15. If the striker plays with his adversary's ball, and misses, he loses one point; and if his adversary discovers that he has played with the wrong ball, he may break the balls and take the lead."

16. In all the before-mentioned cases of playing with the wrong ball, if the error of the striker is not discovered, his adversary must play with the ball the striker played at throughout the hazard, or break the balls and take the lead.

17. Whoever proposes to break the balls, and his adversary agrees to it, the proposer thereof loses the lead.

The remaining Rules are the same in the Winning and Losing Game.

SECTION II.—*General Instructions.*

The general principles of the red winning game may be applied with little variation to the white. Vide Chap. 5, Sect. 2.

CHAPTER IX.

RULES OF THE WHITE LOSING GAME.

The white losing game is the reverse of the white winning, the points in it being reckoned by losing and double hazards. Like the white winning game it is played with the two white balls, and is twelve up.

SECTION I.—*Orders for the White losing Game.*

1. At the beginning you must string for the lead, and for the choice of the balls as in the other games.

2. If the striker misses the ball he loses one, and if he hole his own ball by the same stroke, he loses three points.

3. If the striker holes his adversary's ball, he loses **two** points.

4. Forcing either or both the balls over the table, or on a cushion, reckons nothing, but the striker loses the lead.

5. If the striker misses the adversary's ball, and forces his own ball over the table, &c. he loses one point and the lead.

6. If the striker holes his own ball, he wins two points.

7. If the striker holes both balls, he wins four points*.

8. If the striker holes either of the balls, and forces the other over the table, &c., he loses the lead only.

N.B. The rest of the regulations, &c. as in the winning and losing, and winning games, are likewise to be observed.

SECTION II.—*General Observations.*

Vide the general observations on the Red Losing Game, Chap. 6, Sect. 2.

RULES FOR THE GAMES OF POOL.

There are several ways of playing Pool,—namely, with as many balls as there are players; or with two balls only, the players playing in turns, and playing with the alternate balls; playing at the nearest ball; playing at the last player; or the player playing at whichever ball he choose. But the most popular and perhaps the fairest mode is that in which each has his own ball of a distinguishing colour, and plays at the last player.

The following are the rules, according to this last method.

1. When coloured balls are used, the players must play progressively in the order in which the colours are placed on the Pool marking-board, the top colour being No. 1.

2. Each player has three lives at starting. No. 1 places his ball on the winning and losing spot. No. 2 plays at No. 1. No. 3 at No. 2, and so on, each person playing at the last ball; unless it should be in hand, then the player plays at the nearest ball.

3. If a striker should lose a life in any way, the next player plays at the nearest ball to his own; but if his (the player's)

* This rule does not seem consistent, but is so given by White and Kentfield.

ball be in hand, he plays at the nearest ball to the centre of the baulk line, whether in or out of baulk.

4. Should a doubt arise respecting the distance of balls, it must (if at the commencement of the game, or if the player's ball be in hand,) be measured from the centre spot in the circle; but if the striker's ball be not in hand, the measurement must be made from his ball to the others; and in both cases it must be decided by the marker, or by a majority of the company; but should the distances be equal, then the parties must draw lots.

5. The baulk is no protection at Pool under any circumstances.

6. The player may lose a life by any of the following means:—by pocketing his own ball; by running a coup; by missing the ball; by forcing his ball off the table; by playing with the wrong ball; by playing at the wrong ball; by playing out of his turn; or by having his ball pocketed, or forced off the table by another player.

7. Should the striker pocket the ball he plays at, and by the same stroke pocket his own, or force it over the table, *he* loses the life, and not the person whose ball he pocketed.

8. Should the player strike the wrong ball, he pays the same forfeit to the person whose ball he should have played at, as he would have done if he had pocketed it.

9. If the striker misses the ball he ought to play at, and strikes another and pockets it, *he* loses a life, and not the person whose ball he pocketed; in which case the striker's ball must be taken off the table, and both balls should remain in hand, until it be their turn to play.

10. If the striker, whilst taking his aim, inquires which is the ball he ought to play at, and should be misinformed by any one of the players or by the marker, he does not lose a life, but the balls must be replaced, and the stroke played again. He is not, however, at liberty to take a life, but must play for safety.

11. If information is required by the player, as to which is his ball, or when it is his turn to play, he has a right to an answer from the marker or from the players.

12. If a ball, or balls, should be in the way of, or touch, the striker's ball, so as to prevent his hitting any part of the object ball, he may have them taken up until the stroke be played, and after the balls have ceased running they must be replaced.

13. If a ball or balls are in the way of a striker's cue, so that he cannot play at his ball, he can have them taken up.

14. When the striker takes a life, he may continue to play on as long as he can make a hazard, or until the balls are all off the table, in which latter case he plays from the baulk, or places his ball on the spot as at the commencement.

15. The first person who loses his three lives is entitled to purchase, or, as it is called, to star (a star being the mark placed against his lives on the board, to denote that he has purchased), by paying into the pool the same sum as at the commencement, for which he receives lives equal to the lowest number on the board.

16. If the first person out refuse to star, the second person may do it, but if the second refuse, the third may do it, and so on, until only two persons are left in the pool, in which case the privilege of starring ceases.

17. Only one star is allowed in a Pool.

18. If the striker should move another ball whilst in the act of striking his own ball, the stroke is considered foul; and if, by the same stroke, he pocket a ball, or force it off the table, the owner of that ball does not lose a life, and the ball must be placed on its original spot; but if, by that stroke, he should pocket his own ball, or force it off the table, he loses a life.

19. If the striker's ball touch the ball he has to play at, he is then at liberty either to play at it or at any other ball on the table, and it is not to be considered a foul stroke; in this case, however, the striker is liable to lose a life, by going into a pocket or over the table.

20. After making a hazard, if the striker should take up his ball, or stop it, before it has done running, he cannot claim the life, or the hazard, from the person whose ball was pocketed; it being possible that his own ball might have gone into a pocket, if he had not stopped it.

21. If, before a star, two or more balls are pocketed by the same stroke, including the ball played at, each having one life, the owner of the ball first struck has the option of starring; but should he refuse, and more than one remain, the persons to whom they belong must draw lots for the star.

22. Should the striker's ball stop on the spot of a ball removed, the ball which has been removed must remain in hand until the spot is unoccupied, and then be replaced.

23. If the striker should have his next player's ball removed, and stop on the spot it occupied, the next player must give a miss from the baulk to any part of the table he thinks proper, for which miss he does not lose a life.

24. If the striker has a ball removed, and any other than the next player's ball should stop on the spot it occupied, the ball removed must remain in hand, till the one on its place be played, unless it should happen to be the turn of the one removed to play before the one on its place, in which case that ball must give place to the one originally taken up; after which it may be replaced.

25. If the corner of the cushion should prevent the striker from playing in a direct line, he can have any ball removed for the purpose of playing at it from a cushion.

26. The two last players cannot star or purchase; but they may divide, if they are left with an equal number of lives each; the striker, however, is entitled to his stroke before the division.

27. All disputes to be decided by a majority of the players.

28. The charge for the table to be taken out of the pool before it is handed over to the winner.

Rules for Pool-playing at the last Player.

When coloured balls are used in playing this game, the players must play progressively as the colours are placed on the marking-board, the top colour being No. 1.

THE NEAREST BALL POOL.

In this Pool the players always play at the nearest ball out of the baulk; for in this Pool the baulk is a protection.

1. If all the balls be in the baulk, and the striker's ball in hand, he must lead to the top cushion, or place the ball on the winning and losing spot.

2. If the striker's ball be within the baulk line, and he has to play at a ball out of the baulk, he is allowed to have any ball taken up that may chance to lie in his way.

3. If all the balls be within the baulk, and the striker's ball not in hand, he plays at the nearest ball.

All the other rules of the former pool are to be observed at this.

BAGATELLE GAMES.

THE following games are played on a board, which is usually from six to ten feet in length, and from one foot nine inches to three feet wide, lined with green cloth; a slip of thin wood being placed round the inside of its upper end, to form a semicircle.

There are nine cups let in level with the cloth, numbered one to nine, into which the balls are to be driven in playing the two first mentioned games. (La Bagatelle and Sans Egal.)

There is also a bridge with small arches likewise numbered from 1 to 9, and through which the balls are to be driven in playing the two last mentioned games (Mississippi and Trou Madame) when the cups are not used.

There are likewise two small cushions placed against the sides, to be used in the game of Mississippi; or instead of these the boards are sometimes stuffed round the sides.

Tables of the best manufacture are usually charged at from thirteen to fifteen guineas each, and may be purchased of Mr. Thurston, Catherine Street, Strand.

LA BAGATELLE.

ANY number of players may join in this game, and use either the mace or cue as may be agreed.

Each player strikes a ball up the board, and whoever gets the highest number is entitled to the lead, and takes possession of the nine balls.

The black ball (which counts for double) is placed on the white spot in front of the holes, at the beginning of every round, and must in the first instance be struck by one of the other balls before there can be any score.

The striker's ball must be placed on the white spot nearest the other end of the board, and is to be struck with the mace or cue at the black ball, the object being to put it into one of the holes. The rest of the balls are to be played up in the same manner, either at the outstanding balls, or for the holes.

Any number of rounds may be played for the game, as may be agreed upon at its commencement.

The player who obtains the greatest number—counting the holes into which he puts the balls, according to the figures marked within them—wins the game.

The holes along the edges of the board are for the purpose of marking the game.

Any ball that rebounds beyond the centre, or that is driven off the board, cannot be used again during that round.

SANS EGAL.

This is played by two persons.

The player who leads, which is decided as in bagatelle, chooses four balls of either colour, and places the black ball on the mark in front of the holes, and begins by striking one of his balls up the board.

The other player then strikes one of his balls in the same manner, and so on alternately.

He that holes the black ball counts it towards his game, and also all that he may hole of his own colour.

If a player should hole any of his adversary's balls, it counts for the owner of the balls.

The player who makes the greatest number of points in each round, takes the lead in the next. The game is 21, to 31, according to the arrangement between the players.

MISSISSIPPI.

Place the bridge close up to the circle, and the small cushions against the sides.

Each player is then to strike one ball through the bridge, and he who gets the highest number, has the lead, and plays the nine balls in succession

All balls must strike one of the cushions, previous to entering the bridge, otherwise the number reckons for the adversary.

The game to consist of as many points as may be agreed on at its commencement.

TROU MADAME.

This is played in the same way as the preceding game, except that the balls are played straight from the end of the board through the bridge.

RUSSIAN BAGATELLE,

OR

COCKAMAROO TABLE.

Elevated end of the board which is an inclined plane, lowest at the striking end.

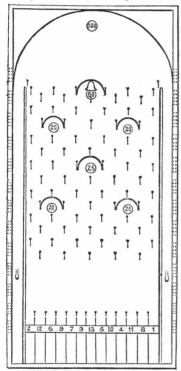

DESCRIPTION OF THE BOARD.

A cavity for the red ball to be placed in, at the commencement of the game *only*. It counts double, *i.e.* 100, as marked inside.

An arch with a bell suspended within it, which if rung by any ball in passing through, counts double for whatever that ball may score by the stroke. If it does not pass through, but merely falls into the cup underneath, it counts only as marked, *i.e.* 50.

The remaining arches with cups beneath them, count respectively as marked, viz. 20 on the sides, and 25 in the centre.

The pegs are brass pins standing up, about 1¼ inches in height.

These are slightly indented spots (one on each side of the board) from which the balls are projected.

Cavities into which the balls run; they count according to the numbers placed above.

The board, which is generally four feet six inches in length, and two feet four inches in width, is lined with superfine green cloth. Those of the best description cost about fifteen guineas, and are made, if wished, to shut up so as to have the appearance of a Pembroke table. They are sold by Mr. Thurston of Catherine Street, and other respectable makers.

Rules of the Game.

I. Commence the game by stringing for the lead, as well as for choice of balls and side of board; the player who gets the highest number takes the lead.

II. The leader must place his ball in the cavity on the side of the board he selects, and play it up, counting the points he may make by the stroke; after which, his opponent plays from the opposite side of the board; and so on, alternately.

III. When a ball lodges on the board without going into a hole or running down to the bottom, the game must be continued with the other ball, each player using it alternately—whoever removes the ball so lodged, scores the number of points made by both the balls, and the game proceeds as at first. Should both the balls be lodged on the board, that ball which was last stopped must be taken up and used to continue the game.

IV. The player continues to lead, as long as he can hole his ball in any of the *cups*.

V. The game to consist of one hundred or more, as may be agreed upon at the commencement.

VI. If the player's ball ring the *bell*, that is passes through the bell arch, he scores double the number he would otherwise gain by the stroke.

VII. Playing into the top hole (marked 100) is the game at once.

VIII. Should the ball go round to the opponent's side, the striker loses five points and the lead; or should he play his ball up, and it returns without going on the board, he loses one point and the lead.

IX. The winner of the game, takes the lead in the next.

AMERICAN BOWLS.

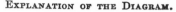

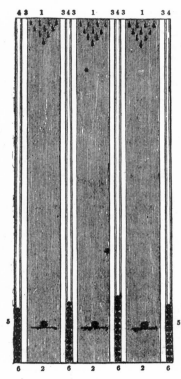

EXPLANATION OF THE DIAGRAM.

1. Ten pins, something in the shape of large hock bottles, arranged in a triangle, its apex being nearest the player.

2. Platforms, (called alleys,) about sixty feet in length and four feet in width, on which the balls are propelled. The surface must be perfectly smooth and level.

3. The white margins on each side of the platforms are channels into which the balls drop, when not dexterously propelled.

4. The intermediate dark spaces or lines are grooves, elevated on frames about three feet above the level of the platform, with a slight inclination towards the bowler's end. By means of these grooves the balls are returned to the bowlers, boys being placed for that purpose on raised seats beyond the pins.

5. The balls here laid on the marked line at the bowler's end of the platform shew whence they are delivered by the player after he has taken his run along five or six feet of the platform.

6. The balls lying in the grooves shew how they are delivered to the bowler. They are returned to him at every setting up of the pins.

At the further end of the platform is a recess of a few feet for the pins to fall in, and beyond this (to stop the balls) is a cushion covered with hide, which swings on hinges, and is reverberated by springs.

On one side of the room are sofas for the spectators, and at the bowling end seats for the bowlers; also refreshment tables,

In the American Bowling Saloon, (393, Strand), whence by the civility of Mr. Thomas Robson, the proprietor, the present particulars have been collected, there are six platforms (running parallel to each other), and sometimes as many as forty or fifty players engaged on them at one time; especially of an evening, when the saloon is brilliantly lighted, and enlivened by music.

The chief art in playing at this somewhat athletic game seems to consist in hitting the apex or point-pin a half ball, (the larger the ball, the greater the chance of success,) but dexterity is only to be acquired by practice. Some players are so expert as to throw down the whole ten pins at one blow several times in succession, and as they are allowed three balls to each division, or setting up of the pins, those which are spared count in addition; thus if a player at starting should knock down all the ten pins at one blow, this would count ten, and would leave a *double spare* or two spare balls, with which if he threw down eight more, he would add that number to his score and count eighteen in the first division, and then go on to the second division with his next three balls. If by a run of luck or skill the player should knock all ten pins with single balls, six times in the course of his ten *divisions*, he would have twelve balls to spare and would therefore be entitled to add to his score whatever he could make with them. When the ten pins are thrown down with two balls, one ball is spared, and counted after the same manner. The highest number it is possible to make with the balls allotted to the ten divisions, is three hundred, *i. e.* ten for each of thirty balls. The mode of keeping count is on a chequered slate of ten times ten squares, numbered from one to ten down the left or front side, the initials of the different players being placed at the head of the columns. It is usual either for players to follow alternately in single divisions, or to play two, three, or five divisions, at a standing, as may be agreed.

The Americans have several varieties of this game, one of which is to play it with only three pins instead of ten, and as the three can scarcely be brought down at one blow, the interest is kept up by betting on the success of each particular aim.

The uninitiated had better not be too fierce in his first onslaught, especially if he play with heavy balls, as the exercise is likely to try the muscles of his arm rather severely, and may leave a reminiscence for some days afterwards.

The balls are usually of four different kinds, varying in size from four to eight inches in diameter, and from four or five to ten or eleven pounds weight.

RULES OF THE GAME, FROM THE PRINTED SET SUSPENDED IN THE AMERICAN BOWLING SALOON, 393, STRAND.

I. Each player to pay sixpence per game, and be allowed three balls for each of the ten divisions; but when spare balls are obtained, then to play on to the extent of them.

II. Any number of players (not exceeding ten) can play together; the lowest half-division paying the game of the highest.

III. Gambling strictly prohibited.

IV. In playing, all pins knocked down considered fair, whether obtained by a front or back (*i. e.* reverberated) ball.

V. No gentleman allowed to stand on the platform in front of the alleys except the players

VI. All ties to be decided by a single ball.

VII. The marked line on the alleys is the utmost limit allowed to players in advancing to deliver the ball.

VIII. Should any dispute arise between players, the Marker to be called as umpire, and his decision to be final.

IX. The sofas behind the players to be reserved exclusively for their use.

X. Two players cannot retain any alley exclusively to themselves when other parties are waiting to play.

XI. Pitching the balls is not permitted, and any player doing so (after notice) forfeits his game from that point.

FINIS.